# 4th Linguistic Annotation Workshop 2010

# (LAW IV)



**Held at ACL 2010**

## Uppsala, Sweden
## 15-16 July 2010

**ISBN: 978-1-61738-817-0**

**Printed from e-media with permission by:**

Curran Associates, Inc.
57 Morehouse Lane
Red Hook, NY 12571

**Some format issues inherent in the e-media version may also appear in this print version.**



Printed by Curran Associates, Inc. (2010)



Association for Computational Linguistics
209 N. Eighth Street
Stroudsburg, Pennsylvania 18360

Phone: 1-570-476-8006
Fax: 1-570-476-0860

acl@aclweb.org

**Additional copies of this publication are available from:**

Curran Associates, Inc.
57 Morehouse Lane
Red Hook, NY 12571 USA
Phone: 845-758-0400
Fax: 845-758-2634
Email: curran@proceedings.com
Web: www.proceedings.com

# Introduction

The Linguistic Annotation Workshop (The LAW) provides a forum to facilitate the exchange and propagation of research results concerned with the annotation, manipulation, and exploitation of corpora; work towards the harmonization and interoperability from the perspective of the increasingly large number of tools and frameworks for annotated language resources; and work towards a consensus on all issues crucial to the advancement of the field of corpus annotation. Although this year's LAW is officially the fourth edition, LAW itself is the convergence of several previous workshops—including NLPXML, FLAC, LINC, and Frontiers in Corpus Annotation—dating back to the first NLPXML in 2001. This series of workshops attests to the rapid developments in the creation and use of annotated data in both language technology and empirical approaches to linguistic studies over the past 10 years.

The response to this year's Call for Papers was enthusiastic: 60 submissions were received. After careful review, the program committee accepted 20 long papers and 24 posters. Selection of the papers was not an easy task, as the papers cover the full range of linguistic facts and their corresponding annotation frameworks, from predicate-argument to discourse structure, speech to social networks, and learner corpus to CVs. The papers also deal with a range of annotation levels, from the macro perspective on infrastructure for international collaboration and interoperability, to the micro perspective on tools to deal with inter-annotator inconsistencies. It is this richness of the topics that attest to the growing maturity of field. We would like to thank SIGANN for its continuing endorsement of the LAW workshops, as well as the support and comments from the ACL-IJCNLP 2009 workshop committee chairs: Pushpak Bhattacharyia and David Weir. We would also like to thank the ACL publication chairs Jing-Shin Chang and Philipp Koehn for their help in producing the LAW IV proceedings. Most of all, we would like to thank all our program committee members and reviewers for their dedication and helpful review comments. Without them, LAW IV could not be implemented successfully.

Nianwen Xue and Massimo Poesio, Program Committee Co-chairs

Nancy Ide and Adam Meyers, Organizers

**Organizers:**

Nancy Ide (Vassar College)
Adam Meyers (New York University)
Chu-Ren Huang (The Hong Kong Polytechnic University)
Antonio Pareja-Lora (SIC, UCM / OEG, UPM)
Sameer Pradhan (BBN Technologies)
Manfred Stede (Universität Potsdam)
Nianwen Xue (Brandeis University)

**Program Committee:**

Program Co-chairs:

Nianwen Xue (Brandeis University)
Massimo Poesio (University of Trento)

Members:

Nicoletta Calzolari (ILC/CNR)
Steve Cassidy (Macquarie University)
Tomaz Erjavec (Josef Stefan Institute)
Katrin Erk (University of Texas at Austin)
Alex Chengyu Fang (City University of Hong Kong)
Christiane Fellbaum (Princeton University)
Chu-Ren Huang (The Hong Kong Polytechnic University)
Nancy Ide (Vassar College)
Richard Johansson (University of Trento)
Aravind Joshi (University of Pennsylvania)
Sandra Kübler (Indiana University)
Seth Kulick (University of Pennsylvania)
Adam Meyers (New York University)
Olga Babko-Malaya (BAE Systems)
Eleni Miltsakaki (University of Pennsylvania)
Antonio Pareja-Lora (SIC, UCM / OEG, UPM)
Martha Palmer (University of Colorado)
Rebecca J. Passonneau (Columbia University)
Marta Recasens Potau (Universitat de Barcelona)
Sameer Pradhan (BBN Technologies)
Rashmi Prasad (University of Pennsylvania)
Arndt Riester (IMS Universität Stuttgart)
James Pustejovsky (Brandeis University)
Kepa Rodriguez (University of Trento)
Anna Rumshisky (Brandeis University)
Manfred Stede (Universität Potsdam)

Marc Verhagen (Brandeis University)
Theresa Wilson (University of Edinburgh)
Andreas Witt (Universität Tübingen)
Anja Nedoluzhko (Charles University)

# Table of Contents


*EmotiBlog: A Finer-Grained and More Precise Learning of Subjectivity Expression Models*
Ester Boldrini, Alexandra Balahur, Patricio Martínez-Barco and Andrés Montoyo .............. 1

*Error-Tagged Learner Corpus of Czech*
Jirka Hana, Alexandr Rosen, Svatava Škodová and Barbora Štindlová .......................... 11

*Annotation Scheme for Social Network Extraction from Text*
Apoorv Agarwal, Owen C. Rambow and Rebecca J. Passonneau .............................. 20

*Agile Corpus Annotation in Practice: An Overview of Manual and Automatic Annotation of CVs*
Bea Alex, Claire Grover, Rongzhou Shen and Mijail Kabadjov .............................. 29

*Consistency Checking for Treebank Alignment*
Markus Dickinson and Yvonne Samuelsson .............................................. 38

*Anveshan: A Framework for Analysis of Multiple Annotators' Labeling Behavior*
Vikas Bhardwaj, Rebecca Passonneau, Ansaf Salleb-Aouissi and Nancy Ide ................... 47

*Influence of Pre-Annotation on POS-Tagged Corpus Development*
Karën Fort and Benoît Sagot ........................................................ 56

*To Annotate More Accurately or to Annotate More*
Dmitriy Dligach, Rodney Nielsen and Martha Palmer ....................................... 64

*Annotating Underquantification*
Aurelie Herbelot and Ann Copestake .................................................. 73

*PropBank Annotation of Multilingual Light Verb Constructions*
Jena D. Hwang, Archna Bhatia, Claire Bonial, Aous Mansouri, Ashwini Vaidya, Nianwen Xue and Martha Palmer ............................................................... 82

*Retrieving Correct Semantic Boundaries in Dependency Structure*
Jinho Choi and Martha Palmer ....................................................... 91

*Complex Predicates Annotation in a Corpus of Portuguese*
Iris Hendrickx, Amália Mendes, Sílvia Pereira, Anabela Gonçalves and Inês Duarte .......... 100

*Using an Online Tool for the Documentation of Edo Language*
Ota Ogie .......................................................................... 109

*Cross-Lingual Validity of PropBank in the Manual Annotation of French*
Lonneke van der Plas, Tanja Samardzic and Paola Merlo ................................. 113

*Characteristics of High Agreement Affect Annotation in Text*
Cecilia Ovesdotter Alm ............................................................. 118

*The Deep Re-Annotation in a Chinese Scientific Treebank*
Kun Yu, Xiangli Wang, Yusuke Miyao, Takuya Matsuzaki and Junichi Tsujii ................. 123

*The Unified Annotation of Syntax and Discourse in the Copenhagen Dependency Treebanks*
Matthias Buch-Kromann and Iørn Korzen .............................................. 127

*Identifying Sources of Inter-Annotator Variation: Evaluating Two Models of Argument Analysis*
Barbara White . . . . . 132

*Dependency-Based PropBanking of Clinical Finnish*
Katri Haverinen, Filip Ginter, Timo Viljanen, Veronika Laippala and Tapio Salakoski . . . . . 137

*Building the Syntactic Reference Corpus of Medieval French Using NotaBene RDF Annotation Tool*
Nicolas Mazziotta . . . . . 142

*Chunking German: An Unsolved Problem*
Sandra Kübler, Kathrin Beck, Erhard Hinrichs and Heike Telljohann . . . . . 147

*Proposal for MWE Annotation in Running Text*
Iris Hendrickx, Amália Mendes and Sandra Antunes . . . . . 152

*A Feature Type Classification for Therapeutic Purposes: A Preliminary Evaluation with Non-Expert Speakers*
Gianluca E. Lebani and Emanuele Pianta . . . . . 157

*Annotating Korean Demonstratives*
Sun-Hee Lee and Jae-young Song . . . . . 162

*Creating and Exploiting a Resource of Parallel Parses*
Christian Chiarcos, Kerstin Eckart and Julia Ritz . . . . . 166

*From Descriptive Annotation to Grammar Specification*
Lars Hellan . . . . . 172

*An Annotation Schema for Preposition Senses in German*
Antje Müller, Olaf Hülscher, Claudia Roch, Katja Keßelmeier, Tobias Stadtfeld, Jan Strunk and Tibor Kiss . . . . . 177

*OTTO: A Transcription and Management Tool for Historical Texts*
Stefanie Dipper, Lara Kresse, Martin Schnurrenberger and Seong-Eun Cho . . . . . 182

*Multimodal Annotation of Conversational Data*
Philippe Blache, Roxane Bertrand, Emmanuel Bruno, Brigitte Bigi, Robert Espesser, Gaelle Ferre, Mathilde Guardiola, Daniel Hirst, Ning Tan, Edlira Cela, Jean-Claude Martin, Stéphane Rauzy, Mary-Annick Morel, Elisabeth Murisasco and Irina Nesterenko . . . . . 186

*Combining Parallel Treebanks and Geo-Tagging*
Martin Volk, Anne Goehring and Torsten Marek . . . . . 192

*Challenges of Cheap Resource Creation*
Jirka Hana and Anna Feldman . . . . . 197

*Discourse Relation Configurations in Turkish and an Annotation Environment*
Berfin Aktaş, Cem Bozşahin and Deniz Zeyrek . . . . . 202

*An Overview of the CRAFT Concept Annotation Guidelines*
Michael Bada, Miriam Eckert, Martha Palmer and Lawrence Hunter . . . . . 207

*Syntactic Tree Queries in Prolog*
Gerlof Bouma . . . . . 212

*An Integrated Tool for Annotating Historical Corpora*
Pablo Picasso Feliciano de Faria, Fabio Natanael Kepler and Maria Clara Paixão de Sousa . . . . 217

*The Revised Arabic PropBank*
Wajdi Zaghouani, Mona Diab, Aous Mansouri, Sameer Pradhan and Martha Palmer . . . . . . . . . . 222

*PackPlay: Mining Semantic Data in Collaborative Games*
Nathan Green, Paul Breimyer, Vinay Kumar and Nagiza Samatova . . . . . . . . . . . . . . . . . . . . . . . . 227

*A Proposal for a Configurable Silver Standard*
Udo Hahn, Katrin Tomanek, Elena Beisswanger and Erik Faessler . . . . . . . . . . . . . . . . . . . . . . . . . 235

*A Hybrid Model for Annotating Named Entity Training Corpora*
Robert Voyer, Valerie Nygaard, Will Fitzgerald and Hannah Copperman . . . . . . . . . . . . . . . . . . . . 243

*Anatomy of Annotation Schemes: Mapping to GrAF*
Nancy Ide and Harry Bunt . . . . . . . . . . . . . . . . . . . . . . . . . . . . . . . . . . . . . . . . . . . . . . . . . . . . . . . . . . 247

*Annotating Participant Reference in English Spoken Conversation*
John Niekrasz and Johanna Moore . . . . . . . . . . . . . . . . . . . . . . . . . . . . . . . . . . . . . . . . . . . . . . . . . . . 256

*Design and Evaluation of Shared Prosodic Annotation for Spontaneous French Speech: From Expert Knowledge to Non-Expert Annotation*
Anne Lacheret-Dujour, Nicolas Obin and Mathieu Avanzi . . . . . . . . . . . . . . . . . . . . . . . . . . . . . . . . 265

*Depends on What the French Say - Spoken Corpus Annotation with and beyond Syntactic Functions*
José Deulofeu, Lucie Duffort, Kim Gerdes, Sylvain Kahane and Paola Pietrandrea . . . . . . . . . . . 274

*The Annotation Scheme of the Turkish Discourse Bank and an Evaluation of Inconsistent Annotations*
Deniz Zeyrek, Işin Demirşahin, Ayişiği Sevdik-Çalli, Hale Ögel Balaban, and Ümit Deniz Turan
282

# Conference Program

**Thursday, July 15, 2010**

**08:40–08:50 Opening remarks**

08:50–10:30 Session I (Chair: Nianwen Xue)

08:50–09:15 *EmotiBlog: A Finer-Grained and More Precise Learning of Subjectivity Expression Models*
Ester Boldrini, Alexandra Balahur, Patricio Martínez-Barco and Andrés Montoyo

09:15–09:40 *Error-Tagged Learner Corpus of Czech*
Jirka Hana, Alexandr Rosen, Svatava Škodová and Barbora Štindlová

09:40–10:05 *Annotation Scheme for Social Network Extraction from Text*
Apoorv Agarwal, Owen C. Rambow and Rebecca J. Passonneau

10:05–10:30 *Agile Corpus Annotation in Practice: An Overview of Manual and Automatic Annotation of CVs*
Bea Alex, Claire Grover, Rongzhou Shen and Mijail Kabadjov

10:30–11:00 Break

11:00–12:40 Session II (Chair: Martha Palmer)

11:00–11:25 *Consistency Checking for Treebank Alignment*
Markus Dickinson and Yvonne Samuelsson

11:25–11:50 *Anveshan: A Framework for Analysis of Multiple Annotators' Labeling Behavior*
Vikas Bhardwaj, Rebecca Passonneau, Ansaf Salleb-Aouissi and Nancy Ide

11:50–12:15 *Influence of Pre-Annotation on POS-Tagged Corpus Development*
Karën Fort and Benoît Sagot

12:15–12:40 *To Annotate More Accurately or to Annotate More*
Dmitriy Dligach, Rodney Nielsen and Martha Palmer

12:40–13:50 Lunch

**Thursday, July 15, 2010 (continued)**

13:50–15:30 Session III (Chair: Manfred Stede)

13:50–14:15 *Annotating Underquantification*
Aurelie Herbelot and Ann Copestake

14:15–14:40 *PropBank Annotation of Multilingual Light Verb Constructions*
Jena D. Hwang, Archna Bhatia, Claire Bonial, Aous Mansouri, Ashwini Vaidya, Nianwen Xue and Martha Palmer

14:40–15:05 *Retrieving Correct Semantic Boundaries in Dependency Structure*
Jinho Choi and Martha Palmer

15:05–15:30 *Complex Predicates Annotation in a Corpus of Portuguese*
Iris Hendrickx, Amália Mendes, Sílvia Pereira, Anabela Gonçalves and Inês Duarte

15:30–16:00 Break

16:00–17:30 Poster session (Chair: Nianwen Xue)

*Using an Online Tool for the Documentation of Edo Language*
Ota Ogie

*Cross-Lingual Validity of PropBank in the Manual Annotation of French*
Lonneke van der Plas, Tanja Samardzic and Paola Merlo

*Characteristics of High Agreement Affect Annotation in Text*
Cecilia Ovesdotter Alm

*The Deep Re-Annotation in a Chinese Scientific Treebank*
Kun Yu, Xiangli Wang, Yusuke Miyao, Takuya Matsuzaki and Junichi Tsujii

*The Unified Annotation of Syntax and Discourse in the Copenhagen Dependency Treebanks*
Matthias Buch-Kromann and Iørn Korzen

*Identifying Sources of Inter-Annotator Variation: Evaluating Two Models of Argument Analysis*
Barbara White

*Dependency-Based PropBanking of Clinical Finnish*
Katri Haverinen, Filip Ginter, Timo Viljanen, Veronika Laippala and Tapio Salakoski

*Building the Syntactic Reference Corpus of Medieval French Using NotaBene RDF Annotation Tool*
Nicolas Mazziotta

*Chunking German: An Unsolved Problem*
Sandra Kübler, Kathrin Beck, Erhard Hinrichs and Heike Telljohann

*Proposal for MWE Annotation in Running Text*
Iris Hendrickx, Amália Mendes and Sandra Antunes

*A Feature Type Classification for Therapeutic Purposes: A Preliminary Evaluation with Non-Expert Speakers*
Gianluca E. Lebani and Emanuele Pianta

*Annotating Korean Demonstratives*
Sun-Hee Lee and Jae-young Song

*Creating and Exploiting a Resource of Parallel Parses*
Christian Chiarcos, Kerstin Eckart and Julia Ritz

*From Descriptive Annotation to Grammar Specification*
Lars Hellan

*An Annotation Schema for Preposition Senses in German*
Antje Müller, Olaf Hülscher, Claudia Roch, Katja Keßelmeier, Tobias Stadtfeld, Jan Strunk and Tibor Kiss

*OTTO: A Transcription and Management Tool for Historical Texts*
Stefanie Dipper, Lara Kresse, Martin Schnurrenberger and Seong-Eun Cho

*Multimodal Annotation of Conversational Data*
Philippe Blache, Roxane Bertrand, Emmanuel Bruno, Brigitte Bigi, Robert Espesser, Gaelle Ferre, Mathilde Guardiola, Daniel Hirst, Ning Tan, Edlira Cela, Jean-Claude Martin, Stéphane Rauzy, Mary-Annick Morel, Elisabeth Murisasco and Irina Nesterenko

*Combining Parallel Treebanks and Geo-Tagging*
Martin Volk, Anne Goehring and Torsten Marek

**Thursday, July 15, 2010 (continued)**

*Challenges of Cheap Resource Creation*
Jirka Hana and Anna Feldman

*Discourse Relation Configurations in Turkish and an Annotation Environment*
Berfin Aktaş, Cem Bozşahin and Deniz Zeyrek

*An Overview of the CRAFT Concept Annotation Guidelines*
Michael Bada, Miriam Eckert, Martha Palmer and Lawrence Hunter

*Syntactic Tree Queries in Prolog*
Gerlof Bouma

*An Integrated Tool for Annotating Historical Corpora*
Pablo Picasso Feliciano de Faria, Fabio Natanael Kepler and Maria Clara Paixão de Sousa

*The Revised Arabic PropBank*
Wajdi Zaghouani, Mona Diab, Aous Mansouri, Sameer Pradhan and Martha Palmer

**Friday, July 16, 2010**

08:50–10:30 Session IV (Chair: Massimo Poesio)

08:50–09:15 *PackPlay: Mining Semantic Data in Collaborative Games*
Nathan Green, Paul Breimyer, Vinay Kumar and Nagiza Samatova

09:15–09:40 *A Proposal for a Configurable Silver Standard*
Udo Hahn, Katrin Tomanek, Elena Beisswanger and Erik Faessler

09:40–10:05 *A Hybrid Model for Annotating Named Entity Training Corpora*
Robert Voyer, Valerie Nygaard, Will Fitzgerald and Hannah Copperman

10:05–10:30 *Anatomy of Annotation Schemes: Mapping to GrAF*
Nancy Ide and Harry Bunt

10:30–11:00 Break

**Friday, July 16, 2010 (continued)**

11:00–12:40 Session V (Chair: Nancy Ide)

11:00–11:25 *Annotating Participant Reference in English Spoken Conversation*
John Niekrasz and Johanna Moore

11:25–11:50 *Design and Evaluation of Shared Prosodic Annotation for Spontaneous French Speech: From Expert Knowledge to Non-Expert Annotation*
Anne Lacheret-Dujour, Nicolas Obin and Mathieu Avanzi

11:50–12:15 *Depends on What the French Say - Spoken Corpus Annotation with and beyond Syntactic Functions*
José Deulofeu, Lucie Duffort, Kim Gerdes, Sylvain Kahane and Paola Pietrandrea

12:15–12:40 *The Annotation Scheme of the Turkish Discourse Bank and an Evaluation of Inconsistent Annotations*
Deniz Zeyrek, Işin Demirşahin, Ayişiği Sevdik-Çalli, Hale Ögel Balaban, and Ümit Deniz Turan

12:40–13:00 Closing remarks

# EmotiBlog: a finer-grained and more precise learning of subjectivity expression models

**Ester Boldrini**
University of Alicante, Department of Software and Computing Systems
eboldrini@dlsi.ua.es

**Alexandra Balahur**
University of Alicante, Department of Software and Computing Systems
abalahur@dlsi.ua.es

**Patricio Martínez-Barco**
University of Alicante, Department of Software and Computing Systems
patricio@dlsi.ua.es

**Andrés Montoyo**
University of Alicante, Department of Software and Computing Systems
montoyo@dlsi.ua.es

## Abstract

The exponential growth of the subjective information in the framework of the Web 2.0 has led to the need to create Natural Language Processing tools able to analyse and process such data for multiple practical applications. They require training on specifically annotated corpora, whose level of detail must be fine enough to capture the phenomena involved. This paper presents *EmotiBlog* – a fine-grained annotation scheme for subjectivity. We show the manner in which it is built and demonstrate the benefits it brings to the systems using it for training, through the experiments we carried out on opinion mining and emotion detection. We employ corpora of different textual genres –a set of annotated reported speech extracted from news articles, the set of news titles annotated with polarity and emotion from the SemEval 2007 (Task 14) and ISEAR, a corpus of real-life self-expressed emotion. We also show how the model built from the EmotiBlog annotations can be enhanced with external resources. The results demonstrate that *EmotiBlog*, through its structure and annotation paradigm, offers high quality training data for systems dealing both with opinion mining, as well as emotion detection.

## 1 Credits

This paper has been supported by Ministerio de Ciencia e Innovación- Spanish Government (grant no. TIN2009-13391-C04-01), and Conselleria d'Educación-Generalitat Valenciana (grant no. PROMETEO/2009/119 and A-COMP/2010/288).

## 2 Introduction

The exponential growth of the subjective information with Web 2.0 created the need to develop new Natural Language Processing (NLP) tools to automatically process and manage the content available on the Internet. Apart from the traditional textual genres, at present we have new ones such as blogs, forums and reviews. The main difference between them is that the latter are predominantly subjective, containing personal judgments. At the moment, NLP tools and methods for analyzing objective information have a better performance than the new ones the research community is creating for managing the subjective content. The survey called "*The State of the Blogosphere 2009*", published by Technorati[1], demonstrates that users are blogging more than ever. Furthermore, in contrast to the general idea about bloggers, each day it is more and more the number of professionals who decide to use this means of communication, contradicting the common belief about the predominance of an informal editing (Balahur et al., 2009). Due to the growing interest in this text type, the subjective data of the Web is increasing on a daily basis, becoming a reflection of people's opinion about a wide range of topics. (Cui, Mittal and Datar, 2006). Blogs represent an important source of real-time, unbiased information, useful for the development of many applications for concrete purposes. Given the proved importance of automatically processing this data, a new task has appeared in NLP task, dealing with the treatment of subjective data: Sentiment Analysis (SA). The main objective of this paper is to present *EmotiBlog* (Boldrini et al., 2009), a fine-grained annotation scheme for labeling subjectivity in the new textual genres. Subjectivity

[1] http://technorati.com/



*Proceedings of the Fourth Linguistic Annotation Workshop, ACL 2010*, pages 1–10,
Uppsala, Sweden, 15-16 July 2010. ©2010 Association for Computational Linguistics

can be reflected in text through expressions of emotions beliefs, views (a way of considering something)[2] and opinions, generally denominated "private states" (Uspensky, 1973), not open to verification (Wiebe, 1994). We performed a series of experiments focused on demonstrating that *EmotiBlog* represents a step forward to previous research in this field; its use allows a finer-grained and more precise learning of subjectivity expression models. Starting form (Wiebe, Wilson and Cardie, 2005) we created an annotation schema able to capture a wide range and key elements, which give subjectivity, moving a step forward the mere polarity recognition. In particular, the experiments concern expressions of emotion, as a finer-grained analysis of affect in text and a subsequent task to opinion mining (OM) and classification. To that aim, we employ corpora of different textual genres– a set of annotated reported speech extracted from news articles (denominated JRC quotes) (Balahur et al., 2010) and the set of news titles annotated with polarity and emotion from the SemEval 2007 Task No. 14 (Strapparava and Mihalcea, 2007), as well as a corpus of real-life self-expressed emotion entitled ISEAR (Scherer and Walbott, 1999). We subsequently show, through the quality of the results obtained, that *EmotiBlog*, through its structure and annotation paradigm, offers high quality training for systems dealing both with opinion mining, as well as emotion detection.

## 3 Motivation and Contribution

The main motivation of this research is the demonstrated necessity to work towards the harmonization and interoperability of the increasingly large number of tools and frameworks that support the creation, instantiation, manipulation, querying, and exploitation of annotated resource. This necessity is stressed by the new tools and resources, which have been recently created for processing the subjectivity in the new-textual genres born with the Web 2.0. Such predominantly subjective data is increasing at an exponential rate (about 75000 new blogs are reported to be created every day) and contains opinions on the most diverse set of topics. Given its worldwide availability, the subjective data on the Web has become a primary source of information (Balahur et al., 2009). As a consequence, new mechanisms have to be implemented so that this data is effectively analyzed and processed. The main challenge of the opinionated content is that, unlike the objective one, which presents facts, the subjective information is most of the times difficult and complex to extract and classify using in grammatically static and fixed rules. Expression of subjectivity is more spontaneous and even if the majority is quite formal, new means of expressivity can be encountered, such as the use of colloquialisms, sayings, collocations or anomalies in the use of punctuation; this is motivated by the fact that subjectivity expression is part of our daily life. For example, at the time of taking a decision, people search for information and opinions expressed on the Web on their matter of interest and base their final decision on the information found. At the same time, when using a product, people often write reviews on it, so that others can have a better idea of the performance of that product before purchasing it. Therefore, on the one hand, the growing volume of opinion information available on the Web allows for better and more informed decisions of the users. On the other hand, the amount of data to be analyzed requires the development of specialized NLP systems that automatically extract, classify and summarize the data available on the Web on different topics. (Esuli and Sebastiani, 2006) define OM as a recent discipline at the crossroads of Information Retrieval and Computational Linguistics, which is concerned not with the topic a document is about, but with the opinion it expresses. Research in this field has proven the task to be very difficult, due to the high semantic variability of affective language. Different authors have addressed the problem of extracting and classifying opinion from different perspectives and at different levels, depending on a series of factors which can be level of interest (overall/specific), querying formula *("Nokia E65"/"Why do people buy Nokia E65?")*, type of text (review on forum/blog/dialogue/press article), and manner of expression of opinion - directly (using opinion statements, e.g. *"I think this product is wonderful!"/"This is a bright initiative"*), indirectly (using affect vocabulary, e.g. *"I love the pictures this camera takes!"/"Personally, I am shocked one can propose such a law!"*) or implicitly (using adjectives and evaluative expressions, e.g. "It's light *as a feather and fits right into my pocket!"*). While determining the overall opinion on a movie is sufficient for taking the decision to watch it or not, when buying a product, people are interested in the individual opinions on the different prod-

[2] http://dictionary.cambridge.org/

uct characteristics. When discussing a person, one can judge and give opinion on the person's actions. Moreover, the approaches taken can vary depending on the manner in which a user asks for the data (general formula such as *"opinions on X" or* a specific question *"Why do people like X?"* and the text source that needs to be queried). Retrieving opinion information in newspaper articles or blogs posts is more complex, because it involves the detection of different discussion topics, the subjective phrases present and subsequently their classification according to polarity. Especially in the blog area, determining points of view expressed in dialogues together with the mixture of quotes and pastes from newspapers on a topic can, additionally, involve determining the persons present and whether or not the opinion expressed is on the required topic or on a point previously made by another speaker. This difficult NLP problem requires the use of specialized data for system training and tuning, gathered, annotated and tested within the different text spheres. At the present moment, these specialized resources are scarce and when they exist, they are rather simplistically annotated or highly domain-dependent. Moreover, most of these resources created are for the English. The contribution we describe in this paper intends to propose solutions to the above-mentioned problems, and consists of the following points: first of all, we overcome the problem of corpora scarcity in other languages except English and also improve the English ones; we present the manner in which we compiled a multilingual corpus of blog posts on different topics of interest in three languages-Spanish, Italian and English. The second issue we tried to solve was the coarse-grained annotation schemas employed in other annotation schema. Thus, we describe the new annotation model, EmotiBlog built up in order to capture the different subjectivity/objectivity, emotion/opinion/attitude aspects we are interested in at a finer-grained level. We justify the need for a more detailed annotation model, the sources and the reasons taken into consideration when constructing the corpus and its annotation. Thirdly, we address an aspect strongly related to blogs annotation: due the presence of "copy and pastes" from news articles or other blogs, the frequent quotes, we include the annotation of both the directly indicated source, as well as the anaphoric references at cross-document level. We discuss on the problems encountered at different stages and comment upon some of the conclusions we have reached while performing this research. this research. Finally, we conclude on our approach and propose the lines for future work.

## 4 Related Work

In recent years, different researchers have addressed the needs and possible methodologies from the linguistic, theoretical and practical points of view. Thus, the first step involved resided in building lexical resources of affect, such as WordNet Affect (Strapparava and Valitutti, 2004), SentiWordNet (Esuli and Sebastiani, 2006), Micro-WNOP (Cerini et. Al, 2007) or "emotion triggers" (Balahur and Montoyo, 2009). All these lexicons contain single words, whose polarity and emotions are not necessarily the ones annotated within the resource in a larger context. We also employed the ISEAR corpus, consisting of phrases where people describe a situation when they felt a certain emotion. Our work, therefore, concentrates on annotating larger text spans, in order to consider the undeniable influence of the context. The starting point of research in emotion is represented by (Balahur and Montoyo, 2008), who centered the idea of subjectivity around that of private states, and set the benchmark for subjectivity analysis as the recognition of opinion-oriented language in order to distinguish it from objective language and giving a method to annotate a corpus depending on these two aspects – MPQA (Wiebe, Wilson and Cardie, 2005). Furthermore, authors show that this initial discrimination is crucial for the sentiment task, as part of Opinion Information Retrieval (last three editions of the TREC Blog tracks[3] competitions, the TAC 2008 competition[4]), Information Extraction (Riloff and Wiebe, 2003) and Question Answering (Stoyanov et al., 2004) systems. Once this discrimination is done, or in the case of texts containing only or mostly subjective language (such as e-reviews), opinion mining becomes a polarity classification task. Our work takes into consideration this initial discrimination, but we also add a deeper level of emotion annotation. Since expressions of emotion are also highly related to opinions, related work also includes customer review classification at a document level, sentiment classification using unsupervised methods (Turney, 2002), Machine Learning techniques (Pang and Lee, 2002), scoring of features (Dave, Lawrence and Pennock, 2003), using PMI, syntactic relations

[3] http://trec.nist.gov/data/blog.html

[4] http://www.nist.gov/tac/

and other attributes with SVM (Mullena and Collier, 2004), sentiment classification considering rating scales (Pang and Lee, 2002), supervised and unsupervised methods (Chaovalit and Zhou, 2005) and semisupervised learning (Goldberg and Zhou, 2006). Research in classification at a document level included sentiment classification of reviews (Ng, Dasgupta and Arifin, 2006), sentiment classification on customer feedback data (Gamon, Aue, Corston-Oliver, Ringger, 2005), comparative experiments (Cui, Mittal and Datar, 2006). Other research has been conducted in analysing sentiment at a sentence level using bootstrapping techniques (Riloff, Wiebe, 2003), considering gradable adjectives (Hatzivassiloglou, Wiebe, 2000), semisupervised learning with the initial training some strong patterns and then applying NB or self-training (Wiebe and Riloff, 2005) finding strength of opinions (Wolson, Wiebe, Hwa, 2004) sum up orientations of opinion words in a sentence (or within some word window) (Kim and Hovy, 2004), (Wilson and Wiebe, 2004), determining the semantic orientation of words and phrases (Turney and Littman, 2003), identifying opinion holders (Stoyanov and Cardie, 2006), comparative sentence and relation extraction and feature-based opinion mining and summarization (Turney, 2002). Finally, fine-grained, feature-based opinion summarization is defined in (Hu and Liu, 2004) and researched in (Turney, 2002) or (Pang and Lee, 2002). All these approaches concentrate on finding and classifying the polarity of opinion words, which are mostly adjectives, without taking into account modifiers or the context in general. Our work, on the other hand, represents the first step towards achieving a contextual comprehension of the linguistic roots of emotion expression.

## 5 Corpora

It is well known that nowadays blogs are the second way of communication most used after the e-mail. They are extremely useful and a poll for discussing about any topic with the world. For this reason, the first corpus object of our study is a collection of blog posts extracted from the Web. The texts we selected have distinctive features, extremely different from traditional textual ones. In fact people writing a post can use an informal language colloquialism, emoticons, etc. to express their feelings and it is not rare to find a mix of sources in the same post; people usually mention some facts or discourses and then they give their opinion about them. As we can deduce, the source detection represents one of the most complex tasks. As we mentioned above, we carried out a multilingual research, collecting texts in three languages: Spanish, Italian, and English about three subjects of interest. The first one contains blog posts commenting upon the signing of the Kyoto Protocol against global warming, the second collection consists of blog entries about the Mugabe government in Zimbabwe, and finally we selected a series of blog posts discussing the issues related to the 2008 USA presidential elections. For each of the abovementioned topics, we have gathered 100 texts, summing up a total of 30.000 words approximately for each language. However in this research we start with English but consider as future work labeling the other languages we have. The second corpus we employed for this research is a collection of 1592 quotes extracted from the news in April 2008. As a consequence they are about many different topics and in English (Balahur and Steinberg, 2009). Both of these corpora have been annotated with *EmotiBlog* that is presented in the next section.

## 6 EmotiBlog Annotation Model

Our annotation schema can be defined as a fine-grained model for labelling subjectivity of the new-textual genres born with the Web 2.0. As mentioned above, it represents a step forward to previous research and it is focused on detecting the linguistic elements, which give subjectivity to the text. The *EmotiBlog* annotation is divided into different levels (Figure 1).

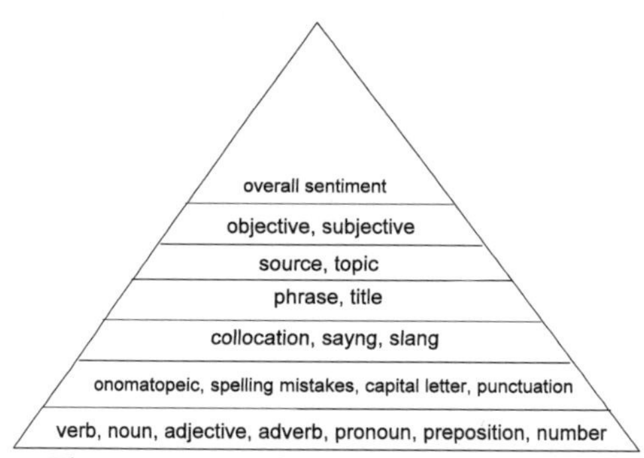

Figure 1: General structure of *EmotiBlog*.

As we can observe in Figure 1, the first distinction to be made is between objective and subjective speech. If we are labelling an objective sentence, we insert the source element, while if we are annotating a subjective discourse, a list of elements with the corresponding attributes have to be added. We select among the list of subjective elements and specify the element's attributes. Table 1 presents the annotation model in detail.

| Elem. | Description |
|---|---|
| Obj. speech | Confidence, comment, source, target. |
| Subj. speech | Confidence, comment, level, emotion, phenomenon, polarity, source and target. |
| Adjectives | Confidence, comment, level, emotion, phenomenon, modifier/not, polarity, source and target. |
| Adverbs | Confidence, comment, level, emotion, phenomenon, modifier/not, polarity, source and target. |
| Verbs | Confidence, comment, level, emotion, phenomenon, polarity, mode, source and target. |
| Anaphora | Confidence, comment, type, source and target. |
| Capital letter | Confidence, comment, level, emotion, phenomenon, modifier/not, polarity, source and target. |
| Punctuation | Confidence, comment, level, emotion, phenomenon, modifier/not, polarity, source and target. |
| Names | Confidence, comment, level, emotion, phenomenon, modifier/not, polarity, and source. |
| Phenomenon | Confidence, comment, type: collocation, saying, slang, title, and rhetoric. |
| Reader Interpretation | Confidence, comment, level, emotion, phenomenon, polarity, source and target. |
| Author Interpretation | Confidence, comment, level, emotion, phenomenon, polarity, source and target. |
| Emotions | Confidence, comment, accept, anger, anticipation, anxiety, appreciation, bad, bewilderment, comfort, … |

Table 1: *EmotiBlog* structure

Each element of the discourse has its own attributes with a series of features, which have to be annotated. Due to space reasons it is impossible to detail each one of them, however we would like to underline the most innovative and relevant. For each element we are labelling the annotator has to insert his level of confidence. In this way we will assign each label a weight that will be computed for future evaluations. Moreover, the annotator has to insert the polarity, which can be positive or negative, the level (high, medium, low) and also the sentiment this element is expressing. Table 2 presents a complete list of the emotions we selected to be part of *EmotiBlog*. We grouped all sentiments into subgroups in order to help the evaluation process. In fact emotions of the same subgroup will have less impact when calculating the inter-annotation agreement. In order to make this subdivision proper and effective division, we were inspired by (Scherer, 2005) who created an alternative dimensional structure of the semantic space for emotions. The graph below represents the mapping of the term Russell (1983) uses for his claim of an emotion circumflex in two-dimensional valence by activity/arousal space (upper-case terms). As we can appreciate, the circle is divided by 4 axes. Moreover, Scherer distinguishes between positive and negative sentiments and after that between active and passive. Furthermore emotions are grouped between obstructive and conductive, and finally between high power and low power control. We started form this classification, grouping sentiments into positive and negative, but we divided them as high/low power control, obstructive/conductive and active/passive. Further on, we distributed the sentiments within our list into the Scherer slots creating other smaller categories included in the abovementioned general ones. The result of this division is shown in Table 2:

| Group | Emotions |
|---|---|
| Criticism | Sarcasm, irony, incorrect, criticism, objection, opposition, scepticism. |
| Happiness | Joy, joke. |
| Support | Accept, correct, good, hope, support, trust, rapture, respect, patience, appreciation, excuse. |
| Importance | Important, interesting, will, justice, longing, anticipation, revenge. |
| Gratitude | Thank. |
| Guilt | Guilt, vexation. |
| Fear | Fear, fright, troubledness, anxiety. |
| Surprise | Surprise, bewilderment, disappointment, consternation. |
| Anger | Rage, hatred, enmity, wrath, force, anger, revendication. |
| Envy | Envy, rivalry, jealousy. |
| Indifference | Unimportant, yield, sluggishness. |
| Pity | Compassion, shame, grief. |
| Pain | Sadness, lament, remorse, mourning, depression, despondency. |
| Shyness | Timidity. |
| Bad | Bad, malice, disgust, greed. |

Table 2: Alternative dimensional structures of the semantic space for emotions

Following with the description of the model, we said that the first distinction to be made is between objective and subjective speech. Analysing the texts we collected, we realised that even if the writer uses an objective speech, sometimes it is just apparently objective and for this reason we added two elements: reader and author interpretation. The first one is the impression/feeling/reaction the reader has reading the intervention and what s/he can deduce from the piece of text and the author interpretation is what we can understand from the author (politic orientation, preferences). All this information can be deduced form some linguistic elements that apparently are not so objective as they may appear. Another innovative element we inserted in the model is the coreference but just at a cross-post level. It is necessary because blogs are composed by posts linked between them and thus cross-document coreference can help the reader to follow the conversations. We also label the unusual usage of capital letters and repeated punctuation. In fact, it is very common in blogs to find words written in capital letter or with no conventional usage of punctuation; these features usually mean shouts or a particular mood of the writer. Using EmotiBlog, we annotate the single elements, but we also mark sayings or collocations, representative of each language. A saying is a well-known and wise statement, which often has a meaning, different from the simple meanings of the words it contains[5]; while a collocation is a word or phrase, which is frequently used with another word or phrase, in a way that sounds correct to native speakers, but might not be expected from the individual words' meanings6. Finally we insert for each element the source and topic. An example of annotation can be: <phenomenon target="Kyoto Protocol" category="phrase" degree="medium" source="w" polarity="positive" emotion="good">The Onion has a <adjective target="Kyoto Protocol" phenomenon="phrase" degree="medium" polarity="positive" emotion="good" source="w" ismodifier="yes">great</adjective> story today titled "Bush Told to Sign Birthday Treaty for Someone Named Kyoto." </phenomenon>

## 7 Experiments and Evaluation

In order to evaluate the appropriateness of the *EmotiBlog* annotation scheme and to prove that the fine-grained level it aims at has a positive impact on the performance of the systems employing it as training, we performed several experiments. Given that a) *EmotiBlog* contains annotations for individual words, as well as for multi-word expressions and at a sentence level, and b) they are labeled with polarity, but also emotion, our experiments show how the annotated elements can be used as training for the opinion mining and polarity classification task, as well as for emotion detection. Moreover, taking into consideration the fact that *EmotiBlog* labels the intensity level of the annotated elements, we performed a brief experiment on determining the sentiment intensity, measured on a three-level scale: low, medium and high. In order to perform these three different evaluations, we chose three different corpora. The first one is a collection of quotes (reported speech) from newspaper articles presented in (Balahur et al., 2010), enriched with the manual fine-grained annotation of *EmotiBlog*[7]; the second one is the collection of newspaper titles in the test set of the SemEval 2007 task number 14 – Affective Text. Finally, the third one is a corpus of self-reported emotional response – ISEAR (Scherer and Walbott, 1999). The intensity classification task is evaluated only on the second corpus, given that it is the only one in which scores between -100 and 0 and 0 and 100, respectively, are given for the polarity of the titles.

### 6.1 Creation of training models

For the OM and polarity classification task, we first extracted the Named Entities contained in the annotations using Lingpipe and united through a "_" all the tokens pertaining to the NE. All the annotations of punctuation signs that had a specific meaning together were also united under a single punctuation sign. Subsequently, we processed the annotated data, using Minipar. We compute, for each word in a sentence, a series of features (some of these features are used in (Choi et al., 2005):

- the part of speech (POS)
- capitalization (if all letters are in capitals, if only the first letter is in capitals, and if it is a NE or not)
- opinionatedness/intensity/emotion - if the word is annotated as opinion word, its polarity, i.e. 1 and -1 if the word is positive or negative, respectively and 0 if it is not an opinion word, its intensity (1.2 or 3) and 0 if it is not a subjective word, its emotion (if it has, none otherwise)
- syntactic relatedness with other opinion word – if it is directly dependent of an opinion word or modifier (0 or 1), plus the polarity/intensity and emotion of this word (0 for all the components otherwise)
- role in 2-word, 3-word and 4-word annotations: opinionatedness, intensity and emotion of the other words contained in the annotation, direct dependency relations with them if they exist and 0 otherwise.

We compute the length of the longest sentence in *EmotiBlog*. The feature vector for each of the sentences contains the feature vectors of each of its words and 0s for the corresponding feature vectors of the words, which the current sentence has less than the longest annotated sentence. Finally, we add for each sentence as feature binary features for subjectivity and polarity, the value corresponding to the intensity of opinion and the

[5] Definition according to the Cambridge Advanced Learner's Dictionary

[6] Definition according to the Cambridge Advanced Learner's Dictionary

[7] Freely available on request to the authors.

general emotion. These feature vectors are fed into the Weka[8] SVM SMO ML algorithm and a model is created (EmotiBlog I). A second model (EmotiBlog II) is created by adding to the collection of single opinion and emotion words annotated in EmotiBlog, the Opinion Finder lexicon and the opinion words found in MicroWordNet, the General Inquirer resource and WordNet Affect.

### 6.2 Evaluation of models on test sets

In order to evaluate the performance of the models extracted from the features of the annotations in *EmotiBlog*, we performed different tests. The first one regarded the evaluation of the polarity and intensity classification task using the *Emoitblog* I and II constructed models on two test sets – the JRC quotes collection and the SemEval 2007 Task Number 14 test set. Since the quotes often contain more than a sentence, we consider the polarity and intensity of the entire quote as the most frequent result in each class, corresponding to its constituent sentences. Also, given the fact that the SemEval Affective Text headlines were given intensity values between -100 and 100, we mapped the values contained in the Gold Standard of the task into three categories: [-100, -67] is high (value 3 in intensity) and negative (value -1 in polarity), [-66, 34] medium negative and [33, 1] is low negative. The values between [1 and 100] are mapped in the same manner to the positive category. 0 was considered objective, so containing the value 0 for intensity. The results are presented in Table 3 (the values I and II correspond to the models EmotiBlog I and EmotiBlog II):

| Test Corpus | Evaluation type | Precision | Recall |
|---|---|---|---|
| JRC quotes I | Polarity | 32.13 | 54.09 |
| | Intensity | 36.00 | 53.2 |
| JRC quotes II | Polarity | 36.4 | 51.00 |
| | Intensity | 38.7 | 57.81 |
| SemEval I | Polarity | 38.57 | 51.3 |
| | Intensity | 37.39 | 50.9 |
| SemEval II | Polarity | 35.8 | 58.68 |
| | Intensity | 32.3 | 50.4 |

Table 3. Results for polarity and intensity classification using the models built from the EmotiBlog annotations

The results shown in Table 2 show a significantly high improvement over the results obtained in the SemEval task in 2007. This is explainable, on the one hand, by the fact that systems performing the opinion task did not have at their disposal the lexical resources for opinion employed in the *EmotiBlog* II model, but also because of the fact that they did not use machine learning on a corpus comparable to *EmotiBlog* (as seen from the results obtained when using solely the *EmotiBlog* I corpus). Compared to the NTCIR 8 Multilingual Analysis Task this year, we obtained significant improvements in precision, with a recall that is comparable to most of the participating systems. In the second experiment, we tested the performance of emotion classification using the two models built using EmotiBlog on the three corpora – JRC quotes, SemEval 2007 Task No.14 test set and the ISEAR corpus. The JRC quotes are labeled using EmotiBlog; however, the other two are labeled with a small set of emotions – 6 in the case of the SemEval data (joy, surprise, anger, fear, sadness, disgust) and 7 in ISEAR (joy, sadness, anger, fear, guilt, shame, disgust). Moreover, the SemEval data contains more than one emotion per title in the Gold Standard, therefore we consider as correct any of the classifications containing one of them. In order to unify the results and obtain comparable evaluations, we assessed the performance of the system using the alternative dimensional structures defined in Table 1. The ones not overlapping with the category of any of the 8 different emotions in SemEval and ISEAR are considered as "Other" and are not included either in the training, nor test set. The results of the evaluation are presented in Table 4. Again, the values I and II correspond to the models EmotiBlog I and II. The "Emotions" category contains the following emotions: joy, sadness, anger, fear, guilt, shame, disgust, surprise.

| Test corpus | Evaluation type | Precision | Recall |
|---|---|---|---|
| JRC quotes I | Emotions | 24.7 | 15.08 |
| JRC quotes II | Emotions | 33.65 | 18.98 |
| SemEval I | Emotions | 29.03 | 18.89 |
| SemEval II | Emotions | 32.98 | 18.45 |
| ISEAR I | Emotions | 22.31 | 15.01 |
| ISEAR II | Emotions | 25.62 | 17.83 |

Table 4. Results for emotion classification using the models built from the EmotiBlog annotations.

The best results for emotion detection were obtained for the "anger" category, where the precision was around 35 percent, for a recall of 19 percent. The worst results obtained were for the ISEAR category of "shame", where precision was around 12 percent, with a recall of 15 per-

[8] http://www.cs.waikato.ac.nz/ml/weka/

cent. We believe this is due to the fact that the latter emotion is a combination of more complex affective states and it can be easily misclassified to other categories of emotion. Moreover, from the analysis performed on the errors, we realized that many of the affective phenomena presented were more explicit in the case of texts expressing strong emotions such as "joy" and "anger", and were mostly related to common-sense interpretation of the facts presented in the weaker ones. As it can be seen in Table 3, results for the texts pertaining to the news category obtain better results, most of all news titles. This is due to the fact that such texts, although they contain a few words, have a more direct and stronger emotional charge than direct speech (which may be biased by the need to be diplomatic, find the best suited words etc.). Finally, the error analysis showed that emotion that is directly reported by the persons experiencing is more "hidden", in the use of words carrying special signification or related to general human experience. This fact makes emotion detection in such texts a harder task. Nevertheless, the results in all corpora are comparable, showing that the approach is robust enough to handle different text types. All in all, the results obtained using the fine and coarse-grained annotations in *EmotiBlog* increased the performance of emotion detection as compared to the systems in the SemEval competition.

### 6.3 Discussion on the overall results

From the results obtained, we can see that this approach combining the features extracted from the EmotiBlog fine and coarse-grained annotations helps to balance between the results obtained for precision and recall. The impact of using additional resources that contain opinion words is that of increasing the recall of the system, at the cost of a slight drop in precision, which proves that the approach is robust enough so that additional knowledge sources can be added. Although the corpus is small, the results obtained show that the phenomena it captures is relevant in the OM task, not only for the blog sphere, but also for other types of text (newspaper articles, self-reported affect).

## 8 Conclusions and future work

Due to the exponential increase of the subjective information result of the high-level usage of the Internet and the Web 2.0, NLP able to process this data are required. In this paper we presented the procedure by which we compiled a multilingual corpus of blog posts on different topics of interest in three languages: Spanish, Italian and English. Further on, we explained the need to create a finer-grained annotation schema that can be used to improve the performance of subjectivity mining systems. Thus, we presented the new annotation model, *EmotiBlog* and justified the benefits of this detailed annotation schema, presenting the sources and the reasons taken into consideration when building up the corpus and its labeling. Furthermore, we addressed the presence of "copy and pastes" from news articles or other blogs, the frequent quotes. For solving this possible ambiguity we included the annotation of both the directly indicated source, as well as the anaphoric references at cross-document level. We performed several experiments on three different corpora, aimed at finding and classifying both the opinion, as well as the expressions of emotion they contained; we showed that the fine and coarse-grained levels of annotation that EmotiBlog contains offers important information on the structure of affective texts, leading to an improvement of the performance of systems trained on it. Although the EmotiBlog corpus is small, the results obtained are promising and show that the phenomena it captures are relevant in the OM task, not only for the blog sphere, but also for other textual-genres. It is well known that OM is an extremely challenging task and a young discipline, thus there is room for improvement above all to solve linguistic phenomena such as the correference resolution at a cross document level, temporal expression recognition. In addition to this, more experiments would need to be done in order to verify the complete robustness of *EmotiBlog*. Last but not least, our idea is to include the existing tools for a more effective semi-supervised annotation. After the training of the ML system we obtain automatically some markables which have to be validated or not by the annotator and the ideal option would be to connect these terms the system detects automatically with tools, such as the mapping with an opinion lexicon based on WordNet (SentiWordNet, WordNet Affect, MicroWordNet), in order to automatically annotate all the synonyms and antonyms with the same or the opposite polarity respectively and assigning them some other elements contemplated into the *EmotiBlog* annotation schema. This would mean an important step forward for saving time during the annotation process and it will also assure a high quality annotation due to the human supervision.

## References


Balahur A., Steinberger R., Kabadjov M., Zavarella V., van der Goot E., Halkia M., Pouliquen B., and Belyaeva J. 2010. *Sentiment Analysis in the News.* In Proceedings of LREC 2010.

Balahur A., Boldrini E., Montoyo A., Martínez-Barco P. 2009. *A Comparative Study of Open Domain and Opinion Question Answering Systems for Factual and Opinionated Queries.* In Proceedings of the Recent Advances in Natural Language Processing.

Balahur A., Montoyo A. 2008. *Applying a Culture Dependent Emotion Triggers Database for Text Valence and Emotion Classification.* In Proceedings of the AISB 2008 Symposium on Affective Language in Human and Machine, Aberdeen, Scotland.

Balahur A., Steinberger R., *Rethinking Sentiment Analysis in the News: from Theory to Practice and back.* In Proceeding of WOMSA 2009. Seville.

Balahur A., Boldrini E., Montoyo A., Martínez-Barco P. 2009. *Summarizing Threads in Blogs Using Opinion Polarity.* In Proceedings of ETTS workshop. RANLP. 2009.

Boldrini E., Balahur A., Martínez-Barco P., Montoyo A. 2009. *EmotiBlog: a fine-grained model for emotion detection in non-traditional textual genres.* In Proceedings of WOMSA. Seville, Spain.

Boldrini E., Fernández J., Gómez J.M., Martínez-Barco P. 2009. *Machine Learning Techniques for Automatic Opinion Detection in Non-Traditional Textual Genres.* In Proceedings of WOMSA 2009. Seville, Spain.

Chaovalit P, Zhou L. 2005. *Movie Review Mining: a Comparison between Supervised and Unsupervised Classification Approaches.* In Proceedings of HICSS-05.

Carletta J. 1996. *Assessing agreement on classification task: the kappa statistic.* Computational Linguistics, 22(2): 249–254.

Cui H., Mittal V., Datar M. 2006. *Comparative Experiments on Sentiment Classification for Online Product Reviews.* In Proceedings of the 21st National Conference on Artificial Intelligence AAAI.

Cerini S., Compagnoni V., Demontis A., Formentelli M., and Gandini G. 2007. *Language resources and linguistic theory: Typology, second language acquisition.* English linguistics (Forthcoming), chapter Micro-WNOp: A gold standard for the evaluation of automatically compiled lexical resources for opinion mining. Franco Angeli Editore, Milano, IT.

Choi Y., Cardie C., Rilloff E., Padwardhan S. 2005. *Identifying Sources of Opinions with Conditional Random Fields and Extraction Patterns.* In Proceedings of the HLT/EMNLP.

Dave K., Lawrence S., Pennock, D. "Mining the Peanut Gallery: Opinion Extraction and Semantic Classification of Product Reviews". In Proceedings of WWW-03. 2003.

Esuli A., Sebastiani F. 2006. *SentiWordNet: A Publicly Available Resource for Opinion Mining.* In Proceedings of the 6th International Conference on Language Resources and Evaluation, LREC 2006, Genoa, Italy.

Gamon M., Aue S., Corston-Oliver S., Ringger E. 2005. *Mining Customer Opinions from Free Text.* Lecture Notes in Computer Science.

Goldberg A.B., Zhu J. 2006. *Seeing stars when there aren't many stars: Graph-based semi-supervised learning for sentiment categorization.* In HLT-NAACL 2006 Workshop on Textgraphs: Graph-based Algorithms for Natural Language Processing.

Hu M., Liu B. 2004. *Mining Opinion Features in Customer Reviews.* In Proceedings of Nineteenth National Conference on Artificial Intelligence AAAI.

Hatzivassiloglou V., Wiebe J. 2000. *Effects of adjective orientation and gradability on sentence subjectivity.* In Proceedings of COLING.

Kim S.M., Hovy E. 2004. *Determining the Sentiment of Opinions.* In Proceedings of COLING.

Mullen T., Collier N. 2006. *Sentiment Analysis Using Support Vector Machines with Diverse Information Sources.* In Proceedings of EMNLP. 2004. Lin, W.H., Wilson, T., Wiebe, J., Hauptman, A. "Which Side are You On? Identifying Perspectives at the Document and Sentence Levels". In Proceedings of the Tenth Conference on Natural Language Learning CoNLL.2006.

Ng V., Dasgupta S. and Arifin S. M. 2006. *Examining the Role of Linguistics Knowledge Sources in the Automatic Identification and Classification of Reviews.* In the proceedings of the ACL, Sydney.

Pang B., Lee L., Vaithyanathan S. 2002. *Thumbs up? Sentiment classification using machine learning techniques.* In Proceedings of EMNLP-02, the Conference on Empirical Methods in Natural Language Processing.

Riloff E., Wiebe J. 2003. *Learning Extraction Patterns for Subjective Expressions.* In Proceedings of the 2003 Conference on Empirical Methods in Natural Language Processing.

Strapparava C. Valitutti A. 2004. *WordNet-Affect: an affective extension of WordNet.* In Proceedings ofthe 4th International Conference on Language Resources and Evaluation, LREC.

Russell J.A. 1983. *Pancultural aspects of the human conceptual organization of emotions.* Journal of Personality and Social Psychology 45: 1281–8.

Scherer K. R. 2005. *What are emotions? And how can they be measured?* Social Science Information, 44(4), 693–727.

Stoyanov V. and Cardie C. 2006. *Toward Opinion Summarization: Linking the Sources.* COLING-ACL. Workshop on Sentiment and Subjectivity in Text.

Stoyanov V., Cardie C., Litman D., and Wiebe J. 2004. *Evaluating an Opinion Annotation Scheme Using a New Multi-Perspective Question and An-*

*swer Corpus*. AAAI Spring Symposium on Exploring Attitude and Affect in Text.

Strapparava and Mihalcea, 2007 - SemEval 2007 Task 14: Affective Text. In Proceedings of the ACL.

Turney P. 2002. *Thumbs Up or Thumbs Down? Semantic Orientation Applied to Unsupervised Classification of Reviews*. ACL 2002: 417-424.

Turney P., Littman M. 2003. *Measuring praise and criticism: Inference of semantic orientation from association*. ACM Transactions on Information Systems 21.

Uspensky B. 1973. *A Poetics of Composition*. University of California Press, Berkeley, California.

Wiebe J. M. 1994. *Tracking point of view in narrative*. Computational Linguistics, vol. 20, pp. 233–287.

Wiebe J., Wilson T. and Cardie C. 2005. *Annotating expressions of opinions and emotions in language*. Language Resources and Evaluation.

Wilson T., Wiebe J., Hwa R. 2004. *Just how mad are you? Finding strong and weak opinion clauses*. In: Proceedings of AAAI.

Wiebe J., Wilson T. and Cardie C. 2005. *"Annotation Expressions of Opinions and Emotions in Language*. Language Resources and Evaluation.

Wiebe J., Riloff E. 2005. *Creating Subjective and Objective Sentence Classifiers from Unannotated Texts*. In Proceedings of the 6th International Conference on Computational Linguistics and Intelligent Text Processing (CICLing).

# Error-tagged Learner Corpus of Czech

**Jirka Hana**
Charles University
Prague, Czech Republic
first.last@gmail.com

**Alexandr Rosen**
Charles University
Prague, Czech Republic
alexandr.rosen@ff.cuni.cz

**Svatava Škodová**
Technical University
Liberec, Czech Republic
svatava.skodova@tul.cz

**Barbora Štindlová**
Technical University
Liberec, Czech Republic
barbora.stindlova@tul.cz

## Abstract

The paper describes a learner corpus of Czech, currently under development. The corpus captures Czech as used by non-native speakers. We discuss its structure, the layered annotation of errors and the annotation process.

## 1 Introduction

Corpora consisting of texts produced by non-native speakers are becoming an invaluable source of linguistic data, especially for foreign language educators. In addition to morphosyntactic tagging and lemmatisation, common in other corpora, learner corpora can be annotated by information relevant to the specific nonstandard language of the learners. Cases of deviant use can be identified, emended and assigned a tag specifying the type of the error, all of which helps to exploit the richness of linguistic data in the texts. However, annotation of this kind is a challenging tasks, even more so for a language such as Czech, with its rich inflection, derivation, agreement, and largely information-structure-driven constituent order. A typical learner of Czech makes errors across all linguistic levels, often targeting the same form several times.

The proposed annotation scheme is an attempt to respond to the requirements of annotating a deviant text in such a language, striking a compromise between the limitations of the annotation process and the demands of the corpus user. The three-level format allows for successive emendations, involving multiple forms in discontinuous sequences. In many cases, the error type follows from the comparison of the faulty and corrected forms and is assigned automatically, sometimes using information present in morphosyntactic tags, assigned by a tagger. In more complex cases, the scheme allows for representing relations making phenomena such as the violation of agreement rules explicit.

After an overview of issues related to learner corpora in §2 and a brief introduction to the project of a learner corpus of Czech in §3 we present the concept of our annotation scheme in §4, followed by a description of the annotation process in §5.

## 2 Learner corpora

A learner corpus, also called interlanguage or L2 corpus, is a computerised textual database of language as produced by second language (L2) learners (Leech, 1998). Such a database is a very powerful resource in research of second language acquisition. It can be used to optimise the L2 learning process, to assist authors of textbooks and dictionaries, and to tailor them to learners with a particular native language (L1).

More generally, a learner corpus – like other corpora – serves as a repository of authentic data about a language (Granger, 1998). In the domain of L2 acquisition and teaching of foreign languages, the language of the learners is called *interlanguage* (Selinker, 1983).[1] An interlanguage includes both correct and deviant forms. The possibility to examine learners' errors on the background of the correct language is the most important aspect of learner corpora (Granger, 1998).

Investigating the interlanguage is easier when the deviant forms are annotated at least by their correct counterparts, or, even better, by tags making the nature of the error explicit. Although

[1] *Interlanguage* is distinguished by its highly individual and dynamic nature. It is subject to constant changes as the learner progresses through successive stages of acquiring more competence, and can be seen as an individual and dynamic continuum between one's native and target languages.



*Proceedings of the Fourth Linguistic Annotation Workshop, ACL 2010*, pages 11–19,
Uppsala, Sweden, 15-16 July 2010. 

learner corpora tagged this way exist, the two decades of research in this field have shown that designing a tagset for the annotation of errors is a task highly sensitive to the intended use of the corpus and the results are not easily transferable from one language to another.

Learner corpora can be classified according to several criteria:

- Target language (TL): Most learner corpora cover the language of learners of English as a second or foreign language (ESL or EFL). The number of learner corpora for other languages is smaller but increasing.
- Medium: Learner corpora can capture written or spoken texts, the latter much harder to compile, thus less common.
- L1: The data can come from learners with the same L1 or with various L1s.
- Proficiency in TL: Some corpora gather texts of students at the same level, other include texts of speakers at various levels. Most corpora focus on advanced students.
- Annotation: Many learner corpora contain only raw data, possibly with emendations, without linguistic annotation; some include part-of-speech (POS) tagging. Several include error tagging. Despite the time-consuming manual effort involved, the number of error-tagged learner corpora is growing.

Error-tagged corpora use the following taxonomies to classify the type of error:

- Taxonomies marking the source of error: The level of granularity ranges from broad categories (morphology, lexis, syntax) to more specific ones (auxiliary, passive, etc.).
- Taxonomies based on formal types of alternation of the source text: omission, addition, misformation, mis-ordering.
- Hierarchical taxonomies based on a combination of various aspects: error domain (formal, grammatical, lexical, style errors), error category (agglutination, diacritics, derivation inflection, auxiliaries, gender, mode, etc.), word category (POS).
- Without error taxonomies, using only correction as the implicit explanation for an error.

In Table 1 we present a brief summary of existing learner corpora tagged by POS and/or error types, including the size of the corpus (in millions of words or Chinese characters), the mother tongue of the learners, or – in case of learners with different linguistic backgrounds – the number of mother tongues (L1), the TL and the learners' level of proficiency in TL. For an extensive overview see, for example (Pravec, 2002; Nesselhauf, 2004; Xiao, 2008).

| Size | L1 | TL | TL proficiency |
|---|---|---|---|
| ***ICLE*** – *Internat'l Corpus of Learner English* | | | |
| 3M | 21 | English | advanced |
| ***CLC*** – *Cambridge Learner Corpus* | | | |
| 30M | 130 | English | all levels |
| ***PELCRA*** – *Polish Learner English Corpus* | | | |
| 0.5M | Polish | English | all levels |
| ***USE*** – *Uppsala Student English Corpus* | | | |
| 1.2M | Swedish | English | advanced |
| ***HKUST*** – *Hong Kong University of Science and Technology Corpus of Learner English* | | | |
| 25M | Chinese | English | advanced |
| ***CLEC*** – *Chinese Learner English Corpus* | | | |
| 1M | Chinese | English | 5 levels |
| ***JEFLL*** – *Japanese EFL Learner Corpus* | | | |
| 0.7M | Japanese | English | advanced |
| ***FALKO*** – *Fehlerannotiertes Lernerkorpus* | | | |
| 1.2M | various | German | advanced |
| ***FRIDA*** – *French Interlanguage Database* | | | |
| 0.2M | various | French | intermediate |
| ***CIC*** – *Chinese Interlanguage Corpus* | | | |
| 2M | 96 | Chinese | intermediate |

Table 1: Some currently available learner corpora

## 3 A learner corpus of Czech

In many ways, building a learner corpus of Czech as a second/foreign language is a unique enterprise. To the best of our knowledge, the CzeSL corpus (Czech as a Second/Foreign Language) is the first learner corpus ever built for a highly inflectional language, and one of the very few using multi-layer annotation (together with FALKO – see Table 1). The corpus consists of 4 subcorpora according to the learners' L1:

- The Russian subcorpus represents an interlanguage of learners with a Slavic L1.
- The Vietnamese subcorpus represents a numerous minority of learners with very few points of contact between L1 and Czech.
- The Romani subcorpus represents a linguistic minority with very specific traits in the Czech cultural context.
- The "remnant" subcorpus covers texts from speakers of various L1s.

The whole extent of CzeSL will be two million words (in 2012). Each subcorpus is again divided into two subcorpora of written and spoken texts;[2] this division guarantees the representative character of the corpus data. The corpus is based on texts covering all language levels according to the Common European Framework of Reference for Languages, from real beginners (A1 level) to advanced learners (level B2 and higher). The texts are elicited during various situations in classes; they are not restricted to parts of written examination. This spectrum of various levels and situations is unique in the context of other learner corpora.

Each text is equipped with the necessary background information, including sociological data about the learner (age, gender, L1, country, language level, other languages, etc.) and the situation (test, homework, school work without the possibility to use a dictionary, etc.).

## 4 Annotation scheme

### 4.1 The feasible and the desirable

The error tagging system for CzeSL is designed to meet the requirements of Czech as an inflectional language. Therefore, the scheme is:

- Detailed but manageable for the annotators.
- Informative – the annotation is appropriate to Czech as a highly inflectional language.
- Open to future extensions – it allows for more detailed taxonomy to be added in the future.

The annotators are no experts in Czech as a foreign language or in 2L learning and acquisition, and they are unaware of possible interferences between languages the learner knows. Thus they may fail to recognise an interferential error. A sentence such as *Tokio je pěkný hrad* 'Tokio is a nice castle' is grammatically correct, but its author, a native speaker of Russian, was misled by 'false friends' and assumed *hrad* 'castle' as the Czech equivalent of Russian *gorod* 'town, city'.[3] Similarly in *Je tam hodně sklepů* 'There are many cellars.' The formally correct sentence may strike the reader as implausible in the context, but it is impossible to identify and emend the error without the knowledge that *sklep* in Russian means 'grave', not 'cellar' (= *sklep* in Czech).

For some types of errors, the problem is to define the limits of interpretation. The clause *kdyby citila na tebe zlobna* is grammatically incorrect, yet roughly understandable as 'if she felt angry at you'. In such cases the task of the annotator is interpretation rather than correction. The clause can be rewritten as *kdyby se na tebe cítila rozzlobená* 'if she felt angry at you', or *kdyby se na tebe zlobila* 'if she were angry at you'; the former being less natural but closer to the original, unlike the latter. It is difficult to provide clear guidelines.

Errors in word order represent another specific type. Czech constituent order reflects information structure and it is sometimes difficult to decide (even in a context) whether an error is present. The sentence *Rádio je taky na skříni* 'A radio is also on the wardrobe' suggests that there are at least two radios in the room, although the more likely interpretation is that among other things, there is also a radio, which happens to sit on the wardrobe. Only the latter interpretation would require a different word order: *Taky je na skříni rádio*. Similarly difficult may be decisions about errors labelled as **lexical** and **modality**.

The phenomenon of Czech diglossia is reflected in the problem of annotating non-standard language, usually individual forms with colloquial morphological endings. The learners may not be aware of their status and/or an appropriate context for their use, and the present solution assumes that colloquial Czech is emended under the rationale that the author expects the register of his text to be perceived as unmarked.

On the other hand, there is the primary goal of the corpus: to serve the needs of the corpus users. The resulting error typology is a compromise between the limitations of the annotation process and the demands of research into learner corpora.

The corpus can be used for comparisons among learner varieties of Czech, studied as national interlanguages (Russian, Vietnamese, Romani etc.) using a matrix of statistic deviations. Similarly interesting are the heterogeneous languages of learners on different stages of acquisition. From the pedagogical point of view, corpus-based analyses have led to a new inductive methodology of data-driven learning, based on the usage of concordances in exercises or to support students' independent learning activities.

### 4.2 The framework

Annotated learner corpora sometimes use data formats and tools developed originally for annotating speech. Such environments allow for an arbitrary

[2] Transcripts of the spoken parts will be integrated with the rest of the corpus at a later stage of the project.

[3] All examples are authentic.

segmentation of the input and multilevel annotation of segments (Schmidt, 2009). Typically, the annotator edits a table with columns corresponding to words and rows to levels of annotation. A cell can be split or more cells merged to allow for annotating smaller or larger segments. This way, phenomena such as agreement or word order can be emended and tagged (Lüdeling et al., 2005).

However, in the tabular format vertical correspondences between the original word form and its emended equivalents or annotations at other levels may be lost. It is difficult to keep track of links between forms merged into a single cell, spanning multiple columns, and the annotations of a form at other levels (rows). This may be a problem for successive emendations involving a single form, starting from a typo up to an ungrammatical word order, but also for morphosyntactic tags assigned to forms, whenever a form is involved in a multi-word annotation and its equivalent or tag leaves the column of the original form.

While in the tabular format the correspondences between elements at various levels are captured only implicitly, in our annotation scheme these correspondences are explicitly encoded. Our format supports the option of preserving correspondences across levels, both between individual word forms and their annotations, while allowing for arbitrary joining and splitting of any number of non-contiguous segments. The annotation levels are represented as a graph consisting of a set of parallel paths (annotation levels) with links between them. Nodes along the paths always stand for word tokens, correct or incorrect, and in a sentence with nothing to correct the corresponding word tokens in every pair of neighbouring paths are linked 1:1. Additionally, the nodes can be assigned morphosyntactic tags, syntactic functions or any other word-specific information. Whenever a word form is emended, the type of error can be specified as a label of the link connecting the incorrect form at level $S_i$ with its emended form at level $S_{i+1}$. In general, these labelled relations can link an arbitrary number of elements at one level with an arbitrary number of elements at a neighbouring level. The elements at one level participating in this relation need not form a contiguous sequence. Multiple words at any level are thus identified as a single segment, which is related to a segment at a neighbouring level, while any of the participating word forms can retain their 1:1 links with their counterparts at other levels. This is useful for splitting and joining word forms, for changing word order, and for any other corrections involving multiple words. Nodes can also be added or omitted at any level to correct missing or odd punctuation signs or syntactic constituents. See Figure 1 below for an example of this multi-level annotation scheme.

The option of relating multiple nodes as single segments across levels could also be used for treating morphosyntactic errors in concord and government. However, in this case there is typically one correct form involved, e.g., the subject in subject-predicate agreement, the noun in adjective-noun agreement, the verb assigning case to a complement, the antecedent in pronominal reference. Rather than treating both the correct and the incorrect form as equals in a 2:2 relation between the levels, the incorrect form is emended using a 1:1 link with an option to refer to the correct form. Such references link pairs of forms at neighbouring levels rather than the forms themselves to enable possible references from a multi-word unit (or) to another multi-word unit. See Figure 1 below again, where such references are represented by arrows originating in labels **val**.

A single error may result in multiple incorrect forms as shown in (1). The adjective *velký* 'big-NOM-SG-M(ASC)' correctly agrees with the noun *pes* 'dog-NOM-SG-MASC'. However, the case of the noun is incorrect – it should be in accusative rather than nominative. When the noun's case is corrected, the case of the adjective has to be corrected as well. Then multiple references are made: to the verb as the case assigner for the noun, and to the noun as the source of agreement for the adjective.

(1) a. *Viděl velký pes.
saw big-NOM-SG-M dog-NOM-SG-M
b. Viděl velkého psa.
saw big-ACC-SG-M dog-ACC-SG-M
'He saw a big dog'

Annotation of learners' texts is often far from straightforward, and alternative interpretations are available even in a broader context. The annotation format supports alternatives, but for the time being the annotation tool does not support local disjunctions. This may be a problem if the annotator has multiple target hypotheses in mind.

### 4.3 Three levels of annotation

A multi-level annotation scheme calls for some justification, and once such a scheme is adopted, the question of the number of levels follows.

After a careful examination of alternatives, we have arrived at a two-stage annotation design, based on three levels. A flat, single-stage, two-level annotation scheme would be appropriate if we were interested only in the original text and in the annotation at some specific level (fully emended sentences, or some intermediate stage, such as emended word forms). The flat design could be used even if we insisted on registering some intermediate stages of the passage from the original to a fully emended text, and decided to store such information with the word-form nodes. However, such information might get lost in the case of significant changes involving deletions or additions (e.g., in Czech as a pro-drop language, the annotator may decide that a misspelled personal pronoun in the subject position should be deleted and the information about the spelling error would lost). The decision to use a multi-level design was mainly due to our interest in annotating errors in single forms as well as those spanning (potentially discontinuous) strings of words.

Once we have a scheme of multiple levels available, we can provide the levels with theoretical significance and assign a linguistic interpretation to each of them. In a world of unlimited resources of annotators' time and experience, this would be the optimal solution. The first annotation level would be concerned only with errors in graphemics, followed by levels dedicated to morphemics, morphosyntax, syntax, lexical phenomena, semantics and pragmatics. More realistically, there could be a level for errors in graphemics and morphemics, another for errors in morphosyntax (agreement, government) and one more for everything else, including word order and phraseology.

Our solution is a compromise between corpus users' expected demands and limitations due to the annotators' time and experience. The annotator has a choice of two levels of annotation, and the distinction, based to a large extent on formal criteria, is still linguistically relevant.

At the level of transcribed input (Level 0), the nodes represent the original strings of graphemes. At the level of orthographical and morphological emendation (Level 1), only individual forms are treated. The result is a string consisting of correct Czech forms, even though the sentence may not be correct as a whole. The rule of "correct forms only" has a few exceptions: a faulty form is retained if no correct form could be used in the context or if the annotator cannot decipher the author's intention. On the other hand, a correct form may be replaced by another correct form if the author clearly misspelled the latter, creating an unintended homograph with another form. All other types of errors are emended at Level 2.

### 4.4 Captured errors

A typical learner of Czech makes errors all along the hierarchy of theoretically motivated linguistic levels, starting from the level of graphemics up to the level of pragmatics. Our goal is to emend the input conservatively, modifying incorrect and inappropriate forms and expressions to arrive at a coherent and well-formed result, without any ambition to produce a stylistically optimal solution. Emendation is possible only when the input is comprehensible. In cases where the input or its part is not comprehensible, it is left with a partial or even no annotation.

The taxonomy of errors is rather coarse-grained, a more detailed classification is previewed for a later stage and a smaller corpus sample. It follows the three-level distinction and is based on criteria as straightforward as possible. Whenever the error type can be determined from the way the error is emended, the type is supplied automatically by a post-processing module, together with morphosyntactic tags and lemmas for the correct or emended forms (see § 5.3).

Errors in individual word forms, treated at Level 1, include misspellings (also diacritics and capitalisation), misplaced word boundaries, missing or misused punctuation, but also errors in inflectional and derivational morphology and unknown stems. These types of errors are emended manually, but the annotator is not expected label them by their type – the type of most errors at Level 1 is identified automatically. The only exception where the error type must be assigned manually is when an unknown stem or derivation affix is used.

Whenever the lexeme (its stem and/or suffix) is unknown and can be replaced by a suitable form, it is emended at Level 1. If possible, the form should fit the syntactic context. If no suitable form can be found, the form is retained and marked as unknown. When the form exists, but is not appropriate in context, it is emended at Level 2 – the reason may be the violation of a syntactic rule or semantic incompatibility of the lexeme.

Table 2 gives a list of error types emended at Level 1. Some types actually include subtypes: words can be incorrectly split or joined, punctuation, diacritics or character(s) can be missing, superfluous, misplaced or of a wrong kind. The Links column gives the maximum number of positions at Level 0, followed by the maximum number of position at Level 1 that are related by links for this type of error. The Id column says if the error type is determined automatically or has to be specified manually.

| Error type | Links | Id |
|---|---|---|
| Word boundary | m:n | A |
| Punctuation | 0:1, 1:0 | A |
| Capitalisation | 1:1 | A |
| Diacritics | 1:1 | A |
| Character(s) | 1:1 | A |
| Inflection | 1:1 | A |
| Unknown lexeme | 1:1 | M |

Table 2: Types of errors at Level 1

Emendations at Level 2 concern errors in agreement, valency and pronominal reference, negative concord, the choice of a lexical item or idiom, and in word order. For the agreement, valency and pronominal reference cases, there is typically an incorrect form, which reflects some properties (morphological categories, valency requirements) of a correct form (the agreement source, syntactic head, antecedent). Table 3 gives a list of error types emended at Level 2. The Ref column gives the number of pointers linking the incorrect form with the correct "source".

| Error type | Links | Ref | Id |
|---|---|---|---|
| Agreement | 1:1 | 1 | M |
| Valency | 1:1 | 1 | M |
| Pronominal reference | 1:1 | 1 | M |
| Complex verb forms | m:n | 0,1 | M |
| Negation | m:n | 0,1 | M |
| Missing constituent | 0:1 | 0 | M |
| Odd constituent | 1:0 | 0 | M |
| Modality | 1:1 | 0 | M |
| Word order | m:n | 0 | M |
| Lexis & phraseology | m:n | 0,1 | M |

Table 3: Types of errors at Level 2

The annotation scheme is illustrated in Figure 1, using an authentic sentence, split in two halves for space reasons. There are three parallel strings of word forms, including punctuation signs, representing the three levels, with links for corresponding forms. Any emendation is labelled with an error type.[4] The first line is Level 0, imported from the transcribed original, with English glosses below (forms marked by asterisks are incorrect in any context, but they may be comprehensible – as is the case with all such forms in this example). Correct words are linked directly with their copies at Level 1, for emended words the link is labelled with an error type. In the first half of the sentence, **unk** for unknown form, **dia** for an error in diacritics, **cap** for an error in capitalisation. According to the rules of Czech orthography, the negative particle *ne* is joined with the verb using an intermediate node **bnd**. A missing comma is introduced at Level 1, labelled as a **p**unctuation error. All the error labels above can be specified automatically in the post-processing step.

Staying with the first half of the sentence, most forms at Level 1 are linked directly with their equivalents at Level 2 without emendations. The reflexive particle *se* is misplaced as a second position clitic, and is put into the proper position using the link labelled **wo** for a word-order error.[5] The pronoun *ona* – 'she' in the nominative case – is governed by the form *líbit se*, and should bear the dative case: *jí*. The arrow to *líbit* makes the reason for this emendation explicit. The result could still be improved by positioning *Praha* after the clitics and before the finite verb *nebude*, resulting in a word order more in line with the underlying information structure of the sentence, but our policy is to refrain from more subtle phenomena and produce a grammatical rather than a perfect result.

In the second half of the sentence, there is only one Level 1 error in diacritics, but quite a few errors at Level 2. *Proto* 'therefore' is changed to *protože* 'because' – a **lex**ical emendation. The main issue are the two finite verbs *bylo* and *vadí*. The most likely intention of the author is best expressed by the conditional mood. The two non-contiguous forms are replaced by the conditional

[4] The labels for error types used here are simplified for reasons of space and mnemonics.

[5] In word-order errors it may be difficult to identify a specific word form violating a rule. The annotation scheme allows for both *se* and *jí* to be blamed. However, here we prefer the simpler option and identify just one, more prominent word form. Similarly with *mi* below.

auxiliary and the content verb participle in one step using a 2:2 relation. The intermediate node is labelled by **cplx** for complex verb forms. The prepositional phrase *pro mně* 'for me' is another complex issue. Its proper form is *pro mě* (homonymous with *pro mně*, but with 'me' bearing accusative instead of dative), or *pro mne*. The accusative case is required by the preposition *pro*. However, the head verb requires that this complement bears bare dative – *mi*. Additionally, this form is a second position clitic, following the conditional auxiliary (also a clitic) in the clitic cluster. The change from PP to the bare dative pronoun and the reordering are both properly represented, including the pointer to the head verb. What is missing is an explicit annotation of the faulty case of the prepositional complement, which is lost during the Level 1 – Level 2 transition, the price for a simpler annotation scheme with fewer levels. It might be possible to amend the PP at Level 1, but it would go against the rule that only forms wrong in isolation are emended at Level 1.

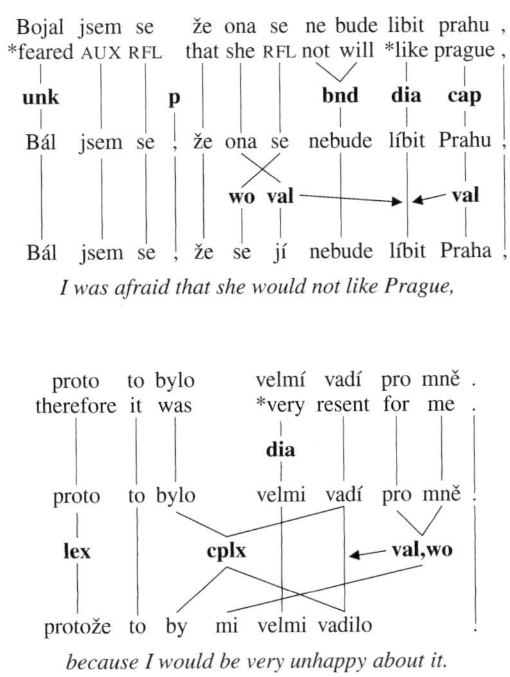


Figure 1: Annotation of a sample sentence

### 4.5 Data Format

To encode the layered annotation described above, we have developed an annotation schema in the Prague Markup Language (PML).[6] PML is a generic XML-based data format, designed for the representation of rich linguistic annotation organised into levels. In our schema, each of the higher levels contains information about words on that level, about the corrected errors and about relations to the tokens on the lower levels. Level 0 does not contain any relations, only links to the neighbouring Level 1. In Figure 2, we show a portion (first three words and first two relations) of the Level 1 of the sample sentence encoded in our annotation schema.

```
<?xml version="1.0" encoding="UTF-8"?>
<adata xmlns="http://utkl.cuni.cz/czesl/">
  <head>
    <schema href="adata_schema.xml" />
    <references>
      <reffile id="w" name="wdata" href="r049.w.xml" />
    </references>
  </head>
  <doc id="a-r049-d1" lowerdoc.rf="w#w-r049-d1">
    ...
    <para id="a-r049-d1p2" lowerpara.rf="w#w-r049-d1p2">
      ...
      <s id="a-r049-d1p2s5">
        <w id="a-r049-d1p2w50">
          <token>Bál</token>
        </w>
        <w id="a-r049-d1p2w51">
          <token>jsem</token>
        </w>
        <w id="a-r049-d1p2w52">
          <token>se</token>
        </w>
        ...
      </s>
      ...
      <edge id="a-r049-d1p2e54">
        <from>w#w-r049-d1p2w46</from>
        <to>a-r049-d1p2w50</to>
        <error>
          <tag>unk</tag>
        </error>
      </edge>
      <edge id="a-r049-d1p2e55">
        <from>w#w-r049-d1p2w47</from>
        <to>a-r049-d1p2w51</to>
      </edge>
      ...
    </para>
    ...
  </doc>
</adata>
```

Figure 2: Portion of the Level 1 of the sample sentence encoded in the PML data format.

## 5 Annotation process

The whole annotation process proceeds as follows:

- A handwritten document is transcribed into html using off-the-shelf tools (e.g. Open Office Writer or Microsoft Word).
- The information in the html document is used to generate Level 0 and a default Level 1 encoded in the PML format.
- An annotator manually corrects the document and provides some information about errors using our annotation tool.
- Error information that can be inferred automatically is added.

[6]http://ufal.mff.cuni.cz/jazz/pml/index_en.html

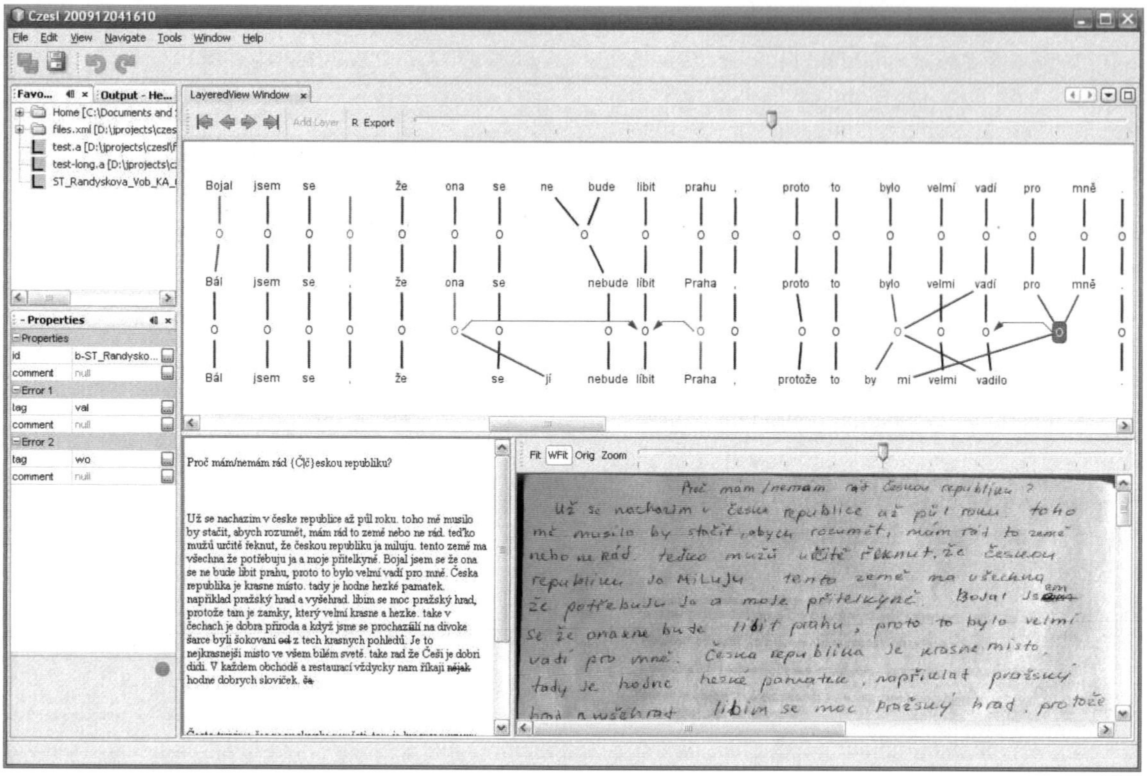

Figure 3: Sample sentence in the annotation tool.

### 5.1 Transcription

The original documents are hand-written, usually the only available option, given that their most common source are language courses and exams. The avoidance of an electronic format is also due to the concern about the use of automatic text-editing tools by the students, which may significantly distort the authentic interlanguage.

Therefore, the texts must be transcribed, which is very time consuming. While we strive to capture only the information present in the original hand-written text, often some interpretation is unavoidable. For example, the transcribers have to take into account specifics of hand-writing of particular groups of students and even of each individual student (the same glyph may be interpreted as *l* in the hand-writing of one student, *e* of another, and *a* of yet another). When a text allows multiple interpretation, the transcribers may provide all variants. For example, the case of initial letters or word boundaries are often unclear. Obviously, parts of some texts may be completely illegible and are marked as such.

Also captured are corrections made by the student (insertions, deletions, etc.), useful for investigating the process of language acquisition.

The transcripts are not spell-checked automatically. In a highly inflectional language, deviations in spelling very often do not only reflect wrong graphemics, but indicate an error in morphology.

### 5.2 Annotation

The manual portion of annotation is supported by an annotation tool we have developed. The annotator corrects the text on appropriate levels, modifies relations between elements (by default all relations are 1:1) and annotates relations with error tags as needed. The context of the annotated text is shown both as a transcribed html document and as a scan of the original document. The tool is written in Java on top of the Netbeans platform.[7] Figure 3 shows the annotation of the sample sentence as displayed by the tool.

### 5.3 Postprocessing

Manual annotation is followed by automatic postprocessing, providing the corpus with additional information:

[7] `http://platform.netbeans.org/`

- Level 1: lemma, POS and morphological categories (this information can be ambiguous)
- Level 2: lemma, POS and morphological categories (disambiguated)
- Level 1: type of error (by comparing the original and corrected strings), with the exception of lexical errors that involve lemma changes (e.g. **kadeřnička – kadeřnice* 'hair-dresser')
- Level 2: type of morphosyntactic errors caused by agreement or valency error (by comparing morphosyntactic tags at Level 1 and 2)
- Formal error description: missing/extra expression, erroneous expression, wrong order
- In the future, we plan to automatically tag errors in verb prefixes, inflectional endings, spelling, palatalisation, metathesis, etc.

## 6 Conclusion

Error annotation is a very resource-intensive task, but the return on investment is potentially enormous. Depending on the annotation scheme, the corpus user has access to detailed error statistics, which is difficult to obtain otherwise. An error-tagged corpus is an invaluable tool to obtain a reliable picture of the learners' interlanguage and to adapt teaching methods and learning materials by identifying the most frequent error categories in accordance with the learner's proficiency level or L1 background.

We are expecting plentiful feedback from the error annotation process, which is just starting. As the goal of a sizable corpus requires a realistic setup, we plan to experiment with more and less detailed sets of error types, measuring the time and inter-annotator agreement. A substantially more elaborate classification of errors is previewed for a limited subset of the corpus.

At the same time, the feedback of the annotators will translate into the ongoing tuning of the annotation guidelines, represented by a comprehensive error-tagging manual. We hope in progress in dealing with thorny issues such as the uncertainty about the author's intended meaning, the inference errors, the proper amount of interference with the original, or the occurrence of colloquial language. In all of this, we need to make sure that annotators handle similar phenomena in the same way.

However, the real test of the corpus will come with its usage. We are optimistic – some of the future users are a crucial part of our team and their needs and ideas are the driving force of the project.

## 7 Acknowledgements

We wish to thank other members of the project team, namely Milena Hnátková, Tomáš Jelínek, Vladimír Petkevič, and Hana Skoumalová for their numerous stimulating ideas, acute insight and important feedback. We are especially grateful to Karel Šebesta, for all of the above and for initiating and guiding this enterprise.

The work described in this paper is funded by the European Social Fund and the government of the Czech Republic within the operational programme 'Education for Competitiveness' as a part of the project 'Innovation in Education in the Field of Czech as a Second Language' (project no. CZ.1.07/2.2.00/07.0259).

## References

Sylviane Granger, editor. 1998. *Learner English on Computer*. Addison Wesley Longman, London and New York.

Geoffrey Leech. 1998. Preface. In Granger Sylviane, editor, *Learner English on Computer*, pages xiv–xx. Addison Wesley Longman, London and New York.

Anke Lüdeling, Maik Walter, Emil Kroymann, and Peter Adolphs. 2005. Multi-level error annotation in learner corpora. In *Proceedings of Corpus Linguistics 2005*, Birmingham.

Nadja Nesselhauf. 2004. Learner corpora and their potential for language teaching. In John McHardy Sinclair, editor, *How to use corpora in language teaching*, Studies in corpus linguistics, pages 125–152. Benjamins, Amsterdam/Philadelphia.

Norma A. Pravec. 2002. Survery of learner corpora. *ICAME Journal*, 26:81–114.

Thomas Schmidt. 2009. Creating and working with spoken language corpora in EXMARaLDA. In *LULCL II: Lesser Used Languages & Computer Linguistics II*, pages 151–164.

Larry Selinker. 1983. Interlanguage. In Betty W. Robinett and Jacquelyn Schachter, editors, *Second Language Learning: Contrastive analysis, error analysis, and related aspects*, pages 173–196. The University of Michigan Press, Ann Arbor, MI.

Richard Xiao. 2008. Well-known and influential corpora. In Anke Lüdeling and Merja Kytö, editors, *Corpus Linguistics. An International Handbook*, volume 1 of *Handbooks of Linguistics and Communication Science [HSK] 29.1*, pages 383–457. Mouton de Gruyter, Berlin and New York.

# Annotation Scheme for Social Network Extraction from Text

**Apoorv Agarwal**
Computer Science Department
Columbia University
New York, U.S.A.
apoorv@cs.columbia.edu

**Owen Rambow**
CCLS
Columbia University
New York, U.S.A.
rambow@ccls.columbia.edu

**Rebecca J. Passonneau**
CCLS
Columbia University
New York, U.S.A.
becky@cs.columbia.edu

## Abstract

We are interested in extracting social networks from text. We present a novel annotation scheme for a new type of event, called *social event*, in which two people participate such that at least one of them is cognizant of the other. We compare our scheme in detail to the ACE scheme. We perform a detailed analysis of inter-annotator agreement, which shows that our annotations are reliable.

## 1 Introduction

Our task is to extract a social network from written text. The extracted social network can be used for various applications such as summarization, question answering, or the detection of main characters in a story. We take a "social network" to be a network consisting of individual human beings and groups of human beings who are connected to each other through various relationships by the virtue of participating in events. A text can describe a social network in two ways: explicitly, by stating the type of relationship between two individuals (Example **??**); or implicitly, by describing an event which creates or perpetuates a social relationship (Example 2). We are interested in the implicit description of social relations through events. We will call these types of events *social events*. Crucially, many social relations are described in text largely implicitly, or even entirely implicitly. This paper presents an annotation project for precisely such social events.

To introduce the terminology and conventions we use throughout the paper, consider the following Example 2. In this example, there are two entities: **Iraqi officials** and **Timothy McVeigh**. These entities are present in text as nominal and named entity mentions respectively (within [...]). Furthermore, these entities are related by an event, whose type we call INR.NONVERBAL-NEAR (a non-verbal interaction that occurs in physical proximity), and whose textual mention is the extent (or span of text) *provided money and training*.[1]

(1) [[Sharif]'s {wife} Tahari Shad Tabussum], 27, (...) made no application for bail at the court, according to local reports. **PER-SOC**

(2) The suit claims [Iraqi officials] {provided money and training} to [convicted bomber Timothy McVeigh] (...) **INR.Nonverbal-Near**

One question that immediately comes to mind is how would these annotations be useful? Let us consider the problem of finding the hierarchy of people in the Enron Email corpus (Klimt and Yang, 2004; Diesner et al., 2005). Much work to solve this problem has focused on using social network analysis algorithms for calculating the graph theoretical quantities (like degree centrality, clustering coefficient (Wasserman and Faust, 1994)) of people in the email sender-receiver network (Rowe et al., 2007). Attempts have been made to incorporate the content of emails usually by using topic modeling techniques (McCallum et al., 2007; Pathak et al., 2008). These techniques consider a distribution of words in emails to classify the interaction between people into topics and then cluster together people that talk about the same topic. Researchers also map relationships among individuals based on their patterns of word use in emails (Keila and Skillicorn, 2005). But these techniques do not attempt to create an accurate social network in terms of interaction or cognitive states of people. In comparison, our data allows

[1]Throughout this paper we will follow this representation scheme for examples – entity mentions will be enclosed in square brackets [...] and relation mentions will be enclosed in set brackets {...}



*Proceedings of the Fourth Linguistic Annotation Workshop, ACL 2010*, pages 20–28,
Uppsala, Sweden, 15-16 July 2010. 

| Sender → Receiver | Email content |
|---|---|
| **Kate → Sam** | [Jacob], the City attorney had a couple of questions which [I] will {attempt to relay} without having a copy of the documents. |
| **Sam → Kate, Mary** | Can you obtain the name of Glendale's bond counsel (lawyer's name, phone number, email, etc.)? |
| **Kate → Sam** | Glendale's City Attorney is Jacob. Please let [me] {know} if [you] need anything else. |
| **Mary → Sam** | I do not see a copy of an opinion in the file nor have we received one since [I] {sent} the execution copies of the ISDA to [Jacob]. |
| **Kate → Jacob** | Jacob, could you provide the name, phone number, etc. of your bond council for our attorney, Sam? |
| **Kate → Sam** | [I] will {work on this for} [you] - and will be in touch. |

Figure 1: An email thread from the Enron Email Corpus. (For space concerns some part of the conversation is removed. The missing conversation does not affect our discussion.)

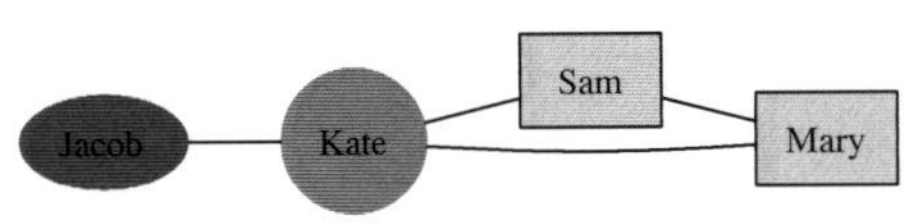


Figure 2: Network formed by considering email exchanges as links. Identical color or shape implies structural equivalence. Only **Sam** and **Mary** are structurally equivalent

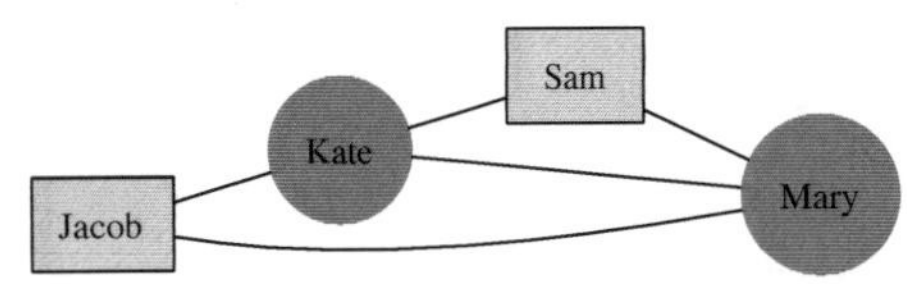


Figure 3: Network formed by augmenting the email exchange network above with links that occur in the content of the emails. Now, **Kate** and **Mary** are structurally equivalent, as are **Sam** and **Jacob**.

for such a technique to be created. This is because our annotations capture interactions described in the content of the email such as face-to-face meetings, physical co-presence and cognizance.

To explore if this is useful, we analyzed an Enron thread which is presented in Figure 1. Figure 2 shows the network formed when only the email exchange is considered. It is easy to see that **Sam** and **Mary** are structurally equivalent and thus have the same role and position in the social network. When we analyze the content of the thread, a link gets added between **Mary** and **Jacob** since **Mary** in her email to **Sam** talks about sending something to **Jacob**. This link changes the roles and positions of people in the network. In the new network, Figure 3, **Kate** and **Mary** appear structurally equivalent to each other, as do **Sam** and **Jacob**. Furthermore, **Mary** now emerges as a more important player than the email exchange on its own suggests. This rather simple example is an indication of the degree to which a link may affect the social network analysis results. In emails where usually a limited number of people are involved, getting an accurate network seems to be crucial to the hierarchal analysis.

There has been much work in the past on annotating entities, relations and events in free text, most notably the ACE effort (Doddington et al., 2004). We intend to leverage this work as much as possible. The task of social network extraction can be broadly divided into 3 tasks: 1) entity extraction; 2) social relation extraction; 3) social event extraction. We are only interested in the third task, social event extraction. For the first two tasks, we can simply use the annotation guidelines developed by the ACE effort. Our social events, however, do not clearly map to the ACE events: we introduce a comprehensive set of social events which are very different from the event annotation that already exists for ACE. This paper is about the annotation of social events.

The structure of the paper is as follows. In Section 2 we present a list of social relations that we annotate. We also talk about some design decisions and explain why we took them. We compare this annotation to existing annotation, notably the ACE annotation, in Section 3. In section 4 we present the procedure of annotation. Section 5 gives details of our inter-annotator agreement calculation procedure and shows the inter-annotator agreement on our task. We conclude in section 6 and mention future direction of research.

## 2 Social Event Annotation

In this section we define the social events that the annotators were asked to annotate. Here, we are interested in the meaning of the annotation; details of the annotation procedure can be found in Section 4. Note that in this annotation effort, we do not consider issues related to the truth of the claims made in the text we are analyzing — we are interested in finding social events whether they are claimed as being true, presented as speculation, or presented as wishful thinking. We assume that other modules will be able to determine the factive status of the described social events, and that social events do not differ from other types of events in this respect.

A social event is an event in which two or more entities relate, communicate or are associated such that for at least one participant, the interaction is **deliberate** and **conscious**. Put differently, at least one participant must be aware of relating to the other participant. In this definition, what constitutes a social relation is an aspect of cognitive state: an agent is aware of being in a particular relation to another agent. While two people passing each other on a street without seeing each other may be a nice plot device in a novel, it is not a social event in our sense, since it does not entail a social relation.

Following are the four types of social events that were annotated:[2]

Interaction event (INR): When both entities participating in an event have each other in their cognitive state (i.e., are aware of the social relation) we say they have an INR relation. The requirement is actually deeper: it extends to the transitive closure under mutual awareness, what in the case of belief is called "mutual belief". An INR event could either be of sub-type VERBAL or NONVERBAL. Note that a verbal interaction event does not mean that all participants must actively communicate verbally, it is enough if one participant communicates verbally and the others are aware of this communication.[3] Furthermore, the interaction can be in physical proximity or from a distance. Therefore, we have further subtypes of INR relation: NEAR and FAR. In all, INR has four subtypes: VERBAL-NEAR, VERBAL-FAR, NONVERBAL-NEAR, NONVERBAL-FAR. Consider the following Example (3). In this sentence, our annotators recorded an INR.VERBAL-FAR between entities **Toujan Faisal** and the **committee**.

(3) [Toujan Faisal], 54, {said} [she] was {informed} of the refusal by an [Interior Ministry committee] overseeing election preparations. **INR.Verbal-Far**

As is intuitive, if one person *informs* the other about something, both have to be cognizant of each other and of the *informing* event. Also, the event of *informing* involves words, therefore, it is a verbal interaction. From the context it is not clear if **Toujan** was informed personally, in which case it would be a NEAR relation, or not. We decided to default to FAR in case the physical proximity is unclear from the context. We decided this because, on observation, we found that if the author of the news article was reporting an event that occurred in close proximity, the author would explicitly say so or give an indication. INR is the only relation which is bi-directional.

Cognition event (COG): When only one person (out of the two people that are participating in an event) has the other in his or her cognitive state, we say there exists a cognition relationship between entities. Consider the aforementioned Example (3). In this sentence, the event *said* marks a COG relation between **Toujan Faisal** and the **committee**. This is because, when one person talks about the other person, the other person must be present in the first person's cognitive state. COG is a directed event from the entity which has the other entity in its cognitive state to the other entity. In the example under consideration, it would be from **Toujan Faisal** to the **committee**. There are no subtypes of this relation.

Physical Proximity event (PPR): We record a PPR event when both the following conditions hold: 1) exactly one entity has the other entity in their cognitive state (this is the same requirement as that for COG) and 2) both the entities are physically proximate. Consider the following Example (4). Here, one can reasonably assume that **Asif Muhammad Hanif** was aware of being in physical proximity to the **three people** killed, while the inverse was not necessarily true.

[2] Details of the annotation guidelines can be found in the unpublished annotation manual, which we will refer to in the final version of the paper.

[3] For this reason we explicitly annotate legal events as VERBAL because legal interactions usually involve words

(4) [Three people] were killed when (...), [Asif Muhammad Hanif], (...), {detonated explosives strapped to [his] body} **PPR**

PPR is a directed event like COG. There are no subtypes of this relation. Note that if there exists a PPR event then of course there would also be a COG event. In such cases, the PPR event subsumes COG, and we do not separately record a COG event.

Perception event (PCR): The Perception Relationship is the distant equivalent of the Physical Proximity event. The point is not physical distance; rather, the important ingredient is the awareness required for PPR, except that physical proximity is not required, and in fact physical distance is required. This kind of relationship usually exists if one entity is watching the other entity on TV broadcast, listening to him or her on the radio or using a listening device, or reading about the other entity in a newspaper or magazine etc. Consider the following Example (5). In this example, we record a PCR relation between the **pair** and the **Nepalese babies**. This is because, the babies are of course not aware of the pair. Moreover, the pair heard about the babies so there is no physical proximity. It is not COG because there was an explicit external information source which brought the babies to the attention of the pair.

(5) [The pair] flew to Singapore last year after {hearing} of the successful surgery on [Nepalese babies] [Ganga] and [Jamuna Shrestha], (...). **PCR**

PCR is a directed event like COG. There are no subtypes of this relation. Note that if there exists a PCR event then we do not separately record a COG event.

Figure 4 represents the series of decisions that an annotator is required to take before reaching a terminal node (or an event annotation label). The interior nodes of the tree represent questions that annotators answer to progress downwards in the tree. Each question has a binary answer. For example, the first question the annotators answer to get to the type and subtype of an event is: "Is the relation directed (1-way) or bi-directional (2-way)?" Depending on the answer, they move to the left or the right in the tree respectively. If its a 2-way relation, then it has to one of the sub-types of INR because only INR requires that both entities be aware of each other.

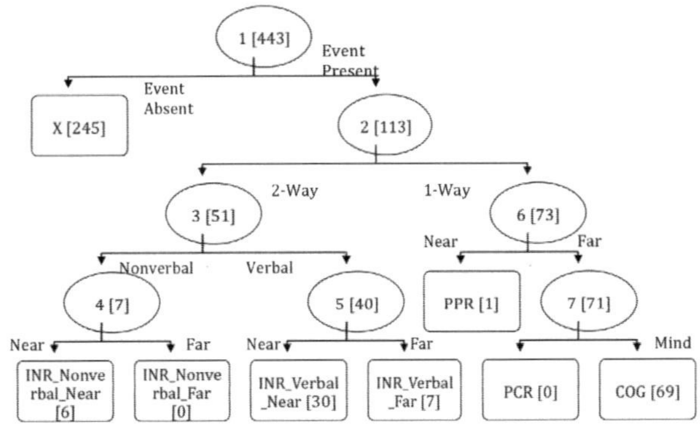


Figure 4: Tree representation of decision points for selecting an event type/subtype out of the list of social events. Each decision point is numbered for easy reference. We refer to these number later when we present our results. The numbers in braces ([...]) are the number of examples that reach a decision point.

## 3 Comparison Between Social Events and ACE Annotations

In this section, we compare our annotations with existing annotation efforts. To the best of our knowledge, no annotation effort has been geared towards extracting social events, or towards extracting expressions that convey social relations in text. The Automated Content Extraction (ACE) annotations are the most similar to ours because ACE also annotates Person Entities (PER.Individual, PER.Group), Relations between people (PER-SOC), and various types of Events. Our annotation scheme is different, however, because the focus of our event annotation is on events that occur only between people. Furthermore, we annotate text that expresses the cognitive states of the people involved, or allows the annotator to infer it. Therefore, at the top level of classification we differentiate between events in which only one entity is cognizant of the other versus events when both entities are cognizant of each other. This distinction is, we believe, novel in event or relation annotation. In the remainder of this section, we will present statistics and detailed examples to highlight differences between our event annotations and the ACE event annotations.

The statistics we present are based on 62 documents from the ACE-2005 corpus that one of our annotator also annotated.[4] Since our event types and subtypes are not directly comparable to the

[4]Due to space constraints we do not give statistics for the other annotator.

ACE event types, we say there is a "match" when both the following conditions hold:

1. The span of text that represents an event in the ACE event annotations overlap with ours.

2. The entities participating in the ACE event are same as the entities participating in our event.[5]

Our annotator recorded a total of 212 events in 62 documents. We found a total of 63 candidate ACE events that had at least two Person entities involved. Out of these 63 candidate events, 54 match both the aforementioned conditions and hence our annotations. A classification of all of the events (those found by our annotators and the ACE events involving at least two persons) into our social event categories and into the ACE categories is given in Figure 5. The figure shows that the majority of social events that match the ACE events are of type INR.VERBAL-NEAR. On analysis, we found that most of these correspond to the ACE type/subtype CONTACT.MEET. It should be noted, however, our type/subtype INR.VERBAL-NEAR has a broader definition than ACE type/subtype CONTACT.MEET, as will become apparent later in this section. In the following, we discuss the 9 ACE events that are not social events, and then we discuss the 158 social events that are not ACE events.

Out of the nine candidate ACE events which did not match our social event annotation, we found five are our annotation errors, i.e. when we analyzed manually and looked for ACE events that did not correspond to our annotations, we found that our annotator missed these events. The remaining four, in contrast, are useful for our discussion because they highlight the differences in ACE and our annotation perspectives. This will become clearer with the following example:

(6) In central Baghdad, [a Reuters cameraman] and [a cameraman for Spain's Telecinco] died when an American tank fired on the Palestine Hotel

ACE has annotated the above example as an event of type CONFLICT-ATTACK in which there are two entities that are of type person: the **Reuters cameraman** and the **cameraman for Spain's Telecinco**, both of which are arguments of type "Victim". Being an event that has two person entities involved makes the above sentence a valid candidate (or potential) ACE event that we match with our annotations. However, it fails to match our annotations, since we do not annotate an event in this sentence. The reason is that this example does not reveal the cognitive states of the two entities – we do not know whether one was aware of the other.

We now discuss social events that are not ACE events. From Figure 5 we see that most of the events that did not overlap with ACE event annotations were Cognition (COG) social events. In the following, our annotator records a COG relation between **Digvijay Singh** and **Abdul Kalam** (also **Atal Behari Vajpayee** and **Varuna**). The reason is that by virtue of talking about the two entities, **Digvijay Singh's** cognitive state contains those entities. However, the sentence does not reveal the cognitive states of the other two entities and therefore it is not an INR event. In contrast, ACE does not have any event annotation for this sentence.

(7) The Times of India newspaper quoted [Digvijay Singh] as {saying} that [Prime Minister Atal Behari Vajpayee] and [President Abdul Kalam] had offended [the Hindu rain God Varuna] by remaining bachelors. **COG**

It is easy to see why COG relations are not usually annotated as ACE events. But it is counterintuitive for INR social events not to be annotated as ACE events. We explain this using Example (3) in Section 2. Our annotator recorded an INR relation between **Toujan Faisal** and the **committee** (event span: *informed*). ACE did not record any event between the two entities.[6] This example highlights the difference between our definition of Interaction events and ACE's definition of Contact events. For this reason, in Figure 5, 51 of our INR relations do not overlap with ACE event categories.

## 4 Annotation Procedure

We used Callisto (a configurable workbench) (Day et al., 2004) to annotate the ACE-2005 corpus for

[5]Recall that our event annotations are between exactly two entities of type PER.Individual or PER.Group.

[6]The ACE event annotated in the sentence is of type "Personell-Elect" (span *election*) which is not recorded as an event between two or more entities and is not relevant here.

| 62 Documents | | | Conflict (5) | Contact (32) | | Justice-* (13) | Life (7) | | | Transaction (2) | Not Found |
|---|---|---|---|---|---|---|---|---|---|---|---|
| | | | Attack | Meet | Phone-Write | | Die | Divorce | Injure | Transfer-Money | |
| INR | Verbal | Near (66) | 0 | 26 | 0 | 9 | 0 | 0 | 0 | 0 | 31 |
| | | Far (17) | 0 | 0 | 3 | 3 | 0 | 1 | 0 | 0 | 10 |
| | NonVerbal | Near (14) | 3 | 0 | 0 | 0 | 2 | 0 | 0 | 1 | 8 |
| | | Far (3) | 0 | 0 | 0 | 0 | 0 | 0 | 0 | 1 | 2 |
| COG (109) | | | 2 | 0 | 0 | 0 | 1 | 0 | 0 | 0 | 106 |
| PPR (2) | | | 0 | 0 | 0 | 0 | 1 | 0 | 1 | 0 | 0 |
| PCR (1) | | | 0 | 0 | 0 | 0 | 0 | 0 | 0 | 0 | 1 |
| Errors | | | 0 | 3 | 0 | 1 | 1 | 0 | 0 | 0 | |

Figure 5: This table maps the type and subtype of ACE events to our types and subtypes of social events. The columns have ACE event types and sub-types. The rows represent our social event types and sub-types. The last column is the number of our events that are not annotated as ACE events. The last row has the number of social events that our annotator missed but are ACE events.

the social events we defined earlier. The ACE-2005 corpus has already been annotated for entities as part of the ACE effort. The entity annotation is therefore not part of this annotation effort. We hired two annotators. Annotators opened ACE-2005 files one by one in Callisto. They could see the whole document at one time (top screen of Figure 6) with entities highlighted in blue (bottom screen of Figure 6). These entities were only of type PER.Individual and PER.Group and belonged to class SPC. All other ACE entity annotations were removed. The annotators were required to read the whole document (not just the part that has entities) and record a social event span (highlighted in dark blue in Figure 6), social event type, subtype and the two participating entities in the event.

The span of a event mention is the *minimum* span of text that *best* represents the presence of the type of event being recorded. It can also be viewed as the span of text that evokes the type of event being recorded. The span may be a word, a phrase or the whole sentence. For example, the span in Example (4) in Section 2 includes *strapped to his body* because that confirms the physical proximity of the two entities. We have, however, not paid much attention to the annotation of the span, and will not report inter-annotator agreement on this part of the annotation. The reason for this is that we are interested in annotating the underlying semantics; we will use machine learning to find the linguistics clues to each type of social event, rather than relying on the annotators' ability to determine these. Also note that we did not give precise instructions on which entity mentions to choose in case of multiple mentions of the same entity. Again, this is because we are interested in annotating the underlying semantics, and we will rely on later analysis to determine which mentions participate in signaling the annotated social events.

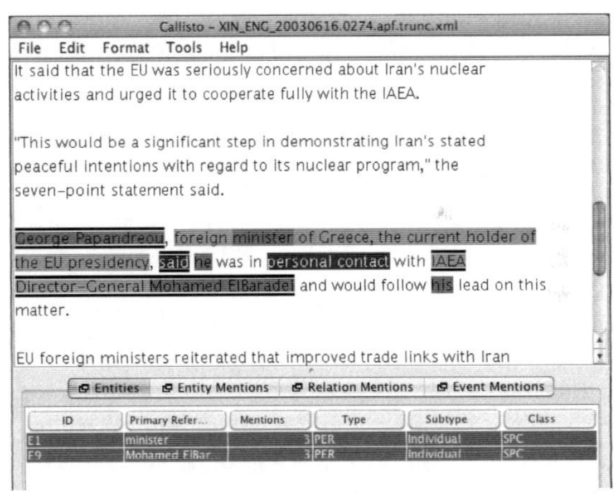


Figure 6: Snapshot of Callisto. Top screen has the text from a document. Bottom screen has tabs for Entities, Entity Mentions etc. An annotator selected text *said*, highlighted in dark blue, as an event of type COG between Entities with entity ID E1 and E9.

Both our annotators annotated 46 common documents. Out these, there was one document that had no entity annotations, implying no social event annotation. The average number of entities in the remaining 45 documents was 6.82 per document, and the average number of entity mentions per document was 23.78. The average number of social events annotated per document by one annotator was 3.43, whereas for the other annotator it was 3.69. In the next section we present our inter-annotator agreement calculations for these 45 documents.

## 5 Inter-annotator Agreement

Annotators consider all sentences that contain at least two person entities (individuals or group), but do not always consider all possible labels, or annotation values. As represented in the decision tree in Figure 5, many of the labels are conditional. At each next depth of the tree, the number of instances can become considerably pruned. Due to the novelty of the annotation task, and the conditional nature of the labels, we want to assess the reliability of the annotation of each decision point. For this, we report Cohen's Kappa (Cohen, 1960) for each independent decision. We use the standard formula for Cohen's Kappa given by:

$$Kappa = \frac{P(a) - P(e)}{1 - P(e)}$$

where $P(a)$ is probability of agreement and $P(e)$ is probability of chance agreement. These probabilities can be calculated from the confusion matrix represented as follows:

| | $Yes_{Ann_2}$ | $No_{Ann_2}$ |
|---|---|---|
| $Yes_{Ann_1}$ | A | B |
| $No_{Ann_1}$ | C | D |

In addition, we present the confusion matrix for each decision point to show the absolute number of cases considered, and F-measure to show the proportion of cases agreed upon. For most decision points, the Kappa scores are at or above the 0.67 threshold recommended by Krippendorff (1980) with F-measures above 0.90. Where Kappa is low, F-measure remains high. As discussed below, we conclude that the annotation schema is reliable.

We note that in the ACE annotation effort, inter-annotator agreement (IAA) was measured by a single number, but this number did not take chance agreement into account: it simply used the evaluation metric to compare systems against a gold standard. Furthermore, this metric is composed of distinct parts which were weighted in accordance with research goals from year to year, meaning that the results of applying the metric changed from year to year. We have also performed an ACE-style IAA evaluation, which we report at the end of this section.

Figure 7 shows the results for the seven binary decision points, considered separately. The number of the decision point in the table corresponds to the decision points in Figure 4. The (flattened) confusion matrices in column two present annotator two's choices by annotator one's, with positive agreement in the upper left (cell A) and negative agreement in the lower right (cell D). In all cases the cell values on the agreement diagonal (A, D) are much higher than the cells for disagreement (B, C). The upper left cell (A) of the matrix for decision 1 represents the positive agreements on the presence of a social event (N=133), and these are the cases considered for decision 2. For the remaining decisions, agreement is always unbalanced towards agreement on the positive cases, with few negative cases. In the case of decision 4, for example, this reflects the inherent unlikelihood of the NONVERBAL-FAR event. In other cases, it reflects a property of the genre. For example, when we apply this annotation schema to fiction, we find a much higher frequency of physically proximate events (PPR), corresponding to the lower left cell (D) of the confusion matrix for decision 6.

For decision 4 (NONVERBAL-NEAR) and 7 (PCR/COG), kappa scores are low but the confusion matrices and high F-measures demonstrate that the absolute agreement is very high. Kappa measures the amount of agreement that would not have occurred by chance, with values in [-1,1]. For binary data and two annotators, values of -1 can occur, indicating that the annotators have perfectly non-random disagreements. The probability of an annotation value is estimated by its frequency in the data (the marginals of the confusion matrix). It does not measure the actual amount of agreement among annotators, as illustrated by the rows for decisions 4 and 7. Because NONVERBAL-FAR is chosen so rarely by either annotator (never by annotator 2), the likelihood that both annotators will agree on NONVERBAL-NEAR is close to one. In this case, there is little room for agreement above chance, hence the Kappa score of zero. We should point out, however, that this skewness was revealed from the annotated corpus. We did not bias our annotators to look for a particular type of relation.

The five cases of high Kappa and high F-measure indicate aspects of the annotation where annotators generally agree, and where the agreement is unlikely to be accidental. We conclude that these aspects of the annotation can be carried out reliably as independent decisions. The two cases of low Kappa and high F-measure indicate aspects of the annotation where, for this data, there is relatively little opportunity for disagreement.

| Decision Point | Confusion Matrix | | | | Kappa | F1 |
|---|---|---|---|---|---|---|
| | A | B | C | D | | |
| 1 (+/- Relation) | 133 | 31 | 34 | 245 | 0.68 | 0.80 |
| 2 (1 or 2 way) | 51 | 8 | 1 | 73 | 0.86 | 0.91 |
| 3 (Verbal/NonV) | 40 | 4 | 0 | 7 | 0.73 | 0.95 |
| 4 (NonV-Near/Far) | 6 | 0 | 1 | 0 | 0.00 | 0.92 |
| 5 (Verbal-Near/Far) | 30 | 1 | 2 | 7 | 0.77 | 0.95 |
| 6 (+/- PPR) | 71 | 0 | 1 | 1 | 0.66 | 0.99 |
| 7 (PCR/COG) | 69 | 1 | 1 | 0 | -0.01 | 0.98 |

Figure 7: This table presents the Inter-annotator agreement measures. Column 1 is the decision point corresponding to the decision tree. Column 2 represents a flattened confusion matrix where A corresponds to top left corner, D corresponds to the bottom right corner, B corresponds to top right corner and C corresponds to the bottom left corner of the confusion matrix. We present values for Cohen's Kappa in column 3 and F-measure in the last column.

Now, we present a measure of % agreement for our annotators by using the ACE evaluation scheme.[7] We considered one annotator to be the gold standard and the other to be a system being evaluated against the gold standard. For the calculation of this measure we first take the union of all event spans. As in the ACE evaluation scheme, we associate penalties with each wrong decision annotators take about the entities participating in an event, type and sub-type of an event. Since these penalties are not public, we assign our own penalties. We choose penalties that are not biased towards any particular event type or subtype. We decide the penalty based on the number of options an annotator has to consider before taking a certain decision. For example, we assign a penalty of 0.5 if one annotator records an event which the other annotator does not. If annotators disagree on the relation type, the penalty is 0.25 because there are four options to select from (INR, COG, PPR, PCR). Similarly, we assign a penalty of 0.2 if the annotators disagree on the relation sub-types (VERBAL-NEAR, VERBAL-FAR, NONVERBAL-NEAR, NONVERBAL-FAR, No sub-type). We assign a penalty of 0.5 if the annotators disagree on the participating entities (incorporating the directionality in directed relations). Using these penalties, we get % agreement of 69.74%. This is a high agreement rate as compared to that of ACE's event annotation, which was reported to be 31.5% at the ACE 2005 meeting.

[7]http://www.itl.nist.gov/iad/mig//tests/ace/2007/doc/ace07-evalplan.v1.3a.pdf

## 6 Conclusion and Future Work

We have presented a new annotation scheme for extracting social networks from text. We have argued, social network created by the sender - receiver links in Enron Email corpus can benefit from social event links extracted from the content of emails where people talk about their "implicit" social relations. Our annotation task is novel in that we are interested in the cognitive states of people: who is aware of interacting with whom, and who is aware of whom without interacting. Though the task requires detection of events followed by conditional classification of events into four types and subtypes, we achieve high Kappa (0.66-0.86) and F-measure (0.8-0.9). We also achieve a high global agreement of 69.74% which is inspired by Automated Content Extraction (ACE) inter-annotator agreement measure. These measures indicate that our annotations are reliable.

In future work, we will apply our annotation effort to other genres, including fiction, and to text from which larger social networks can be extracted, such as extended journalistic reporting about a group of people.

Please contact the second author of the paper about the availability of the corpus.

## Acknowledgments

This work was funded by NSF grant IIS-0713548. We thank Dr. David Day for help with adapting the annotation interface (Callisto) to our requirements. We would like to thank David Elson for extremely useful discussions and feedback on the annotation manual and the inter-annotator calculation scheme. We would also like to thank the Natural Language Processing group at Columbia University for their feedback on our classification of social events.

## References

Jacob Cohen. 1960. A coeffiecient of agreement for nominal scales. *Educational and Psychological Measurement*, 20:37–46.

David Day, Chad McHenry, Robyn Kozierok, and Laurel Riek. 2004. Callisto: A configurable annotation workbench. *International Conference on Language Resources and Evaluation.*

Jana Diesner, Terrill L Frantz, and Kathleen M Carley. 2005. Communication networks from the enron email corpus it's always about the people. enron is no different. *Computational & Mathematical Organization Theory*, 11(3):201–228.

G Doddington, A Mitchell, M Przybocki, L Ramshaw, S Strassel, and R Weischedel. 2004. The automatic content extraction (ace) program–tasks, data, and evaluation. *LREC*, pages 837–840.

P S Keila and D B Skillicorn. 2005. Structure in the enron email dataset. *Computational & Mathematical Organization Theory*, 11 (3):183–199.

Bryan Klimt and Yiming Yang. 2004. Introducing the enron corpus. *In First Conference on Email and Anti-Spam (CEAS).*

Klaus Krippendorff. 1980. *Content Analysis: An Introduction to Its Methodology.* Sage Publications.

Andrew McCallum, Xuerui Wang, and Andres Corrada-Emmanuel. 2007. Topic and role discovery in social networks with experiments on enron and academic email. *Journal of Artificial Intelligence Research*, 30 (1):249–272.

Nishith Pathak, Colin DeLong, Arindam Banerjee, and Kendric Erickson. 2008. Social topic models for community extraction. *Proceedings of SNA-KDD.*

Ryan Rowe, German Creamer, Shlomo Hershkop, and Salvatore J Stolfo. 2007. Automated social hierarchy detection through email network analysis. *Proceedings of the 9th WebKDD and 1st SNA-KDD 2007 workshop on Web mining and social network analysis*, pages 109–117.

Stanley Wasserman and Katherine Faust. 1994. *Social Network Analysis: Methods and Applications.* New York: Cambridge University Press.

# Agile Corpus Annotation in Practice: An Overview of Manual and Automatic Annotation of CVs

**Bea Alex Claire Grover Rongzhou Shen**
School of Informatics
University of Edinburgh
Edinburgh, EH8 9AB, UK

**Mijail Kabadjov**
Joint Research Centre
European Commission
Via E. Fermi 2749, Ispra (VA), Italy

Contact: balex@staffmail.ed.ac.uk

## Abstract

This paper describes work testing agile data annotation by moving away from the traditional, linear phases of corpus creation towards iterative ones and by recognizing the potential for sources of error occurring throughout the annotation process.

## 1 Introduction

Annotated data sets are an important resources for various research fields, including natural language processing (NLP) and text mining (TM). While the detection of annotation inconsistencies in different data sets has been investigated (e.g. Novák and Razímová, 2009) and their effect on NLP performance has been studied (e.g. Alex et al. 2006), very little work has been done on deriving better methods of annotation as a whole process in order to maximize both the quality and quantity of annotated data. This paper describes our annotation project in which we tested the relatively new approach of agile corpus annotation (Voormann and Gut, 2008) of moving away from the traditional, linear phases of corpus creation towards iterative ones and of recognizing the fact that sources of error can occur throughout the annotation process.

We explain agile annotation and discuss related work in Section 2. Section 3 describes the entire annotation process and all its aspects. We provide details on the data collection and preparation, the annotation tool, the annotators and the annotation phases. Section 4 describes the final annotation scheme and Section 5 presents inter-annotator-agreement (IAA) figures measured throughout the annotation. In Section 6, we summarize the performance of the machine-learning (ML)-based TM components which were trained and evaluated on the annotated data. We discuss our findings and conclude in Section 7.

## 2 Background and Related Work

The manual and automatic annotation work described in this paper was conducted as part of the TXV project. The technology used was based on TM components that were originally developed for the biomedical domain during its predecessor project (Alex et al., 2008b). In TXV we adapted the tools to the recruitment domain in a short time frame. The aim was to extract key information from curricula vitae (CVs) for matching applicants to job adverts and to each other. The TM output is visualized in a web application with search navigation that captures relationships between candidates, their skills and organizations etc. This web interface allows recruiters to find hidden information in large volumes of unstructured text.

Both projects were managed using agile, test-driven software development, i.e. solutions were created based on the principles of rapid-prototyping and iterative development cycles of deliverable versions of the TM system and the web application.[1] The same principles were also applied to other project work, including the manual annotation. The aim of this annotation was to produce annotated data for training ML-based TM technology as well as evaluating system components.

Collecting data, drawing up annotation guidelines and getting annotators to annotate this data in sequential steps is similar to the waterfall model in software engineering (Royce, 1970). This approach can be inefficient and costly if annotators unknowingly carried out work that could have been avoided and it can lead to difficulties if at the end of the process the requirements no longer match the annotations. Instead we applied agile software engineering methods to the process of creating annotated data. This is a relatively recent philosophy in software

[1] The agile software development principles are explained in the Agile Manifesto: http://agilemanifesto.org/



*Proceedings of the Fourth Linguistic Annotation Workshop, ACL 2010*, pages 29–37,
Uppsala, Sweden, 15-16 July 2010. 

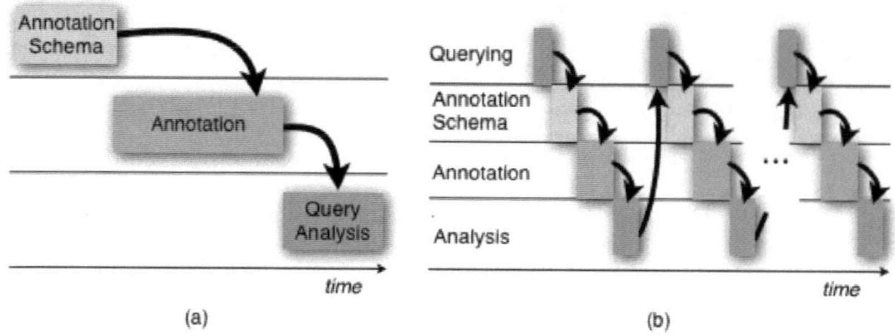


Figure 1: The phases of traditional corpus creation (a) and the cyclic approach in agile corpus creation (b). Reproduction of Figure 2 in Voormann and Gut (2008).

development which was inspired to overcome the drawbacks of the waterfall model. The idea of applying agile methods to corpus creation and annotation was first inspired by Voormann and Gut (2008) but was not tested empirically. Cyclic annotation was already proposed by Atkins et al. (1992) and Biber (1993) with a focus on data creation rather than data annotation. In this paper, we describe a way of testing this agile annotation in practice.

The idea behind an agile annotation process is to produce useable manually annotated data fast as well as discover and correct flaws in either the annotation guidelines or the annotation setup early on. Voormann and Gut (2008) propose query-driven annotation, a cyclic corpus creation and annotation process that begins with formulating a query. The main advantages of this approach are:

- The annotation scheme evolves over time which ensures that annotations are consistent and remain focussed on the research that is carried out. An iterative annotation process therefore improves the annotation guidelines but keeps the annotations suitable to the relevant research questions.
- Problems with the annotation guidelines, errors in the annotation and issues with the setup become apparent immediately and can be corrected early on. This can avoid difficulties later on and will save time and cost.
- Some annotation data is available early on.

Voormann and Gut compare the cyclical approach in agile annotation to traditional linear-phrase corpus creation depicted in Figure 1. In the following section we describe the annotation process in our project which followed the principles of agile corpus creation.

## 3 Annotation Process

This section provides an overview of all aspect involved in the annotation of a data set of CVs for various types of semantic information useful to recruiters when analysing CVs and placing candidates with particular jobs or organizations. We provide information on the data collection, the document preparation, the annotation tool and the annotation process following agile methods.

### 3.1 Data Collection

We automatically collected a set of CVs of software engineers and programmers which are publicly available online. This data set was created by firstly querying Google using the Google API[2] for word documents containing either the terms *"CV"*, *"resume"* or *"curriculum vitae"* as well as the terms *"developer"*, *"programmer"* or *"software"* but excluding documents containing the word *"template"* or *"sample"*. Furthermore, the query was restricted to a 3-month period from 30/03 to 30/06/2008.[3]

We automatically downloaded the Word documents returned by this query, resulting in a pool of 1,000 candidate CVs available for annotation. We split these documents randomly into a TRAIN, a DEVTEST and a TEST set in a ratio of approximately 64:16:20. We used the annotated TRAIN data for training ML-based models and deriving rules and the DEVTEST data for system development and optimization. We set aside the blind TEST set for evaluating the final performance of our named entity recognition (NER) and relation extraction (RE)

[2] `http://code.google.com/apis/ajaxsearch`

[3] The exact Google query is: '(CV OR resume OR "curriculum vitae") AND (developer OR programmer OR software) AND filetype:doc AND -template AND -sample AND daterange:2454466-2454647'.

| CV data set | | | | |
|---|---|---|---|---|
| Set | TRAIN | DEVTEST | TEST | ALL |
| Files | 253 | 72 | 78 | 403 |
| Annotations | 279 | 84 | 91 | 454 |

Table 1: Number of files and annotated files in each section of the CV data set.

components (see Section 6).

The final manually annotated data set contains 403 files, of which 352 are singly and 51 doubly annotated, resulting in an overall total of 454 annotations (see Table 1). This does not include the files used during the pilot annotation. The doubly annotated CVs were used to determine inter-annotator agreement (IAA) in regular intervals (see Section 5).

Some of the documents in the pool were not genuine CVs but either job adverts or CV writing advice. We let the annotators carry out the filtering process of only choosing genuine CVs of software developers and programmers for annotation and reject but record any documents that did not fit this category. The annotators rejected 99 files as being either not CVs at all (49) or being out-of-domain CVs from other types of professionals (50). Therefore, just over 50% of the documents in the pool were used up during the annotation process.

### 3.2 Document Preparation

Before annotation, all candidate CVs were then automatically converted from Word DOC format to OpenOffice ODT as well as to Acrobat PDF format in a batch process using OpenOffice macros. The resulting contents.xml files for each ODT version of the documents contain the textual information of the original CVs. An XSLT stylesheet was used to simplify this format to a simpler in-house XML format, as the input into our pre-processing pipeline. We retained all formatting and style information in span elements for potential later use.

The pre-processing includes tokenization, sentence boundary detection, part-of-speech tagging, lemmatization, chunking, abbreviation detection and rule-based NER for person, location names and dates. This information extraction system is a modular pipeline built around the LT-XML2[4] and LT-TTT2[5] toolsets. The NER output is stored as standoff annotations in the XML. These pre-processed files were used as the basis for annotation.

### 3.3 Annotation Tool

For annotating the text of the CVs we chose MMAX2, the Java-based open source tool (Müller and Strube, 2006).[6] MMAX2 supports multiple levels of annotation by way of stand-off annotation. As a result MMAX2 creates one separate file for each level of annotation for each given base data file. Only the annotation level files get edited during the annotation phase. The base data files which contain the textual information of the documents do not change. In our project, we were interested in three levels of annotation, one for named entities (NEs), one for zones and one for relations between NEs. The MMAX2 GUI allows annotators to mark up nested structures as well as intra- and inter-sentential relations. Both of these functionalities were crucial to our annotation effort.

As the files used for annotation already contained some NEs which were recognized automatically using the rule-based NER system and stored in standoff XML, the conversion into and out of the MMAX2 format was relatively straightforward. For each file to be annotated, we created one base file containing the tokenized text and one entity file containing the rule-based NEs.[7]

### 3.4 Annotation Phases

We employed 3 annotators with various degrees of experience in annotation and computer science and therefore familiar with software engineering skills and terminology. The lead researcher of the project, the first author of this paper, managed the annotators and organized regular meetings with them.

We followed the agile corpus creation approach and carried out cycles of annotations, starting with a simple paper-based pilot annotation. This first annotation of 10 documents enabled us to get a first impression of the type of information contained in CVs of software engineers and programmers as well as the type of information we wanted to capture in the manual and automatic annotation. We drew up a first set of potential types of zones that occur within

[4]http://www.ltg.ed.ac.uk/software/ltxml2

[5]http://www.ltg.ed.ac.uk/software/lt-ttt2

[6]`http://mmax2.sourceforge.net`

[7]For more information on how this is done see Müller and Strube (2006).

CVs and the types of NEs that can be found within each zone (e.g. an EDUCATION zone containing NEs of type LOC, ORG and QUAL).

Using this set of potential markables, we decided on a subset of NEs and zones to be annotated in future rounds. Regarding the zones, we settled on annotating zone titles in a similar way as NEs. Our assumption was that recognizing the beginning of a zone can sufficiently identify zone boundaries. We did not include relations between NEs at this stages, as we wanted to get a clearer idea of the definitions of relevant NEs first before proceeding to relations.

We then carried out a second pilot annotation using 10 more CVs selected from the candidate pool. We used the revised annotation scheme and this time the annotation was done electronically using MMAX2. The annotators also had access to the PDF and DOC versions of each file in case crucial structural or formatting information was lost in the conversion. Files were annotated for NEs and zone titles. We also asked the annotators to answer the following questions:

- Does it make sense to annotate the proposed markables and what are the difficulties in doing so?
- Are there any interesting markables missing from the list?
- Are there are any issues with using the annotation tool?

Half way through the second pilot we scheduled a further meeting to discuss their answers, addressed any question, comments or issues with regard to the annotation and adjusted the annotation guidelines accordingly. At this point, as we felt that the definitions of NEs were sufficiently clear and added guidelines for annotating various types of binary relations between NEs, for example a LOC-ORG relation referring to a particular organization situated at a particular location, e.g. Google - Dublin. We list the final set of markables as defined at the end of the annotation process in Tables 2 and 3.

During the second half of the second pilot we asked the annotators to time their annotation and established that it can take between 30 minutes and 1.5 hours to annotate a CV. We then calculated pairwise IAA for two doubly annotated files which allowed us to get some evidence for which definition of NEs, zone titles and relations were still ambiguous or not actually relevant.

In parallel with both pilots, we also liaised closely with a local recruitment company to gain a first-hand understanding of what information recruiters are interested in when matching candidates to employments or employers. This consultation as well as the conclusions made after the second pilot led to further adaptions of the annotation scheme before the main annotation phase began.

Based on the feedback from the second pilot annotation, we also made some changes to the data conversion and the annotation tool setup to reduce the amount of work for annotators but without restricting the set of markables. In the case of some nested NEs, we propagated relations between embedded NEs that could be referred from the relations of the containing NEs. For example, two DATE entities nested within a DATERANGE entity, the latter of which the annotator related to an ORG entity, were related to the same ORG entity automatically. We also introduced a general GROUP entity which could be used by the annotators to mark up lists of NEs, for example, if they were all related to a different NE mention of type X. In that case, the annotators only had to mark up a relation between the GROUP and X. All implicit relations between the NEs nested in the GROUP and X were propagated during the conversion from the MMAX2 format back into the in-house XML format. This proved particularly useful for annotating relations between SKILL entities and other types of NEs.

Once those changes had been made, the main annotation phase began. Each in-domain CV that was loaded into the annotation tool already contained some NEs pre-annotated by the rule-based NER system (see Section 3.2). The annotators had to correct the annotations in case they were erroneous. Overall, the annotators reported this pre-annotation to be useful rather than hindering as they did not have to do too many corrections. At the end of each day, the annotators checked in their work into the project's subversion (SVN) repository. This provided us with additional control and backup in case we needed to go back to previous versions at later stages.

The annotation guidelines still evolved during the main annotation. Regular annotation meetings were held in case the annotators had questions on the guidelines or if they wanted to discuss specific examples. If a change was made to the annotation guidelines, all annotators were informed and asked to update their annotations accordingly. Moreover, IAA was calculated regularly on sub-sections of the doubly annotated data. This provided more empirical evidence for the types of markables the annotators found difficult to mark up and where clarifications where necessary. The reasons for this were that their definitions were ambiguous or underspecified.

We deliberately kept the initial annotation scheme simple. The idea was for the annotators to shape the annotation scheme based on evidence in the actual data. We believe that this approach made the data set more useful for its final use to train and evaluate TM components. As a result of this agile annotation approach, we became aware of any issues very early on and were able to correct them accordingly.

## 4 Annotation Scheme

In this section, we provide a summary of the final annotation scheme as an overview of all the markables present in the annotated data set.

### 4.1 Named Entities

In general, we asked the annotators to mark up every mention of all NE types throughout the entire CV, even if they did not refer to the CV owner. With some exceptions (DATE in DATERANGE and LOC or ORG in ADDRESS), annotators were asked to avoid nested NEs and aim for a flat annotation. Discontinuous NEs in coordinated structures had to be marked as such, i.e. the NE should only contain strings that refer to it. Finally, abbreviations and their definitions had to be annotated as two separate NEs. The NE types in the final annotation guidelines are listed in Table 2. While carrying out the NE annotation, the annotators were also asked to set the NE attribute of type CANDIDATE (by default set to `true`) to `false` if a certain NE was not an attribute of the CV owner (e.g. the ADDRESS of a referee).

### 4.2 Zone Titles

Regarding the zone titles, we provided a list of synonyms for each type as context (see Table 2). The annotators were asked only to annotate main zone titles, ignoring sub-zones. They were also asked to mark up only the relevant sub-string of the text referring to the zone title and not the entire title if it contained irrelevant information.

| Entity Type | Description |
|---|---|
| ADDRESS | Addresses with streets or postcodes. |
| DATE | Absolute (e.g. 10/04/2010), underspecified (e.g. April 2010) or relative dates (e.g. to date) including DATE entities within DATERANGE entities. |
| DATERANGE | Date ranges with a specific start and end date including ones with either point not explicitly stated (e.g. since 2008). |
| DOB | Dates of birth. |
| EMAIL | Email addresses. |
| JOB | Job titles and roles referring to the official name a post (e.g. software developer) but not a skill (e.g. software development). |
| LOC | Geo-political place names. |
| ORG | Names of companies, institutions and organizations. |
| PER | Person names excluding titles. |
| PHONE | Telephone and fax numbers. |
| POSTCODE | Post codes. |
| QUAL | Qualifications achieved or working towards. |
| SKILL | Skills and areas of expertise incl. hard skills (e.g. Java, C++, French) or general areas of expertise (e.g. software development) but not soft or interpersonal skills (e.g. networking, team work). |
| TIMESPAN | Durations of time (e.g. 7 years, 2 months, over 2 years). |
| URL | URLs |
| GROUP | Dummy NE to group several NEs for annotating multiple relations at once. The individual NEs contained within the group still have to be annotated. |
| **Zone Title Type** | **Synonyms** |
| EDUCATION | Education, Qualifications, Training, Certifications, Courses |
| SKILLS | Skills, Qualifications, Experience, Competencies |
| SUMMARY | Summary, Profile |
| PERSONAL | Personal Information, Personal Data |
| EMPLOYMENT | Employment, Employment History, Work History, Career, Career Record |
| REFERENCES | References, Referees |
| OTHER | Other zone titles not covered by this list, e.g. Publications, Patents, Grants, Associations, Interests, Additional. |

Table 2: The types of NEs and zone titles annotated.

### 4.3 Relations

The binary relations that were annotated (see Table 3) always link two different types of NE mentions. Annotators were asked to mark up relations within the same zone but not across zones.

| Relation Type | Description |
|---|---|
| TEMP-SKILL | A skill related to a temporal expression (e.g. Java - 7 years). TEMP includes any temporal NE types (DATE, DATERANGE and TIMESPAN). |
| TEMP-LOC | A location related to a temporal expression (e.g. Dublin - summer 2004). |
| TEMP-ORG | An organization related to a temporal expression (e.g. Google - 2001-2004). |
| TEMP-JOB | A job title related to a temporal expression (e.g. Software Engineer - Sep. 2001 to Jun. 2004). |
| TEMP-QUAL | A qualification related to a temporal expression (e.g. PhD - June 2004). |
| LOC-ORG | An organization related to a location (e.g. Google - Dublin). |
| LOC-JOB | A job title related to a location (e.g. Software Engineer - Dublin). |
| LOC-QUAL | A qualification related to a location (e.g. PhD - Dublin). |
| ORG-JOB | A job title related to an organization (e.g. Software Engineer - Google). |
| ORG-QUAL | A qualification related to an organization (e.g. PhD - University of Toronto). |
| GROUP-X | A relation that can be assigned in case a group of NEs all relate to another NE X. GROUP-X can be any of the relation pairs mentioned in this list. |

Table 3: The types of relations annotated.

## 5 Inter-Annotator Agreement

We first calculated pairwise IAA for all markables at the end of the 2nd pilot and continued doing so throughout the main annotation phase. For each pair of annotations on the same document, IAA was calculated by scoring one annotator against another using precision (P), recall (R) and $F_1$.[8] An overall IAA was calculated by micro-averaging across all annotated document pairs.[9] We used $F_1$ rather than the Kappa score (Cohen, 1960) to measure IAA as the latter requires comparison with a random baseline, which does not make sense for tasks such as NER.

Table 4 compares the IAA figures we obtained for 2 doubly annotated documents during the 2nd pilot phase, i.e. the first time we measured IAA, to those we obtained on 9 different files once the main annotation was completed. For NEs and zone titles, IAA was calculated using P, R and $F_1$, defining two mentions as equal if they had the same left and right boundaries and the same type. Although this comparison is done over different sub-sets of the corpus, it is still possible to conclude that the NE IAA improved considerably over the course of the annotation process.

The IAA scores for the majority of NEs were increased considerably at the end, with the exception of SKILL for which the IAA ended up being slightly lower as well as DOB and PER of which there are not sufficient examples in either sets to obtain reliably results.[10] There are very large increases in IAA for JOB and ORG entities, as we discovered during the pilot annotation that the guidelines for those markables were not concrete enough regarding their boundaries and definitions. Their final IAA figures show that both of these types of NEs were still most difficult to annotate at the end. However, a final total IAA of 84.8 $F_1$ for all NEs is a relatively high score. In comparison, the final IAA score of 97.1 $F_1$ for the zone titles shows that recognizing zone titles is an even easier task for humans to perform compared to recognizing NEs.

When calculating IAA for relations, only those relations for which both annotators agreed on the NEs were included. This is done to get an idea of the difficulty of the RE task independently of NER. Relation IAA was also measured using $F_1$, where relations are counted as equal if they connect exactly the same NE pair. The IAA for relations between NEs within CVs is relatively high both during the pilot annotation and at the end of the main annotation and only increased slightly over this time. These figures show that this task is much easier than annotating relations in other domains, e.g. in biomedical research papers (Alex et al., 2008a).

The IAA figures show that even with cyclic annotation, evolving guidelines and continuous updating, human annotators can find it challenging to annotate some markables consistently. This has an effect on the results of the automatic annotation where the annotated data is used to train ML-based models and to evaluate their performance.

[8] P, R and $F_1$ are calculated in standard fashion from the number of true positives, false positives and false negatives.

[9] Micro-averaging was chosen over macro-averaging, since we felt that the latter would give undue weight to documents with fewer markables.

[10] The reason why there are no figures for POSTCODE and TIMESPAN entities for the pilot annotation is that none appeared in those documents.

| | (1) 2nd Pilot Annotation | | | | (2) End of Main Annotation | | | | (3) Automatic Annotation | | | |
|---|---|---|---|---|---|---|---|---|---|---|---|---|
| Type | P | R | $F_1$ | TPs | P | R | $F_1$ | TPs | P | R | $F_1$ | TPs |
| **Named Entities** | | | | | | | | | | | | |
| ADDRESS | 100.0 | 100.0 | 100.0 | 1 | 100.0 | 100.0 | 100.0 | 10 | 13.8 | 16.0 | 14.8 | 8 |
| DATE | 62.5 | 92.6 | 74.6 | 25 | 98.5 | 98.5 | 98.5 | 191 | 94.1 | 95.7 | 94.9 | 1,850 |
| DATERANGE | 91.3 | 95.5 | 93.3 | 21 | 98.6 | 97.3 | 97.9 | 71 | 91.4 | 87.0 | 89.2 | 637 |
| DOB | 100.0 | 100.0 | 100.0 | 1 | 75.0 | 100.0 | 85.7 | 3 | 70.8 | 70.8 | 70.8 | 17 |
| EMAIL | 100.0 | 100.0 | 100.0 | 2 | 100.0 | 100.0 | 100.0 | 8 | 95.9 | 100.0 | 97.9 | 93 |
| JOB | 39.1 | 52.9 | 45.0 | 9 | 72.5 | 69.9 | 71.2 | 95 | 70.5 | 61.4 | 65.6 | 742 |
| LOC | 88.9 | 100.0 | 94.1 | 16 | 100.0 | 95.8 | 97.9 | 137 | 83.2 | 87.3 | 85.2 | 1,259 |
| ORG | 68.0 | 81.0 | 73.9 | 17 | 93.4 | 86.4 | 89.8 | 171 | 57.1 | 44.7 | 50.2 | 749 |
| PER | 100.0 | 100.0 | 100.0 | 2 | 100.0 | 95.0 | 97.4 | 19 | 69.8 | 40.5 | 51.2 | 196 |
| PHONE | 100.0 | 100.0 | 100.0 | 4 | 100.0 | 100.0 | 100.0 | 16 | 90.9 | 85.7 | 88.2 | 90 |
| POSTCODE | - | - | - | - | 90.9 | 90.9 | 90.9 | 10 | 98.3 | 71.3 | 82.6 | 57 |
| QUAL | 9.1 | 7.7 | 8.3 | 1 | 68.4 | 81.3 | 74.3 | 13 | 53.9 | 27.2 | 36.1 | 56 |
| SKILL | 76.6 | 86.8 | 81.4 | 210 | 79.3 | 79.0 | 79.2 | 863 | 67.9 | 66.5 | 67.2 | 5,645 |
| TIMESPAN | - | - | - | - | 91.7 | 91.7 | 91.7 | 33 | 74.0 | 76.8 | 75.4 | 179 |
| URL | 100.0 | 100.0 | 100.0 | 2 | 100.0 | 100.0 | 100.0 | 43 | 97.2 | 90.5 | 93.7 | 209 |
| All | 73.0 | 84.1 | 78.1 | 311 | 85.4 | 84.2 | 84.8 | 1,683 | 73.5 | 69.4 | 71.4 | 11,787 |
| **Zone Titles** | | | | | | | | | | | | |
| EDUCATION | 100.0 | 100.0 | 100.0 | 3 | 100.0 | 100.0 | 100.0 | 9 | 86.3 | 75.0 | 80.3 | 63 |
| EMPLOYMENT | 100.0 | 100.0 | 100.0 | 1 | 100.0 | 88.9 | 94.1 | 8 | 83.1 | 69.7 | 75.8 | 69 |
| OTHER | 100.0 | 100.0 | 100.0 | 1 | - | - | - | - | 39.3 | 28.2 | 32.8 | 22 |
| PERSONAL | 25.0 | 25.0 | 25.0 | 1 | 100.0 | 100.0 | 100.0 | 4 | 65.4 | 53.1 | 58.6 | 17 |
| REFERENCES | 100.0 | 100.0 | 100.0 | 1 | 100.0 | 100.0 | 100.0 | 3 | 94.4 | 89.5 | 91.9 | 17 |
| SKILLS | 33.3 | 40.0 | 36.4 | 2 | 100.0 | 100.0 | 100.0 | 7 | 63.8 | 38.9 | 48.4 | 44 |
| SUMMARY | - | - | - | - | 75.0 | 100.0 | 85.7 | 3 | 82.2 | 64.9 | 72.6 | 37 |
| All | 56.3 | 60.0 | 58.1 | 9 | 97.1 | 97.1 | 97.1 | 34 | 72.7 | 55.8 | 63.2 | 269 |
| **Relations** | | | | | | | | | | | | |
| DATE-JOB | - | - | - | - | 100.0 | 83.3 | 90.9 | 10 | 28.1 | 44.7 | 34.5 | 110 |
| DATE-LOC | - | - | - | - | 88.9 | 72.7 | 80.0 | 8 | 71.3 | 52.7 | 60.6 | 223 |
| DATE-ORG | - | - | - | - | 100.0 | 88.2 | 93.8 | 15 | 53.0 | 51.5 | 52.3 | 218 |
| DATE-QUAL | - | - | - | - | 100.0 | 100.0 | 100.0 | 6 | 60.6 | 73.1 | 66.3 | 57 |
| DATERANGE-JOB | 77.8 | 100.0 | 87.5 | 7 | 91.7 | 100.0 | 95.7 | 66 | 80.4 | 72.5 | 76.2 | 663 |
| DATERANGE-LOC | 91.7 | 100.0 | 95.7 | 11 | 85.4 | 79.6 | 82.4 | 70 | 82.0 | 82.7 | 82.4 | 735 |
| DATERANGE-ORG | 93.8 | 100.0 | 96.8 | 15 | 80.2 | 76.2 | 78.2 | 77 | 72.2 | 76.4 | 74.2 | 644 |
| DATERANGE-QUAL | 100.0 | 100.0 | 100.0 | 1 | 100.0 | 100.0 | 100.0 | 21 | 71.1 | 62.1 | 66.3 | 59 |
| DATERANGE-SKILL | 89.0 | 98.1 | 93.3 | 105 | 82.2 | 100.0 | 90.5 | 352 | 61.1 | 33.7 | 43.4 | 1,574 |
| DATE-SKILL | 100.0 | 9.1 | 16.7 | 1 | 95.0 | 67.1 | 78.6 | 57 | 23.6 | 54.5 | 33.0 | 368 |
| JOB-LOC | NaN | 0.0 | NaN | 0 | 91.8 | 65.6 | 76.5 | 78 | 77.0 | 69.1 | 72.8 | 932 |
| JOB-ORG | 87.5 | 100.0 | 93.3 | 7 | 86.8 | 73.3 | 79.5 | 99 | 64.6 | 50.7 | 56.8 | 758 |
| JOB-TIMESPAN | - | - | - | - | 85.7 | 54.6 | 66.7 | 6 | 56.0 | 61.8 | 58.8 | 47 |
| LOC-ORG | NaN | 0.0 | NaN | 0 | 89.6 | 71.4 | 79.5 | 120 | 79.7 | 78.9 | 79.3 | 1,044 |
| LOC-QUAL | NaN | 0.0 | NaN | 0 | 100.0 | 100.0 | 100.0 | 19 | 75.6 | 78.7 | 77.1 | 133 |
| LOC-TIMESPAN | - | - | - | - | 100.0 | 75.0 | 85.7 | 3 | 48.2 | 36.1 | 41.3 | 13 |
| ORG-QUAL | NaN | 0.0 | NaN | 0 | 95.2 | 95.2 | 95.2 | 20 | 77.8 | 71.4 | 74.5 | 140 |
| ORG-TIMESPAN | - | - | - | - | 83.3 | 55.6 | 66.7 | 5 | 55.9 | 33.3 | 41.8 | 19 |
| SKILL-TIMESPAN | - | - | - | - | 86.1 | 74.0 | 79.6 | 37 | 59.5 | 52.6 | 55.8 | 280 |
| All | 85.5 | 83.1 | 84.2 | 147 | 86.8 | 82.6 | 84.6 | 1,069 | 63.1 | 55.3 | 59.0 | 8,017 |

Table 4: IAA for NEs, zone titles and relations in precision (P), recall (R) and $F_1$ at two stages in the annotation process: (1) at the end of the second pilot annotation and (2) at the end of the main annotation phase; as well as automatic annotation scores (3) on the blind TEST set. The total number of true positives (TPs) is shown to provide an idea of the quantities of markables in each set.

## 6 Automatic Annotation

Table 4 also lists the final scores of the automatic ML-based NER and RE components (Alex et al., 2008b) which were adapted to the recruitment domain during the TXV project. Following agile methods, we trained and evaluated models very early into the annotation process. During the system optimization, learning curves helped to investigate for which markables having more training data available would improve performance.

The NER component recognizes NEs and zone titles simultaneously with an overall $F_1$ of 71.4 (84.2% of IAA) and 63.2 (65.0% of IAA), respectively. Extremely high or higher than average scores were obtained for DATE, DATERANGE, EMAIL, LOC, PHONE, POSTCODE, TIMESPAN and URL entities. Mid-range to lower scores were obtained for ADDRESS, DOB, JOB, ORG, PER, QUAL and SKILL entities. One reason is the similarity between NE types, e.g. DOB is difficult to differentiate from DATE. The layout of CVs and the lack of full sentences also pose a challenge as the NER component is trained using contextual features surrounding NEs that are often not present in CV data. Finally, the strict evaluation counts numerous boundary errors for NEs which can be considered correct, e.g. the system often recognizes organization names like "Sun Microsystems, Inc" whereas the annotator included the full stop at the end ("Sun Microsystems, Inc.").

The RE component (Haddow, 2008) performs with an overall $F_1$ of 59.0 on the CV TEST set (69.7% of IAA). It yields high or above average scores for 10 relation types (DATE-LOC, DATE-QUAL, DATERANGE-JOB, DATERANGE-LOC, DATERANGE-ORG, DATERANGE-QUAL, JOB-LOC, LOC-ORG, LOC-QUAL, ORG-QUAL). It yields mid-range to low scores for the other relation types (DATE-JOB, DATE-ORG, DATERANGE-SKILL, DATE-SKILL, JOB-ORG, JOB-TIMESPAN, LOC-TIMESPAN, ORG-TIMESPAN, SKILL-TIMESPAN). The most frequent type is DATERANGE-SKILL, a skill obtained during a particular time period. Its entities tend to be found in the same zone but not always in immediate context. Such relations are inter-sentential, i.e. their entities are in different sentences or what is perceived as sentences by the system. Due to nature of the data, there are few intra-sentential relations, relations between NEs in the same sentence. The further apart two related NEs are, the more difficult it is to recognize them. Similarly to NER, one challenge for RE from CVs is their diverse structure and formatting.

## 7 Discussion and Conclusion

The increase in the IAA figures for the markables over time show that agile corpus annotation resulted in more qualitative annotations. It is difficult to prove that the final annotation quality is higher than it would have been had we followed the traditional way of annotation. Comparing two such methods in parallel is very difficult to achieve as the main aim of annotation is usually to create a corpus and not to investigate the best and most efficient method.

However, using the agile approach we identified problems early on and made improvements to the annotation scheme and the setup during the process rather than at the end. Given a fixed annotation time frame and the proportion of time we spent on correcting errors throughout the annotation process, one might conclude that we annotated less data than we may have done, had we not followed the agile approach. However, Voormann and Hut (2008) argue that agile annotation actually results in more useable data at the end and in less data being thrown away.

Had we followed the traditional approach, we would unlikely have planned a correction phase at the end. The two main reason for that are cost and the general belief that the more annotated data the better. A final major correction phase is usually viewed as too expensive during an annotation project. In order to avoid this cost, the traditional approach taken tends to be to create a set of annotation guidelines when starting out and hold off the main annotation until the guidelines are finalized and considered sufficiently defined. This approach does not lend itself well to changes and adjustments later on which are inevitable when dealing with natural language. As a result the final less accurate annotated corpus tends to be accepted as the ground truth or gold standard and may not be as suitable and useful for a given purpose as it could have been following the agile annotation approach. Besides changing the way in which annotators work, we recognize the need for more flexible annotation tools that allow annotators to implement changes more rapidly.

## References

Beatrice Alex, Malvina Nissim, and Claire Grover. 2006. The impact of annotation on the performance of protein tagging in biomedical text. In *Proceedings of the 5th International Conference on Language Resources and Evaluation (LREC 2006)*, Genoa, Italy.

Bea Alex, Claire Grover, Barry Haddow, Mijail Kabadjov, Ewan Klein, Michael Matthews, Richard Tobin, and Xinglong Wang. 2008a. The ITI TXM corpora: Tissue expressions and protein-protein interactions. In *Proceedings of the Workshop on Building and Evaluating Resources for Biomedical Text Mining at LREC 2008*, Marrakech, Morocco.

Beatrice Alex, Claire Grover, Barry Haddow, Mijail Kabadjov, Ewan Klein, Michael Matthews, Richard Tobin, and Xinglong Wang. 2008b. Automating curation using a natural language processing pipeline. *Genome Biology*, 9(Suppl 2):S10.

Sue Atkins, Jeremy Clear, and Nicholas Ostler. 1992. Corpus design criteria. *Literary and Linguistic Computing*, 7(1):1–16.

Douglas Biber. 1993. Representativeness in corpus design. *Literary and Linguistic Computing*, 8(4):243–257.

Jacob Cohen. 1960. A coefficient of agreement for nominal scales. *Educational and Psychological Measurement*, 20:37–46.

Barry Haddow. 2008. Using automated feature optimisation to create an adaptable relation extraction system. In *Proceedings of BioNLP 2008*, Columbus, Ohio.

Christoph Müller and Michael Strube. 2006. Multi-level annotation of linguistic data with MMAX2. In Sabine Braun, Kurt Kohn, and Joybrato Mukherjee, editors, *Corpus Technology and Language Pedagogy. New Resources, New Tools, New Methods.*, pages 197–214. Peter Lang, Frankfurt. (English Corpus Linguistics, Vol.3).

Václav Novák and Magda Razímová. 2009. Unsupervised detection of annotation inconsistencies using apriori algorithm. In *Proceedings of the Third Linguistic Annotation Workshop (LAW III)*, pages 138–141, Suntec, Singapore.

Winston Royce. 1970. Managing the development of large software systems. In *Proceedings of IEEE WESCON*, pages 1–9.

Holger Voormann and Ulrike Gut. 2008. Agile corpus creation. *Corpus Linguistics and Linguistic Theory*, 4(2):235–251.

# Consistency Checking for Treebank Alignment

**Markus Dickinson**
Indiana University
md7@indiana.edu

**Yvonne Samuelsson**
Stockholm University
yvonne.samuelsson@ling.su.se

## Abstract

This paper explores ways to detect errors in aligned corpora, using very little technology. In the first method, applicable to any aligned corpus, we consider alignment as a string-to-string mapping. Treating the target string as a label, we examine each source string to find inconsistencies in alignment. Despite setting up the problem on a par with grammatical annotation, we demonstrate crucial differences in sorting errors from legitimate variations. The second method examines phrase nodes which are predicted to be aligned, based on the alignment of their yields. Both methods are effective in complementary ways.

## 1 Introduction

Parallel corpora—texts and their translations—have become essential in the development of machine translation (MT) systems. Alignment quality is crucial to these corpora; as Tiedemann (2003) states, "[t]he most important feature of texts and their translations is the correspondence between source and target segments" (p. 2). While being useful for translation studies and foreign language pedagogy (see, e.g., Botley et al., 2000; McEnery and Wilson, 1996), PARALLEL TREEBANKS—syntactically-annotated parallel corpora—offer additional useful information for machine translation, cross-language information retrieval, and word-sense disambiguation (see, e.g., Tiedemann, 2003),

While high-quality alignments are desirable, even gold standard annotation can contain annotation errors. For other forms of linguistic annotation, the presence of errors has been shown to create various problems, from unreliable training and evaluation of NLP technology (e.g., Padro and Marquez, 1998) to low precision and recall of queries for already rare linguistic phenomena (e.g., Meurers and Müller, 2008). Even a small number of errors can have a significant impact on the uses of linguistic annotation, e.g., changing the assessment of parsers (e.g., Habash et al., 2007). One could remove potentially unfavorable sentence pairs when training a statistical MT system, to avoid incorrect word alignments (Okita, 2009), but this removes all relevant data from those sentences and does not help evaluation.

We thus focus on detecting errors in the annotation of alignments. Annotation error detection has been explored for part-of-speech (POS) annotation (e.g., Loftsson, 2009) and syntactic annotation (e.g., Ule and Simov, 2004; Dickinson and Meurers, 2005), but there have been few, if any, attempts to develop general approaches to error detection for aligned corpora. Alignments are different in nature, as the annotation does not introduce abstract categories such as POS, but relies upon defining translation units with equivalent meanings.

We use the idea that variation in annotation can indicate errors (section 2), for consistency checking of alignments, as detailed in section 3. In section 4, we outline language-independent heuristics to sort true ambiguities from errors, and evaluate them on a parallel treebank in section 5. In section 6 we turn to a complementary method, exploiting compositional properties of aligned treebanks, to align more nodes. The methods are simple, effective, and applicable to any aligned treebank. As far as we know, this is the first attempt to thoroughly investigate and empirically verify error detection methods for aligned corpora.



*Proceedings of the Fourth Linguistic Annotation Workshop, ACL 2010*, pages 38–46,
Uppsala, Sweden, 15-16 July 2010. 

## 2 Background

### 2.1 Variation $N$-gram Method

As a starting point for an error detection method for aligned corpora, we use the variation $n$-gram approach for syntactic annotation (Dickinson and Meurers, 2003, 2005). The approach is based on detecting strings which occur multiple times in the corpus with varying annotation, the so-called VARIATION NUCLEI. The nucleus with repeated surrounding context is referred to as a VARIATION $n$-GRAM. The basic heuristic for detecting annotation errors requires one word of recurring context on each side of the nucleus, which is sufficient for detecting errors in grammatical annotation with high precision (Dickinson, 2008).

The approach detects bracketing and labeling errors in constituency annotation. For example, the variation nucleus *last month* occurs once in the Penn Treebank (Taylor et al., 2003) with the label NP and once as a non-constituent, handled through a special label NIL. As a labeling error example, *next Tuesday* occurs three times, twice as NP and once as PP (Dickinson and Meurers, 2003). The method works for discontinuous constituency annotation (Dickinson and Meurers, 2005), allowing one to apply it to alignments, which may span over several words.

### 2.2 Parallel Treebank Consistency Checking

For the experiments in this paper we will use the SMULTRON parallel treebank of Swedish, German, and English (Gustafson-Čapková et al., 2007), containing syntactic annotation and alignment on both word and phrase levels.[1] Additionally, alignments are marked as showing either an EXACT or a FUZZY (approximate) equivalence.

Corpora with alignments often have undergone some error-checking. Previous consistency checks for SMULTRON, for example, consisted of running one script for comparing differences in length between the source and target language items, and one script for comparing alignment labels, to detect variation between EXACT and FUZZY links. For example, the pair *and* (English) and *samt* (German, 'together with') had 20 FUZZY matches and 1 (erroneous) EXACT match. Such methods are limited, in that they do not, e.g., handle missing alignments.

The TreeAligner[2] tool for annotating and querying aligned parallel treebanks (Volk et al., 2007) employs its own consistency checking, recently developed by Torsten Marek. One method uses $2 \times 2$ contingency tables over words, looking, e.g., at the word-word or POS-POS combinations, pinpointing anomalous translation equivalents. While potentially effective, this does not address the use of alignments in context, i.e., when we might expect to see a rare translation.

A second, more treebank-specific method checks for so-called *branch link locality*: if two nodes are aligned, any node dominating one of them can only be aligned to a node dominating the other one. While this constraint can flag erroneous links, it too does not address missing alignments. The two methods we propose in this paper address these limitations and can be used to complement this work. Furthermore, these methods have not been evaluated, whereas we evaluate our methods.

## 3 Consistency of Alignment

To adapt the variation $n$-gram method and determine whether strings in a corpus are consistently aligned, we must: 1) define the units of data we expect to be consistently annotated (this section), and 2) define which information effectively identifies the erroneous cases (section 4).

### 3.1 Units of Data

Alignment relates words in a source language and words in a target language, potentially mediated by phrase nodes. Following the variation $n$-gram method, we define the units of data, i.e., the variation nuclei, as strings. Then, we break the problem into two different source-to-target mappings, mapping a source variation nucleus to a target language label. With a German-English aligned corpus, for example, we look for the consistency of aligning German words to their English counterparts and separately examine the consistency of aligning English words with their German "labels." Because a translated word can be used in different parts of a sentence, we also normalize all target labels into lower-case, preventing variation between, e.g., *the* and *The*.

[1] SMULTRON is freely available for research purposes, see http://www.cl.uzh.ch/kitt/smultron/.

[2] http://www.cl.uzh.ch/kitt/treealigner

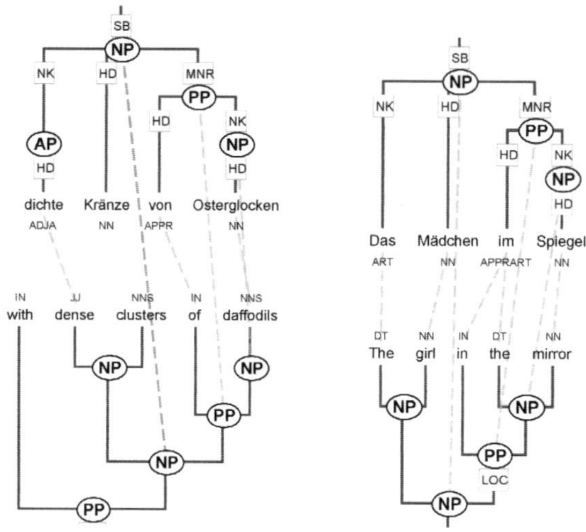


Figure 1: Word and phrase alignments span the same string on the left, but not on the right.

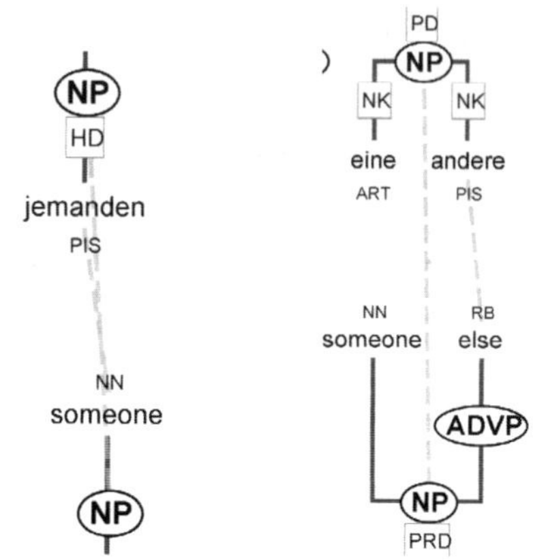


Figure 2: The word *someone* aligned as a phrase on the left, but not a phrase by itself on the right.

Although alignment maps strings to strings for this method, complications arise when mediated by phrase nodes: if a phrase node spans over only one word, it could have two distinct mappings, one as a word and one as a phrase, which may or may not result in the same yield. Figure 1 illustrates this. On the left side, *Osterglocken* is aligned to *daffodils* at the word level, and the same string is aligned on the phrase level (NP to NP). In contrast, on the right side, the word *Spiegel* is aligned to the word *mirror*, while at the phrase level, *Spiegel* (NP) is aligned to *the mirror* (NP). As word and phrase level strings can behave differently, we split error detection into word-level and phrase-level methods, to avoid unnecessary variation. By splitting the problem first into different source-to-target mappings and then into words and phrases, we do not have to change the underlying way of finding consistency.

**Multiple Alignment** The mapping between source strings and target labels handles $n$-to-$m$ alignments. For example, if *Gärten* maps to *the gardens*, *the* and *gardens* is considered one string. Likewise, in the opposite direction, *the gardens* maps as a unit to *Gärten*, even if discontinuous.

**Unary Branches** With syntactic annotation, unary branches present a potential difficulty, in that a single string could have more than one label, violating the assumption that the string-to-label mapping is a function. For example, in Penn Treebank-style annotation, an NP node can dominate a QP (quantifier phrase) node via a unary branch. Thus, an annotator could (likely erroneously) assign different alignments to each phrasal node, one for the NP and one for the QP, resulting in different target labels.

We handle all the (source) unary branch alignments as a conjunction of possibilities, ordered from top to bottom. Just as the syntactic structure can be relabeled as NP/QP (Dickinson and Meurers, 2003), we can relabel a string as, e.g., *the man/man*. If different unary nodes result in the same string (*the man/the man*), we combine them (*the man*). Note that unary branches are unproblematic in the target language since they always yield the same string, i.e., are still one label.

### 3.2 Consistency and Completeness

Error detection for syntactic annotation finds inconsistencies in constituent labeling (e.g., NP vs. QP) and inconsistencies in bracketing (e.g., NP vs. NIL). Likewise, we can distinguish inconsistency in labeling (different translations) from inconsistency in alignment (aligned/unaligned). Detecting inconsistency in alignment deals with the completeness of the annotation, by using the label NIL for unaligned strings.

We use the method from Dickinson and Meurers (2005) to generate NILs, but using NIL for unaligned strings is too coarse-grained for phrase-level alignment. A string mapping to NIL might be a phrase which has no alignment, or it might not be a phrase and thus could not possibly have an alignment. Thus, we create NIL-C as a new label, indicating a constituent with no alignment, differing from NIL strings which do not even form a phrase. For example, on the left side of Figure 2, the string *someone* aligns to *jemanden* on the phrase level. On the right side of Figure 2, the string *someone* by itself does not constitute a phrase (even though the alignment in this instance is correct) and is labeled NIL. If there were instances of *someone* as an NP with no alignment, this would be NIL-C. NIL-C cases seem to be useful for inconsistency detection, as we expect consistency for items annotated as a phrase.

### 3.3 Alignment Types

Aligned corpora often specify additional information about each alignment, e.g., a "sure" or "possible" alignment (Och and Ney, 2003). In SMULTRON, for instance, an EXACT alignment means that the strings are considered direct translation equivalents outside the current sentence context, whereas a FUZZY one is not as strict an equivalent. For example, *something* in English EXACT-aligns with *etwas* in German. However, if *something* and *irgend etwas* ('something or other') are constituents on the phrase level, <*something*, *irgend etwas*> is an acceptable alignment (since the corpus aligns as much as possible), but is FUZZY.

Since EXACT alignments are the ones we expect to consistently align with the same string across the corpus, we attach information about the alignment type to each corpus position. This can be used to filter out variations involving, e.g., FUZZY alignments (see section 4.4). When multiple alignments form a single variation nucleus, there could be different types of alignment for each link, e.g., *dog* EXACT-aligning and *the* FUZZY-aligning with *Hund*. We did not observe this, but one can easily allow for a mixed type (EXACT-FUZZY).

### 3.4 Algorithm

The algorithm first splits the data into appropriate units (SL=source language, TL=target language):

1. Divide the alignments into two SL-to-TL mappings.
2. Divide each SL-to-TL alignment set into word-level and phrase-level alignments.

For each of the four sets of alignments:

1. Map each string in SL with an alignment to a label
   - Label = <(lower-cased) TL translation, EXACT|FUZZY|EXACT-FUZZY>
   - (For phrases) Constituent phrases with no alignment are given the special label, NIL-C.
   - (For phrases) Constituent phrases which are unary branches are given a single, normalized label representing all target strings.
2. Generate NIL alignments for string tokens which occur in SL, but have no alignment to TL, using the method described in Dickinson and Meurers (2005).
3. Find SL strings which have variation in labeling.
4. Filter the variations from step 3, based on likelihood of being an error (see section 4).

## 4 Identifying Inconsistent Alignments

As words and phrases have acceptable variants for translation, the method in section 3 will lead to detecting acceptable variations. We use several heuristics to filter the set of variations.

### 4.1 NIL-only Variation

As discussed in section 3.2, we use the label NIL-C to refer to syntactic constituents which do not receive an alignment, while NIL refers to non-constituent strings without an alignment. A string which varies between NIL and NIL-C, then, is not really varying in its alignment—i.e., it is always unaligned. We thus remove cases varying only between NIL and NIL-C.

### 4.2 Context-based Filtering

The variation $n$-gram method has generally relied upon immediate lexical context around the variation nucleus, in order to sort errors from ambiguities (Dickinson, 2008). However, while useful for grammatical annotation, it is not clear how useful the surrounding context is for translation tasks, given the wide range of possible translations for the same context. Further, requiring identical context around source words is very strict, leading to sparse data problems, and it ignores alignment-specific information (see sections 4.3 and 4.4).

We test three different notions of context. Matching the variation $n$-gram method, we first employ a filter identifying those nuclei which share the "shortest" identical context, i.e., one word of context on every side of a nucleus. Secondly, we relax this to require only one word of context, on either the left or right side. Finally, we require no identical context in the source language and rely only on other filters. For example, with the nucleus *come* in the context *Where does the world come from*, the first notion requires *world come from* to recur, the second either *world come* or *come from*, and the third only requires that the nucleus itself recur (*come*).

### 4.3 Target Language Filtering

Because translation is open-ended, there can be different translations in a corpus. We want to filter out cases where there is variation in alignment stemming from multiple translation possibilities. We implement a TARGET LANGUAGE FILTER, which keeps only the variations where the target words are present in the same sentence. If word $x$ is sometimes aligned to $y_1$ and sometimes to $y_2$, and word $y_2$ occurs in at least one sentence where $y_1$ is the chosen target, then we keep the variation. If $y_1$ and $y_2$ do not occur in any of the same sentences, we remove the variation: given the translations, there is no possibility of having the same alignment.

This also works for NIL labels, given sentence alignments.[3] For NILs, the check is in only one direction: the aligned sentence must contain the target string used as the label elsewhere in the corpus. For instance, the word *All* aligns once with *alle* and twice with NIL. We check the two NIL cases to see whether one of them contains *alle*.

Sentences which are completely unaligned lead to NILs for every word and phrase, and we always keep the variation. In practice, the issue of having no alignment should be handled separately.

### 4.4 Alignment Type Filtering

A final filter relies on alignment type information. Namely, the FUZZY label already indicates that the alignment is not perfect, i.e., not necessarily applicable in other contexts. For example, the English word *dead* FUZZY-aligns with the German *verschwunden* ('gone, missing'), the best translation in its context. In another part of the corpus, *dead* EXACT-aligns with *leblosen* ('lifeless'). While this is variation between *verschwunden* and *leblosen*, the presence of the FUZZY label alerts us to the fact that it should vary with another word. The ALIGNMENT TYPE FILTER removes cases varying between one EXACT label and one or more FUZZY labels.

| | word | phrase |
|---|---|---|
| all | 540 | 251 |
| oneword | 340 | 182 |
| shortest | 96 | 21 |
| all-TL | 194 | 140 |
| oneword-TL | 130 | 94 |
| shortest-TL | 30 | 16 |

Table 1: Number of variations across contexts

## 5 Evaluation

Evaluation was done for English to German on half of SMULTRON (the part taken from the novel *Sophie's World*), with approximately 7500 words from each language and 7600 alignments (roughly 4800 word-level and 2800 phrase-level). Basic statistics are in Table 1. We filter based on the target language (*TL*) and provide three different contextual definitions: no context, i.e., all variations (*all*); one word of context on the left *or* right (*oneword*); and one word of context on the left *and* right, i.e., the shortest surrounding context (*shortest*). The filters reduce the number of variations, with a dramatic loss for the shortest contexts.

A main question concerns the impact of the filtering conditions on error detection. To gauge this, we randomly selected 50 (*all*) variations for the word level and 50 for the phrase level, each corresponding to just under 400 corpus instances. The variations were checked manually to see which were true variations and which were errors.

We report the effect of different filters on precision and recall in Table 2, where *recall* is with respect to the *all* condition.[4] Adding too much lexical context in the source language (i.e., the *shortest* conditions) results in too low a recall to be practically effective. Using one word of context on either side has higher recall, but the precision is no better than using no source language context at all. What seems to be most effective is to only use the target language filter (*all-TL*). Here, we find higher precision—higher than any source language filter—and the recall is respectable.

[3] In SMULTRON, sentence alignments are not given directly, but can be deduced from the set of word alignments.

[4] Future work should test for recall of all alignment errors, by first manually checking a small section of the corpus.

| | Word | | | | Phrase | | | |
|---|---|---|---|---|---|---|---|---|
| | Cases | Errors | P | R | Cases | Errors | P | R |
| all | 50 | 17 | 34% | 100% | 50 | 15 | 30% | 100% |
| oneword | 33 | 12 | 36% | 71% | 33 | 8 | 24% | 53% |
| shortest | 8 | 2 | 25% | 12% | 4 | 1 | 25% | 7% |
| all-TL | 20 | 11 | 55% | 65% | 27 | 12 | 44% | 80% |
| oneword-TL | 15 | 6 | 40% | 35% | 14 | 7 | 50% | 47% |
| shortest-TL | 2 | 1 | 50% | 6% | 3 | 1 | 33% | 7% |

Table 2: Error precision and recall

**TL filter** An advantage of the target language filter is its ability to handle lexical (e.g., case) variations. One example of this is the English phrase *a dog*, which varies between German *einem Hund* (dative singular), *einen Hund* (accusative singular) and *Hunde* (accusative plural). Similar to using lower-case labels, one could map strings to canonical forms. However, the target language filter naturally eliminates such unwanted variation, without any language-specific information, because the other forms do not appear across sentences.

Several of the variations which the target language filter incorrectly removes would, once the error is fixed, still have variation. As an example, consider *cat*, which varies between *Katze* (5 tokens) and NIL (2 tokens). In one of the NIL cases, the word needs to be FUZZY-aligned with the German *Tigerkatze*. The variation points out the error, but there would still be variation (between *Katze*, *Tigerkatze*, and NIL) after correction. This shows the limitation of the heuristic in identifying the required non-exact alignments.

Another case the filter misses is the variation nucleus *heard*, which varies between *gehört* (2 tokens) and *hören* (1 token). In this case, one of the instances of <*heard*, *gehört*> should be <*heard*, *gehört hatte*>. Note that here the erroneous case is not variation-based at all; it is a problem with the label *gehört*. What is needed is a method to detect more translation possibilities.

As an example of a problem for phrases, consider the variation for the nucleus *end* with 5 instances of NIL and 1 of *ein Ende*. In one NIL instance, the proper alignment should be <*the end*, *Ende*>, with a longer source string. Since the target label is *Ende* and not *ein Ende*, the filter removes this variation. One might explore more fuzzily matching NIL strings, so that *Ende* matches with *ein Ende*. We explore a different method for phrases next, which deals with some of these NIL cases.

## 6 A Complementary Method

Although it works for any type of aligned corpus, the string-based variation method of detecting errors is limited in the types of errors it can detect. There might be ways to generalize the variation $n$-gram method (cf. Dickinson, 2008), but this does not exploit properties inherent to aligned treebanks. We pursue a complementary approach, as this can fill in some gaps a string-based method cannot deal with (cf. Loftsson, 2009).

### 6.1 Phrase Alignment Based on Word Links

Using the existing word alignments, we can search for missing or erroneous phrase alignments. If the words dominated by a phrase are aligned, the phrases generally should be, too (cf. Lavie et al., 2008). We take the yield of a constituent in one side of a corpus, find the word alignments of this yield, and use these alignments to predict a phrasal alignment for the constituent. If the predicted alignment is not annotated, it is flagged as a possible error. This is similar to the branch link locality of the TreeAligner (see section 2.2), but here as a prediction, rather than a restriction, of alignment.

For example, consider the English VP *choose her own friends* in (1). Most of the words are aligned to words within *Ihre Freunde vielleicht wählen* ('possibly choose her friends'), with no alignment to words outside of this German VP. We want to predict that the phrases be aligned.

(1) a. [$_{VP}$ choose$_1$ her$_2$ own friends$_3$]
    b. [$_{VP}$ Ihre$_2$ Freunde$_3$ vielleicht wählen$_1$]

The algorithm works as follows:

1. For every phrasal node $s$ in the source treebank:
   (a) Predict a target phrase node $t$ to align with, where $t$ could be non-alignment (NIL):

i. Obtain the yield (i.e., child nodes) of the phrase node $s$: $s_1, \ldots s_n$.
ii. Obtain the alignments for each child node $s_i$, resulting in a set of child nodes in the target language ($t_1, \ldots t_m$).
iii. Store every mother node $t'$ covering all the target child nodes, i.e., all $<s, t'>$ pairs.

(b) If a predicted alignment ($<s, t'>$) is not in the set of actual alignments ($<s, t>$), add it to the set of potential alignments, $A_{S \mapsto T}$.

i. For nodes which are predicted to have non-alignment (but are actually aligned), output them to a separate file.

2. Perform step 1 with the source and target reversed, thereby generating both $A_{S \mapsto T}$ and $A_{T \mapsto S}$.

3. Intersect $A_{S \mapsto T}$ and $A_{T \mapsto S}$, to obtain the set of predicted phrasal alignments not currently aligned.

The main idea in 1a is to find the children of a source node and their alignments and then obtain the target nodes which have all of these aligned nodes as children. A node covering all these target children is a plausible candidate for alignment.

Consider example (2). Within the 8-word English ADVP (*almost twice* ...), there are six words which align to words in the corresponding German sentence, all under the same NP.[5] It does not matter that some words are unaligned; the fact that the English ADVP and the German NP cover basically the same set of words suggests that the phrases should be aligned, as is the case here.

(2) a. Sophie lived on$_2$ [$_{NP_1}$ the$_2$ outskirts$_3$ of a$_4$ sprawling$_{5*}$ suburb$_{6*}$] and had [$_{ADVP}$ almost$_7$ twice$_8$ as$_9$ far$_{10}$ to school as$_{11}$ Joanna$_{12*}$] .

b. Sophie wohnte am$_2$ [$_{NP_1}$ Ende$_3$ eines$_4$ ausgedehnten$_{5*}$ Viertels$_{6*}$ mit Einfamilienhäusern] und hatte [$_{NP}$ einen fast$_7$ doppelt$_8$ so$_9$ langen$_{10}$ Schulweg wie$_{11}$ Jorunn$_{12*}$] .

The prediction of an aligned node in 1a allows for multiple possibilities: in 1aiii, we only check that a mother node $t'$ covers all the target children, disregarding extra children, since translations can contain extra words. In general, many such dominating nodes exist, and most are poor candidates for alignment of the node in question. This is the reason for the bidirectional check in steps 2 and 3.

For example, in (3), we correctly predict alignment between the NP dominating *you* in English and the NP dominating *man* in German. From the word alignment, we generate a list of mother nodes of *man* as potential alignments for the *you* NP. Two of these (six) nodes are shown in (3b). In the other direction, there are eight nodes containing *you*; two are shown in (3a). These are the predicted alignment nodes for the NP dominating *man*. In either direction, this overgenerates; the intersection, however, only contains alignment between the lowest NPs.

(3) a. But it 's just as impossible to realize [$_S$ [$_{NP}$ **you**$_1$] have to die without thinking how incredibly amazing it is to be alive ] .

b. [$_S$ Und es ist genauso unmöglich , darüber nachzudenken , dass [$_{NP}$ **man**$_1$] sterben muss , ohne zugleich daran zu denken , wie phantastisch das Leben ist . ]

While generally effective, certain predictions are less likely to be errors. In figure 3, for example, the sentence pair is an entire rephrasing; <*her, ihr*> is the only word alignment. For each phrasal node in the SL, the method only requires that all its words be aligned with the words under the TL node. Thus, the English PP *on her*, the VP *had just been dumped on her*, and the two VPs in between are predicted as possible alignments with the German VP *ihr einfach in die Wiege gelegt worden* or its immediate VP daughter: they all have *her* and *ihr* aligned, and no contradicting alignments. Sparse word alignments lead to multiple possible phrase alignments. After intersecting, we mark cases with more than one predicted source or target phrase and do not evaluate them.

If in step 1aiii, no target mother ($t'$) exists, but there is alignment in the corpus, then in step 1bi, we output predicted non-alignment. In Example (2), for instance, the English NP *the outskirts of a sprawling suburb* is (incorrectly) predicted to have no alignment, although most words align to words within the same German NP. This prediction arises because *the* aligns to a word (*am*) outside of the German NP, due to *am* being a contraction of the preposition *an* and the article *dem*, (cf. *on* and *the*, respectively). The method for predicting phrase alignments, however, relies upon words being within the constituent. We thus conclude that: 1) the cases in step 1bi are unlikely to be errors, and 2) there are types of alignments which we simply will not find, a problem also for automatic alignment based on similar assumptions (e.g., Zhechev and Way, 2008). In (2), for instance, were there not already alignment between

[5] FUZZY labels are marked by an asterisk, but are not used.

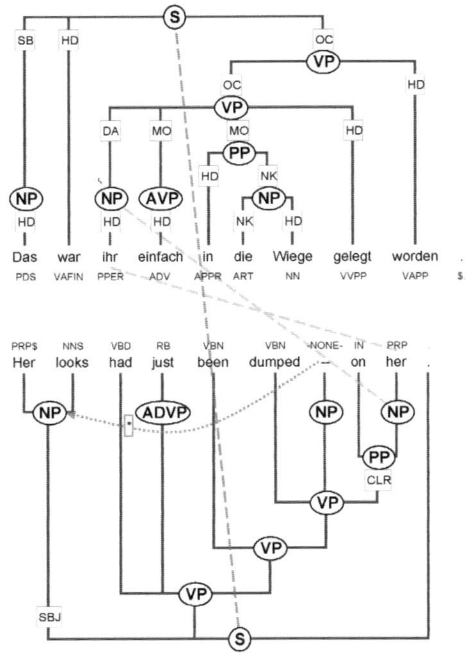


Figure 3: A sentence with minimal alignment

the NPs, we would not predict it.

### 6.2 Evaluation

The method returns 318 cases, in addition to 135 cases with multiple source/target phrases and 104 predicted non-alignments. To evaluate, we sampled 55 of the 318 flagged phrases and found that 25 should have been aligned as suggested. 21 of the phrases have zero difference in length between source and target, while 34 have differences of up to 9 tokens. Of the phrases with zero-length difference, 18 should have been aligned (precision=85.7%), while only 7 with length differences should have been aligned. This is in line with previous findings that length difference can help predict alignment (cf., e.g., Gale and Church, 1993). About half of all phrase pairs that should be aligned should be EXACT, regardless of the length difference.

The method is good at predicting the alignment of one-word phrases, e.g., pronouns, as in (3). Of the 11 suggested alignments where both source and target have a length of 1, all were correct suggestions. This is not surprising, since all words under the phrases are (trivially) aligned. Although shorter phrases with short length differences generally means a higher rate of correct suggestions, we do not want to filter out items based on phrase length, since there are outliers that are correct suggestions, e.g., phrase pairs with lengths of 15 and 13 (difference=2) or 31 and 36 (difference=5). It is worth noting that checking the suggestions took very little time.

## 7 Summary and Outlook

This paper explores two simple, language-independent ways to detect errors in aligned corpora. In the first method, applicable to any aligned corpus, we consider alignment as a string-to-string mapping, where a string could be the yield of a phrase. Treating the target string as a label, we find inconsistencies in the labeling of each source string. Despite setting the problem up in a similar way to grammatical annotation, we also demonstrated that new heuristics are needed to sort errors. The second method examines phrase nodes which are predicted to be aligned, based on the alignment of their yields. Both methods are effective, in complementary ways, and can be used to suggest alignments for annotators or to suggest revisions for incorrect alignments.

The wide range of possible translations and the linguistic information which goes into them indicate that there should be other ways of finding errors. One possibility is to use more abstract source or target language representations, such as POS, to overcome the limitations of string-based methods. This will likely also be a useful avenue to explore for language pairs more dissimilar than English and German. By investigating different ways to ensure alignment consistency, one can begin to provide insights into automatic alignment (Zhechev and Way, 2008). Additionally, by correcting the errors, one can determine the effect on machine translation evaluation.

## Acknowledgments

We would like to thank Martin Volk and Thorsten Marek for useful discussion and feedback of earlier versions of this paper and three anonymous reviewers for their comments.

## References


Botley, S. P., McEnery, A. M., and Wilson, A., editors (2000). *Multilingual Corpora in Teaching and Research*. Rodopi, Amsterdam, Atlanta GA.

Dickinson, M. (2008). Representations for category disambiguation. In *Proceedings of COLING-08*, pages 201–208, Manchester.

Dickinson, M. and Meurers, W. D. (2003). Detecting inconsistencies in treebanks. In *Proceedings of TLT-03*, pages 45–56, Växjö, Sweden.

Dickinson, M. and Meurers, W. D. (2005). Detecting errors in discontinuous structural annotation. In *Proceedings of ACL-05*, pages 322–329.

Gale, W. A. and Church, K. W. (1993). A program for aligning sentences in bilingual corpora. *Computational Linguistics*, 19(1):75–102.

Gustafson-Čapková, S., Samuelsson, Y., and Volk, M. (2007). SMULTRON (version 1.0) - The Stockholm MULtilingual parallel TReebank. www.ling.su.se/dali/research/smultron/index.htm.

Habash, N., Gabbard, R., Rambow, O., Kulick, S., and Marcus, M. (2007). Determining case in Arabic: Learning complex linguistic behavior requires complex linguistic features. In *Proceedings of EMNLP-CoNLL-07*, pages 1084–1092.

Lavie, A., Parlikar, A., and Ambati, V. (2008). Syntax-driven learning of sub-sentential translation equivalents and translation rules from parsed parallel corpora. In *Proceedings of the ACL-08: HLT Second Workshop on Syntax and Structure in Statistical Translation (SSST-2)*, pages 87–95, Columbus, OH.

Loftsson, H. (2009). Correcting a POS-tagged corpus using three complementary methods. In *Proceedings of EACL-09*, pages 523–531, Athens, Greece.

McEnery, T. and Wilson, A. (1996). *Corpus Linguistics*. Edinburgh University Press, Edinburgh.

Meurers, D. and Müller, S. (2008). Corpora and syntax (article 44). In Lüdeling, A. and Kytö, M., editors, *Corpus Linguistics. An International Handbook*, Handbooks of Linguistics and Communication Science. Mouton de Gruyter, Berlin.

Och, F. J. and Ney, H. (2003). A systematic comparison of various statistical alignment models. *Computational Linguistics*, 29(1):19–51.

Okita, T. (2009). Data cleaning for word alignment. In *Proceedings of the ACL-IJCNLP 2009 Student Research Workshop*, pages 72–80, Suntec, Singapore.

Padro, L. and Marquez, L. (1998). On the evaluation and comparison of taggers: the effect of noise in testing corpora. In *Proceedings of ACL-COLING-98*, pages 997–1002, San Francisco, California.

Taylor, A., Marcus, M., and Santorini, B. (2003). The penn treebank: An overview. In Abeillé, A., editor, *Treebanks: Building and using syntactically annotated corpora*, chapter 1, pages 5–22. Kluwer, Dordrecht.

Tiedemann, J. (2003). *Recycling Translations - Extraction of Lexical Data from Parallel Corpora and their Application in Natural Language Processing*. PhD thesis, Uppsala university.

Ule, T. and Simov, K. (2004). Unexpected productions may well be errors. In *Proceedings of LREC-04*, Lisbon, Portugal.

Volk, M., Lundborg, J., and Mettler, M. (2007). A search tool for parallel treebanks. In *Proceedings of the Linguistic Annotation Workshop (LAW) at ACL*, pages 85–92, Prague, Czech Republic. Association for Computational Linguistics.

Zhechev, V. and Way, A. (2008). Automatic generation of parallel treebanks. In *Proceedings of Coling 2008*, pages 1105–1112, Manchester, UK.

# Anveshan: A Framework for Analysis of Multiple Annotators' Labeling Behavior

**Vikas Bhardwaj,**
**Rebecca J. Passonneau** and **Ansaf Salleb-Aouissi**
Columbia University
New York, NY, USA
vsb2108@columbia.edu
(becky@cs|ansaf@ccls).columbia.edu

**Nancy Ide**
Vassar College
Poughkeepsie, NY, USA
ide@cs.vassar.edu

## Abstract

Manual annotation of natural language to capture linguistic information is essential for NLP tasks involving supervised machine learning of semantic knowledge. Judgements of meaning can be more or less subjective, in which case instead of a single correct label, the labels assigned might vary among annotators based on the annotators' knowledge, age, gender, intuitions, background, and so on. We introduce a framework "Anveshan," where we investigate annotator behavior to find outliers, cluster annotators by behavior, and identify confusable labels. We also investigate the effectiveness of using trained annotators versus a larger number of untrained annotators on a word sense annotation task. The annotation data comes from a word sense disambiguation task for polysemous words, annotated by both trained annotators and untrained annotators from Amazon's Mechanical turk. Our results show that Anveshan is effective in uncovering patterns in annotator behavior, and we also show that trained annotators are superior to a larger number of untrained annotators for this task.

## 1 Credits

This work was supported by a research supplement to the National Science Foundation CRI award 0708952.

## 2 Introduction

Manual annotation of language data in order to capture linguistic knowledge has become increasingly important for semantic and pragmatic annotation tasks. A very short list of a few such tasks illustrates the range of types of annotation, in varying stages of development: predicate argument structure (Palmer et al., 2005b), dialogue acts (Hu et al., 2009), discourse structure (Carbone et al., 2004), opinion (Wiebe and Cardie, 2005), emotion (Alm et al., 2005). The number of efforts to create corpus resources that include manual annotations has also been growing. A common approach in assessing the resulting manual annotations is to report a single quantitative measure reflecting the quality of the annotations, either a summary statistic such as percent agreement, or an agreement coefficient from the family of metrics that include Krippendorff's alpha (Krippendorff, 1980) and Cohen's kappa (Cohen, 1960). We present some new assessment methods to use in combination with an agreement coefficient for understanding annotator behavior when there are multiple annotators and many annotation values.

Anveshan (Annotation Variance Estimation)[1] is a suite of procedures for analyzing patterns of agreement and disagreement among annotators, as well as the distributions of annotation values across annotators. Anveshan thus makes it possible to explore annotator behavior in more detail. Currently, it includes three types of analysis: interannotator agreement (IA) among all subsets of annotators, leverage of annotation values for outlier detection, and metrics for comparing annotators' distributions of annotation values (e.g., Kullbach-Liebler divergence).

As an illustration of the utility of Anveshan, we compare two groups of annotators on the same annotation word sense annotation tasks: a half dozen trained annotators and fourteen Mechanical Turkers. Previous work has argued that it can be cost effective to collect multiple labels from untrained labelers at a low cost per label, and to combine the multiple labels through a voting method, rather than to collect single labels from highly trained la-

[1] Anveshan is a Sanskrit word which literally means search or exploration.



*Proceedings of the Fourth Linguistic Annotation Workshop, ACL 2010*, pages 47–55,
Uppsala, Sweden, 15-16 July 2010. ©2010 Association for Computational Linguistics

belers (Snow et al., 2008; Sheng et al., 2008; Lam and Stork, 2003). The tasks included in (Snow et al., 2008), for example, include word sense annotation; in contrast to our case, where the average number of senses per word is 9.5, the one word sense annotation task had three senses. We find that the same half dozen trained annotators can agree well or not on sense labels for polysemous words. When they agree less well, we find that it is possible to distinguish between problems in the labels (e.g., confusable senses) and systematic differences of interpretation among annotators. When we use twice the number of Mechanical Turkers as trained annotators for three of our ten polysemous words, we find inconsistent results.

The next section of the paper presents the motivation for Anveshan and its relevance to the word sense annotation task, followed by a section on related work. The word sense annotation data is given in section 5. Anveshan is described in the subsequent section, followed by the results of its application to the two data sets. We discuss the comparison of trained annotators and Mechanical Turkers, as well as differences among words, in section 7. Section 7 concludes with a short recap of Anveshan in general, and its application to word sense annotations in particular.

## 3 Beyond Interannotator Agreement (IA)

Assessing the reliability of an annotation typically addresses the question of whether different annotators (effectively) assign the same annotation labels. Various measures can be used to compare different annotators, including agreement coefficients such as Krippendorff's alpha (Krippendorff, 1980). Extensive reviews of the properties of such coefficients have been presented elsewhere, e.g., (Artstein and Poesio, 2008). Briefly, an agreement produce values in the interval [-1,1] indicating how much of the observed agreement is above (or below) agreement that would be predicted by chance (value of 0). To measure reliability in this way is to assume that for most of the instances in the data, there is a single correct response. Here we present the use of reliability metrics and other measures for word sense annotation, and we assume that in some cases there may not be a single correct response. When annotators have less than excellent agreement, we aim to examine possible causes.

We take word sense to be a problematic annotation to perform, thus requiring a deeper understanding of the conditions under which annotators might disagree. The many reasons can only be touched on here. For example, word senses are not discrete, atomic units that can be delimited and enumerated. While dictionaries and other lexical resoures, such as WordNet (Miller et al., 1993) or the Hector lexicon (cf. SENSEVAL-1 (Kilgarriff and Palmer, 2000)), do provide enumerations of the senses for a given word, and their interrelations (e.g., a list of senses, a tree of senses), it is widely agreed that this is a convenient abstraction, if for no other reason than the fact that words shift meanings along with the communicative needs of the groups of individuals who use them. The context in which a word is used plays a significant role in restricting the current sense. As a result, it is often argued that the best representation for word meaning would consist in clustering the contexts in which words are used (Kilgarriff, 1997). Yet even this would be insufficient because new communities arise, new behaviors and artifacts emerge along with them, hence new contexts of use and new clusters. At the same time, contexts of use and the senses that go along with them can fade away (cf. the use of *handbag* discussed in (Kilgarriff, 1997) pertaining to disco dancing). Because an enumeration of word senses is somewhat artificial, annotators might disagree on word senses because they disagree on the boundaries between one sense and another, just as professional lexicographers do.

Apart from the artificiality of creating flat or hierarchical sense inventories, the meanings of words can vary in their subjectivity, due to differences in the perception or experience of individuals. This can be true for word senses that are inherently relative, such as *cold* (as in, *turn up the thermostat, it's too cold in here*); or that derive their meaning from cultural norms that may differ from community to community, such as *justice*; or that change as one grows older, e.g., whether a *long time to wait* pertains to hours versus days.

Despite the arguments against using word sense inventories, until they are replaced with an equally convenient and more representative abstraction, they are an extremely convenient computational representation. We rely on WordNet senses, which are presented to annotators with a gloss (definition) and with example uses. In order to better understand reasons for disagreement on senses, we collect labels from multiple annotators. When annotators agree, having multiple annotators is redundant. But when annotators disagree, having multiple annotators is necessary in order to determine whether the disagreement is due to noise based on insufficiently clear sense definitions versus a systematic difference between individuals, e.g., those who see a glass as half empty where others see it as half full. To insure the opportunity to observe how varied the labeling of a single word can be, we collect word sense annotations from multiple annotators. One potential benefit of such investigation might be a better understanding of how to model word meaning.

In sum, we hypothesize the following cases:

- Outliers: A small proportion of annotators may assign senses in a manner that differs markedly from the remaining annotators.
- Confusability of senses: If multiple annotators assign multiple senses in an apparently random fashion, it may be that the senses are not sufficiently distinct.
- Systematic differences among subsets of annotators: If the same 50% of annotators always pick sense *X* where the remaining annotators always pick sense *Y*, it may be that properties of the annotators, such as their age cohort, account for the disagreement.

## 4 Related Work

There has been a decade-long community-wide effort to evaluate word sense disambiguation (WSD) systems across languages in the four Senseval efforts (1998, 2001, 2004, and 2007, cf. (Kilgarriff, 1998; Pedersen, 2002a; Pedersen, 2002b; Palmer et al., 2005a)), with a corollary effort to investigate the issues pertaining to preparation of manually annotated gold standard corpora tagged for word senses (Palmer et al., 2005a).

Differences in IA and system performance across part-of-speech have been examined, as in (Ng et al., 1999; Palmer et al., 2005a). Factors that have been proposed as affecting agreement include whether annotators are allowed to assign multilabels (Véronis, 1998; Ide et al., 2002; Passonneau et al., 2006), the number or granularity of senses (Ng et al., 1999), merging of related senses (Snow et al., 2007), sense similarity (Chugur et al., 2002), entropy (Diab, 2004; Palmer et al., 2005a), and reactions times required to distinguish senses (Klein and Murphy, 2002; Ide and Wilks, 2006).

We anticipate that one of the ways in which the data will be used will be to train machine learning approaches to WSD. Noise in labeling and the impact on machine learning has been discussed from various perspectives. In (Reidsma and Carletta, 2008), it is argued that machine learning performance does not vary consistently with interannotator agreement. Through a simulation study, the authors find that machine learning performance can degrade or not with lower agreement, depending on whether the disagreement is due to noise or systematic behavior. Noise has relatively little impact compared with systematic disagreements. In (Passonneau et al., 2008), a similar lack of correlation between interannotator agreement and machine learning performance is found in an empirical investigation.

## 5 Word Sense Annotation Data

### 5.1 Trained Annotator data

The Manually Annotated Sub-Corpus (MASC) project (Ide et al., 2010) is creating a small, representative corpus of American English written and spoken texts drawn from the Open American National Corpus (OANC).[2] The MASC corpus includes hand-validated or manual annotations for a variety of linguistic phenomena. The first MASC release, available as of May 2010, consists of 82K words.[3] One of the goals of MASC is to support efforts to harmonize WordNet (Miller et al., 1993) and FrameNet (Ruppenhofer et al., 2006), in order to bring the sense distinctions each makes into better alignment.

We chose ten fairly frequent, moderately polysemous words for sense tagging. One hundred occurrences of each word were sense annotated by five or six trained annotators. The ten words are shown in Table 1, the words are grouped by part of speech, with the number of WordNet senses, the number of senses used by the trained annotators (TAs), the number of annotators, and Alpha. We call this the Trained annotator (TA) data.

We find that interannotator agreement (IA) among half a dozen annotators varies depending on the word. For ten words nearly balanced with

[2]http://www.anc.org

[3]http://www.anc.org/MASC/Home.html

| | Senses | | | |
|---|---|---|---|---|
| Word-pos | Avail. | Used | Ann | Alpha |
| long-j | 9 | 4 | 6 | 0.67 |
| fair-j | 10 | 6 | 5 | 0.54 |
| quiet-j | 6 | 5 | 6 | 0.49 |
| time-n | 10 | 8 | 5 | 0.68 |
| work-n | 7 | 7 | 5 | 0.62 |
| land-n | 11 | 9 | 6 | 0.49 |
| show-v | 12 | 10 | 5 | 0.46 |
| tell-v | 8 | 8 | 6 | 0.46 |
| know-v | 11 | 10 | 5 | 0.37 |
| say-v | 11 | 10 | 6 | 0.37 |

Table 1: Interannotator agreement on ten polysemous words: three adjectives, three nouns and four verbs among trained annotators

| | Senses | | | |
|---|---|---|---|---|
| Word-pos | Avail. | Used | Ann | Alpha |
| long-j | 9 | 9 | 14 | 0.15 |
| fair-j | 10 | 10 | 14 | 0.25 |
| quiet-j | 6 | 6 | 15 | 0.08 |

Table 2: Interannotator agreement on adjectives among Mechanical Turk annotators

respect to part of speech, we find a range of about 0.50 to 0.70 for nouns and adjectives, and about 0.37 to 0.46 for verbs. Table 1 shows the ten words and the alpha scores for the same five or six annotators. The layout of the table illustrates both that verbs have lower agreement than adjectives or nouns, and that within each part of speech, annotators achieve varying levels of agreement, depending on the word. The annotators, their level of training, the number of sense choices, the annotation tool, and other factors remain constant from word to word. Thus we hypothesize that the differences in IA reflect differences in the degree of subjectivity of the sense choices, the sense similarity, or both. Anveshan is a data exploration framework to help understand the differences in the ability of the same annotators to agree well on sense annotation for some words and not others.

As shown, annotators achieve respectable agreement on *long*, *time* and *work*, and lower agreement on the remaining words. Verbs have lower agreement overall.

Figure 1 shows WordNet senses for *long* in the form displayed to annotators, who used an annotation GUI developed in Java. The sense number appears in the first column, followed by the glosses, then sample phrases; only three senses are shown, to conserve space. Note that annotators did not see the WordNet synsets (sets of synonymous words) for a given sense.

### 5.2 Mechanical Turk data

Amazon's Mechanical Turk is a crowd-sourcing marketplace where Human Intelligence Tasks (HITs) such as sense annotation for words in a sentence, can be set up and results from a large number of annotators (or turkers) can be obtained quickly. We used Mechanical Turk to obtain annotations from 14 annotators on the set of adjectives to analyze IA for a larger set of untrained annotators.

The task was set up to get 150 occurrences annotated for each of the three adjectives: *fair*, *long* and *quiet*, by 14 mechanical turk annotators each. 100 of these occurrences were the same as those done by the trained annotators. For each word, the 150 instances were divided into 15 HITs of 10 instances each. The average submit time of a HIT was 200 seconds. We report the IA among the Mechanical Turk annotators using Krippendorff's Alpha in Table 2. As shown, the turkers have poor agreement, particularly on *long* and *quiet*, which is at the chance level.

## 6 Anveshan

**Anveshan:** *Annotation Variance Estimation*, is our approach to perform a more subtle analysis of inter-annotator agreement. Anveshan uses simple statistical methods to achieve the three goals identified in section 3: outlier detection, confusable senses, and distinct subsets of annotators that agree with each other.

### 6.1 Method

This section uses the following notation to explain Anveshan's methodology:

We assume that we have $n$ annotators annotating $m$ senses. The probability of annotator $a$ using sense $s_i$ is given by

$$P_a(S = s_i) = \frac{count(s_i, a)}{\sum_{j=1}^{m} count(s_j, a)}$$

where, $count(s_i, a)$ is number of times $s_i$ was used by $a$.

1 *primarily temporal sense; being or indicating a relatively great or greater than average duration or passage of time or a duration as specified*: "a long life"; "a long boring speech"; "a long time"; "a long friendship"; "a long game"; "long ago"; "an hour long"

2 *primarily spatial sense; of relatively great or greater than average spatial extension or extension as specified*: "a long road"; "a long distance"; "contained many long words"; "ten miles long"

3 *of relatively great height*: "a race of long gaunt men" (Sherwood Anderson); "looked out the long French windows"

Figure 1: Three of the WordNet senses for "Long"

Anveshan uses the Kullbach-Liebler divergence (KLD), Jensen-Shannon divergence (JSD) and Leverage to compare probability distributions. The KLD of two probability distributions $P$ and $Q$ is given by:

$$KLD(P,Q) = \sum_i P(i) \log \frac{P(i)}{Q(i)}$$

JSD is a modified version of KLD, it is also known as *total divergence to the average*, and is given by:

$$JSD(P,Q) = \frac{1}{2}KLD(P,M) + \frac{1}{2}KLD(Q,M)$$

where

$$M = (P+Q)/2$$

We define Leverage $Lev$ of probability distribution P over Q as:

$$Lev(P,Q) = \sum_k |P(k) - Q(k)|$$

We now compute the following statistics:

- For each annotator $a_i$, we compute $P_{a_i}$.
- We compute $P_{avg}$, which is $(\sum_i P_{a_i})/n$.
- We compute $Lev(P_{a_i}, P_{avg}), \forall i$
- Then we compute $JSD(P_{a_i}, P_{a_j})$ $\forall(i,j)$, where $i,j \leq n$ and $i \neq j$
- Lastly, we compute a distance measure for each annotator, by computing the KLD between each annotator and the average of the remaining annotators, i.e. we get $\forall i, D_{a_i} = KLD(P_{a_i}, Q)$, where $Q = (\sum_{j \neq i} P_{a_j})/(n-1)$

These statistics give us a deeper understanding of annotator behavior. Looking at the sense usage probabilities, we can identify how frequently senses are used by an annotator. We can see how much an annotator deviates from the average sense usage distribution by looking at Leverage. JSD between two annotators gives us a measure of how close they are to each other. KLD of an annotator with the remaining annotators shows us how different the annotator is from the rest. In the following section we show results, which illustrate the effectiveness of Anveshan in identifying useful patterns in the data from the trained annotators (TAs) and Mechanical Turkers (MTs).

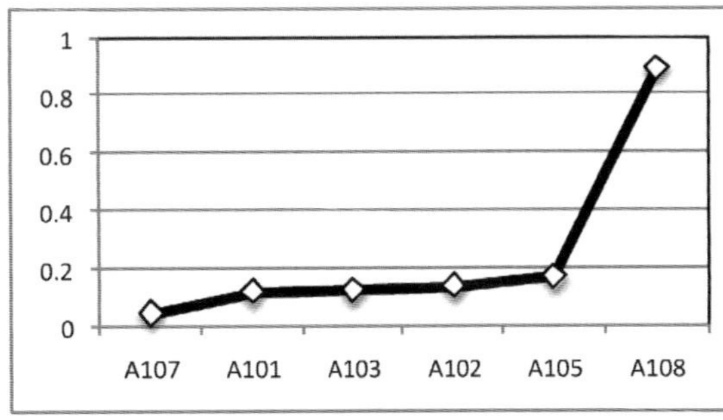


Figure 2: Distance measure (KLD) for Annotators of *long* in TA Data

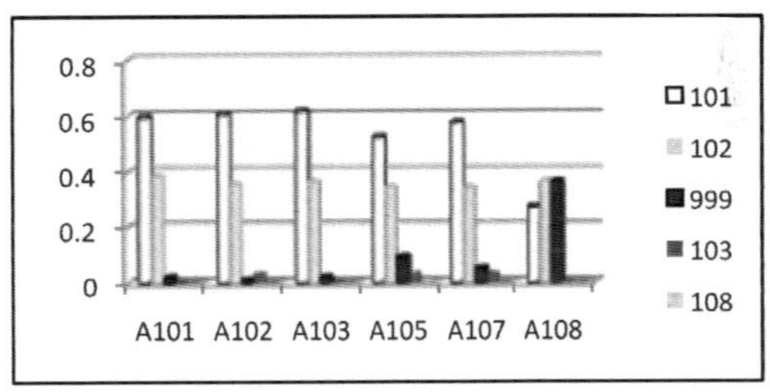


Figure 3: Sense Usage distribution for *long* by annotators in TA Data

### 6.2 Results

We used Anveshan on all data from TAs and MTs. We were successful in correctly identifying outliers on many words. Also, analyzing the sense usage patterns and observing the JSD and KLD scores gave us useful insights on annotator differences. In the figures for this section, the six TAs are represented by their unique identifiers (A101, A102, A103, A105, A107, A108). Word senses are identified by adding 100 to the WordNet sense

| Word | Old Alpha | Ann Dropped | New Alpha |
|---|---|---|---|
| *long* | 0.67 | 1 | 0.80 |
| *land* | 0.49 | 1 | 0.54 |
| *know* | 0.377 | 1 | 0.48 |
| *tell* | 0.45 | 2 | 0.52 |
| *say* | 0.37 | 2 | 0.44 |
| *fair* | 0.54 | 2 | 0.63 |

Table 3: Increase in IA score by dropping annotators (TA Data)

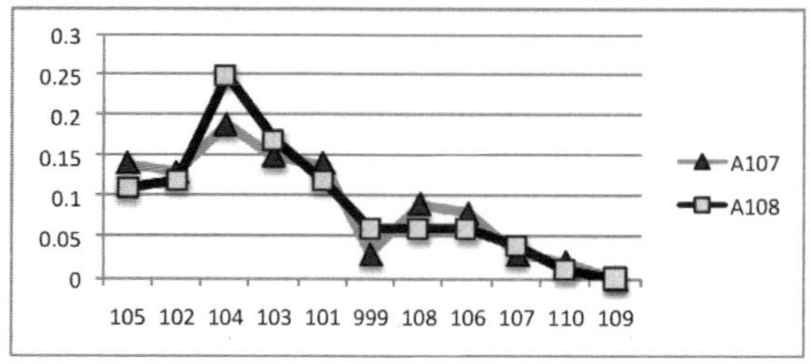


Figure 5: Sense usage patterns of annotators '107' and '108' for *show* in TA Data

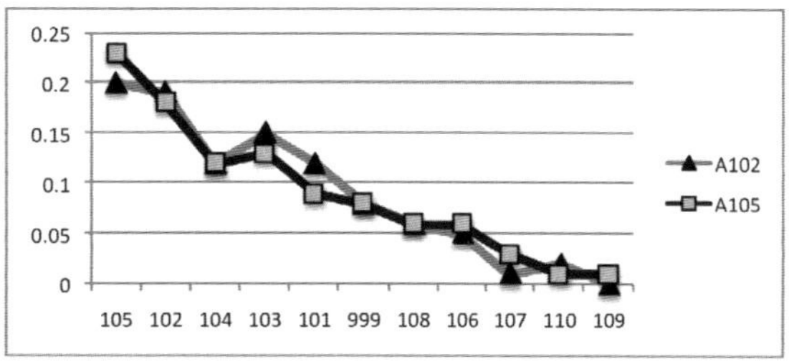


Figure 4: Sense usage patterns of annotators '102' and '105' for *show* in TA Data

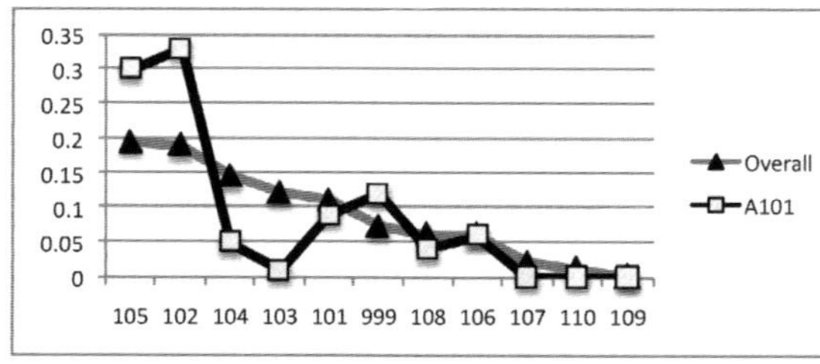


Figure 6: Sense usage distribution of annotator '101' vs. the average of all annotators for *show* in TA Data

number. An additional "*None of the Above*" label is represented as 999; annotators select this when no sense applies, when the word occurs as part of a large lexical unit (collocation) with a clearly distinct meaning, or when the sentence is not a correct example for other reasons (e.g., wrong part of speech).

Figure 2 shows the distance measure (KLD) for each annotator from the rest of the annotators for the word *long* with respect to the probability for each of the four senses used (cf. Table 1). It can be clearly seen that annotator A108 is an outlier. A108 differs in her excessive use of label 999, as shown in Figure 3. Indeed, by dropping A108, we see that the IA score (Alpha) jumps from 0.67 to 0.8 for *long*. Similar results were obtained for annotations for other words as well. Table 3 shows the jump in IA score after outlier(s) were dropped.

Anveshan helps us differentiate between noisy disagreement versus systematic disagreement. The word *show* with 5 annotators has a low agreement score of 0.45. By looking at the sense distributions for the various annotators, and observing annotation preferences for each annotator, we can see that annotators A102 and A105 have similar behavior (Figure 4, with a pairwise alpha of 0.52 versus 0.46 for all five annotators), and annotators A107 and A108 have similar behavior (Figure 5, with a pairwise alpha of 0.53). In contrast, Annotator A101 has very distinct preferences (Figure 6). This behavior is captured by computing JSD scores among all pairs of annotators. As can be seen in Figure 7, the pairs A102-A105 and A107-A108 have very low JSD values, indicating similarity in annotator behavior. At the same time we also see the pairs having A101 in them have a much higher JSD score, which is attributed to the fact that A101 is different from everyone else. If we look at corresponding Alpha scores, we see that pairs having low JSD values have higher agreement scores and vice versa.

Observing the sense usage distributions also helps us identify confusable senses. For example, Figure 8 shows us the differences in sense usage patterns of A101, A103 and the average of all annotators for the word *say*. We can see that A101 and A103 deviate in distinct ways from the average. A101 prefers sense 101 whereas A103 prefers sense 102. This indicates that sense 101 and 102 might be confusable. Sense 1 is given as "*expressing words*"; sense 2 as "*report or maintain*".

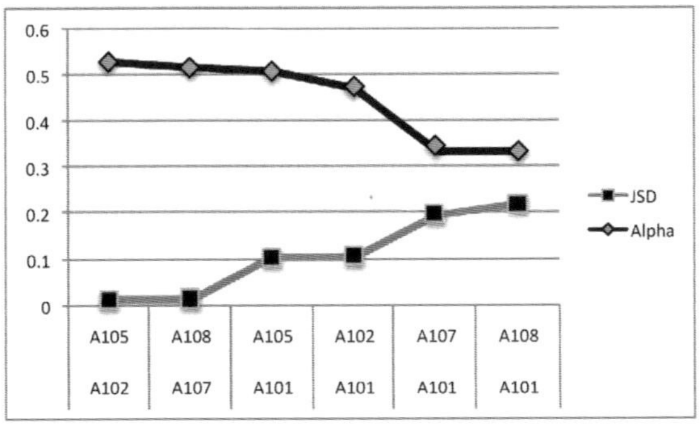


Figure 7: JSD and Alpha scores for pairs of annotators for *show* in TA Data

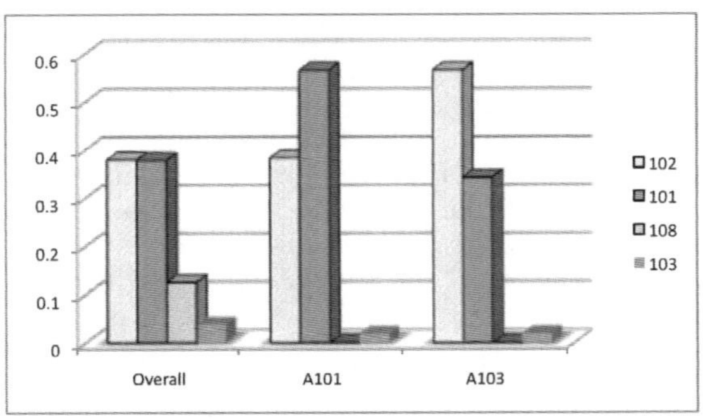


Figure 8: Sense usage distribution for *say* in TA Data for annotators '101' and '103'

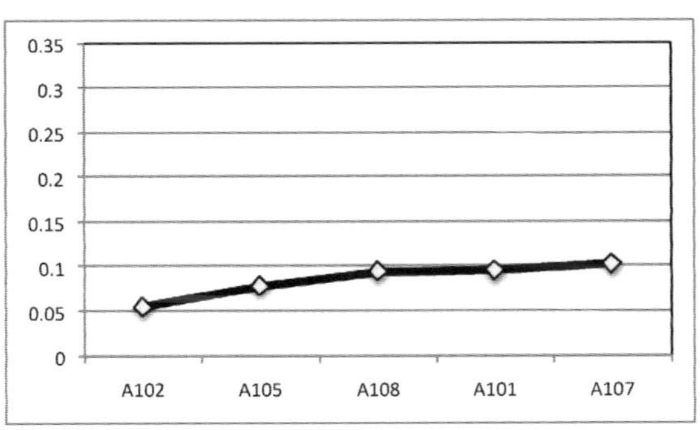


Figure 9: Distance measure (KLD) for annotators of *work* in TA Data

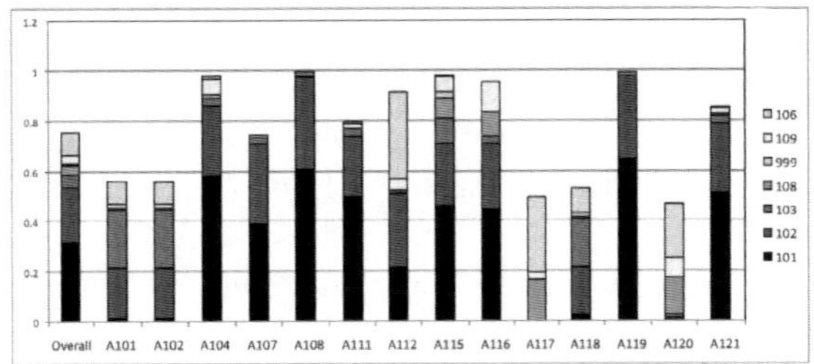

Figure 10: Sense usage distribution among MTs for *long*

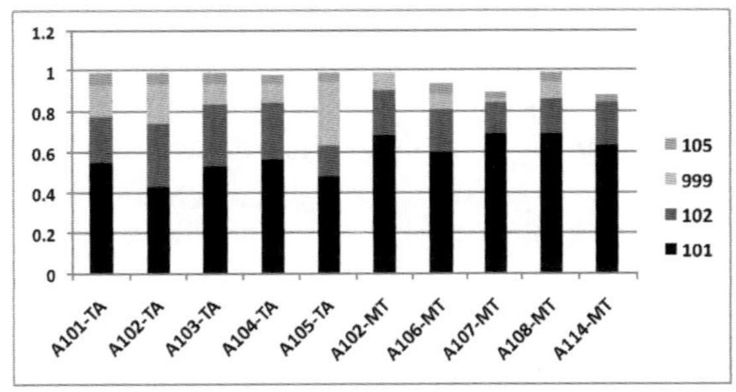


Figure 11: Sense usage distribution among TAs and MTs for *fair*

Anveshan not only helps us understand underlying patterns in annotator behavior and remove noise from IA scores, but also helps identify cases where there is no noise and no systematic subsets of annotators that agree with each other. An example can be seen in for the noun *work*. We observed that the annotators do not have largely different behavior, which is reflected in Figure 9. As none of the annotators are significantly different from the others, the KLD scores are low and the plotted line does not have any steep rises, as seen in Figure 2.

Similar to the results for TA data, Anveshan was successful in identifying outliers in Mechanical Turk data as well. In order to compare the agreement among TAs and MTs, we looked at IA scores of all subsets of annotators for the three adjectives in the Mechanical Turk data. We observed that MTs used much more senses than TAs for all words and that there was a lot of noise in sense usage distribution. Figure 10 illustrates the sense usage statistics for *long* among MTs, for frequently used senses.

We also looked at agreement scores among all subsets of MTs to see if there are any subsets of annotators who agree as much as TAs, and we observed that for both *long* and *quiet*, there were no subsets of MT annotators whose agreement was comparable or greater than the same number of the TAs, however for *fair*, we found one set of 5 annotators whose IA score (0.61) was greater than the IA score (0.54) of trained annotators. We also observed that among both these pairs of annotators, the frequently used senses were the same, as illustrated in Figure 11. Still, the two groups of annotators have sufficiently distinct sense usage that the overall IA for the combined set drops to 0.43.

## 7 Conclusion and Future Work

For annotations on a subjective task, there are cases where there is no single correct label. In this paper, we presented Anveshan, an approach to study annotator behavior and to explore datasets with multiple annotators, and with a large set of annotation values. Here we looked at data from half a dozen trained annotators and fourteen untrained Mechanical Turkers on word sense annotation for polysemous words. The analysis using Anveshan provided many insights into sources of disagreement among the annotators.

We learn that IA Scores do not give us a complete picture and it is necessary to delve deeper and study annotator behavior in order to identify noise possibly due to sense confusability, to eliminate noise due to outliers, and to identify systematic differences where subsets of annotators have much higher IA than the full set.

The results from Anveshan are encouraging and the methodology can be readily extended to study patterns in human behavior. We plan to extend our work by looking at JSD scores of all subsets of annotators instead of pairs, to identify larger subsets of annotators who have similar behavior. We also plan to investigate other statistical methods of outlier detection such as the orthogonalized Gnanadesikan-Kettenring estimator.

## References


Cecilia Ovesdotter Alm, Dan Roth, and Richard Sproat. 2005. Emotions from text: machine learning for text-based emotion prediction. In *HLT '05: Proceedings of the conference on Human Language Technology and Empirical Methods in Natural Language Processing*, pages 579–586, Morristown, NJ, USA. Association for Computational Linguistics.

Ron Artstein and Massimo Poesio. 2008. Inter-coder agreement for computational linguistics. *Computational Linguistics*, 34(4):555–596.

Marco Carbone, Yaakov Gal, Stuart Shieber, and Barbara Grosz. 2004. Unifying annotated discourse hierarchies to create a gold standard. In *Proceedings of the 5th Sigdial Workshop on Discourse and Dialogue.*

Irina Chugur, Julio Gonzalo, and Felisa Verdejo. 2002. Polysemy and sense proximity in the senseval-2 test suite. In *Proceedings of the SIGLEX/SENSEVAL Workshop on Word Sense Disambiguation: Recent Successes and Future Directions*, pages 32–39, Philadelphia.

Jacob Cohen. 1960. A coeffiecient of agreement for nominal scales. *Educational and Psychological Measurement*, 20:37–46.

Mona Diab. 2004. Relieving the data acquisition bottleneck in word sense disambiguation. In *Proceedings of the 42nd Annual Meeting on Association for Computational Linguistics*, pages 303–311.

Jun Hu, Rebecca J. Passonneau, and Owen Rambow. 2009. Contrasting the interaction structure of an email and a telephone corpus: A machine learning approach to annotation of dialogue function units. In *Proceedings of the 10th SIGDIAL on Dialogue and Discourse.*

Nancy Ide and Yorick Wilks. 2006. Making sense about sense. In E. Agirre and P. Edmonds, editors, *Word Sense Disambiguation: Algorithms and Applications*, pages 47–74, Dordrecht, The Netherlands. Springer.

Nancy Ide, Tomaz Erjavec, and Dan Tufis. 2002. Sense discrimination with parallel corpora. In *Proceedings of ACL'02 Workshop on Word Sense Disambiguation: Recent Successes and Future Directions*, pages 54–60, Philadelphia.

Nancy Ide, Collin Baker, Christiane Fellbaum, and Rebecca Passonneau. 2010. The manually annotated sub-corpus: A community resource for and by the people. In *Proceedings of the 48th Annual Meeting of the Association for Computational Linguistics*, Uppsala, Sweden.

Adam Kilgarriff and Martha Palmer. 2000. Introduction to the special issue on senseval. *Computers and the Humanities*, 34:1–2.

Adam Kilgarriff. 1997. I don't believe in word senses. *Computers and the Humanities*, 31:91–113.

Adam Kilgarriff. 1998. SENSEVAL: An exercise in evaluating word sense disambiguation programs. In *Proceedings of the First International Conference on Language Resources and Evaluation (LREC)*, pages 581–588, Granada.

Devra Klein and Gregory Murphy. 2002. Paper has been my ruin: Conceptual relations of polysemous words. *Journal of Memory and Language*, 47:548–70.

Klaus Krippendorff. 1980. *Content Analysis: An Introduction to Its Methodology*. Sage Publications, Beverly Hills, CA.

Chuck P. Lam and David G. Stork. 2003. Evaluating classifiers by means of test data with noisy labels. In *Proceedings of the 18th International Joint Conference on Artificial Intelligence (IJCAI-03)*, pages 513–518, Acapulco.

George A. Miller, Richard Beckwith, Christiane Fellbaum, Derek Gross, and Katherine Miller. 1993. Introduction to WordNet: An on-line lexical database (revised). Technical Report Cognitive Science Laboratory (CSL) Report 43, Princeton University, Princeton. Revised March 1993.

Hwee Tou Ng, Chung Yong Lim, and Shou King Foo. 1999. A case study on inter-annotator agreement for word sense disambiguation. In *SIGLEX Workshop On Standardizing Lexical Resources*.

Martha Palmer, Hoa Trang Dang, and Christiane Fellbaum. 2005a. Making fine-grained and coarse-grained sense distinctions. *Journal of Natural Language Engineering*, 13.2:137–163.

Martha Palmer, Daniel Gildea, and Paul Kingsbury. 2005b. The proposition bank: An annotated corpus of semantic roles. *Comput. Linguist.*, 31(1):71–106.

Rebecca J. Passonneau, Nizar Habash, and Owen Rambow. 2006. Inter-annotator agreement on a multilingual semantic annotation task. In *Proceedings of the International Conference on Language Resources and Evaluation (LREC)*, pages 1951–1956, Genoa, Italy.

Rebecca Passonneau, Tom Lippincott, Tae Yano, and Judith Klavans. 2008. Relation between agreement measures on human labeling and machine learning performance: results from an art history domain. In *Proceedings of the Sixth International Conference on Language Resources and Evaluation (LREC)*, pages 2841–2848.

Ted Pedersen. 2002a. Assessing system agreement and instance difficulty in the lexical sample tasks of Senseval-2. In *Proceedings of the ACL-02 Workshop on Word Sense Disambiguation: Recent Successes and Future Directions*, pages 40–46.

Ted Pedersen. 2002b. Evaluating the effectiveness of ensembles of decision trees in disambiguating SENSEVAL lexical samples. In *Proceedings of the ACL-02 Workshop on Word Sense Disambiguation: Recent Successes and Future Directions*, pages 81–87.

Dennis Reidsma and Jean Carletta. 2008. Reliability measurement without limits. *Comput. Linguist.*, 34(3):319–326.

Josef Ruppenhofer, Michael Ellsworth, Miriam R. L. Petruck, Christopher R. Johnson, and Jan Scheffczyk. 2006. Framenet ii: Extended theory and practice. Available from http://framenet.icsi.berkeley.edu/index.php.

Victor S. Sheng, Foster Provost, and Panagiotis G. Ipeirotis. 2008. Get another label? improving data quality and data mining using multiple, noisy labelers. In *Proceeding of the 14th ACM SIG KDD International Conference on Knowledge Discovery and Data Mining*, pages 614–622, Las Vegas.

Rion Snow, Daniel Jurafsky, and Andrew Y. Ng. 2007. Learning to merge word senses. In *Proceedings of the 2007 Joint Conference on Empirical Methods in Natural Language Processing and Computational Natural Language Learning*, pages 1005–1014, Prague.

Rion Snow, Brendan O'Connor, Daniel Jurafsky, and Andrew Y. Ng. 2008. Cheap and fast - but is it good? evaluating non-expert annotations for natural language tasks. In *Proceedings of Empirical Methods in Natural Language Processing (EMNLP)*, pages 254–263, Honolulu.

Jean Véronis. 1998. A study of polysemy judgements and inter-annotator agreement. In *SENSEVAL Workshop*, pages Sussex, England.

Janyce Wiebe and Claire Cardie. 2005. Annotating expressions of opinions and emotions in language. language resources and evaluation. In *Language Resources and Evaluation (formerly Computers and the Humanities*, page 2005.

# Influence of Pre-annotation on POS-tagged Corpus Development

**Karën Fort**
INIST CNRS / LIPN
Nancy / Paris, France.
karen.fort@inist.fr

**Benoît Sagot**
INRIA Paris-Rocquencourt / Paris 7
Paris, France.
benoit.sagot@inria.fr

## Abstract

This article details a series of carefully designed experiments aiming at evaluating the influence of automatic pre-annotation on the manual part-of-speech annotation of a corpus, both from the quality and the time points of view, with a specific attention drawn to biases. For this purpose, we manually annotated parts of the Penn Treebank corpus (Marcus et al., 1993) under various experimental setups, either from scratch or using various pre-annotations. These experiments confirm and detail the gain in quality observed before (Marcus et al., 1993; Dandapat et al., 2009; Rehbein et al., 2009), while showing that biases do appear and should be taken into account. They finally demonstrate that even a not so accurate tagger can help improving annotation speed.

## 1 Introduction

Training a machine-learning based part-of-speech (POS) tagger implies manually tagging a significant amount of text. The cost of this, in terms of human effort, slows down the development of taggers for under-resourced languages.

One usual way to improve this situation is to automatically pre-annotate the corpus, so that the work of the annotators is limited to the validation of this pre-annotation. This method proved quite efficient in a number of POS-annotated corpus development projects (Marcus et al., 1993; Dandapat et al., 2009), allowing for a significant gain not only in annotation time but also in consistency. However, the influence of the pre-tagging quality on the error rate in the resulting annotated corpus and the bias introduced by the pre-annotation has been little examined. This is what we propose to do here, using different parts of the Penn Treebank to train various instances of a POS tagger and experiment on pre-annotation. Our goal is to assess the impact of the quality (i.e., accuracy) of the POS tagger used for pre-annotating and to compare the use of pre-annotation with purely manual tagging, while minimizing all kinds of biases. We quantify the results in terms of error rate in the resulting annotated corpus, manual annotation time and inter-annotator agreement.

This article is organized as follows. In Section 2, we mention some related work, while Section 3 describes the experimental setup, followed by a discussion on the obtained results (Section 4) and a conclusion.

## 2 Related Work

### 2.1 Pre-annotation for POS Tagging

Very few manual annotation projects give details about the campaign itself. One major exception is the Penn Treebank project (Marcus et al., 1993), that provided detailed information about the manual annotation methodology, evaluation and cost. Marcus et al. (1993) thus showed that manual tagging took twice as long as correcting pre-tagged text and resulted in twice the inter-annotator disagreement rate, as well as an error rate (using a gold-standard annotation) about 50% higher. The pre-annotation was done using a tagger trained on the Brown Corpus, which, due to errors introduced by an automatic mapping of tags from the Brown tagset to the Penn Treebank tagset, had an error rate of 7–9%. However, they report neither the influence of the training of the annotators on the potential biases in correction, nor that of the quality of the tagger on the correction time and the obtained quality.

Dandapat et al. (2009) went further and showed that, for complex POS-tagging (for Hindi and Bangla), pre-annotation of the corpus allows for a gain in time, but not necessarily in consis-



*Proceedings of the Fourth Linguistic Annotation Workshop, ACL 2010*, pages 56–63,
Uppsala, Sweden, 15-16 July 2010. ©2010 Association for Computational Linguistics

tency, which depends largely on the pre-tagging quality. They also noticed that untrained annotators were more influenced by pre-annotation than the trained ones, who showed "consistent performance". However, this very complete and interesting experiment lacked a reference allowing for an evaluation of the quality of the annotations. Besides, it only took into account two types of pre-tagging quality, high accuracy and low accuracy.

### 2.2 Pre-annotation in Other Annotation Tasks

Alex et al. (2008) led some experiments in the biomedical domain, within the framework of a "curation" task of protein-protein interaction. Curation consists in reading through electronic version of papers and entering retrieved information into a template. They showed that perfectly pre-annotating the corpus leads to a reduction of more than 1/3 in curation time, as well as a better recall from the annotators. Less perfect pre-annotation still leads to a gain in time, but less so (a little less than 1/4th). They also tested the effect of higher recall or precision of pre-annotation on one annotator (curator), who rated recall more positively than precision. However, as they notice, this result can be explained by the curation style and should be tested on more annotators.

Rehbein et al. (2009) led quite thorough experiments on the subject, in the field of semantic frame assignment annotation. They asked 6 annotators to annotate or correct frame assignment using a task-specific annotation tool. Here again, pre-annotation was done using only two types of pre-tagging quality, state-of-the-art and enhanced. The results of the experiments are a bit disappointing as they could not find a direct improvement of annotation time using pre-annotation. The authors reckon this might be at least partly due to "an interaction between time savings from pre-annotation and time savings due to a training effect." For the same reason, they had to exclude some of the annotation results for quality evaluation in order to show that, in line with (Marcus et al., 1993), quality pre-annotation helps increasing annotation quality. They also found that noisy and low quality pre-annotation does not overall corrupt human judgment.

On the other hand, Fort et al. (2009) claim that pre-annotation introduces a bias in named entity annotation, due to the preference given by annotators to what is already annotated, thus preventing them from noticing entities that were not pre-annotated. This particular type of bias should not appear in POS-tagging, as all the elements are to be annotated, but a pre-tagging could influence the annotators, preventing them from asking themselves questions about a specific pre-annotation.

In a completely different field, Barque et al. (2010) used a series of NLP tools, called MACAON, to automatically identify the central component and optional peripheral components of dictionary definitions. This pre-processing gave disappointing results as compared to entirely manual annotation, as it did not allow for a significant gain in time. The authors consider that the bad results are due to the quality of the tool that they wish to improve as they believe that "an automatic segmentation of better quality would surely yield some gains."

Yet, the question remains: is there a quality threshold for pre-annotation to be useful? and if so, how can we evaluate it? We tried to answer at least part of these questions for a quite simple task for which data is available: POS-tagging in English.

## 3 Experimental Setup

The idea underlying our experiments is the following. We split the Penn Treebank corpus (Marcus et al., 1993) in a usual manner, namely we use Sections 2 to 21 to train various instances of a POS tagger, and Section 23 to perform the actual experiments. In order to measure the impact of the POS tagger's quality, we trained it on subcorpora of increasing sizes, and pre-annotated Section 23 with these various POS taggers. Then, we manually annotated parts of Section 23 under various experimental setups, either from scratch or using various pre-annotations, as explained below.

### 3.1 Creating the Taggers

We used the MElt POS tagger (Denis and Sagot, 2009), a maximum-entropy based system that is able to take into account both information extracted from a training corpus and information extracted from an external morphological lexicon.[1] It has been shown to lead to a state-of-the-art POS tagger for French. Trained on Sections 2 to 21

[1]MElt is freely available under LGPL license, on the web page of its hosting project (`http://gforge.inria.fr/projects/lingwb/`).

of the Penn Treebank ($\text{MElt}_{\text{en}}^{\text{ALL}}$), and evaluated on Section 23, MElt exhibits a 96.4% accuracy, which is reasonably close to the state-of-the-art (Spoustová et al. (2009) report 97.4%). Since it is trained without any external lexicon, $\text{MElt}_{\text{en}}^{\text{ALL}}$ is very close to the original maximum-entropy based tagger (Ratnaparkhi, 1996), which has indeed a similar 96.6% accuracy.

We trained MElt on increasingly larger parts of the POS-tagged Penn Treebank,[2] thus creating different taggers with growing degrees of accuracy (see table 1). We then POS-tagged the Section 23 with each of these taggers, thus obtaining for each sentence in Section 23 a set of pre-annotations, one from each tagger.

| Tagger | Nb train. sent. | Nb tokens | Acc. (%) |
|---|---|---|---|
| $\text{MElt}_{\text{en}}^{10}$ | 10 | 189 | 66.5 |
| $\text{MElt}_{\text{en}}^{50}$ | 50 | 1,254 | 81.6 |
| $\text{MElt}_{\text{en}}^{100}$ | 100 | 2,774 | 86.7 |
| $\text{MElt}_{\text{en}}^{500}$ | 500 | 12,630 | 92.1 |
| $\text{MElt}_{\text{en}}^{1000}$ | 1,000 | 25,994 | 93.6 |
| $\text{MElt}_{\text{en}}^{5000}$ | 5,000 | 126,376 | 95.8 |
| $\text{MElt}_{\text{en}}^{10000}$ | 10,000 | 252,416 | 96.2 |
| $\text{MElt}_{\text{en}}^{\text{ALL}}$ | 37,990 | 944,859 | 96.4 |

Table 1: Accuracy of the created taggers evaluated on Section 23 of the Penn Treebank

### 3.2 Experiments

We designed different experimental setups to evaluate the impact of pre-annotation and pre-annotation accuracy on the quality of the resulting corpus. The subparts of Section 23 that we used for these experiments are identified by sentence ids (e.g., 1–100 denotes the 100 first sentences in Section 23).

Two annotators were involved in the experiments. They both have a good knowledge of linguistics, without being linguists themselves and had only little prior knowledge of the Penn Treebank POS tagset. One of them had previous expertise in POS tagging (Annotator1). It should also be noticed that, though they speak fluent English, they are not native speakers of the language. They were asked to keep track of their annotation time, noting the time it took them to annotate or correct each series of 10 sentences. They were also asked to use only a basic text editor, with no macro or specific feature that could help them, apart from the usual ones, like `Find`, `Replace`, etc. The set of 36 tags used in the Penn Treebank and quite a number of particular cases is a lot to keep in mind. This implies a heavy cognitive load in short-term memory, especially as no specific interface was used to help annotating or correcting the pre-annotations.

It was demonstrated that training improves the quality of manual annotation in a significant way as well as allows for a significant gain in time (Marcus et al., 1993; Dandapat et al., 2009; Mikulová and Štěpánek, 2009). In particular, Marcus et al. (1993) observed that it took the Penn Treebank annotators 1 month to get fully efficient on the POS-tagging correction task, reaching a speed of 20 minutes per 1,000 words. The speed of annotation in our experiments cannot be compared to this, as our annotators only annotated and corrected small samples of the Penn Treebank. However, the annotators' speed and correctness did improve with practice. As explained below, we took this learning curve into account, as previous work (Rehbein et al., 2009) showed it has an significant impact on the results.

Also, during each experiment, sentences were annotated sequentially. Moreover, the experiments were conducted in the order we describe them below. For example, both annotators started their first annotation task (sentences 1–100) with sentence 1.

We conducted the following experiments:

1. **Impact of the pre-annotation accuracy on precision and inter-annotator agreement:** In this experiment, we used sentences 1–400 with random pre-annotation: for each sentence, one pre-annotation is randomly selected among its possible pre-annotations (one for each tagger instance). The aim of this is to eliminate the bias caused by the annotators' learning curve. Annotation time for each series of 10 consecutive sentences was gathered, as well as precision w.r.t. the reference and inter-annotator agreement (both annotators annotated sentences 1–100 and 301–400, while only one annotated 101–200 and the other 201–300).

2. **Impact of the pre-annotation accuracy on annotation time:** This experiment is based on sentences 601–760, with pre-annotation. We divided them in series of 10 sentences.

[2] More precisely, $\text{MElt}_{\text{en}}^{i}$ is trained on the $i$ first sentences of the overall training corpus, i.e. Sections 2 to 21.

For each series, one pre-annotation is selected (i.e., the pre-annotation produced by one of the 8 taggers), in such a way that each pre-annotation is used for 2 series. We measured the manual annotation time for each series and each annotator.

3. **Bias induced by pre-annotation:** In this experiment, both annotators annotated sentences 451–500 fully manually.[3] Later, they annotated sentences 451–475 with the pre-annotation from $\text{MElt}_{\text{en}}^{\text{ALL}}$ (the best tagger) and sentences 476–500 with the pre-annotation from $\text{MElt}_{\text{en}}^{50}$ (the second-worst tagger). We then compared the fully manual annotations with those based on pre-annotations to check if and how they diverge from the Penn Treebank "gold-standard"; we also compared annotation times, in order to get a confirmation of the gain in time observed in previous experiments.

## 4 Results and Discussion

### 4.1 Impact of the Pre-annotation Accuracy on Precision and Inter-annotator Agreement

The quality of the annotations created during experiment 1 was evaluated using two methods. First, we considered the original Penn Treebank annotations as reference and calculated a simple precision as compared to this reference. Figure 1 gives an overview of the obtained results (note that the scale is not regular).

However, this is not sufficient to evaluate the quality of the annotation as, actually, the reference annotation is not perfect (see below). We therefore evaluated the reliability of the annotation, calculating the inter-annotator agreement between Annotator1 and Annotator2 on the 100-sentence series they both annotated. We calculated this agreement on some of the subcorpora using $\pi$, aka Carletta's Kappa (Carletta, 1996)[4]. The results of this are shown in table 2.

| **Subcorpus** | $\pi$ |
|---|---|
| 1-100 | 0.955 |
| 301-400 | 0.963 |

Table 2: Inter-annotator agreement on subcorpora

The results show a very good agreement according to all scales (Krippendorff, 1980; Neuendorf, 2002; Krippendorff, 2004) as $\pi$ is always superior to 0.9. Besides, it improves with training (from 0.955 at the beginning to 0.963 at the end).

We also calculated $\pi$ on the corpus we used to evaluate the pre-annotation bias (Experiment 3). The results of this are shown in table 3.

| **Subcorpus** | **Nb sent.** | $\pi$ |
|---|---|---|
| No pre-annotation | 50 | 0.947 |
| $\text{MElt}_{\text{en}}^{50}$ | 25 | 0.944 |
| $\text{MElt}_{\text{en}}^{\text{ALL}}$ | 25 | 0.983 |

Table 3: Inter-annotator agreement on subcorpora used to evaluate bias

Here again, the results are very good, though a little bit less so than at the beginning of the mixed annotation session. They are almost perfect with $\text{MElt}_{\text{en}}^{\text{ALL}}$.

Finally, we calculated $\pi$ throughout Experiment 2. The results are given in Figure 2 and, apart from a bizarre peak at $\text{MElt}_{\text{en}}^{50}$, they show a steady progression of the accuracy and the inter-annotator agreement, which are correlated. As for the $\text{MElt}_{\text{en}}^{50}$ peak, it does not appear in Figure 1, we therefore interpret it as an artifact.

### 4.2 Impact of the Pre-annotation Accuracy on Annotation Time

Before discussing the results of Experiment 2, annotation time measurements during Experiment 3 confirm that using a good quality pre-annotation (say, $\text{MElt}_{\text{en}}^{\text{ALL}}$) strongly reduces the annotation time as compared with fully manual annotation. For example, Annotator1 needed an average time of approximately 7.5 minutes to annotate 10 sentences without pre-annotation (Experiment 3), whereas Experiment 2 shows that it goes down to approximately 2.5 minutes when using $\text{MElt}_{\text{en}}^{\text{ALL}}$ pre-annotation. For Annotator2, the corresponding figures are respectively 11.5 and 2.5 minutes.

Figure 3 shows the impact on the pre-annotation type on annotation times. Surprisingly, only the worst tagger ($\text{MElt}_{\text{en}}^{10}$) produces pre-annotations that lead to a significantly slower annotation. In

[3]During this manual annotation step (with no pre-annotation), we noticed that the annotators used the `Find/Replace all` feature of the text editor to fasten the tagging of some obvious tokens like *the* or *Corp.*, which partly explains that the first groups of 10 sentences took longer to annotate. Also, as no specific interface was use to help annotating, a (very) few typographic errors were made, such as *DET* instead of *DT*.

[4]For more information on the terminology issue, refer to the introduction of (Artstein and Poesio, 2008).

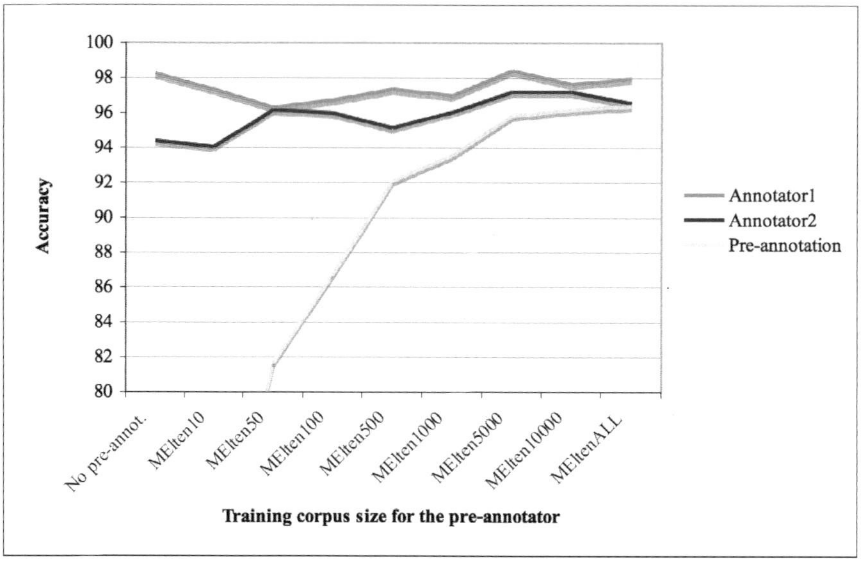


Figure 1: Accuracy of annotation

other words, a 96.4% accurate pre-annotation does not significantly speed up the annotation process with respect to a 81.6% accurate pre-annotation. This is very interesting, since it could mean that the development of a POS-annotated corpus for a new language with no POS tagger could be drastically sped up. Annotating approximately 50 sentences could be sufficient to train a POS tagger such as MElt and use it as a pre-annotator, even though its quality is not yet satisfying.

One interpretation of this could be the following. Annotation based on pre-annotations involves two different tasks: reading the pre-annotated sentence and replacing incorrect tags. The reading task takes a time that does not really depends on the pre-annotation quality. But the correction task takes a time that is, say, linear w.r.t. the number of pre-annotation errors. Therefore, when the number of pre-annotation errors is below a certain level, the correction task takes significantly less time than the reading task. Therefore, below this level, variations in the pre-annotation error rate do not lead to significant overall annotation time. Apparently, this threshold is between 66.5% and 81.6% pre-annotation accuracy, which can be reached with a surprisingly small training corpus.

### 4.3 Bias Induced by Pre-annotation

We evaluated both the bias induced by a pre-annotation with the best tagger, $\text{MElt}_{\text{en}}^{\text{ALL}}$, and the one induced by one of the least accurate taggers, $\text{MElt}_{\text{en}}^{50}$. The results are given in table 4 and 5, respectively.

They show a very different bias according to the annotator. Annotator2's accuracy raises from 94.6% to 95.2% with a 81.6% accuracy tagger ($\text{MElt}_{\text{en}}^{50}$) and from 94.1% to 97.1% with a 96.4% accuracy tagger ($\text{MElt}_{\text{en}}^{\text{ALL}}$). Therefore, Annotator2, whose accuracy is less than that of Annotator1 under all circumstances (see figure 1), seems to be positively influenced by pre-annotation, whether it be good or bad. The gain is however much more salient with the best pre-annotation (plus 3 points).

As for Annotator1, who is the most accurate annotator (see figure 1), the results are more surprising as they show a significant degradation of accuracy, from 98.1 without pre-annotation to 95.8 with pre-annotation using $\text{MElt}_{\text{en}}^{50}$, the less accurate tagger. Examining the actual results allowed us to see that, first, Annotator1 non pre-annotated version is better than the reference, and second, the errors made in the pre-annotated version with $\text{MElt}_{\text{en}}^{50}$ are so obvious that they can only be due to a lapse in concentration.

The results, however, remain stable with pre-annotation using the best tagger (from 98.4 to 98.2), which is consistent with the results obtained by Dandapat et al. (2009), who showed that better trained annotators are less influenced by pre-annotation and show stable performance.

When asked about it, both annotators say they felt they concentrated more without pre-

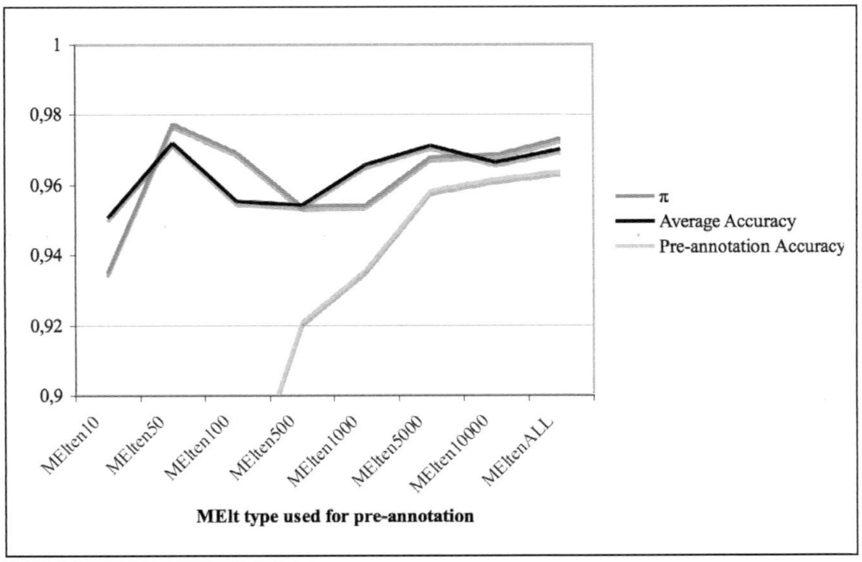


Figure 2: Annotation accuracy and $\pi$ depending on the type of pre-annotation

| Annotator | No pre-annotation | with $\mathrm{MElt}_{\mathrm{en}}^{\mathrm{ALL}}$ |
|---|---|---|
| Annotator1 | 98.4 | 98.2 |
| Annotator2 | 94.1 | 97.1 |

Table 4: Accuracy with or without pre-annotation with $\mathrm{MElt}_{\mathrm{en}}^{\mathrm{ALL}}$ (sentences 451-475)

| Annotator | No pre-annotation | with $\mathrm{MElt}_{\mathrm{en}}^{50}$ |
|---|---|---|
| Annotator1 | 98.1 | 95.8 |
| Annotator2 | 94.6 | 95.2 |

Table 5: Accuracy with or without pre-annotation with $\mathrm{MElt}_{\mathrm{en}}^{50}$ (sentences 476-500)

annotation. It seems that the rather good results of the taggers cause the attention of the annotators to be reduced, even more so as the task is repetitive and tedious. However, annotators also had the feeling that fully manual annotation could be more subject to oversights.

These impressions are confirmed by the comparison of the contingency tables, as can be seen from Tables 6, 7 and 8 (in these tables, lines correspond to tags from the annotation and columns to reference tags; only lines containing at least one cell with 2 errors or more are shown, with all corresponding columns). For example, Annotator1 makes more random errors when no pre-annotation is available and more systematic errors when $\mathrm{MElt}_{\mathrm{en}}^{\mathrm{ALL}}$ pre-annotations are used (typically, *JJ* instead of *VBN*, i.e., adjective instead of past participle, which corresponds to a systematic trend in $\mathrm{MElt}_{\mathrm{en}}^{\mathrm{ALL}}$'s results).

| | JJ | VBN |
|---|---|---|
| JJ | 36 | 4 |

(Annotator 1)

| | JJ | NN | NNP | NNPS | VB | VBN |
|---|---|---|---|---|---|---|
| JJ | 36 | | | | | 4 |
| NN | 1 | 68 | | | 2 | |
| NNP | | | 24 | 2 | | |

(Annotator 2)

Table 6: Excerpts of the contingency tables for sentences 451–457 (512 tokens) with $\mathrm{MElt}_{\mathrm{en}}^{\mathrm{ALL}}$ pre-annotation

| | IN | JJ | NN | NNP | NNS | RB | VBD | VBN |
|---|---|---|---|---|---|---|---|---|
| JJ | | 30 | 2 | | | | | 2 |
| NNS | | | 1 | 2 | 40 | | | |
| RB | 2 | | | | | 16 | | |
| VBD | 1 | | | | | | 17 | 2 |
| WDT | 2 | | | | | | | |

(Annotator 1)

| | JJ | NN | RB | VBN |
|---|---|---|---|---|
| JJ | 28 | 3 | | |
| NN | 2 | 75 | 1 | |
| RB | 2 | | 16 | |
| VBN | 2 | | | 10 |

(Annotator 2)

Table 7: Excerpts of the contingency tables for sentences 476–500 (523 tokens) with $\mathrm{MElt}_{\mathrm{en}}^{50}$ pre-annotation

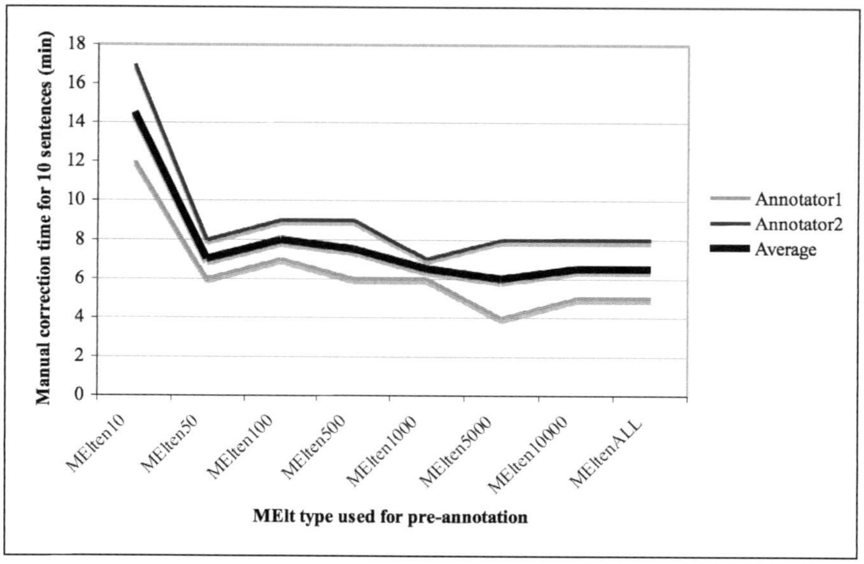


Figure 3: Annotation time depending on the type of pre-annotation

| | CD | DT | JJ | NN | NNP | NNS |
|---|---|---|---|---|---|---|
| CD | 30 | | | 2 | | |
| JJ | | 2 | 72 | | | |
| NN | | | 2 | 148 | | |
| NNS | | | | | 3 | 68 |

(Annotator 1)

| | CD | DT | IN | JJ | JJR | NN | NNP | NNS | RB | VBN |
|---|---|---|---|---|---|---|---|---|---|---|
| IN | | | 104 | | | | | | 2 | |
| JJ | | 2 | | 61 | | 2 | | | 1 | 9 |
| NN | 1 | | | 4 | | 145 | | | | |
| NNPS | | | | | | | 2 | | | |
| NNS | | | | | | 1 | 2 | 68 | | |
| RBR | | | | | 2 | | | | | |

(Annotator 2)

Table 8: Excerpts of the contingency tables for sentences 450–500 (1,035 tokens) without pre-annotation

## 5 Conclusion and Further Work

The series of experiments we detailed in this article confirms that pre-annotation allows for a gain in quality, both in terms of accuracy w.r.t. a reference and in terms of inter-annotator agreement, i.e., reliability. We also demonstrated that this comes with biases that should be identified and notified to the annotators, so that they can be extra careful during correction. Finally, we discovered that a surprisingly small training corpus could be sufficient to build a pre-annotation tool that would help drastically speeding up the annotation.

This should help developing taggers for under-resourced languages. In order to check that, we intend to use this method in a near future to develop a POS tagger for Sorani Kurdish.

We also want to experiment on other, more precision-driven, annotation tasks, like complex relations annotation or definition segmentation, that are more intrinsically complex and for which there exist no automatic tool as accurate as for POS tagging.

## Acknowledgments

This work was partly realized as part of the Quaero Programme[5], funded by OSEO, French State agency for innovation.

## References

Beatrice Alex, Claire Grover, Barry Haddow, Mijail Kabadjov, Ewan Klein, Michael Matthews, Stuart Roebuck, Richard Tobin, and Xinglong Wang. 2008. Assisted Curation: Does Text Mining Really Help? In *Pacific Symposium on Biocomputing*.

Ron Artstein and Massimo Poesio. 2008. Inter-coder Agreement for Computational Linguistics. *Computational Linguistics*, 34(4):555–596.

Lucie Barque, Alexis Nasr, and Alain Polguère. 2010. From the Definitions of the Trésor de la Langue Française to a Semantic Database of the French Language. In *Proceedings of the 14th EURALEX International Congress*, Leeuwarden.

Jean Carletta. 1996. Assessing Agreement on Classification Tasks: the Kappa Statistic. *Computational Linguistics*, 22:249–254.

[5] http://quaero.org/

Sandipan Dandapat, Priyanka Biswas, Monojit Choudhury, and Kalika Bali. 2009. Complex Linguistic Annotation - No Easy Way Out! a Case from Bangla and Hindi POS Labeling Tasks. In *Proceedings of the third ACL Linguistic Annotation Workshop*.

Pascal Denis and Benoît Sagot. 2009. Coupling an Annotated Corpus and a Morphosyntactic Lexicon for State-of-the-art POS Tagging with Less Human Effort. In *Proceedings of PACLIC 2009*, Hong-Kong, China.

Karën Fort, Maud Ehrmann, and Adeline Nazarenko. 2009. Vers une méthodologie d'annotation des entités nommées en corpus ? In *Actes de la 16ème Conférence sur le Traitement Automatique des Langues Naturelles 2009 Traitement Automatique des Langues Naturelles 2009*, Senlis, France.

Klaus Krippendorff, 1980. *Content Analysis: An Introduction to Its Methodology*, chapter 12. Sage, Beverly Hills, CA.

Klaus Krippendorff, 2004. *Content Analysis: An Introduction to Its Methodology, second edition*, chapter 11. Sage, Thousand Oaks, CA.

Mitchell Marcus, Beatrice Santorini, and Mary Ann Marcinkiewicz. 1993. Building a Large Annotated Corpus of English: the Penn Treebank. *Computational Linguistics*, 19(2):313–330.

Marie Mikulová and Jan Štěpánek. 2009. Annotation Quality Checking and its Implications for Design of Treebank (in Building the Prague Czech-English Dependency Treebank). In *Proceedings of the Eight International Workshop on Treebanks and Linguistic Theories*, volume 4-5, Milan, Italy, December.

Kimberly Neuendorf. 2002. *The Content Analysis Guidebook*. Sage, Thousand Oaks CA.

Adwait Ratnaparkhi. 1996. A Maximum Entropy Model for Part-Of-Speech Tagging. In *Proceedings of International Conference on Empirical Methods in Natural Language Processing*, pages 133–142.

Ines Rehbein, Josef Ruppenhofer, and Caroline Sporleder. 2009. Assessing the Benefits of Partial Automatic Pre-labeling for Frame-semantic Annotation. In *Proceedings of the Third Linguistic Annotation Workshop*, pages 19–26, Suntec, Singapore, August. Association for Computational Linguistics.

Drahomíra "Johanka" Spoustová, Jan Hajič, Jan Raab, and Miroslav Spousta. 2009. Semi-supervised Training for the Averaged Perceptron POS Tagger. In *EACL '09: Proceedings of the 12th Conference of the European Chapter of the Association for Computational Linguistics*, pages 763–771, Morristown, NJ, USA.

# To Annotate More Accurately or to Annotate More

**Dmitriy Dligach**
Department of Computer Science
University of Colorado at Boulder
Dmitriy.Dligach@colorado.edu

**Rodney D. Nielsen**
The Center for Computational Language and Education Research
University of Colorado at Boulder
Rodney.Nielsen@colorado.edu

**Martha Palmer**
Department of Linguistics
Department of Computer Science
University of Colorado at Boulder
Martha.Palmer@colorado.edu

## Abstract

The common accepted wisdom is that blind double annotation followed by adjudication of disagreements is necessary to create training and test corpora that result in the best possible performance. We provide evidence that this is unlikely to be the case. Rather, the greatest value for your annotation dollar lies in single annotating more data.

## 1 Introduction

In recent years, supervised learning has become the dominant paradigm in Natural Language Processing (NLP), thus making the creation of hand-annotated corpora a critically important task. A corpus where each instance is annotated by a single tagger unavoidably contains errors. To improve the quality of the data, an annotation project may choose to annotate each instance twice and adjudicate the disagreements, thus producing the (largely) error-free gold standard. For example, OntoNotes (Hovy et al., 2006), a large-scale annotation project, chose this option.

However, given a virtually unlimited supply of unlabeled data and limited funding – a typical set of constraints in NLP – an annotation project must always face the realization that for the cost of double annotation, more than twice as much data can be *single* annotated. The philosophy behind this alternative says that modern machine learning algorithms can still generalize well in the presence of noise, especially when given larger amounts of training data.

Currently, the commonly accepted wisdom sides with the view that says that blind double annotation followed by adjudication of disagreements is necessary to create annotated corpora that leads to the best possible performance. We provide empirical evidence that this is unlikely to be the case. Rather, the greatest value for your annotation dollar lies in single annotating more data. There may, however, be other considerations that still argue in favor of double annotation.

In this paper, we also consider the arguments of Beigman and Klebanov (2009), who suggest that data should be multiply annotated and then filtered to discard all of the examples where the annotators do not have perfect agreement. We provide evidence that single annotating more data for the same cost is likely to result in better system performance.

This paper proceeds as follows: first, we outline our evaluation framework in Section 2. Next, we compare the single annotation and adjudication scenarios in Section 3. Then, we compare the annotation scenario of Beigman and Klebanov (2009) with the single annotation scenario in Section 4. After that, we discuss the results and future work in section 5. Finally, we draw the conclusion in Section 6.

## 2 Evaluation

### 2.1 Data

For evaluation we utilize the word sense data annotated by the OntoNotes project. The OntoNotes data was chosen because it utilizes full double-blind annotation by human annotators and the disagreements are adjudicated by a third (more expe-



*Proceedings of the Fourth Linguistic Annotation Workshop, ACL 2010*, pages 64–72,
Uppsala, Sweden, 15-16 July 2010. 

rienced) annotator. This allows us to

- Evaluate single annotation results by using the labels assigned by the first tagger
- Evaluate double annotation results by using the labels assigned by the second tagger
- Evaluate adjudication results by using the labels assigned by the the adjudicator to the instances where the two annotators disagreed
- Measure the performance under various scenarios against the double annotated and adjudicated gold standard data

We selected the 215 most frequent verbs in the OntoNotes data. To make the size of the dataset more manageable, we randomly selected 500 examples of each of the 15 most frequent verbs. For the remaining 200 verbs, we utilized all the annotated examples. The resulting dataset contained 66,228 instances of the 215 most frequent verbs. Table 1 shows various important characteristics of this dataset averaged across the 215 verbs.

| | |
|---|---|
| Inter-tagger agreement | 86% |
| Annotator1-gold standard agreement | 93% |
| Share of the most frequent sense | 70% |
| Number of classes (senses) per verb | 4.74 |

Table 1: Data used in evaluation at a glance

### 2.2 Cost of Annotation

Because for this set of experiments we care primarily about the cost effectiveness of the annotation dollars, we need to know how much it costs to blind annotate instances and how much it costs to adjudicate disagreements in instances. There is an upfront cost associated with any annotation effort to organize the project, design an annotation scheme, set up the environment, create annotation guidelines, hire and train the annotators, etc. We will assume, for the sake of this paper, that this cost is fixed and is the same regardless of whether the data is single annotated or the data is double annotated and disagreements adjudicated.

In this paper, we focus on a scenario where there is essentially no difference in cost to collect additional data to be annotated, as is often the case (e.g., there is virtually no additional cost to download 2.5 versus 1.0 million words of text from the web). However, this is not always the case (e.g., collecting speech can be costly).

To calculate a cost per annotated instance for blind annotation, we take the total expenses associated with the annotators in this group less training costs and any costs not directly associated with annotation and divide by the total number of blind instance annotations. This value, \$0.0833, is the per instance cost used for single annotation. We calculated the cost for adjudicating instances similarly, based on the expenses associated with the adjudication group. The adjudication cost is an additional \$0.1000 per instance adjudicated. The per instance cost for double blind, adjudicated data is then computed as double the cost for single annotation plus the per instance cost of adjudication multiplied by the percent of disagreement, 14%, which is \$0.1805.

We leave an analysis of the extent to which the up front costs are truly fixed and whether they can be altered to result in more value for the dollar to future work.

### 2.3 Automatic Word Sense Disambiguation

For the experiments we conduct in this study, we needed a word sense disambiguation (WSD) system. Our WSD system is modeled after the state-of-the-art verb WSD system described in (Dligach and Palmer, 2008). We will briefly outline it here.

We view WSD as a supervised learning problem. Each instance of the target verb is represented as a vector of binary features that indicate the presence (or absence) of the corresponding features in the neighborhood of the target verb. We utilize all of the linguistic features that were shown to be useful for disambiguating verb senses in (Chen et al., 2007).

To extract the **lexical features** we POS-tag the sentence containing the target verb and the two surrounding sentences using MXPost software (Ratnaparkhi, 1998). All open class words (nouns, verbs, adjectives, and adverbs) in these sentences are included in our feature set. In addition to that, we use as features two words on each side of the target verb as well as their POS tags.

To extract the **syntactic features** we parse the sentence containing the target verb with Bikel's constituency parser and utilize a set of rules to identify the features in Table 2.

Our **semantic features** represent the semantic classes of the target verb's syntactic arguments

| Feature | Explanation |
|---|---|
| Subject and object | - Presence of subject and object<br>- Head word of subject and object NPs<br>- POS tag of the head word of subject and object NPs |
| Voice | - Passive or Active |
| PP adjunct | - Presence of PP adjunct<br>- Preposition word<br>- Head word of the preposition's NP argument |
| Subordinate clause | - Presence of subordinate clause |
| Path | - Parse tree path from target verb to neighboring words<br>- Parse tree path from target verb to subject and object<br>- Parse tree path from target verb to subordinate clause |
| Subcat frame | - Phrase structure rule expanding the target verb's parent node in parse tree |

Table 2: Syntactic features

such as subject and object. The semantic classes are approximated as

- WordNet (Fellbaum, 1998) hypernyms
- NE tags derived from the output of IdentiFinder (Bikel et al., 1999)
- Dynamic dependency neighbors (Dligach and Palmer, 2008), which are extracted in an unsupervised way from a dependency-parsed corpus

Our WSD system uses the Libsvm software package (Chang and Lin, 2001) for classification. We accepted the default options (C = 1 and linear kernel) when training our classifiers. As is the case with most WSD systems, we train a separate model per verb.

## 3 Experiment One

The results of experiment one show that in these circumstances, better performance is achieved by single annotating more data than by deploing resources towards ensuring that the data is annotated more accurately through an adjudication process.

### 3.1 Experimental Design

We conduct a number of experiments to compare the effect of single annotated versus adjudicated data on the accuracy of a state of the art WSD system. Since OntoNotes does not have a specified test set, for each word, we used repeated random partitioning of the data with 10 trials and 10% into the test set and the remaining 90% comprising the training set.

We then train an SVM classifier on varying fractions of the data, based on the number of examples that could be annotated per dollar. Specifically, in increments of $1.00, we calculate the number of examples that can be single annotated and the number that can be double blind annotated and adjudicated with that amount of money.

The number of examples computed for single annotation is selected at random from the training data. Then the adjudicated examples are selected at random from this subset. Selecting from the same subset of data approaches pair statistical testing and results in a more accurate statistical comparison of the models produced.

Classifiers are trained on this data using the labels from the first round of annotation as the single annotation labels and the final adjudicated labels for the smaller subset. This procedure is repeated ten times and the average results are reported.

For a given verb, each classifier created throughout this process is tested on the same double annotated and adjudicated held-out test set.

### 3.2 Results

Figure 1 shows a plot of the accuracy of the classifiers relative to the annotation investment for a typical verb, *to call*. As can be seen, the accuracy is always higher when training on the larger amount of single annotated data than when training on the amount of adjudicated data that had the equivalent cost of annotation.

Figures 2 and 3 present results averaged over all 215 verbs in the dataset. First, figure 2 shows the average accuracy over all verbs by amount invested. These accuracy curves are not smooth be-

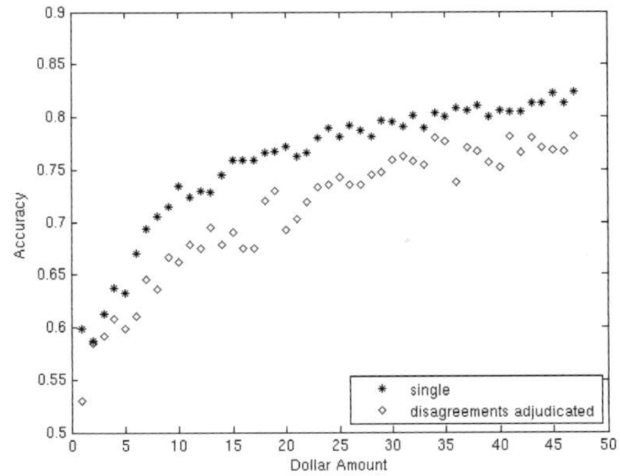


Figure 1: Performance of single annotated vs. adjudicated data by amount invested for *to call*

cause the verbs all have a different number of total instances. At various annotation cost values, all of the instances of one or more verbs will have been annotated. Hence, the accuracy values might jump or drop by a larger amount than seen elsewhere in the graph.

Toward the higher dollar amounts the curve is dominated by fewer and fewer verbs. We only display the dollar investments of up to $60 due to the fact that only five verbs have more than $60's worth of instances in the training set.

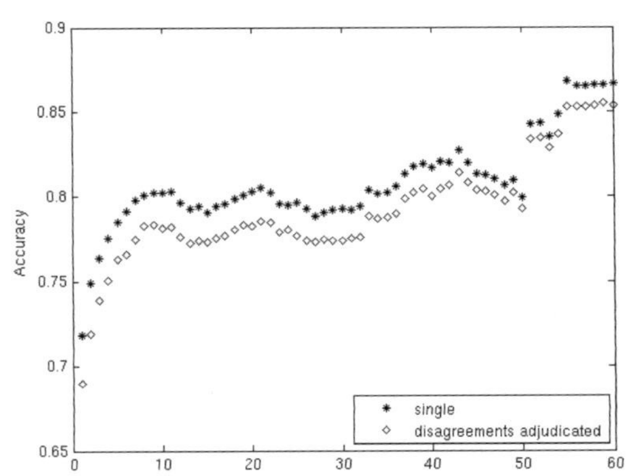


Figure 2: Average performance of single annotated vs. adjudicated data by amount invested

The average difference in accuracy for Figure 2 across all amounts of investment is 1.64%.

Figure 3 presents the average accuracy relative to the percent of the total cost to single annotate all of the instances for a verb. The accuracy at a given percent of total investment was interpolated for each verb using linear interpolation and then averaged over all of the verbs.

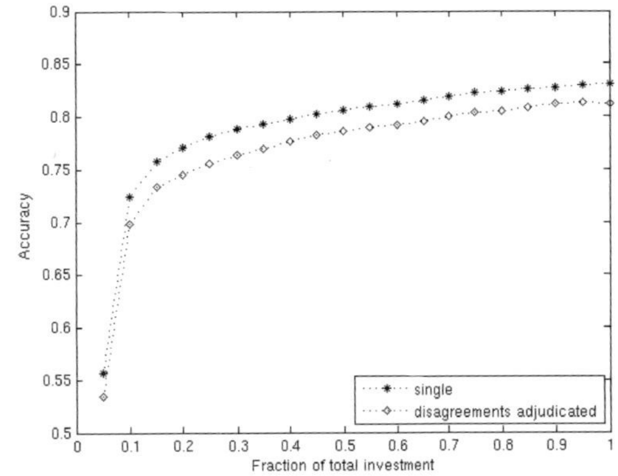


Figure 3: Average performance of single annotated vs. adjudicated data by fraction of total investment

The average difference in accuracy for Figure 3 across each percent of investment is 2.10%.

Figure 4 presents essentially the same information as Figure 2, but as a reduction in error rate for single annotation relative to full adjudication.

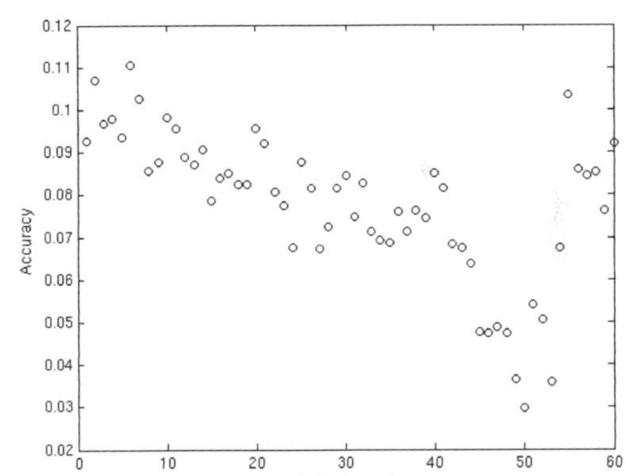


Figure 4: Reduction in error rate from adjudication to single annotation scenario based on results in Figure 2

The relative reduction in error rate averaged over all investment amounts in Figure 2 is 7.77%.

Figure 5 presents the information in Figure 3 as a reduction in error rate for single annotation relative to full adjudication.

The average relative reduction in error rate over the fractions of total investment in Figure 5 is 9.32%.

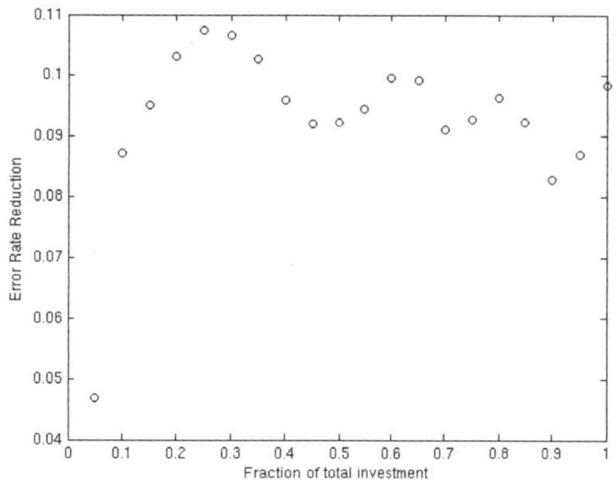


Figure 5: Reduction in error rate from adjudication to single annotation scenario based on results in Figure 3

### 3.3 Discussion

First, it is worth noting that, when the amount of annotated data is the *same* for both scenarios, adjudicated data leads to slightly better performance than single annotated data. For example, consider Figure 3. The accuracy at 100% of the total investment for the double annotation and adjudication scenario is 81.13%. The same number of examples can be *single* annotated for 0.0833 / 0.1805 = 0.4615 of this dollar investment (using the costs from Section 2.2). The system trained on that amount of single annotated data shows a lower accuracy, 80.21%. Thus, in this case, the adjudication scenario brings about a performance improvement of about 1%.

However, the main thesis of this paper is that instead of double annotating and adjudicating, it is often better to single annotate more data because it is a more cost-effective way to achieve a higher performance. The results of our experiments support this thesis. At every dollar amount invested, our supervised WSD system performs better when trained on single annotated data comparing to double annotated and adjudicated data.

The maximum annotation investment amount for each verb is the cost of single annotating all of its instances. When the system is trained on the amount of double annotated data possible at this investment, its accuracy is 81.13% (Figure 3). When trained on single annotated data, the system attains the same accuracy much earlier, at approximately 60% of the total investment. When trained on the entire available single annotated data, the system reaches an accuracy of 82.99%, nearly a 10% relative reduction in error rate over the same system trained on the adjudicated data obtained for the same cost.

Averaged over the 215 verbs, the single annotation scenario outperformed adjudication at every dollar amount investigated.

## 4 Experiment Two

In this experiment, we consider the arguments of Beigman and Klebanov (2009). They suggest that data should be at least double annotated and then filtered to discard all of the examples where there were any annotator disagreements.

The main points of their argument are as follows. They first consider the data to be dividable into two types, *easy* (to annotate) *cases* and *hard cases*. Then they correctly note that some annotators could have a systematic bias (i.e., could favor one label over others in certain types of hard cases), which would in turn bias the learning of the classifier. They show that it is theoretically possible that a band of misclassified hard cases running parallel to the true separating hyperplane could mistakenly shift the decision boundary past up to $\sqrt{N}$ easy cases.

We suggest that it is extremely unlikely that a consequential number of easy cases would exist nearer to the class boundary than the hard cases. The hard cases are in fact generally considered to define the separating hyperplane.

In this experiment, our goal is to determine how the accuracy of classifiers trained on data labeled according to Beigman and Klebanov's *discard disagreements* strategy compares empirically to the accuracy resulting from single annotated data. As in the previous experiment, this analysis is performed relative to the investment in the annotation effort.

### 4.1 Experimental Design

We follow essentially the same experimental design described in section 3.1, using the same state of the art verb WSD system. We conduct a number of experiments to compare the effect of single annotated versus double annotated data. We utilized the same training and test sets as the previous experiment and similarly trained an SVM on fractions of the data representing increments of $1.00 investments.

As before, the number of examples designated

for single annotation is selected at random from the training data and half of that subset is selected as the training set for the double annotated data. Again, selecting from the same subset of data results in a more accurate statistical comparison of the models produced.

Classifiers for each annotation scenario are trained on the labels from the first round of annotation, but examples where the second annotator disagreed are thrown out of the double annotated data. This results in slightly less than half as much data in the double annotation scenario based on the disagreement rate. Again, the procedure is repeated ten times and the average results are reported.

For a given verb, each classifier created throughout this process is tested on the same double annotated and adjudicated held-out test set.

### 4.2 Results

Figure 6 shows a plot of the accuracy of the classifiers relative to the annotation investment for a typical verb, *to call*. As can be seen, the accuracy for a specific investment performing single annotation is always higher than it is for the same investment in double annotated data.

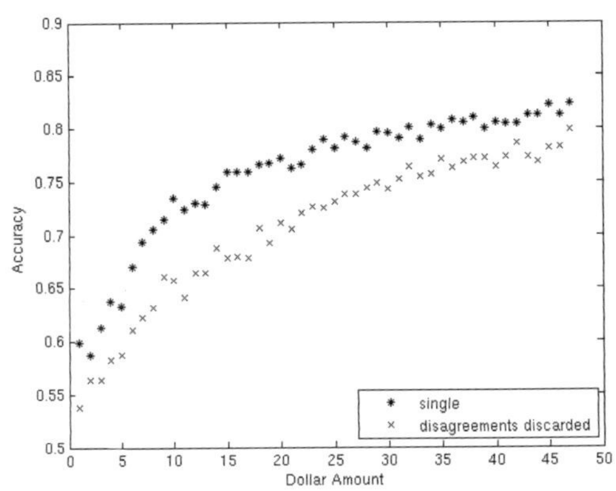


Figure 6: Performance of single annotated vs. double annotated data with disagreements discarded by amount invested for *to call*

Figures 7 and 8 present results averaged over all 215 verbs in the dataset. First, figure 7 shows the average accuracy over all verbs by amount invested. Again, these accuracy curves are not smooth because the verbs all have a different number of total instances. Hence, the accuracy values might jump or drop by a larger amount at the points where a given verb is no longer included in the average.

Toward the higher dollar amounts the curve is dominated by fewer and fewer verbs. As before, we only display the results for investments of up to $60.

The average difference in accuracy for Figure 7 across all amounts of investment is 2.32%.

Figure 8 presents the average accuracy relative to the percent of the total cost to single annotate all of the instances for a verb. The accuracy at a given percent of total investment was interpolated for each verb and then averaged over all of the verbs.

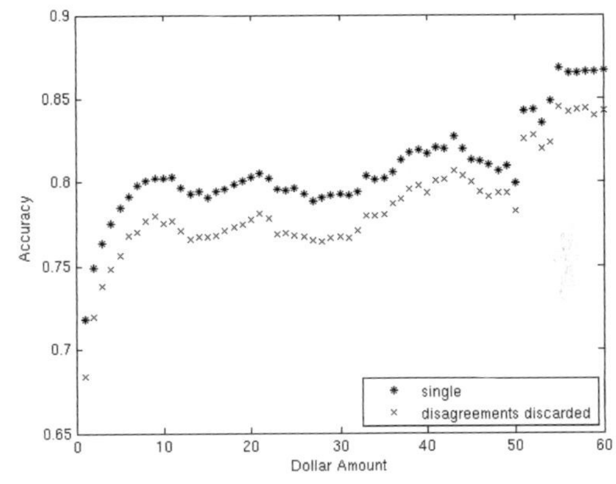


Figure 7: Average performance of single annotated vs. double annotated data with disagreements discarded by amount invested

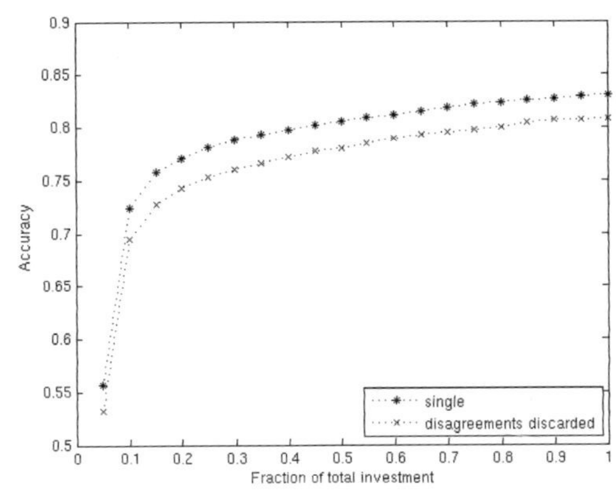


Figure 8: Average performance of single annotated vs. adjudicated data by fraction of total investment

The average difference in accuracy for Figure 8 across all amounts of investment is 2.51%.

Figures 9 and 10 present this information as a reduction in error rate for single annotation relative to full adjudication.

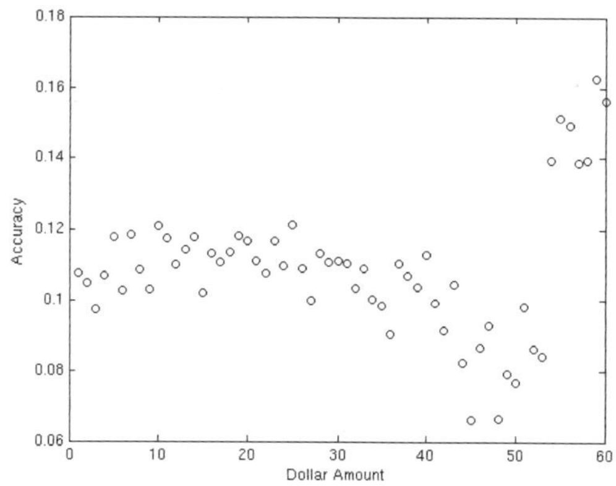


Figure 9: Reduction in error rate from adjudication to single annotation scenario based on results in Figure 7

The relative reduction in error rate averaged over all investment amounts in Figure 9 is 10.88%.

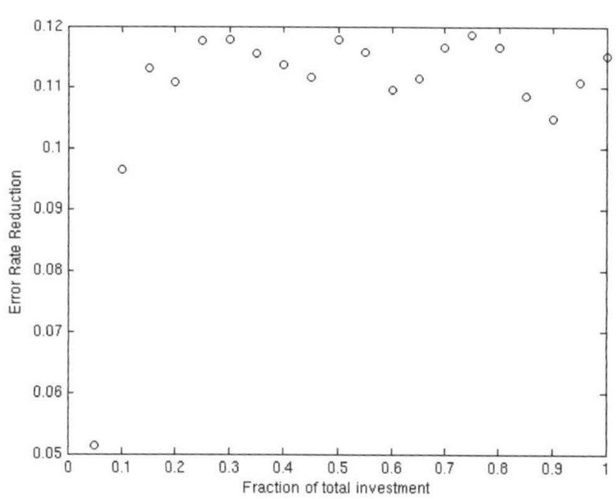


Figure 10: Reduction in error rate from adjudication to single annotation scenario based on results in Figure 8

The average relative reduction in error rate over the fractions of total investment in Figure 10 is 10.97%.

### 4.3 Discussion

At every amount of investment, our supervised WSD system performs better when trained on single annotated data comparing to double annotated data with discarded cases of disagreements.

The maximum annotation investment amount for each verb is the cost of single annotating all of its instances. When the system is trained on the amount of double annotated data possible at this investment, its accuracy is 80.78% (Figure 8). When trained on single annotated data, the system reaches the same accuracy much earlier, at approximately 52% of the total investment. When trained on the entire available single annotated data, the system attains an accuracy of 82.99%, an 11.5% relative reduction in error rate compared to the same system trained on the double annotated data obtained for the same cost.

The average accuracy of the single annotation scenario outperforms the double annotated with disagreements discarded scenario at every dollar amount investigated.

While this empirical investigation only looked at verb WSD, it was performed using 215 distinct verb type datasets. These verbs each have contextual features that are essentially unique to that verb type and consequently, 215 distinct classifiers, one per verb type, are trained. Hence, these could loosely be considered 215 distinct annotation and classification tasks.

The fact that for the 215 classification tasks the single annotation scenario on average performed better than the discard disagreements scenario of Beigman and Klebanov (2009) strongly suggests that, while it is theoretically possible for annotation bias to, in turn, bias a classifier's learning, it is more likely that you will achieve better results by training on the single annotated data.

It is still an open issue whether it is generally best to adjudicate disagreements in the test set or to throw them out as suggested by (Beigman Klebanov and Beigman, 2009).

## 5 Discussion and Future Work

We investigated 215 WSD classification tasks, comparing performance under three annotation scenarios each with the equivalent annotation cost, single annotation, double annotation with disagreements adjudicated, and double annotation with disagreements discarded. Averaging over the 215 classification tasks, the system trained on single annotated data achieved 10.0% and 11.5% relative reduction in error rates compared to training on the equivalent investment in adjudicated and disagreements discarded data, respectively. While we believe these results will generalize to other annotation tasks, this is still an open question to be determined by future work.

There are probably similar issues in what were considered fixed costs for the purposes of this paper. For example, it may be possible to train fewer annotators, and invest the savings into annotating more data. Perhaps more appropriately, it may be feasible to simply cut back on the amount of training provided per annotator and instead annotate more data.

On the other hand, when the unlabeled data is not freely obtainable, double annotation may be more suitable as a route to improving system performance. There may also be factors other than cost-effectiveness which make double annotation desirable. Many projects point to their ITA rates and corresponding kappa values as a measure of annotation quality, and of the reliability of the annotators (Artstein and Poesio, 2008). The OntoNotes project used ITA rates as a way of evaluating the clarity of the sense inventory that was being developed in parallel with the annotation. Lexical entries that resulted in low ITA rates were revised, usually improving the ITA rate. Calculating these rates requires double-blind annotation. Annotators who consistently produced ITA rates lower than average were also removed from the project. Therefore, caution is advised in determining when to dispense with double annotation in favor of more cost effective single annotation.

Double annotation can also be used to shed light on other research questions that, for example, require knowing which instances are "hard." That knowledge may help with designing additional, richer annotation layers or with cognitive science investigations into human representations of language.

Our results suggest that systems would likely benefit more from the larger training datasets that single annotation makes possible than from the less noisy datasets resulting from adjudication. Regardless of whether single or double annotation with adjudication is used, there will always be noise. Hence, we see the further investigation of algorithms that generalize despite the presence of noise to be critical to the future of computational linguistics. Humans are able to learn in the presence of noise, and our systems must follow suit.

## 6 Conclusion

Double annotated data contains less noise than single annotated data and thus improves the performance of supervised machine learning systems that are trained on a specific amount of data. However, double annotation is expensive and the alternative of single annotating more data instead is on the table for many annotation projects.

In this paper we compared the performance of a supervised machine learning system trained on double annotated data versus single annotated data obtainable for the same cost. Our results clearly demonstrate that single annotating more data can be a more cost-effective way to improve the system performance in the many cases where the unlabeled data is freely available and there are no other considerations that necessitate double annotation.

## 7 Acknowledgements

We gratefully acknowledge the support of the National Science Foundation Grant NSF-0715078, Consistent Criteria for Word Sense Disambiguation, and the GALE program of the Defense Advanced Research Projects Agency, Contract No. HR0011-06-C-0022, a subcontract from the BBN-AGILE Team. Any opinions, findings, and conclusions or recommendations expressed in this material are those of the authors and do not necessarily reflect the views of the National Science Foundation.

## References

Ron Artstein and Massimo Poesio. 2008. Inter-coder agreement for computational linguistics. *Comput. Linguist.*, 34(4):555–596.

Eyal Beigman and Beata Beigman Klebanov. 2009. Learning with annotation noise. In *ACL-IJCNLP '09: Proceedings of the Joint Conference of the 47th Annual Meeting of the ACL and the 4th International Joint Conference on Natural Language Processing of the AFNLP: Volume 1*, pages 280–287, Morristown, NJ, USA. Association for Computational Linguistics.

Beata Beigman Klebanov and Eyal Beigman. 2009. From annotator agreement to noise models. *Comput. Linguist.*, 35(4):495–503.

Daniel M. Bikel, Richard Schwartz, and Ralph M. Weischedel. 1999. An algorithm that learns what's in a name. *Mach. Learn.*, 34(1-3):211–231.

Chih-Chung Chang and Chih-Jen Lin, 2001. *LIBSVM: a library for support vector machines.* Software available at `http://www.csie.ntu.edu.tw/~cjlin/libsvm`.

J. Chen and M. Palmer. 2005. Towards robust high performance word sense disambiguation of english verbs using rich linguistic features. pages 933–944. Springer.

Jinying Chen, Dmitriy Dligach, and Martha Palmer. 2007. Towards large-scale high-performance english verb sense disambiguation by using linguistically motivated features. In *ICSC '07: Proceedings of the International Conference on Semantic Computing*, pages 378–388, Washington, DC, USA. IEEE Computer Society.

Dmitriy Dligach and Martha Palmer. 2008. Novel semantic features for verb sense disambiguation. In *HLT '08: Proceedings of the 46th Annual Meeting of the Association for Computational Linguistics on Human Language Technologies*, pages 29–32, Morristown, NJ, USA. Association for Computational Linguistics.

Christiane Fellbaum. 1998. *WordNet: An electronic lexical database*. MIT press Cambridge, MA.

Eduard Hovy, Mitchell Marcus, Martha Palmer, Lance Ramshaw, and Ralph Weischedel. 2006. Ontonotes: the 90% solution. In *NAACL '06: Proceedings of the Human Language Technology Conference of the NAACL, Companion Volume: Short Papers on XX*, pages 57–60, Morristown, NJ, USA. Association for Computational Linguistics.

A. Ratnaparkhi. 1998. *Maximum entropy models for natural language ambiguity resolution*. Ph.D. thesis, University of Pennsylvania.

# Annotating Underquantification

**Aurelie Herbelot**
University of Cambridge
Cambridge, United Kingdom
ah433@cam.ac.uk

**Ann Copestake**
University of Cambridge
Cambridge, United Kingdom
aac10@cam.ac.uk

## Abstract

Many noun phrases in text are ambiguously quantified: syntax doesn't explicitly tell us whether they refer to a single entity or to several, and what portion of the set denoted by the Nbar actually takes part in the event expressed by the verb. We describe this ambiguity phenomenon in terms of underspecification, or rather **underquantification**. We attempt to validate the underquantification hypothesis by producing and testing an annotation scheme for quantification resolution, the aim of which is to associate a single quantifier with each noun phrase in our corpus.

## 1 Quantification resolution

We are concerned with **ambiguously quantified** noun phrases (NPs) and their interpretation, as illustrated by the following examples:

1. Cats are mammals = *All* cats...
2. Cats have four legs = *Most* cats...
3. Cats were sleeping by the fire = *Some* cats...
4. The beans spilt out of the bag = *Most/All of the* beans...
5. Water was dripping through the ceiling = *Some* water...

We are interested in **quantification resolution**, that is, the process of giving an ambiguously quantified NP a formalisation which expresses a *unique* set relation appropriate to the semantics of the utterance. For instance, we wish to arrive at:

6. All cats are mammals.
   $|\phi \cap \psi| = |\phi|$ where $\phi$ is the set of all cats and $\psi$ the set of all mammals.

Resolving the quantification value of NPs is important for many NLP tasks. Let us imagine an information extraction system having retrieved the triples 'cat – is – mammal' and 'cat – chase – mouse' for inclusion in a factual database about felines. The problem with those representation-poor triples is that they do not contain the necessary information about quantification to answer such questions as 'Are all cats mammals?' or 'Do all cats chase mice?' Or if they attempt to answer those queries, they give the same answer to both. Ideally, we would like to annotate such triples with quantifiers which have a direct mapping to probability adverbs:

7. *All* cats are mammals AND Tom is a cat $\rightarrow$ Tom is *definitely* a mammal.
8. *Some* cats chase mice AND Tom is a cat $\rightarrow$ Tom *possibly* chases mice.

Adequate quantification is also necessary for inference based on word-level entailment: an existentially quantified NP can be replaced by a suitable hypernym but this is not possible in non-existential cases: *(Some) cats are in my garden* entails *(Some) animals are in my garden* but *(All) cats are mammals* doesn't imply that *(All) animals are mammals*.

In Herbelot (to appear), we provide a formal semantics for ambiguously quantified NPs, which relies on the idea that those NPs exhibit an underspecified quantifier, i.e. that for each NP in a corpus, a set relation can be agreed upon. Our formalisation includes a placeholder for the quantifier's set relation. In line with inference requirements, we assume a three-fold partitioning of the quantificational space, corresponding to the natural language quantifiers *some*, *most* and *all* (in addition to *one*, for the description of singular, unique entities). The corresponding set relations are:

9. $some(\phi, \psi)$ is true iff $0 < |\phi \cap \psi| < |\phi - \psi|$
10. $most(\phi, \psi)$ is true iff $|\phi - \psi| \leq |\phi \cap \psi| < |\phi|$
11. $all(\phi, \psi)$ is true iff $|\phi \cap \psi| = |\phi|$

This paper is an attempt to show that our formalisation lends itself to evaluation by human annotation. The labels produced will also serve as training and test sets for an automatic quantification resolution system.



*Proceedings of the Fourth Linguistic Annotation Workshop, ACL 2010*, pages 73–81,
Uppsala, Sweden, 15-16 July 2010. 

## 2 Under(specified) quantification

Before we present our annotation scheme, we will spell out the essential idea behind what we call **underquantification**.

The phenomenon of ambiguous quantification overlaps with **genericity** (see Krifka et al, 1995, for an introduction to genericity). Generic NPs are frequently expressed syntactically as bare plurals, although they occur in definite and indefinite singulars too, as well as bare singulars. There are many views on the semantics of generics (e.g. Carlson, 1995; Pelletier and Asher, 1997; Heyer, 1990; Leslie, 2008) but one of them is that they quantify (Cohen, 1996), although, puzzlingly enough, not always with the same quantifier:

12. Frenchmen eat horsemeat = *Some/Relatively-many* Frenchmen... (For the *relatively many* reading, see Cohen, 2001.)
13. Cars have four wheels = *Most* cars...
14. Typhoons arise in this part of the Pacific = *Some* typhoons... OR *Most/All* typhoons...

This behaviour has so far prevented linguists from agreeing on a single formalisation for all generics. The only accepted assumption is that an operator $GEN$ exists, which acts as a silent quantifier over the restrictor (subject) and matrix (verbal predicate) of the generic statement. The formal properties of $GEN$ are however subject to debate: in particular, it is not clear which natural language quantifier it would map onto (some view it as *most*, but this approach requires some complex domain restriction to deal with sentences such as 12).

In this paper, we take a different approach which sidesteps some of the intractable problems associated with the literature on generics and which also extends to definite plurals. Instead of talking of ambiguous quantification, we will talk of **underspecified quantification**, or **underquantification**. By this, we mean that the bare plural, rather than exhibiting a silent, $GEN$ quantifier, simply features a placeholder in the logical form which must be filled with the appropriate quantifier (e.g., $uq(x, \text{cat}'(x), \text{sleep}'(x))$, where $uq$ is the placeholder quantifier). This account caters for the facts that so-called generics can so easily be quantified via traditional quantifiers, that $GEN$ is silent in all known languages, and it explains also why it is the bare form which has the highest productivity, and can refer to a range of quantified sets, from existentials to universals. Using the underquantification hypothesis, we can paraphrase any generic of the form 'X does Y' as 'there is a set of things X, *a certain number of which* do Y' (note the partitive construction). Such a paraphrase allows us to also resolve ambiguously quantified definite plurals, which have traditionally been associated with universals, outside of the genericity phenomenon (e.g. Lyons, 1999).

Because of space constraints, we will not give our formalisation for underquantification in this paper (see Herbelot,to appear, for details). It involves a representation of the partitive construct exemplified above and requires knowledge of the distributive or collective status of the verbal predicate. We also argue that if generics can always be quantified, their semantics may involve more than quantification. So we claim that in certain cases, a double formalisation of the NP as a quantified entity and a kind is desirable. We understand kinds in the way proposed by Chierchia (1998), that is as the plurality of all instances denoted by a given word in the world under consideration. Under the kind reading, we can interpret 12 as meaning *Collectively, the group of all Frenchmen has the property of eating horsemeat.*

## 3 Motivation

### 3.1 Linguistic motivation

It is usual to talk of 'annotation' generically, to cover any process that involves humans using a set of guidelines to mark some specific linguistic phenomenon in some given text. However, we would argue that, when considering the aims of an annotation task and its relation to the existing linguistic literature, it becomes possible to distinguish between various types of annotation. Further, we will show that our own effort situates itself in a little studied relation to formal semantics.

The most basic type of annotation is the one where computational linguists mark large amounts of textual data with well-known and well-understood labels. The production of tree banks like the Penn Treebank (Marcus et al, 1993) makes use of undisputed linguistic categories such as parts of speech. The aim is to make the computer learn and use irrefutable bits of linguistics. (Note that, despite agreement, the representation of those categories may differ: see for example the range of available parts of speech tag sets.) This type of task mostly involves basic syntactic knowledge, but can be taken to areas of syntax and semantics where the studied phenomena have a (somewhat) clear, agreed upon definition (Kingsbury et al, 2002). We must clarify that in those cases, the choice of a formalism may already imply a certain theoretical position – leading to potential incompatibilities between formalisms. However, the categories for such annotation are themselves fixed: there is a generally agreed broad understanding of concepts such as noun phrases and coordination.

Another type of annotation concerns tasks where the linguistic categories at play are not fixed. One example is discourse annotation according to rhetorical function (Teufel et al, 2006) where humans are asked to differentiate between several discursive categories such as 'contrast' or 'weakness'. In such a task, the computational linguist develops a theory where different states or values are associated with various phenomena. In order to show that the world functions according to the model presented, experimentation is required. This usually takes the form of an annotation task where several human subjects are required to mark pieces of text following guidelines inferred from the model. The intuition behind the annotation effort is that agreement between humans support the claims of the theory (Teufel, in press). In particular, it may confirm that the phenomena in question indeed exist and that the values attributed to them are clearly defined and distinguishable. The work is mostly of a descriptive nature – it creates phenomenological definitions that encompass bits of observable language.

Our own work is similar to the latter type of annotation in that it is trying to capture a phenomenon that is still under investigation in the linguistic literature. However, it is also different because the categories we use are fixed by language: the quantifiers *some*, *most* and *all* exist and we assume that their definition is agreed upon by speakers of English. What we are trying to investigate is whether those quantifiers should be used at all in the context of ambiguous quantification.

The type of annotation carried out in this paper can be said to have more formal aims than the tasks usually attempted in computational linguistics. In particular, it concerns itself with some of the broad claims made by formal semantics: its model-theoretical view and the use of generalised quantifiers to formalise noun phrases.

In Section 1, we assumed that quantifiers denote relations between sets and presented the task of quantification resolution as choosing the 'correct' set relation for a particular noun phrase in a particular sentence – implying some sort of truth value at work throughout the process: the correct set relation produces the sentence with truth value 1 while the other set relations produce a truth value of 0. What we declined to discuss, though, is the way that those reference sets were selected in natural language, i.e. we didn't make claims about what model, or models, are used by humans when they compute the truth value of a given quantified statement. The annotation task may not answer this question but it should help us ascertain to what extent humans share a model of the world.

In Section 2, we also argued that all subject generic noun phrases could be analysed in terms of quantification. That is, an (underspecified) generalised quantifier is at work in sentences that contain such generic NPs. It is expected that if the annotation is feasible and shows good agreement between annotators, the quantification hypothesis would be confirmed. Thus, annotation may allow us to make semantic claims such as 'genericity does quantify'. Note that the categories we assume are intuitive and do not depend on a particular representation: it is possible to reuse our annotation with a different formalism as long as the theoretical assumption of quantification is agreed upon.

We are not aware of any annotation work in computational linguistics that contributes to validating (or invalidating) a particular formal theory. In that respect, the experiments presented in this paper are of a slightly different nature than the standard research on annotation (despite the fact that, as we will show in the next section, they also aim at producing data for a language analysis system).

### 3.2 Previous work on genericity annotation

The aim of our work being the production of an automatic quantification resolution system, we need an annotated corpus to train and test our machine learning algorithm. There is no corpus that we know of which would give us the required data. The closest contestants are the ACE corpus (2008) and the GNOME corpus (Poesio, 2000) which both focus on the phenomenon of genericity, as described in the linguistic literature. Unfortunately, neither of those corpora are suitable for use in a general quantification task.

The ACE corpus only distinguishes between

'generic' and 'specific' entities. The classification proposed by the authors of the corpus is therefore a lot broader than the one we are attempting here and there is no direct correspondence between their labels and natural language quantifiers: we have shown in Section 2 that genericity didn't map to a particular division of the quantificational space. Furthermore, the ACE guidelines contradict to some extent the literature on genericity. They require for instance that a generic mention be quantifiable with *all*, *most* or *any*. This implies that statements such as *Mosquitoes carry malaria* either refer to a kind only (i.e. they are not quantified) or are not generic at all. Further, despite the above reference to quantification, the authors seem to separate genericity and universal quantification as two antithetical phenomena, as shown by the following quote: "Even if the author may intend to use a GEN reading, if he/she refers to all members of the set rather than the set itself, use the SPC tag".

The GNOME annotation scheme is closer in essence to the literature on genericity and much more detailed than the ACE guidelines. However, the scheme distinguishes only between generic and non-generic entities, as in the ACE corpus case, and the corpus itself is limited to three genres: museum labels, pharmaceutical leaflets, and tutorial dialogues. The guidelines are therefore tailored to the domains under consideration; for instance, bare noun phrases are said to be typically generic. This restricted solution has the advantage of providing good agreement between annotators (Poesio, 2004 reports a Kappa value of 0.82 for this annotation).

## 4 Annotation corpus

We use as corpus a snapshot of the English version of the online encyclopaedia Wikipedia.[1] The choice is motivated by the fact that Wikipedia can be taken as a fairly balanced corpus: although it is presented as an encyclopaedia, it contains a wide variety of text ranging from typical encyclopaedic descriptions to various types of narrative texts (historical reconstructions, film 'spoilers', fiction summaries) to instructional material like rules of games. Further, each article in Wikipedia is written and edited by many contributors, meaning that speaker heterogeneity is high. We would also expect an encyclopaedia to contain relatively many generics, allowing us to assess how our quantificational reading fares in a real annotation task. Finally, the use of an open resource means that the corpus can be freely distributed.[2]

In order to create our annotation corpus, we first isolated the first 100,000 pages in our snapshot and parsed them into a Robust Minimal Recursion Semantics (RMRS) representation (Copestake, 2004) using first the RASP parser (Briscoe et al, 2006) and the RASP to RMRS converter (Ritchie, 2004). We then extracted all constructions of the type Subject-Verb-Object from the obtained corpus and randomly selected 300 of those 'triples' to be annotated. Another 50 random triples were selected for the purpose of annotation training (see Section 7.1).

We show in Figure 1 an example of an annotation instance produced by the parser pipeline. The data provided by the system consists of the triple itself, followed by the argument structure of that triple, including the direct dependents of its constituents, the number and tense information for each constituent, the file from which the triple was extracted and the original sentence in which it appeared. The information provided to annotators is directly extracted from that representation. (Note that the examples were not hand-checked, and some parsing errors may have remained.)

## 5 Evaluating the annotation

In an annotation task, two aspects of agreement are important when trying to prove or refute a particular linguistic model: stability and reproducibility (Krippendorf, 1980). Reproducibility refers to the consistency with which humans apply the scheme guidelines, i.e. to the so-called **inter-annotator agreement**. Stability relates to whether the same annotator will consistently produce the same annotations at different points in time. The measure for stability is called **intra-annotator agreement**. Both measures concern the repeatability of an annotation experiment.

In this work, agreement is calculated for each pair of annotators according to the Kappa measure. There are different versions of Kappa depending on how multiple annotators are treated and how the probabilities of classes are calculated to establish the expected agreement between annotators, $Pr(e)$: we use Fleiss' Kappa (Fleiss, 1971), which allows us to compute agreement between

[1] http://www.wikipedia.org

[2] For access, contact the first author.

```
digraph G211 {
"TRIPLE: weed include pigra" [shape=box];
include -> weed [label="ARG1 n"];
include -> pigra [label="ARG2 n"];
invasive -> weed [label="ARG1 n"];
compound_rel -> pigra [label="ARG1 n"];
compound_rel -> mimosa [label="ARG2 n"];
"DNT INFO: lemma::include() tense::present lpos::v  (arg::ARG1 var::weed() num::pl pos::)
           (arg::ARG2 var::pigra() num::sg pos::)"  [shape=box];
"FILE: /anfs/bigtmp/newr1-50/page101655"  [shape=box];
"ORIGINAL: Invasive weeds include Mimosa  pigra, which covers 80,000 hectares
of the Top End, including vast areas of  Kakadu. " [shape=box]; }
```

Figure 1: Example of annotation instance

multiple annotators.

# 6 An annotation scheme for quantification resolution

## 6.1 Scheme structure

Our complete annotation scheme can be found in Herbelot (to appear). The scheme consists of five parts. The first two present the annotation material and the task itself. Some key definitions are given. The following part describes the various quantification classes to be used in the course of the annotation. Participants are then given detailed instructions for the labelling of various grammatical constructs. Finally, in order to keep the demand on the annotators' cognitive load to a minimum, the last part reiterates the annotation guidelines in the form of diagrammatic decision trees.

In the next sections, we give a walk-through of the guidelines and definitions provided.

## 6.2 Material

Our annotators are first made familiar with the material provided to them. This material consists of 300 entries comprising a single sentence and a triple Subject-Verb-Object which helps the annotator identify which subject noun phrase in the sentence they are requested to label (the 'ORIGINAL' and 'TRIPLE' lines in the parser output – see Figure 1). No other context is provided. This is partly to make the task shorter (letting us annotate more instances) and partly to allow for some limited comparison between human and machine performance (by restricting the amount of information given to our annotators, we force them – to some extent – to use the limited information that would be available to an automatic quantification resolution system, e.g. syntax).

## 6.3 Definitions

In our scheme, we introduce the annotators to the concepts of **quantification** and **kind**.[3]

**Quantification** is described in simple terms, as the process of 'paraphrasing the noun phrase in a particular sentence using an unambiguous term expressing some quantity'. An example is given.

15. *Europeans* discovered the Tuggerah Lakes in 1796 = *Some Europeans* discovered the Tuggerah Lakes in 1796.

We only allow the three quantifiers *some*, *most* and *all*. In order to keep the number of classes to a manageable size, we introduce the additional constraint that the process of quantification must yield a single quantifier. We force the annotator to choose between the three proposed options and introduce priorities in cases of doubt: *most* has priority over *all*, *some* has priority over the other two quantifiers. This ensures we keep a conservative attitude with regard to inference (see Section 1).

**Kinds** are presented as denoting 'the group including all entities described by the noun phrase under consideration', that is, as a supremum. (As mentioned in Section 2, the verbal predicate applies collectively to that supremum in the corresponding formalisation.)

Quantification classes are introduced in a separate part of the scheme. We define the five labels SOME, MOST, ALL, ONE and QUANT (for already quantified noun phrases) and give examples for each one of them.

We try, as much as possible, to keep annotators away from performing complex reference resolution. Their first task is therefore to simply attempt

[3]Distributivity and collectivity are also introduced in the scheme because they are a necessary part of our proposed formalisation. However, as this paper focuses on the annotation of quantification itself, we will not discuss this side of the annotation task.

to paraphrase the existing sentence by appending a relevant quantifier to the noun phrase to be annotated. In some cases, however, this is impossible and no quantifier yields a correct English sentence (this often happens in collective statements). To help our annotators make decisions in those cases, we ask them to distinguish what the noun phrase might refer to when they first hear it and what it refers to at the end of the sentence, i.e., when the verbal predicate has imposed further constraints on the quantification of the NP.

### 6.4 Guidelines

Guidelines are provided for five basic phrase types: quantified noun phrases, proper nouns, plurals, non-bare singulars and bare singulars.

#### 6.4.1 Quantified noun phrases

This is the simplest case: a noun phrase that is already quantified such as *some people*, *6 million inhabitants* or *most of the workers*. The annotator simply marks the noun phrase with a QUANT label.

#### 6.4.2 Proper nouns

Proper nouns are another simple case. But because what annotators understand as a proper noun varies, we provide a definition. We note first that proper nouns are often capitalised. It should however be clear that, while capitalised entities such as *Mary*, *Easter Island* or *Warner Bros* refer to singular, unique objects, others refer to groups or instances of those groups: *The Chicago Bulls*, *a Roman*. The latter can be quantified:

16. The Chicago Bulls won last week. (ALL – collective)
17. A Roman shows courage in battle. (MOST – distributive)

We define proper nouns as noun phrases that 'contain capitalised words and refer to a concept which doesn't have instances'. All proper nouns are annotated as ONE.

#### 6.4.3 Plurals

Plurals must be appropriately quantified and the annotators must also specify whether they are kinds or not. This last decision can simply be made by attempting to paraphrase the sentence with either a definite singular or an indefinite singular – potentially leading to a typical generic statement.

#### 6.4.4 (Non-bare) singulars

Like plurals, singulars must be tested for a kind reading. This is done by attempting to pluralise the noun phrase. If pluralisation is possible, then the kind interpretation is confirmed and quantification is performed. If not (certain non-mass terms have no identifiable parts), the singular refers to a single entity and is annotated as ONE.

#### 6.4.5 Bare singulars

We regard bare singulars as essentially plural, under the linguistic assumption of non-overlapping atomic parts – for instance, water is considered a collection of $H_2O$ molecules, rice is regarded as a collection of grains of rice, etc (see Chierchia, 1998). In order to make this relation clear, we ask annotators to try and paraphrase bare singulars with an (atomic part) plural equivalent and follow, as normal, the decision tree for plurals:

18. *Free software* allows users to co-operate in enhancing and refining the programs they use $\approx$ *Open source programs* allow users...

When the paraphrase is impossible (as in certain non-mass terms which have no identifiable parts), the noun phrase is deemed a unique entity and labelled ONE.

## 7 Implementation and results

### 7.1 Task implementation

Three annotators were used in our experiment. One annotator was one of the authors; the other two annotators were graduate students (non-linguists), both fluent in English. The two graduate students were provided with individual training sessions where they first read the annotation guidelines, had the opportunity to ask for clarifications, and subsequently annotated, with the help of the author, the 50 noun phrases in the training set. The actual annotation task was performed without communication with the scheme author or the other annotators.

### 7.2 Kappa evaluation

We made an independence assumption between quantification value and kind value, and evaluated agreement separately for each type of annotation.

Intra-annotator agreement was calculated over the set of annotations produced by one of the authors. The original annotation experiment was reproduced at three months' interval and Kappa was

| Class | Kind | Quantification |
|---|---|---|
| Kappa | 0.85 | 0.84 |

Table 1: Intra-annotator agreements for both tasks

| Class | Kind | Quantification |
|---|---|---|
| Kappa | 0.67 | 0.72 |

Table 2: Inter-annotator agreements for both tasks

computed between the original set and the new set. Table 1 shows results over 0.8 for both tasks, corresponding to 'perfect agreement' according to the Landis and Koch classification (1977). This indicates that the stability of the scheme is high.

Table 2 shows inter-annotator agreements of over 0.6 for both tasks, which correspond to 'substantial agreement'. This result must be taken with caution, though. Although it shows good agreement overall, it is important to ascertain in what measure it holds for separate classes. In an effort to report such per class agreement, we calculate Kappa values for each label by evaluating each class against all others collapsed together (as suggested by Krippendorf, 1980).

Table 3 indicates that substantial agreement is maintained for separate classes in the kind annotation task. Table 4, however, suggests that, if agreement is perfect for the ONE and QUANT classes, it is very much lower for the SOME, MOST and ALL classes. While it is clear that the latter three are the most complex to analyse, we can show that the lower results attached to them are partly due to issues related to Kappa as a measure of agreement. Feinstein and Cicchetti (1990), followed by Di Eugenio and Glass (2004) proved that Kappa is subject to the effect of prevalence and that different marginal distributions can lead to very different Kappa values for the same observed agreement. It can be shown, in particular, that an unbalanced, symmetrical distribution of the data produces much lower figures than balanced or unbalanced, asymmetrical distributions because the expected agreement gets inflated. Our confusion matrices indicate that our data falls into the category of unbalanced, symmetrical distribution: the classes are not evenly distributed but annotators agree on the relative prevalence of each class. Moreover, in the quantification task itself, the ONE class covers roughly 50% of the data. This means that, when calculating per class agreement, we get an approximately balanced distribution for the ONE label and an unbalanced, but still symmetrical, distribution for the other labels. This leads to the expected agreement being rather low for the ONE class and very high for the other classes. Table 5 reproduces the per class agreement figures obtained for the quantification task but shows, in addition, the observed and expected agreements for each label. Although the observed agreement is consistently close to, or over, 0.9, the Kappa values differ widely in conjunction with expected agreement. This results in relatively low results for SOME, MOST and ALL (the QUANT label has nearly perfect agreement and therefore doesn't suffer from prevalence).

| Class | KIND | NOT-KIND | QUANT |
|---|---|---|---|
| Kappa | 0.63 | 0.71 | 0.88 |

Table 3: Per class inter-annotator agreement for the kind annotation

| Class | ONE | SOME | MOST | ALL | QUANT |
|---|---|---|---|---|---|
| Kappa | 0.81 | 0.45 | 0.44 | 0.51 | 0.88 |

Table 4: Per class inter-annotator agreement for the quantification annotation

| Class | Kappa | Pr(a) | Pr(e) |
|---|---|---|---|
| ONE | 0.814 | 0.911 | 0.521 |
| SOME | 0.445 | 0.893 | 0.808 |
| MOST | 0.438 | 0.931 | 0.877 |
| ALL | 0.509 | 0.867 | 0.728 |
| QUANT | 0.884 | 0.987 | 0.885 |

Table 5: The effect of prevalence on per class agreement, quantification task. $Pr(a)$ is the observed agreement between annotators, $Pr(e)$ the expected agreement.

With regard to the purpose of creating a gold standard for a quantification resolution system, we also note that out of 300 quantification annotations, there are only 14 cases in which a majority decision cannot be found, i.e., at least two annotators agreed in 95% of cases. Thus, despite some low Kappa results, the data can adequately be used for the production of training material.[4]

[4]As far as such data ever can be: Reidsma and Carletta, 2008, show that systematic disagreements between annotators will produce bad machine learning, regardless of the Kappa obtained on the data.

In Section 8, we introduce difficulties encountered by our subjects, as related in post-annotation discussions. We focus on quantification.

## 8 Annotation issues

### 8.1 Reference

Although we tried to make the task as simple as possible for the annotators by asking them to paraphrase the sentences that they were reading, they were not free from having to work out the referent of the NP (consciously or unconsciously) and we have evidence that they did not always pick the same referent, leading to disagreements at the quantification stage. Consider the following:

19. Subsequent annexations by Florence in the area have further diminished the likelihood of incorporation.

In the course of post-annotation discussions, it became clear that not all annotators had chosen the same referent when quantifying the subject NP in the first clause. One annotator had chosen as referent *subsequent annexations*, leading to the reading *Some subsequent annexations, conducted by Florence in the area, have further diminished the likelihood of incorporation.* The other two annotators had kept the whole NP as referent, leading to the reading *All the subsequent annexations conducted by Florence in the area have further diminished the likelihood of incorporation.*

### 8.2 World knowledge

Being given only one sentence as context for the NP to quantify, annotators sometimes lacked the world knowledge necessary to make an informed decision. This is illustrated by the following:

20. The undergraduate schools maintain a non-restrictive Early Action admissions programme.

Discussion revealed that all three annotators had a different interpretation of what the mentioned Early Action programme might refer to, and of the duties of the undergraduate schools with regard to it. This led to three different quantifications: SOME, MOST and ALL.

### 8.3 Interaction with time

The existence of interactions between NP quantification and what we will call temporal quantification is not surprising: we refer to the literature on genericity and in particular to Krifka et al (1995) who talk of characteristic predication, or habituality, as a phenomenon encompassed by genericity. We do not intend to argue for a unified theory of quantification, as temporal quantification involves complexities which are beyond the scope of this work. However, the interactions observed between temporality and NP quantification might explain further disagreements in the annotation task. The following is a sentence that contains a temporal adverb (*sometimes*) and that produced some disagreement amongst annotators:

21. Scottish fiddlers emulating 18th-century playing styles sometimes use a replica of the type of bow used in that period.

Two annotators labelled the subject of that sentence as MOST, while the third one preferred SOME. In order to understand the issue, consider the following, related, statement:

22. Mosquitoes sometimes carry malaria.

This sentence has the possible readings: *Some mosquitoes carry malaria* or *Mosquitoes, from time to time in their lives, carry malaria.* The first reading is clearly the preferred one.

The structure of (21) is identical to that of (22) and it should therefore be taken as similarly ambiguous: it either means that some of the Scottish fiddlers emulating 18th-century playing styles use a replica of the bow used in that period, or that a Scottish fiddler who emulates 18th-century playing styles, from time to time, uses a replica of such a bow. The two readings may explain the labels given to that sentence by the annotators.

## 9 Conclusion

Taking prevalence effects into account, we believe that our agreement results can be taken as evidence that underquantification is analysable in a consistent way by humans. We also consider them as strong support for our claim that 'genericity quantifies'. Our scheme could however be refined further. In a future version, we would add guidelines regarding the selection of the referent of the noun phrase, encourage the use of external resources to obtain the context of a given sentence (or simply provide the actual context of the sentence), and give some pointers as to how to resolve issues or ambiguities caused by temporal quantification.

## References


ACE. 2008. *ACE (Automatic Content Extraction) English Annotation Guidelines for Entities*, Version 6.6 2008.06.13. Linguistic Data Consortium.

Edward Briscoe, John Carroll and Rebecca Watson. 2006. 'The Second Release of the RASP System'. In *Proceedings of the COLING/ACL 2006 Interactive Presentation Sessions*, Sydney, Australia, 2006.

Gregory Carlson. 1995. 'Truth-conditions of Generics Sentences: Two Contrasting Views'. In Gregory N. Carlson and Francis Jeffrey Pelletier, Editors, *The Generic Book*, pages 224 – 237. Chicago University Press.

Gennaro Chierchia. 1998. 'Reference to kinds across languages'. *Natural Language Semantics*, 6:339–405.

Ariel Cohen. 1996. *Think Generic: The Meaning and Use of Generic Sentences*. Ph.D. Dissertation. Carnegie Mellon University at Pittsburgh. Published by CSLI, Stanford, 1999.

Ann Copestake. 2004. 'Robust Minimal Recursion Semantics'. `www.cl.cam.ac.uk/~aac10/papers/rmrsdraft.pdf`.

Barbara Di Eugenio and Michael Glass. 2004. 'The kappa statistic: a second look'. *Computational Linguistics*, 30(1):95–101.

Alvan R. Feinstein and Domenic V. Cicchetti. 1990. 'High agreement but low kappa: I. The problems of two paradoxes'. *Journal of Clinical Epidemiology*, 43(6):543–549.

Joseph Fleiss. 1971. 'Measuring nominal scale agreement among many raters'. *Psychological Bulletin*, 76(5):378-382.

Aurelie Herbelot. To appear. *Underspecified quantification*. Ph.D. Dissertation. Computer Laboratory, University of Cambridge, United Kingdom.

Gerhard Heyer. 1990. 'Semantics and Knowledge Representation in the Analysis of Generic Descriptions'. *Journal of Semantics*, 7(1):93–110.

Paul Kingsbury, Martha Palmer and Mitch Marcus. 2002. 'Adding Semantic Annotation to the Penn TreeBank'. In *Proceedings of the Human Language Technology Conference (HLT 2002)*, San Diego, California, pages 252–256.

Manfred Krifka, Francis Jeffry Pelletier, Gregory N. Carlson, Alice ter Meulen, Godehard Link and Gennaro Chierchia. 1995. 'Genericity: An Introduction'. In Gregory N. Carlson and Francis Jeffry Pelletier, Editors. *The Generic Book*, pages 1–125. Chicago: Chicago University Press.

Klaus Krippendorff. 1980. *Content Analysis: An Introduction to Its Methodology*. Newbury Park, CA: Sage.

J. Richard Landis and Gary G. Koch. 1977. 'The Measurement of Observer Agreement for Categorical Data'. *Biometrics*, 33:159–174.

Sara-Jane Leslie. 2008. 'Generics: Cognition and Acquisition.' *Philosophical Review*, 117(1):1–47.

Christopher Lyons. 1999. *Definiteness*. Cambridge University Press, Cambridge, UK.

Mitchell P. Marcus, Beatrice Santorini, and Mary Ann Marcinkiewicz. 1993. 'Building a large annotated corpus of english: The penn treebank'. *Computational Linguistics*, 19(2):313–330.

Francis Jeffry Pelletier and Nicolas Asher. 1997. 'Generics and defaults'. In: Johan van Benthem and Alice ter Meulen, Editors, *Handbook of Logic and Language*, pages 1125–1177. Amsterdam: Elsevier.

Massimo Poesio. 2000. 'The GNOME annotation scheme manual', Fourth Version. `http://cswww.essex.ac.uk/Research/nle/corpora/GNOME/anno_manual_4.htm`

Massimo Poesio. 2004. 'Discourse Annotation and Semantic Annotation in the GNOME Corpus'. In: *Proceedings of the ACL Workshop on Discourse Annotation*, Barcelona, Spain.

Dennis Reidsma and Jean Carletta. 2008. 'Reliability measurement without limits'. *Computational Linguistics*, 34(3), pages 319–326.

Anna Ritchie. 2004. 'Compatible RMRS Representations from RASP and the ERG'. `http://www.cl.cam.ac.uk/TechReports/UCAM-CL-TR-661`.

Simone Teufel, Advaith Siddharthan, Dan Tidhar. 2006. 'An annotation scheme for citation function'. In: *Proceedings of Sigdial-06*, Sydney, Australia, pages 80–87.

Simone Teufel. 2010. *The Structure of Scientific Articles: Applications to Summarisation and Citation Indexing*. CSLI Publications. In press.

# PropBank Annotation of Multilingual Light Verb Constructions

**Jena D. Hwang[1], Archna Bhatia[3], Clare Bonial[1], Aous Mansouri[1], Ashwini Vaidya[1], Nianwen Xue[2], and Martha Palmer[1]**

[1]Department of Linguistics, University of Colorado at Boulder, Boulder CO 80309
[2]Department of Computer Science, Brandeis University, Waltham MA 02453
[3]Department of Linguistics, University of Illinois at Urbana-Champaign, Urbana IL 61801

{hwangd,claire.bonial,aous.mansouri,ashwini.vaidya,martha.palmer}
@colorado.edu, bhatia@illinois.edu, xuen@brandeis.edu

## Abstract

In this paper, we have addressed the task of PropBank annotation of light verb constructions, which like multi-word expressions pose special problems. To arrive at a solution, we have evaluated 3 different possible methods of annotation. The final method involves three passes: (1) manual identification of a light verb construction, (2) annotation based on the light verb construction's Frame File, and (3) a deterministic merging of the first two passes. We also discuss how in various languages the light verb constructions are identified and can be distinguished from the non-light verb word groupings.

## 1 Introduction

One of the aims in natural language processing, specifically the task of semantic role labeling (SRL), is to correctly identify and extract the different semantic relationships between words in a given text. In such tasks, verbs are considered important, as they are responsible for assigning and controlling the semantic roles of the arguments and adjuncts around it. Thus, the goal of the SRL task is to identify the arguments of the predicate and label them according to their semantic relationship to the predicate (Gildea and Jurafsky, 2002; Pradhan et al., 2003).

To this end, PropBank (Palmer et. al., 2005) has developed semantic role labels and labeled large corpora for training and testing of supervised systems. PropBank identifies and labels the semantic arguments of the verb on a verb-by-verb basis, creating a separate Frame File that includes verb specific semantic roles to account for each subcategorization frame of the verb. It has been shown that training supervised systems with PropBank's semantic roles for shallow semantic analysis yield good results (see CoNLL 2005 and 2008).

However, semantic role labeling tasks are often complicated by multiword expressions (MWEs) such as idiomatic expressions (e.g., 'Stop *pulling my leg*!'), verb particle constructions (e.g., 'You must *get over* your shyness.'), light verb constructions (e.g., '*take a walk*', '*give a lecture*'), and other complex predicates (e.g., V+V predicates such as Hindi's निकल गया *nikal gayaa*, lit. 'exit went', means 'left' or 'departed'). MWEs that involve verbs are especially challenging because the subcategorization frame of the predicate is no longer solely dependent on the verb alone. Rather, in many of these cases the argument structure is assigned by the union of two predicating elements. Thus, it is important that the manual annotation of semantic roles, which will be used by automatic SRL systems, define and label these MWEs in a consistent and effective manner.

In this paper we focus on the PropBank annotation of light verb constructions (LVCs). We have developed a multilingual schema for annotating LVCs that takes into consideration the similarities and differences shared by the construction as it appears in English, Arabic, Chinese, and Hindi. We also discuss in some detail the practical challenges involved in the crosslinguistic analysis of LVCs, which we hope will bring us a step closer to a unified crosslinguistic analysis.

Since NomBank, as a companion to PropBank, provides corresponding semantic role



*Proceedings of the Fourth Linguistic Annotation Workshop, ACL 2010*, pages 82–90,
Uppsala, Sweden, 15-16 July 2010. 

labels for noun predicates (Meyers et al., 2004), we would like to take advantage of NomBank's existing nominalization Frame Files and annotations as much as possible. A question that we must therefore address is, "Are nominalization argument structures exactly the same whether or not they occur within an LVC?" as will be discussed in section 6.1.

## 2 Identifying Light Verb Constructions

Linguistically LVCs are considered a type of a complex predicate. Many studies from differing angles and frameworks have characterized complex predicates as a fusion of two or more predicative elements. For example, Rosen (1997) treats complex structures as complementation structures, where the argument structure of elements in a complex predicate are fused together. Goldberg (1993) takes a constructional approach to complex predicates and arrives at an analysis that is comparable to viewing complex predicates as a single lexical item. Similarly, Mohanan (1997) assumes different levels of linguistic representation for complex predicates in which the elements, such as the noun and the light verb, functionally combine to give a single clausal nucleus. Alsina (1997) and Butt (1997) suggest that complex predicates may be formed by syntactically independent elements whose argument structures are brought together by a predicate composition mechanism.

While there is no clear-cut definition of LVCs, let alone the whole range of complex predicates, for the purposes of this study, we have adapted our approach largely from Butt's (2004) criteria for defining LVCs. LVCs are characterized by a light verb and a predicating complement (henceforth, *true predicate*) that "combine to predicate as a single element." (Ibid.) In LVC, the verb is considered semantically bleached in such a way that the verb does not hold its full predicating power. Thus, the light verb plus its true predicate can often be paraphrased by a verbal form of the true predicate without loss of the core meaning of the expression. For example, the light verb 'gave' and the predicate 'lecture' in 'gave a lecture', together form a single predicating unit such that it can be paraphrased by 'lectured'.

True predicates in LVCs can be a noun (the object of the verb or the object of the preposition in a prepositional phrase), an adjective, or a verb. One light verb plus true predicate combination found commonly across all our PropBank languages (i.e., English, Arabic, Chinese, and Hindi) is the noun as the object of the verb as in 'Sara **took [a stroll]** along the beach'. In Hindi, true predicates can be adjectives or verbs, in addition to the nouns.

मुझे तुम **[अच्छे] लगे** (Adjective)
to-me you [**nice**] **seem**
lit. 'You seem nice to me'
'You (are) liked to me (=I like you).'

मैंने सब कुछ **[कर] लिया** (Verb)
I-ERG everything [**do**] **took**
lit. 'I took do everything'
'I have done everything.'

As for Arabic, the LVCs come in verb+noun pairings. However, they surface in two syntactic forms. It can either be the object of the verb just like in English:

**القى** جورج **[محاضرة]** عن لبنان
**gave.he** Georges [**lecture**] PREP Lebanon
lit.'Georges gave a lecture about Lebanon'
'Georges lectured about Lebanon'

or the complement can be the object of a preposition:

**سأقوم [بزيارة]** سيدنا إلياس
**conduct.I [PREP-visit]** our.saint Ilias
lit. 'I will conduct with visit Saint Ilias's'
'I will visit Saint Ilias's'

## 3 Standard PropBank Annotation Procedure

The PropBank annotation process can be broken down into two major steps: creation of the Frame Files for verbs occurring in the data and annotation of the data using the Frame Files. During the creation of the Frame Files, the usages of the verbs in the data are examined by linguists (henceforth, "framers"). Based on these observations, the framers create a Frame File for each verb containing one or more framesets, which correspond to coarse-grained senses of the predicate lemma. Each frameset specifies the PropBank labels (i.e., ARG0, ARG1,...ARG5) corresponding to the argument structure of the verb. Additionally, illustrative examples are included for each frameset, which will later be referenced by the annotators. These examples also include the use of the ARGM labels.

Thus, the framesets are based on the examination of the data, the framers' linguistic knowledge and native-speaker intuition. At times, we also make use of the syntactic and semantic behavior of the verb as described by certain lexical resources. These resources include VerbNet (Kipper et. al., 2006) and FrameNet (Baker et. al., 1998) for English, a number of monolingual and bilingual dictionaries for Arabic, and Hindi WordNet and DS Parses (Palmer et. al., 2009) for Hindi. Additionally, if available, we consult existing framesets of words with similar meanings across different languages.

The data awaiting annotation are passed onto the annotators for a double-blind annotation process using the previously created framesets. The double annotated data is then adjudicated by a third annotator, during which time the differences of the two annotations are resolved to produce the Gold Standard.

Two major guiding considerations during the framing and annotating process are data consistency and annotator productivity. During the frameset creation process, verbs that share similar semantic and syntactic characteristics are framed similarly. During the annotation process, the data is organized by verbs so that each verb is tackled all at once. In doing so, we firstly ensure that the framesets of similar verbs, and in turn, the annotation of the verbs, will both be consistent across the data. Secondly, by tackling annotation on verb-by-verb basis, the annotators are able to concentrate on a single verb at a time, making the process easier and faster for the annotators.

## 4 Annotating LVC

A similar process must be followed when annotating light verb constructions The first step is to create consistent Frame Files for light verbs. Then in order to make the annotation process produce consistent data at a reasonable speed, we have decided to carry out the light verb annotation in three passes (Table 1): (1) annotate the light verb, (2) annotate the true predicate, and (3) merge the two annotations into one.

The first pass involves the identification of the light verb. The most important parts of this step are to identify a verb as having bleached meaning, thereafter assign a generic light verb frameset and identify the true predicating expression of the sentence, which would be marked with ARG-PRX (i.e., ARGument-PRedicating eXpression). For English, for example, annotators were instructed to use Butt's (2004) criteria as described in Section 2. These criteria required that annotators be able to recognize whether or not the complement of a potential light verb was itself a predicating element. To make this occasionally difficult judgment, annotators used a simple heuristic test of whether or not the complement was headed by an element that has a verbal counterpart. If so, the light verb frameset was selected.

The second pass involves the annotation of the sentence with the true predicate as the relation. During this pass, the true predicate is annotated with an appropriate frameset. In the third pass, the arguments and the modifiers of the two previous passes are reconciled and merged into a single annotation. In order to reduce the number of hand annotation, it is preferable for this last pass, the Pass 3, to be done automatically.

Since the nature of the light verb is different from that of other verbs as described in Section 2, the advantage of doing the annotation of the light verb and the true predicate on separate passes is that in the light verb pass the annotators will be able to quickly dispose of the verb as a light verb and in the second pass, they will be allowed to solely focus on the annotation of the light verb's true predicate.

The descriptions of how the arguments and modifiers of the light verbs and their true predicates are annotated are mentioned in Table 1, but notably, none of the examples in it currently include the annotation of arguments

| | Pass 1:<br>Light Verb Annotation | Pass 2:<br>True Predicate Annotation | Pass 3:<br>Merge of Pass1&2 Annotation |
|---|---|---|---|
| Relation | Light verb | True predicate | Light verb + true predicate |
| Arguments and Modifiers | - Predicating expression is annotated with ARG-PRX<br>- Arguments and modifiers of the light verb are annotated | - Arguments and modifiers of the true predicate are annotated | - Arguments and modifiers found in the two passes are merged, preferably automatically. |
| Frameset | Light verb frameset | True predicate's frameset | LVC's frameset |
| Example | ***"John took a brisk walk through the park."*** | | |
| | REL: took<br>ARG-PRX: a brisk walk | ARG-MNR: brisk<br>REL: walk | REL: took walk<br>ARG-MNR: brisk |

Table 1. Preliminary Annotation Scheme

and modifiers. This is intentional, as coming to an agreement concerning the details of what exactly each of the three passes looks like while meeting the needs of the four PropBank languages is quite challenging. Thus, for the rest of the paper we will discuss the strengths and weaknesses of the two trial methods of annotation we have considered and discarded in Section 5, as well as the final annotation scheme we chose in Section 6.

## 5 Trials

### 5.1 Method 1

As our first attempt, the annotation of argument and adjuncts was articulated in the following manner (Table 2).

| Pass 1: | Pass 2: |
|---|---|
| Light verb | True predicate |
| - Predicating expression is labeled ARG-PRX<br>- *Annotate the Subject argument of the light verb as the Arg0.*<br>- *Annotate the rest of the arguments and modifiers of the light verb with ARGM labels.* | - *Annotate arguments and modifiers of the true predicate within its domain of locality.* |
| Generic light verb Frame File | True predicate's Frame File |
| **"John took a brisk walk through the park."** | |
| ARG0: John<br>REL: took<br>ARG-PRX: a brisk walk<br>ARG-DIR: through the park | ARG-MNR: brisk<br>REL: walk |

Table 2. Method 1 for annotation for Passes 1 and 2. Revised information is in italics.

In Pass 1, in addition to annotating the predicating expression of the light verb with ARG-PRX, the subject argument was marked with an ARG0. The choice of ARG0, which corresponds to a proto-typical agent, was guided by the observation that English LVCs tend to lend a component of agentivity to the subject even in cases where the true predicate would not necessarily assign an agent as its subject. The rest of the arguments and modifiers were labeled with corresponding ARGM (i.e., modifier) labels. The assumption here is that the arguments of the light verb will also be the arguments of the true predicate.

In Pass 2, then, the annotation of the arguments of the true predicate was restricted to its domain of locality (i.e., the span of the ARG-PRX as marked in Pass1). That is, in the example 'John took a brisk walk through the park', the labeled spans for the true predicate would be limited to the NP 'a brisk walk' and neither 'John' nor through the park' would be annotated as the arguments of the true predicate 'walk'.

**Frame Files:** This method would require three Frame Files: a generic light verb Frame File, a true predicate Frame File, and an LVC Frame File. The Frame File for the light verb would not be specific to the form of the light verb (e.g., same frame for *take* and *make*). Rather, it would indicate a skeletal argument structure in order to reduce the amount of Frame Files made, including only Arg0 as its argument[1].

### 5.2 Weakness of Method 1

This method has one glaring problem: the assumption that the semantic roles of the arguments as assigned by the light verb uniformly coincide with those assigned by the true predicate does not always hold. Consider the following English sentence[2].

> whether <u>Wu Shu-Chen</u> would **make** another **[appearance]** in court was subject to observation

In this example, 'Wu Shu-Chen' is the agent argument (Arg0) of the light verb 'make' and is the theme or patient argument (Arg1) of a typical 'appearance' event. Also consider the following example from Hindi.

It is possible that in a light verb construction, the light verb actually modifies the standard underlying semantics of a nominalization like appearance. In any event, we cannot assume that the expected argument labels for the light verb and for the standard interpretation of the nominalization will always coincide. Thus, we could say that Pass 2's true predicate annotation is only partial and is not representative of the complete argument structure. In particular, we are left with a very difficult merging problem, because the argument labels of the two separate passes conflict as seen in the above examples.

### 5.3 Method 2

In order to remedy the problem of conflicting argument labels, we revised Method 1's Pass 2 annotation scheme. This is shown in Table 3. Pass 1 remains unchanged from Method 1.

In this method, both the light verb and the true predicate of the sentence receive complete sets of

[1] This is why the rest of the argument/modifiers would be annotated using ARGM modifier labels.

[2] The light verb is in boldface, the true predicate is in bold and square brackets, and the argument/adjunct under consideration is underlined.

| Pass 2: |
|---|
| True predicate |
| - *Annotate the Subject argument of the light verb with the appropriate role of the true predicate* <br> - Annotate arguments and modifiers of the true predicate *without limitation as to the domain of locality.* |
| True predicate's Frame File |
| **"He made another appearance at the party"** |
| ARG1: He <br> ARG-ADV: another <br> REL: appearance <br> ARG-DIR: at court |

Table 3. Method 2 for annotation for Pass 2. Pass 1 as presented in Table 2 remains unchanged. Revised information for Pass 2 is in italics

argument and modifier labels. In Pass 2, the limitation of annotating within the domain of locality is removed. That is, the arguments and modifiers inside and outside the true predicate's domain of control are annotated with respect to their *semantic relationship to the true predicate* (e.g., in the English example of Section 5.2, 'Wu Shu-Chen' would be considered ARG1 of 'appearance').

**Frame Files:** This method would also require three Frame Files. The major difference is that with this method the Frame File for the true predicate includes arguments that are sisters to the light verb.

### 5.4 Weaknesses of Method 2

If in Method 1 we have committed the error of semantic unfaithfulness due to omission, in Method 2 we are faced with the problem of including too much. In the following sentence, consider the role of the underlined adjunct:

> A New York audience … **gave** it a big round of **applause** when the music started to play.

By the annotation in Method 2, the underlined temporal adjunct 'when the music started to play' is labeled as both the argument of 'give' and of 'applause'. The question here is does the argument apply to both the giving and the applauding event? In other words, does the adjunct play an equal role in both passes?

Since it could be easily said that the temporal phrase applies to both the applauding and the giving of the applause events, this example may not be particularly compelling. However, what if a syntactic complement of the light verb is a semantic argument of the true predicate and the true predicate only? This is seen more frequently in the cases where the light verb is less bleached than in the case of 'give' above. Consider the following Arabic example.

> **أخذنا في [الاعتبار]** في تحضيراتنا إمكان تكبدهم خسائر
> took.we PREP DEF-consideration PREP prepertations.our possibility sustain.their losses
> 'We **took** into **[consideration]** during our preparations the possibility of them sustaining losses'

Here, even though the constituent 'of them sustaining losses' is the syntactic complement of the verb 'to take;' semantically, it modifies only the nominal object of the PP 'consideration.'

There are similar phenomena in Chinese light verb constructions. Syntactic modifiers of the light verb are semantic arguments of the true predicate, which is usually a nominalization that serves as its complement.

> 我们 正 对 这 个 问题 **[进行] 讨论。**
> we now regarding this CL issue [**conduct**] **discussion**.
> lit."We are conducting a discussion on this issue."
> "We are discussing this issue."

The prepositional phrase 对这个问题 'regarding this issue' is a sister to the light verb but semantically it is an argument of the nominalized predicate 讨论 'discussion'.

The logical next question would be: does the annotation of the arguments, adjuncts and modifiers have to be all or nothing? It could conceivably be possible to assign a selected set of arguments at the light verb or true predicate level. For example, in the Chinese sentence, the modifier 'regarding this CL issue', though a syntactic adjunct to the light verb, could be left out from the semantic annotation in Pass 1 and included only in the Pass 2.

However, the objection to this treatment comes from a more practical need. As mentioned above, in order to keep the manual annotation to a minimum, it would be necessary to keep Pass 3 completely deterministic. As is, with the unmodified Method 2, there would be the need to choose between Pass 1 or Pass 2 annotation to when doing the automatic Pass 3. If we modify Method 2 by annotating only a selected set of syntactic arguments for the light verb or the true predicate, then this issue is exacerbated. In such a case there we would have to develop with strict rules for which arguments of which pass should be included in Pass 3. Pass 3 would no longer be automatic, and should be done manually.

| | Pass 1:<br>Light Verb Identification | Pass 2:<br>LVC Annotation | Pass 3:<br>Deterministic relation merge |
|---|---|---|---|
| Relation | Light verb | True predicate | Light verb + true predicate |
| Arguments & Modifiers | - Predicating expression is annotated with ARG-PRX | - Arguments and modifiers of the LVCs are annotated | - Arguments and modifiers are taken from Pass 2 |
| Frame File | <no Frame File needed> | LVC's Frame File | LVC's Frame File |
| Example | ***"John took a brisk walk through the park."*** | | |
| | REL: took<br>ARG-PRX: a brisk walk | ARG0: John<br>ARG-MNR: brisk<br>REL: walk<br>ARGM-DIR: through the park | ARG0: John<br>ARG-MNR: brisk<br>REL: [took][walk]<br>ARGM-DIR: through the park |

Table 4. Final Annotation Scheme

## 6 Final Annotation Scheme

### 6.1 Semantic Fidelity

Many of the objections so far to Methods 1 and 2 have centered on the issue of semantic fidelity during the annotation of each of the two passes. The debate of whether both passes should be annotated and to what extent has practical implications for the third Pass, as described above. However, more importantly it comes down to whether or not the semantics of the final *light verb plus true predicate combination* is indeed distinct from the semantics of its parts (i.e. light verb and true predicate, separately). This may be a fascinating linguistic question, but it is not something our annotators can be debating for each and every instance.

Instead, we argue that the semantic argument structure of the *light verb plus true predicate combination* can in practice be different from that of the expressions taken independently as has been proposed by various studies (Butt, 2004; Rosen, 1997; Grimshaw & Mester, 1988). Thus, we resolve the cases in which the differences in argument roles as assigned by the light verb and the nominalization (Section 5.2) by handling the argument structure of the standard nominalization separately from that of the nominalization participating in the LVC. In the example 'Chen made another appearance in court', we annotate 'Chen' as the Agent (ARG0) of the full predicate '[make] [appearance]', which is different from the argument structure of the standard nominalization which would label 'Chen' to be the Patient argument (ARG1).

### 6.2 Method 3: Final Method

Our final method of light verb annotation reflects the notion that the noun, verb, or adjective as a true predicate within an LVC can have a different argument structure from that of the word alone. Table 4 shows the final annotation scheme for light verb construction.

During Pass 1, the LVCs and their predicating expressions are identified in the data. Instances identified as LVCs in Pass 1 are then manually annotated during Pass 2, annotating the arguments and adjuncts of the light verb and the true predicate with roles that reflect their semantic relationships to the *light verb plus true predicate*. In practice, Pass 1 becomes a way of simply manually identifying the light verb usages. It is in Pass 2 that we make the final choice of argument labels for all of the arguments. Thus in Pass 3, the light verb and the true predicate lemmas from Pass 1 and 2 are joined into a single unit (e.g., in the example found in Table 4, the light verb 'took' would be joined with the true predicate 'walk' into 'took+walk')[3]. In this final method, Pass 3 can be achieved completely deterministically.

The major difference in this annotation scheme from that of Methods 1 and 2 is that instead of annotating in terms of the semantics of the bare noun, adjective or verb, the argument structure is determined for the entire predicate or the full event: semantics of the *light verb plus the true predicate*. This means that for the sentences where the argument roles of the verb and the nominalization disagree like 'Chen' in 'Chen

3 The order of Pass 2 and Pass 3 as presented in Table 4 is arguably a product of how the annotation tools for PropBank are set up for Arabic, Chinese, and English. That is, the order of the Pass 2 and Pass 3 could potentially be flipped provided that the tools and procedures of annotation support it, as is the case for Hindi PropBank. After the LVC and ARG-PRX are identified in Pass 1, the light verb and the true predicate can be deterministically joined into a single relation in Pass 2, leaving the manual annotation of LVC for Pass 3. The advantage of this alternative ordering is that because the annotation of LVC is done around light verb plus the true predicate as a single relation, rather than the true predicate alone as in Table 4, the argument annotation may in actuality be more intuitive for annotators even with less training.

made another[4] appearance in court', we label the argument with the role that is consistent with the entire predicate (i.e. Agent, ARG0).

**Frame Files:** The final advantage to this method is that only one Frame File is needed. Since Pass 1 is an identification round, no Frame File is required. A single Frame File for LVC that includes the argument structure with respect to the *light verb plus true predicate combination* will suffice for Pass 2 and Pass 3.

## 7 Distinguishing LVCs from MWEs

As we have discussed in Section 2, we adapted our approach from Butt's (2004) definition of LVCs. That is, an LVC is characterized by a semantically bleached light verb and a true predicate. These elements combine as a single predicating unit, in such a way that the light verb plus its true predicate can be paraphrased by a verbal form of the true predicate without loss of the core meaning of the expression (e.g. 'lectured' for 'gave a lecture'). Also, as discussed in Section 6.1, our approach advocates the notion that the semantic argument structure of the *light verb plus true predicate* is different from that of the expressions taken independently (as also proposed by Butt, 2004; Rosen, 1997; Grimshaw & Mester, 1988 among others).

While these definitions are appropriate for the PropBank annotation task as we have presented it, there are still cases that merit closer attention. Even English with a rather limited set of verbs that are commonly cited as LVCs, includes a problematic mixture of what could arguably be termed either LVCs or idiomatic expressions: 'make exception', 'take charge'. This difficulty in part is the effect of frequency and entrenchment of particular constructions. The light verbs themselves do not diminish in form over time in a manner similar to auxiliaries (Butt, 2004), although the complements of common LVCs can change over time such that it is no longer clear that the complement is a predicating element.

In the case of English, the expressions 'take charge' may be more commonly found today as a LVC than independently in its verbal form. As we discovered with our annotators, native English speakers are uncomfortable using the verb 'charge' (i.e. to burden with a responsibility) as an independent matrix verb. A similar phenomenon can be seen in Arabic, where the predicate أطلق اسم lit. 'release name' exemplifies a prototypical LVC that means 'to name'. However, in our data we see cases in which the complement is missing, while the semantics of the LVC remains intact:

أو ما يطلق عليه "القطاع العام"
CONJ REL be released.he PREP-him/it
DEF-sector DEF-public
lit 'Or what is released to it "the public sector"'
'Or what is called/named "the public sector."'

This raises the question of: when does a construction that may have once been an LVC become more properly defined as an idiomatic expression due to such entrenchment? Idiomatic expressions can potentially be distinguished from LVCs through judgments of how fixed or syntactically variable a construction is, and on the basis of how semantically transparent or decomposable the construction is (Nunberg et. al., 1994). However, sometimes the dividing line is hard to draw.

A similar problem arises in determining whether a construction is a case of an LVC or simply a usage with a distinct sense of the verb. Take, for example, the following Arabic sentence.

تناول الغذاء
take.he DEF-food
lit. '(he) took food'
'he ate'

Here, the Arabic word غذاء 'food' is the noun derivation of the root shared by the verb تغذى 'to eat', in such a way that the sentence could be rephrased as تغذى '(he) ate'. This example falls neatly into the LVC category. However, further examples suggest that the example is a case of a distinct sense of 'to take orally' where the restrictions on the object are that the theme must be something that can be taken by mouth:

| | |
|---|---|
| تناول الدواء | تناول الحساء |
| take.he DEF-medicine | take.he DEF-soup |
| 'he took medicine' | 'he took soup' |

Finally, determining the appropriate criteria to distinguish between a truly semantically bleached verb and verbs that seem to be participating in complex predication but contribute more to the semantics of the construction is a challenge for all languages. For example, in English data, there are potential LVCs with verbs that are not often thought of as light verbs, such as 'produce an alteration' and

[4] The adjective 'another' is annotated as the modifier of the full predicate '[make][appearance]' as it can be interpreted to mean that the make appearance event happened a previous appearance has been made.

'issue a complaint'. Although most English speakers would agree that the verbs in these constructions do not contribute to the semantics of the construction (e.g. 'issue a complaint' can be paraphrased to 'to complain'), there are similar constructions such as 'register a complaint,' wherein the verb cannot be considered light. For the purposes of annotation, where it is necessary for annotators to understand clear criteria for distinguishing light verbs, such cases are highly problematic because there is no deterministic way to measure the extent to which the verbal element contributes to the semantics of the construction. In turn, there is not a good way to distinguish some of these borderline verbs from their normal, heavy usages.

Such problems can be resolved by establishing language-specific semantic or syntactic tests that can be used for taking care of the borderline cases of LVCs. However, there is one other plausible manner we have identified that could help in detecting such atypical LVCs. This can be done by focusing on the argument structures of predicating complements rather than focusing on the verbs themselves. Grimshaw & Mester (1988) suggest that the formation of LVCs involves argument transfer from the predicating complement to the verb, which is semantically bleached and thematically incomplete and assigns no thematic roles itself. Similarly, Stevenson *et al.* (2004) suggest that the acceptability of a potential LVC depends on the semantic properties of the complement. Thus, atypical LVCs, such as the English construction 'issue a complaint,' can potentially be detected during the annotation of eventive nouns, planned for all PropBank languages.

This process will make our treatment of LVCs more comprehensive. Used with our language-specific semantic and syntactic criteria relating to both the verb and the predicating complement, it will help us to more effectively capture as many types of LVCs as possible, including those of the V+ADJ and V+V varieties.

## 8 Usefulness of our Approach

Two basic approaches have previously been taken to handle all types of MWEs, including LVCs in natural language processing applications. The first is to treat MWEs quite simply as fixed expressions or long strings of words with spaces in between; the second is to treat MWEs as purely compositional (Sag et al., 2002). The words-with-spaces approach is adequate for handling fixed idiomatic expressions, but issues of lexical proliferation and flexibility quickly arise when this approach is applied to light verbs, which are syntactically flexible and can number in the tens of thousands for a given language (Stevenson et al., 2004; Sag et al., 2002). Nonetheless, large-scale lexical resources such as FrameNet (Baker et al., 1998) and WordNet (Fellbaum, 1999) continue to expand with entries that are MWEs.

The purely compositional approach is also problematic for light verbs because it is notoriously difficult to predict which light verbs can grammatically combine with other predicating elements; thus, this approach leads to problems of overgeneration (Sag et al., 2002). In order to overcome this problem, Stevenson et al. (2004) attempted to determine which nominalizations could form a valid complement to the English light verbs *take, give* and *make,* using Levin's (1993) verb classes to group similar nominalizations. This approach was rather successful for *take* and *give*, but inconclusive for the verb *make*.

Our approach can help to develop a resource that is useful whether one takes a words-with-spaces approach or a compositional approach. Specifically, for those implementing a words-with-spaces approach, the resulting PropBank annotation can serve as a lexical resource listing for LVCs. For those interested in implementing a compositional approach the PropBank annotation can serve to assist in predicting likely combinations. Moreover, information in the PropBank Frame Files can be used to generalize across classes of nouns that can occur with a given light verb with the help of lexical resources such as WordNet (Fellbaum, 1998), FrameNet (Baker et. al., 1998), and VerbNet (Kipper-Schuler, 2005) (in a manner similar to the approach of Stevenson et al. (2004)).

## Acknowledgements

We also gratefully acknowledge the support of the National Science Foundation Grant CISE-CRI 0709167, Collaborative: A Multi-Representational and Multi-Layered Treebank for Hindi/Urdu, and a grant from the Defense Advanced Research Projects Agency (DARPA/IPTO) under the GALE program, DARPA/CMO Contract No HR0011-06-C-0022, subcontract from BBN, Inc.

Any opinions, findings, and conclusions or recommendations expressed in this material are those of the authors and do not necessarily reflect the views of the National Science Foundation.

## Reference


Alsina, A. 1997. Causatives in Bantu and Romance. In A. Alsina, J. Bresnan, and P. Sells eds. *Complex Predicates.* Stanford, California: CSLI Publications, p. 203-246.

Baker, Collin F., Charles J. Fillmore, and John B. Lowe. 1998. The Berkeley FrameNet Project. In Proceedings of the 17th International Conference on Computational Linguistics (COLING/ACL-98), pages 86–90, Montreal. ACL.

Butt, M. 2004. The Light Verb Jungle. In G. Aygen, C. Bowern & C. Quinn eds. *Papers from the GSAS/Dudley House Workshop on Light Verbs.* Cambridge, Harvard Working Papers in Linguistics, p. 1-50.

Butt, M. 1997. Complex Predicates in Urdu. In A. Alsina, J. Bresnan, and P. Sells eds. *Complex Predicates.* Stanford, California: CSLI Publications, p. 107-149.

Fellbaum, Christine, ed.: 1998, *WordNet: An Electronic Lexical Database,* Cambridge, MA: MIT Press.

Grimshaw, J., and A. Mester. 1988. Light verbs and θ-marking. Linguistic Inquiry 19(2):205–232.

Gildea, Daniel and Daniel Jurafsky. 2002. Automatic Labeling of Semantic Roles. Computational Linguistics 28:3, 245-288.

Goldberg, Adele E. 2003. "Words by Default: Inheritance and the Persian Complex Predicate Construction." In E. Francis and L. Michaelis (eds). Mismatch: Form-Function Incongruity and the Architecture of Grammar. CSLI Publications. 84-112.

Kipper-Schuler, Karin. 2005. VerbNet: A broad coverage, comprehensive verb lexicon. Ph.D. thesis, University of Pennsylvania.

Levin, B. 1993. *English Verb Classes and Alternations: A Preliminary Investigation.* Chicago: Chicago Univ. Press.

Meyers, A., R. Reeves, C. Macleod, R. Szekely, V. Zielinska, B. Young, and R. Grishman. 2004. The NomBank Project: An interim report. In Proceedings of the HLT-NAACL 2004 Workshop: Frontiers in Corpus Annotation, pages 24- 31, Boston, MA. pages 430–437, Barcelona, Spain.

Mohanan, T. 1997. Multidimensionality of Representation: NV Complex Predicates in Hindi. In A. Alsina, J. Bresnan, and P. Sells eds. *Complex Predicates.* Stanford, California: CSLI Publications, p. 431-471.

Martha Palmer, Rajesh Bhatt, Bhuvana Narasimhan, Owen Rambow, Dipti Misra Sharma, Fei Xia, Hindi Syntax: Annotating Dependency, Lexical Predicate-Argument Structure, and Phrase Structure, In the Proceedings of the 7th International Conference on Natural Language Processing, ICON-2009, Hyderabad, India, Dec 14-17, 2009

Palmer, Martha, Daniel Gildea, and Paul Kingsbury. 2005. The Proposition Bank: An Annotated Corpus of Semantic Roles. Computational Linguistics, 31(1):71–106.

Pradhan, Sameer, Kadri Hacioglu, Valerie Krugler, Wayne Ward, James H. Martin, Daniel Jurafsky. 2004. Shallow Semantic Parsing using Support Vector Machines. University of Colorado Technical Report: TR-CSLR 2003-03.

Rosen, C. 1997. Auxiliation and Serialization: On Discerning the Difference. In A. Alsina, J. Bresnan, and P. Sells eds. *Complex Predicates.* Stanford, California: CSLI Publications, p. 175-202.

Sag, I., Baldwin, T. Bond, F., Copestake, A., Flickinger, D. 2002. Multiword expressions: A pain in the neck for NLP. In Proceedings of teh Third International Conference on Intelligent Text processing and Computatinal Linguistics (CICLING 2002), p. 1-15, Mexico City, Mexico. ACL.

Stevenson, S., Fazly, A., and North, R. (2004). Statistical measures of the semi-productivity of light verb constructions. In Proceedings of the ACL-04 Workshop on Multiword Expressions: Integrating Processing, p. 1–8.

# Retrieving Correct Semantic Boundaries in Dependency Structure

**Jinho D. Choi**
Department of Computer Science
University of Colorado at Boulder
choijd@colorado.edu

**Martha Palmer**
Department of Linguistics
University of Colorado at Boulder
martha.palmer@colorado.edu

## Abstract

This paper describes the retrieval of correct semantic boundaries for predicate-argument structures annotated by dependency structure. Unlike phrase structure, in which arguments are annotated at the phrase level, dependency structure does not have phrases so the argument labels are associated with head words instead: the subtree of each head word is assumed to include the same set of words as the annotated phrase does in phrase structure. However, at least in English, retrieving such subtrees does not always guarantee retrieval of the correct phrase boundaries. In this paper, we present heuristics that retrieve correct phrase boundaries for semantic arguments, called semantic boundaries, from dependency trees. By applying heuristics, we achieved an F1-score of 99.54% for correct representation of semantic boundaries. Furthermore, error analysis showed that some of the errors could also be considered correct, depending on the interpretation of the annotation.

## 1 Introduction

Dependency structure has recently gained wide interest because it is simple yet provides useful information for many NLP tasks such as sentiment analysis (Kessler and Nicolov, 2009) or machine translation (Gildea, 2004). Although dependency structure is a kind of syntactic structure, it is quite different from phrase structure: phrase structure gives phrase information by grouping constituents whereas dependency structure gives dependency relations between pairs of words. Many dependency relations (e.g., subject, object) have high correlations with semantic roles (e.g., agent, patient), which makes dependency structure suitable for representing semantic information such as predicate-argument structure.

In 2009, the Conference on Computational Natural Language Learning (CoNLL) opened a shared task: the participants were supposed to take dependency trees as input and produce semantic role labels as output (Hajič et al., 2009). The dependency trees were automatically converted from the Penn Treebank (Marcus et al., 1993), which consists of phrase structure trees, using some heuristics (cf. Section 3). The semantic roles were extracted from the Propbank (Palmer et al., 2005). Since Propbank arguments were originally annotated at the phrase level using the Penn Treebank and the phrase information got lost during the conversion to the dependency trees, arguments are annotated on head words instead of phrases in dependency trees; the subtree of each head word is assumed to include the same set of words as the annotated phrase does in phrase structure. Figure 1 shows a dependency tree that has been converted from the corresponding phrase structure tree.

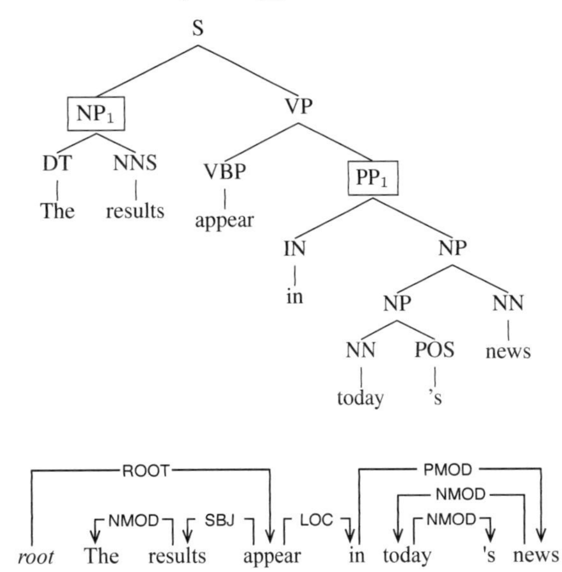


Figure 1: Phrase vs. dependency structure



*Proceedings of the Fourth Linguistic Annotation Workshop, ACL 2010*, pages 91–99,
Uppsala, Sweden, 15-16 July 2010. 

In the phrase structure tree, arguments of the verb predicate *appear* are annotated on the phrases: NP$_1$ as ARG$_0$ and PP$_1$ as ARGM-LOC. In the dependency tree, the arguments are annotated on the head words instead: *results* as the ARG$_0$ and *in* as the ARGM-LOC. In this example, both PP$_1$ and the subtree of *in* consist of the same set of words $\{$*in, today, 's, news*$\}$ (as is the case for NP$_1$ and the subtree of *results*); therefore, the phrase boundaries for the semantic arguments, called semantic boundaries, are retrieved correctly from the dependency tree.

Retrieving the subtrees of head words usually gives correct semantic boundaries; however, there are cases where the strategy does not work. For example, if the verb predicate is a gerund or a past-participle, it is possible that the predicate becomes a syntactic child of the head word annotated as a semantic argument of the predicate. In Figure 2, the head word *plant* is annotated as ARG$_1$ of the verb predicate *owned*, where *owned* is a child of *plant* in the dependency tree. Thus, retrieving the subtree of *plant* would include the predicate itself, which is not the correct semantic boundary for the argument (the correct boundary would be only $\{$*The, plant*$\}$).

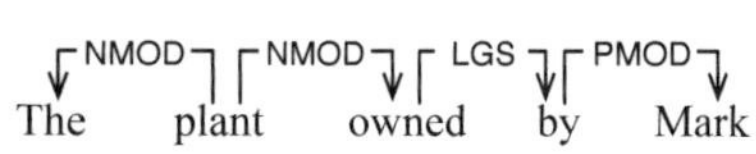


Figure 2: Past-participle example

For such cases, we need some alternative for retrieving the correct semantic boundaries. This is an important issue that has not yet been thoroughly addressed. In this paper, we first show how to convert the Penn Treebank style phrase structure to dependency structure. We then describe how to annotate the Propbank arguments, already annotated in the phrase structure, on head words in the dependency structure. Finally, we present heuristics that correctly retrieve semantic boundaries in most cases. For our experiments, we used the entire Penn Treebank (Wall Street Journal). Our experiments show that it is possible to achieve an F1-score of 99.54% for correct representation of the semantic boundaries.

## 2 Related work

Ekeklint and Nivre (2007) tried to retrieve semantic boundaries by adding extra arcs to dependency trees, so the structure is no longer a tree but a graph. They experimented with the same corpus, the Penn Treebank, but used a different dependency conversion tool, Penn2Malt.[1] Our work is distinguished from theirs because we keep the tree structure but use heuristics to find the boundaries. Johansson (2008) also tried to find semantic boundaries for evaluation of his semantic role labeling system using dependency structure. He used heuristics that apply to general cases whereas we add more detailed heuristics for specific cases.

## 3 Converting phrase structure to dependency structure

We used the same tool as the one used for the CoNLL'09 shared task to automatically convert the phrase structure trees in the Penn Treebank to the dependency trees (Johansson and Nugues, 2007). The script gives several options for the conversion; we mostly used the default values except for the following options:[2]

- **splitSlash=false**: do not split slashes. This option is taken so the dependency trees preserve the same number of word-tokens as the original phrase structure trees.

- **noSecEdges=true**: ignore secondary edges if present. This option is taken so all siblings of verb predicates in phrase structure become children of the verbs in dependency structure regardless of empty categories. Figure 3 shows the converted dependency tree, which is produced when the secondary edge (*ICH*) is not ignored, and Figure 4 shows the one produced by ignoring the secondary edge. This option is useful because NP* and PP-2* are annotated as separate arguments of the verb predicate *paid* in Propbank (NP* as ARG$_1$ and PP-2* as ARGM-MNR).

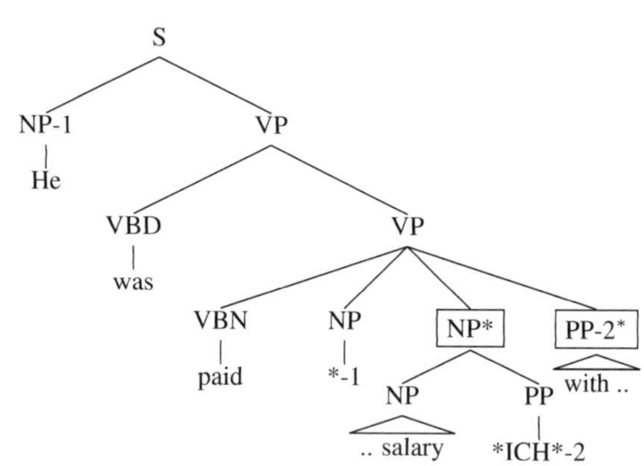


[1]http://stp.lingfil.uu.se/ nivre/research/Penn2Malt.html

[2]http://nlp.cs.lth.se/software/treebank_converter/

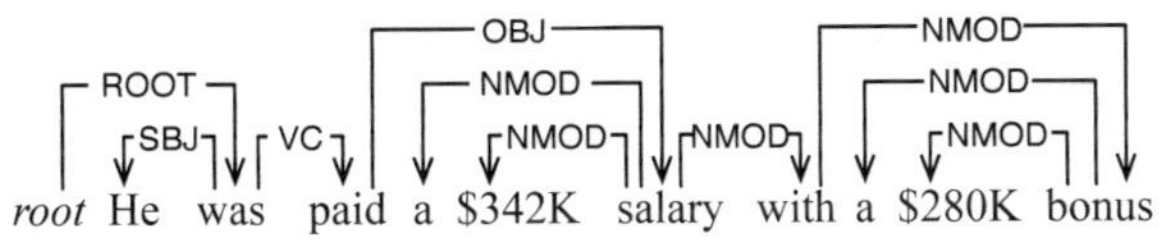


Figure 3: When the secondary edge is not ignored

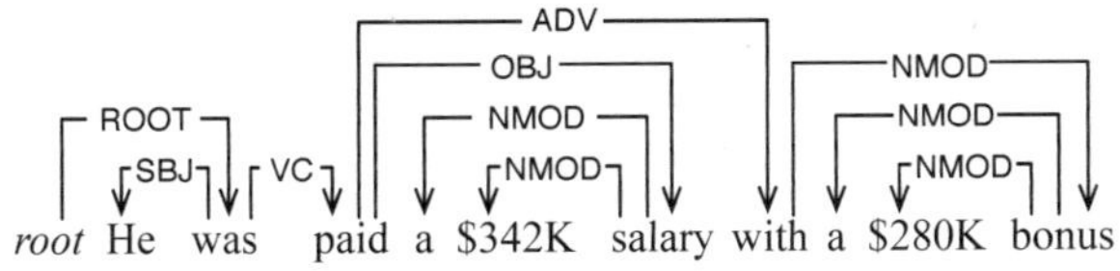


Figure 4: When the secondary edge is ignored

Total 49,208 dependency trees were converted from the Penn Treebank. Although it was possible to apply different values for other options, we found them not helpful in finding correct semantic boundaries of Propbank arguments. Note that some of non-projective dependencies are removed by ignoring the secondary edges. However, it did not make all dependency trees projective; our methods can be applied for either projective or non-projective dependency trees.

## 4 Adding semantic roles to dependency structure

### 4.1 Finding the head words

For each argument in the Propbank annotated on a phrase, we extracted the set of words belonging to the phrase. Let this set be $S_p$. In Figure 1, $PP_1$ is the ARGM-LOC of *appear* so $S_p$ is $\{$*in*, *today*, *'s*, *news*$\}$. Next, we found a set of head words, say $S_d$, whose subtrees cover all words in $S_p$ (e.g., $S_d = \{$*in*$\}$ in Figure 1). It would be ideal if there existed one head word whose subtree covers all words in $S_p$, but this is not always the case. It is possible that $S_d$ needs more than one head word to cover all the words in $S_p$.

Figure 5 shows an algorithm that finds a set of head words $S_d$ whose subtrees cover all words in $S_p$. For each word $w$ in $S_p$, the algorithm checks if $w$'s subtree gives the maximum coverage (if $w$'s subtree contains more words than any other subtree); if it does, the algorithm adds $w$ to $S_d$, removes all words in $w$'s subtree from $S_p$, then repeats the search. The search ends when all words in $S_p$ are covered by some subtree of a head word in $S_d$. Notice that the algorithm searches for the minimum number of head words by matching the maximum coverages.

**Input**: $S_p$ = a set of words for each argument in the Propbank
**Output**: $S_d$ = a set of head words whose subtrees cover all words in $S_p$

**Algorithm:**getHeadWords($S_p$)
$S_d = \{\}$
**while** $S_p \neq \emptyset$ **do**
    $max$ = None
    **foreach** $w \in S_p$ **do**
        **if** $|subtree(w)| > |subtree(max)|$ **then**
            $max = w$
    **end**
    $S_d$.add($max$)
    $S_p$.removeAll($subtree(max)$)
**end**
**return** $S_d$

Figure 5: Finding the min-set of head words

The algorithm guarantees to find the min-set $S_d$ whose subtrees cover all words in $S_p$. This gives 100% recall for $S_d$ compared to $S_p$; however, the precision is not guaranteed to be as perfect. Section 5 illustrates heuristics that remove the over-generated words so we could improve the precision as well.

### 4.2 Ignoring empty categories

As described in Figures 3 and 4, dependency trees do not include any empty categories (e.g., null elements, traces, PRO's): the empty categories are dropped during the conversion to the dependency trees. In the Penn Treebank, 11.5% of the Propbank arguments are annotated on empty categories. Although this is a fair amount, we decided to ignore them for now since dependency structure is not naturally designed to handle empty categories. Nonetheless, we are in the process of finding ways of automatically adding empty categories to dependency trees so we can deal with the remaining of 11.5% Propbank arguments.

### 4.3 Handling disjoint arguments

Some Propbank arguments are disjoint in the phrase structure so that they cannot be represented as single head words in dependency trees. For example in Figure 6, both NP-1* and S* are $ARG_1$ of the verb predicate *continued* but there is no head word for the dependency tree that can represent both phrases. The algorithm in Figure 5 naturally handles this kind of disjoint arguments. Although words in $S_p$ are not entirely consecutive ({*Yields*, *on*, *mutual*, *funds*, *to*, *slide*}), it iteratively finds both head words correctly: *Yields* and *to*.

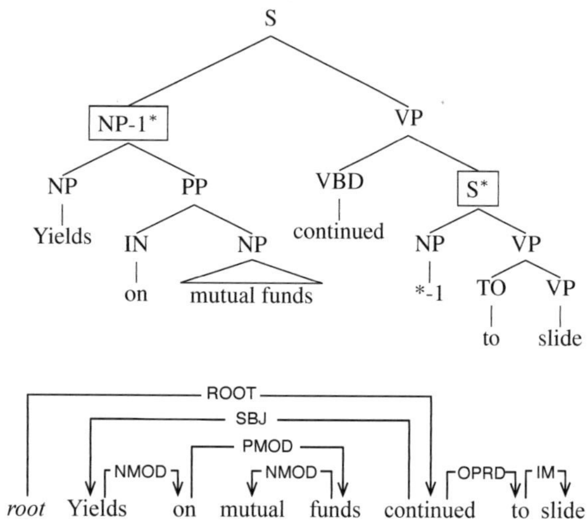


Figure 6: Disjoint argument example

## 5 Retrieving fine-grained semantic boundaries

There are a total of 292,073 Propbank arguments in the Penn Treebank, and only 88% of them map to correct semantic boundaries from the dependency trees by taking the subtrees of head words. The errors are typically caused by including more words than required: the recall is still 100% for the error cases whereas the precision is not. Among several error cases, the most critical one is caused by verb predicates whose semantic arguments are the parents of themselves in the dependency trees (cf. Figure 2). In this section, we present heuristics to handle such cases so we can achieve precision nearly as good as the recall.

### 5.1 Modals

In the current dependency structure, modals (e.g., *will*, *can*, *do*) become the heads of the main verbs. In Figure 7, *will* is the head of the verb predicate *remain* in the dependency tree; however, it is also an argument (ARGM-MOD) of the verb in Propbank. This can be resolved by retrieving only the head word, but not the subtree. Thus, only *will* is retrieved as the ARGM-MOD of *remain*.

Modals can be followed by conjuncts that are also modals. In this case, the entire coordination is retrieved as ARGM-MOD (e.g., {*may*, *or*, *may*, *not*} in Figure 8).

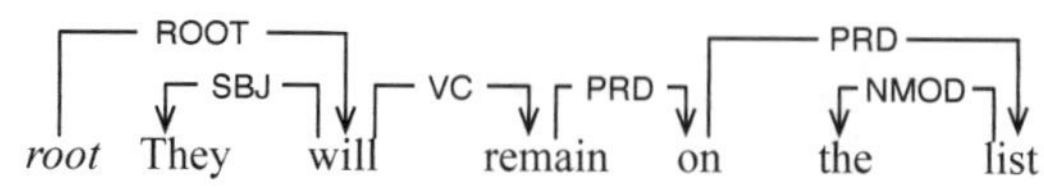


Figure 7: Modal example 1

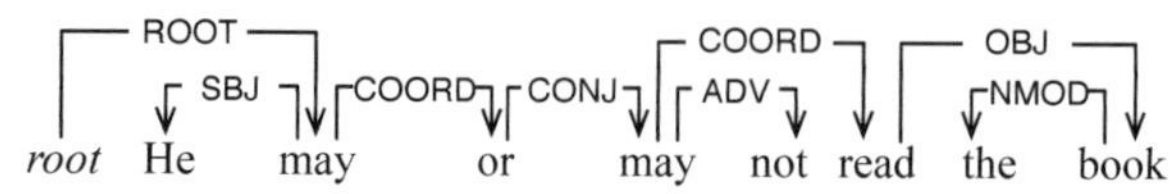


Figure 8: Modal example 2

### 5.2 Negations

Negations (e.g., *not*, *no longer*) are annotated as ARGM-NEG in Propbank. In most cases, negations do not have any child in dependency trees, so retrieving only the negations themselves gives the correct semantic boundaries for ARGM-NEG, but there are exceptions. One is where a negation comes after a conjunction; in which case, the negation becomes the parent of the main verb. In Figure 9, *not* is the parent of the verb predicate *copy* although it is the ARGM-NEG of the verb.

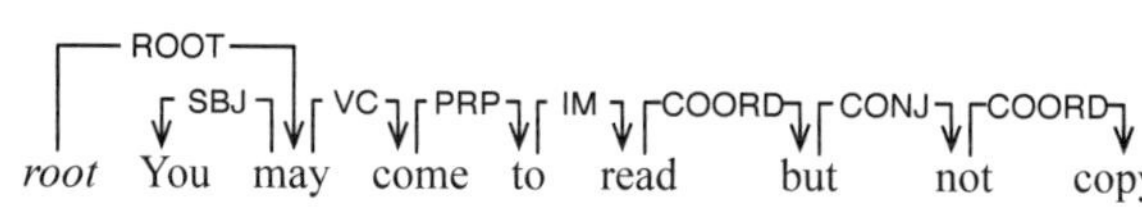


Figure 9: Negation example 1

The other case is where a negation is modified by some adverb; in which case, the adverb should also be retrieved as well as the negation. In Figure 10, both *no* and *longer* should be retrieved as the ARGM-NEG of the verb predicate *oppose*.

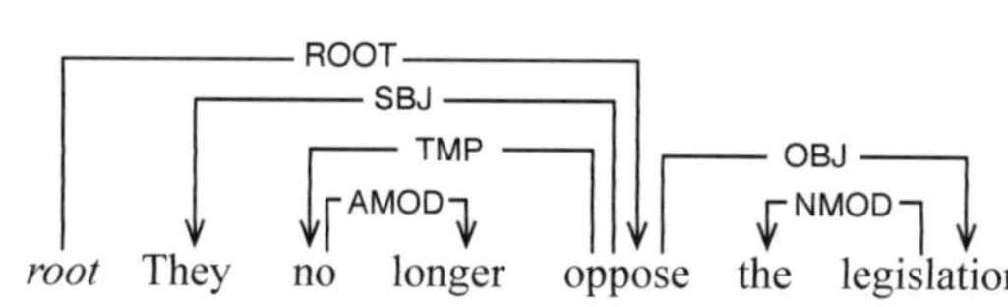


Figure 10: Negation example 2

### 5.3 Overlapping arguments

Propbank does not allow overlapping arguments. For each predicate, if a word is included in one argument, it cannot be included in any other argument of the predicate. In Figure 11, *burdens* and *in the region* are annotated as $ARG_1$ and ARGM-LOC of the verb predicate *share*, respectively. The arguments were originally annotated as two separate phrases in the phrase structure tree; however, *in* became the child of *burdens* during the conversion, so the subtree of *burdens* includes the subtree of *in*, which causes overlapping arguments.

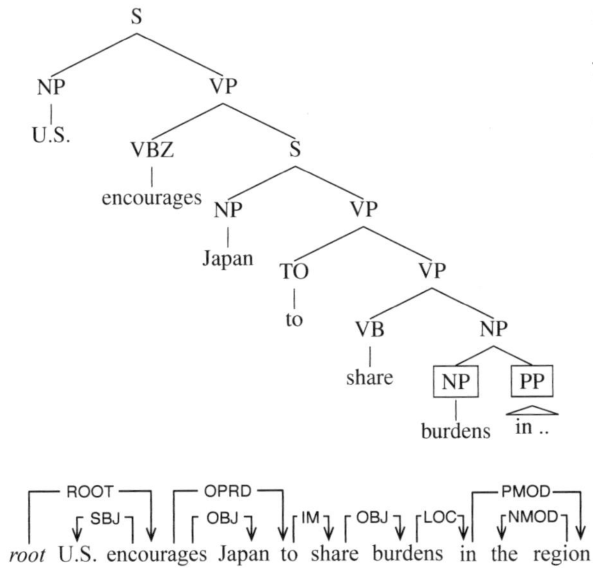


Figure 11: Overlapping argument example 1

When this happens, we reconstruct the dependency tree so *in* becomes the child of *share* instead of *burdens* (Figure 12). By doing so, taking the subtrees of *burdens* and *in* no longer causes overlapping arguments.[3]

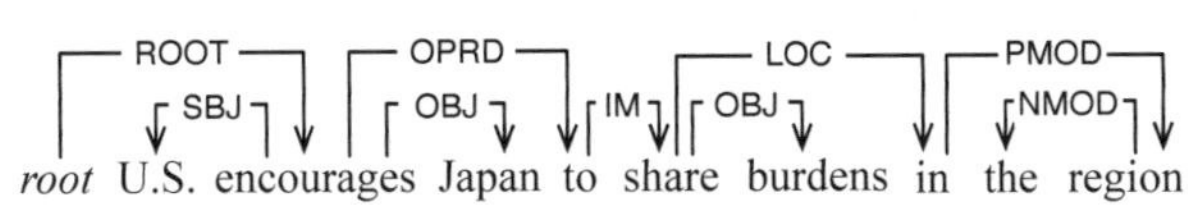


Figure 12: Overlapping argument example 2

## 5.4 Verb predicates whose semantic arguments are their syntactic heads

There are several cases where semantic arguments of verb predicates become the syntactic heads of the verbs. The modals and negations in the previous sections are special cases where the semantic boundaries can be retrieved correctly without compromising recall. The following sections describe other cases, such as relative clauses (Section 5.4.2), gerunds and past-participles (Section 5.4.3), that may cause a slight decrease in recall by finding more fine-grained semantic boundaries. In these cases, the subtree of the verb predicates are excluded from the semantic arguments.

[3]This can be considered as a Treebank/Propbank disagreement, which is further discussed in Sectino 6.2.

### 5.4.1 Verb chains

Three kinds of verb chains exist in the current dependency structure: auxiliary verbs (including modals and *be*-verbs), infinitive markers, and conjunctions. As discussed in Section 5.1, verb chains become the parents of their main verbs in dependency trees. This indicates that when the subtree of the main verb is to be excluded from semantic arguments, the verb chain needs to be excluded as well. This usually happens when the main verbs are used within relative clauses. In addition, more heuristics are needed for retrieving correct semantic boundaries for relative clauses, which are further discussed in Section 5.4.2.

The following figures show examples of each kind of verb chain. It is possible that multiple verb chains are joined with one main verb. In this case, we find the top-most verb chain and exclude its entire subtree from the semantic argument. In Figure 13, *part* is annotated as $\text{ARG}_1$ of the verb predicate *gone*, chained with the auxiliary verb *be*, and again chained with the modal *may*. Since *may* is the top-most verb chain, we exclude its subtree so only *a part* is retrieved as the $\text{ARG}_1$ of *gone*.

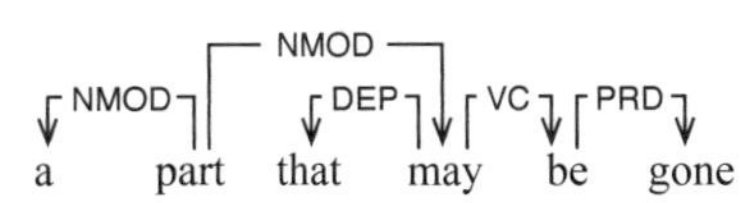


Figure 13: Auxiliary verb example

Figure 14 shows the case of infinitive markers. *those* is annotated as $\text{ARG}_0$ of the verb predicate *leave*, which is first chained with the infinitive marker *to* then chained with the verb *required*. By excluding the subtree of *required*, only *those* is retrieved as the $\text{ARG}_0$ of *leave*.

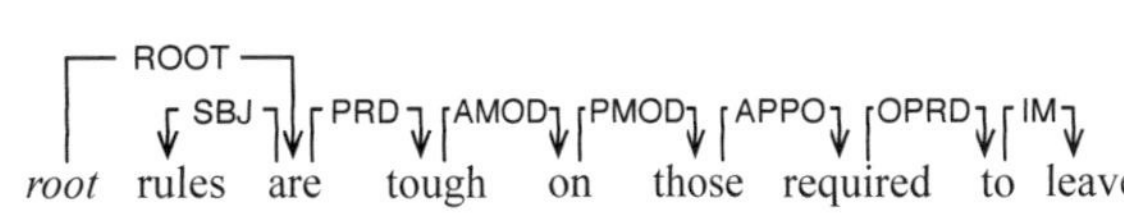


Figure 14: Infinitive marker example

Figure 15 shows the case of conjunctions. *people* is annotated as $\text{ARG}_0$ of the verb predicate *exceed*, which is first chained with *or* then chained with *meet*. By excluding the subtree of *meet*, only *people* is retrieved as the $\text{ARG}_0$ of *exceed*.

When a verb predicate is followed by an object complement (OPRD), the subtree of the object complement is not excluded from the semantic argument. In Figure 16, *distribution* is annotated as

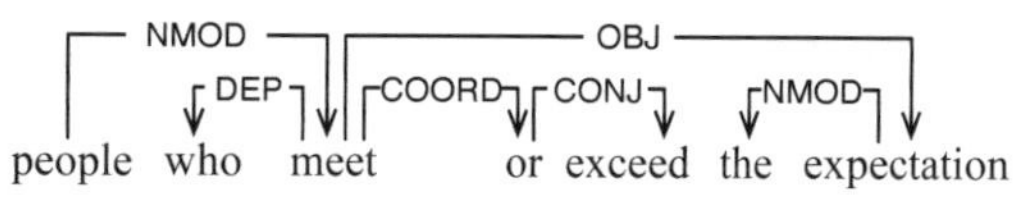


Figure 15: Conjunction example

ARG$_1$ of the verb predicate *expected*. By excluding the subtree of *expected*, the object complement *to occur* would be excluded as well; however, Propbank annotation requires keeping the object complement as the part of the argument. Thus, *a distribution to occur* is retrieved as the ARG$_1$ of *expected*.

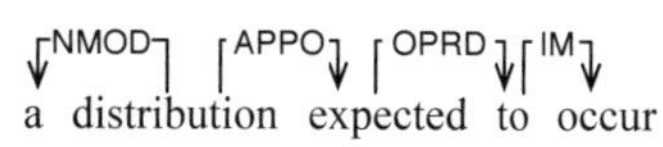


Figure 16: Object complement example

### 5.4.2 Relative clauses

When a verb predicate is within a relative clause, Propbank annotates both the relativizer (if present) and its antecedent as part of the argument. For example in Figure 15, *people* is annotated as ARG$_0$ of both *meet* and *exceed*. By excluding the subtree of *meet*, the relativizer *who* is also excluded from the semantic argument, which is different from the original Propbank annotation. In this case, we keep the relativizer as part of the ARG$_0$; thus, *people who* is retrieved as the ARG$_0$ (similarly, *a part that* is retrieved as the ARG$_0$ of *gone* in Figure 13).

It is possible that a relativizer is headed by a preposition. In Figure 17, *climate* is annotated as ARGM-LOC of the verb predicate *made* and the relativizer *which* is headed by the preposition *in*. In this case, both the relativizer and the preposition are included in the semantic argument. Thus, *the climate in which* becomes the ARGM-LOC of *made*.

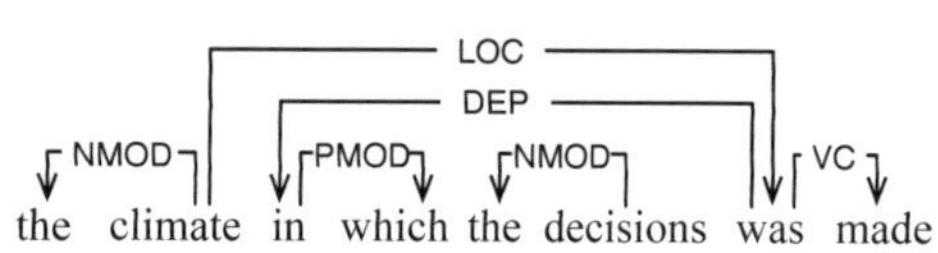


Figure 17: Relativizer example

### 5.4.3 Gerunds and past-participles

In English, when gerunds and past-participles are used without the presence of *be*-verbs, they often function as noun modifiers. Propbank still treats them as verb predicates; however, these verbs become children of the nouns they modify in the dependency structure, so the heuristics discussed in Section 5.4 and 5.4.1 need to be applied to find the correct semantic boundaries. Furthermore, since these are special kinds of verbs, they require even more rigorous pruning.

When a head word, annotated to be a semantic argument of a verb predicate, comes after the verb, every word prior to the verb predicate needs to be excluded from the semantic argument. In Figure 18, *group* is annotated as ARG$_0$ of the verb predicate *publishing*, so all words prior to the predicate (*the Dutch*) need to be excluded. Thus, only *group* is retrieved as the ARG$_0$ of *publishing*.

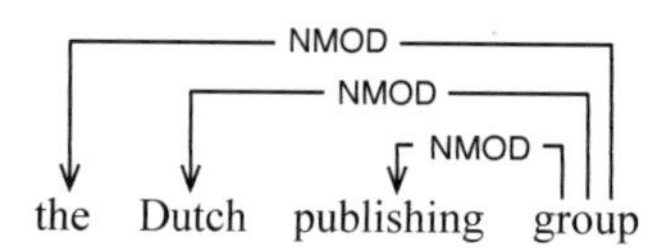


Figure 18: Gerund example

When the head word comes before the verb predicate, the subtree of the head word, excluding the subtree of the verb predicate, is retrieved as the semantic argument. In Figure 19, *correspondence* is annotated as ARG$_1$ of the verb predicate *mailed*, so the subtree of *correspondence*, excluding the subtree of *mailed*, is retrieved to be the argument. Thus, *correspondence about incomplete 8300s* becomes the ARG$_1$ of *mailed*.

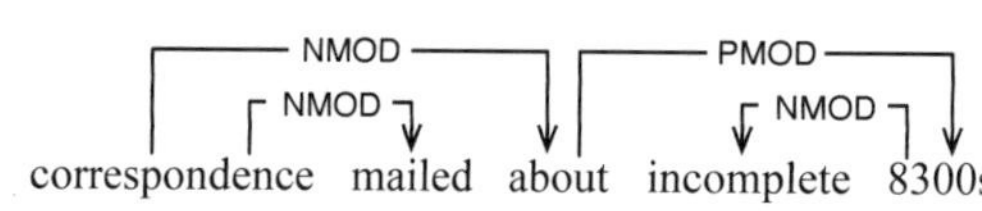


Figure 19: Past-participle example 1

When the subtree of the verb predicate is immediately followed by comma-like punctuation (e.g., comma, colon, semi-colon, etc.) and the head word comes before the predicate, every word after the punctuation is excluded from the semantic argument. In Figure 20, *fellow* is annotated as ARG$_1$ of the verb predicate *named*, so both the subtree of the verb (*named John*) and every word after the comma (*, who stayed for years*) are excluded from the semantic argument. Thus, only *a fellow* is retrieved as the ARG$_1$ of *named*.

### 5.5 Punctuation

For evaluation, we built a model that excludes punctuation from semantic boundaries for two reasons. First, it is often not clear how punctuation

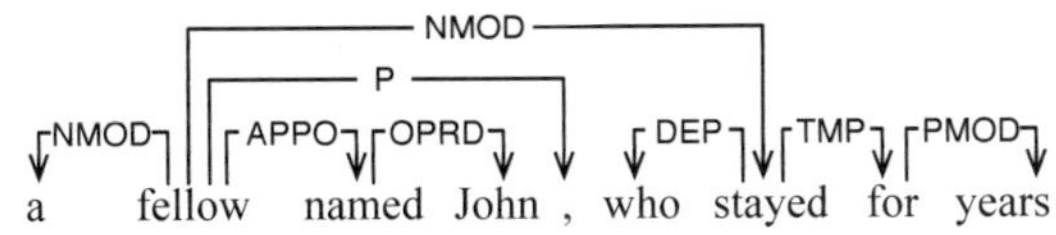


Figure 20: Past-participle example 2

needs to be annotated in either Treebank or Propbank; because of that, annotation for punctuation is not entirely consistent, which makes it hard to evaluate. Second, although punctuation gives useful information for obtaining semantic boundaries, it is not crucial for semantic roles. In fact, some of the state-of-art semantic role labeling systems, such as ASSERT (Pradhan et al., 2004), give an option for omitting punctuation from the output. For these reasons, our final model ignores punctuation for semantic boundaries.

## 6 Evaluations

### 6.1 Model comparisons

The following list describes six models used for the experiments. Model I is the baseline approach that retrieves all words in the subtrees of head words as semantic boundaries. Model II to VI use the heuristics discussed in the previous sections. Each model inherits all the heuristics from the previous model and adds new heuristics; therefore, each model is expected to perform better than the previous model.

- I - all words in the subtrees (baseline)
- II - modals + negations (Sections 5.1, 5.2)
- III - overlapping arguments (Section 5.3)
- IV - verb chains + relative clauses (Sections 5.4.1, 5.4.2)
- V - gerunds + past-participles (Section 5.4.3)
- VI - excluding punctuations (Section 5.5)

The following list shows measurements used for the evaluations. $gold(arg)$ is the gold-standard set of words for the argument $arg$. $sys(arg)$ is the set of words for $arg$ produced by our system. $c(arg_1, arg_2)$ returns 1 if $arg_1$ is equal to $arg_2$; otherwise, returns 0. $T$ is the total number of arguments in the Propbank.

$$
\begin{aligned}
Accuracy &= \frac{1}{T} \cdot \sum_{\forall arg} c(gold(arg), sys(arg)) \\
Precision &= \frac{1}{T} \cdot \sum_{\forall arg} \frac{|gold(arg) \cap sys(arg)|}{|sys(arg)|} \\
Recall &= \frac{1}{T} \cdot \sum_{\forall arg} \frac{|gold(arg) \cap sys(arg)|}{|gold(arg)|} \\
F1 &= \frac{2 \cdot Precision \cdot Recall}{Precision + Recall}
\end{aligned}
$$

Table 1 shows the results from the models using the measurements. As expected, each model shows improvement over the previous one in terms of accuracy and F1-score. The F1-score of Model VI shows improvement that is statistically significant compared to Model I using $t$-test ($t = 149.00$, $p < 0.0001$). The result from the final model is encouraging because it enables us to take full advantage of dependency structure for semantic role labeling. Without finding the correct semantic boundaries, even if a semantic role labeling system did an excellent job finding the right head words, we would not be able to find the actual chunks for the arguments. By using our approach, finding the correct semantic boundaries is no longer an issue for using dependency structure for automatic semantic role labeling.

| Model | Accuracy | Precision | Recall | F1 |
|---|---|---|---|---|
| I | 88.00 | 92.51 | 100 | 96.11 |
| II | 91.84 | 95.77 | 100 | 97.84 |
| III | 92.17 | 97.08 | 100 | 98.52 |
| IV | 95.89 | 98.51 | 99.95 | 99.23 |
| V | 97.00 | 98.94 | 99.95 | 99.44 |
| VI | **98.20** | 99.14 | 99.95 | **99.54** |

Table 1: Model comparisons (in percentage)

### 6.2 Error analysis

Although each model consistently shows improvement on the precision, the recall is reduced a bit for some models. Specifically, the recalls for Models II and III are not 100% but rather 99.9994% and 99.996%, respectively. We manually checked all errors for Models II and III and found that they are caused by inconsistent annotations in the gold-standard. For Model II, Propbank annotation for ARGM-MOD was not done consistently with conjunctions. For example in Figure 8, instead of annotating *may or may not* as the ARGM-MOD, some annotations include only *may* and *may not* but not the conjunction *or*. Since our system consistently included the conjunctions, they appeared to be different from the gold-standard, but are not errors.

For Model III, Treebank annotation was not done consistently for adverbs modifying negations. For example in Figure 10, *longer* is sometimes (but rarely) annotated as an adjective where it is supposed to be an adverb. Furthermore, *longer* sometimes becomes a child of the verb predicate *oppose* (instead of being the child of *no*). Such annotations made our system exclude *longer* as a part of ARGM-NEG, but it would have found them correctly if the trees were annotated consistently.

There are a few cases that caused errors in Models IV and V. The most critical one is caused by PP (prepositional phrase) attachment. In Figure 21, *enthusiasm* is annotated as $\text{ARG}_1$ of the verb predicate *showed*, so our system retrieved the subtree of *enthusiasm*, excluding the subtree of *showed*, as the semantic boundary for the $\text{ARG}_1$ (e.g., *the enthusiasm*). However, Propbank originally annotated both *the enthusiasm* and *for stocks* as the $\text{ARG}_1$ in the phrase structure tree (so the prepositional phrase got lost in our system).

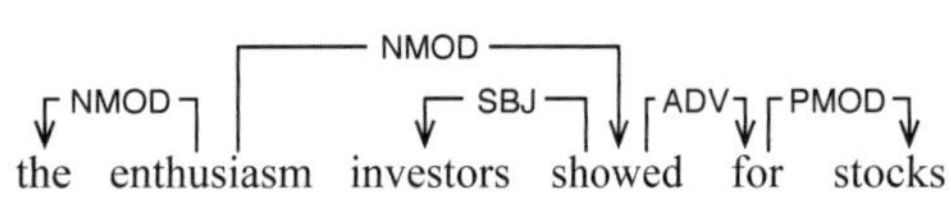


Figure 21: PP-attachment example 1

This happens when there is a disagreement between Treebank and Propbank annotations: the Treebank annotation attached the PP (*for stocks*) to the verb (*showed*) whereas the Propbank annotation attached the PP to the noun (*enthusiasm*). This is a potential error in the Treebank. In this case, we can trust the Propbank annotation and reconstruct the tree so the Treebank and Propbank annotations agree with each other. After the reconstruction, the dependency tree would look like one in Figure 22.

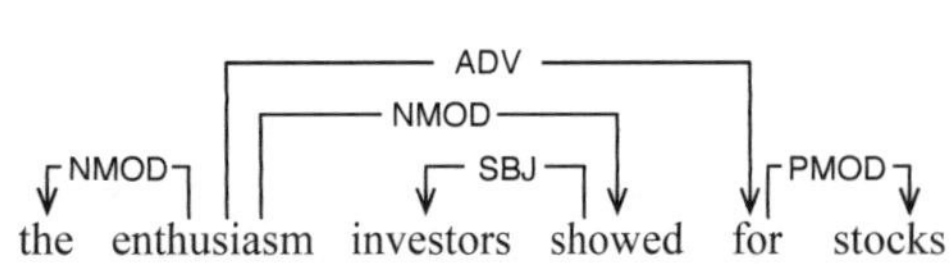


Figure 22: PP-attachment example 2

## 7 Conclusion and future work

We have discussed how to convert phrase structure trees to dependency trees, how to find the minimum-set of head words for Propbank arguments in dependency structure, and heuristics for retrieving fine-grained semantic boundaries. By using our approach, we correctly retrieved the semantic boundaries of 98.2% of the Propbank arguments (F1-score of 99.54%). Furthermore, the heuristics can be used to fix some of the inconsistencies in both Treebank and Propbank annotations. Moreover, they suggest ways of reconstructing dependency structure so that it can fit better with semantic roles.

Retrieving correct semantic boundaries is important for tasks like machine translation where not only the head words but also all other words matter to complete the task (Choi et al., 2009). In the future, we are going to apply our approach to other corpora and see how well the heuristics work. In addition, we will try to find ways of automatically adding empty categories to dependency structure so we can deal with the full set of Propbank arguments.

## Acknowledgments

Special thanks are due to Professor Joakim Nivre of Uppsala University and Claire Bonial of the University of Colorado at Boulder for very helpful insights. We gratefully acknowledge the support of the National Science Foundation Grants CISE-CRI-0551615, Towards a Comprehensive Linguistic Annotation and CISE-CRI 0709167, Collaborative: A Multi-Representational and Multi-Layered Treebank for Hindi/Urdu, and a grant from the Defense Advanced Research Projects Agency (DARPA/IPTO) under the GALE program, DARPA/CMO Contract No. HR0011-06-C-0022, subcontract from BBN, Inc. Any opinions, findings, and conclusions or recommendations expressed in this material are those of the authors and do not necessarily reflect the views of the National Science Foundation.

## References

Jinho D. Choi, Martha Palmer, and Nianwen Xue. 2009. Using parallel propbanks to enhance word-alignments. In *Proceedings of ACL-IJCNLP workshop on Linguistic Annotation (LAW'09)*, pages 121–124.

Susanne Ekeklint and Joakim Nivre. 2007. A dependency-based conversion of propbank. In *Proceedings of NODALIDA workshop on Building Frame Semantics Resources for Scandinavian and Baltic Languages (FRAME'07)*, pages 19–25.

Daniel Gildea. 2004. Dependencies vs. constituents for tree-based alignment. In *Proceedings of the Conference on Empirical Methods in Natural Language Processing (EMNLP'04)*, pages 214–221.

Jan Hajič, Massimiliano Ciaramita, Richard Johansson, Daisuke Kawahara, Maria Antònia Martí, Lluís Màrquez, Adam Meyers, Joakim Nivre, Sebastian Padó, Jan Štěpánek, Pavel Straňák, Mihai Surdeanu, Nianwen Xue, and Yi Zhang. 2009. The conll-2009 shared task: Syntactic and semantic dependencies in multiple languages. In *Proceedings of the 13th Conference on Computational Natural Language Learning (CoNLL'09)*, pages 1–18.

Richard Johansson and Pierre Nugues. 2007. Extended constituent-to-dependency conversion for english. In *Proceedings of the 16th Nordic Conference of Computational Linguistics (NODALIDA'07)*.

Richard Johansson. 2008. *Dependency-based Semantic Analysis of Natural-language Text*. Ph.D. thesis, Lund University.

Jason S. Kessler and Nicolas Nicolov. 2009. Targeting sentiment expressions through supervised ranking of linguistic configurations. In *Proceedings of the 3rd International AAAI Conference on Weblogs and Social Media (ICWSM'09)*.

Mitchell P. Marcus, Mary Ann Marcinkiewicz, and Beatrice Santorini. 1993. Building a large annotated corpus of english: The penn treebank. *Computational Linguistics*, 19(2):313–330.

Martha Palmer, Daniel Gildea, and Paul Kingsbury. 2005. The proposition bank: An annotated corpus of semantic roles. *Computational Linguistics*, 31(1):71–106.

Sameer S. Pradhan, Wayne Ward, Kadri Hacioglu, James H. Martin, and Daniel Jurafsky. 2004. Shallow semantic parsing using support vector machines. In *Proceedings of the Human Language Technology Conference/North American chapter of the Association for Computational Linguistics annual meeting (HLT/NAACL'04)*.

# Complex Predicates annotation in a corpus of Portuguese

**Iris Hendrickx, Amália Mendes, Sílvia Pereira, Anabela Gonçalves and Inês Duarte**
Centro de Linguística da Universidade de Lisboa, Lisboa, Portugal
`{iris, amalia.mendes}@clul.ul.pt`

**Abstract**

We present an annotation scheme for the annotation of complex predicates, understood as constructions with more than one lexical unit, each contributing part of the information normally associated with a single predicate. We discuss our annotation guidelines of four types of complex predicates, and the treatment of several difficult cases, related to ambiguity, overlap and coordination. We then discuss the process of marking up the Portuguese CINTIL corpus of 1M tokens (written and spoken) with a new layer of information regarding complex predicates. We also present the outcomes of the annotation work and statistics on the types of CPs that we found in the corpus.

## 1 Introduction

Complex predicates are predicates composed of more than one element but functionally equivalent to a single predicate. Examples of complex predicates (CPs) are constructions of verb+noun, like *have a rest*, *take a walk*, and constructions verb+verb, like the constructions with a causative verb in Portuguese, like *mandar ler o livro a alguém* 'make read the book to someone'. These constructions raise interesting questions regarding the aspectual, semantic and syntactic properties which underlie the relationship between the elements of the CP. There are different theoretical perspectives on the compositional nature of CPs. For example, in the case of constructions of the type verb+noun, the verb is either considered a light verb (Jespersen, 1949) or a support verb (Gross, 1981), in the sense that it has lost part or all of its meaning and has no predicative value in the construction, or as an auxiliary verb with aspectual properties (Abeillé et al., 1998).

Our hypothesis is that both elements of the CP seem to contribute to the properties of complex predicates, in such a way that the argument structure and the attribution of thematic roles are determined by both constituents through the combination of their thematic structures (Grimshaw, 1988). One has to address several important questions: is there a systematic relationship between the syntactic and semantic selection properties of the two elements? How do the argument structure of the light verb and the derived noun combine and contribute to define the complex predicate? To study these questions we annotated the Portuguese CINTIL corpus (Barreto et al., 2006) with a new layer on CPs. By taking into consideration different types of CPs and by using corpus data for our analysis of their properties, the objective is to present a unified approach to CP formation, along which the CP constructions available in Portuguese may be accounted for, namely in what concerns their lexico-syntactic properties and their interpretation.

Here we focus on the corpus annotation of complex predicates. This paper is structured as follows. In section 2 we discuss related work on the annotation of CPs in other languages. In section 3 we present a typology of complex predicates. In section 4 we detail our the annotation schema and also focus on several specific cases of CPs and the annotation labels for these cases. In section 5 we give more information about the CINTIL corpus and in 6 we show the outcomes of the annotations and present statistics on the types of CPs that we found in the corpus. We conclude in section 7.

## 2 Related Work

For other languages, people have proposed different representations for CPs and for some languages there are corpora available enhanced with CP labeling. The Prague TreeBank for Czech, which is based on a dependency grammar, labels CPs explicitly. A complex predicate is represented



*Proceedings of the Fourth Linguistic Annotation Workshop, ACL 2010*, pages 100–108,
Uppsala, Sweden, 15-16 July 2010. 

by two nodes: the verb node is assigned a functor according to the function of the entire complex predicate in the sentence structure; the nominal node is assigned the CPHR functor, which signals that it is a part of a multi-word predicate, and is represented as an immediate daughter of the node for the verbal component (Mikulová et al., 2006; Cinková and Kolářová, 2005).

For German there is an example corpus annotated with verb phrases and light verbs (Fellbaum et al., 2006). However, only idiomatic expressions are labeled in this German corpus while we focus on non-idiomatic CPs. Calzolari et al. (2002) treat support verb constructions (verb+noun), and focus their attention, just like we did in our approach, on constructions where the subject of the verb is a participant in the event denoted by the noun. Their objective is however not corpus annotation, but the creation of a computational lexicon of MWEs with both syntactic and semantic information.

Also the field of semantic or thematic role labeling investigates constructions of verb+noun, but it focuses on predicate-argument structures in general, while we focus on a specific type of relations. FrameNet uses frame semantics theory to represent such predicate-argument structures which also includes handling complex predicates (e.g. (Johnson and Fillmore, 2000)). For German, there exists a fully annotated corpus with semantic frames (Erk et al., 2003). The basis of the Framenet semantic annotation are conceptual *frames* expressing an event or object and the semantic arguments (*frame elements*) that are (obligatory or optional) parts of the frames. They also specifically address support verbs and observe that support verbs often occur with nouns expressing an event (Johansson and Nugues, 2006). In a Framenet semantic annotation, support verbs are not considered as parts of frames or as part of the frame elements, they are annotated with a specific 'support verb' label. We, on the contrary, view CP as one semantic and syntactic unit.

In Nombank, a distinction is made between idioms (which in principle are not marked) and light verb plus noun combinations, which are to be annotated, and criteria are given to make such distinction (English (Meyers, 2007), Chinese (Xue, 2006)). In (1) we show a NomBank annotation example of the sentence with a complex predicate.

Usually, CPs of the type verb+verb are treated as infinitive dependent clauses and are not annotated as CPs (cf. the Penn Treebank (Marcus et al., 1993) and the Portuguese treebank Cordial-SIN (Carrilho and Magro, 2009)).

(1) 'The campaign takes advantage of the eye-catching photography.'
SUPPORT = takes
REL = advantage
ARG0 = the campaign
ARG1 = of the eye-catching photography

## 3 Typology of complex predicates

We consider CPs as constructions sharing certain properties defined in Butt (1995). A complex predicate has: a multi-headed and complex argument structure; more than one lexical unit, each contributing part of the information normally associated with a single predicate and a grammatical functional structure equal to the one of a simple predicate. Several types of constructions are in accordance to this definition of CPs: (i) two main verbs, forming a restructuring construction, like *querer estudar* 'to want to study' (ii) two main verbs in a causative construction, like *fazer rir* 'to make laugh'; (iii) a light verb followed by a noun: *dar um passeio* 'to take a walk', *ter medo* 'to have fear'; (iv) a light verb followed by a secondary predicate: either an adjective, like *tornar a história credível* 'make the story believable', or a prepositional phrase, like *fazer x em pedaços* 'to make x into pieces'; (v) two concatenated verbs (serial verb constructions), like *O Pedro pegou e despediu-se* (lit: 'Pedro took and said goodbye'). This last construction is mostly restricted to the informal spoken register. Regarding constructions (i) and (ii) with two main verbs, it is generally assumed that these CPs include at least two verbs which behave as a single constituent under local phenomena such as Clitic Climbing or Long Object Movement (Kayne, 1975; Gonçalves, 2002; Gonçalves, 2003). Each one of the verbs preserves its own argument structure.

In the case of constructions (iii) involving a light verb and a noun derived from a verb, one of the most frequently referred property is the possibility of being paraphrased by the main verb from which the noun is derived (see example 2), although this is not a necessary condition.

(2) (a) *dar um contributo /contribuir*
'to give a contribution' / 'to contribute'
(b) *ter um desmaio / desmaiar*
'to have a blackout' / 'to faint'

Light verbs occurring in these constructions have a rather similar semantics across different languages and involve mostly verbs like *have*, *take* and *give* in English (Bowern, 2006) and *ter* 'to have', *dar* 'to give', *fazer* 'to make' in Portuguese. Furthermore, both the light verb and the derived noun contribute to predicate information and argument structure and theta-role assignment appear to be determined simultaneously by the two constituents. It is important to determine the exact nature of the semantic contribution of light verbs to the whole predicate and the similarities and differences between the light verb construction and its lexicalized verbal counterpart, if it exists.

## 4 Annotation system

The corpus annotation focused on four of the types of CPs listed in the previous section, excluding type (iv): constructions where a main verb is followed by a secondary predicate, due to time limitations. Constructions with a light verb (type (iii)) were consequently restricted to verb+noun. We only annotated constructions in which the subject of the CP controlled the event denotated by the noun. For example, constructions like *Mary gave a talk* where Mary is the one who is presenting, and not any other entity. We excluded cases where the subject does not seem to obligatorily control the event (e.g. *dar um título* 'to give a title').

We further restricted our annotation to a particular set of nouns:

- nouns derived from a verb, like *dar um passeio* 'to take a walk' (lit: 'to give a walk');
- nouns expressing an emotion, i.e., psych-nouns like *ter medo* 'to be afraid' (lit: 'to have fear');

Nouns derived from a verb are very common. For example, half of the nouns in the English Nombank corpus that have semantic frame elements are actually nominalizations from verbs as stated on the NomBank homepage[1].

The restrictions on the type of noun occurring in CPs lead to the exclusion of constructions with idiomatic meaning (like *dar a mão* 'to give a hand')[2].

The annotation guidelines follow the results of our study of CPs under a generative grammar framework, and are consequently theory-oriented. We didn't include for the moment semantic and aspectual information in our annotation of CPs. We have undertaken some work on the aspectual information conveyed by both light verb and noun and on the aspectual restrictions that hold between the two elements (Duarte et al. 2009) and we plan to latter partially integrate those findings in our annotation system.

We divided the annotation of the CPs in two main groups: verb+verb constructions (type (i), (ii), (v) as described in section 3) and verb+noun constructions (type (iii)). The verb+verb constructions are denoted with the tag [CV] and the noun+verb constructions with [CN]. Furthermore, inside the verb+verb category, we make distinctions between restructuring constructions (tagged as [CVR]), causative constructions ([CVC]) and constructions with coordinated verbs ([CVE]). Example 3 gives an illustration of each of these subtypes. For the verb+noun constructions we distinguish contexts with bare nouns ([CNB]) and contexts where a determiner precedes the noun (just tagged as [CN]) (cf.example 4).

(3) (a) porque nos [CVR]*queriam convidar*
because [they] us wanted to invite
'because they wanted to invite us'

(b) veio abalar estes alicerces espirituais [CVC]*fazendo traduzir* ao rapaz "Pucelle" de Voltaire
he shacked these spiritual foundations by making translate to the boy "Pucelle" by Voltaire
'he shacked these spiritual foundations by making the boy translate "Pucelle" by Voltaire'

(c) e [CVE]*vai* um *e conta* ao outro
and goes one and tells to the other
'and he tells the other'

(4) (a) Facto que leva a CGD a considerar que não [CNB]*tem obrigações* em relação aos trabalhadores.
'The fact that leads the CGD to believe that it doesn't have obligations towards the workers.'

(b) o erro de [CN]*fazer uma interpretação* literal
'the error of making a literal interpretation'

[1] http://nlp.cs.nyu.edu/ meyers/NomBank.html

[2] These are currently under study in the scope of a project on multi-word expressions in Portuguese.

There is also information on the typical position of the element inside the CP (position 1, 2, etc.), as well as on its contextual position in the corpus (B=Beginning, I=Intermediate, E=End). With typical position we refer to the ordering of elements of the CP in its canonical form, corresponding to the descriptions and examples given in section 3. The typical and contextual position can differ as is illustrated in example 5.

(5) depois de *um*[CN2_B] *aviso*[CN3_I] *dado*[CN1_E]
'after a warning was given'

The elements forming the CP may not be contiguous and in that case only the elements pertaining to the CP are annotated. In example 6 the adverb *logo* 'immediately' is not a part of the CP and consequently is not annotated. Also, only the main verb is annotated and not the auxiliary verbs which might occur (cf. the auxiliary *tinha* 'had' is not tagged in 7).

(6) *dar*[CN1_B] logo *uma*[CN2_I] *ajuda*[CN3_E]
give immediately an help
'give help immediately'

(7) tinha *dado*[CN1_B] *uma*[CN2_I] *ajuda*[CN3_E]
had given an help
'had given help'

The categories and tags which compose our annotation system provide an overview of different contexts of CP constructions encountered in authentic data, which is a major goal of this annotation project.

The process of annotation was based on concordances extraction using lists of verbs entering restructuring constructions (type (i)), given in 8 and lists of causative verbs (type (ii)), shown in 9. Considering the large candidate list of possible CPs with light verbs, the annotation first focused on constructions with verbs *ter*, *dar* and *fazer* followed by a noun. For CPs with coordinated verbs (type (v)), a list of typical verbs entering the construction was elaborated, shown in 10, and applied to a search pattern (two verbs separated by a conjunction and possibly by some other lexical element). Concordances retrieved were then manually evaluated.

(8) *querer* 'want'
*desejar* 'desire'
*costumar* 'use to'
*tentar* 'try'
*pretender* 'want'
*tencionar* 'make plan to'
*conseguir* 'succeed'

(9) *mandar* 'order'
*deixar* 'let'
*fazer* 'make'

(10) *ir* 'go'
*agarrar* 'grab'
*pegar* 'hold'

Information on the categories, tags, restrictions and special cases (discussed in section 4.1) were described in the annotation guidelines.

### 4.1 Special cases

The observation of corpus data pointed to a range of specific situations requiring new categories and tags.

#### 4.1.1 Ambiguity

Some contexts in the corpus are clearly cases of CPs and are straightforwardly annotated as CPs, like restructuring constructions with clitic climbing (cf. 3a) and causative constructions with two internal arguments like in example 3b. Also example 11 is a clear case where the subject of the lower verb occurs as an indirect object (*aos cidadãos em geral*) and the that-clause which is the direct object of the lower verb (*que a fotocópia corresponde a um acto de pirataria inaceitável*) is reanalyzed as the direct object of the CP. Other clear cases of CPs are pronominal passives where the direct object of the second verb occurs as subject of the higher verb (Long Object Movement), producing subject-verb agreement (this construction was not encountered in the corpus, a possible example would be (12)).

(11) *fazer perceber* aos cidadãos em geral, que a fotocópia corresponde a um acto de pirataria inaceitável
'make understand to all citizens that a photocopy corresponds to an act of unacceptable piratery'

(12) *Querem-se estudar* os problemas.
'want-3PL.PASS study the problems'

Other contexts are clearly not instances of CPs and as such are not annotated. This is the case of constructions with a restructuring verb without clitic climbing, as in example 13.

(13) *querem perpetuá* -lo
'[they] want to perpetuate it'

But many CPs can have an ambiguous interpretation between a complex predicate construction and a construction with a main verb and an embedded infinitive clause, and we found it relevant to mark those constructions with the information of ambiguity (tag [_VINF]). For example, contexts similar to (12) but with a singular NP, as in example 14a, can receive two possible structural interpretations: the NP *justiça* 'justice' can be interpreted as the subject of the higher verb (a long object movement construction and consequently a CP construction) or as the direct object of the second verb (an impersonal construction). In (14b) we show how we annotated this example using a label expressing the ambiguity.

(14) (a) Pretende-se cometer justiça.
Aims-IMP to commit justice [IMP = Impersonal]
'One wants to commit justice'
(b) Pretende[CVR_VINF1_B]-se cometer[CVR_VINF2_E] (...) justiça

### 4.1.2 Overlapping CPs

Beside these examples, the corpus includes constructions in which one of the elements of a CP (restructuring type) is also part of another CP (causative type), so that two CPs are in fact superposed. In these cases, the element which is part of both CPs receives a double tag (see the verb *deixar* in example 15).

(15) não o queriam[CVR1_B]
deixar[CVR2_E][CVC_VINF1_B]
fugir[CVC_VINF2_E]
not him want to let escape
'they didn't want to let him escape'

## 4.2 Coordination inside CPs

There are also occurrences of coordination inside the CP, possible when two CPs share the same higher verb (light verb, restructuring or causative verb). The coordinated elements of the CP are tagged with extra information on their first or second position in the coordinated structure (tags [CVR2_1] and [CVR2_2], cf. 16). The coordination is usually marked with a conjunction, like in example 16 with a restructuring construction, equivalent in fact to two CPs *querer ouvir* and *querer registar*. However, in the spoken subpart of the corpus there may be no overt connector and just a slight pause as in example 17 (the pause is marked by "/").

(16) para quem o quis[CVR1_B]
ouvir[CVR2_1_E] e eventualmente
registar[CVR2_2_E]
to whom him wanted to listen and eventually register
'to whom wanted to listen and eventually register him'

(17) nós temos[CN1_B] uma[CN2_1_I]
tristeza[CN3_1_E] / uma[CN2_2_I]
frustração[CN3_2_E] muito grande
'we have a sadness / a frustration very deep'

## 5 Corpus constitution

The CINTIL corpus[3] contains 1 million tokens and was compiled using different existing resources developed at the Centre of Linguistics of the University of Lisbon (CLUL): the written corpus Parole (Bacelar do Nascimento et al., 1998), the spoken corpus C-ORAL-ROM (Bacelar do Nascimento et al., 2005) and new written texts from the Reference Corpus of Contemporary Portuguese-CRPC (Bacelar do Nascimento, 2000), a large monitor corpus with over 300M words. One third of the corpus is composed of transcribed spoken materials (both formal and informal) and the remaining two thirds are composed of written materials.

This corpus has been previously annotated and manually revised (Barreto et al., 2006), in a joint project of NLX-FCUL[4] and CLUL. The CINTIL corpus has important features, compared to other resources for Portuguese, namely the depth of its linguistic information, its size, range of domains and sources, and level of accuracy. The annotation comprises information on part-of-speech (POS), lemma and inflection, multi-word expressions pertaining to the class of adverbs and to the closed POS classes, and multi-word proper names (for

[3]The CINTIL corpus is available for online queries (//cintil.ul.pt) through the use of a concordancer adapted to Portuguese.
[4]http://nlx.di.fc.ul.pt

named entity recognition), together with specific categories for spoken texts (like Emphasis (/EMP), Extra-linguistic (/EL), Fragment (/FRG)). Below is an excerpt of the POS annotation and lemmatization where tags follow the order [lemma/ POS category # inflected features [named entity] ].

(18) pretende/PRETENDER/vpi#3s[O]
reconverter/RECONVERTER/inf-nifl[O]
o/O/da#ms[O]
centro/CENTRO/cn#ms[B-LOC]
de/de/prep[I-LOC]
Matosinhos/MATOSINHOS/pnm[I-LOC]

In the next section we present the results of the addition of a new layer of information on complex predicates to this corpus.

## 6 Annotation results

The annotation of the whole corpus was done manually by one MA student who was well familiar with the task. A concordancer was used to identify possible complex predicate structures. Difficult cases were picked out and discussed with two other persons to reach an agreement on the annotation. Several of such hard cases were then added to the annotation guidelines. After manual annotation, the annotations were checked with a script to check the consistency of the labels and to correct some minor errors.

To validate the annotations we performed a small experiment. A second person annotated a small sample of sentences independently of the first annotator. Next we compute the inter-annotator agreement on the two different annotations. This gives us some indication of the difficulty of the task and the consistency of the labeling of the first annotator. We computed the kappa statistics (Cohen, 1960) on the complex predicates labeled by the two annotators in 50 sentences. We acknowledge that this is just a very small sample, yet this gave us a kappa value of .81 which indicates a high overlap between both annotations.

In Table 1 we list the frequencies of the complex predicates found in the CINTIL corpus. In total we found 1981 CPs, the majority (1292 CPs) are combinations of a verb with a noun. For the verb predicates the table clearly shows that these cases are mostly ambiguous. We also looked at the occurrences of the more complex events described in section 4.1 presented in table 2. We encountered 28 cases of coordinated complex predicates

| label | written | spoken | total |
|---|---|---|---|
| CV total | 470 | 219 | 689 |
| CVR | 34 | 47 | 81 |
| CVC | 13 | 3 | 16 |
| CVE | 0 | 1 | 1 |
| CVR_VINF | 300 | 143 | 443 |
| CVC_VINF | 123 | 25 | 148 |
| CN total | 706 | 586 | 1292 |
| CNB | 353 | 213 | 566 |
| CN_ | 353 | 373 | 726 |
| total | 1176 | 805 | 1981 |

Table 1: Number of annotated complex predicates in the spoken and written parts of the CINTIL corpus.

| label | written | spoken | total |
|---|---|---|---|
| CV ambiguity | 423 | 168 | 591 |
| coordination | 15 | 13 | 28 |
| overlap | 6 | 10 | 16 |

Table 2: Zooming in on the frequencies of the special cases (sec. 4.1) in the CINTIL corpus.

and 14 times a verb was part of two different CPs at the same time. The CPs with verb+verb constructions show a very high number of ambiguous occurrences. It is clear that in most cases the context of such a construction does not provide sufficient evidence to disambiguate it. We only found a handful of cases in which the context did resolve the ambiguity.

We also looked into the ordering of the CPs in the corpus. To what extent do the CPs occur in their canonical form? Table 3 shows the results. We found a change in ordering only for the verb+noun CPs. For the CPs with a bare noun we found only 9 cases of non-canonical order. For CPs with an NP with a determiner-noun combination we did see more variation in order, of the total number of 726 occurrences, 16.9% had a different word order.

We also wanted to see if all the verbs used to identify CP constructions (verbs listed in 8 9, 10 plus the 3 light verbs) were equally present in the CINTIL corpus or if there was any significant lexical difference. We present the results of the frequencies of the verbs of each CP type in Tables 4, 5, 7 and 6. When comparing the list in

| label | written | spoken | total | % of occ |
|---|---|---|---|---|
| CN | 86 | 37 | 123 | 16.9 |
| CNB | 7 | 2 | 9 | 1.6 |

Table 3: Number of complex predicates that do not follow their canonical form. The last column presents the percentage of the total number of CN or CNB occurrences that are not in their canonical form.

| CVC | written | spoken |
|---|---|---|
| deixar | 1 | 0 |
| fazer | 11 | 0 |
| mandar | 1 | 3 |
| total | 13 | 3 |

Table 5: frequencies of the main verb in CVC complex predicates.

8 with the verbs in Table 4, we can see that the verbs *desejar* and *tencionar* were included for the query of restructuring predicates but do not occur in the corpus in CP constructions. Out of the five verbs, *querer* 'want' is clearly the most frequent in both written and spoken sub-parts of the corpus. Apart from *conseguir* 'succeed', the rest of the verbs have very low frequencies, and *costumar* 'use to' is only present in the spoken corpus, while the opposite is true for *pretender* 'want', a verb associated to a more formal register. In causative constructions with CPs (Table 5 ), the verb *fazer* 'make' is clearly prominent in the written corpus, although it does not occur in the spoken one. The only causative verb in CP constructions in the spoken corpus is *mandar* 'order'. In causative constructions, contrary to restructuring ones, the genre seems to influence the lexical choice of the higher verb of the complex predicate.

| CVR | written | spoken |
|---|---|---|
| conseguir | 6 | 7 |
| costumar | 0 | 3 |
| pretender | 2 | 0 |
| querer | 25 | 34 |
| tentar | 1 | 3 |
| total | 34 | 47 |

Table 4: frequencies of the main verb in CVR complex predicates.

The verb+noun constructions are divided in two different tables, according to our categorization in bare nouns (Table 6) and nouns preceded by a determiner (Table 7). The same three verbs enter the constructions although their frequencies are different in the two different structures: the verb *fazer* is clearly dominant when followed by a noun preceded by a determiner, while the verb *ter* is the more frequent light verb with bare nouns.

| CNB | written | spoken |
|---|---|---|
| dar | 69 | 27 |
| fazer | 87 | 52 |
| ter | 197 | 134 |
| total | 353 | 213 |

Table 6: frequencies of the main verb in CNB complex predicates

| CN | written | spoken |
|---|---|---|
| dar | 79 | 34 |
| fazer | 193 | 231 |
| ter | 81 | 108 |
| total | 353 | 373 |

Table 7: frequencies of the main verb in CN complex predicates.

## 7 Final remarks

We presented the annotation process of complex predicates in the CINTIL corpus. We first explained our theoretical framework and gave a broad typology of CPs. Next we detailed the annotation schema that we used and zoomed in on some difficult cases. We presented the outcomes of the annotation work. We gave a first broad statistical analysis of the annotations, and next we zoomed in on some insights in characteristics of CPs in Portuguese that this new annotation layer has offered. This new resource provides diversified authentic data that will enable a general overview of CP constructions and can shed new light on the Syntax-Semantics interface. It is also an important part for forthcoming tasks of syntactic and semantic corpus annotation.

In the future we plan to further analyze the results of the verb+verb types of CPs. The large number of ambiguous cases and the few contexts which give us definite clues for categorizing the sequence as a CP challenges our concept of complex predicates. The causative and restructuring constructions require more attention and further study. As to the verb+noun constructions, we want to examine the contexts with and without determiner to see if the same CP can occur in both structures. We also want to look further into the high frequency of specific light verbs with bare nouns and the possible relationship with the semantics of the light verbs. In this study we restricted the annotation to a particular group of light verbs. In a next step we would like to look at a broader list to try to establish the necessary properties to categorize a verb as a light verb. We plan to address, for example, certain contexts of psych-nouns like *sentir medo* 'feel fear', *experienciar uma profunda emoção* 'experience a deep emotion', where the predicative nature of the verb is unclear. We also plan to enlarge our description and annotation of CPs to include idiomatic expressions with light verbs.

## References


A. Abeillé, D. Godard, and I. Sag, 1998. *Complex Predicates in Nonderivational Syntax*, volume 30 of *Syntax and Semantics*, chapter Two Kinds of Composition in French Complex predicates. San Diego Academic Press, San Diego.

M. F. P. Bacelar do Nascimento, P. Marrafa, L.A.S. Pereira, R. Ribeiro, R. Veloso, and L. Wittmann. 1998. Le-parole - do corpus à modelização da informação lexical num sistema-multifunção. In *Actas do XIII Encontro da Associação Portuguesa de Linguística, APL*, pages 115–134, Lisboa.

M. F. Bacelar do Nascimento, J. Bettencourt Gonçalves, R. Veloso, S. Antunes, F. Barreto, and R. Amaro, 2005. *C-ORAL-ROM: Integrated Reference Corpora for Spoken Romance Languages*, chapter The Portuguese Corpus, pages 163–207. Amsterdam/Philadelphia: John Benjamins Publishing Company, Studies in Corpus Linguistics. Editors: E. Cresti and M. Monegnia.

M. F. Bacelar do Nascimento, 2000. *Corpus, Méthodologie et Applications Linguistiques*, chapter Corpus de Référence du Portugais Contemporain, pages 25–30. H. Champion et Presses Universitaires de Perpignan, Paris. Editor: M. Bilger.

F. Barreto, A. Branco, E. Ferreira, A. Mendes, M. F. P. Bacelar do Nascimento, F. Nunes, and J. Silva. 2006. Open resources and tools for the shallow processing of portuguese. In *Proceedings of the 5th International Conference on Language Resources and Evaluation (LREC2006)*, Genoa, Italy.

C. Bowern. 2006. Inter theorical approaches to complex verb constructions: position paper. In *The Eleventh Biennal Rice University Linguistics Symposium*.

E. Carrilho and C. Magro, 2009. *Syntactic Annotation System Manual of corpus CORDIAL-SIN*. http://www.clul.ul.pt/sectores/variacao/cordialsin/Syntactic%20annotation%20manual.html.

S. Cinková and V. Kolářová. 2005. Nouns as components of support verb constructions in the prague dependency treebank. In *Insight into Slovak and Czech Corpus Linguistics*. Veda Bratislava.

J. Cohen. 1960. A coefficient of agreement for nominal scales. *Education and Psychological Measuremen*, 20:37–46.

K. Erk, A. Kowalski, S. Padó, and M. Pinkal. 2003. Towards a resource for lexical semantics: A large german corpus with extensive semantic annotation. In *Proceedings of the 41st Annual Meeting of the Association for Computational Linguistics*, pages 537–544, Sapporo, Japan, July. Association for Computational Linguistics.

C. Fellbaum, A. Geyken, A. Herold, F. Koerner, and G. Neumann. 2006. Corpus-based studies of german idioms and light verbs. *International Journal of Lexicography*, 19(4):349–360.

A. Gonçalves. 2002. The causee in the faire-inf construction of portuguese. *Journal of Portuguese Linguistics*.

A. Gonçalves. 2003. Defectividade funcional e predicados complexos em estruturas de controlo do português. In I. Castro and I. Duarte, editors, *Miscelnea de estudos em homenagem a Maria Helena Mira Mateus*, volume I. Imprensa Nacional-Casa da Moeda.

J. Grimshaw. 1988. Light verbs and marking. *Linguistic Inquiry*, 19(2):205–232.

M. Gross. 1981. Les bases empiriques de la notion de prédicat sémantique. *Langages*, 63:7–52.

O. Jespersen. 1949. *A Modern English Grammar on Historical Principles*. Londres: George Allen & Unwin; Copenhaga: Ejnar Munksgaard.

R. Johansson and P. Nugues. 2006. Automatic annotation for all semantic layers in FrameNet. In *Proceedings of EACL-2006*, Trento, Italy, April 15-16.

C. R. Johnson and C. J. Fillmore. 2000. The framenet tagset for frame-semantic and syntactic coding of predicate-argument structure. In *Proceedings of the 1st Meeting of the North American Chapter of the Association for Computational Linguistics (ANLP-NAACL 2000)*, pages 56–62, Seattle WA.

R. Kayne. 1975. *French Syntax: the Transformational Cycle*. The MIT Press, Cambridge, Mass.

M. Marcus, S. Santorini, and M. Marcinkiewicz. 1993. Building a Large Annotated Corpus of English: the Penn Treebank. *Computational Linguistics*, 19(2):313–330.

M.Butt. 1995. *The Structure of Complex Predicates in Urdu*. Stanford, CA: CSLI Publications.

A. Meyers. 2007. Annotation guidelines for nombank – noun argument structure for propbank. Technical report, New York University. http://nlp.cs.nyu.edu/meyers/nombank/nombank-specs-2007.pdf.

M. Mikulová, A. Bémová, J. Hajič, E. Hajicková, and J. Havelka et al. 2006. Annotation on the tectogrammatical level in the prague dependency treebank annotation manual. technical report. Technical Report UFAL CKL Technical Report TR-2006-35, ÚFAL MFF UK, Prague, Czech Rep.

N. Xue. 2006. Annotating the predicate-argument structure of chinese nominalizations. In *Proceedings of the LREC 2006*, pages 1382–1387, Genoa, Italy.

# Using an online tool for the documentation of Ȩdó language

**Ota Ogie**
Norwegian University of Science and Technology (NTNU)
ota.ogie@hf.ntnu.no

**Abstract**

Language documentation is important as a tool for preservation of endangered languages and making data available to speakers and researchers of a language. A data base such as TypeCraft is important for typology studies both for well documented languages as well as little documented languages and is a valid tool for comparison of languages. This requires that linguistic elements must be coded in a manner that allows comparability across widely varying language data. In this paper, I discuss how I have used the coding system in TypeCraft for the documentation of data from Ȩdó language, a language belonging to the Edoid group of the Benue-Congo subfamily of the Volta-Congo language family and spoken in Mid-Western Nigeria, West Africa. The study shows how syntactic, semantic and morphological properties of multi-verb constructions in Ȩdó (Benue-Congo) can be represented in a relational database.

## 1. Introduction

In this paper[1], I show some ways in which I am using a shared methodology in my research on multi-verb constructions. My research is centered around the language Ȩdó, spoken in Mid-Western Nigeria, Ga and Akan (kwa), and the tool is the system TypeCraft, which has been developed in the ISK department, NTNU and first documented in Beermann and Prange (2006).

Ȩdó language belongs to the Niger-Congo, Atlantic-Congo, Volta-Congo, Benue-Congo-Edoid language family. The Ediod language family consists of 33 languages and 19 of these languages have either very little documentation or no documentation available.

Multi-verb constructions are constructions in which the verbs in series must function as independent verbs in simple constructions, with at least one shared argument and no marking of syntactic dependency.

The paper shows how syntactic, semantic and morphological properties of multi-verb constructions in Ȩdó (Benue-Congo) can be represented in a relational database and the development of annotation standards that contribute to contrastive and typological research. The analysis is extended to multi-verb constructions in the following languages of the Niger-Congo: Ga and Akan (Kwa).

## 2. TypeCraft

TypeCraft is a tool for typological analysis that allows for annotation, classification and search of data along different morphological, syntactic, semantic and pragmatic criteria. In annotating it is important to have annotation schemes that allow for typological and contrastive studies.

In this paper I use an annotation scheme for verbal constructions currently being developed at NTNU and documented in Hellan and Dakubu (2009). Syntactic and semantic information about construction types are provided by templates composed by labels. The basic structural parts of a template are referred to as **slots** that are separated by hyphens. A template with a verbal head can consist of maximal 7 slots; (1) POS of the head, and diathesis information; (2) valence specification; (3) dependent specification; (4) participant roles; (5) aspect and aktionsart; (6)

[1] I thank Professor Lars Hellan, NTNU Norway for his comments on earlier versions of this paper.



*Proceedings of the Fourth Linguistic Annotation Workshop, ACL 2010*, pages 109–112,
Uppsala, Sweden, 15-16 July 2010. 

situation type; (7) provides a linking type between slot 6 situation type and the specifications in slots 2-4. Slots 1 and 2 are obligatorily filled, the others not. (cf. Hellan and Dakubu, 2009). At present annotation of the construction labels is manual and not incorporated into the TypeCraft. However TypeCraft provides a construction tier where this information can be incorporated.

## 3. Sentence level and word level annotation

TypeCraft provides a set of glosses for syntactic and semantic coding and a set of parameters along which sentences may be classified that allow for standardized annotation and cross linguistic comparison as illustrated in figure1:

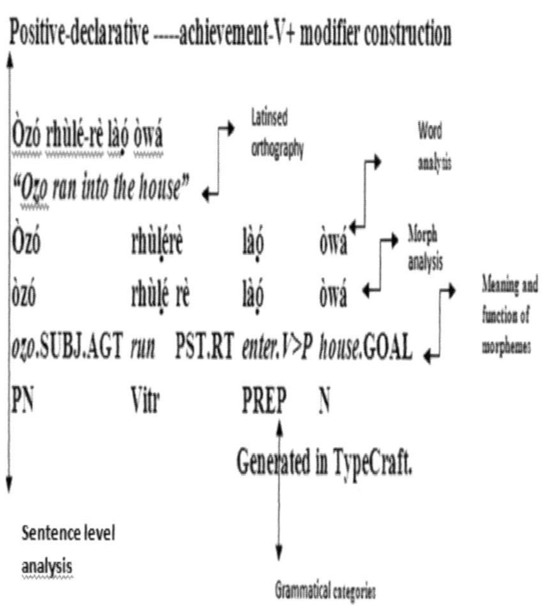


figure1: Word and sentence level annotation

### 3.1 Word level

Word level annotation allows for analysis of predicates in terms of syntactic and semantic properties including information about the subcategorization properties and argument structure of predicates.

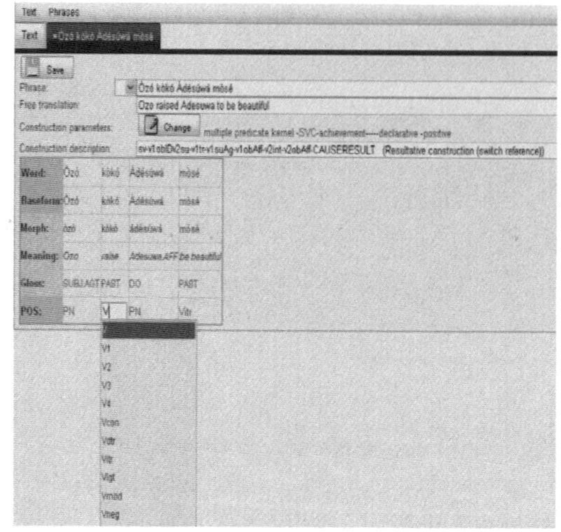

Figure2: Text editor in TypeCraft showing word level annotation

Type craft features 7 tiers that provide information at the word level as shown in the Ẹ̀dó example below.

(1). Ẹ̀dó
Construction parameters: TransitiveVerb-accomplishment-----declarative -positive
Construction labels: v-tr-suAg_obThincrem-COMPLETED_MONODEVMT

**Ọ̀ gbẹ̀n-nẹ́ èbé**

*"He/she wrote books"*

| | | | |
|---|---|---|---|
| Ọ̀ | gbẹ̀nnẹ́ | | èbé |
| ọ̀ | gbẹ̀n | nẹ́ | èbé |
| 3SG.SUBJ.NOM.AGT | *write* | PL.PST.H | *book*.DO.TH |
| PRON | V | | CN |

Generated in TypeCraft

The construction labels are explained as follows: *v* in Slot1 in the example above states that the head of the construction is a verb. *tr* in Slot2 states that the verb is transitive, *suAg_obThincrem* in Slot 4 states that the NP that is the subject of the construction bears an agent theta role and the object an incremental theme theta role. Lastly slot 5 gives the information that the aktionsart of the construction is completed monodevelopment.

### 3.2 Sentence level

TypeCraft provides a set of global tags at the sentence level that allows for classification in terms of syntactic and semantic automatically generated construction parameters such as constituent type, core constituent vs adjunct, transitivity, thematic roles, situation and aspect types, propositional types and polarity. Polarity is based on the assumption that States Of Affairs (SOA) comes in pairs: positive and negative. Figure 3 is used as illustration:

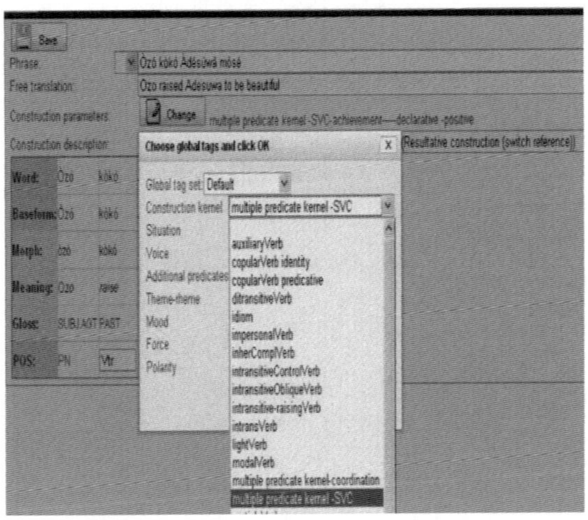

Figure3: Text editor in TypeCraft showing sentence level annotation

(2). **Ẹ̀dó**

Construction parameters: multiple predicate kernel -SVC-achievement-----declarative -positive

Construction labels: *svSuObIDALLsuAgobAff*-v1tr-v2tr-EVENTSEQ

**Òzó lé ìzé khiẹ́n**

*"Ozo cooked rice and sold"*

| | | | |
|---|---|---|---|
| Òzó | lé | ìzé | khiẹ́n |
| òzó | lé | ìzé | khiẹ́n |
| *Ozo*.SUBJ.AGT | *cook*.PST.H | *rice.AFF*.DO | *sell*.PST.H |
| PN | V | N | V |

Generated in TypeCraft.

The construction parameter is explained as follows: the global tags *multiple predicate kernel -SVC-* provides information about constituent type, *achievement* provides information about situation and aspect types, *declarative* provides information about propositional types and *positive* about polarity.

The construction labels have the following structure: Area1 (in italics for ease of exposition) gives the global labels, the number of verbs in series *(ie sv, sv3, sv4 )* as well as argument sharing information (coded by the label *IDALL*) and information about thematic relations holding across the verb in series. Area 2 gives the valence information as well as information about grammatical function and thematic roles (underlined for ease of exposition). Information about the situation type of the construction is provided by Area 3 and is written in capital letters.

Information about tense, aspect, mood and negation is also provided by area 1 in the construction labels. Sharing of these features across verbs in series is represented as with sharing of arguments as in example (3) from Akan below.

(3). **Akan**

Construction parameters: multiple predicate kernel -SVC-achievement-----declarative -positive

Construction labels:

*svsuAspIDALLsuAgaspCompl*-v1tr-v1obAff-v2intr- CAUSERESULT

**Ama twe-e Kofi hwe-e fam**

*"Ama pulled Kofi and fell (Ama fell) (covert reference subject sharing) "*

| | | | | |
|---|---|---|---|---|
| Ama | twee | Kofi | hwee | fam |
| ama | twe e | kofi | hwe e | fam |
| *Ama*.SUBJ.AGT | *pull* COMPL | *kofi.AFF*.DO | *fall*.COMPL | *under* |
| PN | Vtr | PN | Vitr | |

Generated in TypeCraft.

With respect to the global labels in area 1, Hellan and Dakubu (2009) uses also the global label *ev* to represent Extended Verb Complexes and the label *pv* for preverbs in EVCs. In addition, to the labeling conventions used by Hellan and Dakubu (2009) for SVCs (*sv*) and EVCs (*ev, pv*), the following global labels are introduced to account for the range of multi-verb constructions in my data.

- cc – covert co-ordination
- mvc- multi-verb construction
- mc- modifier construction

## 4. Text , phrasal and construction search

TypeCraft allows for search using different word level and sentence level parameters. This facilitates comparative analysis in multi-verb constructions. For example, argument sharing is a property that identifies types of multi-verb constructions. A search using the construction label *svsuObIDALL* is used as illustration. The result gives an output of serial verb constructions in Ẹ̀dó and Ga consisting of two verbs in series with the subject and object arguments of the verbs in series sharing reference:

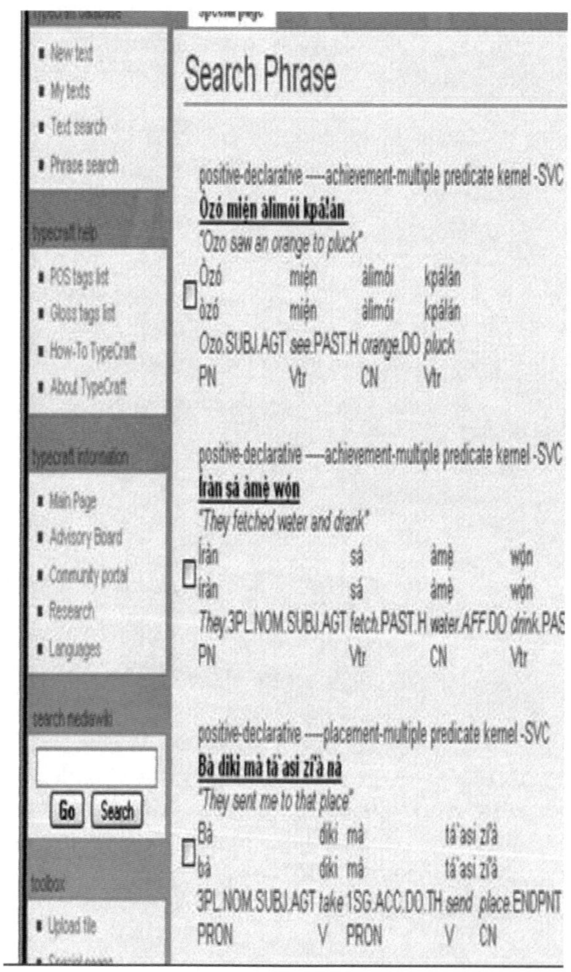


Figure 4: Search for phrase using global tag *svsuObIDALL*

The standardized annotation, search parameters and online nature of TypeCraft makes it advantageous compared to toolbox, a linguistic data management file based system used by many linguists in the documentation of African languages.

## 5. Conclusion

Standardized annotations and online databases such as TypeCraft aid linguists and speakers of a language in research, preservation of languages and in producing literacy materials that aid education and literacy. My research on multi-verb constructions in Ẹ̀dó is the first in-depth annotation for Ẹ̀dó and will be easily available for language researchers/teachers/students all over the world.

## 6. References

Beermann, Dorothee and Atle Prange. 2006. "Annotating and archiving Natural Language Paradigms online", presentation at the *Texas Linguistic Society Annual Conference.* Austin, Texas. 2006.

Hellan, Lars and Dakubu , Mary Esther Kropp. 2009. Identifying verb constructions cross-linguistically,*Studies in the Languages of the Volta Basin 6. Part 3.* Accra Ghana University Press 2009.

Ogie, Ota 2009. Multi-verb constructions in Edo. PhD dissertation. Norwegian University of Science and Technology. Trondheim. Norway. Also to appear in VDM publishers. Germany.

Ogie, Ota . 2009. In-depth annotation of multi-verb constructions in Èdó. http://www.typecraft.org.NTNU.

Ogie, Ota . 2009. Multi-verb constructions in Edo. http://www.typecraft.org.NTNU.

Ogie, Ota 2009. An annotation tool for less-resourced languages. Presented at The Nordic African Days 2009. Africa- in search for alternatives. Trondheim 1-3 October 2009. The Nordic African Institute.

Ogie, Ota & Dorothee Beermann 2009.Typecraft Software for the documentation of minority languages. Presented at ISFITovation February 26th 2009. Slides 29- 44. http://itovation.wordpress.com/2009/02/26/watch-isfitovation-live/. NTNU, Trondheim, Norway

# Cross-lingual Validity of PropBank in the Manual Annotation of French

**Lonneke van der Plas** **Tanja Samardžić** **Paola Merlo**

Linguistics Department
University of Geneva
Rue de Candolle 5, 1204 Geneva
Switzerland
{Lonneke.vanderPlas,Tanja.Samardzic,Paola.Merlo}@unige.ch

## Abstract

Methods that re-use existing mono-lingual semantic annotation resources to annotate a new language rely on the hypothesis that the semantic annotation scheme used is cross-lingually valid. We test this hypothesis in an annotation agreement study. We show that the annotation scheme can be applied cross-lingually.

## 1 Introduction

It is hardly a controversial statement that elegant language subtleties and powerful linguistic imagery found in literary writing are lost in translation. Yet, translation preserves enough meaning across language pairs to be useful in many applications and for many text genres.

The belief that this layer of meaning which is preserved across languages can be formally represented and automatically calculated underlies methods that use parallel corpora for the automatic generation of semantic annotations through cross-lingual transfer (Padó, 2007; Basili et al., 2009).

A methodology similar in spirit — re-use of the existing resources in a different language — has also been applied in developing manually annotated resources. Monachesi et al. (2007) annotate Dutch sentences using the PropBank annotation scheme (Palmer et al., 2005), while Burchardt et al. (2009) use the FrameNet framework (Fillmore et al., 2003) to annotate a German corpus. Instead of building special lexicons containing the specific semantic information needed for the annotation for each language separately, which is a complex and time-consuming endeavour in itself, these approaches rely on the lexicons already developed for English.

In this paper, we hypothesize that the level of abstraction that is necessary to develop a semantic lexicon/ontology for a *single language* based on *observable linguistic behaviour* — that is a mono-lingual, item-specific annotation — is cross-linguistically valid. We test this hypothesis by manually annotating French sentences using the PropBank frame files developed for English.

It has been claimed that semantic parallelism across languages is smaller when using the PropBank semantic annotations instead of the FrameNet scheme, because FrameNet is more abstract and less verb-specific (Padó, 2007). We are working with the PropBank annotation scheme, contrary to other works that use the FrameNet scheme, such as Padó (2007) and Basili et al. (2009). We choose this annotation for two main reasons. First, the primary use of our annotation is to serve as a gold standard in the task of syntactic-semantic parsing. FrameNet does not have a properly sampled hand-annotated corpus of English, by design. So we cannot use it for this task. Second, in Merlo and Van der Plas (2009), the semantic annotations schemes of PropBank and VerbNet (Kipper, 2005) are compared, based on annotation of the SemLink project (Loper et al., 2007). The authors conclude that PropBank is the preferred annotation for a joint syntactic-semantic setting.

If the PropBank annotation scheme is cross-lingually valid, annotators can reach a consensus and can do so swiftly. Thus, cross-lingual validity is measured by how well-defined the manual annotation task is (inter-annotator agreement) and by how hard it is to reach an agreement (pre- and post-consensus inter-annotator agreement). In addition, we measure the impact of the level of abstraction of the predicate labels. Conversely, how often labels do not transfer and distributions of disagreements are indicators of lack of parallelism across languages that we study both by quantitative and qualitative analysis.

To preview the results, we find that the PropBank annotation scheme developed for English can be applied for a large portion of French sen-



*Proceedings of the Fourth Linguistic Annotation Workshop, ACL 2010*, pages 113–117,
Uppsala, Sweden, 15-16 July 2010. 

tences without adjustments, which confirms its cross-lingual validity. A high level of inter-annotator agreement is reached when the verb-specific PropBank labels are replaced by less fine-grained verb classes after annotating. Non-parallel cases are mostly due to idioms and collocations.

## 2 Materials and Methods

Our choices of formal representation and of labelling scheme are driven by the goal of producing useful annotations for syntactic-semantic parsing in a setting based on an aligned corpus. In the following subsections we describe the annotation scheme and procedure, the corpus, and phases of annotation.

### 2.1 The PropBank Annotation Framework

We use the PropBank scheme for the manual annotations. PropBank is a linguistic resource that contains information on the semantic structure of sentences. It consists of a one-million-word corpus of naturally occurring sentences annotated with semantic structures and a lexicon (the PropBank frame files) that lists all the predicates (verbs) that can be found in the annotated sentences and the sets of semantic roles they introduce.

Predicates are marked with labels that specify the sense of the verb in the particular sentence. Arguments are marked with the labels A0 to A5. The labels A0 and A1 have approximately the same value with all verbs. They are used to mark instances of typical AGENTS (A0) and PATIENTS (A1). The value of other numbers varies across verbs. Modifiers are annotated in PropBank with the label AM. This label can have different extensions depending on the semantic type of the constituent, for example *locatives* and *adverbials*.

### 2.2 Annotation Procedure

Annotators have access to PropBank frame files and guidelines adapted for the current task. The frame files provide verb-specific descriptions of all possible semantic roles and illustrate these roles with examples as shown for the verb *paid* in (1) and the verb senses of *pay* in Table 1. Annotators need to look up each verb in the frame files to be able to label it with the right verb sense and to be able to allocate the arguments consistently.

(1) [$_{A0}$ The Latin American nation] has [$_{REL-PAY.01}$ paid] [$_{A1}$ very little] [$_{A3}$ on its debt] [$_{AM-TMP}$ since early last year].

| Frame | Semantic roles |
|---|---|
| pay.01 | A0: payer or buyer<br>A1: money or attention<br>A2: person being paid, destination of attention<br>A3: commodity, paid for what |
| pay.02<br>*pay off* | A0: payer<br>A1: debt<br>A2: owed to whom, person paid |
| pay.03<br>*pay out* | A0: payer or buyer<br>A1: money or attention<br>A2: person being paid, destination of attention<br>A3: commodity, paid for what |
| pay.04 | A1: thing succeeding or working out |
| pay.05<br>*pay off* | A1: thing succeeding or working out |
| pay.06<br>*pay down* | A0: payer<br>A1: debt |

Table 1: The PropBank lexicon entry for *pay*.

In our cross-lingual setting, annotators used the English PropBank frame files to annotate the French sentences. This means that for every predicate they find in the French sentence, they need to translate it, and find an English verb sense that is applicable to the French verb. If an appropriate entry cannot be found in the frame files for a given predicate, the annotator is instructed to use the "dummy" label for the predicate and fill in the roles according to their own insights.

For the annotation of sentences we use an adaptation of the user-friendly, freely available Tree Editor (TrEd, Pajas and Štěpánek, 2008). The tool shows the syntactic analysis and the plain sentence in the same window allowing the user to add semantic arcs and labels to the nodes in the syntactic dependency tree.

The decision to show syntactic information is merely driven by the fact that we want to guide the annotator in selecting the heads of phrases during the annotation process. The sentences are parsed by a syntactic parser (Titov and Henderson, 2007) that we trained on syntactic dependency annotations for French (Candito et al., 2009). Although the parser is state-of-the-art (87.2% Labelled Attachment Score), in case of parse errors, we ask annotators to ignore the errors of the parser and put the label on the actual head.

### 2.3 Corpus

We selected the French sentences for the manual annotation from the parallel Europarl corpus (Koehn, 2005). Because translation shifts are known to pose problems for the automatic cross-lingual transfer of semantic roles (Padó, 2007) and for machine translation (Ozdowska and Way,

2009), and these are more likely to appear in indirect translations, we decided to select only those parallel sentences, for which we can infer from the labels used in Europarl that they are direct translations from English to French, or vice versa. We selected 1040 sentences for annotation (40 in total for the two training phases, 100 for calibration, and 900 for the main annotation phase.)[1]

### 2.4 Annotation Phases

The training procedure described in Figure 1 is inspired by the methodology indicated in Padó (2007). A set of 130 sentences were annotated manually by four annotators with very good proficiency in both French and English for the training and the calibration phase. The remaining 900 sentences are annotated by one annotator (out of those four), a trained linguist. Inter-annotator agreement was measured at several points in the annotation process marked with an arrow in Figure 1. The guidelines were adjusted after the training phase.

- Training phase
  -TrainingA: 10 sentences, all annotators together
  -TrainingB: 30 sentences, all annotators individually⇐
  -Reach consensus on Training B ⇐
- Calibration phase
  -100 sentences by main annotator, one third of those by each of the other 3 annotators ⇐
- Main annotation phase
  -900 sentences by main annotator

Figure 1: The annotation phases.

## 3 Results

Cross-lingual validity is measured by comparing inter-annotator agreement at several stages in the annotation, by measuring the agreement on less specific predicate labelling, and by a quantitative and qualitative analysis of non-parallel cases.

### 3.1 Inter-annotator Agreement for Several Annotation Phases

To assess the quality of the manual annotations we measured the agreement between annotators as the average F-measure of all pairs of annotators after each phase of the annotation procedure.[2] The first row of Table 2 shows that the task is hard. But the difference between the first row and the second row shows that there were many differences between annotators that could be resolved. After discussions and individual corrections the scores are between 91% and 95%. This indicates that the task is well-defined. Row three shows that the agreement in the calibration phase increases a lot compared to the last training phase (row 1). This might in part be due to the fact that the guidelines were adjusted by the end of the training phase, but could also be because the annotators are getting more acquainted to the task and the software.

| | Predicates | | Arguments | |
|---|---|---|---|---|
| | Lab. F | Unl. F | Lab. F | Unl. F |
| TrainingB | 46 | 85 | 62 | 75 |
| TrainingB(cons.) | 95 | 97 | 91 | 95 |
| Calibration | 59 | 93 | 69 | 84 |

Table 2: Percent inter-annotator agreement (F-measure) for labelled/unlabelled predicates and for labelled/unlabelled arguments

As expected, because annotators used the English PropBank frame files to annotate French verbs, the task of labelling predicates proved more difficult than labelling semantic roles. It results in the lowest agreement scores overall. In the following subsections we study the sources of disagreement in predicate labelling in more detail.

### 3.2 Inter-annotator Agreement in Predicate Labellings

Predicate labels in PropBank apply to particular verb senses, for example *walk.01* for the first sense of the verb *walk*. Even though the senses are coarser than, for example, the senses in WordNet (Fellbaum, 1998), the labels are rather specific. This specificity possibly poses problems when working in a cross-lingual setting.

We compare the agreement reached using PropBank verb sense labels with the agreement reached using the verb classifications from VerbNet (Kipper, 2005) and the mapping to PropBank labels as provided in the type mappings of the SemLink project[3] (Loper et al., 2007). If two annotators used two different predicate labels to annotate the

[1] As usual practice in preprocessing for automatic alignment, the datasets were tokenised and lowercased and only sentence pairs corresponding to a 1-to-1 alignment with lengths ranging from 1 to 40 tokens on both French and English sides were considered.

[2] It is a known fact that measuring annotator agreement using the kappa score is problematic in categorisation tasks that do not have a fixed number of items and categories (Burchardt et al., 2006). The F-measure is a well-known measure used for the evaluation of many task such as syntactic-semantic parsing, the task that is the motivation for this paper. The choice of the F-measure makes the comparison to the performance of the future parser easier.

[3] (http://verbs.colorado.edu/semlink/)

same verb, but those verb senses belong to the same verb class, we count those as correct[4].

The average inter-annotator agreement is relatively low when we compare the annotations on the PropBank verb sense level: 59%. However, at the level of verb classes, the inter-annotator agreement increases to 81%. This raises the issue of whether we should not label the predicates with verb classes instead of verb senses. By using PropBank labels for the manual annotation and replacing these with verb classes in post-processing, the benefits are two-fold: We are able to reach a high level of cross-lingual parallelism on the annotations, while keeping the manual annotation task as specific and less abstract as possible.

### 3.3 Analysis of Non-Parallel Cases

For a single annotator, the main measure of cross-lingual validity is the percentage of dummy predicates in the annotation. In the sentences from the calibration and the main annotation phase from the main annotator (1000 sentences in total), we find 130 predicates (tokens) for which the annotator used the "dummy" label.

Manual inspection reveals that the "dummy" label is mainly used for French multi-word expressions (82%), most of which can be translated by a single English verb (47%), whereas others cannot, because they are translated by a combination that includes a form of 'be' that is not annotated in PropBank (25%). The 47% of multi-word expressions that receive the "dummy" label show the annotator's reluctance to put a single verb label on a French multi-word expression. The annotation guidelines could be adapted to instruct annotators not to hesitate in such cases.

Similarly, collocations and idiomatic expressions are the main sources of disagreement in predicate labellings among annotators. We can conclude that, as shown in studies on other language pairs (Burchardt et al., 2009), collocations and idiomatic expressions were identified as verb uses where the verb's predicate label cannot be transferred directly from one language to another.

## 4 Discussion and Related Work

Burchardt et al. (2009) use English FrameNet to annotate a corpus of German sentences manually. They find that the vast majority of frames can be applied to German directly. However, around one third of the verb senses identified in the German corpus were not covered by FrameNet. Also, a number of German verbs were found to be underspecified. Finally, some problems related to treating particular verb uses were identified, such as idioms, metaphors, and support verb constructions.

Monachesi et al. (2007) use PropBank labels for semi-automatic annotation of a corpus of Dutch sentences. Semantic roles were first annotated using a rule-based semantic parser and then corrected by one annotator. Although not all Dutch verbs could be translated to an equivalent verb sense in English, these cases were assessed as relatively rare. What proved to be problematic was identifying the correct label for modifiers.

Bittar (2009) makes use of cross-lingual lexical transfer in annotating French verbs with event types, by adapting a small-scale English verb lexicon with specified event structure (TimeML).

The inter-annotator agreement in labelling predicates reported in Burchardt et al. (2009) reaches 85%, while our best score (when falling back to verb classes) is 81%. However, unlike Burchardt et al. (2009) we did not introduce any new French labels. We find, like Monachesi et al. (2007), that non-parallel cases are less frequent than what is reported in Burchardt et al. (2009), which could be due to the properties of the annotations schemes.

## 5 Conclusions

We can conclude that the general task of annotating French sentences using English PropBank frame files is well-defined. Nevertheless, it is a hard task that requires linguistic training. With respect to the disagreements on labelling predicates, we can conclude that a large part can be resolved if we compare the annotations at the level of verb classes instead of at the very fine-grained level of verb senses. Non-parallel cases are mostly due to idioms and collocations. Their rate is relatively low and can be further reduced by adapting annotation guidelines.

## Acknowledgments

The research leading to these results has received funding from the EU FP7 programme (FP7/2007-2013) under grant agreement nr 216594 (CLASSIC project: www.classic-project.org). We would like to thank Goljihan Kashaeva and James Henderson for valuable comments.

[4]The mappings from PropBank verb sense labels to VerbNet verb classes are one-to-many and not complete. We counted a pair as matching if there exists a class to which both verb senses belong. We found a verb class for both verb senses in about 78% of the cases and discarded the rest.

## References

R. Basili, D. De Cao, D. Croce, B. Coppola, and A. Moschitti, 2009. *Computational Linguistics and Intelligent Text Processing*, chapter Cross-Language Frame Semantics Transfer in Bilingual Corpora, pages 332–345. Springer Berlin / Heidelberg.

A. Bittar. 2009. Annotation of events and temporal expressions in French texts. In *Proceedings of the third Linguistic Annotation Workshop (LAW III)*, pages 48–51, Suntec, Singapore.

A. Burchardt, K. Erk, A. Frank, A. Kowalski, S. Padó, and M. Pinkal. 2006. The SALSA corpus: a German corpus resource for lexical semantics. In *Proceedings of the 5th International Conference on Language Resources and Evaluation (LREC 2006)*, pages 969–974, Genoa, Italy.

A. Burchardt, K. Erk, A. Frank, A. Kowalski, S. Pado, and M. Pinkal, 2009. *Multilingual FrameNets in Computational Lexicography: Methods and Applications*, chapter FrameNet for the semantic analysis of German: Annotation, representation and automation, pages 209–244. De Gruyter Mouton, Berlin.

M.-H. Candito, B. Crabbé, P. Denis, and F. Guérin. 2009. Analyse syntaxique du français : des constituants aux dépendances. In *Proceedings of la Conférence sur le Traitement Automatique des Langues Naturelles (TALN'09)*, Senlis, France.

C. Fellbaum. 1998. WordNet, an electronic lexical database. MIT Press.

C. J. Fillmore, R. Johnson, and M.R.L. Petruck. 2003. Background to FrameNet. *International journal of lexicography*, 16.3:235–250.

K. Kipper. 2005. *VerbNet: A broad-coverage, comprehensive verb lexicon*. Ph.D. thesis, University of Pennsylvnia.

P. Koehn. 2005. Europarl: A parallel corpus for statistical machine translation. In *Proceedings of the MT Summit*, pages 79–86, Phuket, Thailand.

E. Loper, S-T Yi, and M. Palmer. 2007. Combining lexical resources: Mapping between PropBank and VerbNet. In *Proceedings of the 7th International Workshop on Computational Semantics (IWCS-7)*, pages 118–129, Tilburg, The Netherlands.

P. Merlo and L. van der Plas. 2009. Abstraction and generalisation in semantic role labels: PropBank, VerbNet or both? In *Proceedings of the Joint Conference of the 47th Annual Meeting of the ACL and the 4th International Joint Conference on Natural Language Processing of the AFNLP*, pages 288–296, Suntec, Singapore.

P. Monachesi, G. Stevens, and J. Trapman. 2007. Adding semantic role annotation to a corpus of written Dutch. In *Proceedings of the Linguistic Annotation Workshop (LAW)*, pages 77–84, Prague, Czech republic.

S. Ozdowska and A. Way. 2009. Optimal bilingual data for French-English PB-SMT. In *Proceedings of the 13th Annual Conference of the European Association for Machine Translation (EAMT'09)*, pages 96–103, Barcelona, Spain.

S. Padó. 2007. *Cross-lingual Annotation Projection Models for Role-Semantic Information*. Ph.D. thesis, Saarland University.

P. Pajas and J. Štěpánek. 2008. Recent advances in a feature-rich framework for treebank annotation. In *Proceedings of the 22nd International Conference on Computational Linguistics (Coling 2008)*, pages 673–680, Manchester, UK.

M. Palmer, D. Gildea, and P. Kingsbury. 2005. The Proposition Bank: An annotated corpus of semantic roles. *Computational Linguistics*, 31:71–105.

I. Titov and J. Henderson. 2007. A latent variable model for generative dependency parsing. In *Proceedings of the International Conference on Parsing Technologies (IWPT-07)*, pages 144–155, Prague, Czech Republic.

# Characteristics of high agreement affect annotation in text

**Cecilia Ovesdotter Alm**
Cornell University, USA
cissioalm@gmail.com

## Abstract

The purpose of this paper is to present an unusual English dataset for affect exploration in text. It describes a corpus of fairy tales from three sources that have been annotated for affect at the sentence level. Special attention is given to data marked by high annotator agreement. A qualitative analysis of characteristics of high agreement sentences from H. C. Andersen reveals several interesting trends, illustrated by examples.

## 1 Introduction

Meaning is essential to language. The importance of expressive, attitudinal/emotive, or social/interpersonal meaning has been noted by prominent linguists (Bühler, 1934; Lyons, 1977; Jakobson, 1996; Halliday, 1996). However, affect is still an understudied phenomenon in linguistics, although many affective computing applications actually apply to language (Picard, 1997).

The motivation behind this discussion is to bring a special and rather unique dataset to the attention of reseachers in the field of natural language processing, affective computing, and related areas. This paper discusses affect representation, presents an affect dataset, and then focuses on clear-cut cases of affective meaning and expression in text with a summary of an analysis of data for which human annotators highly agreed on the assignment of affect labels. For dataset results in supervised classification (including experimentation on high agreement data), cf. Alm (2009).[1]

## 2 Affect representation

Affect can be modeled, e.g. as categories (Ekman, 1994), dimensions (Osgood, 1969), by focus on appraisal (Ortony et al, 1988), or on experience of physical and bodily responses (Cornelius, 2000). There is a lack of consensus on a model of affect (Picard, 1997; Scherer, 2003) and controversy surrounds such modeling. Pragmatically, different views of affect complement each other and jointly create a basis for understanding affective language phenomena. Affect modeling decisions are arguably application dependent. For a detailed literature review on previous work on how to characterize affect, affect in text-based linguistics and in subjective NLP or speech technology, and tales and oral narratives, see Alm (2009). Also see http://emotion-research.net/.

Resulting originally from an interest in text analysis for child-directed expressive text-to-speech synthesis, this dataset relies on a categorical annotation scheme of basic emotions; a model supported by the compelling observation that emotive facial expressions were cross-culturally recognized well above chance (Ekman and Friesen, 1998). In vision and speech research "the Big Six" (Cornelius, 2000) (i.e. *happiness, fear, anger, surprise, disgust*, and *sadness*) appear quite often. Nevertheless, the Ekmanian view remains controversial. For instance, Russel and Fernández-Dols (1998) have critiqued the relevance, methods, and rigor of the "Facial Expression Program" for emotion. One alternative is free labeling (i.e. annotators may come up with their own labels), but that may result in impractical, large label sets. A study grouping items from open-ended responses to a perception test on characterizing certain fairy tale sentences noted that although other cases occurred, Big Six emotions were frequent in answers (Bralè et al, 2005).

As regards the dataset's use of affect categories, several empirical studies have shown above chance performance for recognition of categorical emotions in classification tasks involving prosody. Categorical labels may be more straightforward

[1]For details on this dataset and experimentation conducted with it, readers should consult my book (Alm, 2009), which exceeds this paper in scope and depth.



*Proceedings of the Fourth Linguistic Annotation Workshop, ACL 2010*, pages 118–122,
Uppsala, Sweden, 15-16 July 2010. 

for annotators to conceptualize compared to dimensional scales, as participants pointed out in a study (Francisco and Gervas, 2006). Also, categories are arguably suitable for pedagogy, and they naturally fit computational classification. A basic affect category is also broad enough to span related affect states, e.g. the *emotion family* (Ekman, 1994) of *angry* could also cover concepts such as *irritated, annoyed* and *enraged*.[2] Finally, the foundational nature of basic, categorical affects intuitively seems to fit a child-directed context and fairy tales contents, which may include certain canonical topics and behaviors, compared to more spontaneous discourse.[3]

## 3 Corpus data overview

The affect dataset consists of 176 stories (more than 15,000 sentences) by Beatrix Potter, the Brothers Grimm and H. C. Andersen, manually annotated at the sentence level by pairs of annotators.[4] For the annotation process, annotators read tales and had to make a choice from a set of affect categories for sentences. Each sentence was given four affect labels since each of two annotators assigned both a *primary emotion* (guided by the prence of a *feeler*, mostly a character or character type in the text) and a background *mood* to a sentence. The four labels were then combined into a sentence's affect labels. For more details on the annotation process, cf. (Alm, 2009). The label set consisted of a set of categorical affect labels. Prior to the analysis below, ANGRY and DISGUSTED were merged (motivated by data sparsity and related semantics) into one category, as were POSITIVELY and NEGATIVELY SURPRISED, yielding a merged set of affect labels: ANGRY-DISGUSTED, FEARFUL, HAPPY, NEUTRAL, SAD, SURPRISED.

Interannotator agreement can be an artifact of annotation scheme and procedure. For example, pairs might be trained to annotate similarly, across-the-board rules (e.g. *questions* are negative) might ignore subtle decisions, or problematic items might be removed. Such approaches may yield higher agreement, cleaner data, and perhaps better performance and more consistent

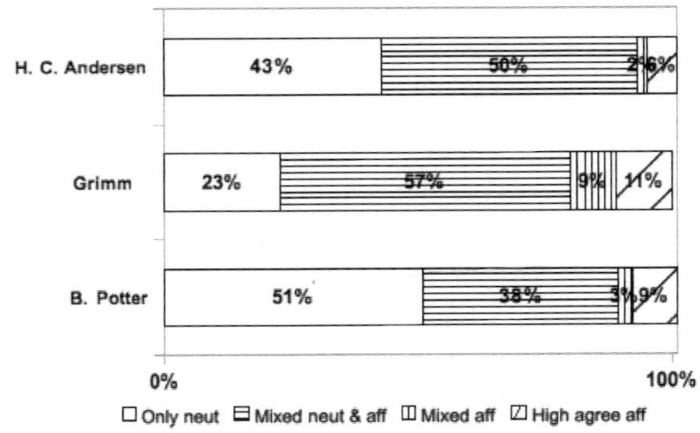


Figure 1: *(Dis)agreement: merged labels*

trained applications. But, the relevance of that for study of linguistic behavior is less clear. Zaenen (2006) noted that "[f]or interannotator agreement, it suffices that all annotators do the same thing. But even with full annotator agreement it is not sure that the task captures what was originally intended" (577); this should not be confused with understanding a linguistic issue. Fig. 1 reports on a diagnostic alternative with the ratios of (dis)agreement types. This avoids the concept of *ground truth*, which may not hold for all language phenomena. Affect, which is highly subjective, is arguably better captured by flexible *acceptability*.[5]

Fig. 1 shows that sentences only labeled NEUTRAL were frequent, as were disagreements, which were more common for sentences marked both with NEUTRAL and one or more affect classes. This parallels findings for polarity expressions in subjective texts (Wilson et al, 2005), and shows that the border between affective and neutral is fuzzy. (Affect perception lacks clear definitions and is subjective, and neutrality suffers from the same dilemma.) A sentence with *high agreement* affect was defined as all four primary emotion and mood labels having the same *affective* label (given the merged label set). These were more common than mixed affective labels.

## 4 High agreement in H. C. Andersen

This section examines the subset of high agreement sentences in the H. C. Andersen data from a qualitative-interpretive perspective. The analysis is not intended as rigid categorization, but rather to get an overall idea of why high agreement might occur on affect labels across annotators. Isolated sentences were extracted and mostly examined that way, rarely considering context. This

[2]Categories do not exclude adding intensity for approximating an arousal dimension, arguably relevant for speech.

[3]Naturally, tales also encompass narrative complexity.

[4]The annotated data are available at the author's website (both the full dataset and the high agreement subsets). For instance, for the high agree affect data, a storyname is followed by its corresponding high agree affective sentences in the following format: `sentence-id-in-story@label-code@sentence`.

[5]Regular agreement scores for the corpus would be low.

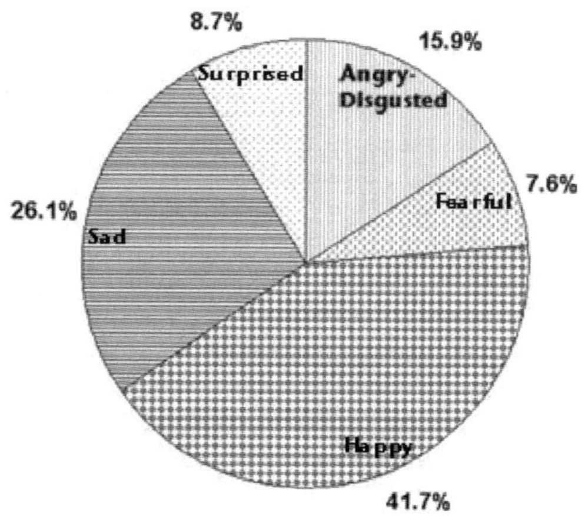


Figure 2: *Distribution of 460 H. C. Andersen high agreement affective sentences across affect labels*

focused the analytical scope.[6] Five annotators engaged with the overall H. C. Andersen subcorpus of 77 tales. 460 sentences were marked by affective high agreement, given the five affective classes. The distribution of affective classes for this subset is in Fig. 2, with HAPPY and SAD being most frequent.

### 4.1 Characteristics: high agreement affect

The below overview lists characteristics observed in an analysis on the H. C. Andersen high agreement data. It briefly describes each characteristic and lets an example illustrate it. For more discussion, examples, word lists etc., see Alm (2009). The characteristics occur in some and not all sentences; some frequently, others more rarely. Often, several jointly characterize a sentence.

The illustrative sentence examples in this section use the following format: Affect labels are in small caps and sentences are in italics. Also, phrases in bold-face illustrate the discussed characteristic, whereas phrases that annotators noted are underlined (single underscore for non-overlapping vs. double underscore for overlapping mark-up), and their *feeler/s* for the primary emotion annotation is/are included (with annotator subscripts to show if they had indicated the same or not) in parenthesis in small caps.

#### 4.1.1 Affect words

Content words that directly name an affective state (e.g. reflecting a particular intensity) are common in high agreement sentences, cf.:

ANGRY-DISGUSTED: *They buzzed round the prince and stung his face and hands;* ***angrily*** *he drew his sword and brandished it, but he only touched the air and did not hit the gnats.* (VILLAIN$_{1,2}$)

That narration can directly announce affective states is an indication of the important narrative role affect can play in stories. Also, Wilson and Wiebe (2003) interestingly noted that annotators agreed more strongly with strong subjective expressions, which affect words are examples of. Some illustrative affect words from the examined data are (for SURPRISED): *alarmed, astonished, astonishment, shocked, shocking, startled, surprised.* Special cases include *negation* (e.g. *not happy* for SAD); *figurative/idiomatic phrases* (e.g. *one of his heartstrings had broken* for SAD); or appearance with more than one affect (e.g. *anguish* for SAD or FEARFUL).

#### 4.1.2 Words for related/contrastive affect states

Expressions in the sentential context naming related or contrastive affective states not in the label set (e.g. *dull, pride, relief,* or *shame*) may also help evoke a particular affect, as in:

HAPPY: *They looked at Little Claus ploughing with his five horses, and he was so* ***proud*** *that he smacked his whip, and said, "Gee-up, my five horses."* (HERO$_{1,2}$)

#### 4.1.3 Affect related words or expressions

Lexical items or phrases which describe actions, properties, behaviors, cognitive states, or objects associated with particular affects occur frequently in the examined high agreement subset, e.g. as in:

HAPPY: *They* ***laughed*** *and they* ***wept****; and Peter* ***embraced*** *the old Fire-drum.* (HERO$_1$, (TRUE) MOTHER$_2$, (TRUE) FATHER$_2$)

Some more prominent affect related lexical items include *weep, kiss, laugh, cry* (= *weep*), and forms of *pleasure, tears,* and *smile.* Expressions of weeping or tears often appear with sadness, but may also depict happiness. *Negations* may occur.

#### 4.1.4 Polarity words and expressions

Words or expressions of positive or negative polarity can help to set the scene with a particular affective mode, in particular with relation to context and acquired knowledge. Expressions of opposing polarity may be used as a contrast, as in:

HAPPY: *It became a* ***splendid*** *flower-garden*

[6] Annotators' noted *feeler* and emotional/connotative phrases for the sentences were inspected.

*to the **sick** boy, and his little **treasure** upon earth.* (SICK BOY$_{1,2}$)

Modifiers can intensify the affective load. Lexical words and phrases may have *permanent* vs. *occasional* attitudinal meaning (Hedquist, 1978).

#### 4.1.5 Knowledge and human experience

Readers may from experience associate aquired knowledge about situations, visualizations, and behaviors with particular affects. For example, it is common knowledge that starving is traumatic:
SAD: *He was **hungry and thirsty**, yet no one gave him anything; and when it became dark, and they were about to close the gardens, the porter **turned him out**.* (HERO$_{1,2}$).

Story worlds tend to involve canonical representations of characters, actions, functions, situations and objects. Surrounding *context* can be important for affective interpretations. Scenarios may include, e.g. *an inspiration from weather, flowers, nature, or God; singing (or dancing, jumping); physical lack and need; sleep deprivation or allowance; addiction; incapability; unexpected observation; appearance/posture (or intonation); contextual guidance;* or relate to *marriage* (see (Alm, 2009) for examples). In fact, arguably most discussed characteristics can be traced to acquired knowledge, experience, associations, or context.

#### 4.1.6 Speech acts

Speech acts reflect a certain kind of communicative knowledge that can have affective meaning (such as *cursing, insulting, commanding*), e.g.:
ANGRY-DISGUSTED:
***Let her be expelled from** the congregation and the Church.* (VILLAIN$_{1,2}$)

#### 4.1.7 Types of direct speech

Direct speech may be used by characters in tales to express affect. This might include *speaking excitedly, (WH)-exclamations* or *(WH)-questions, short utterances, interjections* (and *sound effects*), such as *ah, alas, hurrah, o God, sorry, thump, ugh*. Direct speech can be introduced by words of speaking, as in:
FEARFUL: *"**Mercy!**" cried Karen.* (HEROINE$_{1,2}$)

#### 4.1.8 Mixed emotions

Affective high agreement sentences also include cases of mixed emotions, e.g. affect or affect-related words referring to more than one affect. The 'winning' affect may be inferred. Contrast might make it more prominent, as in:
HAPPY (mixed SAD): *He now **felt glad** at having **suffered sorrow and trouble**, because it enabled him to **enjoy** so much better all the **pleasure and happiness** around him; for the great swans swam round the new-comer, and stroked his neck with their beaks, as a welcome.* (MAIN CHARACTER/HERO$_{1,2}$)

### 4.2 Tendencies of particular affect categories

Lastly, there may be trends for particular characteristics associating more or less with a particular affect. For example, in this subset, FEARFUL sentences seem often to contain affect or affect related words, whereas SURPRISED sentences may quite often be characterized by various types of direct speech or involve unexpected observations.

## 5 Conclusion

This paper brought attention to an affect dataset, and discussed (mostly surface) characteristics in its H. C. Andersen high agreement subset, illustrating the complexity of affect cues, without claiming an exhaustive analysis. It also tentatively hypothesized that some characteristics may show particular affinity with certain affects.

The high agreement sentence data may be particularly interesting for affect research, while other parts of the annotated, larger corpus may reveal insights on affect variation in text and perception thereof (bearing in mind that the dataset is not necessarily representative across domains and text types, nor of contemporary texts).

Lastly, as noted above, developed knowledge, experience, associations, and context appear very important for affect understanding. This is also a substantial part of what makes the problem of automatically predicting affect from text so challenging; it involves levels of deep cognitive understanding rather than just extractable surface features. Whereas the discussed characteristics naturally do not consistute the answer to affect understanding, they may inform future search for it. Deep understanding and continuous, as opposed to static, computational development of affective understanding remain crucial areas of future work for expressive NLP applications.

### Acknowledgments

Thanks to R. Sproat, R. Proaño, and reviewers. Project funded by NSF (award ITR-#0205731).

## References


Alm, Cecilia Ovesdotter. 2009. *Affect in Text and Speech*. VDM Verlag: Saarbrcken.

Bralè, Véronique, Valérie Maffiolo, Ioannis Kanellos, and Thierry Moudenc. 2005. Towards an expressive typology in storytelling: A perceptive approach. In Jianhua Tao, Tieniu Tan, and Rosalind W. Picard (Eds.), *Affective Computing and Intelligent Interaction, First International Conference, ACII 2005, Beijing, China, October 22-24, 2005, Proceedings*, 858-865.

Bühler, Karl. 1934. *Sprachtheorie: Die Darstellungsfunktion der Sprache*. Stuttgart: Gustav Fischer Verlag.

Cahn, Janet E. 1990. The generation of affect in synthesized speech. *Journal of the American Voice I/O Society* 8, 1-19.

Cornelius, Randolph R. 2000. Theoretical approaches to emotion. In *Proceedings of the ISCA Workshop on Speech and Emotion*, 3-10.

Ekman, Paul. 1994. All emotions are basic. In P. Ekman and R. J. Davidson (Eds.), *The Nature of Emotion: Fundamental Questions*. Oxford: Oxford University Press, 15-19.

Ekman, Paul and Wallace V. Friesen. 1998 [1971] Constants across culture in the face and emotion. Jenkins, Jennifer M and Oatley, Keith and Stein, Nancy L. (eds). *Human Emotions: A Reader*. Malden, Massachussetts: Blackwell, 63-72.

Francisco, Virginia and Pablo Gervás 2006. Exploring the compositionality of emotions in text: Word emotions, sentence emotions and automated tagging. In *AAAI-06 Workshop on Computational Aesthetics: Artificial Intelligence Approaches to Beauty and Happiness*.

Halliday, Michael A. K. 1996. Linguistic function and literary style: An inquiry into the language of William Golding's *The Inheritors*. Weber, Jean Jacques (ed). *The Stylistics Reader: From Roman Jakobson to the Present*. London: Arnold, 56-86.

Hedquist, Rolf. 1978. *Emotivt språk: En studie i dagstidningarnas ledare*. Ph.D. Thesis. Umeå.

Jakobson, Roman. 1996. Closing statement: Linguistics and poetics. Weber, Jean Jacques (ed). *The Stylistics Reader: From Roman Jakobson to the Present*. London: Arnold, 10-35.

Lyons, John. 1977. *Semantics* volumes 1, 2. Cambridge: Cambridge University Press.

Ortony, Andrew, Gerlad L. Clore, and Allan Collins. 1988. *The Cognitive Structure of Emotions*. Cambridge: Cambridge University Press.

Osgood, Charles E. 1969. On the whys and wherefores of E, P, and A. *Journal of Personality and Social Psychology* 12 (3), 194-199.

Picard, Rosalind W. 1997. *Affective computing*. Cambridge, Massachusetts: MIT Press.

Russell, James A. and José M. Fernández-Dols 1998 [1997]. What does a facial expression mean? Jenkins, Jennifer M and Oatley, Keith and Stein, Nancy L. (eds). *Human Emotions: A Reader*. Malden, Massachussetts: Blackwell, 63-72.

Scherer, Klaus R. 2003. Vocal communication of emotion: A review of research paradigms. *Speech Communication* 40 (1-2), 227256.

Wilson, Theresa, Janyce Wiebe, and Paul Hoffman. 2005. Recognizing contextual polarity in phrase-level sentiment analysis. *Proceedings of HLT/EMNLP*, 347-354.

Wilson, Theresa and Janyce Wiebe. 2003. Annotating opinions in the world press. *4th SigDial workshop on Discourse and Dialogue*.

Zaenen, Annie. 2006. Mark-up barking up the wrong tree. *Journal of Computational Linguistics* 32 (4), 577-580.

# The Deep Re-annotation in a Chinese Scientific Treebank

**Kun Yu**[1] **Xiangli Wang**[1] **Yusuke Miyao**[2] **Takuya Matsuzaki**[1] **Junichi Tsujii**[1,3]
1. The University of Tokyo, Hongo 7-3-1, Bunkyo-ku, Tokyo, 113-0033, Japan
{kunyu, xiangli, matuzaki, tsujii}@is.s.u-tokyo.ac.jp
2. National Institute of Informatics, Hitotsubashi 2-1-2, Chiyoda-ku, Tokyo, 101-8430, Japan
yusuke@nii.ac.jp
3. The University of Manchester, Oxford Road, Manchester, M13 9PL, UK

**Abstract**

In this paper, we introduce our recent work on re-annotating the deep information, which includes both the grammatical functional tags and the traces, in a Chinese scientific treebank. The issues with regard to re-annotation and its corresponding solutions are discussed. Furthermore, the process of the re-annotation work is described.

## 1 Introduction

A Chinese scientific Treebank (called the *NICT Chinese Treebank*) has been developed by the National Institute of Information and Communications Technology of Japan (NICT). This treebank annotates the word segmentation, pos-tags, and bracketing structures according to the annotation guideline of the Penn Chinese Treebank (Xia, 2000(a); Xia, 2000(b); Xue and Xia, 2000). Contrary to the Penn Chinese Treebank in news domain, the NICT Chinese Treebank includes sentences that are manually translated from Japanese scientific papers. Currently, the NICT Chinese Treebank includes around 8,000 Chinese sentences. The annotation of more sentences in the science domain is ongoing.

The current annotation of the NICT Chinese Treebank is informative for some language analysis tasks, such as syntactic parsing and word segmentation. However, the deep information, which includes both the grammatical functional tags and the traces, are omitted in the annotation. Without grammatical functions, the simple bracketing structure is not informative enough to represent the semantics for Chinese. Furthermore, the traces are critical elements in detecting long-distance dependencies.

Gabbard et al. (2006) and Blaheta and Charniak (2000) applied machine learning models to automatically assign the empty categories and functional tags to an English treebank. However, considering about the different domains that the Penn Chinese Treebank and the NICT Chinese Treebank belong to, the machine learning model trained on the Penn Chinese Treebank may not work successfully on the NICT Chinese Treebank. In order to guarantee the high annotation quality, in our work, we manually re-annotate both the grammatical functional tags and the traces to the NICT Chinese Treebank. With the deep re-annotation, the NICT Chinese Treebank could be used not only for the shallow natural language processing tasks, but also as a resource for deep applications, such as the lexicalized grammar development from treebanks (Miyao 2006; Guo 2009; Xia 1999; Hockenmaier and Steedman 2002).

Considering that the translation quality of the sentences in the NICT Chinese Treebank may affect the quality of re-annotation, in the current phase, we only selected 2,363 sentences that are of good translation quality, for re-annotation. In the future, with the expansion of the NICT Chinese Treebank, we will continue this re-annotation work on large-scale sentences.

## 2 Content of Re-annotation

Because the NICT Chinese Treebank follows the annotation guideline of the Penn Chinese Treebank, our re-annotation uses similar annotation criteria in the Penn Chinese Treebank.

Figure 1 exemplifies our re-annotation to a sentence in the NICT Chinese Treebank. In this example, we first re-annotate the trace (as indicated by the italicized part in Figure 1(b)) for the extracted head noun '词/word'. Furthermore, we re-annotate the functional tag of the trace (as indicated by the dashed-box in Figure 1(b)), to indicate that the extracted head noun should be restored into the relative clause as a topic.

There are 26 functional tags in the Penn Chinese Treebank (Xue and Xia, 2000), in which seven functional tags describe the grammatical



*Proceedings of the Fourth Linguistic Annotation Workshop, ACL 2010*, pages 123–126,
Uppsala, Sweden, 15-16 July 2010. ©2010 Association for Computational Linguistics

roles and one functional tag (i.e. LGS) indicates a logical subject. Since the eight functional tags are crucial for obtaining the grammatical function of constituents, we re-annotate the eight functional tags (refer to Table 1) to the NICT Chinese Treebank.

```
(NP (CP (IP (NP (NN 单词)
                (NN 亲密度))
            (VP (VA 高)))
        (DEC 的))
    (NP (NN 词)))
```

*(the word of which the word cohesion is high)*

(a) A relative clause in the NICT Chinese Treebank

```
(NP (CP (WHNP-1 (-NONE- *OP*)
        (CP (IP (NP-TPC (-NONE- *T*-1))
                (NP (NN 单词)
                    (NN 亲密度))
                (VP (VA 高)))
            (DEC 的)))
    (NP (NN 词)))
```

(b) The relative clause after re-annotation

Figure 1. Our re-annotation to a relative clause.

| Functional Tag | Description |
|---|---|
| IO | indirect object |
| OBJ | direct object |
| EXT | post-verbal complement that describes the extent, frequency, or quantity |
| FOC | object fronted to a pre-verbal but post-subject position |
| PRD | non-verbal predicate |
| SBJ | surface subject |
| TPC | topic |
| LGS | logical subject |

Table 1. Functional tags that we re-annotate.

```
(IP (NP-TPC-1 (NN 信息))
    (VP (ADVP (AD 比较))
        (VP (ADVP (AD 容易))
            (VP (VV 获得)
                (NP-OBJ (-NONE- *T*-1))))))
```

*(It is easier to obtain information.)*

(a) A topic construction with long-distance dependency after re-annotation of functional tag and trace

```
(IP (NP-TPC (DP (DT 该))
            (NP (NN 算法)))
    (NP-SBJ (NP (PN 其))
            (NP (NN 合理性)))
    (VP (ADVP (AD 已))
        (VP (VV 得到)
            (VV 证实))))
```

*(The rationality of this algorithm has been verified.)*

(b) A topic construction without long-distance dependency after re-annotation of functional tag

Figure 2. Our re-annotation to topic constructions.

In addition, in the annotation guideline of the Penn Chinese Treebank, four constructions are annotated with traces: *BA-construction*, *BEI-construction*, *topic construction* and *relative clause*. The *BEI-construction* and *relative clause* introduce long-distance dependency. Therefore, we re-annotate the traces for the two constructions. The *topic construction* introduces the topic phrase. For the topic constructions that contain long-distance dependency, we re-annotate both the traces and the functional tags (refer to the italicized part in Figure 2(a)). Some topic constructions, however, do not include long-distance dependency. In such cases, we only re-annotate the functional tag to indicate that it is a topic (refer to the italicized part in Figure 2(b)). In addition, the *BA-construction* moves the object to a pre-verbal position. Although the *BA-construction* does not contain long-distance dependency, we still re-annotate the trace to acquire the original position of the moved object in the sentence.

## 3 Issues and Solutions

### 3.1 Trace re-annotation in the BA/BEI construction

The NICT Chinese Treebank follows the word segmentation and pos-tag annotation guideline of the Penn Chinese Treebank. Therefore, there are some BA-constructions and BEI-constructions that cannot be re-annotated with traces. The principle reason for this is that the moved object has semantic relations with only part of the verb. For example, in the sentence shown in Figure 3(a), the moved head noun '家乡/hometown' is the object of '建/construct', but not for '建成/construct to be'.

```
(VP (BA 把)
    (IP (NP (NN 家乡))
        (VP (VV 建成)
            (NP (NN 花园)))))
```

*(construct the hometown to be a garden)*

(a) The annotation in the NICT Chinese Treebank

```
(VP (BA 把)
    (IP (NP-SBJ-1 (NN 家乡))
        (VP (VV 建)
            (NP-OBJ (-NONE- *-1))
            (AM 成)
            (NP (NN 花园)))))
```

(b) Our proposed re-annotation of functional tag and trace

Figure 3. Our re-annotation to a BA construction with split verb.

Our analysis of the Penn Chinese Treebank shows that only a closed list of characters (such as '成/to be') can be attached to verbs in such a case. Therefore, we solve the problem by following four steps (for an example, refer to Figure 3(b)):

(1) A linguist manually collects the characters that can be attached to verbs in such a case from the Penn Chinese Treebank and assigns them a new pos-tag 'AM (argument marker)'.

(2) The annotators use the character list as a reference during the re-annotation. When the verb in a BA/BEI construction ends with a character in the list, and the annotators think the verb should be split, the annotators record the sentence ID without performing any re-annotation.

(3) The linguist collects all of the recorded sentences, and defines pattern rules to automatically split the verbs in the BA/BEI constructions.

(4) The annotators annotate trace for the sentences with the split verbs. This step will be finished in our future work.

### 3.2 Topic detection

In the annotation guideline of the Penn Chinese Treebank, a topic is defined as '*the element that appears before the subject in a declarative sentence*'. However, the NICT Chinese Treebank does not annotate the omitted subject. Therefore, we could not use the position of the subject as a criterion for topic detection.

In order to resolve this issue, we define some heuristic rules based on both the meaning and the bracketing structure of phrases, to help detect the topic phrase. Only the phrase that satisfies all the rules will be re-annotated as a topic. The following exemplifies some rules:

(1) If there is a phrase before a subject, the phrase is probably a topic.

(2) A topic phrase must be parallel to the following verb phrase.

(3) The preposition phrase and localization phrase describing the location or time are not topics.

### 3.3 Inconsistent annotation in the NICT Chinese Treebank

There are some inconsistent annotations in the NICT Chinese Treebank, which makes our re-annotation work difficult.

These inconsistencies include:

(1) Inconsistent word segmentation, such as segmenting the word '相对应/corresponding' into two words '相对/opposite' and '应/ought'.

(2) Inconsistent pos-tag annotation. For example, when the word '的' exists between two noun phrases, it should be tagged as an associative marker (i.e. DEG), according to the guideline of the Penn Chinese Treebank. However, in the NICT Chinese Treebank, sometimes it is tagged as a nominalizer (i.e. DEC).

(3) Inconsistent bracketing annotation. Figure 4(a) shows the annotation of a relative clause in the NICT Chinese Treebank. In this annotation, the noun phrase '大阪/Osaka 地铁/subway' is incorrectly treated as the extracted head; furthermore, the adverb '人工/by hand' that modifies the verb '制作/make' is incorrectly annotated as an adjective that modifies the noun '变形图/deformation graph'. After correcting these inconsistencies, the relative clause should be annotated as shown in Figure 4(b).

```
(NP (QP (CD 很多))
    (ADJP (JJ 人工))
    (DNP (NP (CP (IP (VP (VV 制作)))
                 (DEC 的))
             (NP (NR 大阪)
                 (NN 地铁)))
         (DEG 的))
    (NP (NN 变形图)))
```

*(many deformation graphs of Osaka subway that are made by hand)*

(a) The inconsistent annotation of a relative clause

```
(NP (QP (CD 很多))
    (NP (CP (IP (VP (ADVP (AD 人工))
                    (VP (VV 制作))))
            (DEC 的))
        (NP (DNP (NP (NR 大阪)
                     (NN 地铁))
                 (DEG 的))
            (NP (NN 变形图)))))
```

(b) The annotation after correcting the inconsistencies

Figure 4. An inconsistent annotation in the NICT Chinese Treebank and its correction.

In our re-annotation, these inconsistently annotated sentences in the NICT Chinese Treebank were recorded by the annotators. We then sent them back to NICT for further verification.

## 4 Process of Re-annotation

### 4.1 Annotation Guideline

During the re-annotation, we basically follow the annotation guideline of the Penn Chinese Treebank (Xue and Xia, 2000). However, in order to fit with the characteristics of scientific sentences in the NICT Chinese Treebank, some constraints are added to the guideline.

For example, in the science domain, the relative clause is often used to describe a phenomenon, in which the extracted head noun is usually an abstract noun, and the relative clause is an appositive of the extracted head noun. Figure 5 shows an example in which the relative clause '系统/system 停止/stop 工作/working' is a description of the extracted head noun '现象 /phenomenon'. In such a case, the head noun cannot be restored into the clause. Therefore, we add the following restriction in our re-annotation guideline: *Do not re-annotate the trace when the head noun of a relative clause is an abstract noun and it is an appositive of the relative clause.*

```
(NP (CP (IP (NP (NN 系统))
            (VP (VV 停止)
                (NP (NN 工作))))
        (DEC 的))
    (NP (NN 现象)))
```

(*the phenomenon that the system stops working*)

Figure 5. A relative clause in the NICT Chinese Treebank.

### 4.2 Quality Control

Several processes were undertaken to guarantee the quality of our re-annotation:

(1) We chose graduate students who major in Chinese for all of the annotators.

(2) A visualization tool - XConc Suite (Kim et al., 2008) was used as assistance during the re-annotation.

(3) Only 2,363 sentences with good translation quality in the NICT Chinese Treebank were chosen for re-annotation in the current phase.

(4) Before starting the re-annotation, a linguist selected 200 representative sentences, which contain all the linguistic phenomena that we want to re-annotate, from among the 2,363 sentences in the NICT Chinese Treebank. The selected 200 sentences were manually re-annotated by the linguist, and were split into two sets for training the annotators sequentially. We evaluated the annotation quality of the annotators during training. The average annotation quality of all the annotators after training is shown in Table 2.

| Annotation Quality | | Inter-annotator Consistency | |
|---|---|---|---|
| Precision | Recall | Precision | Recall |
| 70.71% | 70.75% | 61.59% | 61.59% |

Table 2. The average annotation quality of the annotators after training.

(5) After training, the remaining sentences were split into several parts and assigned to the annotators for re-annotation. In each part, there were around 20% sentences that were shared by all of the annotators. These shared sentences were used to check and guarantee inter-annotator consistency during the re-annotation.

## 5 Conclusion and Future Work

We re-annotated the deep information, which includes eight types of grammatical functional tags and the traces in four constructions, to a Chinese scientific treebank, i.e. the NICT Chinese Treebank. Since the NICT Chinese Treebank is based on manually translated sentences, only 2,363 sentences with good translation quality were re-annotated in the current phase to guarantee the re-annotation quality.

In the future, we will finish the trace annotation for the BA and BEI constructions with split verbs. Furthermore, we will continue our re-annotation on more sentences in the NICT Chinese Treebank.


## Acknowledgments

We would like to thank Dr. Kiyotaka Uchimoto and Dr. Junichi Kazama for providing the NICT Chinese Treebank.


## References


Don Blaheta and Eugene Charniak. 2000. Assigning Function Tags to Parsed Text. *Proceedings of NAACL 2000.*

Ryan Gabbard, Seth Kulick and Mitchell Marcus. 2006. Fully Parsing the Penn Treebank. *Proceedings of HLT-NAACL 2006.*

Yuqing Guo. 2009. *Treebank-based acquisition of Chinese LFG Resources for Parsing and Generation.* Ph.D. Thesis. Dublin City University.

Julia Hockenmaier and Mark Steedman. 2002. Acquiring Compact Lexicalized Grammars from a Cleaner Treebank. *Proceedings of the 3rd LREC.*

Jindong Kim, Tomoko Ohta, and Junichi Tsujii. 2008. Corpus Annotation for Mining Biomedical Events from Literature. *BMC Bioinformatics*, 9(10).

Yusuke Miyao. 2006. From Linguistic Theory to Syntactic Analysis: Corpus-oriented Grammar Development and Feature Forest Model. Ph.D Thesis. The University of Tokyo.

Fei Xia. 1999. Extracting Tree Adjoining Grammars from Bracketed Corpora. *Proceedings of the 5th NLPRS.*

Fei Xia. 2000 (a). The Segmentation Guidelines for the Penn Chinese Treebank (3.0).

Fei Xia. 2000 (b). The Part-of-speech Tagging Guidelines for the Penn Chinese Treebank (3.0).

Nianwen Xue, Fudong Chiou, and Martha Palmer. 2002. Building a Large-Scale Annotated Chinese Corpus. *Proceedings of COLING 2002.*

Nianwen Xue and Fei Xia. 2000. The Bracketing Guidelines for the Penn Chinese Treebank.

Shiwen Yu et al. 2002. The Basic Processing of Contemporary Chinese Corpus at Peking University Specification. *Journal of Chinese Information Processing*, 16 (5).

Qiang Zhou. 2004. Annotation Scheme for Chinese Treebank. *Journal of Chinese Information Processing*, 18 (4).

# The unified annotation of syntax and discourse in the Copenhagen Dependency Treebanks

Matthias Buch-Kromann          Iørn Korzen

Center for Research and Innovation in Translation and Translation Technology
Copenhagen Business School

## Abstract

We propose a unified model of syntax and discourse in which text structure is viewed as a tree structure augmented with anaphoric relations and other secondary relations. We describe how the model accounts for discourse connectives and the syntax-discourse-semantics interface. Our model is dependency-based, ie, words are the basic building blocks in our analyses. The analyses have been applied cross-linguistically in the Copenhagen Dependency Treebanks, a set of parallel treebanks for Danish, English, German, Italian, and Spanish which are currently being annotated with respect to discourse, anaphora, syntax, morphology, and translational equivalence.

## 1 Introduction

The Copenhagen Dependency Treebanks, CDT, consist of five parallel open-source treebanks for Danish, English, German, Italian, and Spanish.[1] The treebanks are annotated manually with respect to syntax, discourse, anaphora, morphology, as well as translational equivalence (word alignment) between the Danish source text and the target texts in the four other languages.

The treebanks build on the syntactic annotation in the 100,000-word Danish Dependency Treebank (Kromann 2003) and Danish-English Parallel Dependency Treebank (Buch-Kromann *et al.* 2007). Compared to these treebanks, which are only annotated for syntax and word alignment, the new treebanks are also annotated for discourse, anaphora, and morphology, and the syntax annotation has been revised with a much more fine-grained set of adverbial relations and a number of other adjustments. The underlying Danish PAROLE text corpus (Keson and Norling-Christensen 1998) consists of a broad mixture of 200-250 word excerpts from general-purpose texts.[2] The texts were translated into the other languages by professional translators who had the target language as their native language.

The final treebanks are planned to consist of approximately 480 fully annotated parallel texts for Danish and English, and a subset of approximately 300 fully annotated parallel texts for German, Italian, and Spanish, with a total of approximately 380,000 (2·100,000 + 3·60,000) annotated word or punctuation tokens in the five treebanks in total. So far, the annotators have made complete draft annotations for 67% of the texts for syntax, 40% for word alignments, 11% for discourse and anaphora, and 3% for morphology. The annotation will be completed in 2010.

In this paper, we focus on how the CDT treebanks are annotated with respect to syntax and discourse, and largely ignore the annotation of anaphora, morphology, and word alignments. In sections 2 and 3, we present the syntax and discourse annotation in the CDT. In section 4, we present our account of discourse connectives. In section 5, we briefly discuss the syntax-discourse-semantics interface, and some criticisms against tree-based theories of discourse.

## 2 The syntax annotation of the CDT

The syntactic annotation of the CDT treebanks is based on the linguistic principles outlined in the dependency theory Discontinuous Grammar (Buch-Kromann 2006) and the syntactic annotation principles described in Kromann (2003), Buch-Kromann *et al.* (2007), and Buch-Kromann et al (2009). All linguistic relations are represented as directed labelled relations between words or morphemes. The model operates with a primary dependency tree structure in which each word or morpheme is assumed to act as a complement or adjunct to another word or morpheme, called the *governor* (or *head*), except for the top node

[1]The treebanks, the annotation manual, and the relation hierarchy can be downloaded from the web site: http://code.google.com/p/copenhagen-dependency-treebank

[2]In practice, the use of text excerpts has not been a problem for our discourse annotation: we mainly annotate text excerpts that have a coherent discourse structure, which includes 80% of the excerpts in our text corpus. Moreover, given the upper limit on the corpus size that we can afford to annotate, small text excerpts allow our corpus to have a diversity in text type and genre that may well offset the theoretical disadvantage of working with reduced texts.



*Proceedings of the Fourth Linguistic Annotation Workshop, ACL 2010*, pages 127–131,
Uppsala, Sweden, 15-16 July 2010. 

of the sentence or unit, typically the finite verb. This structure is augmented with secondary relations, e.g., between non-finite verb forms and their subjects, and in antecedent-anaphor relations. Primary relations are drawn above the nodes and secondary below, all with directed arrows pointing from governor to dependent. The relation label is written at the arrow tip, or in the middle of the arrow if a word has more than one incoming arrow.

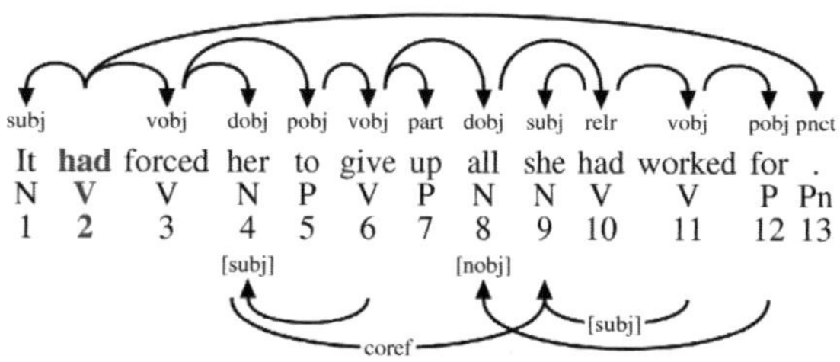


Figure 1. Primary dependency tree (top) and secondary relations (bottom) for the sentence "It had forced her to give up all she had worked for".

An example is given in Figure 1 above. Here, the arrow from "had$_2$" to "It$_1$" identifies "It" as the subject of "had", and the arrow from "forced$_3$" to "to$_5$" identifies the phrase headed by "to" as the prepositional object of "forced". Every word defines a unique phrase consisting of the words that can be reached from the head word by following the downward arrows in the primary tree.[3] For example, in Figure 1, "worked$_{11}$" heads the phrase "worked$_{11}$ for$_{12}$", which has a secondary noun object *nobj* in "all$_8$"; "had$_{10}$" heads the phrase "she$_9$ had$_{10}$ worked$_{11}$ for$_{12}$"; and "It$_1$" heads the phrase "It$_1$". Examples of secondary dependencies include the coreferential relation between "her$_4$" and "she$_9$", and the anaphoric relation in Figure 2. Part-of-speech functions are written in capital letters under each word. The inventory of relations is described in detail in our annotation manual (posted on the CDT web site).

Dependency arrows are allowed to cross, so discontinuous word orders such as topicalisations and extrapositions do not require special treatment. This is exemplified by the discontinuous dependency tree in Figure 2, in which the relative clause headed by "was$_7$" has been extraposed from the direct object and placed after the time adverbial "today$_5$".[4]

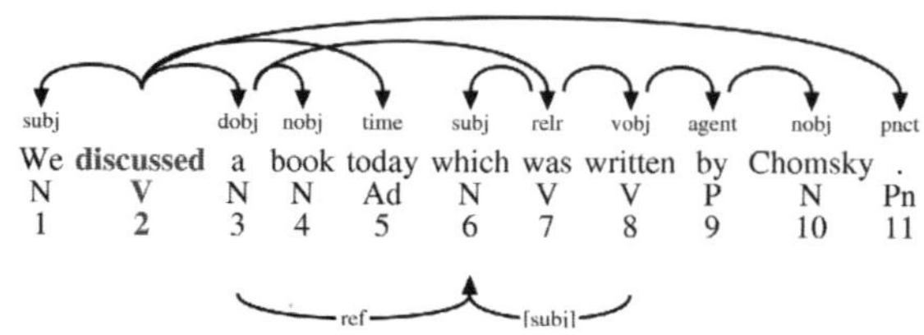


Figure 2. Primary dependency tree and secondary relations for the sentence "We discussed a book today which was written by Chomsky".

Buch-Kromann (2006) provides a detailed theory of how the dependency structure can be used to construct a word-order structure which provides fine-grained control over the linear order of the sentence, and how the dependency structure provides an interface to compositional semantics by determining a unique functor-argument structure given a particular modifier scope (ie, a specification of the order in which the adjuncts are applied in the meaning construction).[5]

## 3 The discourse annotation of the CDT

Just like sentence structures can be seen as dependency structures that link up the words and morphemes within a sentence (or, more precisely, the phrases headed by these words), so discourse structures can be viewed as dependency structures that link up the words and morphemes within an entire discourse. In Figures 1 and 2, the top nodes of the analysed sentences (the only words without incoming arrows) are the finite verbs "had$_2$" and "discussed$_2$" respectively, and these are shown in boldface. Basically, the CDT discourse annotation consists in linking up each such sentence top node with its nucleus (understood as the unique word within another sentence that is deemed to govern the relation) and labelling the relations between the two nodes.

The inventory of discourse relations in CDT is described in the CDT manual. It borrows heavily from other discourse frameworks, in particular Rhetorical Structure Theory, RST (Mann and Thompson, 1987; Tabaoda and Mann, 2006; Carlson et al, 2001) and the Penn Discourse Treebank, PDTB (Webber 2004; Dinesh *et al.*, 2005, Prasad *et al.*, 2007, 2008), as well as (Korzen, 2006, 2007), although the inventory had to be extended to accommodate the great

[3]Because of this isomorphism between phrases and head words, a dependency tree can always be represented as a phrase-structure tree in which every phrase has a unique lexical head; the resulting phrase-structure tree is allowed to contain crossing branches.

[4]In our current syntax annotation, we analyze the initial connective or conjunction as the head of the subordinate clause; in relative clauses, the relative verb functions as the head, i.e., the arrow goes from "a (book)" to "was (written)".

[5]In terms of their formal semantics, complements function as arguments to their governor, whereas adjuncts function as modifiers; i.e., semantically, the governor (type X) acts as an argument with the modifier (type X/X) as its functor.

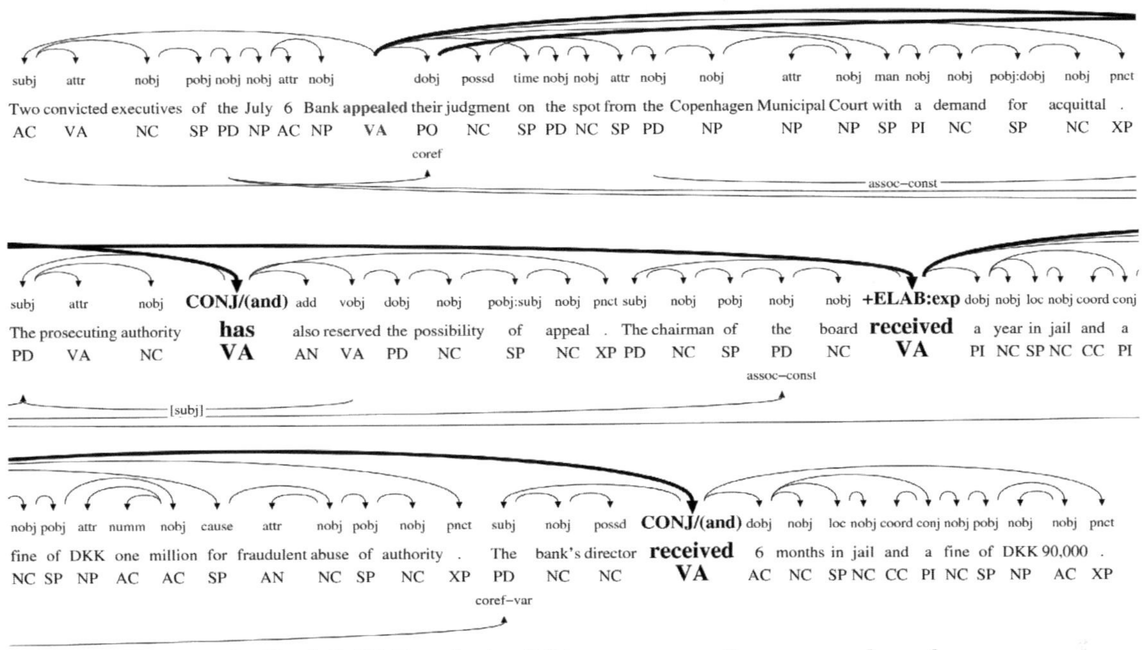


Figure 3. The full CDT analysis of (1) wrt. syntax, discourse, and anaphora.

variety of text types in the CDT corpus other than news stories. The inventory allows relation names to be formed as disjunctions or conjunctions of simple relation names, to specify multiple relations or ambiguous alternatives.

One of the most important differences between the CDT framework and other discourse frameworks lies in the way texts are segmented. In particular, CDT uses words as the basic building blocks in the discourse structure, while most other discourse frameworks use clauses as their atomic discourse units, including RST, PDTB, GraphBank (Wolf and Gibson, 2005), and the Pottsdam Commentary Corpus, PCC (Stede 2009).[6] This allows the nucleus and satellite in a discourse relation to be identified precisely by means of their head words, as in the example (1) below from the CDT corpus, where the second paragraph is analyzed as an elaboration of the deverbal noun phrase "their judgment" (words that are included in our condensed CDT analysis in Figure 4 are indicated with boldface and subscripted with numbers that identify them):

(1) Two convicted executives of the July 6 Bank **appealed$_1$ their$_2$** judgment on the spot from the Copenhagen Municipal Court with a demand for acquittal. The prosecuting authority **has$_3$** also reserved the possibility of appeal.

The chairman of the board **received$_4$** a year in jail and a fine of DKK one million for fraudulent abuse of authority [...]. The bank's director **received$_5$** 6 months in jail and a fine of DKK 90,000. *(Text 0531)*

The full CDT analysis of (1) is given in Figure 3, a more readable condensed version in Figure 4. The last sentence of the first paragraph, "The prosecuting authority has$_3$ also reserved the possibility of appeal", is a conjunct to the first sentence, and its top node "has$_3$" is linked to the top node of the first sentence, "appealed$_1$". The slash after a relation name indicates an explicit or implicit discourse connective used by the annotators to support their choice of relation type.

As in CDT's syntax annotation, the primary syntax and discourse relations must form a tree that spans all the words in the text, possibly supplemented by secondary relations that encode anaphoric relations and other secondary dependencies. Apart from this, CDT does not place any restrictions on the relations; in particular, a word

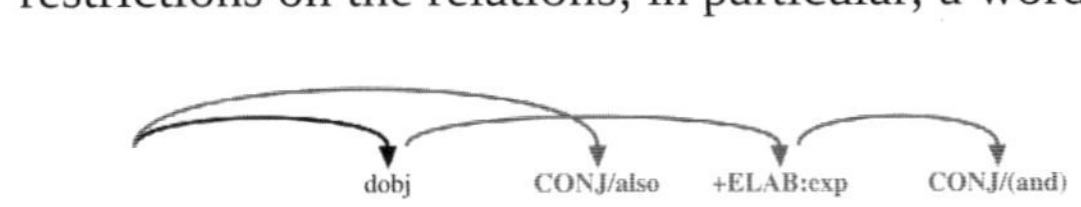


Figure 4. Condensed version of Figure 3.

[6]As noted by Carlson and Marcu (2001), the boundary between syntax and discourse is rather unclear: the same meaning can be expressed in a continuum of ways that range from clear discourse constructions ("He laughed. That annoyed me.") to clear syntactic constructions ("His laugh annoyed me."). Moreover, long discourse units may function as objects of attribution verbs in direct or indirect speech, or as parenthetical remarks embedded within an otherwise normal sentence. CDT's use of words as basic building blocks, along with a primary tree structure that spans syntax and discourse, largely eliminates these problems.

may function as nucleus for several different satellites, discourse relations may join non-adjacent clauses, and are allowed to cross; and secondary discourse relations are used to account for the distinction between story line level and speech level in attributions.

## 4 Discourse connectives

Discourse connectives play a prominent role in PDTB, and inspire the analysis of connectives in CDT. However, there are important differences in analysis, which affect the way discourse structures are construed. In a construction of the form "*X C Y*" where *X* and *Y* are clauses and *C* is a discourse connective (such as "because", "since", "when"), three dependency analyses suggest themselves, as summarized in Table 5.

| | **Head** | **Conjunction** | **Marker** |
|---|---|---|---|
| **Syntax** | comp comp<br>X C Y | mod comp<br>X C Y | mod mod<br>X C Y |
| **Semantics** | *C'*(*X'*,*Y'*) | [*C'*(*Y'*)] (*X'*) | [*Y'*(*C'*)] (*X'*) |

Table 5. Three analyses of discourse connectives.

When analyzed as the head of the construction, *C* takes *X* and *Y* as its (discourse) complements; semantically, the meaning *C'* of *C* acts as functor, and the meanings *X'*,*Y'* of *X*,*Y* act as arguments of *C'*. When analyzed as a subordinating conjunction, *C* subcategorizes for *Y* and modifies *X*; semantically, *C'* computes a meaning *C'*(*Y'*) from *Y'*, which acts as functor with *X'* as argument. Finally, analyzed as a marker, *C* modifies *Y* which in turn modifies *X*; semantically, *Y'* selects its meaning *Y'*(*C'*) based on the marker *C'* (i.e., the marker merely helps disambiguate *Y'*); *Y'*(*C'*) then acts as functor with argument *X'*.

The three analyses are markedly different in terms of their headedness, but quite similar in terms of their semantics. CDT opts for the marker analysis, with the obvious benefit that there is no need to postulate the presence of a phonetically empty head for implicit connectives. This analysis also implies that since discourse markers always modify the satellite, explicit and implicit discourse markers can be used to determine the discourse relation and its direction.

It is interesting that almost all theories of discourse structure, including RST, PDTB, GraphBank, PCC, and the dependency-based discourse analysis proposed by Mladová (2008), seem to analyze connectives as heads – even in the case where *C*+*Y* is an adverbial clause modifying X, where virtually all mainstream theories of syntax opt for one of the two other analyses. Perhaps current theories of discourse structure perceive discourse structure as a semantic rather than syntactic structure. In any case, it is not clear that this is the most fruitful analysis. A clear distinction between syntactic structure and semantic structure has proved crucial to the understanding of headedness in syntax (e.g. Croft 1995, Manning 1995), and it is one of the hardwon insights of syntax that semantic centrality or prominence is not directly reflected in the syntactic surface structure. Something similar might be true for discourse structure as well.

## 5 Syntax-discourse-semantics interface

CDT models discourse structure as a primary dependency tree supplemented by secondary relations. We believe that a tree-based view of discourse provides many important benefits, most importantly a clear interface to syntax and compositional semantics. There has been several attempts to refute the tree hypothesis on empirical grounds, though, including Wolf and Gibson (2005), Prasad et al (2005), Lee et al (2008), and Stede (2009), who have put forward important criticisms. Our framework addresses many of these objections, including the many problems related to attribution verbs, which do require a complicated treatment in our framework with secondary dependencies. A full discussion of this topic is, however, beyond the scope of this paper.

## 6 Conclusion

In this paper, we have presented a dependency-based view of discourse and syntax annotation where the syntax and discourse relations in a text form a primary dependency tree structure linking all the words in the text, supplemented by anaphoric relations and other secondary dependencies. The framework forms the basis for the annotation of syntax, discourse, and anaphora in the Copenhagen Dependency Treebanks. In future papers, we will address some of the criticisms that have been raised against tree-based theories of discourse.

## 7 Acknowledgments

This work was supported by a grant from the Danish Research Council for the Humanities. Thanks to Bonnie Webber, Henrik Høeg Müller, Per Anker Jensen, Peter Colliander, and our three reviewers for their valuable commments.

## References


Matthias Buch-Kromann 2006. *Discontinuous Grammar. A dependency-based model of human parsing and language learning*. Copenhagen: Copenhagen Business School.

Matthias Buch-Kromann, Iørn Korzen, and Henrik Høeg Müller. 2009. Uncovering the 'lost' structure of translations with parallel treebanks. *Copenhagen Studies in Language* 38: 199-224.

Matthias Buch-Kromann, Jürgen Wedekind, and Jakob Elming. 2007. The Copenhagen Danish-English Dependency Treebank v. 2.0. http://code.google.com/p/copenhagen-dependency-treebank

Lynn Carlson and Daniel Marcu. 2001. *Discourse Tagging Reference Manual*. ISI Technical Report ISI-TR-545.

Lynn Carlson, Daniel Marcu, and Mary Ellen Okurowski. 2001. Building a Discourse-Tagged Corpus in the Framework of Rhetorical Structure Theory. In *Proc. of the 2nd SIGdial Workshop on Discourse and Dialogue*. Association for Computational Linguistics: 1-10.

William Croft. 1995. What's a head? In J. Rooryck and L. Zaring (eds.). *Phrase Structure and the Lexicon*. Kluwer.

Nikhil Dinesh, Alan Lee, Eleni Miltsakaki, Rashmi Prasad, Aravind Joshi, and Bonnie Webber. 2005. Attribution and the (Non-)Alignment of Syntactic and Discourse Arguments of Connectives. *Proc. of the Workshop on Frontiers in Corpus Annotation II: Pie in the Sky*, pp. 29-36.

Britt Keson and Ole Norling-Christensen. 1998. PA-ROLE-DK. The Danish Society for Language and Literature.

Iørn Korzen. 2006. Endocentric and Exocentric Languages in Translation. *Perspectives: Studies in Translatology*, 13 (1): 21-37.

Iørn Korzen. 2007. Linguistic typology, text structure and appositions. In I. Korzen, M. Lambert, H. Vassiliadou. *Langues d'Europe, l'Europe des langues. Croisements linguistiques. Scolia* 22: 21-42.

Matthias T. Kromann. 2003. The Danish Dependency Treebank and the DTAG treebank tool. In *Proc. of Treebanks and Linguistic Theories (TLT 2003), 14-15 November, Växjö*. 217–220.

Alan Lee, Rashmi Prasad, Aravind Joshi, and Bonnie Webber 2008. Departures from Tree Structures in Discourse: Shared Arguments in the Penn Discourse Treebank. *Proceedings of the Constraints in Discourse III Workshop.*

Willliam C. Mann and Sandra A. Thompson 1987. *Rhetorical Structure Theory. A Theory of Text Organization*. ISI: Information Sciences Institute, Los Angeles, CA, ISI/RS-87-190, 1-81.

Christopher D. Manning. 1995. Dissociating functor-argument structure from surface phrase structure: the relationship of HPSG Order Domains to LFG. Ms., Carnegie Mellon University.

Lucie Mladová, Šarka Zikánová, and Eva Hajičová. 2008. From Sentence to Discourse: Building an Annotation Scheme for Discourse Based on Prague Dependency Treebank. In *Proc. 6th International Conference on Language Resources and Evaluation (LREC 2008).*

Rashmi Prasad, Eleni Miltsakaki, Nikhil Dinesh, Alan Lee, Aravind Joshi, Livio Robaldo, and Bonnie Webber. 2007. The Penn Discourse TreeBank 2.0. Annotation Manual. The PDTB Research Group. http://www.seas.upenn.edu/~pdtb/PDTBAPI/pdtb-annotation-manual.pdf

Rashmi Prasad, Nikhil Dinesh, Alan Lee, Eleni Miltsakaki, Livio Robaldo, Aravind Joshi, and Bonnie Webber. 2008. The Penn Discourse TreeBank 2.0. In *Proc. 6th Int. Conf. on Language Resources and Evaluation*, Marrakech, Morocco.

Manfred Stede. 2008. Disambiguating Rhetorical Structure. *Research on Language and Computation* (6), pp. 311-332..

Maite Taboada and William C. Mann. 2006a. Rhetorical Structure Theory: looking back and moving ahead. *Discourse Studies* 8/3/423.

Maite Taboada and William C. Mann. 2006b. Applications of Rhetorical Structure Theory. *Discourse Studies* 8/4/567. http://dis.sagepub.com

Bonnie Webber. 2004. D-LTAG: extending lexicalized TAG to discourse. *Cognitive Science* 28: 751-779.

Bonnie Webber. 2006. Accounting for Discourse Relation: Constituency and Dependency. M. Dalrymple (ed.). *Festschrift for Ron Kaplan*. CSLI Publications.

Florian Wolf and Edward Gibson 2005. Representing Discourse Coherence: A Corpus-Based Study. Computational Linguistics 31(2), 249-287.

# Identifying Sources of Inter-Annotator Variation: Evaluating Two Models of Argument Analysis

**Barbara White**
The University of Western Ontario
London, ON, Canada N6A 3K7
bwhite6@uwo.ca

## Abstract

This paper reports on a pilot study where two Models of argument were applied to the Discussion sections of a corpus of biomedical research articles. The goal was to identify sources of systematic inter-annotator variation as diagnostics for improving the Models. In addition to showing a need to revise both Models, the results identified problems resulting from limitations in annotator expertise. In future work two types of annotators are required: those with biomedical domain expertise and those with an understanding of rhetorical structure.

## 1 Introduction

Given the vast and growing body of biomedical research literature being published there is a need to develop automated text mining tools that will assist in filtering out the information most useful to researchers. Previous studies applying Argumentative Zoning (AZ) (Teufel et al. 1999) and Zone Analysis (ZA) (Mizuta et al. 2005) have shown that an analysis of the argumentative structure of a text can be of use in Information Extraction (IE). As an alternative approach, it was believed that Toulmin's work on informal logic and argument structure (1958/2003) could reflect the rhetorical strategies used by the authors of biomedical research articles.

In order to compare and evaluate these approaches two Models of argument were applied to the same set of biomedical research articles. Inter-annotator agreement/disagreement between and within Models was examined. Given that human-annotated data are ultimately to be used for machine learning purposes, there is growing recognition of the need to analyze coder disagreements in order to differentiate between systematic variation and noise (e.g. Reidsma and Carletta 2008). The goal of this study was to identify systematic disagreements as diagnostics for improving the Models of argument.

## 2 Annotation Project

The two Models of rhetoric (argument) in Tables 1 and 2 were applied to a corpus of 12 articles downloaded at random from the *BMC-series* (BioMed Central) of journals. The corpus covered nine different domains, with a total of 400 sentences; the three annotators worked independently. Although the entire articles were read by the annotators, only the sentences in the Discussion section were argumentatively categorized. The annotators were the study coordinator (B, a PhD student in Computational Linguistics and current author) and two fourth year undergraduate students from the Bachelor of Medical Sciences program at The University of Western Ontario (J and K).

Coders annotated one article at a time, applying each of the two Models; no sentence was allowed to be left unannotated. In cases where an annotator was conflicted between categories guidelines for 'trumping' were provided with the Models. (For details on the Models, trumping systems, instructions to annotators, corpus data and a sample annotated article please see www.csd.uwo.ca/~mercer/White_Thesis09.pdf.)

The first model (Model 1) of argumentation to be applied stems from work in AZ and ZA and was adapted by White. It focuses on the content of a text, essentially differentiating 'new' from 'old' information, and results from analysis (Table 1). The second model is based on the concepts and language of Toulmin (1958/2003). Jenicek applied Toulmin to create a guide for writing medical research articles (2006) and Graves (personal communications 2008, 2009) further adapted these ideas to work with our corpus (Model 2). Its main focus is to identify 'Claims' being made by the authors, but it also differentiates between internal and external evidence, as



*Proceedings of the Fourth Linguistic Annotation Workshop, ACL 2010*, pages 132–136,
Uppsala, Sweden, 15-16 July 2010. ©2010 Association for Computational Linguistics

well as categories of explanation and implication (Table 2).

| Category | Specifications |
|---|---|
| CONTEXT (1) | Background, accepted facts, previous work, motivation |
| METHOD (2) | Methods, tools, processes, experimental design |
| CURRENT RESULTS (3) | Findings of current experiment |
| RESULTS COMPARED (4) | Current results support or contradict previous work |
| ANALYSIS (5) | Possible interpretations or implications of current or previous results, significance or limitations of their study |

**Table 1: Model 1 categories (White 2009)**

| Category | Specifications |
|---|---|
| EXTRANEOUS (0) | Statements extraneous to authors' argumentation, not related to a CLAIM |
| CLAIM (1) | Proposition put forward based on analysis of results |
| GROUNDS (2) | Internal evidence from current study |
| WARRANT/ BACKING (3) | Understanding of the problem, or data, from other studies |
| QUALIFIER (4) | Possible explanations for results, comparisons with external evidence |
| PROBLEM IN CONTEXT (5) | Implications for the field, future research directions |

**Table 2: Model 2 categories (Toulmin 1958, Jenicek 2006, Graves 2009)**

### 2.1 Results

Data were compiled on individual annotator's argument category choices for each of the 400 sentences, for each Model of rhetoric. This allowed comparisons to be made between the two Models, within Model by category, and between annotators. Although the coders had different backgrounds, they were treated as equals i.e. there was no 'expert' who served as a benchmark. There were three possible types of inter-annotator agreement: we all agreed on a choice of category, we all differed, or two annotators agreed and the third disagreed. This latter group of two-way agreement (also implying two-way variation) was broken down into its three possibilities: J and K agreed, and differed from B (JK~B), J and B agreed, and differed from K (JB~K), or B and K agreed, and differed from J (BK~J) (Table 3).

| | Model 1 | | Model 2 | |
|---|---|---|---|---|
| All agree | 242 | 60.50% | 157 | 39.25% |
| All disagree | 15 | 3.75% | 33 | 8.25% |
| JK~B | 32 | 8.00% | 71 | 17.75% |
| JB~K | 42 | 10.50% | 68 | 17.00% |
| BK~J | 69 | 17.25% | 71 | 17.75% |
| Total | 400 | 100% | 400 | 100% |

**Table 3 Number of sentences in agreement groups**

The overall (three-way) inter-annotator agreement was higher for Model 1 at 60.5%, with Model 2 at 39.25%. All annotators were less familiar with Model 2 than Model 1, and the former had one more category, thus there was more opportunity to disagree. Although there is no guarantee that three-way agreement implies we were all 'right', it does suggest a shared understanding of what the Model categories describe. On the other hand, there were instances of sentences under both Models where three different categories had been chosen but they could all seem to legitimately apply. In addition, in sentences which are argumentatively and/or grammatically complex, where one is forced to choose only one categorization, it is often difficult to decide which is the most appropriate.

Given the difference in academic background of the annotators, one hypothesis had been that J and K would be more likely to agree with each other and differ from B, the coder who was not knowledgeable in the biomedical sciences. As can be seen in Table 3, however, this did not turn out to be the case.

## 3 Sources of Inter-Annotator Variation

It was crucial to examine inter-annotator disagreements within each Model in order to determine the categories that were particular sources of variation. As a reference point for this, and for looking at individual annotator preferences, I present in Tables 4 and 5 the overall distribution of argument categories within Model. These are calculated on the basis of all 1200 annotation tokens (400 sentences * 3 annotators) across the corpus.

### 3.1 Model 1

| Category | Tokens | Percent |
|---|---|---|
| CONTEXT (1) | 337 | 28.0% |
| METHOD (2) | 128 | 10.7% |
| CURRENT RESULTS (3) | 189 | 15.8% |
| RESULTS COMPARED (4) | 114 | 9.5% |
| ANALYSIS (5) | 432 | 36.0% |
| **Total** | 1200 | 100% |

**Table 4 Overall distribution by category – Model 1**

The CONTEXT category was developed in order to filter out background ('old') material. Although this seemed straightforward, the results showed that CONTEXT was the largest source of inter-annotator variation under Model 1: of the 158 sentences that had some degree of inter-annotator variation, almost two-thirds (100) involved some variation between CONTEXT and another category. The primary reason for this was that frequently sentences in our corpus that included category (1) material also included material suited to other categories (typically ANALYSIS or RESULTS COMPARED) i.e. they were complex sentences. There was also inter-annotator disagreement between CURRENT RESULTS (3) and RESULTS COMPARED (4); this was to be expected given the potential overlap of content when discussing the authors' current study, especially in complex sentences.

### 3.2 Model 2

| Category | Tokens | Percent |
|---|---|---|
| EXTRANEOUS (0) | 250 | 20.8% |
| CLAIM (1) | 185 | 15.4% |
| GROUNDS (2) | 218 | 18.2% |
| WARRANT/ BACKING (3) | 215 | 18.0% |
| QUALIFIER (4) | 256 | 21.3% |
| PROBLEM IN CONTEXT (5) | 76 | 6.3% |
| **Total** | 1200 | 100% |

**Table 5 Overall distribution by category – Model 2**

The EXTRANEOUS category had been developed for sentences of a 'background' nature, which did not fit into the Toulmin argument structure i.e. they did not seem to relate directly to any CLAIM. Of the 243 sentences with some degree of inter-annotator variation under Model 2, 101 involved the EXTRANEOUS category. This variation a) showed that there were problems in understanding argument structure, and b) reflected the differences in annotator preferences (Table 7).

Model 2 is crucially a CLAIMS-based system, so variation between CLAIMS and other categories is particularly significant, especially since it is assumed that this might be the category of greatest interest to biomedical researchers. There were 52 sentences which involved some variation between CLAIM (1) and QUALIFIER (4), a fact which revealed a need to make clearer distinctions between these two categories. Many sentences in our corpus seemed to meet the specifications for both categories at the same time i.e. they were both an explanation and a conclusion. There were 46 sentences involving some disagreement between (4) and WARRANT/BACKING (3). The source of this variation seemed to be the difficulty deciding whether the 'compare and contrast with external evidence' aspect of (4) or the straightforward 'external evidence' of (3) was more appropriate for certain, especially complex, sentences.

### 3.3 Annotators

Under Model 1 the three annotator columns show a relatively similar distribution (Table 6). The exception is that J was less inclined to select the CONTEXT category, and more inclined to select RESULTS COMPARED, than either B or K.

| Category | B | J | K | Total |
|---|---|---|---|---|
| CONTEXT (1) | 121 | 92 | 124 | 337 |
| METHOD (2) | 39 | 43 | 46 | 128 |
| CURRENT RESULTS (3) | 59 | 67 | 63 | 189 |
| RESULTS COMPARED (4) | 36 | 57 | 21 | 114 |
| ANALYSIS (5) | 145 | 141 | 146 | 432 |
| **Total** | 400 | 400 | 400 | 1200 |

**Table 6 Category distribution by annotator – Model 1**

Under Model 2 we see an extreme range among annotators in the number of sentences they identified as EXTRANEOUS with J having more than twice as many as B (Table 7). This degree of annotator bias guaranteed that category

(0) would be involved in considerable inter-annotator disagreement. The other notable skewing occurred in categories (1) and (4) where B and J shared similar numbers as opposed to K: K had 91 sentences as CLAIM, almost twice as many as B or J, and only 50 sentences as QUALIFIER, roughly half as many as B or J.

| Category | B | J | K | Total |
|---|---|---|---|---|
| EXTRANEOUS (0) | 54 | 116 | 80 | 250 |
| CLAIM (1) | 45 | 49 | 91 | 185 |
| GROUNDS (2) | 86 | 61 | 71 | 218 |
| WARRANT/ BACKING (3) | 81 | 49 | 85 | 215 |
| QUALIFIER (4) | 108 | 98 | 50 | 256 |
| PROBLEM IN CONTEXT (5) | 26 | 27 | 23 | 76 |
| **Total** | 400 | 400 | 400 | 1200 |

**Table 7 Category distribution by annotator – Model 2**

In addition to the systematic annotator preferences discussed above there were instances of 'errors', choices which appear to be violations of category specifications. These may be the result of haste or inattention, insufficient training or a lack of understanding of the article's content or the Models.

### 3.4 Corpus Data

It was assumed that longer sentences would be more likely to be complex and thus more likely to involve inter-annotator variation. The results showed that the articles with the smallest (19) and largest (31) average number of words per sentence did exhibit this pattern: the former ranked highly in three-way annotator agreement (first under Model 1 and second under Model 2) and the latter second lowest under both Models. However, between these extremes there was no clear relationship between sentence length and overall coder agreement under either Model. The most striking finding was the wide range of three-way coder agreement among the twelve articles in the corpus: from 36% to 81% under Model 1 and 8% to 69% under Model 2. The averages in Table 3 mask this source of inter-annotator variation.

## 4 Conclusion

The problem of choosing a single argument category for a complex sentence was at the core of much of the inter-annotator variation found under both Models. The issue of sentences which are rhetorically but not grammatically complex e.g. those with a single tensed verb that seemed to qualify as both a CLAIM and a QUALIFIER under Model 2 should be dealt with where possible by revising the category specifications. However sentences that are grammatically complex should be divided into clauses (one for each tensed verb) as a pre-annotating process. Although this creates more units and thus more opportunities for coders to disagree, it is believed that reducing uncertainty by allowing a different argument category for each clause would be worth the trade-off.

Although Model 1 had higher average three-way agreement at 60.5% than Model 2, this was still relatively poor performance. As discussed above the clear problem with this Model is the CONTEXT (1) category. Research scientists are always working within and building on previous work – their own and others'; thus 'old' and 'new' information are inherently intertwined. Therefore this category needs to be revised, possibly separating specific previous studies from statements related to the motivation for or goals of the current experiment. As discussed above, the EXTRANEOUS category of Model 2 needs to be redefined, and the CLAIM and QUALIFIER categories must be clearly distinguished. Despite the relatively poor performance of Model 2, with the above improvements it is believed that a CLAIMS-based Model is still a good candidate for developing future IE tools.

Annotator bias reflects the fact that coders did not have sufficient understanding of rhetorical techniques and structure, but also the problems with category specifications noted above. The extreme 'inter-article' variation (Section 3.4) indicates that when texts are not clearly written, an annotator's lack of knowledge of biomedicine and/or argument are even more problematic. Since the quality of writing in a corpus is a factor that cannot be controlled 'team' annotations are recommended: a biomedical domain expert should work together with an expert in rhetoric.

It must be admitted, however, that even with improvements to the Models of argument and using annotators with more domain expertise, some degree of inter-annotator disagreement will inevitably occur as a result of individual differences. Ultimately annotators are making judgments – about texts and arguments that were created by others – that are somewhat subjective.

## References


Milos Jenicek. 2006. How to read, understand, and write 'Discussion' sections in medical articles: An exercise in critical thinking. *Med Sci Monitor*, 12(6): SR28-SR36.

Yoko Mizuta, Anna Korhonen, Tony Mullen and Nigel Collier. 2005. Zone Analysis in Biology Articles as a Basis for Information Extraction. *International Journal of Medical Informatics*, 75(6): 468-487.

Dennis Reidsma and Jean Carletta. 2008. Reliability Measurement without Limits. *Computational Linguistics*, 34(3): 319-326.

Simone Teufel, Jean Carletta and Mark Moens. 1999. An annotation scheme for discourse-level argumentation in research articles. *Proceedings of the Eighth Meeting of the European Chapter of the Association for Computational Linguistics*: 110-117.

Stephen E. Toulmin. 1958/2003. *The Uses of Argument*. Cambridge University Press, Cambridge, U.K.

Barbara White. 2009. *Annotating a Corpus of Biomedical Research Texts: Two Models of Rhetorical Analysis*. PhD thesis, The University of Western Ontario, Canada. www.csd.uwo.ca/~mercer/White_Thesis09.pdf

# Dependency-based PropBanking of clinical Finnish

**Katri Haverinen,**[1,3] **Filip Ginter,**[1] **Timo Viljanen,**[1]
**Veronika Laippala**[2] **and Tapio Salakoski**[1,3]
[1]Department of Information Technology
[2]Department of French Studies
[3]Turku Centre for Computer Science, TUCS
20014 University of Turku, Finland
first.last@utu.fi

## Abstract

In this paper, we present a PropBank of clinical Finnish, an annotated corpus of verbal propositions and arguments. The clinical PropBank is created on top of a previously existing dependency treebank annotated in the Stanford Dependency (SD) scheme and covers 90% of all verb occurrences in the treebank.

We establish that the PropBank scheme is applicable to clinical Finnish as well as compatible with the SD scheme, with an overwhelming proportion of arguments being governed by the verb. This allows argument candidates to be restricted to direct verb dependents, substantially simplifying the PropBank construction.

The clinical Finnish PropBank is freely available at the address http://bionlp.utu.fi.

## 1 Introduction

Natural language processing (NLP) in the clinical domain has received substantial interest, with applications in decision support, patient managing and profiling, mining trends, and others (see the extensive review by Friedman and Johnson (2006)). While some of these applications, such as document retrieval and trend mining, can rely solely on word-frequency-based methods, others, such as information extraction and summarization require a detailed linguistic analysis capturing some of the sentence semantics. Among the most important steps in this direction is an analysis of verbs and their argument structures.

In this work, we focus on the Finnish language in the clinical domain, analyzing its verbs and their argument structures using the PropBank scheme (Palmer et al., 2005). The choice of this particular scheme is motivated by its practical, application-oriented nature. We build the clinical Finnish PropBank on top of the existing dependency treebank of Haverinen et al. (2009).

The primary outcome of this study is the PropBank of clinical Finnish itself, consisting of the analyses for 157 verbs with 2,382 occurrences and 4,763 arguments, and covering 90% of all verb occurrences in the underlying treebank. This PropBank, together with the treebank, is an important resource for the further development of clinical NLP applications for the Finnish language.

We also establish the applicability of the PropBank scheme to the clinical sublanguage with its many atypical characteristics, and finally, we find that the PropBank scheme is compatible with the Stanford Dependency scheme of de Marneffe and Manning (2008a; 2008b) in which the underlying treebank is annotated.

## 2 The PropBank scheme

Our annotation work is based on the PropBank semantic annotation scheme of Palmer et al. (2005). For each verb, PropBank defines a number of *framesets*, each frameset corresponding to a coarse-grained sense. A frameset consists of a *roleset* which defines a set of *roles* (*arguments* numbered from Arg0 onwards) and their descriptions, and a set of syntactic *frames*. Any element that occurs together with a given verb sufficiently frequently is taken to be its argument. Arg0 is generally a *prototypical Agent* argument and Arg1 is a *prototypical Patient or Theme* argument. The remaining numbered arguments have no consistent overall meanings: they are defined on a verb-by-verb basis. An illustration of a verb with two framesets is given in Figure 1. In addition to the numbered arguments, a verb occurrence can have a number of modifiers, labeled ArgM, each modifier being categorized as one of 14 subtypes, such as *temporal*, *cause* and *location*.



*Proceedings of the Fourth Linguistic Annotation Workshop, ACL 2010*, pages 137–141,
Uppsala, Sweden, 15-16 July 2010. ©2010 Association for Computational Linguistics

| | |
|---|---|
| kestää.0: "tolerate" | kestää.1: "last" |
| Arg0: the one who tolerates | Arg1: the thing that lasts |
| Arg1: what is being tolerated | Arg2: how long it lasts |

Figure 1: The PropBank framesets for *kestää* (translated to English from the original frames file) correspond to two different uses of the verb.

| | |
|---|---|
| Pitkä yövuoro | Long nightshift |
| Jouduttu laittamaan | Had to put to |
| illala bipap:lle, | bipap in the evning, |
| nyt hapettuu hyvin. | now oxidizes well. |
| DIUREESI: riittävää | DIURESIS: sufficient |
| Tajunta: rauhallinen | Consciousness: calm |
| hrhoja ei enää ole | there are no more hllucinations |

Figure 2: Example of clinical Finnish (left column) and its exact translation (right column), with typical features such as spelling errors preserved.

## 3 Clinical Finnish and the clinical Finnish treebank

This study is based on the clinical Finnish treebank of Haverinen et al. (2009), which consists of 2,081 sentences with 15,335 tokens and 13,457 dependencies. The text of the treebank comprises eight complete patient reports from an intensive care unit in a Finnish hospital. An intensive care patient report describes the condition of the patient and its development in time. The *clinical Finnish* in these reports has many characteristics typical of clinical languages, including frequent misspellings, abbreviations, domain terms, telegraphic style and non-standard syntactic structures (see Figure 2 for an illustration). For a detailed analysis, we refer the reader to the studies by Laippala et al. (2009) and Haverinen et al. (2009).

The treebank of Haverinen et al. is annotated in the Stanford Dependency (SD) scheme of de Marneffe and Manning (2008a; 2008b). This scheme is layered, and the annotation variant of the treebank of Haverinen et. al is the *basic* variant of the scheme, in which the analysis forms a tree.

The SD scheme also defines a *collapsed dependencies with propagation of conjunct dependencies* variant (referred to as the *extended* variant of the SD scheme throughout this paper). It adds on top of the *basic* variant a second layer of dependencies which are not part of the strict, syntactic tree. In particular, the *xsubj* dependency marks external subjects, and dependencies involving the heads of coordinations are explicitly duplicated also for the remaining coordinated elements where appropriate. The *extended* variant of the SD scheme is illustrated in Figure 3.

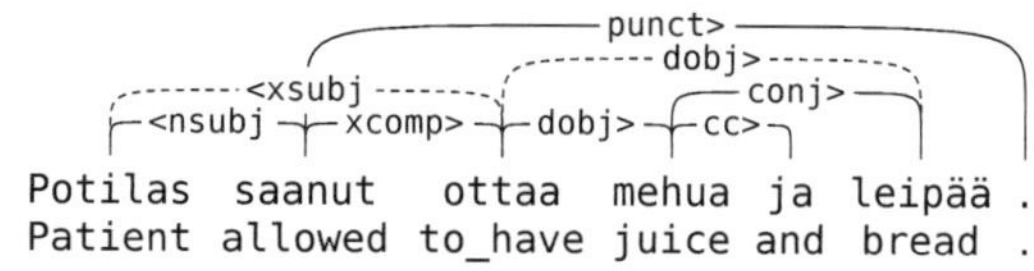


Figure 3: The *extended* SD scheme. The dashed dependencies denote the external subjects and propagated conjunct dependencies that are only part of the *extended* variant of the scheme. The example can be translated as *Patient [has been] allowed to have juice and bread.*

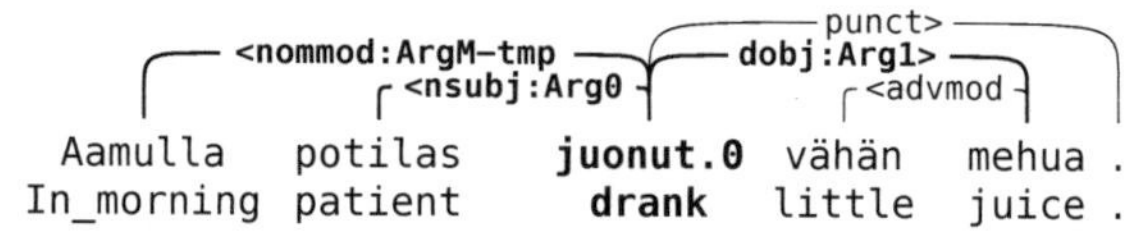


Figure 4: The PropBank annotation scheme on top of the treebank syntactic annotation. The verb *juonut (drank)* is marked with its frameset, in this case the frameset number 0. This frameset specifies that Arg0 marks the agent doing the drinking and Arg1 the liquid being consumed. The ArgM-tmp label specifies that *Aamulla* is a temporal modifier. The example can be translated as *In the morning patient drank a little juice.*

Due to the importance of the additional dependencies for PropBanking (see Section 5 for discussion), we augment the annotation of the underlying treebank to conform to the *extended* variant of the SD scheme by manual annotation, adding a total of 520 dependencies.

The PropBank was originally developed on top of the constituency scheme of the Penn Treebank and requires arguments to correspond to constituents. In a dependency scheme, where there is no explicit notion of constituents, we associate arguments of a verb with dependencies governed by it. The argument can then be understood as the entire subtree headed by the dependent. The annotation is illustrated in Figure 4.

## 4 PropBanking clinical Finnish

When annotating the clinical Finnish PropBank, we consider all verbs with at least three occurrences in the underlying treebank. In total, we analyze 157 verbs with 192 framesets. Since the treebank does not have gold-standard POS infor-

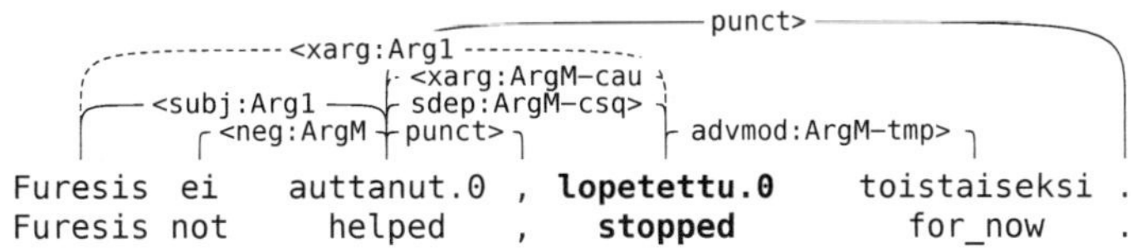


Figure 5: The simplified PropBank annotation strategy. The dashed dependencies labeled with the technical dependency type *xarg* signify arguments and modifiers not in a syntactic relationship to the verb. These arguments and modifiers, as well as those associated with a *conj* or *sdep* dependency (ArgM-csq in this Figure), are only marked in the 100 sentence sample for quantifying unannotated arguments and modifiers. The sentence can be translated as *Furesis did not help, stopped for now.*

mation, we identify all verbs and verbal participles using the FinCG[1] analyzer, which gives a verbal reading to 2,816 tokens. With POS tagging errors taken into account, we estimate the treebank to contain 2,655 occurrences of verbs and verb participles. Of these, 2,382 (90%) correspond to verbs with at least three occurrences and are thus annotated. In total, these verbs have 4,763 arguments and modifiers.

Due to the telegraphic nature of clinical Finnish, omissions of different sentence elements, even main verbs, are very frequent. In order to be able to analyze the syntax of sentences with a missing main verb, Haverinen et al. have added a so called *null verb* to these sentences in the treebank. For instance, the clinical Finnish sentence *Putkesta nestettä (Liquid from the drain)* lacks a main verb, and the insertion of one produces *Putkesta *null* nestettä*. In total, there are 428 null verb occurrences, making the null verb the most common verb in the treebank.

In the clinical PropBank annotation, we treat the null verb in principle as if it was a regular verb, and give it framesets accordingly. For each null verb occurrence, we have determined which regular verb frameset it stands for, and found that, somewhat surprisingly, there were only four common coarse senses of the null verb, roughly corresponding to four framesets of the verbs *olla (to be)*, *tulla (to come)*, *tehdä (to do)* and *laittaa (to put)*. The 26 (6%) null verb occurrences that did not correspond to any of these four framesets were assigned to a "leftover frameset", for which no arguments were marked.

[1]http://www.lingsoft.fi

## 5 Annotating the arguments on top of the SD scheme

In contrast to the original PropBank, where any syntactic constituent could be marked as an argument, we require arguments to be directly dependent on the verb in the SD scheme (for an illustration, see Figure 5). This restriction is to considerably simplify the annotation process — instead of all possible subtrees, the annotator only needs to look for direct dependents of the verb. In addition, this constraint should naturally also simplify possible automatic identification and classification of the arguments.

In addition to restricting arguments to direct dependents of the verb, coordination dependencies *conj* and *sdep* (implicit coordination of top level independent clauses, see Figure 5) are left outside the annotation scope. This is due to the nature of the clinical language, which places on these dependencies cause-consequence relationships that require strong inference. For instance, sentences such as *Patient restless, given tranquilizers* where there is clearly a causal relationship but no explicit marker such as *thus* or *because*, are common.

Naturally, it is necessary to estimate the effect of these restrictions, which can be justified only if the number of lost arguments is minimal. We have conducted a small-scale experiment on 100 randomly selected sentences with at least one verb that has a frameset assigned. We have provided this portion of the clinical PropBank with a full annotation, including the arguments not governed by the verb and those associated with *conj* and *sdep* dependencies. For an illustration, see Figure 5.

There are in total 326 arguments and modifiers (169 arguments and 157 modifiers) in the 100 sentence sample. Of these, 278 (85%) are governed by the verb in the *basic* SD scheme and are thus in a direct syntactic relationship with the verb. Further 19 (6%) arguments and modifiers are governed by the verb in the *extended* SD scheme. Out of the remaining 29 (9%), 23 are in fact modifiers, leaving only 6 numbered arguments not accounted for in the *extended* SD scheme. Thus, 96% (163/169) of arguments and 85% (134/157) of modifiers are directly governed by the verb.

Of the 23 ungoverned modifiers, all are either cause (CAU) or consequence (CSQ)[2]. Of the *sdep* and *conj* dependencies only a small portion (9/68) were associated with an argument or a modifier, all of which were in fact CAU or CSQ modifiers. Both these and the CAU and CSQ modifiers not governed by the verb reflect strongly inferred relationships between clauses.

Based on these figures, we conclude that an overwhelming majority of arguments and modifiers is governed by the verb in the *extended* SD scheme and restricting the annotation to dependents of the verb as well as leaving *sdep* and *conj* outside the annotation scope seems justified. Additionally, we demonstrate the utility of the conjunct dependency propagation and external subject marking in the *extended* SD scheme.

## 6 Related work

Many efforts have been made to capture meanings and arguments of verbs. For instance, the VerbNet project (Kipper et al., 2000) strives to create a broad on-line verb lexicon, and FrameNet (Ruppenhofer et al., 2005) aims to document the range of valences of each verb in each of its senses. The PropBank project (Palmer et al., 2005) strives for a practical approach to semantic representation, adding a layer of semantic role labels to the Penn Treebank (Marcus et al., 1993).

In addition to the original PropBank by Palmer et al., numerous PropBanks have been developed for languages other than English (e.g. Chinese (Xue and Palmer, 2003) and Arabic (Diab et al., 2008)). Also applications attempting to automatically recover PropBank-style arguments have been proposed. For example, the CoNLL shared task has focused on semantic role labeling four times, twice as a separate task (Carreras and Màrquez, 2004; Carreras and Màrquez, 2005), and twice in conjunction with syntactic parsing (Surdeanu et al., 2008; Hajič et al., 2009).

In semantic analysis of clinical language, Paek et al. (2006) have experimented on PropBank-based machine learning on abstracts of Randomized Controlled Trials (RCTs), and Savova et al. (2009) have presented work on temporal relation discovery from clinical narratives.

## 7 Conclusion

In this paper, we have presented a PropBank of clinical Finnish, building a new layer of annotation on top of the existing clinical treebank of Haverinen et al. (2009). This PropBank covers all 157 verbs occurring at least three times in the treebank and accounts for 90% of all verb occurrences.

This work has also served as a test case for the PropBank annotation scheme in two senses. First, the scheme has been tested on a highly specialized language, clinical Finnish, and second, its compatibility with the SD syntactic scheme has been examined. On both accounts, we find the PropBank scheme a suitable choice.

In general, the specialized language did not seem to cause problems for the scheme. For instance, the frequent null verbs could be analyzed similarly to regular verbs, with full 94% belonging to one of only four framesets. This is likely due to the very restricted clinical domain of the corpus.

We also find a strong correspondence between the PropBank arguments and the verb dependents in the *extended* SD scheme, with 96% of arguments and 85% of modifiers being directly governed by the verb. The 15% ungoverned modifiers are cause-consequence relationships that require strong inference. This correspondence allowed us to simplify the annotation task by only considering direct verb dependents as argument candidates.

The new version of the treebank, manually anonymized, including the enhanced SD scheme annotation and the PropBank annotation, is freely available at `http://bionlp.utu.fi`.


## Acknowledgments

We are grateful to Heljä Lundgren-Laine, Riitta Danielsson-Ojala and prof. Sanna Salanterä for their assistance in the anonymization of the corpus. We would also like to thank Lingsoft Ltd. for making FinTWOL and FinCG available to us. This work was supported by the Academy of Finland.


[2]CSQ is a new modifier subtype added by us, due to the restriction of only annotating direct syntactic dependents, which does not allow the annotation of all causal relationships with the type CAU.

## References


Xavier Carreras and Lluís Màrquez. 2004. Introduction to the CoNLL-2004 shared task: Semantic role labeling. In *HLT-NAACL 2004 Workshop: Eighth Conference on Computational Natural Language Learning (CoNLL-2004)*, pages 89–97, Boston, Massachusetts, USA, May 6 - May 7. Association for Computational Linguistics.

Xavier Carreras and Lluís Màrquez. 2005. Introduction to the CoNLL-2005 shared task: Semantic role labeling. In *Proceedings of the Ninth Conference on Computational Natural Language Learning (CoNLL-2005)*, pages 152–164, Ann Arbor, Michigan, June. Association for Computational Linguistics.

Marie-Catherine de Marneffe and Christopher Manning. 2008a. Stanford typed dependencies manual. Technical report, Stanford University, September.

Marie-Catherine de Marneffe and Christopher Manning. 2008b. Stanford typed dependencies representation. In *Proceedings of COLING'08, Workshop on Cross-Framework and Cross-Domain Parser Evaluation*, pages 1–8.

Mona Diab, Mansouri Aous, Martha Palmer, Babko-Malaya Olga, Wadji Zaghouani, Ann Bies, and Mohammed Maamouri. 2008. A pilot Arabic PropBank. In *Proceedings of LREC'08*, pages 3467–3472. Association for Computational Linguistics.

Carol Friedman and Stephen Johnson. 2006. Natural language and text processing in biomedicine. In *Biomedical Informatics*, pages 312–343. Springer.

Jan Hajič, Massimiliano Ciaramita, Richard Johansson, Daisuke Kawahara, Maria A. Martí, Lluís Màrquez, Adam Meyers, Joakim Nivre, Sebastian Padó, Jan Štěpánek, Pavel Straňák, Mihai Surdeanu, Niawen Xue, and Yi Zhang. 2009. The CoNLL-2008 shared task: Syntactic and semantic dependencies in multiple languages. In *Proceedings of CoNLL'09: Shared Task*, pages 1–18. Association for Computational Linguistics.

Katri Haverinen, Filip Ginter, Veronika Laippala, and Tapio Salakoski. 2009. Parsing clinical Finnish: Experiments with rule-based and statistical dependency parsers. In *Proceedings of NODALIDA'09, Odense, Denmark*, pages 65–72.

Karin Kipper, Hoa Trang Dang, and Martha Palmer. 2000. Class-based construction of a verb lexicon. In *Proceedings of the Seventeenth National Conference on Artificial Intelligence and Twelfth Conference on Innovative Applications of Artificial Intelligence*, pages 691–696. AAAI Press / The MIT Press.

Veronika Laippala, Filip Ginter, Sampo Pyysalo, and Tapio Salakoski. 2009. Towards automatic processing of clinical Finnish: A sublanguage analysis and a rule-based parser. *International Journal of Medical Informatics, Special Issue on Mining of Clinical and Biomedical Text and Data*, 78:7–12.

Mitchell Marcus, Beatrice Santorini, and Mary Ann Marcinkiewicz. 1993. Building a large annotated corpus of English: The Penn Treebank. *Computational Linguistics*, 19(2):313–330.

Hyung Paek, Yacov Kogan, Prem Thomas, Seymor Codish, and Michael Krauthammer. 2006. Shallow semantic parsing of randomized controlled trial reports. In *Proceedings of AMIA'06*, pages 604–608.

Martha Palmer, Dan Gildea, and Paul Kingsbury. 2005. The Proposition Bank: an annotated corpus of semantic roles. *Computational Linguistics*, 31(1).

Josef Ruppenhofer, Michael Ellsworth, Miriam R. L. Petruck, Christopher R. Johnson, and Jan Scheffczyk. 2005. FrameNet II: Extended theory and practice. Technical report, ICSI.

Guergana Savova, Steven Bethard, Will Styler, James Martin, Martha Palmer, James Masanz, and Wayne Ward. 2009. Towards temporal relation discovety from the clinical narrative. In *Proceedings of AMIA'09*, pages 568–572.

Mihai Surdeanu, Richard Johansson, Adam Meyers, Lluís Màrquez, and Joakim Nivre. 2008. The CoNLL-2008 shared task on joint parsing on syntactic and semantic dependencies. In *Proceedings of CoNLL'08*, pages 159–177. Association for Computational Linguistics.

Nianwen Xue and Martha Palmer. 2003. Annotating the propositions in the Penn Chinese Treebank. In *Proceedings of the 2nd SIGHAN Workshop on Chinese Language Processing*, pages 47–54, Sapporo, Japan. Association for Computational Linguistics.

# Building the *Syntactic Reference Corpus of Medieval French* Using *NotaBene RDF Annotation Tool*

**Nicolas Mazziotta**
Universität Stuttgart, Institut für Linguistik/Romanistik
nicolas.mazziotta@ulg.ac.be

**Abstract**

In this paper, we introduce the *NotaBene RDF Annotation Tool* free software used to build the *Syntactic Reference Corpus of Medieval French*. It relies on a dependency-based model to manually annotate Old French texts from the *Base de Français Médiéval* and the *Nouveau Corpus d'Amsterdam*.

NotaBene uses OWL ontologies to frame the terminology used in the annotation, which is displayed in a tree-like view of the annotation. This tree widget allows easy grouping and tagging of words and structures. To increase the quality of the annotation, two annotators work independently on the same texts at the same time and NotaBene can also generate automatic comparisons between both analyses. The RDF format can be used to export the data to several other formats: namely, TigerXML (for querying the data and extracting structures) and graphviz dot format (for quoting syntactic description in research papers).

First, we will present the *Syntactic Reference Corpus of Medieval French* project (SRCMF) (1). Then, we will show how the *NotaBene RDF Annotation Tool* software is used within the project (2). In our conclusion, we will stress further developments of the tool (3).

## 1 Introducing the SRCMF Project

### 1.1 Main goals

There currently exists no widely available syntactically annotated corpus for Medieval French. Several syntactic corpora are available for Latin[1] or Old Portuguese.[2] Research for automatic annotation of Medieval French is being carried out by the *Modéliser le changement: les voies du français* project.[3]

SRCMF is an international initiative, gathering French (dir. Sophie Prévost, CNRS, Paris) and German (dir. Achim Stein, Institut für Linguistik/Romanistik, University of Stuttgart) resources and teams. The aim of this project is to provide selected excerpts[4] of the two biggest Medieval French corpora – the *Base de Français Médiéval* (Guillot et al., 2007), and the *Nouveau Corpus d'Amsterdam* (Kunstmann and Stein, 2007a) with a syntactic annotation layer that is meant to follow the same guidelines in both corpora.

It was decided at the very beginning of the project that, at first, the syntactic analysis would be manually added to the corpus by experts, rather than automatically inserted by an automaton.[5]. Accordingly, annotation layers that previously exist are not used to elaborate the new layer. This choice leads to several consequences, when one considers the mistakes that could be made during the annotation procedure: 1/ errors are less systematic than those introduced by an automaton; 2/ the annotation model does not need to be formalised at first; 3/ proofreading is very important. While the first point might be a major advantage in a further statistical exploration of the data (because of the "better" randomness of the errors), the third is a major problem: proofreading is very time-consuming. But as previous automatic POS annotation is provided in both corpora, this tagging can be used *a posteriori*. We plan to perform mutual validation between the POS and the syn-

[1] The *Latin Dependency Treebank* and the *Index Thomisticus Treebank* (Bamman et al., 2008).

[2] *Tycho Brahe* project http://www.tycho.iel.unicamp.br/~tycho/.

[3] Which provide syntactic annotation for 19 texts dating from the 11th to the end of the 13th C. (Martineau, 2008).

[4] There are still legal and technical issues that interfere with the final size of the corpus.

[5] Automatic annotation will be investigated later on.



*Proceedings of the Fourth Linguistic Annotation Workshop, ACL 2010*, pages 142–146,
Uppsala, Sweden, 15-16 July 2010. 

tactic annotations: this procedure is allowed by the independency of their elaborations.

At the time this paper was submitted, the sample annotation of *Le Roman de Tristan* (Defourques and Muret, 1947) (ca 28.000 words, ca 54.000 annotations)[6] has been completed and will be made available soon.

### 1.2 Syntactic Annotation Model

We will not give an in-depth description of the model here: we limit ourselves to a general presentation that will make the rest of the paper more easily understandable.

The deficient nominal flexion in Medieval French makes the task of identifying the head of NPs very difficult, and there is considerable ambiguity. Therefore, the basic annotation we provide only concerns the structure of the clause, and relations at phrase- or word-level (Lazard, 1984) are not described, except by a basic identification of prepositions and conjunctions, and by delimitation, when necessary (e.g., relative clauses occur at phrase-level: we mark their boundaries in order to describe their structure).

It is to be stressed that the added annotations are as genuinely syntactic as possible. This means that neither semantic, nor enunciative analyses are encoded –following the *Théorie des trois points de vue* (Hagège, 1999). On the formal part, as far as morphological features are concerned, only verbal inflexion is taken into account, since it has obvious effects on the syntax of the clause. It is also important to distinguish between *syntactic structures*, which occur at deep level, and *word order*, which is considered as an expression of these structures and does not receive any annotation.

The model is dependency-based (Polguère and Mel'čuk, 2009; Kahane, 2001), and relations are centered on verb forms, which are the main governor nodes of the clauses. Everything in the clause depends on this central verb –including the subject, which is not compulsory in Medieval French, and is therefore described as a complement. The model gives higher priority to morphosyntactic criteria than to semantic ones, and the relation linking it to its satellites can be *qualified* by checking precise criteria. E.g., subjects are identified by verb-subject agreement, objects become subjects in a passive transformation, etc.

[6]We do not provide exact figures, for they are subject to change slightly as we review our annotation work.

### 1.3 Annotation Workflow

Four annotators are currently working on the project.[7] The annotation workflow for each portion of text (ca 2000 words) is the following: 1/ two different annotators perform individual annotation of the same portion of text; 2/ the same people perform a crossed-correction for most obvious errors by the annotators; 3/ two different proofreaders perform a second-step comparison and deal with complex cases.

## 2 NotaBene RDF Annotation Tool

Stein (2008, 165-168) has given a comprehensive specification of what the features of the annotation tool should be. Most importantly, we adopt the principle that the software should provide a convenient interface to manually annotate the syntactic relations between words and also to perform comparisons. *NotaBene RDF Annotation Tool* free software (still in alpha version) focuses on those features.[8] An SRCMF-specific plugin has been designed for manual annotation and annotation comparisons.

### 2.1 General Presentation

As explained in (Mazziotta, forthcoming), NotaBene is an attempt to use Semantic-Web techniques to provide textual data with linguistic annotations. This data has to be valid XML that identifies every taggable token with a unique identifier (e.g.: an `@xml:id` attribute) that is interpreted as a URI. It uses RDF formalisms (Klyne and Carroll, 2004)[9] to store annotations and OWL ontologies to describe terminologies (Bechhofer et al., 2004). NotaBene focuses on multiple conceptualisation and allows concurrent visualisations of the same text/annotation[10]. The use of RDF rather than the more commonly used XML makes it easier to cross several overlapping analysis without having to elaborate complex jointing procedures (Loiseau, 2007).

[7]Currently, the four annotators work part-time on the annotation task, hence, one could say there is the equivalent of two full-time annotators.

[8]It is freely available at `https://sourceforge.net/projects/notabene/`. Note that the documentation is still very sparse; please contact the author if you intend to use the program.

[9]See also the current NotaBene conceptual specification `http://notabene.svn.sourceforge.net/viewvc/notabene/trunk/doc/specification.pdf`, that explains how the RDF model has been restricted.

[10]Furthermore, it can show concurrent terminologies applied to the same text, but we will not discuss it here.

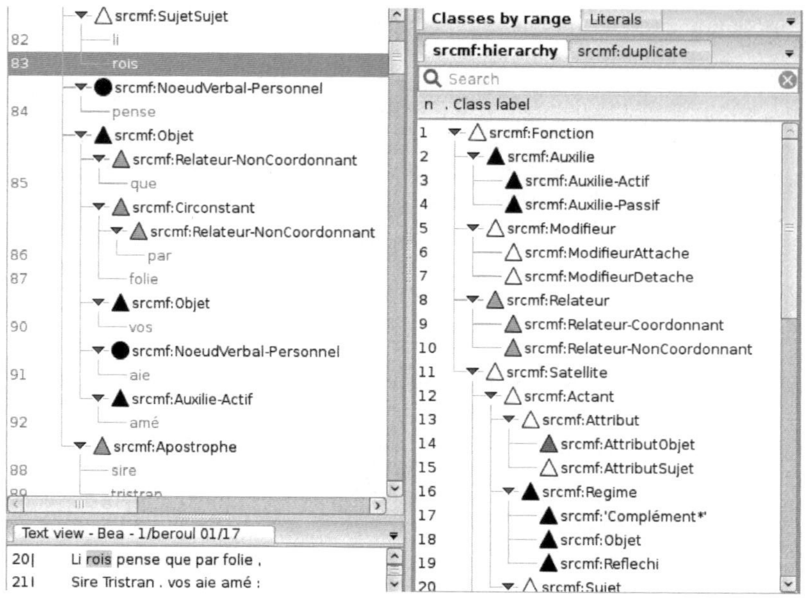


Figure 1: NotaBene SRCMF Working environment

Each visualisation is associated with one or more OWL ontologies. The current terminology is visible on the right panel of the application (see fig. 1, showing some SRCMF-specific classes).[11]

Visualisations are dynamically linked with the RDF data structure, which is updated on-the-fly.

### 2.2 SRCMF Plugin for Syntactic Annotation

For the sake of ergonomics, it turned out to be easier to represent syntactic structures using a constituent-like visualisation. By identifying the governor of each structure, we can use such a visualisation to represent a dependency graph, as there is evidence (Robinson, 1970) of formal equivalence on the two descriptions –we will discuss this later on (see section 2.4). Hence, the main plugin for syntactic annotation is a tree-like widget in which words are displayed vertically from top to bottom in the order of the text. Here is an example of a fully annotated sentence to introduce the interface:

> Li rois pense que par folie, Sire Tristran, vos aie amé ["The king thinks that it was madness that made me love you, Lord Tristan"] –Béroul, in (Defourques and Muret, 1947, v. 20)

As it can be seen on the left panel in fig. 1, the text is wrapped in a hierarchy of folders that mainly represent labelled subtrees[12]. Within each clause, a disc is used to visually identify the main governor, whereas triangles mark its dependents.

At the beginning of the annotation task, the plugin shows a simple list of words, which are selected and wrapped into folders that represent the linguistic analysis of the text. This can be done either by using customisable keyboard shortcuts or by pointing and clicking with the mouse.

A simultaneous view of the running text, preserving references and punctuation, is synchronised with the tree widget (see at the bottom-left corner of fig. 1).

### 2.3 Comparison Procedures

NotaBene's ability to display concurrent annotations of the same text is used to compare the results of the syntactic analysis by two annotators. It identifies structures that differ by not having the same contents or label. As it can be seen in fig. 2, the same structure has not been understood in the same way by the first (who places the *Apostrophe* at the main clause level) and by the second annotator (who places it at the subordinate clause level). At the application level, NotaBene simply sees that the *Objet* folder on the right pane con-

[11] Although the figure shows a tree, the class hierarchy is a graph. See n. 12 for some translations of the labels.

[12] The tag labels translate roughly (the *srcmf* prefix is the namespace of the project): *Phrase* "Clause", *SujetSujet* "Subject", *Objet* "Object", *Circonstant* "Adjunct", *NœudVerbal...* "Finite Verb", *Auxilie...* "Non-finite auxiliated form", *Relateur...* "Conjunction/preposition", *Apostrophe* "Vocative".

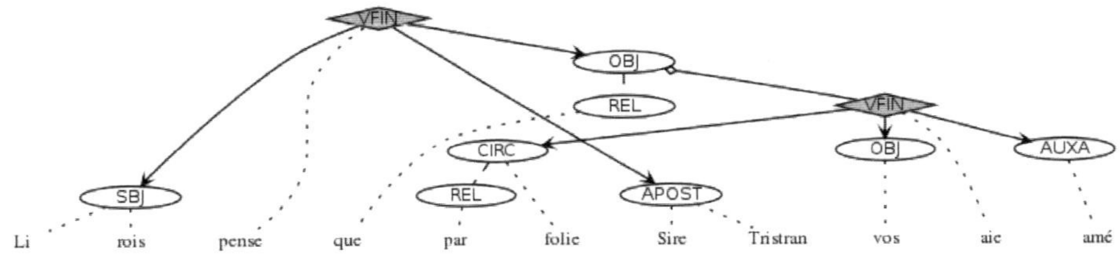


Figure 3: DOT Graph Export

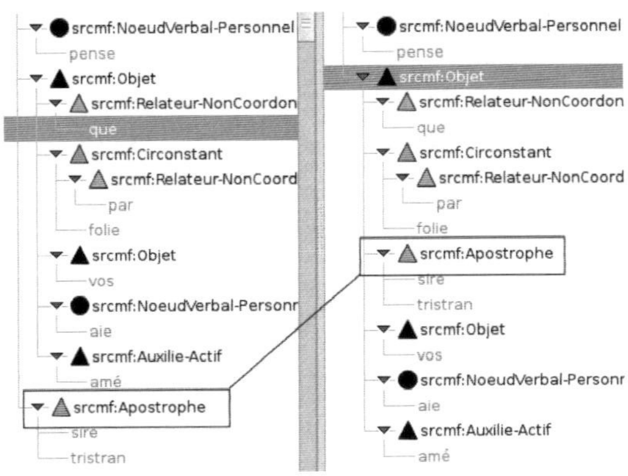

Figure 2: Comparison (boxes manually added)

tains an additional *Apostrophe* and focuses on the *Objet* structure on the right, and the first word of the structure on the left. The person who performs the comparison can immediately choose the right interpretation, and correct the erroneous analysis.

## 2.4 Export Capabilities

The RDF data model underlying the tree widget mimicks the tree structure and needs to be converted to create a genuine dependency graph. As the tree structure identifies SRCMF-specific governors (formally equivalent to heads in Head-Driven Phrase Structure Grammar), the transformation is relatively easy[13]. The resulting dependency RDF graph can be validated against the ontology and additional class restrictions defining the annotation model, but this feature still needs to be implemented in NotaBene.

It is possible to create as many filters as necessary to transform the RDF graph into other data structures, using NotaBene as an interface. At first, we have decided to focus on two objectives: 1/ corpus exploration; 2/ analysis rendering for the purpose of human reading.

The best syntactic corpus exploration tool we know about is TigerSearch (Brants et al., 2002).[14] The TigerSearch documentation defines the TigerXML format to represent dependency or constituency structures. TigerSearch corpora can be queried using a specific formalism and displays the analysis in a tree-like from.

TigerSearch tree display is not sufficient to represent our syntactic model – mainly because complex relations involving coordinations are surimpressed on the tree drawing, creating too many nodes to be conveniently readable. To enhance the readablility of the syntactic relations, we export our RDF graph into graphviz DOT files,[15] to render an elegant representation of the syntactic structures –fig. 3 (node labels are self-explanatory).

# 3 Conclusion and "TODO's"

The use of NotaBene satisfies the annotators of the SRCMF project, providing a convenient means to add manual annotations, compare parallel analyses and export data structures to other formalisms and tools.

In order to increase the quality of the project output, further implementations will at first deal with: 1/ data validation, using OWL reasoners[16]; 2/ *a posteriori* comparisons between POS annotation and syntactic annotation

## Acknowledgements

The project is funded from 2009 to 2012 by the *Agence Nationale de la Recherche*, France and the *Deutsche Forschungsgemeinschaft*, Germany. We would like to thank Brigite Antoine, Beatrice Barbara Bichoff, Tom Rainsford, Achim Stein and Jean-Christophe Vanhalle for proofreading.

[13] Although the description of coordination relations – which is difficult in a dependency-based framework (Kahane, 2001, 6-7)– requires a more complex algorithm.

[14] See `http://www.ims.uni-stuttgart.de/projekte/TIGER/TIGERSearch/`.

[15] `http://www.graphviz.org/`.

[16] Using Integrity Constraint Validation, currently being added to Pellet semantic reasoner software, see `http://clarkparsia.com/`.

## References


David Bamman, Marco Passarotti, Roberto Busa, and Gregory Crane. 2008. The annotation guidelines of the latin dependency treebank and index thomisticus treebank: the treatment of some specific syntactic constructions in latin. In Nicoletta Calzolari, Khalid Choukri, Bente Maegaard, Joseph Mariani, Jan Odjik, Stelios Piperidis, and Daniel Tapias, editors, *Proceedings of the Sixth International Language Resources and Evaluation (LREC'08)*, Marrakech, Morocco, may. European Language Resources Association (ELRA).

Sean Bechhofer, Frank Van Harmelen, Jim Hendler, Ian Horrocks, Deborah L. McGuinness, Peter F. Patel-Schneider, and Lynn Andrea Stein, editors. 2004. *OWL Web Ontology Language Reference. Reference. W3C Recommendation 10 February 2004.*

Sabine Brants, Stefanie Dipper, Silvia Hansen, Wolfgang Lezius, and George Smith. 2002. The TIGER Treebank. In *Proceedings of The First Workshop on Treebanks and Linguistic Theories (TLT2002) 20th and 21st September 2002, Sozopol, Bulgaria.*

L. M. Defourques and E. Muret, editors. 1947. *Béroul. Le roman de Tristan. Poème du XII$^{e}$ siècle.* Champion, Paris, 4 edition.

Céline Guillot, Alexei Lavrentiev, and Christiane Marchello-Nizia. 2007. La Base de Français Médiéval (BFM): états et perspectives. In Kunstmann and Stein (Kunstmann and Stein, 2007b), pages 143–152.

Claude Hagège. 1999. *La structure des langues.* Number 2006 in Que sais-je? Presses Universitaires de France, Paris, 5 edition.

Sylvain Kahane. 2001. Grammaires de dépendance formelles et théorie sens-texte. In *Actes TALN 2001, Tours, 2-5 juillet 2001.*

Graham Klyne and Jeremy J. Carroll, editors. 2004. *Resource Description Framework (RDF): Concepts and Abstract Syntax W3C Recommendation 10 February 2004.*

Pierre Kunstmann and Achim Stein. 2007a. Le Nouveau Corpus d'Amsterdam. (Kunstmann and Stein, 2007b), pages 9–27.

Pierre Kunstmann and Achim Stein, editors. 2007b. *Le Nouveau Corpus d'Amsterdam. Actes de l'atelier de Lauterbad, 23-26 février 2006.* Steiner, Stuttgart.

Gilbert Lazard. 1984. La distinction entre nom et verbe en syntaxe et en morphologie. *Modèles linguistiques*, 6(1):29–39.

Sylvain Loiseau. 2007. Corpusreader: un dispositif de codage pour articuler une pluralité d'interprétations. *Corpus*, 6:153–186.

France Martineau. 2008. Un corpus pour l'analyse de la variation et du changement linguistique. *Corpus*, 7:135–155.

Nicolas Mazziotta. forthcoming. Logiciel *NotaBene* pour l'annotation linguistique. annotations et conceptualisations multiples. *Recherches Qualitatives.*

Alain Polguère and Igor Mel'čuk, editors. 2009. *Dependency in linguistic description.* John Benjamins, Amsterdam and Philadelphia.

Jane Robinson. 1970. Dependency structures and transformational rules. *Language*, 46:259–285.

Achim Stein. 2008. Syntactic annotation of Old French text corpora. *Corpus*, 7:157–171.

# Chunking German: An Unsolved Problem

**Sandra Kübler**
Indiana University
Bloomington, IN, USA
skuebler@indiana.edu

**Kathrin Beck, Erhard Hinrichs, Heike Telljohann**
Universität Tübingen
Tübingen, Germany
{kbeck,eh,telljohann}@sfs.uni-tuebingen.de

## Abstract

This paper describes a CoNLL-style chunk representation for the Tübingen Treebank of Written German, which assumes a flat chunk structure so that each word belongs to at most one chunk. For German, such a chunk definition causes problems in cases of complex prenominal modification. We introduce a flat annotation that can handle these structures via a stranded noun chunk.

## 1 Introduction

The purpose of this paper is to investigate how the annotation of noun phrases in the Tübingen Treebank of Written German (TüBa-D/Z) can be transformed into chunks with no internal structure, as proposed in the CoNLL 2000 shared task (Tjong Kim Sang and Buchholz, 2000). Chunk parsing is a form of partial parsing, in which non-recursive phrases are annotated while difficult decisions, such as prepositional phrase attachment, are left unsolved. Flat chunk representations are particularly suitable for machine learning approaches to partial parsing and are inspired by the IOB approach to NP chunking first proposed by Ramshaw and Marcus (1995). They are particularly relevant for approaches that require an efficient analysis but not necessarily a complete syntactic analysis.

German allows a higher degree of syntactic complexity in prenominal modification of the syntactic head of an NP compared to English. This is particularly evident in written texts annotated in the TüBa-D/Z. The complexity of German NPs that causes problems in the conversion to CoNLL-style chunks also affects PCFG parsing approaches to German.The complexity of NPs is one of the phenomena that have been addressed in tree transformation approaches for German parsing (Trushkina, 2004; Ule, 2007; Versley and Rehbein, 2009).

## 2 Defining Chunks

The notion of a chunk is orginally due to Abney (1991), who considers chunks as non-recursive phrases which span from the left periphery of a phrase to the phrasal head. Accordingly, the sentence "The woman in the lab coat thought you had bought an expensive book." is assigned the chunk structure: "[S [NP The woman] [PP in [NP the lab coat] ] [VP thought] ] [S [NP you] [VP had bought] [NP an [ADJP expensive] book]] .". Abney-style chunk parsing is implemented as cascaded, finite-state transduction (cf. (Abney, 1996; Karlsson et al., 1995)).

Notice that cascaded, finite-state transduction allows for the possibility of chunks containing other chunks as in the above sentence, where the prepositional chunk contains a noun chunk within. The only constraint on such nested chunks is the prohibition on recursive structures. This rules out chunks in which, for example, a noun chunk contains another noun chunk. A much stricter constraint on the internal structure of chunks was subsequently adopted by the shared task on chunk parsing as part of the Conference for Natural Language Learning (CoNLL) in the year 2000 (Tjong Kim Sang and Buchholz, 2000). In this shared task, chunks were defined as non-overlapping, non-recursive phrases so that each word is part of at most one chunk. Based on this definition, the prepositional phrase in the sentence above would be chunked as "[Prep in] [NP the lab coat]". Since the prepositional chunk cannot have an embedded noun chunk, the definition of the CoNLL shared task assumed that the prepositional chunk only contains the preposition, thus taking the definition seriously that the chunk ends with the head. The noun chunk remains separate. Additionally, the noun phrase "an expensive book" is annotated as a noun chunk without internal structure.

The CoNLL shared task definition of chunks is



*Proceedings of the Fourth Linguistic Annotation Workshop, ACL 2010*, pages 147–151,
Uppsala, Sweden, 15-16 July 2010. 

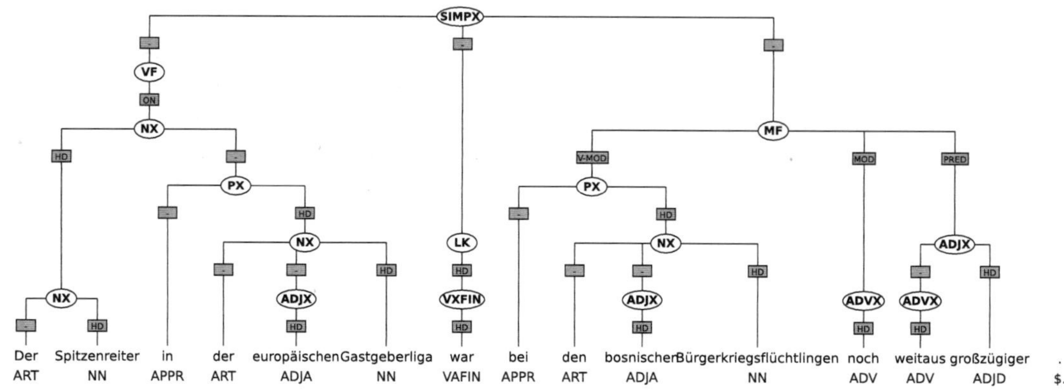


Figure 1: Treebank annotation for the sentence in (2).

useful for machine learning based approaches to chunking since it only requires one level of analysis, which can be represented as IOB-chunking (Tjong Kim Sang and Buchholz, 2000). For English, this definition of chunks has become standard in the literature on machine learning.

For German, chunk parsing has been investigated by Kermes and Evert (2002) and by Müller (2004). Both approaches used an Abney-style chunk definition. However, there is no corresponding flat chunk representation for German because of the complexity of pre-head modification in German noun phrases. Sentence (1) provides a typical example of this kind.

(1) $[_{NC}$ der $[_{NC}$ seinen Sohn$]$ liebende Vater$]$
the his son loving father
'the father who loves his son'

The structure in (1) violates both the Abney-style and the CoNLL-style definitions of chunks – Abney's because it is recursive and the CoNLL-style definition because of the embedding. A single-level, CoNLL-style chunk analysis will have to cope with the separation of the determiner "der" and the head of the outer phrase. We will discuss an analysis in section 5.

## 3 The Treebank: TüBa-D/Z

The Tübingen Treebank of Written German (TüBa-D/Z) is a linguistically annotated corpus based on data of the German newspaper 'die tageszeitung' (taz). Currently, it comprises approximately 45 000 sentences. For the syntactic annotation, a theory-neutral and surface-oriented annotation scheme has been adopted that is inspired by the notion of topological fields and enriched by a level of predicate-argument structure. The annotation scheme comprises four levels of syntactic annotation: the lexical level, the phrasal level, the level of topological fields, and the clausal level. The primary ordering principle of a clause is the inventory of topological fields, which characterize the word order regularities among different clause types of German, and which are widely accepted among descriptive linguists of German (cf. (Drach, 1937; Höhle, 1986)). Below this level of annotation, i.e. strictly within the bounds of topological fields, a phrase level of predicate-argument structure is applied with its own descriptive inventory based on a minimal set of assumptions that has to be captured by any syntactic theory. The context-free backbone of phrase structure (Telljohann et al., 2004) is combined with edge labels specifying the grammatical functions and long-distance relations. For more details on the annotation scheme see Telljohann et al. (2009).

(2) Der Spitzenreiter in der europäischen Gastgeberliga war bei den bosnischen Bürgerkriegsflüchtlingen noch weitaus großzügiger.
'The front-runner in the European league of host countries was far more generous with the Bosnian civil war refugees.'

Figure 1 shows the tree for the sentence in (2). The main clause (SIMPX) is divided into three topological fields: initial field (VF), left sentence bracket (LK), and middle field (MF). The finite verb in LK is the head (HD) of the sentence. The edge labels between the level of topological fields and the phrasal level constitute the grammatical function of the respective phrase: subject (ON), ambiguous modifier (MOD), and predicate (PRED). The label V-MOD specifies the long-distance dependency of the prepositional phrase on the main verb. Below the lexical level, the parts of speech are annotated. The hierarchical annotation of constituent structure and head (HD) / non-head (-) labels capture phrase internal dependencies. While premodifiers are attached directly on the same level, postmodifiers are attached higher in order to keep their modification scope ambiguous. The PP "in der europäischen Gastgeberliga" is the postmodifier of the head-NX and therefore attached on a higher phrase level.

## 4 General Conversion Strategy

The conversion to CoNLL-style chunks starts from the syntactic annotation of the TüBa-D/Z. In general, we directly convert the lowest phrasal projections with lexical content to chunks. For the sentence in (2) above, the chunk annotation is shown in (3). Here, the first noun phrase[1], "Der Spitzenreiter", as well as the finite verb phrase and the adverbial phrase are used as chunks.

(3) [NX Der Spitzenreiter] [PX in der europäischen Gastgeberliga] [VXFIN war] [PX bei den bosnischen Bürgerkriegsflüchtlingen] [ADVX noch] [ADJX weitaus großzügiger].

This sentence also shows exceptions to the general conversion rule: We follow Tjong Kim Sang and Buchholz (2000) in including ADJPs into the NCs, such as in "den bosnischen Bürgerkriegsflüchtlingen". We also include premodifying adverbs into ADJCs, such as in "weitaus großzügiger". But we deviate from Tjong Kim Sang and Buchholz in our definition of the PCs and include the head NP into this chunk, such as in "in der europäischen Gastgeberliga".

(4) a. Allerdings werden wohl Rationalisierungen mit der Modernisierung der Behördenarbeit einhergehen.

'However, rationalizations will accompany modernization in the workflow of civil service agencies.'

b. [ADVX Allerdings] [VXFIN werden] [ADVX wohl] [NX Rationalisierungen] [PX mit der Modernisierung] [NX der Behördenarbeit] [VXINF einhergehen].

In cases of complex, post-modified noun phrases grouped under the prepositional phrase, we include the head noun phrase into the prepositional chunk but group the postmodifying phrase into a separate phrase. The sentence in (4a) gives an example for such a complex noun phrase. This sentence is assigned the chunk annotation in (4b). Here, the head NP "der Modernisierung" is grouped in the PC while the post-modifying NP "der Behördenarbeit" constitutes its own NC.

The only lexical constituent in the treebank that is exempt from becoming a chunk is the *named entity* constituent (EN-ADD). Since these constituents do not play a syntactic role in the tree, they are elided in the conversion to chunks.

## 5 Complications in German

While the conversion based on the phrasal annotation of TüBa-D/Z results in the expected chunk structures, it is incapable of handling a small number of cases correctly. Most of these cases involve complex NPs. We will concentrate here on one case: complex premodified NPs that include the complement of a participle or an adjective, as discussed in section 2. This is a non-trivial problem since the treebank contains 1 497 cases in which an ADJP within an NP contains a PP and 415 cases, in which an ADJP within an NP contains another NP. Sentence (5a) with the syntactic annotation in Figure 2 gives an example for such an embedded PP.

(5) a. Die teilweise in die Erde gebaute Sporthalle wird wegen ihrer futuristischen Architektur auch als "Sport-Ei" bezeichnet.

'The partially underground sports complex is also called the "sports egg" because of its futuristic architecture.'

b. [sNX Die] [ADVX teilweise] [PX in die Erde] [NX gebaute Sporthalle] [VXFIN wird] [PX wegen ihrer futuristischen Architektur] [ADVX auch]

[1] For the sake of convenience, we will use acronyms in the remainder of the paper. Since we use the same labels in the treebank annotation and in the chunk representation (mostly ending in X), we will use labels ending in P (e.g. NP, PP) to talk about phrases in the treebank and labels ending in C (e.g. NC, PC) to talk about chunks.

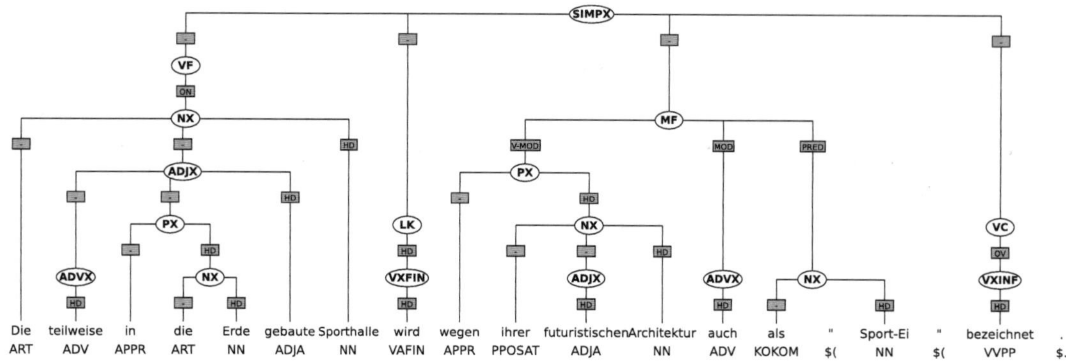


Figure 2: Treebank annotation for the sentence in (5a).

[NX als " Sport-Ei] " [VXINF bezeichnet].

Since we are interested in a flat chunk annotation in which each word belongs to at most one chunk, the Abney-style embedded chunk definition shown in sentence (1) is impossible. If we decide to annotate the PP "in die Erde" as a chunk, we are left with two parts of the embedding NP: the determiner "Die" and the ADVP "teilweise" to the left of the PP and the ADJP "gebaute" and the noun on the right. The right part of the NP can be easily grouped into an NC, and the ADVP can stand on its own. The only remaining problem is the treatment of the determiner, which in German, cannot constitute a phrase on its own. We decided to create a new type of chunk, stranded NC (sNX), which denotes that this chunk is part of an NC, to which it is not adjacent. Thus the sentence in (5a) has the chunk structure shown in (5b).

The type of complex NPs shown in the previous section can become arbitrarily complex. The example in (6a) with its syntactic analysis in Figure 3 shows that the attributively used adjective "sammelnden" can have all its complements and adjuncts. Here, we have a reflexive pronoun "sich" and a complex PP "direkt vor ihrem Sezessions-Standort am Karlsplatz". The chunk analysis based on the principles from section 4 gives us the analysis in (6b). The complex PP is represented as three different chunks: an ADVC, and two PCs.

(6) a. Sie "thematisierten" auf Anraten des jetzigen Staatskurators Wolfgang Zinggl die sich direkt vor ihrem Sezessions-Standort am Karlsplatz sammelnden Fixer.

'On the advice of the current state curator Wolfgang Zinggl, they "broach the issue" of the junkies who gather right in front of their location of secession at the Karlsplatz .'

b. [NX Sie] " [VXFIN thematisierten] " [PX auf Anraten] [NX des jetzigen Staatskurators] [NX Wolfgang Zinggl] [sNX die] [NX sich] [ADVX direkt] [PX vor ihrem Sezessions-Standort] [PX am Karlsplatz] [NX sammelnden Fixer].

## 6 Conclusion

In this paper, we have shown how a CoNLL-style chunk representation can be derived from TüBa-D/Z. For the complications stemming from complex prenominal modification, we proposed an analysis in which the stranded determiner is marked as such. For the future, we are planning to make this chunk representation available to license holders of the treebank.

## References

Steven Abney. 1991. Parsing by chunks. In Robert Berwick, Steven Abney, and Caroll Tenney, editors, *Principle-Based Parsing*, pages 257–278. Kluwer Academic Publishers, Dordrecht.

Steven Abney. 1996. Partial parsing via finite-state cascades. In John Carroll, editor, *ESSLLI Workshop on Robust Parsing*, pages 8–15, Prague, Czech Republic.

Erich Drach. 1937. *Grundgedanken der Deutschen Satzlehre*. Diesterweg, Frankfurt/M.

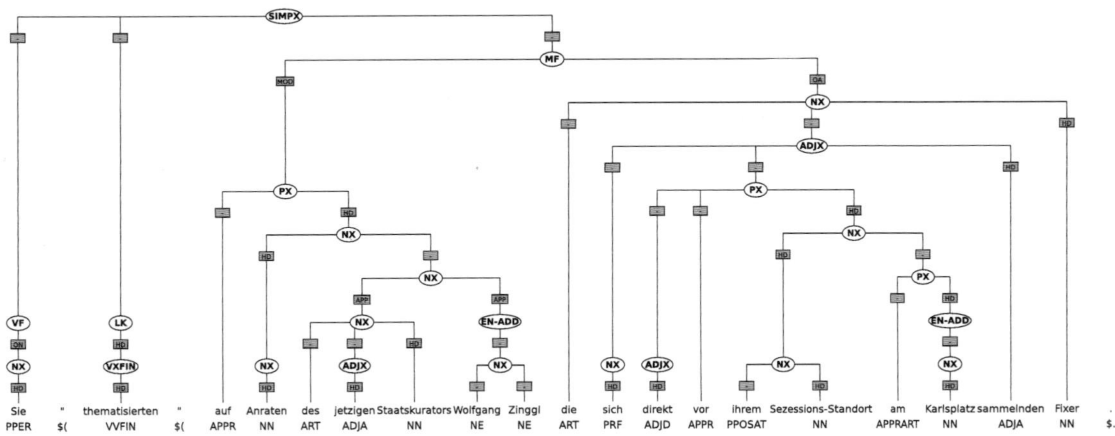


Figure 3: Treebank annotation for the sentence in (6a).


Tilman Höhle. 1986. Der Begriff "Mittelfeld", Anmerkungen über die Theorie der topologischen Felder. In *Akten des Siebten Internationalen Germanistenkongresses 1985*, pages 329–340, Göttingen, Germany.

Fred Karlsson, Atro Voutilainen, J. Heikkilä, and Atro Anttila, editors. 1995. *Constraint Grammar: A Language-Independent System for Parsing Unrestricted Text.* Mouton de Gruyter.

Hannah Kermes and Stefan Evert. 2002. YAC – a recursive chunker for unrestricted German text. In *Proceedings of the Third International Conference on Language Resources and Evaluation (LREC)*, Las Palmas, Gran Canaria.

Frank H. Müller. 2004. Annotating grammatical functions in German using finite-state cascades. In *Proceedings of COLING 2004*, Geneva, Switzerland.

Lance A. Ramshaw and Mitchell P. Marcus. 1995. Text chunking using transformation-based learning. In *Proceedings of the ACL 3rd Workshop on Very Large Corpora*, pages 82–94, Cambridge, MA.

Heike Telljohann, Erhard Hinrichs, and Sandra Kübler. 2004. The TüBa-D/Z treebank: Annotating German with a context-free backbone. In *Proceedings of the Fourth International Conference on Language Resources and Evaluation (LREC)*, pages 2229–2235, Lisbon, Portugal.

Heike Telljohann, Erhard W. Hinrichs, Sandra Kübler, Heike Zinsmeister, and Kathrin Beck, 2009. *Stylebook for the Tübingen Treebank of Written German (TüBa-D/Z).* Seminar für Sprachwissenschaft, Universität Tübingen, Germany.

Erik Tjong Kim Sang and Sabine Buchholz. 2000. Introduction to the CoNLL shared task: Chunking. In *Proceedings of The Fourth Conference on Computational Language Learning, CoNLL'00, and the Second Learning Language in Logic Workshop, LLL'00*, pages 127–132, Lisbon, Portugal.

Julia S. Trushkina. 2004. *Morpho-Syntactic Annotation and Dependency Parsing of German.* Ph.D. thesis, Eberhard-Karls Universität Tübingen.

Tylman Ule. 2007. *Treebank Refinement: Optimising Representations of Syntactic Analyses for Probabilistic Context-Free Parsing.* Ph.D. thesis, Eberhard-Karls Universität Tübingen.

Yannick Versley and Ines Rehbein. 2009. Scalable discriminative parsing for German. In *Proceedings of the International Conference on Parsing Technology (IWPT'09)*, Paris, France.

# Proposal for Multi-Word Expression Annotation in Running Text

**Iris Hendrickx, Amália Mendes and Sandra Antunes**
Centro de Linguística da Universidade de Lisboa, Lisboa, Portugal
{iris, amalia.mendes, sandra.antunes}@clul.ul.pt

**Abstract**

We present a proposal for the annotation of multi-word expressions in a 1M corpus of contemporary portuguese. Our aim is to create a resource that allows us to study multi-word expressions (MWEs) in their context. The corpus will be a valuable additional resource next to the already existing MWE lexicon that was based on a much larger corpus of 50M words. In this paper we discuss the problematic cases for annotation and proposed solutions, focusing on the variational properties of MWEs.

## 1 Introduction

Given the widespread studies of co-occurring words phenomenon, the term 'multi-word expression' (MWE) usually refers to a sequence of words that act as a single unit, embracing all different types of word combinations. Their study is of extreme importance for computational linguistics, where applications find notorious difficulties when dealing with them (Sag et al., 2002).

Having a well-balanced corpus annotated with multi-word expressions offers the possibility to analyze the behavior of MWEs as they appear in running text. Such corpus will contain a rich and diversified set of MWE and also be an excellent resource to evaluate automatic MWE identification systems. Here we propose our approach to the manual annotation of the CINTIL corpus (Barreto et al., 2006) with MWE information. This Portuguese corpus of 1M tokens is a balanced corpus of both spoken and written data from different sources and has been previously annotated with linguistic information such as part-of-speech and lemma and inflection.

As the starting point for our annotation project, we want to use a Portuguese MWE lexicon containing approximately 14,000 entries. The lexicon contains besides idiomatic expressions, also many collocations: expressions of frequently co-occurring words that do not show syntactic or semantic fixedness. We are mostly interested in the idiomatic expressions and will only mark up these in the corpus.

## 2 Related Work

There is already quite some work about the creation and representation of MWE lexicons (Baldwin and Kim, 2010). Most of the currently available corpora annotated with MWE information consist of a collection of extracted sentences containing a MWE (for example the data sets in the MWE 2008 shared task[1]). Fellbaum et al. (2006) report on a larger German example corpus consisting of MWEs with their surrounding sentences. There are also data sets specifically designed for automatic MWE identification, in which part of the sentences contains an idiomatic expression and the other part expresses a literal meaning (e.g. (Sporleder and Li, 2009)). An example of a balanced corpus fully annotated with MWEs is the Prague Treebank which is enriched with a diverse set of MWE annotations (Böhmová et al., 2005).

## 3 MWE Lexicon

Our annotation proposal uses information from a lexicon of MWE for Portuguese (available online[2]). This lexicon is implemented on a MySQL relational database. The MWEs were extracted from a 50M words balanced corpus of Portuguese. The MWE are organized under canonical forms. Also inflectional variations of the canonical forms are recorded, in total the lexicon contains 14,153 canonical forms and 48,154 MWEs variations. For each of those several examples are collected from the corpus. Each MWE entry is also assigned

[1] More infomation at: http://multiword.sourceforge.net/

[2] MWE lexicon: http://www.clul.ul.pt/sectores/linguistica_de_corpus/manual_combinatorias_online.php



*Proceedings of the Fourth Linguistic Annotation Workshop, ACL 2010*, pages 152–156,
Uppsala, Sweden, 15-16 July 2010. 

to one or multiple word lemmas, of a total number of 1180 single word lemmas. The MWE were selected from a sorted list of n-grams based on the mutual information measure (Church and Hanks, 1990) and validated manually (Mendes et al., 2006; Antunes et al., 2006; Bacelar do Nascimento et al., 2006).

## 4 Proposed annotation

In this section we discuss our approach to the annotation of MWEs in the corpus.

### 4.1 Typology

We want to classify each idiomatic MWE occurring in the CINTIL corpus according to a typology that expresses the typical properties of the MWE. Although the lexicon of MWEs covers a wide range of units, from idiomatic expressions to collocations, we decided to restrict our annotation of the corpus to cases of idiomatic MWEs because those are the problematic ones for any task of semantic annotation and disambiguation. The MWE lexicon does not provide labels for idiomatic vs. compositional expressions, so this information will have to be added during the annotation task. Identifying idiomatic MWEs is not a simple task. For clear cases of idiomatic units, the global meaning can not be recovered by the sum of the individual meanings of the elements that compose the expression.

In other cases, only part of the MWE has an idiomatic meaning, while one or more of the elements are used in their literal meaning (e.g *saúde de ferro* 'iron health'). Deciding if one of the elements of the MWE is literal or not depends in fact of our definition of literal: if we consider it to be the first prototypical meaning of a word, this very restrictive definition will trigger us to label a large number of MWEs as idiomatic. Other MWEs are compositional but receive an additional meaning, like *cartão vermelho* in football, which is literally a red card but has an additional meaning of punishment.

We want to cover these different cases in our annotation, and to establish a typology that takes into account morpho-syntactic and semantic aspects of the MWE: its functional part-of-speech (PoS) category, the PoS categories of its internal elements, its fixed or semi-fixed nature, its global or partial idiomatic property and motivation, and possible additional meanings.

### 4.2 Division by syntactic category

When studying the MWE lexicon, we noticed different properties of MWEs according to their syntactic patterns. Consequently, we propose to divide our annotation guidelines according to each syntactic pattern and to establish different properties that enables us to distinguish literal from idiomatic usage. At the sentence level, MWEs such as proverbs or aphorisms (e.g. *água mole em pedra dura tanto bate até que fura* lit. 'water in hard rock beats so long that it finally breaks') have specific properties: they do not accept any possible syntactic changes like passivization or relativization, they do not accept any inflectional variation, the only possible change is lexical (when speakers substitute one or more elements, like we will discuss in section 4.4). However fixed, the meaning of this example is clearly motivated and compositional in the sense that it is recovered by the meaning of the individual elements. On the contrary, MWEs which are verb phrases will admit much more morpho-syntactic variation. Moreover, noun phrases raise specific issues: the most syntactically fixed units will be very close or identical to compound nouns. For example, the meaning of the prepositional modifier of the noun can be literal but the overall expression will still be used as a compound and will denote a very specific entity, frequently from domain-specific languages (*projecto de lei* 'project of legislation', *contrato de compra e venda* 'sell contract'). Moreover, the prepositional and adjectival modifiers of the noun will express many different semantic relationships (part of, made of, used for) which interact with the meaning (literal or idiomatic) of the noun (Calzolari et al., 2002). Establishing specific guidelines for these different types of MWEs will enable a more accurate annotation. To decide upon the difficult cases of idiomatic and non-idiomatic usage, we plan to use the intuitions of different annotators.

### 4.3 Linking to MWE lexicon

We will annotate each encountered MWE in the corpus with a link to the MWE-entry in the lexicon, instead of labelling each MWE with its typology. This way we link each MWE to its canonical form and other additional information. Moreover, we can easily gather all occurrences of one particular canonical MWE and check its variation in the corpus. It will also allow us to work with a

more detailed typology and will give us the possibility to revise it during the annotation process. It might be difficult to establish beforehand very precise guidelines that will apply to all the MWEs and even to all the MWEs of a specific subtype. Often, guidelines are constantly in need of revision as we encounter slightly different contexts who challenges decisions previously taken.
The corpus annotation will enable us to extend the information in the MWE lexicon with typology labels regarding the whole expression (function, idiomatic meaning) but also regarding individual words of the expression as to whether they are obligatory or not.

We plan to add a meaning to idiomatic expressions using a dictionary. We expect that MWEs will be unambiguous: they have the same meaning each time they are used. In some cases, the synonym or paraphrase proposed for the MWE might not be able to replace the MWE in the corpus context. For example, the MWE *às mãos cheias* means *em grande quantidade* 'in large quantity', but this meaning can not always replace the MWE in context.

The annotation process of fully fixed expressions could be retrieved automatically. For the variable expressions we will combine automatic retrieval with manual validation, Here the automatic retrieval step will aim for a high recall and select all sentences that contain the lemmas of the MWE. Without doubt our corpus will contain many MWEs that are not yet listed in the MWE lexicon. Therefore each sentence will need to be checked manually for MWEs. We can create the links between the lexicon and MWEs in the corpus automatically, but again, as not all MWEs will occur in the lexicon, we will need to do a manual validation of the automatic labelling and also add newly discovered MWEs to the lexicon.

### 4.4 MWE Variation

Corpus analysis clearly shows that MWEs have different types of internal variation. Following Moon (1998), we will also assume that, in most of the cases, these expressions "have fixed or canonical forms and that variations are to some extent derivative or deviant". The canonical forms of (variable) expressions are listed in the MWE lexicon. Mapping MWE occurrences in the corpus to their canonical form can be a hard task depending on the flexibility of the MWE. In the next part we discuss our proposal how to handle the annotation of several types of variation in MWEs: lexical, syntactic and structural variation, lexical insertions and truncation of MWEs.

#### 4.4.1 Lexical diversity

MWEs have a wide range of lexical variation and it can apply to any type of grammatical category, although we do notice that verb variation is the commonest type. Studying the lexicon showed us that there is a group of cases in which a word in a MWE can only be replaced by another word from a very limited set (usually not larger than 10 words) of synonyms or antonyms. For these cases this set is already recorded in the MWE lexicon. We mark these variable words as: 'obligatory parts of the MWE and member of a specified list'. In 1 we show an example: the canonical form followed by a sentence containing this MWE and the English translations.

Many MWEs also contain parts that are almost lexically free or only restricted to a semantic class such as person or named entity. These elements are represented in the MWE lexicon with a pronoun (e.g. *alguém, algum* ('someone', 'something')) or the tag *NOUN* (with possible gender/number restrictions) when a pronoun cannot substitute the free part. When marking up these elements in the corpus, we will label them with a reference to the pronoun used in the canonical form (example 2).

(1) **dizer/ sair** *da boca para fora*
(to say / to get out from the mouth outside)
Arrependeu-se com o que lhe **saiu** *da boca para fora*
'She regretted her slip of the tongue'

(2) *estar nas mãos de* **ALGUÉM**
A nossa vida *está nas mãos de* **Deus**
'Our life is in the hands of God'

MWEs are not always contiguous: it is frequent to encounter insertion of lexical elements which do not belong to the canonical form of the MWE. Often, the function of the inserted elements is adverbial, quantificational or emphatic. Or the MWE occurs in a negative context, by the insertion of the adverb *não*. Such inserted elements that are not part of the MWE are not labelled. This is the case of the quantifier `muitas` in (3), which is not part of the canonical form of the MWE *dar voltas à cabeça* 'to think'.

(3) *Dei* `muitas` *voltas à cabeça* para encontrar uma solução.
'I've been thinking a lot to find a solution.'

Another type of MWE variation is truncation: only a part of the full expression is lexically realized. This phenomenon usually occurs with proverbs and sayings. For example in 4 the bracketed part was not realized in the sentence, but it is part of the canonical form in the MWE lexicon. When marking up such truncated expressions we do not label explicitly this phenomenon, we just mark up the occurring part with a reference link to MWEs in the lexicon.

(4) *mais vale um pássaro na mão* (do que dois a voar)
'bird in the hand is worth (two in the bush)'

#### 4.4.2 Syntactic variation

An obvious form of syntactic variation is inflection of verbs and nouns. Since Portuguese is a highly inflectional language, practically all the verbs that occur in MWEs inflect, except for some fixed sayings. Also shifting from active to passive voice leads to syntactic variation. We do not label auxiliary verbs as part of the MWE.

Several MWEs that have a free part such as example 2 do not only exhibit lexical variation but also syntactic variation: pronominalization (*estar nas mãos dele*) or with a possessive form (*estar nas suas mãos*). In such cases we will mark up possessives as part of the MWE but give them an additional label to signal that they are optional elements. However, possessives are not always optional, sometimes it is an obligatory part of the canonical form and we will annotate it normally (e.g. *o leão mostra a sua raça.* 'the lion shows what he's made off').

Also permutations of the MWE can occur (ex.5). We do not signal this phenomenon in our annotation as this can easily be detected when comparing to the canonical form.

(5) *estar de mãos e pés atados / estar de pés e mãos atados*
'to be tied hand and foot/ foot and hand'

#### 4.4.3 Structural variation

True idioms are both semantically and syntactically fixed. However, language use is creative and can lead to MWEs that only partly match the 'real' MWE as listed in the MWE lexicon. For these cases we mark up the different part with an extra label to clarify which part exactly varies. For example 6.

(6) *no poupar é que está o ganho*
in the saving is the profit
*no* **esperar / provar / comparar** *é que está o ganho*
in waiting / proving / comparing is the profit

(7) já *dei voltas* **e voltas** *à cabeça*
'thoughs went on and on in my mind'

(8) **ALGO** *é a mãe de todas* **NOUN-PL**
'something is the mother of all x'
**a educação** *é a mãe de todas* **as civilizações**
**a liberdade** *é a mãe de todas* **as virtudes**
'education is the mother of all civilizations'
'freedom is the mother of all virtues'

Another interesting case is shown in example 7 in wich a part of the MWE is duplicated for emphasis. This should be treated differently than the example in 3. In these cases we will label the duplicated part as 'part of the MWE but optional' (similar to possessives).

There are cases in which part of the MWE may vary without any apparent limits, while the other part remains fixed. An example can be found in 8. These are actually just an extension of ones we already discussed (see example 2) and we treat them in the same matter.

## 5 Conclusion

In sum, we propose to split the annotation of MWEs to develop separate annotation guidelines for the grammatical categories, as we have observed that e.g. nominal MWEs behave differently than verbal MWEs. Each MWE in the running text will be linked to its canonical form in the lexicon. The lexicon itself will be enhanced with additional information such as typology information and MWE meaning. Special elements of the MWE such as optional or variable parts will be explicitly marked as such both in the lexicon and in the annotation of the MWE in the corpus. We are convinced that the implementation of our proposal will lead to a rich new resource that can help us study the behavior of MWE in more depth. We also plan to use this resource for the development and evaluation of automatic MWE identification systems.

## References


S. Antunes, M. F. Bacelar do Nascimento, J. M. Casteleiro, A. Mendes, L. Pereira, and T. Sá. 2006. A lexical database of portuguese multiword expressions. In *LNAI*, volume 3960, pages 238–243. Springer-Verlag, Berlin, (PROPOR 2006).

M. F. Bacelar do Nascimento, A. Mendes, and S. Antunes, 2006. *Spoken Language Corpus and Linguistic Informatics*, chapter Typologies of MultiWord Expressions Revisited: A Corpus-driven Approach, pages 227–244. Coll. Usage-Based Linguistic Informatics, vol.V. John Benjamins.

T. Baldwin and S. Nam Kim. 2010. Multiword expressions. In Nitin Indurkhya and Fred J. Damerau, editors, *Handbook of Natural Language Processing, Second Edition*. CRC Press, Taylor and Francis Group, Boca Raton, FL. ISBN 978-1420085921.

F. Barreto, A. Branco, E. Ferreira, A. Mendes, M. F. P. Bacelar do Nascimento, F. Nunes, and J. Silva. 2006. Open resources and tools for the shallow processing of portuguese. In *Proceedings of the 5th International Conference on Language Resources and Evaluation (LREC2006)*, Genoa, Italy.

A. Böhmová, S. Cinková, and E. Hajičová. 2005. A Manual for Tectogrammatical Layer Annotation of the Prague Dependency Treebank (English translation). Technical report, ÚFAL MFF UK, Prague, Czech Republic.

N. Calzolari, C. Fillmore, R. Grishman, N. Ide, A. Lenci, C. MacLeod, and A. Zampolli. 2002. Towards best practice for multiword expressions in computational lexicon. In *Proceedings of the Third International Conference on Language Resources and Evaluation (LREC'2002)*, pages 1934–1940, Las Palmas, Spain.

K.W. Church and P. Hanks. 1990. Word association norms, mutual information, and lexicography. *Computational Linguistics*, 16(1):22–29.

C. Fellbaum, A. Geyken, A. Herold, F. Koerner, and G. Neumann. 2006. Corpus-based studies of german idioms and light verbs. *International Journal of Lexicography*, 19(4):349–360.

A. Mendes, M. F. Bacelar do Nascimento, S. Antunes, and L. Pereira. 2006. COMBINA-PT: a large corpus-extracted and hand-checked lexical database of portuguese multiword expressions. In *Proceedings of LREC 2006*, pages 1900–1905, Genoa, Italy.

R. Moon. 1998. Fixed expressions and idioms in english: A corpus-based approach. In *Oxford Studies in Lexicography and Lexicology*. Clarendon Press, Oxford.

I. Sag, T. Baldwin, F. Bond, A. Copestake, and D. Flickinger. 2002. Multiword Expressions: A Pain in the Neck for NLP. In *Proceedings of CICLING-2002*.

C. Sporleder and L. Li. 2009. Unsupervised recognition of literal and non-literal use of idiomatic expressions. In *Proceedings of the 12th Conference of the European Chapter of the ACL (EACL 2009)*, pages 754–762, Athens, Greece, March. Association for Computational Linguistics.

# A Feature Type Classification for Therapeutic Purposes: a preliminary evaluation with non-expert speakers

**Gianluca E. Lebani**
University of Trento
gianluca.lebani@unitn.it

**Emanuele Pianta**
Fondazione Bruno Kessler
pianta@fbk.eu

## Abstract

We propose a feature type classification thought to be used in a therapeutic context. Such a scenario lays behind our need for a easily usable and cognitively plausible classification. Nevertheless, our proposal has both a practical and a theoretical outcome, and its applications range from computational linguistics to psycholinguistics. An evaluation through inter-coder agreement has been performed to highlight the strength of our proposal and to conceive some improvements for the future.

## 1 Introduction

Most common therapeutic practices for anomia rehabilitation rely either on the therapist's intuitive linguistic knowledge or on different kinds of resources that have to be consulted manually (Semenza, 1999; Raymer and Gonzalez-Rothi, 2002; Springer, 2008). STaRS.sys (Semantic Task Rehabilitation Support system) is a tool thought for supporting the therapist in the preparation of a semantic task (cfr. Nickels, 2002).

To be effective, such a system must lean on a knowledge base in which every concept is associated with different kinds of featural descriptions. The notion of feature refers to the linguistic descriptions of a property that can be obtained by asking a subject to describe a concept. Examples of concept-feature pairings will be represented here as *<concept> feature*[1] couples such as *<dog> has a tail* or *<dog> barks*.

As a consequence of this scenario, an intuitive and cognitively plausible classification of the feature types that can be associated with a concept is a vital component of our tool. In this paper, we present a classification that meets such criteria, built by moving from an analysis of the relevant proposals available in the literature.

We evaluated our classification by asking to a group of naive Italian speakers to annotate a test set by using our categories. The resulting agreement has been interpreted both as an index of reliability and as a measure of ease of learning and use by non-expert speakers. In these preliminary phases we focus on Italian, leaving to future evaluations whether or how to extend the domain of our tool to other languages.

These pages are organized as follows: in Section 2 we briefly review the relevant works for the following discussion. In Section 3 we introduce our classification and in the remaining part we evaluate its reliability and usability.

## 2 Related Works

### 2.1 Feature Norms

In the psychological tradition, a collection of feature norms is typically built by asking to a group of speakers to generate short phrases (i.e. features) to describe a given set of concepts.

Even if normative data have been collected and employed for addressing a wide range of issues on the nature of the semantic memory, the only freely available resources are, to our knowledge, those by Garrard et al (2001), those by McRae et al (2005), those by Vinson and Vigliocco (2008), all in English, and the Dutch norms available in the Leuven database (De Deyne et al, 2008).

Moving out of the psychological domain, the only collection built in the lexicographic tradition is that by Kremer et al (2008), collected from Italian and German speakers

[1] Typographical conventions: concepts, categories and features will be printed in *italics courier new* font. When reporting a concept-feature pair, the concept will be further enclosed by *<angled brackets>*. Feature types and classes of types will be both reported in times roman, but while the formers will be written in *italics*, type classes will be in SMALL CAPITALS.



*Proceedings of the Fourth Linguistic Annotation Workshop, ACL 2010*, pages 157–161,
Uppsala, Sweden, 15-16 July 2010. 

### 2.2 Related Classifications

The proposals that constitute our theoretical framework have been chosen for their being either implemented in an extensive semantic resource, motivated by well specified theoretical explanations (on which there is consensus) or effectively used in a specific therapeutic context. They have originated in research fields as distant as lexicography, theoretical linguistics, ontology building, (clinical) neuropsychology and cognitive psychology. Specifically, the works we moved from have been:

- a type classification adopted for clinical purposes in the CIMeC's Center for Neurocognitive Rehabilitation (personal communication);
- the knowledge-type taxonomy proposed by Wu & Barsalou (2009), and the modified version adopted by Cree & McRae (2003);
- the brain region taxonomy proposed by Cree & McRae (2003);
- the semantic (but not lexical) relations implemented in WordNet 3.0 (Fellbaum, 1998) and in EuroWordNet (Alonge et al, 1998);
- the classification of part/whole relations by Winston et al (1987);
- the SIMPLE-PAROLE-CLIPS Extended Qualia Structures (Ruimy et al, 2002).

## 3 STaRS.sys feature types classification

The properties of our classification follow from the practical use scenario of STaRS.sys. In details, the fact that it's thought to be used in a therapeutic context motivates our need for a classification that has to be: (1) intuitive enough to be easily used by therapist and (2) robust and (3) cognitively plausible so as to be used for preparing the relevant kinds of therapeutic tasks.

Furthermore, being focused on features produced by human speakers, the classification applies to the linguistic description of a property, rather than to the property itself. Accordingly, then, pairings like the following:

```
<plane> carries stuff
<plane> is used for carrying stuff
```

are though as instances of different types (respectively, *is involved in* and *is used for*).

Starting from an analysis of the relevant proposals available in the literature, we identified a set of 26 feature types, most of which have been organized into the following six classes:

**TAXONOMIC PROPERTIES:** Two types related to the belonging of a concept to a category have been isolated: the *is-a* and the *coordinate* types.

**PART-OF RELATIONS:** We mainly followed Winston et al's (1987) taxonomy in distinguishing six types describing a relation between a concept and its part(s): *has component*, *has member*, *has portion*, *made-of*, *has phase* and *has geographical part*.

**PERCEPTUAL PROPERTIES:** Inspired by the Cree and McRae's (2003) brain region taxonomy, we isolated six types of perceivable properties: *has size*, *has shape*, *has texture*, *has taste*, *has smell*, *has sound*, *has colour*.

**USAGE PROPERTIES:** This class is composed by three types of an object's use descriptions: *is used for*, *is used by* and *is used with*.

**LOCATIONAL PROPERTIES:** We identified three types describing the typical *situation*, *space* and *time* associated to an object.

**ASSOCIATED EVENTS AND ATTRIBUTES:** This class encompasses three kinds of information that can be associated to an object: its emotive property (*has affective property*), one of its permanent properties (*has attribute*) and the role it plays in an action or in a process (*is involved in*). As a matter of fact, each of the other classes is a specification of one of the two latter types, to which particular relevance has been accorded due to their status from a cognitive point of view.

**Others:** Two feature types fall out of this classification, and constitute two distinct classes on their own. These are the *has domain* type, that specifies the semantic field of a concept, and the dummy *is associated with*, used for classifying all those features that falls out of any other label.

**Comparison and final remarks:** A quick comparison between our types and the other classifications reveals that, apart from the *is used with* type, we didn't introduce any new opposition. Any type of ours, indeed, has a parallel type or relation in at least one of the other proposals. Such a remark shows what is the third major advantage of our classification, together with its usability and its cognitive plausibility: its compatibility with a wide range of well known theoretical and experimental frameworks, that allows it to serve as a common ground for the interplay of theories, insights and ideas originated from the above mentioned research areas.

## 4 Evaluation

Given the aims of our classification, and of STaRS.sys in general, we choose to evaluate our coding scheme by asking to a group of non experts to label a subset of the non-normalized Kremer et al's (2008) norms and measuring the inter-coder agreement between them (Artstein and Poesio, 2008), adhering to the Krippendorff's (2004, 2008) recommendations.

The choice to recruit only naive subjects has the positive consequence of allowing us to draw inferences also on the usability of our proposal. That is, such an evaluation can be additionally seen as a measure of how easily a minimally trained user can understand the oppositions isolated in our classification.

### 4.1 Experimental Setup

**Participants:** 5 Italian speakers with a university degree were recruited for this evaluation. None of them had any previous experience in lexicography, nor any education in lexical semantics.

**Materials:** 300 concept-feature pairs were selected mainly from a non-normalized version of the Kremer et al's (2008) norms. We choose this dataset because (1) it's a collection of descriptions generated by Italian speakers and (2) we wanted to avoid any bias due to a normalization procedure, so as to provide our subjects with descriptions that were as plausible as possible.

The experimental concept-attribute pairs have been chosen so to have the more balanced distribution of concepts and feature types as possible, by not allowing duplicated pairs. As for the concepts, an uniform distribution of features per category (30 feature for all the ten categories of the original dataset) and of features per concept (i.e. between 4 and 7) has been easily obtained.

The attempt to balance feature types, however, has revealed impracticable, mainly due to the nature of the concepts of the Kremer's collection and to the skewness of its type distribution. Therefore, we fixed an arbitrary minimum threshold of ten plausible features per type. Plausible features have been obtained from a pilot annotation experiment performed by one author and an additional subject. We further translated 23 concept-feature pairs from the McRae (11 cases) and from the Leuven (12 cases) datasets for balancing types as much as possible.

Still, it has not been possible to find ten features for the following types: *has Geographical Part*, *has Phase* and *has Member* (no features at all: this is a consequence of the kind of concept represented the dataset), *has Portion* (only four cases, again, this is a consequence of the source dataset), *has Domain* (5) and *has Sound* (6). We nevertheless decided to include these types in the instructions and the relevant features in the test set. Our decision has been motivated by the results of the pilot experiment, in which the subjects made reference to such types as a secondary interpretation in more than ten cases.

**Procedure:** The participants were asked to label every concept-feature pair with the appropriate type label, relying primarily on the linguistic form of the feature. They received a 17-pages booklet providing an explanation of the annotation goals, a definition and some examples for every type class and for every type, a decision flowchart and a reference table.

Every participant was asked to read carefully the instructions, to complete a training set of 30 concept-feature pairs and to discuss his/her decisions with one of the two authors before starting the experimental session. The test set was presented as a unique excel sheet. On the average, labeling the 300 experimental pairs took 2 hours.

### 4.2 Results

The annotations collected from the participants have been normalized by conflating direct (e.g. *is-a*) and reverse (e.g. *is the Category of*) relation labels, and the agreement between their choice has been measured adopting Fleiss' Kappa. The "Kappa: annotators" column of Table 1 reports the general and the type-wise kappa scores[2] for the annotations of the participants.

| Feature Type | *Kappa: annotators* | *Kappa: gold/majority* |
|---|---|---|
| *is-a* | 0.900 | 0.956 |
| *coordination* | 0.788 | 0.913 |
| *has component* | 0.786 | 0.864 |
| *has portion* | 0.558 | 0.747 |
| *made of* | 0.918 | 0.955 |
| *has size* | 0.912 | 1 |
| *has shape* | 0.812 | 1 |
| *has texture* | 0.456 | 0.793 |
| *has taste* | 0.852 | 1 |
| *has smell* | 0.865 | 1 |
| *has sound* | 0.582 | 0.795 |
| *has colour* | 0.958 | 1 |
| *is used for* | 0.831 | 0.727 |
| *is used by* | 0.964 | 1 |
| *is used with* | 0.801 | 0.939 |
| *situation located* | 0.578 | 0.854 |
| *space located* | 0.808 | 0.898 |
| *time located* | 0.910 | 0.946 |
| *is involved in* | 0.406 | 0.721 |
| *has attribute* | 0.460 | 0.746 |
| *has affective property* | 0.448 | 0.855 |
| *has domain* | 0.069 | 0.277 |
| *is associated with* | 0.141 | 0.415 |
| **General** | **0.73** | **0.866** |

Table 1: Type-wise agreement values

[2] All reported Kappa values are associated with $p < 0.001$.

Even if there is no consensus on how to interpret Kappa values in isolation, and despite the fact that, to our knowledge, this is the first work of this kind, we can nevertheless draw interesting conclusions from the pattern in table 1. The general Kappa score has a value of 0.73, and the agreement values are above 0.8 for 12 types, not so distant in 2 cases, and well above 0.67 for 9 types, 5 of which are our "residual" categories, that is, those that are more "general" that at least one of the other types[3].

Such a contrast between the residual and the other types is even more pronounced in the class-wise analysis, where the only Kappa value below the 0.8 threshold is the one obtained for the ASSOCIATED EVENTS AND ATTRIBUTES class ($\kappa$ = 0.766) [4]. Furthermore, the distribution of false positives in a confusion matrix between the performance of the annotators and the "majority" vote[5] shows that part of the low agreement for the residual types is due to the "summation" of the disagreement on the other categories. Obviously, part of this variance is due also to the fact that such types have fuzzier boundaries, and so are more difficult to handle.

As for the remaining four low agreement types, two of them (*has affective property*, *has domain*) have been signaled by the annotators to be difficult to handle, while the remaining two (*has sound*, *has portion*) have been frequently confused with one of the ASSOCIATED EVENTS AND ATTRIBUTES types and with the *has component* type, respectively. Such results are not very puzzling for the *has domain* and *has portion* types, given the technicality of the former and, for the latter, the nature of the described concepts. They do point, however, to a better definition of the remaining two types, the *has sound* and *has affective property* ones, in that most difficulties seem to arise from an unclear definition of their respective scopes.

As pointed out by Artstein and Poesio (2008), agreement doesn't ensure validity. In trying to evaluate how our annotators "did it right", we measured the exact Kappa coefficient (Conger, 1980) between the majority annotation (i.e. what annotators should have done to agree) and the annotation of the same set by one of the two authors. With some approximation, we see this last performance as the "right" one.

Results are reported in the "Kappa: gold/majority" column of Table 1. The general Kappa value is well above 0.8, and so it is for 15 of the 23 types. Only two types (*has domain* and *is associated with*) are below the 0.67 minimal threshold. These data further confirm the difficulties in handling residual types, but, more importantly, seem to suggest that our "gold standard" annotator have been able to learn the classification in a fairly correct way (at least, it did in a way similar as one of the two authors of this classification).

### 4.3 Discussion

We interpret the results of our evaluation as a demonstration of the reliability of our coding scheme as well as of the usability of our classification, at least as the non residual types are concerned. For the future, many improvements are suggested by our data. In particular, they showed the need of the annotators to receive a better training on some relations and distinctions.

This points in the direction of both a more deep training on the types we've dubbed as "residuals", and of a better definition of poorly understood types such as *has domain* and *has affective property* and puzzling distinctions such as the *has smell/is Involved in* ones.

## 5 Conclusions and Future Directions

In this paper we introduced a classification of the information types that can be expressed to describe a concrete concept. Even if we thought this classification mainly for therapeutic purposes, its use can be broadened to include a wide range of possible NLP tasks.

We evaluated our proposal by asking a group of naive speakers to annotate a list of concept-feature pairs with the appropriate label. Even if our results can't be interpreted as absolutely positive, we consider them promising, in that (1) the skeleton of the classification seems to have been validated by the performance of our participants and (2) a great part of the disagreement seems to be solvable through major care in the training phase. In the near future we are going to test our (improved) coding scheme with annotators from the population of the STaRS.sys final users, i.e. therapist with experience in semantic therapy. Finally, further research is needed to assess if and to what extent the semantic model underlying our classification is compatible with those of existing lexical and/or semantic resources.

[3] Our residual labels are *has Attribute*, *has Texture*, *is Associated with*, *is Involved in* and *Situation Located*.

[4] The general Fleiss' Kappa value for the class-wise comparison is 0.766.

[5] That is, the performance obtained by assigning the label chosen by the majority of the annotators.

**Acknowledgments**

We are grateful to the annotators who gave us the data reported in Section 4 and to all the CLICers that commented our classification. In particular, we would like to thank dr. Federica Cavicchio for their statistical advice and Gerhard Kremer for providing us with a non-normalized version of his dataset.

## Reference

Antonietta Alonge, Nicoletta Calzolari, Piek Vossen, Laura Bloksma, Irene Castellon, Maria A. Marti and Wim Peters. 1998. The linguistic design of the EuroWordNet database. *Computer and the Humanities*, 32: 91-115.

Ron Artstein and Massimo Poesio. 2008. Inter-coder agreement for computational linguistics. *Computational Linguistics*, 34 (4): 555-596.

Anthony J. Conger. 1980. Integration and generalisation of Kappas for multiple raters. *Psychological Bulletin*, 88: 322-328.

George S. Cree and Ken MCrae. 2003. Analyzing the factors underlying the structure and computation of the meaning of chipmunk, cherry, chisel, cheese, and cello (and many other such concrete nouns). *Journal of Experimental Psychology: General*, 132 (2): 163-201

Simon De Deyne, Steven Verheyen, Eef Amel, Wolf Vanpaemel, Matthew J. Dry, Wouter Voorspoels and Gert Storm. 2008. Exemplar by feature applicability matrices and other Dutch normative data for semantic concepts. *Behavior Research Methods*, 40 (4): 1030-1048.

Christiane Fellbaum. 1998. *WordNet. An electronic lexical database*. The MIT Press. Cambridge, MA.

Joseph L. Fleiss. 1971. Measuring nominal scale agreement among many raters. *Psychological Bulletin*, 76 (5): 378-382.

Peter Garrard, Matthew A. Lambon Ralph, John R. Hodges and Karalyn Patterson. 2001. Prototypicality, distinctiveness and intercorrelation: analyses of the semantic attributes of living and nonliving concepts. *Cognitive Neuropsychology*, 18 (2): 125-174.

Gerhard Kremer, Andrea Abel and Marco Baroni. 2008. Cognitively salient relations for multilingual lexicography. *Proceedings of COLING-CogALex Workshop 2008*: 94-101.

Klaus Krippendorff. 2004. Reliability in content analysis: some common misconceptions and recommendations. *Human Communication Research*, 30 (3): 411-433.

Klaus Krippendorff. 2008. Testing the reliability of content analysis data: what is involved and why. In K. Krippendorff and M.A. Bock (eds.). *The Content Analysis Reader*. Sage, Thousand Oaks, CA: 350-357.

Ken McRae, George S. Cree, Mark S. Seidenberg and Chris McNorgan. 2005. Semantic feature production norms for a large set of living and nonliving things. *Behavior Research Methods, Instruments & Computers*, 37 (4): 547-559.

Gregory L. Murphy. 2002. *The big book of concepts*. The MIT Press, Cambridge, MA.

Lyndsey Nickels.2002. Therapy for naming disorders: revisiting, revising, and reviewing. *Aphasiology*, 16 (10/11): 935-979

Anastasia M. Raymer and Leslie J. Gonzalez-Rothi. 2002. Clinical diagnosis and treatment of naming disorders. In A.E. Hillis (ed.). *Handbook of Adult Language Disorders*. Psychology Press: 163-182.

Eleanor Rosch and Carolyn B. Mervis. 1975. Family resemblances: studies in the internal structure of categories. *Cognitive Psychology*, 7: 573-605.

Nilda Ruimy, Monica Monachini, Raffaella Distante, Elisabetta Guazzini, Stefano Molino, Marisa Ulivieri, Nicoletta Calzolari and Antonio Zampolli. 2002. Clips, a multi-level Italian computational lexicon: a glimpse to data. *Proceedings LREC 2002*: 792-799.

Carlo Semenza. 1999. Lexical-semantic disorders in aphasia. In G. Denes and L. Pizzamiglio (eds.). *Handbook of clinical and experimental neuropsychology*. Psychology Press, Hove: 215-244.

Luise Springer. 2008. Therapeutic approaches in aphasia rehabilitation. In B. Stemmer and H. Whitaker (eds.) *Handbook of the Neuroscience of Language*. Elsevier Science, : 397-406.

David P. Vinson and Gabriella Vigliocco. 2008. Semantic feature production norms for a large set of objects and events. *Behavior Research Methods*, 40 (1): 183-190.

Morton E. Winston, Roger Chaffin and Douglas Herrman. 1987. A taxonomy of part-whole relation. *Cognitive Science*, 11:417-444.

Ling-ling Wu and Lawrence W. Barsalou. 2009. Perceptual Simulation in conceptual combination: evidence from property generation. *Acta Psychologica*, 132: 173-189.

# Annotating Korean Demonstratives

**Sun-Hee Lee**
Wellesley College
Wellesley, USA
slee6@wellesley.edu

**Jae-young Song**
Yonsei University
Seoul, Korea
jysong@yonsei.ac.kr

## Abstract

This paper presents preliminary work on a corpus-based study of Korean demonstratives. Through the development of an annotation scheme and the use of spoken and written corpora, we aim to determine different functions of demonstratives and to examine their distributional properties. Our corpus study adopts similar features of annotation used in Botley and McEnery (2001) and provides some linguistic hypotheses on grammatical functions of Korean demonstratives to be further explored.

## 1 Introduction

Korean demonstratives are known to have two different functions: anaphoric and deictic reference. Anaphoric demonstratives refer to objects, individuals, events, situations, or propositions in the given linguistic context. Deictic demonstratives refer to physical objects, individuals, or positions (or regions) in the given situational context. Deictic variations commonly signal the speaker's physical distance from specified items. Previous literature on Korean demonstratives has focused on deictic functions in spoken Korean, but a comprehensive approach to their diverse linguistic functions is still lacking. This study examines distinct usages of Korean demonstratives in a spoken and a written corpus through the annotation of relevant linguistic features. Our annotation scheme and features are expected to help clarify grammatical functions of Korean demonstratives, as well as other anaphoric expressions.

English demonstratives show a binary distinction that depends on physical distance; there is a distinction between proximal forms (*this*, *these*, *this N*, *these Ns*) and distal forms (*that*, *those*, *that N*, *those Ns*). In contrast, demonstratives in languages like Korean and Japanese show a three-way distinction: proximal forms, speaker-centered distal forms, and speaker- and hearer-centered distal forms. For example, deictic demonstrative *i* refers to a proximal object relative to the speaker, *ku* refers to a distant object that is close to the hearer, and *ce* refers to a distant object that is far from both the speaker and the hearer. Thus, distinct usage of *ce* and *ku* is associated with how the speaker allocates the deictic center and contextual space, i.e., the speaker-centered space vs. the speaker- and the hearer–centered space. In contrast with deictic usage, previous studies (Chang, 1980; Chang, 1984) assumed that anaphoric demonstratives show only a two-way distinction between proximal forms *i* and distal forms *ku*. However, it is still controversial as to whether the boundaries between anaphora and deixis are clear cut. With our annotation scheme, we aim to capture the linguistic properties contributing to interpretations of demonstratives in Korean. In particular, we aim to determine whether different registers or genres contribute to different functions of demonstratives by comparing their usage in a spoken corpus and a written corpus.

In consideration of a future comparative analysis with English demonstratives, we have designed our annotation scheme by adopting Botley and McEnery's (2001) paradigmatic set of distinctive features for English demonstratives. However, the detailed annotation features have been revised according to language specific features of Korean.

## 2 Corpus Study

For data extraction, we used two Sejong tagged corpora including a 20,343 *eojeol* spoken corpus and 21,023 *eojeol* written corpus.[1] Each corpus is

[1] The term *eojeol* refers to a unit set off by spaces and corresponds to a word unit in English.



*Proceedings of the Fourth Linguistic Annotation Workshop, ACL 2010*, pages 162–165,
Uppsala, Sweden, 15-16 July 2010. ©2010 Association for Computational Linguistics

composed of four conversations/texts with approximately 5000 *eojeol*. The subcorpora of the spoken corpus are everyday conversations without assigned topics and those of the written corpus are three newspaper articles and part of a novel.

Compared to English, Korean demonstratives include more complex grammatical categories with morphological relations. The demonstrative forms *i*, *ku*, and *ce* combine with other words or morphemes and form complex words including nominals (e.g., *i-kes*: this+thing 'this'), adverbs (e.g., *ce-lehkey*: that+way 'that way'), adjectives (e.g., *ku-lehata*: it+is 'is so') and other lexical categories. Thus, it is difficult to determine if they all belong to the same category of demonstratives in Korean. In this study, demonstratives are restricted to words that contain *i*, *ku*, and *ce* maintaining a distinct referentialfunction of pointing. The selected demonstratives include adnouns ( *i* N 'this N', *ku* N 'that N', *ce* 'that N'), pronouns ( *i-es/i-ke* 'this', *ku-kes/ ku-ke* 'it', *ce-kes/ceke* 'that', *i-tul* 'these', *ku-tul* 'they' *ce-tul*), and locative pronouns ( *yeki* 'here', *keki* 'there', *ceki* 'over there'). Although those forms have different lexical categories, strong similarities exist within the same morphological families, which we will refer to as *i* type, *ku* type, and *ce* type demonstratives. Our annotation work aims to extract a generalization of the fundamental usage of the three different types and to use that generalization for developing further research on various morphological variants containing *i, ku,* and *ce.*

### 2.1 The Annotation Scheme

In order to mark referential functions of Korean demonstratives, we first adopt Halliday and Hasan's (1976) classification of the different reference functions of demonstratives: exophoric vs. endophoric usage. We further divide exophora into deixis and background. While the former refers to a physical object or an individual (or location) in the situational context, the latter refers to certain shared information between the speaker and the hearer.

(1)

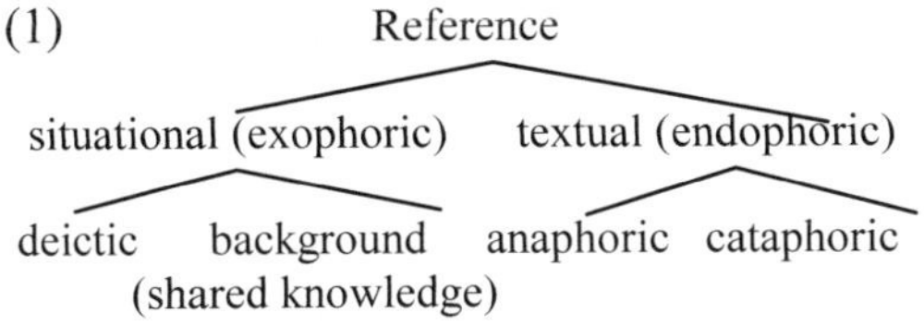


Six distinct features include "Lexical Category of a Demonstrative", "Endophoricity", "Exophoricity", "Syntactic Category of an Antecedent", "Phoric Type", and "Semantic Function of an Antecedent". The first five features are adopted from five features in Botley and McEnery's (2001) annotation work on English demonstratives.[2] The last feature (semantic function) has been added for future work annotating semantic information that facilitates anaphor resolution processes.

Lexical categories of Korean demonstratives in this study include four parts of speech: adnoun, pronoun, locative pronoun (functioning also as an adverb), and exclamatory expressions. While the first three categories show referential functions, the exclamatory expressions do not have reference. Instead, they are used as expressions conveying the speaker's emotion or state, e.g., embarrassment, confusion, hedging. We do not, however, exclude the possibility of linguistic connectivity between demonstrative and exclamatory forms. For instance, the distal demonstrative form *ce* tends to be used as a hedging expression in Korean. Our study includes exclamatory usage as an annotation feature.

Endophoricity refers to two different functions: anaphoric vs. cataphoric. Exophoricity refers to context based vs. deixis. According to Halliday and Hasan's classification in (1), demonstratives with referential function show two major usages: endophoric and exophoric. The first type takes its antecedent within the given text; the latter, within the given situation. Distinction between an anaphor and a cataphor depends on the position of the antecedent. When an endophor follows its antecedent, it is an anaphor; the other case is a cataphor. Demonstratives may have different types of antecedents syntactically. The corresponding values include nominals (including N or NP), clausals (including V, A, VP,

[2] As one of the reviewers pointed out, our study has some limitations as it only refers to two previous studies, Halliday and Hasan (1976) and Botley and McEnery (2001). Although we are aware of the other fundamental work including demonstratives in a broader range of referential expressions such as Gundel et al. (1993), Prince (1981), Nissim et al. (2004), etc., we choose to focus on Korean demonstratives because their exact grammatical functions have not been comprehensively studied in existing literature. In addition, developing a broader classification system for referential expressions in Korean is a challenging task from both theoretical and empirical perspectives; linguistic analyses of Korean nominal expressions must deal with controversial issues such as definiteness without articles, zero elements functioning as anaphors, unsystematic morphological marking of plurality and genericity, etc.

AP, etc.), and sentential elements (S or Ss for more than two sentences).[3]

The feature semantic function of an antecedent includes values of nominal entities, events, and propositions. This feature will be expanded into specified values such as event, process, state, and circumstances in our future study. Phoric type has been adopted from Botley and McEnery (2001) and refers to two distinct relations: reference and substitution. According to Halliday and Hasan, substitution is a relation between linguistic forms, whereas reference is a relation between meanings. The values of phoric type also include non-phoric such as exophora whose antecedents exist outside the text.

The annotation features and values we use are summarized in Table 1.

| Feature | Value1 | Value2 | Value 3 | Value4 |
|---|---|---|---|---|
| Lexical Category (L) | AN (adnoun) | PR (Pronoun) | LPR (Locative pronoun) | EX (Exclamation) |
| Endophoricity (O) | A (anaphor) | C (cataphor) | | |
| Exophoricity (X) | T (situational) | D (deictic) | | |
| Syntactic Function (F) | NO (nominals) | CL (clausal) | S (sentential) | |
| Semantic Function (M) | N (entities) | E (event) | P (propositions) | |
| Phoric Type (H) | R (reference) | U (Substitution) | K (non-phoric) | |

Table 1 Annotation Features and Possible Values

The initial results of inter-annotator agreement between two trained annotators are promising. Cohen's Kappa is 0.76 for the average agreement of six high level categories and it increases following a discussion period (K = 0.83, K=2)[4].

## 3 Results

We identified 1,235 demonstratives in our pilot study. The distributions of demonstratives were significantly different between the spoken and the written corpora. Table 2 shows the raw frequencies in the spoken and the written corpora for each combination of feature and value outlined in Table 1. The raw frequencies are supplemented with the log likelihood in order to show the significance for frequency differences in the two corpora in Table 2. Each demonstrative is followed by a two-character code separated by underscore. The first character denotes the feature and the second the value. For example, the first item *kulen* 'that (kind of)' whose lexical category (L) is adnoun (AN) mostly appeared in the spoken corpus and not in the written corpus.[5]

| Feature | S | W | LL |
|---|---|---|---|
| kulen_L_AN | 183 | 14 | 177.7 |
| kulen_H_R | 178 | 14 | 171.3 |
| kulen_O_A | 163 | 14 | 152.4 |
| kuke(s)_L_PR | 202 | 38 | 128.5 |
| kuke(s)_H_R | 187 | 38 | 112.5 |
| ku_L_EX | 114 | 9 | 109.6 |
| i_O_A | 6 | 105 | 104.0 |
| kuke(s)_O_A | 172 | 38 | 97.0 |
| kulen_F_NO | 69 | 2 | 82.4 |
| ike(s)_H_K | 68 | 3 | 75.7 |
| ike(s)_X_D | 63 | 2 | 74.3 |

Table 2 Frequency of Demonstrative Features

Whereas 931 demonstratives appeared in the spoken corpus, only 304 appeared in the written corpus. The distributions of three different types of demonstratives are listed in Table 3.

| Types | Total Frequency | Written | | Spoken | |
|---|---|---|---|---|---|
| | | Freq. | % | Freq. | % |
| *i* | 398 | 176 | 56 | 222 | 44 |
| *ku* | 773 | 128 | 17 | 645 | 83 |
| *ce* | 64 | 0 | 0 | 64 | 100 |
| Total | 1235 | 304 | 25 | 931 | 75 |

Table 3 Distribution of Three Demonstrative Types

The spoken corpus and the written corpus show different preferences for *i*, *ku*, and *ce* types.

Written: *i* (58%) > *ku* (42%) > *ce* (0%)
Spoken: *ku* (69%) > *i* (24%) > *ce* (7%)

Whereas *ku* demonstratives are preferred to corresponding *i* demonstratives in the spoken corpus, *i* demonstratives are preferred in the written cor-

[3] Although the syntactic category of an antecedent can be differentiated in a more sophisticated way using phrasal categories such as NP, VP, AdvP, etc. (as well as lexical categories), this will render the annotation process nearly impossible unless one uses a corpus with syntactic annotation, such as treebanks. Thus, we use simplified syntactic information such as nominal, clausal, and sentential.

[4] The agreement rate was calculated for each six high level categories separately and then averaged. The syntactic function has the lowest agreement rate even after the discussion (K=0.76). This is due to complex properties of Korean demonstratives with unclear boundaries between exclamatory expressions and other lexical categories.

[5] In Table 2, the log likelihood scores show that the usage of *kulen* is significantly different in the spoken and the written corpus. The log-likelihood scores in Table 2 are significant at a 99 percent confidence level with 1 degree of freedom if they are greater than 6.6. We only show a partial frequency list here due to the space limitations.

pus. This fact is associated with the linguistic function of *ku* that represents a speaker's desire to anchor interpersonal involvement with the hearer by actively inviting the hearer's voluntary understanding of the target referent. In contrast, *i* demonstratives imply that the speaker (writer) intends to incorporate the hearer (reader) within the proximal cognitive distance. In terms of annotation features, our findings are summarized as follows.

**Lexical category:** In both the written and spoken corpora, adnominal demonstratives are more frequently used than pronouns or locative pronouns. Demonstrative forms used as intensifiers, hedges, or personal habitual noise have been marked as exclamatives. Annotators have found that it is often difficult to clearly distinguish them from adnominal demonstratives.

**Endophoricity:** Our written corpus does not include any cataphors, whereas the spoken corpus shows 61 cases (cf. 523 anaphors). This fact seems to be related to the speaker's discourse strategy of intending to call the discourse participants' attention by placing an endophoric element before its antecedent.

**Exophoricity:** Exophoric usage of demonstratives in the written corpus is very limited. Only 17 cases were found (6 deixis vs. 11 context-based). In the spoken corpus, exophoric usages occur more frequently across three types of demonstratives. The deictic usage dominates the context-based usage (151 deixis vs. 79 context-based). As noted in previous literature, *ce* demonstratives mainly appear in deictic context, where its antecedent is visible or exists in the given situation. There seems to be a constraint of deictic usage of *ce* involving physical existence or visibility (or cognitive awareness) of an entity in addition to distance. This hypothesis needs to be further investigated with additional data.

**Syntactic and Semantic Function:** All three types of *i*, *ku*, and *ce* demonstratives refer to nominal entities as their antecedents. Although *i* and *ku* demonstratives are also used to refer to clausals and sentential elements, only a few examples of *ce* replace clausal or sentential elements. Another notable point is that *i* and *ku* demonstratives refer to clausal or sentential elements (corresponding to events or propositions) more frequently than nominal entities in both spoken and written corpora. 59% of the antecedents of *i* demonstratives (56% for *ku* type) in the written corpus are clausals or sentential elements, whereas 53% of the antecedents of *i* type (69% for *ku* type) are in the spoken corpus. This result needs to be tested on a larger corpus in our future study.

**Phoric Type:** In our annotated corpus, we only found referential examples, not substitutional cases. Exophoric examples are marked as non-phoric. In the written corpus, referential demonstratives are predominant (285 cases) and a small number of non-phoric cases are observed (18 cases). In the spoken corpus, referential demonstratives are more frequent (590 cases), whereas non-phoric cases have been more observed than in the written corpus (198 cases).

## 3 Conclusion

In this paper we presented a corpus-based study on Korean demonstratives. Six annotation features were used to mark complex linguistic functions of demonstratives. Using spoken and written corpora, we compared different usages of Korean demonstratives and showed that their usages are different depending on the registers of spoken and written Korean.

In spite of the deictic functions of demonstratives highlighted in previous research, our study indicates that endophoric usage is more predominant. This hypothesis, as well as others in this study, will be tested with a large corpus in our future work. We also plan to incorporate more sophisticated exploitation on semantic types of antecedents. This information will be useful for resolving the meaning of anaphoric demonstratives.

## References


Botley, Simon and Tony McEnery. 2001. Demonstratives in English. *Journal of English Linguistics*, 29(1): 7-33.

Chang, Kyung-Hee. 1980. Semantic Analysis of Demonstrative *i*, *ku*, *ce*. *Ehakyenku,* 16(2):167-0184.

Chang, Seok-Jin 1984. Cisiwa Coung. *Hangul,* 186: 115-149.

Gundel, Jaeanette, Nancy Hedberg, and Ron Zacharski. 1993. Cognitive Status and the Form of Referring Expressions in Discourse. *Language*, 69(2):274-307.

Halliday, M.A.K. and Ruqaiya Hasan. 1976. *Cohesion in English.* London: Longman.

Min, Kyung Mo. 2008. *A Study on Reference Items in Korean*. Ph.D. Dissertation. Yonsei University.

Poesio, Massimo. 2004. The MATE/GNOME Scheme for Anaphoric Annotation, Revisited. In *Proceedings of SIGDIAL*. Boston.

Prince, Ellen. 1981. Toward a Taxonomy of Given-New Information. *Radical Pragmatics*: 223-255. Academic Press. New York.

# Creating and Exploiting a Resource of Parallel Parses

**Christian Chiarcos*** and **Kerstin Eckart**** and **Julia Ritz***

* Collaborative Research Centre 632
"Information Structure"
Universität Potsdam
{chiarcos|jritz}@uni-potsdam.de

** Collaborative Research Centre 732
"Incremental Specification in Context"
Universität Stuttgart
eckartkn@ims.uni-stuttgart.de

## Abstract

This paper describes the creation of a resource of German sentences with multiple automatically created alternative syntactic analyses (parses) for the same text, and how qualitative and quantitative investigations of this resource can be performed using ANNIS, a tool for corpus querying and visualization. Using the example of PP attachment, we show how parsing can benefit from the use of such a resource.

## 1 Introduction

In this paper, we describe the workflow and the infrastructure to create and explore a corpus that contains multiple parses of German sentences. A corpus of alternative parses created by different tools allows us to study structural differences between the parses in a systematic way.

The resource described in this paper is a collection of German sentences with *-ung* nominalizations extracted from the SDEWAC corpus (Faaß et al., 2010), based on the DEWAC web corpus (Baroni and Kilgarriff, 2006). These sentences are employed for the study of lexical ambiguities in German *-ung* nominalizations (Eberle et al., 2009); e.g., German *Absperrung*, derived from *absperren* 'to block', can denote an event ('blocking'), a state ('blockade') or an object ('barrier'). Sortal disambiguation, however, is highly context-dependent, and reliable and detailed analyses of the linguistic context are crucial for a sortal disambiguation of these nominalizations.

More reliable and detailed linguistic analyses can be achieved, for example, by combining the information produced by different parsers: On the basis of qualitative and quantitative analyses, generalized rules for the improvement of the respective parsers can be developed, as well as rules for the mapping of their output to a tool-independent representation, and weights for the parallel application and combination of multiple parsers. This approach has been previously applied to morphological and morphosyntactic annotations (Borin, 2000; Zavrel and Daelemans, 2000; Tufiş, 2000), but only recently to syntax annotation (Francom and Hulden, 2008; de la Clergerie et al., 2008). Because of the complexity of syntax annotations as compared to part of speech tags, however, novel technologies have to be applied that allow us to represent, to visualize and to query multiple syntactic analyses of the same sentence.

This paper describes the workflow from raw text to a searchable representation of the corpus. One of the aims of this new resource is to assess potential weaknesses in the parsers as well as their characteristic strengths. For the example of ambiguities in PP attachment, Sect. 4 shows how linguistic analyses can be improved by combining information from different parsers.

## 2 Parsing

In order to maximize both coverage and granularity of linguistic analyses, we chose parsers from different classes: A probabilistic constituent parser and a rule-based parser that produces semantically enriched dependency parses.

### 2.1 BitPar

BitPar (Schmid, 2006) is a probabilistic context free parser using bit-vector operations (Schmid, 2004). Node categories are annotated along with grammatical functions, part-of-speech tags and morphological information in a parse tree. BitPar analyses are conformant to the TIGER annotation scheme (Brants et al., 2004), and the tool's output format is similar to the list-based bracketing format of the Penn Treebank (Bies et al., 1995). The BitPar analysis of sentence (1) is visualized as the right-most tree in Fig. 1.



*Proceedings of the Fourth Linguistic Annotation Workshop, ACL 2010*, pages 166–171,
Uppsala, Sweden, 15-16 July 2010. ©2010 Association for Computational Linguistics

(1) *Der Dax reagiert derzeit auf die*
the Dax reacts presently on the
*Meldungen aus London.*
messages from London
'Presently, the Dax [German stock index, N.B.] is reacting to the news from London.'

### 2.2 B3 Tool

The second parser applied here is the B3 Tool (Eberle et al., 2008), a rule-based parser that provides syntactic-semantic analyses that combine dependency parsing with FUDRT representations.[1] The B3 Tool is developed on the basis of a research prototype by Lingenio[2] in the context of a project on lexical ambiguities in German nominalizations[3].

For further processing, the output of the B3 Tool is converted into a PTB-style bracketing format similar to that used by BitPar. This transformation involves the generation of a constituency graph from the original dependency analysis: In the first step, rules are used that insert nodes and projections as described by Eberle (2002). Then, another transformation step is necessary: As the B3 Tool aims for an abstract, flat semantics-oriented structure, certain aspects of the surface structure are not represented in its output and need to be restored in order to create analyses that can be aligned with constituent-based representations. For example, punctuation marks do not appear as leaves of the syntactic tree, as their contribution is included in the description of the head verb. Similarly, auxiliaries are not represented as individual words in the B3 output, as their tense and aspect information is integrated with the event description that corresponds to the head verb.[4] As we focus on the integration of multiple syntactic analyses, leaves from the B3 Tool output that represent semantic information were not considered, e.g., information on coreference.

The converted B3 analysis of sentence (1) is visualized as the left tree in Fig. 1.

[1]Flat Underspecified Discourse Representation Theory (Eberle, 1997; Eberle, 2004)

[2]`http://www.lingenio.de/English/`

[3]Project B3 of the Collaborative Research Centre (Sonderforschungsbereich) SFB 732, Stuttgart, Germany.

[4]For the study described here, punctuation marks were added to the surface structure but auxiliaries not yet. There are several possible approaches to dealing with these structural aspects (e.g. inserting empty elements, converting BitPar into B3-like representations, etc.). The discussion of these strategies is, however, beyond the scope of this technical paper.

## 3 Querying and Visualizing Alternative Parses

In order to integrate multiple annotations created by different tools, we employ a generic XML format, PAULA XML (Dipper and Götze, 2005). PAULA XML is an XML linearization of the data model underlying the ANNIS data base.[5] It is comparable to NITE XML (Carletta et al., 2005) and GrAF (Ide, 2007). PAULA XML supports diverse data structures (trees, graphs, and flat spans of tokens) and allows for conflicting hierarchies.

The integrated PAULA representation of the multiple-parses corpus can be accessed using ANNIS, a web interface for querying and visualizing richly annotated corpora. Fig. 1 shows the ANNIS interface: top left is the query field; below that is the 'match count' field (presenting the number of instances matching the query). Below this field is the list of corpora the user choses from. Matches are visualized in the right window. Tokens and token-level annotations are shown in a Key Word In Context (KWIC) view (upper part of the search result pane in Fig. 1), e.g., B3 morphology (2nd row), BitPar parts of speech (3rd row), and BitPar morphology (4th row). Trees are visualized with the Tree view (below KWIC view).

## 4 Exploiting multiple parses

The goal of our research is to develop rules for the combination of BitPar and B3 parses such that the resulting merged parse provides more reliable linguistic analyses than the ones provided by either alone. The rule-based B3 Tool provides deep semantic analyses. B3 parses are thus generally richer in information than BitPar parses. Certain ambiguities, however, are not resolved but rather represented by underspecification. In this section, we explore the possibility to employ BitPar parses to resolve such underspecifications.

### 4.1 Studying PP attachment in ANNIS

The attachment of prepositional phrases is often ambiguous between high attachment (e.g., PP as a clausal adjunct) and low attachment (PP as a nominal modifier). In such cases, the B3 Tool employs underspecification, which is represented by a special edge label `xprep`.[6]

[5]PAULA and ANNIS have been developed at the Collaborative Research Centre 632, `http://www.sfb632.uni-potsdam.de/~d1/annis/`.

[6]The `xprep` label indicates underspecification as to whether the PP has to be attached to its parent node or a node

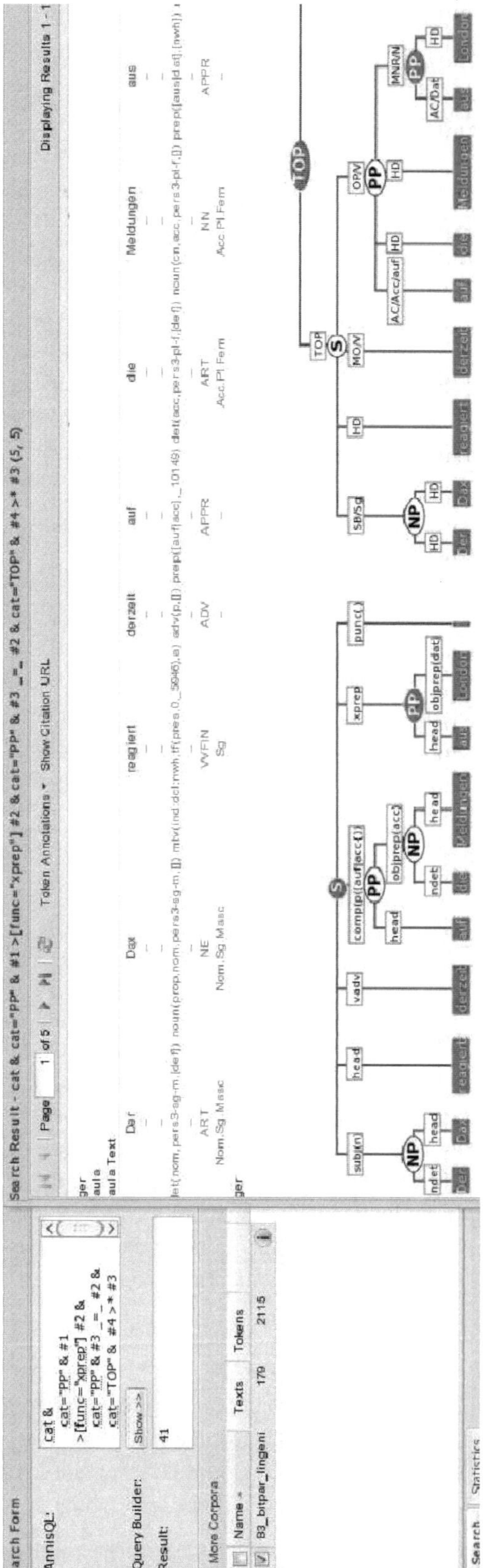

Figure 1: ANNIS2 screenshot with query results for QUERY 1

Using ANNIS, we retrieve all cases where a BitPar PP corresponds to a B3 PP with the edge labeled `xprep` (the query used to accomplish this will be referenced by QUERY 1 in the following). Fig. 1 illustrates an example match: The B3 PP (left tree) is attached to the root node with an edge label `xprep`; in the BitPar analysis (right tree), the prepositional phrase is correctly attached to the other `PP` node.

Using an extended query, we conducted a quantitative analysis comparing the node labels assigned to the parent node of the respective PPs in BitPar parses and B3 parses.

Considering only those matches where the B3 parent node was either VP or S (85%, 35 of 41), high attachment is indicated by BitPar labels VP or S for the BitPar parent node (34%, 12 of 35) and low attachment by labels PP or NP (66%, 23 of 35). BitPar thus distinguishes low and high PP attachment, with a preference for low attachment in our data set.

Results of a subsequent qualitative analysis of the first 20 matches retrieved by this query are summarized in Tab. 1: Only 16% (3 of 19) BitPar predictions are incorrect, 32% (6 of 19) are possible (but different attachment would have produced a felicitous reading), and 53% (10 of 19) are correct. BitPar analyses of PP attachment are thus

| BitPar prediction | correct | possible | incorrect | total |
|---|---|---|---|---|
| low | 57% | 36% | 7% | 14 |
| high | 40% | 20% | 40% | 5 |
| low or high | 53% | 32% | 16% | 19* |

* one match (non-sentence) excluded

Table 1: Qualitative analysis of the first 20 matches

relatively reliable, and where the B3 Tool indicates underspecification with respect to PP attachment, the point of attachment can be adopted from the BitPar parse. With such a merging of BitPar parses and B3 parses, a more detailed and more reliable analysis is possible.

## 4.2 Merging B3 and BitPar parses

With the information from the comparison of BitPar and B3 Tool attachments, a workflow is imaginable where both parsers are applied in parallel, and then their output is merged into a common representation. As opposed to traditional approaches that reduce parse integration to a selec-

dominated by its parent.

tion between entire parses, cf. Crysmann et al. (2002), we employ a full merging between B3 parses and BitPar parses. This merging is based on hand-crafted rules that express preferences between pieces of information from one parse or the other in accordance with the results of quantitative and qualitative analyses as described above.

B3 parses can be enriched with structural information from BitPar, e.g., by the following exemplaric rule:[7] if the B3 parse indicates underspecification with respect to the PP attachment point (QUERY 1), establish a dominance edge between (i) the correspondent of the Bitpar PP (the PP '*from London*' in the example) and (ii) the correspondent of its parent node (the PP '*to the news*'), and delete the original, underspecified B3 edge. The same procedure can also be applied to perform corrections of a parse, if further quantitative and qualitative studies indicate that, for example, the B3 parser systematically fails at a particular phenomenon.

In some cases, we may also want to employ context-dependent rules to exploit the advantageous characteristics of a specific parser, e.g., to preserve ambiguities. Example (2) illustrates that PP attachment has an effect on the sortal interpretation of *Absperrung* 'barrier/blocking/blockade': Different points of attachment can produce different possible readings. The PP *by the police* specifies the subject of the nominalized verb *absperren* 'to block'. This indicates that here, the event/state readings are preferred over the object (=entity) reading.

(2) *Die Feuerwehr unterstützte die*
the fire brigade supported the
*Absperrung durch die Polizei.*
blocking by the police
'The fire brigade supported the police's blockade/blocking.'

## 5 Conclusion

In this paper, we described the creation of a resource of German sentences with parallel parses and the infrastructure employed to exploit this resource. We also identified possible fields of application for this resource: By querying this resource one finds strong tendencies regarding the relative reliability and level of detail of different parsers; on this basis, the strengths of several tools can be weighted, as represented, e.g., by generalized, context-dependent rules to combine the output of multiple parsers. Here, this approach was illustrated for two parsers and their combination to disambiguate PP attachment as part of a study of German *-ung* nominalizations. A future perspective could be to add more tools to the comparison, find out their characteristic strengths and perform a sort of weighted voting to decide when an analysis should be enhanced by the information from another one.

We have shown that the infrastructure provided by the ANNIS data base and the underlying data format PAULA can be employed to conduct this kind of research. Although originally developed for different purposes (representation and querying of richly annotated corpora), its generic character allowed us to apply it with more than satisfactory results to a new scenario.

Subsequent research may further exploit the potential of the ANNIS/PAULA infrastructure and the development of application-specific extensions. In particular, it is possible to register in ANNIS a problem-specific visualization for parallel parses that applies in place of the generic tree/DAG view for the namespaces `bitpar` and `b3`. Another extension pertains to the handling of conflicting tokenizations: The algorithm described by Chiarcos et al. (2009) is sufficiently generic to be applied to any PAULA project, but it may be extended to account for B3-specific deletions (Sect. 2.2). Further, ANNIS supports an annotation enrichment cycle: Matches are exported as WEKA tables, statistical, symbolic or neural classifiers can be trained on or applied to this data, and the modified match table can be reintegrated with the original corpus. This allows, for example, to learn an automatic mapping between B3 and BitPar annotations.

**Acknowledgements**

Collaborative Research Centre 732 (Universität Stuttgart) and Collaborative Research Centre 632 (Humboldt Universität zu Berlin and Universität Potsdam) are funded by Deutsche Forschungsgemeinschaft (DFG).

[7] Other formulations are possible, see Heid et al. (2009) for the enrichment of BitPar parses with lexical knowledge from B3 parses.

## References


Marco Baroni and Adam Kilgarriff. 2006. Large linguistically-processed Web corpora for multiple languages. In *Proceedings of the 11th Conference of the European Chapter of the Association for Computational Linguistics*, pages 87–90, Trento, Italy. EACL.

Ann Bies, Mark Ferguson, Karen Katz, and Robert MacIntyre. 1995. Bracketing guidelines for treebank ii style penn treebank project. `ftp://ftp.cis.upenn.edu/pub/treebank/doc/manual/root.ps.gz` (May 31, 2010). version of January 1995.

Lars Borin. 2000. Something borrowed, something blue: Rule-based combination of POS taggers. In *Proceedings of the 2nd International Conference on Language Resources and Evaluation (LREC 2000)*, Athens, Greece, May, 31st – June, 2nd.

Sabine Brants, Stefanie Dipper, Peter Eisenberg, Silvia Hansen, Esther König, Wolfgang Lezius, Christian Rohrer, George Smith, and Hans Uszkoreit. 2004. TIGER: Linguistic interpretation of a German corpus. *Research on Language and Computation*, 2(4):597–620.

Jean Carletta, Stefan Evert, Ulrich Heid, and Jonathan Kilgour. 2005. The NITE XML Toolkit: data model and query. *Language Resources and Evaluation Journal (LREJ)*, 39(4):313–334.

Christian Chiarcos, Julia Ritz, and Manfred Stede. 2009. By all these lovely tokens...: merging conflicting tokenizations. In *Proceedings of the Third Linguistic Annotation Workshop*, pages 35–43. Association for Computational Linguistics.

Berthold Crysmann, Anette Frank, Kiefer Bernd, Stefan Mueller, Guenter Neumann, Jakub Piskorski, Ulrich Schaefer, Melanie Siegel, Hans Uszkoreit, Feiyu Xu, Markus Becker, and Hans-Ulrich Krieger. 2002. An integrated architecture for shallow and deep processing. In *Proceedings of 40th Annual Meeting of the Association for Computational Linguistics*, pages 441–448, Philadelphia, Pennsylvania, USA, July.

Eric Villemonte de la Clergerie, Olivier Hamon, Djamel Mostefa, Christelle Ayache, Patrick Paroubek, and Anne Vilnat. 2008. PASSAGE: from French Parser Evaluation to Large Sized Treebank. In *Proceedings of the $6^{th}$ Conference on Language Resources and Evaluation (LREC 2008)*, Marrakech, Morocco, May.

Stefanie Dipper and Michael Götze. 2005. Accessing Heterogeneous Linguistic Data — Generic XML-based Representation and Flexible Visualization. In *Proceedings of the 2nd Language & Technology Conference 2005*, pages 23–30, Poznan, Poland, April.

Kurt Eberle, Ulrich Heid, Manuel Kountz, and Kerstin Eckart. 2008. A tool for corpus analysis using partial disambiguation and bootstrapping of the lexicon. In Angelika Storrer, Alexander Geyken, Alexander Siebert, and Kay-Michael Würzner, editors, *Text Resources and Lexical Knowledge – Selected Papers from the $9^{th}$ Conference on Natural Language Processing (KONVENS 2008)*, pages 145–158, Berlin, Germany. Mouton de Gruyter.

Kurt Eberle, Gertrud Faaß, and Ulrich Heid. 2009. Proposition oder Temporalangabe? Disambiguierung von -ung-Nominalisierungen von verba dicendi in nach-PPs. In Christian Chiarcos, Richard Eckart de Castilho, and Manfred Stede, editors, *Von der Form zur Bedeutung: Texte automatisch verarbeiten / From Form to Meaning: Processing Texts Automatically, Proceedings of the Biennial GSCL Conference 2009*, pages 81–91, Tübingen. Gunter Narr Verlag.

Kurt Eberle. 1997. Flat underspecified representation and its meaning for a fragment of German. Arbeitspapiere des Sonderforschungsbereichs 340, Nr. 120, Universität Stuttgart, Stuttgart, Germany.

Kurt Eberle. 2002. Tense and Aspect Information in a FUDR-based German French Machine Translation System. In Hans Kamp and Uwe Reyle, editors, *How we say WHEN it happens. Contributions to the theory of temporal reference in natural language*, pages 97–148. Niemeyer, Tübingen. Ling. Arbeiten, Band 455.

Kurt Eberle. 2004. Flat underspecified representation and its meaning for a fragment of German. Habilitationsschrift, Universität Stuttgart, Stuttgart, Germany.

Gertrud Faaß, Ulrich Heid, and Helmut Schmid. 2010. Design and application of a Gold Standard for morphological analysis: SMOR as an example of morphological evaluation. In *Proceedings of the seventh international conference on Language Resources and Evaluation (LREC)*, Valetta, Malta.

Jerid Francom and Mans Hulden. 2008. Parallel Multi-Theory Annotations of Syntactic Structure. In *Proceedings of the Sixth International Language Resources and Evaluation (LREC 2008)*, Marrakech, Morocco, May.

Ulrich Heid, Kurt Eberle, and Kerstin Eckart. 2009. Towards more reliable linguistic analyses: workflow and infrastructure. Poster presentation at the GSCL 2009 workshop: Linguistic Processing Pipelines, Potsdam.

Nancy Ide. 2007. GrAF: A Graph-based Format for Linguistic Annotations. In *Proceedings of the LAW Workshop at ACL 2007*, Prague.

Helmut Schmid. 2004. Efficient Parsing of Highly Ambiguous Context-Free Grammars with Bit Vectors. In *Proceedings of the 20th International Conference on Computational Linguistics, Coling'04*, volume 1, pages 162–168, Geneva, Switzerland.

Helmut Schmid. 2006. Trace Prediction and Recovery With Unlexicalized PCFGs and Slash Features. In *Proceedings of COLING-ACL 2006*, Sydney, Australia.

Dan Tufiş. 2000. Using a large set of EAGLES-compliant morpho-syntactic descriptors as a tagset for probabilistic tagging. In *Proceedings of the 2nd International Conference on Language Resources and Evaluation (LREC 2000)*, pages 1105–1112, Athens, Greece, May, 31st – June, 2nd.

Jakub Zavrel and Walter Daelemans. 2000. Bootstrapping a Tagged Corpus through Combination of Existing Heterogeneous Taggers. In *Proceedings of the 2nd International Conference on Language Resources and Evaluation (LREC 2000)*, Athens, Greece, May, 31st – June, 2nd.

# From Descriptive Annotation to Grammar Specification

**Lars Hellan**
NTNU
Trondheim, Norway
lars.hellan@hf.ntnu.no

## Abstract

The paper presents an architecture for connecting annotated linguistic data with a computational grammar system. Pivotal to the architecture is an annotational *interlingua* – called the *Construction Labeling* system (CL) - which is notationally very simple, descriptively finegrained, cross-typologically applicable, and formally well-defined enough to map to a state-of-the-art computational model of grammar. In the present instantiation of the architecture, the computational grammar is an HPSG-based system called *TypeGram*. Underlying the architecture is a research program of enhancing the interconnectivity between linguistic analytic subsystems such as grammar formalisms and text annotation systems.

## 1 Introduction

This paper advocates the view that all aspects of descriptive, theoretical, typological, and computational linguistics should hang together in overall precisely defined networks of terminologies and formalisms, but flexibly so such that each field can choose suitable formats, and different traditions can maintain their preferred terminologies and formalisms. Terms and symbols used for linguistic annotation are central in this enterprise, and the paper describes an algorithm by which a code suitable for sentence level annotation can be aligned with a system of attribute-value matrix (AVM) representations. An aim for further development is a similar alignment for PoS/morpheme annotation symbols.

The alignment described has as its theoretical and computational reference point an HPSG-based system, where, aside from AVMs, *types* play a crucial role. Most likely, alignment architectures with similar capacities to the one here described can have other formal frameworks integrated. For such alternatives the present system may serve as a roadmap, and hopefully more: the architecture is sought to be modular such that parts of it – such as the formal framework, or an annotation tag system - can be replaced while keeping other parts constant. At the present point, however, this is a demonstration tied to unique choices for each module in the architecture. It serves as a feasibility demonstration of the design as such, and equally much to motivate the specific annotation code presented, which is pivotal to the system as a whole.

This paper has two parts. The first part presents the sentence-level annotation code. It consists of strings of labels (connected by hyphens) where each label represents a possible *property of a sentential sign*, such as, e.g., 'has Argument structure X', 'has Aspect Y', 'has a Subject with properties Z', 'expresses situation type S', etc. The construction type specification in (1) is a first illustration of the code:

(1) `v-tr-suAg_obAffincrem-COMPLETED_MONODEVMNT`
(Ex.: English: *the boy ate the cake*)

This reads: the sign is headed by *verb*; its syntactic frame is *transitive*; it has a Subject (su) whose thematic role is *agent*, and an Object (ob) whose thematic role is *incrementally affected*; its aspectual type is characterized as a combination of *completed* and *monotonic development*.

Expressions like that in (1), characterizing a sentence from its 'global' perspective, are referred to as *templates*. The code is flexible in having no upward bound on the number of labels used in a template, and expressive in that each label represents a *statement* about some part or aspect of the sign. The code as such will be referred to as the **Construction Labeling** (***CL***) system; see section 2.

The circumstance that each individual label has the logic of a statement, is essential to the transparency of the code. This propositional character of a label also opens for the alignment of CL with a formal grammar system, which is addressed in the second part of the paper. Here we show how templates can be linked to AVMs, like the template in (1) to an AVM like (2) (in mixed HPSG/LFG style),



*Proceedings of the Fourth Linguistic Annotation Workshop, ACL 2010*, pages 172–176,
Uppsala, Sweden, 15-16 July 2010. 

(2)

$$\left[\begin{array}{l} \text{HEAD verb} \\ \text{GF} \left[\begin{array}{l} \text{SUBJ} \left[\text{INDX } \boxed{1} \left[\text{ROLE agent}\right]\right] \\ \text{OBJ} \left[\text{INDX } \boxed{2} \left[\text{ROLE aff-increm}\right]\right] \end{array}\right] \\ \text{INDX ref-index} \\ \text{ASPECT completed} \\ \text{ACTNTS} \left[\begin{array}{l} \text{ACT1 } \boxed{1} \\ \text{ACT2 } \boxed{2} \end{array}\right] \\ \text{SIT-TYPE monotonic\_development} \end{array}\right]$$

and in such a way that each individual label in the template can be seen as inducing its specific part of the AVM, as informally and partially indicated in (3):

(3)

$$\text{v - - -} \quad \left[\text{HEAD verb}\right]$$

$$\text{tr - - -} \quad \left[\begin{array}{l} \text{GF} \left[\begin{array}{l} \text{SUBJ} \left[\text{INDX } \boxed{1}\right] \\ \text{OBJ} \left[\text{INDX } \boxed{2}\right] \end{array}\right] \\ \text{ACTNTS} \left[\begin{array}{l} \text{ACT1 } \boxed{1} \\ \text{ACT2 } \boxed{2} \end{array}\right] \end{array}\right]$$

$$\text{suAg - - -} \quad \left[\text{GF} \left[\text{SUBJ} \left[\text{INDX} \left[\text{ROLE agent}\right]\right]\right]\right]$$

$$\text{obAffincrem - - -} \quad \left[\text{GF} \left[\text{OBJ} \left[\text{INDX} \left[\text{ROLE aff-increm}\right]\right]\right]\right]$$

Thus, while the labels have a descriptive transparency essential to the descriptive functionality of the over-all code, this transparency can be 'cashed out' also in the definition of a linking between CL and grammar formalisms like that illustrated in (2) and (3). Section 3 describes a possible architecture for achieving this, centered around the computational grammar *TypeGram*.

## 2 Construction Labeling

In its first development, the coding system has been based on two typologically very diverse languages: *Norwegian*, and the West African language *Ga*. An overview of the system is given in (Hellan and Dakubu 2010). The end product of its application to a language is called a *construction profile* of the language, abbreviated its *c-profile*. This is an assembly of between 150 and 250 templates encoding the span of variation offered by the language in a fixed number of respects, in a code immediately comparable to c-profiles of other languages. A c-profile for both Ga and Norwegian is given in (Hellan and Dakubu op. cit.); see also (Hellan and Dakubu 2009, Dakubu 2008, Hellan 2008).

The typical method of establishing c-profiles is through *paradigm building*, where, based on one sentence of the language, one establishes the various paradigms relative to which the sentence instantiates choices, and supplements these paradigms with paradigms spun out of other sentences or constructions, ultimately establishing a full network of construction types for the language relative to the discriminants selected. ('Construction' is here used in a theory neutral way.)

The creation of c-profiles is obviously an incremental process, both in the building of templates instantiating possibilities defined by the range of discriminants recognized at any point, and in extending this range reflecting new phenomena and new languages investigated. Thus, while the stage referred to above reflects in depth work on Germanic and Kwa, significant enhancements are currently made through work on Ethio-semitic (especially through the study (Wakjira, to appear) on Kistaninya), Bantu, Indic, and other language groups, mostly not yet having achieved full c-profiles.

Although presentable as networks, in normal displays c-profiles are given as *lists*, with strict principles of ordering. Some c-profiles are also entered in the TypeCraft database (http://www.typecraft.org/), where one can search according to any labels serving as constituents of templates. At present, the number of labels employed in the code is about 40 for valence types, 90 for specifications relating to the syntactic form of specific constituents, 40 for thematic roles of specific constituents, 20 for aspect and Aktionsart values, and 60 for situation types. For valence and grammatical functions, language and framework independence in the code is made possible due to considerable agreement across traditions, whereas for participant roles and situation types, there is much less of a consolidated basis, and in these areas code development and evaluation is still a primary issue.

## 3 TypeGram

TypeGram is in most respects a normal HPSG-based computational grammar built on the LKB platform (Copestake 2002). Crucial to the present discussion, it has some components designed for linking it up with the CL code, which makes it possible for it to

- provide an *AVM display* of any CL template (like (2) above, for (1));
- provide a basis for a *rapid development of a parsing grammar* for any language for which a c-profile has been created;

- provide an *intermediate parsing facility* for sentences of any language even when no grammar specific to the language has been created, as long as the language has been assigned a c-profile.

We will refer to the 'basic' part of TypeGram as its *Core*. Relative to current grammar formalisms using AVMs, such as *LFG* and *HPSG* (cf. Bresnan 2001, Butt et al. 1999, Pollard and Sag 1994), the TypeGram Core borrows from LFG an inventory of *grammatical functions*, and from HPSG the use of *types*, and a design by which all components of a grammar are encoded in AVMs. Unlike most computational grammars, the Core defines analyses for phenomena not restricted to one language, but for the union of all languages for which c-profiles have been defined. (In this respect it resembles the *HPSG Grammar Matrix* ('the Matrix' - see Bender et. al, and http://www.delph-in.net/matrix/ ); we comment on its relationship to this system below.) The mediation between the Core and the c-profiles is induced by special type files:

- one file for each c-profile (of which there are currently three, for Ga, Norwegian and Kistaninya)
- one general file, called *Labeltypes,* for defining CL labels as *types* in terms of the Core *types*.

This architecture can be summed up as follows (with 'Ga c-types' meaning 'types corresponding to the templates constituting the c-profile for Ga', and items in boldface being items defined inside the TypeGram system):

(4)

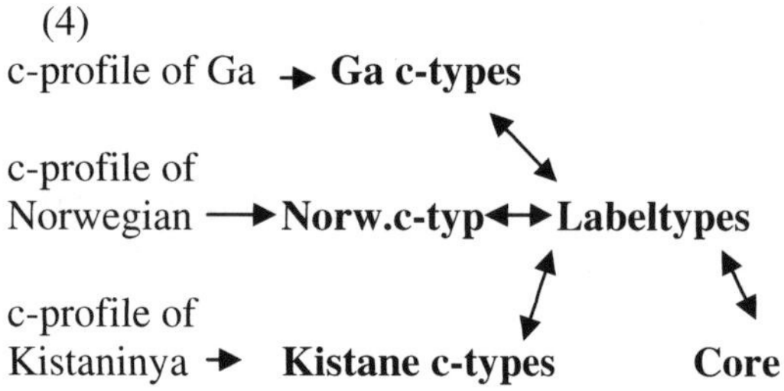


Thus, what communicates between the *Core* and the construction specifications in the CL code is *Labeltypes*, which in turn feeds into the language specific template definition files. The latter files build *only* on *Labeltypes*, which in turn builds *only* on the *Core*. This allows for modularity: the content of the Core can be changed, e.g., to the system of the Matrix (or even an LFG-based system), without affecting the c-profiles or the c-type inventories.

We now describe possibilities offered by the architecture.

### 3.1 Providing AVM displays of templates

In exemplifying this function, we use a template from Ga, along with a glossed example to illustrate the construction type:

(5) `v-ditr-obPostp-suAg_obEndpt_ob2Mover-PLACEMENT`

| | | | | |
|---|---|---|---|---|
| **Amɛ-wo tsɔne** | **lɛ** | **mli** | **yelɛ** | |
| 3P.AOR-put | vehicle | DEF | inside | yam |
| V | N | Art | N | N |

'They put [vehicle's inside] [yam]' = 'They put yams in the lorry.'

Here the two objects represent a *Mover* (the yam) and where the Mover is finally placed (the lorry's inside). This *Endpoint* is characterized as the inside of something, where the expression of this inside is structurally like a possessive NP construction.

In the type-file 'Ga c-types', the template in (5) is turned into a grammatical type by the type definition (6) (where ':=' means 'is a subtype of' and '*&*' is the operation of unification):

(6)
v-ditr-obPostp-suAg_obEndpt_ob2Th-PLACEMENT :=
v & ditr & obPostp & suAg & obEndpt & ob2Th & PLACEMENT.

The way in which the individual types *v*, *ditr*, *obPostp*, etc., are here *unified* to constitute a definition of the type corresponding to the full template, corresponds to the way in which, in (3), the constituent labels of the template (1) are portrayed as contributing to its full AVM.

The defining types in (6) are in turn defined in *labeltypes,* by definitions whose defining terms are in turn defined in the *Core*.

With such type definitions in the background, the template *v-ditr-obPostp-suAg_obEndpt_ob2Th-PLACEMENT* is a type recognized in the grammar. Using the *view type definition* offered in a standard LKB interface, one sees the AVM assigned to this template.

### 3.2 Developing a parsing grammar

Suppose that we want to develop a grammar of Ga – GaGram -, taking advantage of the type apparatus already described. (For Ga, the lexicon (Dakubu 2009) is partly informed by the c-profile and is a resource in building the lexicon of the grammar.) What is missing is defining a lexicon, inflectional rules, derivational rules and syntactic combinatorial rules. The latter is partly deducible from the constructional templates, and for templates which reflect verb subcategorization frames, lexical frame types are fairly directly derivable from the templates. What needs to be done in addition is specifying the lexical root items of Ga, and the inflectional and derivational formatives used in the language.

This 'grammar construction kit' offered by TypeGram clearly resembles the *HPSG Grammar Matrix* ('Matrix'; cf. Bender et al. 2002). It differs from the Matrix most essentially through the way in which the grammar internal specifications are 'semi-automatically' updated as the c-profile grows. This systematic linkage between a cross-linguistic descriptive classification code and a computational grammar code is not yet available in the Matrix. Nothing, though, precludes introducing the TypeGram architecture also there, in this respect.

### 3.3 An intermediate parsing facility

TypeGram has specifications which, in addition to the above, in principle enable it to parse the Ga string in (5) – viz.,

(7) *Amɛ-wo tsɔne lɛ mli yɛlɛ*

as a structure like (8) (AVM not shown):

(8)

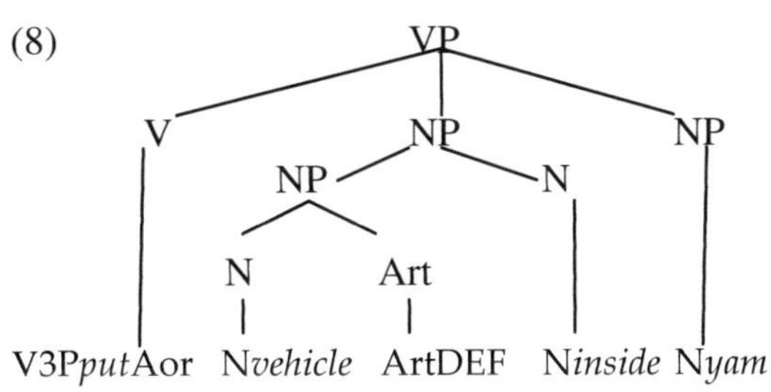


We may informally refer to (8) as an 'x-ray' of (7). As terminal nodes in the parse tree, it has the English glosses corresponding to the Ga roots, and functional morph glosses for the actual formatives of the Ga string. This is achieved through having as input to the parser not the string (7) itself, but the standard *gloss* associated with the string – (9a) – suitably modified to standard LKB parse input format:

(9)

a.

| | | | | |
|---|---|---|---|---|
| 3P.AOR-put | vehicle | DEF | inside | yam |
| V | N | Art | N | N |

b. V3P*put*Aor N*vehicle* ArtDEF N*inside* N*yam*

This is achieved by having the TypeGram lexicon contain all those English roots which ever appear in the glosses of Ga sentences (obviously relative to a limited, but in principle expandable corpus), and having these roots be associated with exactly the frame types which the corresponding Ga roots have relative to Ga. Thus, to produce (8), this lexicon would have to include an entry like (10) (using LKB style format), 'put' being the counterpart to *wo* in this context:

(10)

put := v-ditr-obPostp-suAg_obEndpt_ob2Th-PLACEMENT & [ ORTH <"put">,
ACTANTS.PRED put_rel ].

What this facility amounts to is a parser displaying the structure of sentences of a language for which one has designed a c-profile, but not yet a parsing grammar. It would be useful as a tool for typological comparison. To work, such a system would require a highly disciplined set of conventions for 'standard' glossing, and an interface in addition to LKB where such a glossing would be 'read in' as a string-to-parse; the latter is a facility not yet implemented (the only existing candidate interface for this purpose, to our knowledge, would be *TypeCraft* (cf. Beermann and Mihaylov 2009), while the development of the former (presumably with reference to existing glossing conventions such as the Leipzig Glossing rules, see References) would be part of the over-all initiative described at the outset.

## 4 Conclusion

With the Construction Labeling code and its deployment across languages as a basis, we have shown how this code can be mapped to a grammar formalism, both formally and computationally. We are thereby able to, at one and the same time, develop descriptive sentence level annotations across typologically diverse languages with a unitary code, and derive from these annotations facilities for automatic display of AVMs for any coded annotation, for rapid grammar development for the language concerned, and – so far less robustly - for intermediate 'gloss'-reflecting parsing.

We have thereby provided a system where descriptive, theoretical, typological, and computational concerns are brought together in an over-all precisely defined network of terminologies and formalisms, and flexibly so such that each field – here annotation and grammar development – have their respective suitable formats.

## References


Dorothee Beermann and Pavel Mihaylov 2009. TypeCraft – Glossing and Databasing for Linguists. Proceedings of the 23rd Scandinavian Conference of Linguistics, Uppsala, Sweden, October 2008.

Emily M Bender, Dan Flickinger, and Stephan Oepen. 2002. The Grammar Matrix: An open-source starter kit for the rapid development of cross-linguistically consistent broad-coverage precision grammars. In *Proceedings of the Workshop on Grammar Engineering and Evaluation*, COLING 2002, Taipei.

Joan Bresnan. 2001. *Lexical Functional Grammar*. Oxford: Blackwell.

Miriam Butt, Tracy Holloway King, Maria-Eugenia Nini and Frederique Segond. 1999. *A Grammar-writer's Cookbook*. Stanford: CSLI Publications.

Ann Copestake. 2002. *Implementing Typed Feature Structure Grammars*. CSLI Publications.

Mary Esther Kropp Dakubu,. 2008. The Construction label project: a tool for typological study. Presented at West African Languages Congress (WALC), Winneba, July 2008.

Mary Esther Kropp Dakubu. 2009. Ga-English Dictionary. Accra.

Lars Hellan. 2008. Enumerating Verb Constructions Cross-linguistically. COLING Workshop on Grammar Engineering Across frameworks. Manchester. http://www.aclweb.org/anthology-new/W/W08/#1700

Lars Hellan and Mary Esther Kropp Dakubu. 2009: A methodology for enhancing argument structure specification. In: *Proceedings from the 4th Language Technology Conference (LTC 2009)*, Poznan.

Lars Hellan and Mary Esther Kropp Dakubu. 2010. *Identifying Verb Constructions Cross-linguistically*. SLAVOB series, Univ. of Ghana (http://www.typecraft.org/w/images/d/db/1_Intrulabels_SLAVOB-final.pdf, http://www.typecraft.org/w/images/a/a0/2_Ga_appendix_SLAVOB-final.pdf, http://www.typecraft.org/w/images/b/bd/3_Norwegian_Appendix_plus_3_SLAVOB-final.pdf )

Carl Pollard and Ivan Sag. 1994. *Head-Driven Phrase Structure Grammar*. Chicago University Press.

Bedilu Debela Wakjira. To appear. Kistaninya Verb Morphology and Verb Constructions. PhD dissertation. NTNU.


Some web sites:

Leipzig glossing rules:

http://www.eva.mpg.de/lingua/resources/glossing-rules.php

TypeGram:

http://www.typecraft.org/tc2wiki/TypeGram

TypeCraft:

http://www.typecraft.org/

Construction Labeling site:

http://www.typecraft.org/research/projects/Verbconstructions/

# An Annotation Schema for Preposition Senses in German


Antje Müller, Olaf Hülscher, Claudia Roch, Katja Keßelmeier, Tobias Stadtfeld, Jan Strunk, Tibor Kiss

Sprachwissenschaftliches Institut, Ruhr-Universität Bochum
D-44801 Bochum, Germany
{mueller, roch, kesselmeier, stadtfeld, strunk, tibor}
@linguistics.rub.de, olaf.huelscher@rub.de



## Abstract

Prepositions are highly polysemous. Yet, little effort has been spent to develop language-specific annotation schemata for preposition senses to systematically represent and analyze the polysemy of prepositions in large corpora. In this paper, we present an annotation schema for preposition senses in German. The annotation schema includes a hierarchical taxonomy and also allows multiple annotations for individual tokens. It is based on an analysis of usage-based dictionaries and grammars and has been evaluated in an inter-annotator-agreement study.


## 1 Annotation Schemata for Preposition Senses: A Problem to be Tackled

It is common linguistic wisdom that prepositions are highly polysemous. It is thus somewhat surprising that little attention has been paid to the development of specialized annotation schemata for preposition senses.[1] In the present paper, we present a tagset for the annotation of German prepositions. The need for an annotation schema emerged in an analysis of so-called Preposition-Noun Combinations (PNCs), sometimes called determinerless PPs or bare PPs. PNCs minimally consist of a preposition and a count noun in the singular that appear without a determiner. In (1), examples are given from German.

(1) *auf parlamentarische Anfrage* (after being asked in parliament), *bei absolut klarer Zielsetzung* (given a clearly present aim), *unter sanfter Androhung* (under gentle threat)

The preposition-sense annotation forms part of a larger annotation task of the corpus, where all relevant properties of PPs and PNCs receive either automated or manual annotations. In developing an annotation schema for preposition senses, we pursue two general goals:

I. An annotation schema for preposition senses should provide a basis for manual annotation of a corpus to determine whether the interpretation of prepositions is a grammatical factor.

II. The preposition sense annotations together with the other annotations of the corpus should serve as a reference for the automatic classification of preposition senses.

With regard to the goals formulated, the present paper is an intermediate report. The annotation schema has been developed and the manual annotation of the corpus is well under way. The next logical steps will be to apply the annotations to a wider range of prepositions and eventually to use the annotated corpus for an automated classification system for preposition senses.

As PNCs form the basic rationale for the current investigation, we are only considering prepositions that occur in PPs *and* PNCs in German. We thus systematically exclude prepositions that do not take an NP complement, postpositions, and complex prepositions. Thus, the sense annotation for prepositions currently comprises the following 22 simple prepositions in German:

(2) an, auf, bei, dank, durch, für, gegen, gemäß, hinter, in, mit, mittels, nach, neben, ohne, seit, über, um, unter, vor, während, wegen

As empirical base of the analysis, we use a Swiss German newspaper corpus, which contains about 230 million tokens (Neue Zürcher Zeitung 1993-1999).

The remaining paper is structured as follows: Section 2 is devoted to the characteristics of the annotation schema. In section 3, we present an analysis of the schema in terms of inter-annotator

[1] The Preposition Project is a notable exception (cf. www.clres.com/prepositions.html).




*Proceedings of the Fourth Linguistic Annotation Workshop, ACL 2010*, pages 177–181,
Uppsala, Sweden, 15-16 July 2010.

agreement. It takes into account that the annotation schema is hierarchically ordered and allows for multiple annotations. Section 4 illustrates the application of the schema to the preposition *ohne* ('without') in German.

## 2 Properties of the Annotation Schema

There are no standardized features for an annotation of preposition senses in German. Our work is thus based on several reference works, which we analyzed and combined to develop the schema, namely *Duden Deutsch als Fremdsprache* (Duden, 2002) (a dictionary of German for foreign learners), *Deutsche Grammatik* from Helbig and Buscha (2001) (a grammar of German for foreign learners) (both usage-based), the *Lexikon Deutscher Präpositionen* (Schröder, 1986) (a dictionary of German prepositions) and an analysis of prepositions with a temporal meaning (Durell and Brée, 1993). Prima facie, the dictionary of German prepositions appears to be the most promising starting point because it includes a fine-grained feature-based analysis of preposition senses. However, it turns out that it is too complex for manual annotation, making use of more than 200 binary features to classify preposition meanings.

The annotation schema shows a hierarchically organized, tree-like structure. Beginning with a root node, types of preposition meanings branch to subtrees for different classes (e.g. local, temporal or causal) with differing depths or to individual, non-splitting branches (see Figure 1). For temporal and spatial interpretations, we use decision trees that help to guide the annotator through the annotation process.

Altogether the annotation schema includes the following list of top-level categories: SPATIAL, TEMPORAL, MODAL, CAUSAL, STATE, COMMUNALITY/COMMUTATIVE, TRANSGRESSION, AGENT, REDUCTION/EXTENSION, PARTICIPATION, SUBORDINATION, RECIPIENT, AFFILIATION, CORRELATION/INTERACTION, ORDER, THEME, SUBSTITUTE, EXCHANGE, COMPARISON, RESTRICTIVE, COPULATIVE, ADVERSATIVE, DISTRIBUTIVE, STATEMENT/OPINION, EXISTENCE/PRESENCE, CENTRE OF REFERENCE, and REALIZATION.

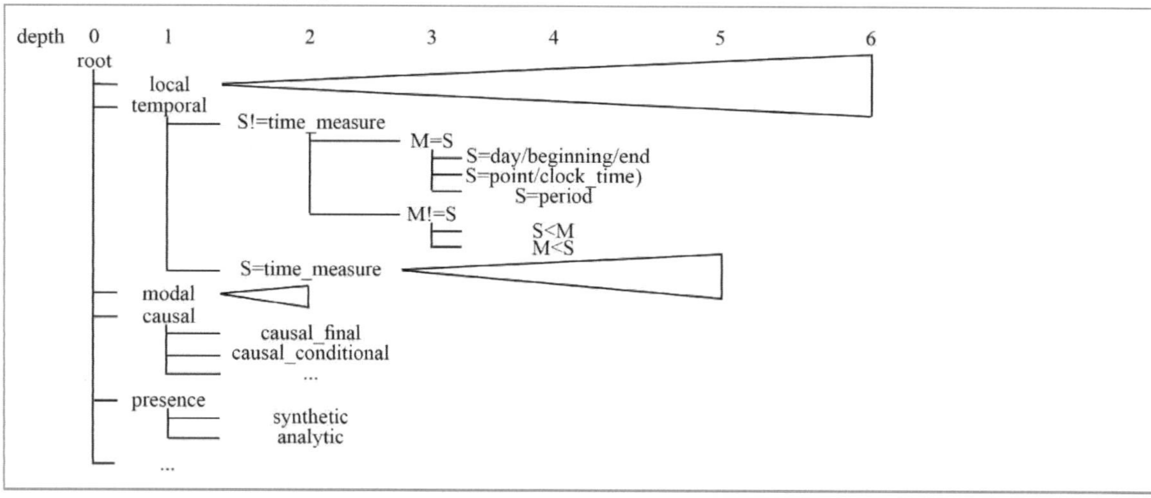


Figure 1: Hierarchical Annotation Schema

The schema allows cross-classification at every level. This is of particular importance for the classification of directional meanings. Directionality is introduced through cross-classification and not through copying the hierarchical structure of the local subtree.[2]

Another important property of the annotation schema is the possibility of multiple annotations for one preposition in context. For instance, a final distinction between a temporal and a causal interpretation cannot be drawn in example (3).

(3) *Feuer nach [temporal/causal] Blitzschlag*
'Fire after/because of lightning stroke'

In addition to the semantic categories, we use a feature 'governed' to label a preposition as governed by a lexical head whenever appropriate. Governed prepositions usually are assumed to be semantically empty but in some cases there is a discernible meaning for the preposition despite its being governed.

The preposition sense annotation is only one part of a bigger annotation project. Annotations on lexical (POS, morphology, countability, preposition meaning, noun meaning), syntactic (chunks), relational (internal and external dependencies), and

[2] During annotation, local and directional interpretations can be distinguished by case assignment in the majority of cases.

global (e.g. marking as a headline or part of a TV program in a newspaper, idiomaticity, telegraphic style) levels will serve as a basis for annotation mining to detect licensing conditions of PNCs.

## 3 An Analysis of Inter-Annotator Agreement in a Hierarchical Annotation Schema

A weighted kappa statistic (κ) forms a standard for assessing the feasibility of annotation schemata. Based on Cohen's seminal work (Cohen, 1968), Artstein and Poesio (2008) suggest the measure in (4), where κ is calculated as the weighted difference between observed and expected *disagreement.*

(4) $\kappa_w = 1 - \frac{D_o}{D_e}$

Two aspects of the present annotation schema prohibit a direct application of this statistic. First, the annotation schema makes use of a hierarchy with subtypes, which leads to overlapping annotation categories. As an illustration, assume that one annotator has annotated a given preposition with the sense PRESENCE, while a second annotator makes use of the annotation ANALYTIC, the latter being a subtype of the first. Secondly, the annotation schema allows more than one annotation for the same token, to cover cases where an ambiguous interpretation cannot be maximally reduced, as in (4).

To deal with the first problem, the hierarchical structure of the annotation schema is included in the calculation of the weight coefficients for κ. Basically, two annotations are more closely related if either both annotations are dominated by the same set of nodes in the hierarchy, or one annotation is a direct subtype of the other one (as usual, we assume domination to be reflexive). Accordingly, the weight coefficient for a given disagreement is reduced in relation to the depth of embedding of the subcategories, based on the cardinality of the set of nodes that dominate both categories.

As an illustration consider two senses A and B in the following configurations: a) A and B are directly dominated by C, a subtype of ROOT; b) A dominates B, A being a subtype of ROOT, and c) ROOT directly dominates A and C, and B is a subtype of C. Intuitively, c) is a case of clear disagreement, while in b) we find that one annotation is more specific than the other one, and in a), the annotators have at least agreed in a common supertype of the categories.

Consequently, the weight coefficient for disagreement should be highest in case c), but should be similar in cases a) and b).

(5)

a) b) c)

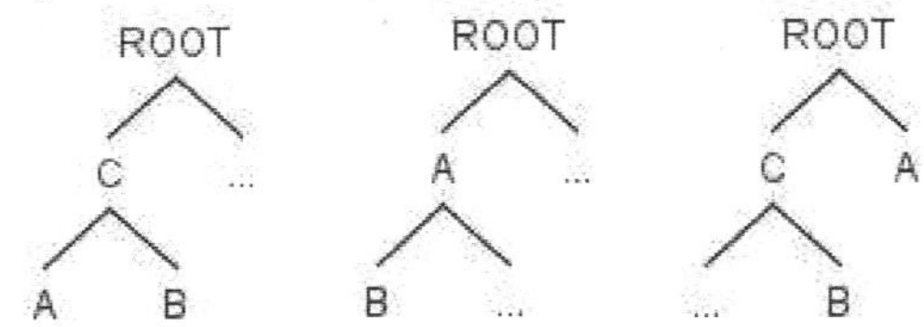


The weight coefficient is determined by the following formula, where $d_{k_j k_l}$ designates the depth of the lowest common dominating node of the two senses (and hence the cardinality of the set of dominating nodes minus 1).

(6) $w_{k_j k_l} = \begin{cases} \frac{1}{2^{d_{k_j k_l}}}, & k_j \neq k_l \\ 0, & k_j = k_l \end{cases}$

For the configuration a), the number of dominating nodes equals 2. Thus $d_{k_j k_l}$ equals 1, resulting in a weight coefficient of 0.5. For the configuration b), the cardinality of dominating nodes also equals 2, and again the weight coefficient is determined as 0.5. For c), however, the set of dominating nodes only contains ROOT, and consequently, the weight is determined as $1/2^0 = 1$.[3]

With regard to multiple annotations, we define new categories consisting of the combination of the used categories. To calculate the weight of disagreement between two combined categories, we compute the weights of all ordered pairs from the Cartesian product of the relevant categories and then calculate the arithmetic mean. As an illustration consider the following configuration: one annotator has assigned the senses A and B to a given preposition, where A and B are subtypes of C, while the second annotator has assigned B only. In this case, we determine the sum of disagreement between A and B and A and A, respectively, and divide it by the number of possible combinations (two in the present case). The following formula captures this idea.

(7) $w_{k_j k_l} = \frac{1}{|k_j||k_l|} \sum_{p \in k_j} \sum_{q \in k_l} w_{pq}$

Now, instead of determining the κ statistic on the basis of non-overlapping, i.e. mutually exclu-

---

[3] As we assume that dominance is reflexive, each supertype is a supertype of itself. Hence, the weights determined for the cases (5a) and (5b) are identical because A is a direct supertype of B. This would be different if A were an indirect supertype of B.

sive categories, the weights are determined by taking the tree structure into account. Based on the weighted kappa statistic, we have carried out an evaluation based on 1.336 annotated examples of the prepositions *an, auf, bei, neben, unter,* and *vor.* The following table summarizes the results for the full set of sense annotations, for senses with subtypes *(local, temporal, causal, modal),* as well as for some individual senses.

Table 1: Subset of Weighted Kappa-values

| **subtree with the following root node** | $\kappa_w$ |
|---|---|
| ROOT | 0.644 |
| local | 0.709 |
| causal | 0.575 |
| modal | 0.551 |
| temporal | 0.860 |
| local_reference_plane | 0.569 |
| temporal_M=S_S=PERIOD | 0.860 |

The overall result of 0.644 provides support for the general feasibility of the annotation schema, and the results for local and temporal senses are particularly promising. The results for modal and causal senses, however, indicate the necessity to take a look at the data again and to identify sources of error.

## 4 Criteria for annotating *ohne* ('without')

The preposition ohne ('without') allows six different interpretations at top level, among them are the interpretations PRESENCE, COMITATIVE, and PARTICIPATION. The rule guided nature of the annotation schema will be illustrated by the following examples:

(8) *Die Anklage wirft dem ersten von*
The prosecution accuses the first of
*drei Angeklagten, einem 32jährigen Mann*
three accused a 32-year-old man
*ohne Beruf, die Mitwirkung an*
without profession the involvement at
*allen drei Tötungsdelikten vor.*
all three homicides PTKVZ

"The prosecution accuses the first of three defendants, a 32 years old man without a profession, of the involvement in all three homicides."

(9) *Ein mobiles Einsatzkommando überwältigte*
A mobile task force defeated
*den Geiselnehmer, als er ohne das*
the hostage-taker, when he without the
*Kind den Gerichtssaal verließ.*
child the court room left.

"A mobile task force defeated the hostage-taker, when he left the court room without the child."

(10) *Ein monetärer Schulterschluss ohne das*
A monetary closing of ranks without the
*westliche Nachbarland wäre nicht*
western neighboring country would be not
*nur in Paris undenkbar.*
only in Paris unthinkable.

"A monetary closing of ranks without involving the western neighbor would be unthinkable not only in Paris."

PARTICIPATION is defined as active or passive participation in an activity; COMITATIVE is defined as an abstract coactivity of two individuals or objects. PRESENCE, finally, characterizes the presence of an object or a property. With regard to *ohne,* the features have to be negated, i.e. denoting a *lack* of participation, co-activity, or *absence* of a feature. From the definition, it already follows that the external argument of a P with the interpretations PARTICIPATION or COMITATIVE is presumably event-like, but object-like with PRESENCE. COMITATIVE and PARTICIPATION, finally, are distinguished by the mutuality present in COMITATIVE, which is not present with PARTICIPATION, giving rise to an assignment of PRESENCE in (8), COMITATIVE in (9), and PARTICIPATION in (10).

## 5 Conclusion

We have presented an annotation schema for preposition senses in German that is based on usage-based grammars and dictionaries. It comprises a restricted set of less than 30 top level sense categories, and allows for multiple annotations of individual token if a maximal sense reduction cannot be achieved. The categories local, temporal, causal, modal and presence introduce hierarchical subtypes, access to the subtypes is partially guided by decision trees in the annotation process. The hierarchical structure of the annotation schema is also reflected in its validation in terms of inter-annotator agreement. Here, it became necessary to modify Cohen's $\kappa$ to allow for overlapping categories and multiple annotations. The results reported here show that the schema is feasible for manual annotation of preposition senses.

## References


Ron Artstein and Massimo Poesio. 2008. Inter-coder agreement for computational linguistics. *Computational Linguistics*, 34 (4): 555-596.

Timothy Baldwin et al. 2006. In search of a systematic treatment of determinerless PPs. In Patrick Saint-Dizier (ed.), *Syntax and Semantics of Prepositions*. Springer, Dordrecht, 163-179.

Christian Chiarcos, Stefanie Dipper, Michael Götze, Ulf Leser, Anke Lüdeling, Julia Ritz, and Manfred Stede. 2008. A flexible framework for integrating annotations from different tools and tagsets. *Traitement Automatique des Langues*. Special Issue Platforms for Natural Language Processing. ATALA, 49 (2).

Jacob Cohen. 1968. Weighted kappa: nominal scale agreement with provision for scaled disagreement or partial credit. *Psychological bulletin,* 70 (4): 213-220.

Florian Dömges, Tibor Kiss, Antje Müller and Claudia Roch. 2007. Measuring the Productivity of Determinerless PPs. *Proceedings of the ACL 2007 Workshop on Prepositions*, Prague, 31-37.

Duden. 2002. *Duden. Deutsch als Fremdsprache.* Bibliographisches Institut and F.A. Brockhaus AG, Mannheim.

Duden. 2005. *Duden. Die Grammatik.* Duden Band 4. Bibliographisches Institut & F.A. Brockhaus AG, Mannheim.

Martin Durell and David Brée. 1993. German temporal prepositions from an English perspective. In Cornelia Zelinsky-Wibbelt (ed.), *The Semantics of Prepositions. From Mental Processing to Natural Language Processing*. De Gruyter, Berlin/New York, 295-325.

Gerhard Helbig and Joachim Buscha. 2001. *Deutsche Grammatik. Ein Handbuch für den Ausländerunterricht*. Leipzig, Langenscheidt.

Jochen Schröder. 1986. *Lexikon deutscher Präpositionen*. Leipzig, VEB Verlag Enzyklopädie.

Laurel S. Stvan. 1998. *The Semantics and Pragmatics of Bare Singular Noun Phrases*. Ph.D. thesis, Northwestern University, Evanston/ Chicago, IL.

# OTTO: A Transcription and Management Tool for Historical Texts

**Stefanie Dipper, Lara Kresse, Martin Schnurrenberger & Seong-Eun Cho**
Institute of Linguistics, Ruhr University Bochum
D – 44780 Bochum
dipper@linguistics.rub.de, lara.kresse@rub.de,
martin.schnurrenberger@rub.de, seong-eun.cho@rub.de

**Abstract**

This paper presents OTTO, a transcription tool designed for diplomatic transcription of historical language data. The tool supports easy and fast typing and instant rendering of transcription in order to gain a look as close to the original manuscript as possible. In addition, the tool provides support for the management of transcription projects which involve distributed, collaborative working of multiple parties on collections of documents.

## 1 Corpora of Historical Languages[1]

The only way to study historical languages is, of course, by looking at texts, or corpora from these languages. Compared to texts from modern languages, early manuscripts or prints pose particular challenges. Depending on physical condition of the manuscripts, passages can be hard to decipher, or pages can be damaged or missing completely. Some texts contain words or passages that have been added later, e.g., to clarify the meaning of a text segment, or to correct (real or assumed) errors.

Moreover, historical texts exhibit a large amount of character peculiarities (special letters, punctuation marks, abbreviations, etc.), which are not easily encoded by, e.g., the ASCII encoding standard. For instance, medieval German texts often use superscribed letters to represent emerging or remnant forms of diphthongs, e.g. *uͦ*. Some texts distinguish two forms of the (modern) letter <s>, the so-called short vs. long s: <s> vs. < >. Conversely, some texts do not differentiate between the (modern) letters <u> and <v>.

The existence of letter variants is often attributed to aesthetic reasons or to save (expensive) space. Thus, when early manuscripts are to be transcribed, it must first be decided whether the differences between such variants are considered irrelevant and, hence, can be safely ignored, or whether they constitute a (possibly) interesting phenomenon and potential research issue.

This discussion relates to the *level of transcription*, i.e. "how much of the information in the original document is included (or otherwise noted) by the transcriber in his or her transcription" (Driscoll, 2006). *Diplomatic transcription* aims at reproducing a large range of features of the original manuscript or print, such as large initials or variant letter forms.

Another important issue with historical corpora is meta-information. A lot of research on historical texts focuses on the text proper and its content, rather than its language. For instance, researchers are interested in the history of a text ("who wrote this text and where?"), its relationship to other texts ("did the writer know about or copy another text?"), its provenance ("who were the owners of this text?"), or its role in the cultural context ("why did the author write about this subject, and why in this way?"). To answer such questions, information about past and current depositories of a manuscript, peculiarities of the material that the text is written on, etc. are collected. In addition, any indicator of the author (or writer) of the text is noted down. Here, the text's language becomes relevant as a means to gather information about the author. Linguistic features can be used to determine the text's date of origin and the author's social and regional affiliation. Usually, this kind of information is encoded in the *header* (see, e.g., the TEI header (TEI Consortium (eds), 2007)).[2]

From the above, we derive the following requirements:

Above all, use of *Unicode* is indispensable, to

[1]The research reported in this paper was financed by Deutsche Forschungsgemeinschaft, Grant DI 1558/1-1.
We would like to thank the anonymous reviewers for their helpful comments.

[2]Text Encoding Initiative, www.tei-c.org



*Proceedings of the Fourth Linguistic Annotation Workshop, ACL 2010*, pages 182–185,
Uppsala, Sweden, 15-16 July 2010. ©2010 Association for Computational Linguistics

be able to encode and represent the numerous special symbols and characters in a reliable and sustainable way. Of course, not all characters that occur in historical texts are already covered by the current version of Unicode. This is especially true of character *combinations*, which are only supported partially (the main reason being that Unicode's Combining Diacritical Marks focus on superscribed diacritics rather than characters in general). Therefore, Unicode's Private Use Area has to be used as well.

Similarly, there are characters without glyphs defined and designed for them. Hence, an ideal transcription tool should support the user in creating new glyphs whenever needed.

Since there are many more characters in historical texts than keys on a keyboard, the transcription tool must provide some means to key in all characters and combinations (similar issues arise from logographic scripts, such as Chinese). In principle, there are two ways to do this:

(i) The transcriber uses a virtual keyboard, which supports various character sets simultaneously and is operated by the mouse. Virtual keyboards are "WYSIWYG" in that their keys are labeled by the special characters, which can then be selected by the user by mouse clicks. As is well known, virtual keyboards are often preferred by casual users, beginners, or non-experts, since they are straightforward to operate and do not require any extra knowledge. However, the drawback is that "typing" with a computer mouse is rather slow and tedious and, hence, not a long-term solution.

(ii) Alternatively, special characters, such as "$", "@", etc., are used as substitutes for historical characters, commonly in combination with ordinary characters, to yield a larger number of characters that can be represented. Regular and advanced users usually prefer substitute characters to virtual keyboards, because once the user knows the substitutes, typing them becomes very natural and fast. Of course, with this solution transcribers have to learn and memorize the substitutes.

Some tools convert substitutes to the actual characters immediately after typing (this is the case, e.g., with shortcuts in Emacs), while others require additional post-processing by interpreters and viewers to display the intended glyphs (e.g., LaTeX encodings converted to postscript). Immediate preview seems advantageous in that it provides immediate feedback to the user. On the other hand, it might be easier to memorize substitutes if the user can actually see them.

Which input method is to be preferred for historical data? Transcription projects often involve both beginners and advanced users: having people (e.g. student assistants) join and leave the team is rather often the case, because transcribing is a very labor- and time-intensive task.

Our transcription tool OTTO faces this fact by combining the advantages of the two methods. The user types and views character substitutes but simultaneously gets feedback in a separate window about whether the input is correct or not. This lessens the uncertainty of new team members and helps avoiding typing mistakes, thus increasing the quality of transcription.

Another important requirement is the possibility to mark additions, deletions, uncertain readings, etc. To encode such information, TEI also provides a standardized representation format.

Finally, projects that involve multiple parties distributed over different sites add a further requirement. In such scenarios, tools are preferably hosted by a server and operated via a web browser. This way, there is no need of multiple installations at different sites, and data on the server does not need to be synchronized but is always up to date.

To our knowledge, there is no transcription tool that (i) would support Unicode, (ii) allow for fast typing, using character substitutes, and (iii) is web-based. In MS Word, special characters are usually inserted by means of virtual keyboards but character substitutes can be defined via macros. However, macros often pose problems when Word is upgraded. Moreover, Word is not web-based. LaTeX, which supports character substitutes, is often considered too complex for non-expert users, does not offer instant preview, and is not web-based.

## 2 The Transcription Tool OTTO[3]

OTTO is an online transcription tool for editing, viewing and storing information of historical language data. OTTO's data model is a directed graph. Nodes point to a (possibly empty) stretch of primary data and are labeled.

The tool is written in PHP and also uses some Java Script; data is stored in a mySQL database.

[3]A prior version of OTTO has been described in Dipper and Schnurrenberger (2009).

Figure 1: Screenshot of the text editor

Any server which runs PHP >5.2 can be a host for OTTO. Users can login to the tool from anywhere using a standard web browser. A live demo of OTTO, with slightly restricted functionality, can be tried out here: `http://underberg.linguistics.rub.de/ottolive`.

## 2.1 Transcribing with OTTO

OTTO integrates a user-definable header editor, to enter meta information about the manuscript, such as its title, author, date of origin, etc. However, the tool's core feature is the text editor. The upper part of the text editor in Fig. 1 displays the lines that have been transcribed and saved already. Each line is preceded by the bibliographic key, *M117_sd2*, the folio and line numbers, which are automatically generated.

The bottom part is dominated by two separate frames. The frame on the left, called *Transcription*, is the currently "active" field, where the user enters the transcription (or edits an existing one). The transcriber can use substitute characters to encode non-ASCII characters. In the figure, the dollar sign (`$`) serves as a substitute for long s (< >, see the first word of the text, *De$*), and `u\o` stands for ů (see *Cu\onrat* in the Transcription field at the bottom).

The frame on the right, called *Unicode*, directly transforms the user input to its diplomatic transcription form, using a set of transcription rules. The diplomatic Unicode view thus provides immediate feedback to the transcriber whether the input is correct or not.

Transcription rules have the form of "search-and-replace" patterns. The first entity specifies the character "to be searched" (e.g. `$`), the second entity specifies the diplomatic Unicode character that "replaces" the actual character. Transcription rules are defined by the user, who can consult a database such as the ENRICH Gaiji Bank[4] to look up Unicode code points and standardized mappings for them, or define new ones. OTTO uses the Junicode font, which supports many of MUFI's medieval characters, partly defined in Unicode's Private Use Area.[5]

Rules can be defined locally—i.e., applying to the current transcription only—or globally, i.e., applying to all documents contained in OTTO's database.[6] The rules are used to map the lines entered in the Transcription frame to the lines in diplomatic form in the Unicode frame.

OTTO allows for the use of comments, which

[4] `http://beta.manuscriptorium.com/`

[5] Junicode: `http://junicode.sourceforge.net/`; MUFI (Medieval Unicode Font Initiative): `http://www.mufi.info/`

[6] Global rules can be thought of as the application of a project's transcription criteria; local rules can be viewed as handy abbreviations defined by individual users.

can be inserted at any point of the text. Since the current version of OTTO does not provide special means to take record of passages that have been added, deleted, or modified otherwise, the comment mechanism could be exploited for this purpose.

The transcription, both in original (typed) and in Unicode version, can be exported to a (customized) TEI-conform XML format. Transcription rules are optionally included in the header.

### 2.2 Transcription Projects

Projects that deal with the creation of historical corpora often involve a cascade of successive processing steps that a transcription has to undergo. For instance, high-quality transcriptions are often entered twice, by two transcribers independently from each other, and their outcomes are compared and adjusted. In the case of diplomatic transcriptions, a further step called *collating* is necessary. Collating means comparing the transcription and the original manuscript in full detail. Often two people are involved: One person reads out the manuscript letter for letter, and also reports on any superscript, white-space, etc. The other person simultaneously tracks the transcription, letter for letter. This way, high-quality diplomatic transcription can be achieved.

To cope with the numerous processing steps, transcription projects often involve a lot of people, who work on different manuscripts (or different pages of the same manuscript), in different processing states.

OTTO supports such transcription projects in several aspects: First, it allows for remote access to the database, via standard web browsers. Second, documents that are currently edited by some user are locked, i.e., cannot be edited or modified otherwise by another user. Third, OTTO provides facilities to support and promote communication among project members. Finally, graphical progress bars show the progress for each transcription, measuring the ratio of the subtasks already completed to all subtasks,

## 3 Conclusion and Future Work

This paper presented OTTO, an online transcription tool for easy and fast typing, by the use of user-defined special characters, and, simultaneously, providing a view on the manuscript that is as close to the original as possible. OTTO also supports distributed, collaborative working of multiple parties on collections of documents.

Future work includes adding further support for transcribing special characters. First, we plan to integrate a virtual keyboard for casual users. The keyboard can also be used in the creation of transcription rules, in order to specify the Unicode replacement characters, or if the user wants to look up the substitute character defined for a specific Unicode character in the set of transcription rules.

We plan to use the TEI *gaiji* module for the representation of transcription rules and substitute characters; similarly, elements from the TEI *transcr* module could be used for the encoding of additions, deletions, etc.[7]

For facilitating the collation process, we plan to integrate transparent overlays. The user would have to rescale an image of the original manuscript and adjust it to the transcription, so that corresponding characters would match.

OTTO is designed as to allow for adding custom functions, by being programmed according to the paradigm of object-oriented programming. Additional functionality can easily be integrated (known as Plug-Ins). We currently work on integrating a normalizer into OTTO which maps spelling and dialectal variants of word forms to a standardized word form (Schnurrenberger, 2010).

OTTO will be made freely available to the research community.

## References


Stefanie Dipper and Martin Schnurrenberger. 2009. OTTO: A tool for diplomatic transcription of historical texts. In *Proceedings of 4th Language & Technology Conference*, Poznan, Poland. To appear.

Matthew J. Driscoll. 2006. Levels of transcription. In Lou Burnard, Katherine O'Brien O'Keeffe, and John Unsworth, editors, *Electronic Textual Editing*, pages 254–261. New York: Modern Language Association of America. URL: `http://www.tei-c.org/About/Archive_new/ETE/Preview/driscoll.xml`.

Martin Schnurrenberger. 2010. Methods for graphemic normalization of unstandardized written lang uage from Middle High German Corpora. Master's thesis, Ruhr University Bochum.

TEI Consortium (eds). 2007. TEI P5: Guidelines for electronic text encoding and interchange. `http://www.tei-c.org/Guidelines/P5/`.


[7] `http://www.tei-c.org/release/doc/tei-p5-doc/html/WD.html` and `PH.html`

# Multimodal Annotation of Conversational Data

**P. Blache**[1], **R. Bertrand**[1], **B. Bigi**[1], **E. Bruno**[3], **E. Cela**[6], **R. Espesser**[1], **G. Ferré**[4], **M. Guardiola**[1], **D. Hirst**[1], **E.-P. Magro**[6], **J.-C. Martin**[2], **C. Meunier**[1], **M.-A. Morel**[6], **E. Murisasco**[3], **I Nesterenko**[1], **P. Nocera**[5], **B. Pallaud**[1], **L. Prévot**[1], **B. Priego-Valverde**[1], **J. Seinturier**[3], **N. Tan**[2], **M. Tellier**[1], **S. Rauzy**[1]

(1) LPL-CNRS-Université de Provence (2) LIMSI-CNRS-Université Paris Sud
(3) LSIS-CNRS-Université de Toulon (4) LLING-Université de Nantes
(5) LIA-Université d'Avignon (6) RFC-Université Paris 3

`blache@lpl-aix.fr`

## Abstract

We propose in this paper a broad-coverage approach for multimodal annotation of conversational data. Large annotation projects addressing the question of multimodal annotation bring together many different kinds of information from different domains, with different levels of granularity. We present in this paper the first results of the OTIM project aiming at developing conventions and tools for multimodal annotation.

## 1 Introduction

We present in this paper the first results of the OTIM[1] project aiming at developing conventions and tools for multimodal annotation. We show here how such an approach can be applied in the annotation of a large conversational speech corpus.

Before entering into more details, let us mention that our data, tools and conventions are described and freely downloadable from our website (http ://www.lpl-aix.fr/ otim/).

The annotation process relies on several tools and conventions, most of them elaborated within the framework of the project. In particular, we propose a generic transcription convention, called *Enriched Orthographic Trancription*, making it possible to annotate all specific pronunciation and speech event, facilitating signal alignment. Different tools have been used in order to prepare or directly annotate the transcription : grapheme-phoneme converter, signal alignment, syllabification, prosodic analysis, morpho-syntactic analysis, chunking, etc. Our ambition is to propose a large corpus, providing rich annotations in all the different linguistic domains, from prosody to gesture. We describe in the following our first results.

[1]OTIM stands for *Outils pour le Traitement de l'Information Multimodale* (Tools for Multimodal Annotation). This project in funded by the French ANR agency.

## 2 Annotations

We present in this section some of the annotations of a large conversational corpus, called CID (Corpus of Interactional Data, see (Bertrand08)), consisting in 8 dialogues, with audio and video signal, each lasting 1 hour.

**Transcription :** The transcription process is done following specific conventions derived from that of the GARS (Blanche-Benveniste87). The result is what we call an *enriched orthographic construction*, from which two derived transcriptions are generated automatically : the standard orthographic transcription (the list of *orthographic tokens*) and a specific transcription from which the *phonetic tokens* are obtained to be used by the grapheme-phoneme converter.

From the phoneme sequence and the audio signal, the aligner outputs for each phoneme its time localization. This aligner (Brun04) is HMM-based, it uses a set of 10 macro-classes of vowel (7 oral and 3 nasal), 2 semi-vowels and 15 consonants. Finally, from the time aligned phoneme sequence plus the EOT, the orthographic tokens is time-aligned.

**Syllables :** The corpus was automatically segmented in syllables. Sub-syllabic constituents (onset, nucleus and coda) are then identified as well as the syllable structure (V, CV, CCV, etc.). Syllabic position is specified in the case of polysyllabic words.

**Prosodic phrasing :** Prosodic phrasing refers to the structuring of speech material in terms of boundaries and groupings. Our annotation scheme supposes the distinction between two levels of phrasing : the level of accentual phrases (AP, (Jun, 2002)) and the higher level of intonational phrases



*Proceedings of the Fourth Linguistic Annotation Workshop, ACL 2010*, pages 186–191,
Uppsala, Sweden, 15-16 July 2010. 

(IP). Mean annotation time for IPs and APs was 30 minutes per minute.

**Prominence :** The prominence status of a syllable distinguishes between accentuability (the possibility for syllable to be prominent) and prominence (at the perception level). In French the first and last full syllables (not containing a schwa) of a polysyllabic word can be prominent, though this actual realization depends on speakers choices. Accentuability annotation is automatic while prominence annotation is manual and perceptually based.

**Tonal layer :** Given a lack of consensus on the inventory of tonal accents in French, we choose to integrate in our annotation scheme three types of tonal events : a/ underlying tones (for an eventual FrenchToBI annotation) ; b/ surface tones (annotated in terms of MOMel-Intsint protocol Hirst et al 2000) ; c/ melodic contours (perceptually annotated pitch movements in terms of their form and function). The interest to have both manual and automatic INTSINT annotations is that it allows the study of their links.

**Hand gestures :** The formal model we use for the annotation of hand gestures is adapted from the specification files created by Kipp (2004) and from the MUMIN coding scheme (Allwood et al., 2005). Among the main gesture types, we annotate iconics, metaphoric, deictics, beats, emblems, butterworths or adaptors.

We used the Anvil tool (Kipp, 2004) for the manual annotations. We created a specification files taking into account the different information types and the addition of new values adapted to the CID corpus description (e.g. we added a separate track *Symmetry*). For each hand, the scheme has 10 tracks. We allowed the possibility of a gesture pertaining to several semiotic types using a boolean notation. A gesture phrase (i.e. the whole gesture) can be decomposed into several gesture phases i.e. the different parts of a gesture such as the preparation, the stroke (the climax of the gesture), the hold and the retraction (when the hands return to their rest position) (McNeill, 1992). The scheme also enables to annotate gesture lemmas (Kipp, 2004), the shape and orientation of the hand during the stroke, the gesture space, and contact. We added the three tracks to code the hand trajectory, gesture velocity and gesture amplitude.

**Discourse and Interaction :** Our discourse annotation scheme relies on multidimensional frameworks such as DIT++ (Bunt, 2009) and is compatible with the guidelines defined by the *Semantic Annotation Framework* (Dialogue Act) working group of ISO TC37/4.

Discourse units include information about their producer, have a form *(clause, fragment, disfluency, non-verbal)*, a content and a communicative function. The same span of raw data may be covered by several discourse units playing different communicative functions. Two discourse units may even have exactly the same temporal extension, due to the multifonctionality that cannot be avoided (Bunt, 2009).

Compared to standard dialogue act annotation frameworks, three main additions are proposed : *rhetorical function*, *reported speech* and *humor*. Our rhetorical layer is an adaptation of an existing schema developed for monologic written data in the context of the ANNODIS project.

**Disfluencies :** Disfluencies are organized around an interruption point, which can occur almost anywhere in the production. Disfluencies can be prosodic (lenghtenings, silent and filled pauses, etc.), or lexicalized. In this case, they appear as a word or a phrase truncation, that can be completed. We distinguish three parts in a disfluency (see (Shriberg, 1994), (Blanche-Benveniste87)) :

- Reparandum : what precedes the interruption point. This part is mandatory in all disfluencies. We indicate there the nature of the interrupted unit (word or phrase), and the type of the truncated word (lexical or grammatical) ;
- Break interval. It is optional, some disfluencies do not bear any specific event there.
- Reparans : the part following the break, repairing the reparandum. We indicate there type of the repair (no restart, word restart, determiner restart, phrase restart, etc.), and its function (continuation, repair without change, repair with change, etc.).

## 3 Quantitative information

We give in this section some indication about the state of development of the CID annotation.

**Hand gestures :** 75 minutes involving 6 speakers have been annotated, yielding a total number of 1477 gestures. The onset and offset of gestures correspond to the video frames, starting from and going back to a rest position.

**Face and gaze :** At the present time, head movements, gaze directions and facial expressions have been coded in 15 minutes of speech yielding a total number of 1144 movements, directions and expressions, to the exclusion of gesture phases. The onset and offset of each tag are determined in the way as for hand gestures.

**Body Posture :** Our annotation scheme considers, on top of chest movements at trunk level, attributes relevant to sitting positions (due to the specificity of our corpus). It is based on the *Posture Scoring System* (Bull, 1987) and the *Annotation Scheme for Conversational Gestures* (Kipp et al., 2007). Our scheme covers four body parts : arms, shoulders, trunk and legs. Seven dimensions at arm level and six dimensions at leg level, as well as their related reference points we take in fixing the spatial location, are encoded.

Moreover, we added two dimensions to describe respectively the arm posture in the sagittal plane and the palm orientation of the forearm and the hand. Finally, we added three dimensions for leg posture : height, orientation and the way in which the legs are crossed in sitting position.

We annotated postures on 15 minutes of the corpus involving one pair of speakers, leading to 855 tags with respect to 15 different spatial location dimensions of arms, shoulder, trunk and legs.

| Annotation | Time (min.) | Units |
|---|---|---|
| Transcript | 480 | - |
| Hands | 75 | 1477 |
| Face | 15 | 634 |
| Gaze | 15 | 510 |
| Posture | 15 | 855 |
| R. Speech | 180 | |
| Com. Function | 6 | 229 |

**Disfluencies** At the moment, this annotation is fully manual (we just developed a tool helping the process in identifying disfluencies, but it has not yet been evaluated). Annotating this phenomenon requires 15mns for 1 minute of the corpus. The following table illustrates the fact that disfluencies are speaker-dependent in terms of quantity and type. These figures also shows that disfluencies affect lexicalized words as well as grammatical ones.

| | Speaker_1 | Speaker_1 |
|---|---|---|
| Total number of words | 1,434 | 1,304 |
| Disfluent grammatical words | 17 | 54 |
| Disfluent lexicalized words | 18 | 92 |
| Truncated words | 7 | 12 |
| Truncated phrases | 26 | 134 |

**Transcription and phonemes** The following table recaps the main figures about the different specific phenomena annotated in the EOT. To the best of our knowledge, these data are the first of this type obtained on a large corpus. This information is still to be analyzed.

| Phenomenon | Number |
|---|---|
| Elision | 11,058 |
| Word truncation | 1,732 |
| Standard liaison missing | 160 |
| Unusual liaison | 49 |
| Non-standard phonetic realization | 2,812 |
| Laugh seq. | 2,111 |
| Laughing speech seq. | 367 |
| Single laugh IPU | 844 |
| Overlaps > 150 ms | 4,150 |

**Syntax** We used the stochastic parser developed at the LPL (Blache&Rauzy, 2008) to automaticaly generate morppho-syntactic and syntactic annotations. The parser has been adapted it in order to account for the specificities of speech analysis. First, the system implements a segmentation technique, identifying large syntactic units that can be considered as the equivalent of sentences in written texts. This technique distinguishes between strong and weak or soft punctuation marks. A second modification concerns the lexical frequencies used by the parser model in order to capture phenomena proper to conversational data.

The categories and chunks counts for the whole corpus are summarized in the following figure :

| Category | Count | Group | Count |
|---|---|---|---|
| adverb | 15123 | AP | 3634 |
| adjective | 4585 | NP | 13107 |
| auxiliary | 3057 | PP | 7041 |
| determiner | 9427 | AdvP | 15040 |
| conjunction | 9390 | VPn | 22925 |
| interjection | 5068 | VP | 1323 |
| preposition | 8693 | Total | 63070 |
| pronoun | 25199 | | |
| noun | 13419 | Soft Pct | 9689 |
| verb | 20436 | Strong Pct | 14459 |
| Total | 114397 | Total | 24148 |

## 4 Evaluations

**Prosodic annotation :** Prosodic annotation of 1 dialogue has been done by 2 experts. The annotators worked separately using Praat. Inter-transcriber agreement studies were done for the annotation of higher prosodic units. First annotator marked 3,159 and second annotator 2,855

Intonational Phrases. Mean percentage of inter-transcriber agreement was 91.4% and mean kappa-statistics 0.79, which stands for a quite substantial agreement.

**Gesture :** We performed a measure of inter-reliability for three independent coders for Gesture Space. The measure is based on Cohen's corrected kappa coefficient for the validation of coding schemes (Carletta96).

Three coders have annotated three minutes for *GestureSpace* including *GestureRegion* and *GestureCoordinates*. The kappa values indicated that the agreement is high for *GestureRegion* of right hand (kappa = 0.649) and left hand (kappa = 0.674). However it is low for *GestureCoordinates* of right hand (k= 0.257) and left hand (k= 0.592). Such low agreement of *GestureCoordinates* might be due to several factors. First, the number of categorical values is important.

Second, three minutes might be limited in terms of data to run a kappa measure. Third, GestureRegion affects GestureCoordinates : if the coders disagree about GestureRegion, they are likely to also annotate GestureCoordinates in a different way. For instance, it was decided that no coordinate would be selected for a gesture in the center-center region, whereas there is a coordinate value for gestures occurring in other parts of the GestureRegion. This means that whenever coders disagree between the center-center or center region, the annotation of the coordinates cannot be congruent.

## 5 Information representation

### 5.1 XML encoding

Our approach consists in first precisely define the organization of annotations in terms of typed-feature structures. We obtain an abstract description from which we automatically generate a formal schema in XML. All the annotations are then encoded following this schema.

Our XML schema, besides a basic encoding of data following AIF, encode all information concerning the organization as well as the constraints on the structures. In the same way as TFS are used as a tree description language in theories such as HPSG, the XML schema generated from our TFS representation also plays the same role with respect to the XML annotation data file. On the one hand, basic data are encoded with AIF, on the other hand, the XML schema encode all higher level information. Both components (basic data + structural constraints) guarantee against information loss that otherwise occurs when translating from one coding format to another (for example from Anvil to Praat).

### 5.2 Querying

To ease the multimodal exploitation of the data, our objective is to provide a set of operators dedicated to concurrent querying on hierarchical annotation. Concurrent querying consists in querying annotations belonging to two or more modalities or even in querying the relationships between modalities. For instance, we want to be able to express queries over gestures and intonation contours (what kind of intonational contour does the speaker use when he looks at the listener ?). We also want to be able to query temporal relationships (in terms of anticipation, synchronization or delay) between both gesture strokes and lexical affiliates.

Our proposal is to define these operators as an extension of XQuery. From the XML encoding and the temporal alignment of annotated data, it will possible to express queries to find patterns and to navigate in the structure. We also want to enable a user to check predicates on parts of the corpus using classical criteria on values, annotations and existing relationships (temporal or structural ones corresponding to inclusions or overlaps between annotations). First, we shall rely on one of our previous proposal called MSXD (MultiStructured XML Document). It is a XML-compatible model designed to describe and query concurrent hierarchical structures defined over the same textual data which supports Allen's relations.

## 6 Conclusion

Multimodal annotation is often reduced to the encoding of gesture, eventually accompanied with another level of linguistic information (e.g. morpho-syntax). We reported in this paper a broad-coverage approach, aiming at encoding all the linguistic domains into a unique framework. We developed for this a set of conventions and tools making it possible to bring together and align all these different pieces of information. The result is the CID (Corpus of Interactional Data), the first large corpus of conversational data bearing rich annotations on all the linguistic domains.

## References


Allen J. (1999) Time and time again : The many way to represent time. International Journal of Intelligent Systems, 6(4)

Allwood, J., Cerrato, L., Dybkjaer, L., Jokinen, K., Navarretta, C., Paggio, P. (2005) The MUMIN Multimodal Coding Scheme, NorFA yearbook 2005.

Baader F., D. Calvanese, D. L. McGuinness, D. Nardi, P. F. Patel-Schneider (2003) The Description Logic Handbook : Theory, Implementation, Applications. Cambridge University Press.

Bertrand, R., Blache, P., Espesser, R., Ferré, G., Meunier, C., Priego-Valverde, B., Rauzy, S. (2008) "Le CID - Corpus of Interactional Data - Annotation et Exploitation Multimodale de Parole Conversationnelle", in revue *Traitement Automatique des Langues*, 49 :3.

Bigi, C. Meunier, I. Nesterenko, R. Bertrand 2010. "Syllable Boundaries Automatic Detection in Spontaneous Speech", in *proceedings of LREC 2010*.

Blache P. and Rauzy S. 2008. "Influence de la qualité de l'étiquetage sur le chunking : une corrélation dépendant de la taille des chunks". in proceedings of *TALN 2008* (Avignon, France), pp. 290-299.

Blache P., R. Bertrand, and G. Ferré 2009. "Creating and Exploiting Multimodal Annotated Corpora : The ToMA Project". In *Multimodal Corpora : From Models of Natural Interaction to Systems and Applications*, Springer.

Blanche-Benveniste C. & C. Jeanjean (1987) *Le français parlé. Transcription et édition*, Didier Erudition.

Blanche-Benveniste C. 1987. "Syntaxe, choix du lexique et lieux de bafouillage", in *DRLAV* 36-37

Browman C. P. and L. Goldstein. 1989. "Articulatory gestures as phonological units". In *Phonology* 6, 201-252

Brun A., Cerisara C., Fohr D., Illina I., Langlois D., Mella O. & Smaili K. (2004- "Ants : Le systÃÍme de transcription automatique du Loria", Actes des *XXV Journées d'Etudes sur la Parole*, Fès.

E. Bruno, E. Murisasco (2006) Describing and Querying hierarchical structures defined over the same textual data, in Proceedings of the *ACM Symposium on Document Engineering* (DocEng 2006).

Bull, P. (1987) *Posture and Gesture*, Pergamon Press.

Bunt H. 2009. "Multifunctionality and multidimensional dialogue semantics." In *Proceedings of DiaHolmia'09*, SEMDIAL.

Bürki A., C. Gendrot, G. Gravier & al.(2008) "Alignement automatique et analyse phonétique : comparaison de différents systèmes pour l'analyse du schwa", in revue TAL ,49 :3

Carletta, J. (1996) "Assessing agreement on classification tasks : The kappa statistic", in *Computational Linguistics* 22.

Corlett, E. N., Wilson,John R. Manenica. I. (1986) "Influence Parameters and Assessment Methods for Evaluating Body Postures", in *Ergonomics of Working Postures : Models, Methods and Cases* , Proceedings of the First International Occupational Ergonomics Symposium.

Di Cristo & Hirst D. (1996) "Vers une typologie des unites intonatives du français", XXIème JEP, 219-222, 1996, Avignon, France

Di Cristo A. & Di Cristo P. (2001) "Syntaix, une approche métrique-autosegmentale de la prosodie", in revue *Traitement Automatique des Langues*, 42 :1.

Dipper S., M. Goetze and S. Skopeteas (eds.) 2007. *Information Structure in Cross-Linguistic Corpora : Annotation Guidelines*, Working Papers of the SFB 632, 7 :07

FGNet Second Foresight Report (2004) Face and Gesture Recognition Working Group. http ://www.mmk.ei.tum.de/ waf/fgnet-intern/3rd-fgnet-foresight-workshop.pdf

Gendner V. et al. 2003. "PEAS, the first instantiation of a comparative framework for evaluating parsers of French". in *Research Notes of EACL 2003* (Budapest, Hungaria).

Hawkins S. and N. Nguyen 2003. "Effects on word recognition of syllable-onset cues to syllable-coda voicing", in *Papers in Laboratory Phonology VI*. Cambridge Univ. Press.

Hirst, D., Di Cristo, A., Espesser, R. 2000. "Levels of description and levels of representation in the analysis of intonation", in *Prosody : Theory and Experiment*, Kluwer.

Hirst, D.J. (2005) "Form and function in the representation of speech prosody", in K.Hirose, D.J.Hirst & Y.Sagisaka (eds) *Quantitative prosody modeling for natural speech description and generation* (*Speech Communication* 46 :3-4.

Hirst, D.J. (2007) "A Praat plugin for Momel and INTSINT with improved algorithms for modelling and coding intonation", in *Proceedings of the XVIth International Conference of Phonetic Sciences*.

Hirst, D. (2007), Plugin Momel-Intsint. Internet : http ://uk.groups.yahoo.com/group/praat-users/files/Daniel_Hirst/plugin_momel-intsint.zip, Boersma, Weenink, 2007.

Jun, S.-A., Fougeron, C. 2002. "Realizations of accentual phrase in French intonation", in *Probus 14*.

Kendon, A. (1980) "Gesticulation and Speech : Two Aspects of the Porcess of Utterance", in M.R. Key (ed.), *The Relationship of Verbal and Nonverbal Communication*, The Hague : Mouton.

Kita, S., Ozyurek, A. (2003) "What does cross-linguistic variation in semantic coordination of speech and gesture reveal ? Evidence for an interface representation of spatial thinking and speaking", in *Journal of Memory and Language*, 48.

Kipp, M. (2004). Gesture Generation by Imitation - From Human Behavior to Computer Character Animation. Boca Raton, Florida, Dissertation.com.

Kipp, M., Neff, M., Albrecht, I. (2007). An annotation scheme for conversational gestures : how to economically capture timing and form. Language Resources and Evaluation, 41(3).

Koiso H., Horiuchi Y., Ichikawa A. & Den Y.(1998) "An analysis of turn-taking and backchannels based on prosodic and syntactic features in Japanese map task dialogs", in *Language and Speech*, 41.

McNeill, D. (1992). Hand and Mind. What Gestures Reveal about Thought, Chicago : The University of Chicago Press.

McNeill, D. (2005). Gesture and Thought, Chicago, London : The University of Chicago Press.

Milborrow S., F. Nicolls. (2008). Locating Facial Features with an Extended Active Shape Model. ECCV (4).

Nesterenko I. (2006) "Corpus du parler russe spontané : annotations et observations sur la distribution des frontières prosodiques", in revue TIPA, 25.

Paroubek P. et al. 2006. "Data Annotations and Measures in EASY the Evaluation Campaign for Parsers in French". in proceedings of the *5th international Conference on Language Resources and Evaluation 2006* (Genoa, Italy), pp. 314-320.

Pierrehumbert & Beckman (1988) Japanese Tone Structure. Coll. Linguistic Inquiry Monographs, 15. Cambridge, MA, USA : The MIT Press.

Platzer, W., Kahle W. (2004) Color Atlas and Textbook of Human Anatomy, Thieme. Project MuDis. Technische Universitat Munchen. http ://www9.cs.tum.edu/research

Scherer, K.R., Ekman, P. (1982) Handbook of methods in nonverbal behavior research. Cambridge University Press.

Shriberg E. 1994. *Preliminaries to a theory of speech disfluencies*. PhD Thesis, University of California, Berkeley

Wallhoff F., M. Ablassmeier, and G. Rigoll. (2006) "Multimodal Face Detection, Head Orientation and Eye Gaze Tracking", in proceedings of *International Conference on Multisensor Fusion and Integration* (MFI).

White, T. D., Folkens, P. A. (1991) Human Osteology. San Diego : Academic Press, Inc.

# Combining Parallel Treebanks and Geo-Tagging

**Martin Volk, Anne Göhring, Torsten Marek**
University of Zurich, Institute of Computational Linguistics
volk@cl.uzh.ch

## Abstract

This paper describes a new kind of semantic annotation in parallel treebanks. We build French-German parallel treebanks of mountaineering reports, a text genre that abounds with geographical names which we classify and ground with reference to a large gazetteer of Swiss toponyms. We discuss the challenges in obtaining a high recall and precision in automatic grounding, and sketch how we represent the grounding information in our treebank.

## 1 Introduction

Treebanks have become valuable resources in natural language processing as training corpora for natural language parsers, as repositories for linguistic research, or as evaluation corpora for different NLP systems. We define a treebank as a collection of syntactically annotated sentences. The annotation can vary from constituent to dependency or tecto-grammatical structures. The term treebank is mostly used to denote manually checked collections, but recently it has been extended to also refer to automatically parsed corpora.

We have built manually checked treebanks for various text genres (see section 3): economy texts, a popular science philosophy novel, and technical user manuals. We are now entering a new genre, mountaineering reports, with the goal to link textual to spatial information. We build French and German treebanks of translated texts from the Swiss Alpine Club. This genre contains a multitude of geographical names (e.g. mountains and valleys, glaciers and rivers). Therefore we need to include the identification and grounding of these toponyms as part of the annotation process.

In this paper we first describe our corpus of alpine texts, then our work on creating parallel treebanks which includes aligning the parallel trees on word and phrase level. We sketch the difficulties in disambiguating the toponyms and describe our integration of the toponym identifiers as a special kind of semantic annotation in the treebank.

## 2 Our Text+Berg Corpus

In our project Text+Berg[1] we digitize alpine heritage literature from various European countries. Currently our group digitizes all yearbooks of the Swiss Alpine Club (SAC) from 1864 until today. Each yearbook consists of 300 to 600 pages and contains reports on mountain expeditions, culture of mountain peoples, as well as the flora, fauna and geology of the mountains.

The corpus preparation presented interesting challenges in automatic OCR correction, language identification, and text structure recognition which we have described in (Volk et al., 2010).

As of March 2010 we have scanned and OCR-converted 142 books from 1864 to 1982, corresponding to nearly 70,000 pages. This resulted in a multilingual corpus of 6101 articles in German, 2659 in French, 155 in Italian, 13 in Romansch, and 3 in Swiss-German. The parallel part of our corpus currently contains 701 translated articles amounting to 2.6 million tokens in French and 2.3 million tokens in German.

## 3 Parallel Treebanks

In recent years the combined research on treebanks and parallel corpora has led to parallel treebanks. We have built a parallel treebank (English, German, Swedish) which contains 1500 sentences in three languages: 500 sentences each from Jostein Gaarder's novel "Sophie's World", from economy texts (e.g. business reports from mechanical engineering company ABB and from the bank SEB), and from a technical manual with

[1] See www.textberg.ch.



*Proceedings of the Fourth Linguistic Annotation Workshop, ACL 2010*, pages 192–196,
Uppsala, Sweden, 15-16 July 2010. 

usage instructions for a DVD player (Göhring, 2009).

We have annotated the English sentences according to the well-established Penn Treebank guidelines. For German we followed the TIGER annotation guidelines, and we adapted these guidelines also for Swedish (see (Volk and Samuelsson, 2004)). For French treebanking we are looking for inspiration from the Le Monde treebank (Abeillé et al., 2003) and from L'Arboratoire (Bick, 2010). The Le Monde treebank is a constituent structure treebank partially annotated with functional labels. L'Arboratoire is based on constraint grammar analysis but can also output constituent trees.

### 3.1 Our Tree Alignment Tool

After finishing the monolingual trees we aligned them on the word level and phrase level. For this purpose we have developed the **TreeAligner** (Lundborg et al., 2007). This program comes with a graphical user interface to insert or modify alignments between pairs of syntax trees.[2]

The TreeAligner displays tree pairs with the trees in mirror orientation (one top-up and one top-down). This has the advantage that the alignment lines cross fewer parts of the lower tree. Figure 1 shows an example of a tree pair with alignment lines. The lines denote translation equivalence. Both trees are constituent structure trees, but the edge labels contain function labels (like subject, object, attribute) which can be used to easily convert the trees to dependency structures (cf. (Marek et al., 2009)).

Recently we have extended the TreeAligner's functionality from being solely an alignment tool to also being a powerful **search tool over parallel treebanks** (Volk et al., 2007; Marek et al., 2008). This enables our annotators to improve the alignment quality by cross-checking previous alignments. This functionality makes the TreeAligner also attractive to a wider user base (e.g. linguists, translation scientists) who are interested in searching rather than building parallel treebanks.

### 3.2 Similar Treebanking Projects

Parallel treebanks have evolved into an active research field in the last decade. Cmejrek et al. (2003) have built a parallel treebank for the specific purpose of machine translation, the Czech-English Penn Treebank with tecto-grammatical dependency trees. Other parallel treebank projects include Croco (Hansen-Schirra et al., 2006) which is aimed at building a English-German treebank for translation studies, LinES an English-Swedish parallel treebank (Ahrenberg, 2007), and the English-French HomeCentre treebank (Hearne and Way, 2006), a hand-crafted parallel treebank consisting of 810 sentence pairs from a Xerox printer manual.

Some researchers have tried to exploit parallel treebanks for example-based or statistical machine translation (Tinsley et al., 2009). Since manually created treebanks are too small for this purpose, various researchers have worked on automatically parsing and aligning parallel treebanks. Zhechev (2009) and Tiedemann and Kotzé (2009) have presented methods for automatic cross-language phrase alignment.

There have been various attempts to enrich treebanks with semantic information. For example, the Propbank project has assigned semantic roles to Penn treebank sentences (Kingsbury et al., 2002). Likewise the SALSA project has added frame-semantic annotations on top of syntax trees from the German TIGER treebank (Burchardt et al., 2006). Frame-semantics was extended to parallel treebanks by (Padó, 2007) and (Volk and Samuelsson, 2007). To our knowledge a treebank with grounded toponym information has not been created yet.

## 4 Geo-Tagging

Named entity recognition is an important aspect of information extraction. But it has also been recognized as important for the access to heritage data.

In a previous project we have investigated methods for named entity recognition in newspaper texts (Volk and Clematide, 2001). In that work we had only distinguished two types of geographical names: city names and country names. This was sufficient for texts that dealt mostly with facts like a company being located in a certain country or having started business in a certain city. In contrast to that, our alpine text corpus deals with much more fine-grained location information: mountains and valleys, glaciers and climbing routes, cabins and hotels, rivers and lakes. In fact the description of movements (e.g. in moun-

[2]The TreeAligner has been implemented in Python by Joakim Lundborg and Torsten Marek and is freely available at http://kitt.cl.uzh.ch/kitt/treealigner.

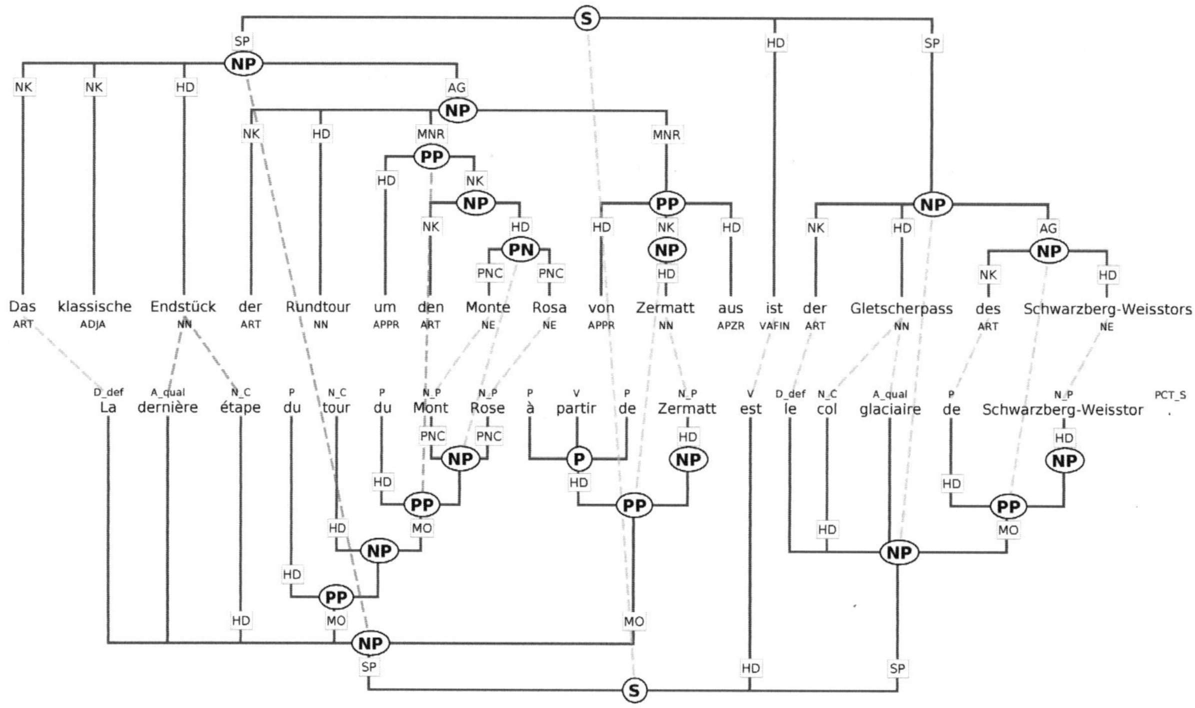


Figure 1: German-French tree pair with alignments in the TreeAligner.

tains) requires all kinds of intricate references to positions and directions in three dimensions.

In order to recognize the geographical names in our corpus we have acquired a large list of Swiss toponyms.

### 4.1 The SwissTopo Name List

The Swiss Federal Office of Topography (`www.swisstopo.ch`) maintains a database of all names that appear on its topographical maps. We have obtained a copy of this database which contains 156,755 names in 61 categories. Categories include settlements (10 categories ranging from large cities to single houses), bodies of water (13 categories from major rivers to ponds and wells), mountains (7 categories from mountain ranges to small hills), valleys, mountain passes, streets and man-made facilities (e.g. bridges and tunnels), and single objects like hotels, mountain cabins, monuments etc. Some objects are subclassified according to size. For example, cities are subdivided into main, large, middle and small cities according to their number of inhabitants.

Every name is listed in the SwissTopo database with its coordinates, its altitude (if applicable and available), the administrative unit to which it belongs (usually the name of a nearby town), and the canton.

### 4.2 A First Experiment: Finding Mountain Names

We selected an article from the SAC yearbook of 1900 to check the precision and recall of automatically identifying mountain names based on the SwissTopo name list. The article is titled "Bergfahrten im Clubgebiet (von Dr. A. Walker)". It is an article in German with a wealth of French mountain names since the author reports about his hikes in the French speaking part of Switzerland. We took the article after OCR without any further manual correction. After our tokenization (incl. the splitting of punctuation symbols) it consisted of 9380 tokens.

We used the SwissTopo mountain names classified as "Massiv, HGipfel, GGipfel, and KGipfel" i.e. the 4 highest mountain classes. They consist of 5588 mountain names. This leads to a recall of 54 mountain names (20 different mountain names) at the expense of erroneously marking 6 nouns *Gendarm, Haupt, Kamm, Stand, Stein, Turm* as mountain names.

How many mountain names have we missed to identify? A manual inspection showed that there are another 92 mountain names (35 different mountain names) missing. So recall of the naive exact matching is below 40% despite the large gazetteer. We have reported on a number of reasons for missed names in (Volk et al., 2010).

We found that spelling variations and partial coreferences account for the majority of recall problems. In addition we need to disambiguate between name-noun and name-name homographs. This leaves the issue on how to represent the geotagging information in our treebank.

## 5 Geonames in Treebanks

Named entity classification can be divided into name recognition, disambiguation and grounding. The first two steps are applicable to all kinds of names. The final step of grounding the names is different depending on the name types. A person name may be grounded by refering to the person's Wikipedia page. The same could be done for a geographical name. The obvious disadvantage are changing URLs and missing Wikipedia pages. The goal of grounding must be to link the name to the most stable and most reliable "ground". Therefore toponyms are often linked to their geographical coordinates. We have chosen to link the toponyms from our alpine texts to unique identifiers in the SwissTopo database. This works well for Swiss names and particularly well for parallel French-German sentence pairs. The cross-language alignment assures that the names are recognized in either language and the classification information can then automatically be transfered to the other language.

In our example in figure 1, the mountain name "Monte Rosa" is listed in SwissTopo with its altitude (4633 m) and its location close to Zermatt. Since "Zermatt" itself occurs in the sentence, this is strong evidence that we have identified the correct mountain, and we will attach its SwissTopo identification number in our treebank. Technically this means we add a reference to the gazetteer and to the identifier within the gazetteer into the XML representation of the linguistic object.

In our German example sentence "Monte Rosa" is annotated as a proper name (PN). This occurrence is phrase 502 in sentence 311 of our treebank. The grounding id (g_id) is taken from SwissTopo which then allows us to access the geographical coordinates, the altitude and neighborhood information.

```
<nt id="s311_502"
    cat="PN"
    g_source="SwissTopo"
    g_id="7355873" >
```

Instead of integrating the grounding pointers directly in the XML file of the treebank, it is possible to use stand-off annotation by connecting the identifier of the geo-name with the identifier from the gazetteer in a separate file.

The alignments in our parallel treebank lead to the advantage that the grounding information needs to be saved only once. In our example, the corresponding mountain name "Mont Rose" in the French translation is listed in SwissTopo only as a building in the municipality of Genthod in the canton Geneva. Since we have strong evidence from the German sentence, we can rule out this option.

Zermatt itself occurs in both the French and German sentences in our example. It is listed in SwissTopo with its altitude (1616 m) and classified as mid-sized municipality (2000 to 10,000 inhabitants). Zermatt is a unique name in SwissTopo and therefore is grounded via its SwissTopo identifier. Likewise we ground "Schwarzberg Weisstor" (spelled without hyphen in SwissTopo) which is listed as foot pass in the municipality of Saas-Almagell. In case of doubt we could verify that Saas-Almagell and Zermatt are neighboring towns, which indeed they are.

## 6 Conclusions

Grounding toponyms in parallel treebanks represents a new kind of semantic annotation. We have sketched the issues in automatic toponym classification and disambiguation. We are working on a French-German parallel treebank of alpine texts which contain a multitude of toponyms that describe way-points on climbing or hiking routes but also panorama views. We are interested in identifying all toponyms in order to enable treebank access via geographical maps. In the future we want to automatically compute and display climbing routes from the textual descriptions. The annotated treebank will then serve as a gold standard for the evaluation of the automatic geo-tagging.

## References


Anne Abeillé, Lionel Clément, and Francois Toussenel. 2003. Building a Treebank for French. In Anne Abeillé, editor, *Building and Using Parsed Corpora*, volume 20 of *Text, Speech and Language Technology*, chapter 10, pages 165–187. Kluwer, Dordrecht.

Lars Ahrenberg. 2007. LinES: An English-Swedish parallel treebank. In *Proc. of Nodalida*, Tartu.

Eckhard Bick. 2010. FrAG, a hybrid constraint grammar parser for French. In *Proceedings of LREC*, Malta.

A. Burchardt, K. Erk, A. Frank, A. Kowalski, S. Padó, and M. Pinkal. 2006. The SALSA corpus: A German corpus resource for lexical semantics. In *Proceedings of LREC 2006*, pages 969–974, Genoa.

Martin Cmejrek, Jan Curin, and Jiri Havelka. 2003. Treebanks in machine translation. In *Proc. Of the 2nd Workshop on Treebanks and Linguistic Theories*, pages 209–212, Växjö.

Anne Göhring. 2009. Spanish expansion of a parallel treebank. Lizentiatsarbeit, University of Zurich.

Silvia Hansen-Schirra, Stella Neumann, and Mihaela Vela. 2006. Multi-dimensional annotation and alignment in an English-German translation corpus. In *Proceedings of the EACL Workshop on Multidimensional Markup in Natural Language Processing (NLPXML-2006)*, pages 35– 42, Trento.

Mary Hearne and Andy Way. 2006. Disambiguation strategies for data-oriented translation. In *Proceedings of the 11th Conference of the European Association for Machine Translation (EAMT)*, pages 59–68, Oslo.

P. Kingsbury, M. Palmer, and M. Marcus. 2002. Adding semantic annotation to the Penn TreeBank. In *Proceedings of the Human Language Technology Conference (HLT'02)*, San Diego.

Joakim Lundborg, Torsten Marek, Maël Mettler, and Martin Volk. 2007. Using the Stockholm TreeAligner. In *Proc. of The 6th Workshop on Treebanks and Linguistic Theories*, Bergen, December.

Torsten Marek, Joakim Lundborg, and Martin Volk. 2008. Extending the TIGER query language with universal quantification. In *Proceeding of KONVENS*, pages 3–14, Berlin.

Torsten Marek, Gerold Schneider, and Martin Volk. 2009. A framework for constituent-dependency conversion. In *Proceedings of the 8th Workshop on Treebanks and Linguistic Theories*, Milano, December.

Sebastian Padó. 2007. *Cross-Lingual Annotation Projection Models for Role-Semantic Information.* Ph.D. thesis, Saarland University, Saarbrücken.

Jörg Tiedemann and Gideon Kotzé. 2009. Building a large machine-aligned parallel treebank. In *Proceedings of the 8th International Workshop on Treebanks and Linguistic Theories*, pages 197–208, Milano.

John Tinsley, Mary Hearne, and Andy Way. 2009. Exploiting parallel treebanks to improve phrase-based statistical machine translation. In *Computational Linguistics and Intelligent Text Processing*. Springer.

Martin Volk and Simon Clematide. 2001. Learn-filter-apply-forget. Mixed approaches to named entity recognition. In Ana M. Moreno and Reind P. van de Riet, editors, *Applications of Natural Language for Information Systems. Proc. of 6th International Workshop NLDB'01*, volume P-3 of *Lecture Notes in Informatics (LNI) - Proceedings*, pages 153–163, Madrid.

Martin Volk and Yvonne Samuelsson. 2004. Bootstrapping parallel treebanks. In *Proc. of Workshop on Linguistically Interpreted Corpora (LINC) at COLING*, Geneva.

Martin Volk and Yvonne Samuelsson. 2007. Frame-semantic annotation on a parallel treebank. In *Proc. of Nodalida Workshop on Building Frame Semantics Resources for Scandinavian and Baltic Languages*, Tartu.

Martin Volk, Joakim Lundborg, and Maël Mettler. 2007. A search tool for parallel treebanks. In *Proc. of Workshop on Linguistic Annotation at ACL*, pages 85–92, Prague.

Martin Volk, Noah Bubenhofer, Adrian Althaus, Maya Bangerter, Lenz Furrer, and Beni Ruef. 2010. Challenges in building a multilingual alpine heritage corpus. In *Proceedings of LREC*, Malta.

Ventsislav Zhechev. 2009. *Automatic Generation of Parallel Treebanks. An Efficient Unsupervised System.* Ph.D. thesis, School of Computing at Dublin City University.

# Challenges of Cheap Resource Creation for Morphological Tagging

**Jirka Hana**
Charles University
Prague, Czech Republic
first.last@gmail.com

**Anna Feldman**
Montclair State University
Montclair, New Jersey, USA
first.last@montclair.edu

## Abstract

We describe the challenges of resource creation for a resource-light system for morphological tagging of fusional languages (Feldman and Hana, 2010). The constraints on resources (time, expertise, and money) introduce challenges that are not present in development of morphological tools and corpora in the usual, resource intensive way.

## 1 Introduction

Morphological analysis, tagging and lemmatization are essential for many Natural Language Processing (NLP) applications of both practical and theoretical nature. Modern taggers and analyzers are very accurate. However, the standard way to create them for a particular language requires substantial amount of expertise, time and money. A tagger is usually trained on a large corpus (around 100,000+ words) annotated with the correct tags. Morphological analyzers usually rely on large manually created lexicons. For example, the Czech analyzer (Hajič, 2004) uses a lexicon with 300,000+ entries. As a result, most of the world languages and dialects have no realistic prospect for morphological taggers or analyzers created in this way.

We have been developing a method for creating morphological taggers and analyzers of fusional languages[1] without the need for large-scale knowledge- and labor-intensive resources (Hana et al., 2004; Hana et al., 2006; Feldman and Hana, 2010) for the target language. Instead, we rely on (i) resources available for a related language and (ii) a limited amount of high-impact, low-cost manually created resources. This greatly reduces cost, time requirements and the need for (language-specific) linguistic expertise.

The focus of our paper is on the creation of resources for the system we developed. Even though we have reduced the manual resource creation to the minimum, we have encountered a number of problems, including training language annotators, documenting the reasoning behind the tagset design and morphological paradigms for a specific language as well as creating support tools to facilitate and speed up the manual work. While these problems are analogous to those that arise with standard resource creation, the approach to their solution is often different as we discuss in the following sections.

## 2 Resource-light Morphology

The details of our system are provided in (Feldman and Hana, 2010). Our main assumption is that a model for the target language can be approximated by language models from one or more related source languages and that inclusion of a limited amount of high-impact and/or low-cost manual resources is greatly beneficial and desirable.

We use TnT (Brants, 2000), a second order Markov Model tagger. We approximate the target-language emissions by combining the emissions from the (modified) source language corpus with information from the output of our resource-light analyzer (Hana, 2008). The target-language transitions are approximated by the source language (Feldman and Hana, 2010).

## 3 Resource creation

In this section we address the problem of collection, selection and creation of resources needed by our system. The following resources must be available:

- a reference grammar book for information

[1] Fusional languages are languages in which several feature values are realized in one morpheme. For example Indo-European languages, including Czech, German, Romanian and Farsi, are predominantly fusional.



*Proceedings of the Fourth Linguistic Annotation Workshop, ACL 2010*, pages 197–201,
Uppsala, Sweden, 15-16 July 2010. ©2010 Association for Computational Linguistics

about paradigms and closed class words,

- a large amount of plain text for learning a lexicon, e.g. newspapers from the Internet,
- a large annotated training corpus of a related language,
- optionally, a dictionary (or a native speaker) to provide analyses of the most frequent words,
- a non-expert (not a linguist and not a native speaker) to create the resources listed below,
- limited access to a linguist (to make non-obvious decisions in the design of the resources),
- limited access to a native speaker (to annotate a development corpus, to answer a limited number of language specific questions).

and these resources must be created:

- a list of morphological paradigms,
- a list of closed class words with their analyses,
- optionally, a list of the most frequent forms,
- a small annotated development corpus.

For evaluation, an annotated test corpus must be also created. As this corpus is not part of the resource-light system per se, it can (and should) be as large as possible.

### 3.1 Restrictions

Since our goal is to create resources cheaply and fast, we intentionally limit (but not completely exclude) the inclusion of any linguist and of anybody knowing the target language. We also limit the time of training and encoding of the basic target-language linguistic information to a minimum.

### 3.2 Tagset

In traditional settings, a tagset is usually designed by a linguist, moreover a native speaker. The constraints of a resource-light system preclude both of these qualifications. Instead, we have standardized the process as much as possible to make it possible to have the tagset designed by a non-expert.

#### 3.2.1 Positional Tagset

All languages we work with are morphologically rich. Naturally, such languages require a large number of tags to capture their morphological properties. An obvious way to make it manageable is to use a structured system. In such a system, a tag is a composition of tags each coming from a much smaller and simpler atomic tagset tagging a particular morpho-syntactic property (e.g. gender or tense). This system has many benefits, including the 1) relative easiness for a human annotator to remember individual positions rather than several thousands of atomic symbols; 2) systematic morphological description; 3) tag decomposability; and 4) systematic evaluation.

#### 3.2.2 Tagset Design: Procedure

Instead of starting from scratch each time a tagset for a new language is created, we have provided an annotated tagset template. A particular tagset can deviate from this template, but only if there is a linguistic reason. The tagset template includes the following items:

- order of categories (POS, SubPOS, gender, animacy, number, case, ...) – not all might be present in that language; additional categories might be needed;
- values for each category (N – nouns, C – numerals, M – masculine);
- which categories we do not distinguish, even though we could (proper vs. common nouns);
- a fully worked out commented example (as mentioned above).

Such a template not only provides a general guidance, but also saves a lot of time, because many of rather arbitrary decisions involved in any tagset creation are done just once (e.g. symbols denoting basic POS categories, should numerals be included as separate POS, etc.). As stated, a tagset may deviate from such a template, but only if there is a specific reason for it.

### 3.3 Resources for the morphological analyzer

Our morphological analyzer relies on a small set of morphological paradigms and a list of closed class and/or most frequent words.

### 3.3.1 Morphological paradigms

For each target language, we create a list of morphological paradigms. We just encode basic facts about the target language morphology from a standard grammar textbook. On average, the basic morphology of highly inflected languages, such as Slavic languages, are captured in 70-80 paradigms. The choices on what to cover involve a balance between precision, coverage and effort.

### 3.3.2 A list of frequent forms

Entering a lexicon entry is very costly, both in terms of time and knowledge needed. While it is usually easy (for a native speaker) to assign a word to one of the major paradigm groups, it takes considerably more time to select the exact paradigm variant differing only in one or two forms (in fact, this may be even idiolect-dependent). For example, in Czech, it is easy to see that the word *atom* 'atom' does not decline according to the neuter paradigm *město* 'town', but it takes more time to decide to which of the hard masculine inanimate paradigms it belongs. On the other hand, entering possible analyses for individual word forms is usually very straightforward. Therefore, our system uses a list of manually provided analyses for the most common forms.

Note that the process of providing the list of forms is not completely manual – the correct analyses are selected from those suggested on the basis of the words' endings. This can be done relatively quickly by a native speaker or by a non-native speaker with the help of a basic grammar book and a dictionary.

## 3.4 Documentation

Since the main idea of the project is to create resources quickly for an arbitrarily selected fusional language, we cannot possibly create annotation and language encoding manuals for each language. So, we created a manual that explains the annotation and paradigm encoding procedure in general and describes the main attributes and possible values that a language consultant needs to consider when working on a specific language. The manual has five parts:

1. How to summarize the basic facts about the morphosyntax of a language;

2. How to create a tagset

3. How to encode morphosyntactic properties of the target language in paradigms;

4. How to create a list of closed class words.

5. Corpus annotation manual

The instructions are mostly language independent (with some bias toward Indo-European languages), but contain a lot of examples from languages we have processed so far. These include suggestions how to analyze personal pronouns, what to do with clitics or numerals.

## 3.5 Procedure

The resource creation procedure involves at least two people: a native speaker who can annotate a development corpus, and a non-native speaker who is responsible for the tagset design, morphological paradigms, and a list of closed class words or frequent forms. Below we describe our procedure in more detail.

### 3.5.1 Tagset and MA resources creation

We have realized that even though we do not need a native speaker, some understanding of at least basic morphological categories the language uses is helpful. So, based on our experience, it is better to hire a person who speaks (natively or not) a language with some features in common. For example, for Polish, somebody knowing Russian is ideal, but even somebody speaking German (it has genders and cases) is much better than a person speaking only English. In addition, a person who had created resources for one language performs much better on the next target language. Knowledge comes with practice.

The order of work is as follows:

1. The annotator is given basic training that usually includes the following: 1) brief explanation of the purpose of the project; 2) tagset design; 3) paradigm creation.

2. The annotator summarizes the basic facts about the morphosyntax of a language,

3. The first version of the tagset is created.

4. The list of paradigms and closed-class words is compiled. During this process, the tagset is further adjusted.

### 3.5.2 Corpus annotation

The annotators do not annotate from scratch. We first run our morphological analyzer on the selected corpus; the annotators then disambiguate the output. We have created a support tool (`http://ufal.mff.cuni.cz/~hana/law.html`) that displays the word to be annotated, its context, the lemma and possible tags suggested by the morphological analyzer. There is an option to insert a new lemma and a new tag if none of the suggested items is suitable. The tags are displayed together with their natural language translation.

## 4 Case studies

Our case studies include Russian via Czech, Russian via Polish, Russian via Czech and Polish, Portuguese via Spanish, and Catalan via Spanish.

We use these languages to test our hypotheses and we do not suggest that morphological tagging of these languages should be designed in the way we do. Actually, high precision systems that use manually created resources already exist for these languages. The main reason for working with them is that we can easily evaluate our system on existing corpora.

We experimented with the direct transfer of transition probabilities, cognates, modifying transitions to make them more target-like, training a battery of subtaggers and combining the results (Reference omitted). Our best result on Russian is 81.3% precision (on the full 15-slot tag, on all POSs), and 92.2% (on the detailed POS). We have also noticed that the most difficult categories are nouns and adjectives. If we improve on these individual categories, we will improve significantly the overall result. The precision of our model on Catalan is 87.1% and 91.1% on the full tag and SubPOS, respectively. The Portuguese performance is comparable as well.

The resources our experiments have relied upon include the following:

1. Russian
   - Tagset, paradigms, word-list: speaker of Czech and linguist, some knowledge of Russian
   - Dev corpus: a native speaker & linguist
2. Catalan
   - Tagset: modified existing tagset (designed by native speaking linguists)
   - paradigms, word-list: linguist speaking Russian and English
   - Dev corpus: a native speaking linguists
3. Portuguese
   - Tagset: modified Spanish tagset (designed by native speaking linguists) by us
   - paradigms, word-list: a native speaking linguist
   - Dev corpus: a native speaking linguist
4. Romanian
   - Tagset, paradigms, word-list: designed by a non-linguist, speaker of English
   - Dev corpus – a native speaker

Naturally, we cannot expect the tagging accuracy to be 100%. There are many factors that contribute to the performance of the model:

1. target language morphosyntactic complexity,
2. source-language–target-language proximity,
3. quality of the paradigms,
4. quality of the cognate pairs (that are used for approximating emissions),
5. time spent on language analysis,
6. expertise of language consultants,
7. supporting tools.

## 5 Summary

We have described challenges of resource creation for resource-light morphological tagging. These include creating clear guidelines for tagset design that can be reusable for an arbitrarily selected language; precise formatting instructions; providing basic linguistic training with the emphasis on morphosyntactic properties of fusional languages; creating an annotation support tool; and giving timely and constructive feedback on intermediate results.

## 6 Acknowledgement

The development of the tagset was supported by the GAČR grant P406/10/P328 and by the U.S. NSF grant # 0916280.

## References


Thorsten Brants. 2000. TnT - A Statistical Part-of-Speech Tagger. In *Proceedings of 6th Applied Natural Language Processing Conference and North American chapter of the Association for Computational Linguistics annual meeting (ANLP-NAACL)*, pages 224–231.

Anna Feldman and Jirka Hana. 2010. *A Resource-light Approach to Morpho-syntactic Tagging*, volume 70 of *Language and Computers: Studies in Practical Linguistics*. Rodopi, Amsterdam/New York.

Jan Hajič. 2004. *Disambiguation of Rich Inflection: Computational Morphology of Czech*. Karolinum, Charles University Press, Prague, Czech Republic.

Jirka Hana, Anna Feldman, and Chris Brew. 2004. A Resource-light Approach to Russian Morphology: Tagging Russian Using Czech Resources. In *Proceedings of Empirical Methods for Natural Language Processing (EMNLP)*, pages 222–229, Barcelona, Spain.

Jirka Hana, Anna Feldman, Luiz Amaral, and Chris Brew. 2006. Tagging Portuguese with a Spanish Tagger Using Cognates. In *Proceedings of the Workshop on Cross-language Knowledge Induction hosted in conjunction with the 11th Conference of the European Chapter of the Association for Computational Linguistics (EACL)*, pages 33–40, Trento, Italy.

Jirka Hana. 2008. Knowledge- and labor-light morphological analysis. *OSUWPL*, 58:52–84.

# Discourse Relation Configurations in Turkish and an Annotation Environment

**Berfin Aktaş**[*] and **Cem Bozsahin**[*†] and **Deniz Zeyrek**[*‡]
[*] Informatics Institute, [†] Computer Eng. and [‡] Foreign Language Education Dept.
Middle East Technical University, Ankara Turkey 06531
berfinaktas@gmail.com {bozsahin,dezeyrek}@metu.edu.tr

## Abstract

In this paper, we describe an annotation environment developed for the marking of discourse structures in Turkish, and the kinds of discourse relation configurations that led to its design.

## 1 Introduction

The property that distinguishes a discourse from a set of arbitrary sentences is defined as coherence (Halliday and Hasan, 1976). Coherence is established by the relations between the units of discourse.

Systematic analysis of coherence requires an annotated corpus in which coherence relations are encoded. Turkish Discourse Bank Project (TDB) aims to produce a large-scale discourse level annotation resource for Turkish (Zeyrek and Weber, 2008). The TDB follows the annotation scheme of the PDTB (Miltsakaki et al, 2004). The lexicalized approach adopted in the TDB assumes that discourse relations are set up by lexical items called discourse connectives. Connectives are considered as discourse level predicates which take exactly two arguments. The arguments are abstract objects like propositions, facts, events, etc. (Asher, 1993). They can be linked either by explicitly realized connectives or by implicit ones recognized by an inferential process. We annotate explicit connectives; implicit connectives are future work. We use the naming convention of the PDTB. Conn stands for the connective, Arg1 and Arg2 for the first and the second argument, respectively. Conn, Arg1 and Arg2 are assumed to be required components of discourse relations. Supplementary materials which are relevant to but not necessary for the interpretation are also annotated.

Our main data is METU Turkish Corpus(MTC) (Say et al, 2002). MTC is a written source of Turkish with approximately 2 million words. The original MTC files include informative tags, such as the author of the text, the paragraph boundaries in the text, etc. We removed these tags to obtain raw text files and set the character encoding of the files to "UTF-8". These conversions are useful for programming purposes such as visualizing the data in different platforms and the use of third-party libraries.

We developed an annotation environment to mark up the discourse relations, which we call DATT (Discourse Annotation Tool for Turkish). DATT produces XML files as annotation data which are generated by the implementation of a stand-off annotation methodology. We present in §2 the data from Turkish discourse, which forced us to use stand-off annotation instead of in-line markup. The key aspect is potential crossing of the markup links. However, stand-off annotation is also advantageous for separate licensing. We present the design of data structure and the functionality of the tool in §3. We report some preliminary results in the conclusion.

## 2 Dependency analysis of discourse relations

The TDB has no a priori assumption on how the predicates and arguments are placed. We need to take into account potential cases to be able to handle overlappings and crossings among relations. We use the terminology proposed by Lee et al (2006), and follow their convention for naming the variations of structures we came across.

We looked at the connective tokens placed close to each other, and made an initial investigation to reveal how these predicates and their arguments are located in the text. Preliminary analysis of the data indicates that the components of two relations are placed in 7 different ways, two of which are special to Turkish (§2.5; §2.6). This section is devoted to the descriptions of observed patterns with



*Proceedings of the Fourth Linguistic Annotation Workshop, ACL 2010*, pages 202–206,
Uppsala, Sweden, 15-16 July 2010. ©2010 Association for Computational Linguistics

representative examples.[1]

In the examples the connective (Conn) is underlined, Arg1 is in *italics* and Arg2 is in **boldface**. A connective's relative order with respect to its own arguments is not shown in the graphical templates. It is made explicit in the subsequent examples.

### 2.1 Independent relations

The predicate-argument structure of the connectives are independent from each other (i.e., there is no overlap between the arguments of different connectives.) The template is (1). An example is provided in (2).

(1) 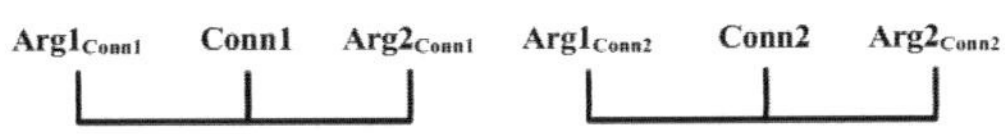


(2) *Akıntıya kapılıp umulmadık bir geceyi bölüştü benimle* ve **bu kadarla kalsın istedi belki.** *Eda açısından olayın yorumu bu kadar yalın olmalı.* Ama eğer böyleyse **benim için yorumlanması olanaksız bir düşten başka kalan yok geriye şimdi.**

*She was drifted with a current and shared an unexpected night with me* and **perhaps she wanted to keep it this much only.** *From the perspective of Eda, the interpretation of the incident should be that simple.* But, *if this is the case,* **now there is nothing left behind for me but a dream impossible to interpret.**

In (2), the relation set up by Ama is fully preceded by the relation set up by ve. There is no overlap between the argument spans of the connectives ve and Ama.

### 2.2 Full embedding

The text span of a relation constitutes an argument of another connective (3). An example is provided in (4).

(3) 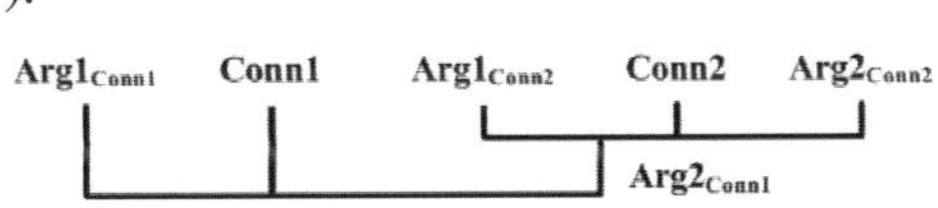


(4)a. [..] madem **yanlış bir yerde olduğumuzu düşünüyoruz da doğru denen yere asla varamayacağımızı biliyoruz** , *senin gibi biri nasıl böyle bir soru sorar* ,[..]

b. [..] madem **yanlış bir yerde olduğumuzu düşünüyoruz** da *doğru denen yere asla varamayacağımızı biliyoruz* , senin gibi biri nasıl böyle bir soru sorar,[..]

[..] if we think that we are in a wrong place, and we know that we will never never reach the right place; how come a person like you ask such a question? [..]

In (4), the span of the relation headed by da constitutes the Arg2 of the connective madem.

### 2.3 Shared argument

Two different connectives can share the same argument (5).

(5) 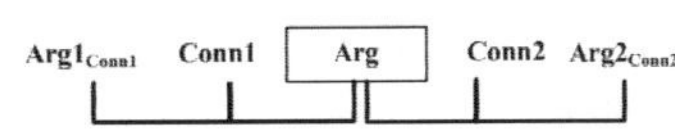


In some situations, different connectives can share both of their arguments as in the case of (6):

(6) Dedektif romanı içinden çıkılmaz gibi görünen esrarlı bir cinayetin çözümünü sunduğu için, *her şeyden önce mantığa güveni ve inancı dile getiren bir anlatı türüdür* ve bundan ötürü de **burjuva rasyonelliğinin edebiyattaki özü haline gelmiştir.**

Unraveling the solution to a seemingly intricate murder mystery, the detective novel is *a narrative genre which primarily gives voice to the faith and trust in reason* and being so, **it has become the epitome of bourgeois rationality in the literature.**

### 2.4 Properly contained argument

The argument span of one connective encapsulates the argument of another connective plus more text (7).

(7) 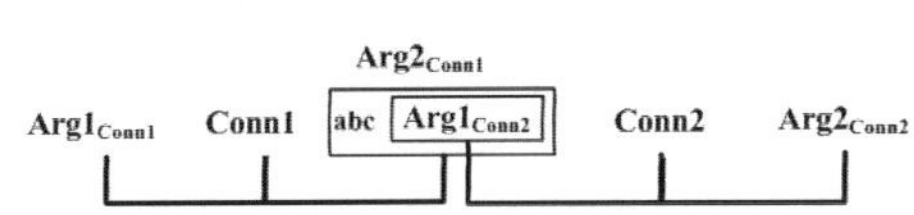


An example is provided in (8), where Arg2 of ve properly contains Arg1 of Tersine.

(8)a. *Kapıdan girdi* ve **söyler misin, hiç etkilenmedin mi yazdıklarından?, dedi.** Tersine, çok etkilendim.

b. Kapıdan girdi ve söyler misin, *hiç etkilenmedin mi yazdıklarından?,* dedi. Tersine, **çok etkilendim.**

[1] All data in this paper are taken from MTC, unless stated otherwise. More examples can be found in Aktaş (2008).

S/he entered through the door and said "Tell me, are you not touched at all by what s/he wrote?". On the contrary, I am very much affected.

### 2.5 Properly contained relation

The argument span of one connective covers the predicate-argument structure of another connective and more text (9), as exemplified in (10).

(9) 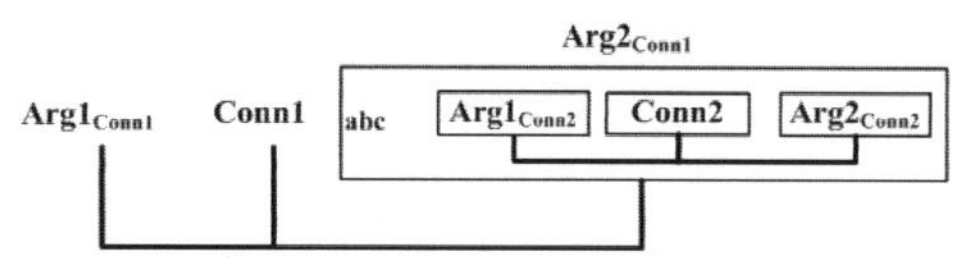


(10)a. *Burada bizce bir ifade bozukluğu veya çeviri yanlışı bahis konusu olabilir,* çünkü **elbiseler sanki giyildiği sürece ve yıpranmamışken yıkanamaz, fakat daha sonra yıkanabilirmiş gibi bir anlam taşımaktadır.**

b. Burada bizce bir ifade bozukluğu veya çeviri yanlışı bahis konusu olabilir, çünkü *elbiseler sanki giyildiği sürece ve yıpranmamışken yıkanamaz,* fakat **daha sonra yıkanabilirmiş** gibi bir anlam taşımaktadır.

Here a mistake of expression or mistranslation might be the case, because the meaning is as if the clothes cannot be washed as long as they are used and not worn out, but can be washed later.

In (10), the second argument of çünkü covers the whole relation headed by fakat and the text "gibi bir anlam taşımaktadır", which is not part of it.

### 2.6 Nested relations

A relation is nested inside the span of another relation (11).

(11) 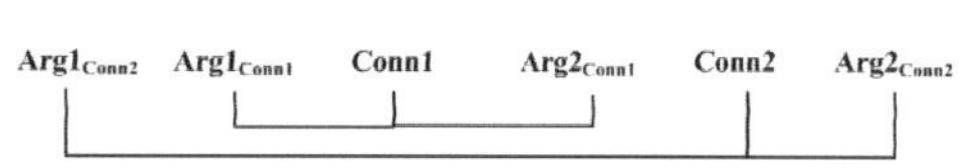


In (12), the relation headed by da is properly nested between the connective ve and its first argument.

(12) *Büyük bir masada günlerce, gecelerce oturup konuşacağız - konuşmayı unuttum diyorum* da **gülüyorlar bana** - ve **biriniz kalkıp şiir okuyacak.**

We will sit and talk around a big table for days and nights - I say I have forgotten how to speak and they laugh at me - and one of you will stand up and recite poetry.

### 2.7 Pure crossing

The dependency structure of a relation interleaves with the arguments, or the connective of another relation (13), as exemplified in (14).

(13) 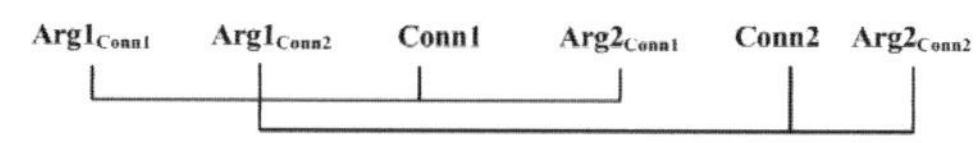


(14)a. (Constructed) *Kitabı okumaya başladım* : Okullar çoktan açılmıştı. Ardından **kapının çaldığını duydum ama yerimden kalkmadan okumaya devam ettim:** Ama bu okula henüz öğretmen atanmamıştı.

b. Kitabı okumaya başladım *Okullar çoktan açılmıştı.* Ardından kapının çaldığını duydum ama yerimden kalkmadan okumaya devam ettim: Ama **bu okula henüz öğretmen atanmamıştı.**

I started to read the book. The schools had long been opened. Then, I heard the door bell ring but I continued reading without getting up: But a teacher had not been appointed to this school yet.

## 3 The tool

DATT is an XML-based infrastructure for text annotation. It aims to produce searchable and trackable data. An initial investigation of connective and argument locations revealed that there is argument sharing of various sorts, and nested and crossing relations in Turkish discourse. The existence of such constructions lead us to use a stand-off annotation rather than an in-line method. These dependencies are violations of tree structure required by XML. Using the OCCURS feature of SGML for this purpose would lead to a less portable markup tool.

### 3.1 Data representation

In stand-off markup, annotations are stored separate from data. Since the base file is not modified during annotation, it is guaranteed that all the annotators are dealing with the same version of the data. The text spans of dependency constructions are represented in terms of character offsets from the beginning of the text file. This is a highly error-prone way of storing annotation data. If there is a shift in the character indexes in the original text file, previously annotated data will be meaningless. To compensate for this, we keep the text spans of annotations for recovery purposes.

Annotation files are well-formed XML files. One can easily add new features to the annotations. XML facilities available as online sources such as the libraries for search and post-processing reduce the implementation effort of adding new features.

### 3.2 Search functionality

In the TDB, the annotation process is organized according to connective types and their tokens. The connective to be annotated is identified, and all the relations which are set up by the instances of that connective are marked. Therefore it is important to be able to find all the instances of a specific connective in the entire data source. DATT has a search functionality which walks through all resource files and shows the annotator which files have the token. We used "Apache Lucene Search Library" for this functionality.

Two distinguishing characteristics of Turkish, the vowel harmony and voicing, motivated us to enhance the search facilities by adding support for allomorphy. In Turkish, suffixes may have many different forms. The ability to search on these forms is crucial if connectives are attached to the inflected forms of words, which is very frequently the case. For instance, the "-dık"(the factive nominal) suffix has eight allomorphs (i.e. -dık, -dik, -duk, -dük, -tık, -tik, -tuk, -tük) depending on the phonological environment.

In Turkish discourse, the meaning of a connective may change according to the inflectional category of the word that precedes it. For example, the word just before the connective"için" can be inflected with "-dık" and "-mak"(the infinitive) suffixes. With "-dık" the connective bears the meaning of causal "since", while in the other case, the connective has the meaning of "so as to"(Zeyrek, Webber, 2008). Because of this semantic difference, it will be important for the annotator to cluster the instances of a connective token preceded by all the forms of a certain inflectional suffix in one search. DATT provides this opportunity with the allomorph search support.

In Turkish, connectives can be inflected. For example, the connective "dolayısıyla" (due to that) is the inflected form of "dolayı"(due to). The support for regular expression search is also added to DATT to retrieve the inflected forms of the same connective.

### 3.3 The user interface

The user interface of DATT is expected to allow the marking of dependency hierarchies mentioned in Section 2 in a user-friendly way. the TDB annotation requires at least three components, which are Arg1, Conn and Arg2. In DATT, in order to guide the annotator, we enforce the labeling of these mandatory components, while marking of the supplementary material is optional.

Another feature of DATT is the ability to mark discontiguous text spans as a unique relation, which is attested in Turkish discourse (15). Its connective-argument structure is shown below. The Arg1 of the connective <u>-erek</u> is interleaved with the second argument Arg2.

(15) *Yürü lan, dedi Katana,* **Ramiz'i kolundan** <u>çekerek</u>, *Miskoye korkuyo!*
"Hey you, move" said Katana, while dragging Ramiz by the arm, "Miskoye is freaked out."

| Conn | Arg1 | Arg2 |
|---|---|---|
| -erek | Yürü ... Kat$ [5], Mis$ korkuyo | Ram$ ... çekerek |

## 4 Conclusion

We adopt a lexical approach to discourse annotation. Connectives are words, and they take two text spans as arguments. An exploration of these structures shows that there is argument-sharing and overlap among relations. We are considering automatic detection of relation types for an appraisal of discourse relation distribution. For the time being, DATT has search support for allomorphy and regular expressions as an aid to finding the connectives.

Approximately 60 connective types and 100 tokens have been determined so far in the annotation process, using 3 annotators. 7,000 relation tokens headed by the connectives have been annotated using DATT, spanning approximately 300,000-word text. Work for agreement statistics is under way. We hope that machine learning techniques can discover more structure in the data once we have reasonable confidence with annotation.

[5] We use the notation "abc$" to refer to the word that begins with the string "abc".

## References


Berfin Aktaş. 2008. Computational Aspects of Discourse Annotation. Informatics Institute, METU. *Unpublished master thesis.*

Nicholas Asher. 1993. *Reference to Abstract Objects in Discourse.* Kluwer Academic Publishers.

M. A. K. Halliday and Ruqaiya Hasan. 1976. *Cohesion in English.* London: Longman.

Alan Lee and Rashmi Prasad and Aravind Joshi and Nikhil Dinesh and Bonnie Webber. 2006. Complexity of dependencies in discourse. In *Proceedings of the 5th International Workshop on Treebanks and Linguistic Theories.*

Eleni Miltsakaki and Rashmi Prasad and Aravind Joshi and Bonnie Webber. 2004. The Penn Discourse TreeBank. *LREC*, Lisbon, Portugal.

Bilge Say and Deniz Zeyrek and Kemal Oflazer and Umut Ozge. 2002. Development of a Corpus and a Treebank for Present-day Written Turkish. *11th International Conference on Turkish Linguistics.*

Deniz Zeyrek and Bonnie Webber. 2008. A Discourse Resource for Turkish: Annotating Discourse Connectives in the METU Corpus. In *Proceedings of IJCNLP.*

# An Overview of the CRAFT Concept Annotation Guidelines

**Michael Bada**
**Lawrence E. Hunter**
University of Colorado Denver
Anschutz Medical Campus
Aurora, CO, USA
mike.bada@ucdenver.edu
larry.hunter@ucdenver.edu

**Miriam Eckert**
**Martha Palmer**
University of Colorado Boulder
Boulder, CO, USA
miriam_eckert@jdpa.com
martha.palmer@colorado.edu

## Abstract

We present our concept-annotation guidelines for an large multi-institutional effort to create a gold-standard manually annotated corpus of full-text biomedical journal articles. We are semantically annotating these documents with the full term sets of eight large biomedical ontologies and controlled terminologies ranging from approximately 1,000 to millions of terms, and, using these guidelines, we have been able to perform this extremely challenging task with a high degree of interannotator agreement. The guidelines have been designed to be able to be used with any terminology employed to semantically annotate concept mentions in text and are available for external use.

## 1 Introduction

Manually annotated gold-standard corpora are becoming increasingly critical for the development of advanced NLP systems. At the same time, the use of ontologies as formal representations of domain-specific knowledge is being seen in a wide range of applications, particularly in the biomedical domain. We are synergistically creating a gold-standard corpus called the Colorado Richly Annotated Full-Text (CRAFT) Corpus that pushes the boundaries of both of these prominent types of resources. For this project, we are manually annotating a collection of 97 full-text biomedical journal articles comprising a total of more than 750,000 words, as opposed to the sentences or abstracts upon which other gold-standard corpora have focused. Additionally, while most other related corpora have used small annotation schemas consisting of a few to several dozen classes for their semantic annotation, we are employing the full sets of terms, ranging from approximately one thousand to several tens of thousands of terms, of select ontologies of the Open Biomedical Ontologies (OBO) Consortium, the most prominent set of biomedical ontologies (Smith *et al.*, 2007), as well as several other significant large biomedical controlled terminologies. The terms of these ontologies and terminologies, which serve as the classes of the semantic annotation schema for the this corpus, are continually under development by biomedical researchers and knowledge engineers and are widely used throughout the biomedical field, as opposed to other annotation schemas that are often idiosyncratic and not likely reusable for other tasks. Furthermore, though these ontologies have been used for a variety of NLP tasks, they have not been used in their entirety toward gold-standard markup of text.

With regard to the CRAFT Corpus project, we have previously written of desiderata in using large ontologies and terminologies for semantic annotation of natural-language documents (Bada and Hunter, 2009a) and of semantic issues in the use of one of the ontologies we are using, the Gene Ontology (Bada and Hunter, 2009b). In this paper, we present a brief overview of the concept[1] annotation guidelines we are using for this corpus and the motivations behind our choices. With these guidelines, our annotators have routinely achieved 90+% agreement with the project lead on all but the one most challenging terminological annotation passes, which currently is more than 80%. The guidelines were designed to be reusable regardless of the

[1] Throughout this document, "concept", "class", and "term" are used interchangeably.



*Proceedings of the Fourth Linguistic Annotation Workshop, ACL 2010*, pages 207–211,
Uppsala, Sweden, 15-16 July 2010. 

ontology/terminology being used for semantic annotation, and we have indeed used them with minimal exceptions for concept annotation of our corpus using eight orthogonal large ontologies and terminologies.

## 2 Overview of the CRAFT Corpus

The CRAFT Corpus is a collection of 97 full-text biomedical journal articles that is being richly annotated both syntactically and semantically and is designed to be an open community resource for the development of advanced bioNLP systems. The 97 articles of the corpus comprise the intersection of articles that are open-access and that have been used as evidential sources for Gene Ontology (GO) annotations of genes and gene products of the laboratory mouse by our collaborators who serve as the official GO curators of the preeminent mouse database. (The GO, the flagship OBO, is an ontology composed of three subontologies representing the specific molecular functions (MF) of genes and gene products, the higher-level biological processes (BP) in which they participate, and the cellular components (CC) in which they localize (Ashburner *et al.*, 2000). GO annotations, which are entirely different from the annotations we discuss in the work presented here, are created by labeling genes and gene products of organisms with GO terms.)

These articles in their entirety are being syntactically annotated by sentence segmentation, tokenization, part-of-speech tagging, and treebanking. The articles' nouns and noun phrases are also being coreferentially annotated (Cohen *et al.*, 2010). Though these branches constitute a significant amount of the annotations of the project, they are outside the scope of this paper. Furthermore, we are working on creating assertional annotations between the concept annotations via relations.

Six ontologies of the OBO library and two additional controlled terminologies have thus far been selected for concept annotation of these articles on the bases that these are relatively well-constructed knowledge representations, are widely used by bioinformaticians and/or biomedical researchers, and represent concepts needed to extract significant biomedical assertions from the literature. In addition to the three aforementioned GO ontologies, the OBOs that were selected for concept annotation are the Cell Type Ontology (CL), which represents types of cells (Bard *et al.*, 2005); the Chemical Entities of Biological Interest (ChEBI) ontology, which represents types of small molecules, parts of molecules, atoms, and subatomic particles (Degtyarenko *et al.*, 2008); and the Sequence Ontology (SO), which represents types of biological macromolecules and their components (Eilbeck *et al.*, 2005). In addition to these ontologies, we are also annotating the articles with the terms of the NCBI Taxonomy, the most widely used Linnaean hierarchy of biological organisms, and the unique identifiers of the Entrez Gene database, the preeminent resource for species-specific genes (Sayers *et al.*, 2009).

The annotation methodology, not presented here due to lack of space, has been presented in a previous publication (Bada and Hunter, 2009a).

## 3 Overview of the CRAFT Concept Annotation Guidelines

Concept annotation entails annotating text with concepts, *i.e.*, classes or terms from ontologies or terminologies. (We use this more expansive term as opposed to named-entity annotation since several of the terminologies we are using contain terms representing processes and functions, which are annotated just as terms representing entities are.) Every mention (including abbreviations and misspellings) of every *explicitly represented* concept of the ontology or terminology is annotated, and the text selected must be as semantically close as possible—essentially semantically equivalent—to the term with with which it is annotated. Thus (as shown later), a mention of platelets is semantically annotated with a term representing platelets as opposed to the more common case of annotating with a more general term (*e.g.*, representing cells) selected from a much smaller annotation schema.

For each concept annotation, any selected text span must be adjacent on each of its boundaries to an appropriate delimiter. A whitespace character most often serves as a delimiter:

> **Ex. 1.** localization: :of: :annexin: :A7: :in: :platelets: :and: :red: :blood: :cells [PMID:12925238[2]]

(Colons indicate possible boundaries of annotations.) Any punctuation mark can also serve as a delimiter indicating a boundary of an annotation:

[2] For each example, the PubMed ID of the biomedical article from which it is extracted is shown.

> **Ex. 2.** To examine this:,: we analyzed the ability of red blood cells derived from the annexin A7 mice :(:*anxA7*:-:/:-:): to form exovesicles:.: [PMID:12925238]

Finally, beginnings and ends of documents can serve as boundaries of annotations.

It is important to note that letters (including non-Latin letters) and numbers can never serve as delimiters. Practically, this means that an annotation text span can never begin or end in between two letters, between two numbers, or between a number and a letter. These delimiters were chosen so that the annotator would not be burdened with the very difficult and time-consuming task of having to figure out what every letter of every abbreviation represented and whether they should be annotated; similarly, this avoids evaluation of any arbitrary part of any word (*e.g.*, whether the "cyto" of "cytological" should be annotated with the term cell[3]). This choice of delimiters sometimes prevents the annotator from creating an annotation that he or she may wish to create, but in our experience, this is a relatively rare occurrence, and it is a small price to pay for greatly simplifying an already extremely large and difficult task. Furthermore, it is a straighforward rule for both human and computational annotators to follow.

One primary motivation behind our strategy of annotating only explicitly represented concepts is the capture of the exact semantics of textual mentions; conversely, annotating a textual mention with a more general term (*e.g.*, annotating "platelet" with cell) entails loss of knowledge. A second motivation is that of making this task of semantic annotation doable: The alternative of annotating every mention of the concepts within the domain of a given terminology including all concepts within the domain that are not explicitly represented in the terminology rapidly becomes an overwhelming task with even a moderately sized terminology. For example, using this alternative strategy to annotate all mentions of ChEBI chemical concepts explicitly represented or not, if an annotator came across a mention of a chemical not represented in the ontology, *e.g.*, iodixanol, assuming he were not intimately familiar with the structure and function of iodixanol, he would have to first research this. From among the thousands of structural terms, he would have to annotate this mention with all relevant terms pertaining to its structure such as amides, polyols, aromatic compounds, and organoiodine compounds since this compound contains the corresponding chemical groups that define these types of molecules (and none of these terms subsumes another). Furthermore, he would have to evaluate annotating with all relevant terms from among the hundreds of ChEBI functional terms (*e.g.*, xenobiotic, base, chromophore, cofactor). This enormous amount of work becomes even more difficult when working with concepts that are not as precisely defined as, for example, the chemical structure terms.

Text spans that can be considered for annotation are dictated by syntax, and the text that is selected must be semantically equivalent to a term in the ontology/terminology. For example, for a noun, any modifying adjective or prepositional phrase can be considered for inclusion in the annotation if its inclusion results in a semantic match to a concept in the ontology/terminology.

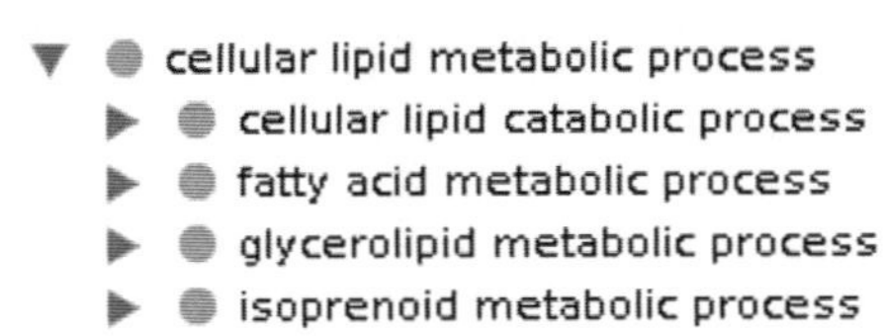


**Fig. 1.** Part of the GO BP cellular lipid metabolic process hierarchy.

> **Ex. 3:** Skeletal muscle is a major site to regulate whole-body fatty-acid and glucose metabolism. [PMID:15328533]

In Ex. 3, "metabolism" along with its premodifying "fatty-acid" (but not with its premodifying "whole-body") are selected for one annotation, as this is a semantic match to the GO term fatty acid metabolic process. Determiners and quantifiers are never included in concept annotation. Note that this is an example of a *discontinuous annotation*—an annotation consisting of two or more discontinuous spans of text, which is unambiguously represented as standoff.

The use of one or more terminologies in the semantic markup of text may result in overlapping and nesting annotations. *Overlapping* refers to the overlapping of the selected text of an annotation, in part or in whole, with the selected text of another annotation. *Nesting* is a type of overlapping in which the selected text of an annotation is a proper subset of the selected text of

[3] Names of ontological concepts are rendered in fixed-width type throughout this document.

another another. A nested annotation is created only if it is to be annotated with a term that is *not* a superclass of the term used in the nesting annotation. This is a trivial evaluation if the terms for the nesting and nested annotations are from different terminologies, as one cannot be a superclass of the other; if the terms are from the same terminology, one may or may not be a superclass of the other. There are no corresponding restrictions for overlapping annotations that are not nesting/nested annotations.

The full CRAFT Corpus annotation guidelines can be viewed at http://bionlp-corpora.sourceforge.net/CRAFT/CRAFT_concept_annotation_guidelines.pdf and are available for use by others under a specified Creative Commons license.

## 4 Results

To date, we have created more than 107,000 concept annotations; these are broken down by terminology in Table 1.

| Terminology | # Annotations | # Articles |
|---|---|---|
| ChEBI | 15,313 | 97 |
| CL | 8,290 | 97 |
| Entrez Gene* | 5,618 | 29 |
| GO BP* | 22,101 | 91 |
| GO CC | 7,247 | 97 |
| GO MF* | 5,563 | 91 |
| NCBI Taxonomy | 11,202 | 97 |
| SO | 32,502 | 97 |
| **Total** | 107,836 | - |

**Table 1.** Current counts of annotations and articles; * indicates an ongoing pass.

To illustrate the utility of our guidelines, we present the IAAs for six terminological passes of the corpus. As seen in Figs. 2 and 3, the annotators quickly reach and with few exceptions remain at a 90+% IAA level for all of the terminological passes except for the extremely challenging (and ongoing) GO BP & MF pass, currently at a typical 80-85%. As presented previously, most of these data points are single-blind statistics; however, as a control, a small number were annotated double-blind, including three articles annotated with the SO, which resulted in an IAA of 89.9%, compared with a single-blind IAA of 90.4% for the previous week, suggesting that these single-blind IAAs are unlikely to be significantly biased.

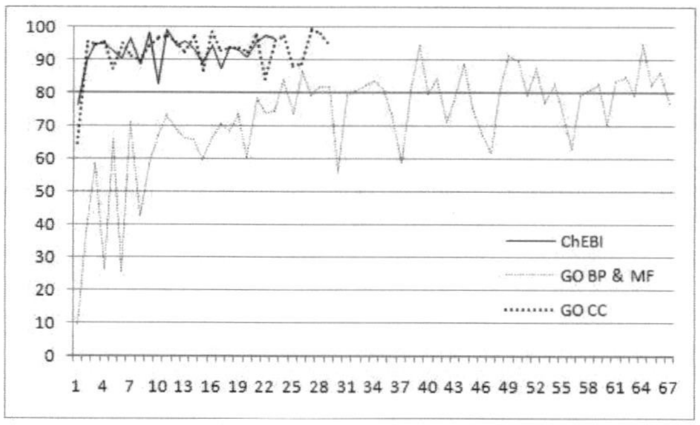


**Fig. 2.** IAA vs. number of training sessions for annotation of the corpus with ChEBI, GO BP & MF, and GO CC.

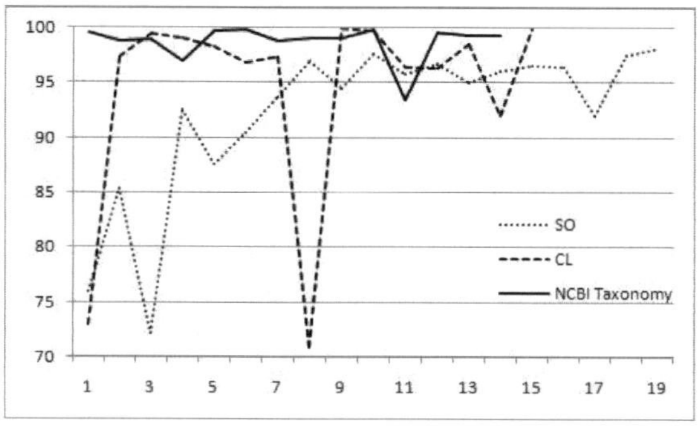


**Fig. 3.** IAA vs. number of training sessions for annotation of the corpus with SO, CL, and NCBI Taxonomy.

## 5 Conclusions

We have succinctly presented our concept-annotation guidelines, with which we routinely achieve high IAAs in the semantic annotation of full-text biomedical journal articles. The decisions behind these guidelines were made to maximally facilitate both manual and programmatic annotation of text with the full term sets of terminologies, particularly large ones. Foremost, the decision to annotate a part of the text with a term is based on whether this text is a direct semantic match to an explicitly represented term, and the specific selection of text is cleanly dictated by syntactic rules. Additionally, to greatly reduce the workload of our human annotators, a nested annotation is created only if the term to be used is not a superclass of the term used to annotate the nesting concept mention. These guidelines were designed to be used with any ontology or terminology and are available for others to use.

**Acknowledgments**
The authors gratefully acknowledge their support by NIH 5G08M009639 and 5T15 LM009451.

## References


Ashburner M, Ball CA, Blake JA, Botstein D, Butler H, Cherry JM, Davis AP, Dolinski K, Dwight SS, Eppig JT, Harris MA, Hill DP, Issel-Tarver L, Kasarskis A, Lewis S, Matese JC, Richardson JE, Ringwald M, Rubin GM, Sherlock G. 2000. Gene Ontology: tool for the unification of biology. Nat Genetics, 25:25-29.

Bada, M. and Hunter, L. 2009a. Using Large Terminologies to Semantically Annotate Concept Mentions in Natural-Language Documents. Proceedings of the International Conference on Knowledge Capture (K-CAP) Semantic Authoring, Annotation and Knowledge Markup (SAAKM) Workshop 2009, Redondo Beach, CA, USA.

Bada, M. and Hunter, L. 2009b. Using the Gene Ontology to Annotate Biomedical Journal Articles. Proceedings of the International Conference on Biomedical Ontology (ICBO) 2009, Buffalo, NY, USA.

Bard, J., Rhee, S. Y., and Ashburner, M. 2005. An ontology for cell types. Genome Biology, 6(2), R21.

Cohen, K. B., Lanfranchi, A., Corvey, W., Baumgartner, Jr., W. A., Roeder, C., Ogren, P. V., Palmer, M., and Hunter, L. E. 2010. Annotation of all coreference in biomedical text: Guideline selection and adaptation. Proceedings of the 7th Language Resources and Evaluation Conference (LREC) Workshop on Building and Evaluating Resources for Biomedical Text Mining (BioTxtM), Valletta, Malta.

Degtyarenko, K., de Matos, P., Ennis, M., Hastings, J., Zbinden, M., McNaught, A., Alcántara, R., Darsow, M., Guedj, M., and Ashburner, M. 2008. ChEBI: a database and ontology for chemical entities of biological interest. Nucleic Acids Research, 36, Database Issue:D344-D350.

Eilbeck, K., Lewis, S. E., Mungall, C. J., Yandell, M., Stein, L., Durbin, R., and Ashburner, M. 2005. The Sequence Ontology: a tool for the unification of genome annotations. Genome Biology 6, R44.

Sayers, E. W., Barrett, T., Benson, D. A., Bryant, S. H., Canese, K., Chetvernin, V., Church, D. M., DiCuccio, M., Edgar, R., Federhen, S., Feolo, M., Geer, L. Y., Helmberg, W., Kapustin, Y., Landsman, D., Lipman, D. J., Madden, T. L., Maglott, D. R., Miller, V., Mizrachi, I., Ostell, J., Pruitt, K. D., Schuler, G. D., Sequeira, E., Sherry, S. T., Shumway, M., Sirotkin, K., Souvarov, A., Starchenko, G., Tatusova, T. A., Wagner, L., Yaschenko, E., and Ye, J. 2009. Database resources of the National Center for Biotechnology Information. Nucleic Acids Research, 37, Database Issue:D5-15.

# Syntactic tree queries in Prolog

**Gerlof Bouma**
Universität Potsdam, Department Linguistik
Campus Golm, Haus 24/35
Karl-Liebknecht-Straße 24–25
14476 Potsdam, Germany
gerlof.bouma@uni-potsdam.de

**Abstract**

In this paper, we argue for and demonstrate the use of Prolog as a tool to query annotated corpora. We present a case study based on the German TüBa-D/Z Treebank to show that flexible and efficient corpus querying can be started with a minimal amount of effort. We end this paper with a brief discussion of performance, that suggests that the approach is both fast enough and scalable.

## 1 Introduction

Corpus investigations that go beyond formulating queries and studying (graphical renderings of) the retrieved annotation very quickly begin to require a general purpose programming language to do things like manipulating and transforming annotation, categorizing results, performing non-trivial counting and even statistical analysis, as query tools only offer a fixed, restricted set of operations. The use of a general purpose programming language has drawbacks, too, however: one has to deal with interfacing with a database, non-deterministic search, definition of linguistically relevant relations and properties in terms of the lower level database relations, etcetera.

As a solution for this dilemma of trading flexibility and power against the ease with which one can query corpora, we propose to use Prolog. Prolog is well suited to query databases (Nilsson and Maluszynski, 1998). Unlike in other general purpose languages, the programmer is relieved of the burden of writing functions to non-deterministically search through the corpus or database.

In comparison to dedicated query languages and their processors, the fact that one can always extend the Prolog predicates that constitute the query language lifts many restrictions on the kinds of queries one can pose. A more specific point is that we can have fine grained control over the scope of negation and quantification in queries in Prolog, something that is sometimes lacking from dedicated languages (for discussion, see Lai and Bird (2004); for a prominent example, König et al. (2003); for an exception, Kepser (2003))

Lai and Bird (2004) formulated a number of queries to compare query languages for syntactically annotated corpora. In this paper, we demonstrate the ease with which a flexible and fast query environment can be constructed by implementing these queries and using them as a rudimentary benchmark for performance.

## 2 Representing the TüBa-D/Z corpus

The TüBa-D/Z treebank of German newspaper articles (Telljohann et al., 2006, v5) comprises about 800k tokens in 45k sentences. We store the corpus as collection of directed acyclic graphs, with edges directed towards the roots of the syntactic trees (Brants, 1997).

```
% node/7 SentId NodeId MotherId
%                             Form Edge Cat Other
node(153, 4, 503, die, -, art, [morph=asf]).
node(153, 503, 508, '$phrase', hd, nx, []).
```

By using the sentence number as the first argument of `node/7` facts, we leverage first argument indexing to gain fast access to any node in the treebank. Provided we know the sentence number, we never need to consider more nodes than the largest tree in the corpus. Since all nodes that stand in a *syntactic* relation are within the same sentence, querying syntactic structure is generally fast. An example tree and its full representation is given in Figure 1. Note that in this paper, we only consider the primary nodes and edges, even though we are in no fundamental way restricted to querying only this annotation level.

A set of interface relations provide a first level of abstraction over this representation. Direct dom-



*Proceedings of the Fourth Linguistic Annotation Workshop, ACL 2010*, pages 212–216,
Uppsala, Sweden, 15-16 July 2010. ©2010 Association for Computational Linguistics

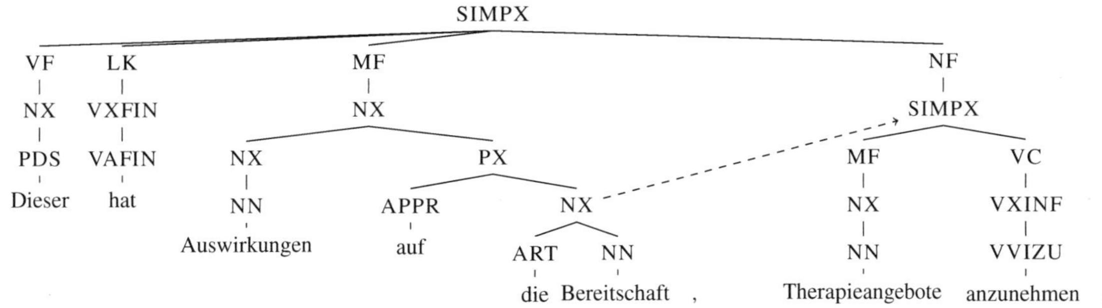


"This has effects on the willingness to accept therapy."

```
node(153, 0, 500, 'Dieser', hd, pds, [morph=nsm]).
node(153, 1, 501, hat, hd, vafin, [morph='3sis']).
node(153, 2, 502, 'Auswirkungen', hd, nn, [morph=apf]).
node(153, 3, 508, auf, -, appr, [morph=a]).
node(153, 4, 503, die, -, art, [morph=asf]).
node(153, 5, 503, 'Bereitschaft', hd, nn, [morph=asf]).
node(153, 6, 0, (','), --, '$,', [morph= --]).
node(153, 7, 504, 'Therapieangebote', hd, nn, [morph=apn]).
node(153, 8, 505, anzunehmen, hd, vvizu, [morph= --]).
node(153, 9, 0, '.', --, $., [morph= --]).


secondary(153,503,512,refint).
```

```
node(153, 515, 0, '$phrase', --, simpx, []).
node(153, 506, 515, '$phrase', -, vf, []).
node(153, 500, 506, '$phrase', on, nx, []).
node(153, 507, 515, '$phrase', -, lk, []).
node(153, 501, 507, '$phrase', hd, vxfin, []).
node(153, 513, 515, '$phrase', -, mf, []).
node(153, 511, 513, '$phrase', oa, nx, []).
node(153, 502, 511, '$phrase', hd, nx, []).
node(153, 508, 511, '$phrase', -, px, []).
node(153, 503, 508, '$phrase', hd, nx, []).
node(153, 514, 515, '$phrase', -, nf, []).
node(153, 512, 514, '$phrase', mod, simpx, []).
node(153, 509, 512, '$phrase', -, mf, []).
node(153, 504, 509, '$phrase', oa, nx, []).
node(153, 510, 512, '$phrase', -, vc, []).
node(153, 505, 510, '$phrase', hd, vxinf, []).
```

Figure 1: A tree from Tüba-D/Z and its Prolog representation.

inance and other simple relations are defined directly in terms of this interface.

```
has_sentid(node(A_s,_,_,_,_,_,_),A_s).
has_nodeid(node(_,A_n,_,_,_,_,_),A_n).
has_mother(node(_,_,A_m,_,_,_,_),A_m).
  has_form(node(_,_,_,A_f,_,_,_),A_f).
has_poscat(node(_,_,_,_,_,A_p,_),A_p).

is_under(A,B):-
    has_mother(A,A_m,A_s),
    is_phrasal(B),
    has_nodeid(B,A_m,A_s).

are_sentmates(A,B):-
    has_sentid(A,A_s),
    has_sentid(B,A_s).

is_phrasal(A):-
    has_form(A,'$phrase').
```

None of these predicates consult the database. Actually looking up a graph involves calling the nodes describing it. So, `is_phrasal(A), A`, will return once for each phrasal node in the corpus. Transitive closures over the relations above define familiar tree navigation predicates like dominance (closure of `is_under/2`). In contrast with the simple relations, these closures *do* look up their arguments.

```
has_ancestor(A,B):-
    has_ancestor(A,B,_).

has_ancestor(A,B,AB_path):-
    are_sentmates(A,B),
    A, is_under(A,A1), A1,
    has_ancestor_rfl(A1,B,AB_path).
```

```
has_ancestor_rfl(A,A,[]).
has_ancestor_rfl(A,B,[A|AB_path]):-
    is_under(A,A1), A1,
    has_ancestor_rfl(A1,B,AB_path).
```

At this point, linear precedence is still undefined for phrases. We define string position of a phrase as its span over the string, which we get by taking indices of the first and last words in its yield.

```
yields_dl(A,Bs):-
    is_phrasal(A)
      -> ( is_above(A,A1),
           findall(A1, A1, A1s),
           map(yields_dl,A1s,Bss),
           fold(append_dl,Bss,Bs)
         )
    ; % is_lexical(A)
      Bs = [A|Cs]\Cs.

spans(A,A_beg,A_end):-
    yields_dl(A,Bs\[]),
    map(has_nodeid,Bs,B_ns),
    fold(min,B_ns,A_beg),
    fold(max,B_ns,B_n_mx),
    A_end is B_n_mx+1
```

Thus, the span of the word *Auswirkungen* in the tree in Figure 1 is 2–3, and the span of the MF-phrase is 2–6. It makes sense to precalculate `spans/3`, as this is an expensive way of calculating linear order and we are likely to need this information frequently, for instance in predicates like:

```
precedes(A,B):-
    are_sentmates(A,B),
    spans(A,_,A_end),
    spans(B,B_beg,_),
    A_end =< B_beg.

directly_precedes(A,B):-
    are_sentmates(A,B),
    spans(A,_,A_end),
    spans(B,A_end,_).

are_right_aligned(A,B):-
    are_sentmates(A,B),
    spans(A,_,A_end),
    spans(B,_,A_end).
```

TIGERSearch implements an alternative definition of linear precedence, where two left-corners are compared (König et al., 2003). It would be straightforward to implement this alternative.

## 3 Application & Comparison

Lai and Bird (2004) compare the expressiveness of query languages by formulating queries that test different aspects of a query language, such as the ability to constrain linear order and dominance, to use negation and/or universal quantification, and to separate context from the returned subgraphs. The queries have thus been designed to highlight strengths and weaknesses of different query languages in querying linguistic structure. Six of these queries – with categories changed to match the Tüba-D/Z corpus – are given in Table 1 and expressed in TIGERSearch query syntax in Table 2. Since TIGERSearch does not allow for negation to outscope existential quantification of nodes, queries Q2 and Q5 are not expressible (also see Marek et al. (2008) for more discussion). In addition, Q7 has two interpretations, depending on whether one wants to return NPs once for each PP in the context or just once altogether. TIGERSearch does not allow us to differentiate between these two interpretations.

**Q1 & Q2** The implementation of domination, `has_ancestor/2`, performs database lookup. We therefore call it last in `q1/1`. To ensure the correct scope of the negation, lookup of `A` in `q2/1` is explicit and *outside* the scope of negation-as-Prolog-failure `\+/1`, whereas `B` is looked up *inside* its scope.

```
q1(A):-
    has_cat(A,simpx),
    has_surf(B,'sah'),
    has_ancestor(B,A).

q2(A):-
    has_cat(A,simpx),
    has_surf(B,sah),
    A, \+ has_ancestor(B,A).
```

| | |
|---|---|
| Q1 | Find sentences that include the word *sah*. |
| Q2 | Find sentences that do not include *sah*. |
| Q3 | Find NPs whose rightmost child is an N. |
| Q4 | Find NPs that contain an AdjP immediately followed by a noun that is immediately followed by a prepositional phrase. |
| Q5 | Find the first common ancestor of sequences of an NP followed by a PP. |
| Q7 | Find an NP dominated by a PP. Return the subtree dominated by that NP only. |

Table 1: Query descriptions

```
Q1 [cat="SIMPX"] >* [word="sah"]
Q2 (not expressible)
Q3 #n1:[cat="NX"] > #n2:[pos="NN"]
   & #n1 >@r #n2
Q4 #nx:[cat="NX"] >* #ax:[cat="ADJX"]
   & #nx >* #n:[pos="NN"]
   & #nx >* #px:[cat="PX"]
   & #px >@l #pxl
   & #ax >@r #axr
   & #axr . #n
   & #n . #pxl
Q5 (not expressible)
Q7 [cat="PX"] >* #nx:[cat="NX"]
```

Table 2: TIGERSearch queries

**Q3, Q4** The implementation of `spans/3` relies on given nodes, which means that database lookup is performed before checking linear order constraints, explicitly in `q3/1` and implicitly in `q4_a/1`. In addition, these constraints are expensive to check, so we make sure we postpone their evaluation as much as possible.

```
q3(A):-
    has_cat(A,nx),
    has_pos(B,nn),
    is_under(B,A),
    A, B, are_right_aligned(A,B).

q4_a(A):-
    has_cat(A,nx),
    has_cat(B,adjx),
    has_pos(C,nn),
    has_cat(D,px),
    has_ancestor(B,A),
    has_ancestor(C,A),
    has_ancestor(D,A),
    directly_precedes(B,C),
    directly_precedes(C,D).
```

If we precalculate `spans/3`, the alternative order of checking dominance and linear precedence constraints becomes viable, as in `q4_b/1`.

```
q4_b(A):-
    has_cat(A,nx,A_s),
    has_cat(B,adjx,A_s),
    has_pos(C,nn,A_s),
    has_cat(D,px,A_s),
    B,C,D,              % (cont. on next page)
```

```
    directly_precedes(B,C),
    directly_precedes(C,D),
    has_ancestor(B,A),
    has_ancestor(C,A),
    has_ancestor(D,A).
```

The procedural sides of Prolog make that these two alternatives are processed with considerable speed differences.

**Q5** The *lowest common ancestor* part of Q5 can be implemented by constraining the paths between two nodes and their common ancestor:

```
q5(A):-
    has_cat(B,nx,A_s),
    has_cat(C,px,A_s),
    B, C,
    precedes(B,C),
    has_ancestor(B,A,BA_path),
    has_ancestor(C,A,CA_path),
    \+ ( last(BA_path,D), last(CA_path,D) ).
```

**Q7** Precise control over the quantification of the two nodes in Q7 is achieved by using the built-in `once/1` predicate (∼existential quantification) and by choosing different moments of database lookup for the two nodes.

```
q7_a(A):-     % once for each np-pp pair
    has_cat(A,nx),
    has_cat(B,px),
    has_ancestor(A,B).

q7_b(A):-    % just once per np
    has_cat(A,nx),
    has_cat(B,px),
    A, once(has_ancestor(A,B)).
```

## 4 Performance

In Table 3, we list wall-clock times for execution of each of the queries. These serve to demonstrate the fact that our straightforward use of Prolog results in a system that is not only flexible and with short development times, but that is also fast enough to be usable. We have also included TIGERSearch execution times for the same queries to give an idea of the speed of querying with Prolog.[1]

Table 3 shows Prolog execution times fall well within useable ranges, provided we precalculate `span/3` facts for queries that rely heavily on linear order. The non-declarative side of Prolog is most clearly seen in the difference between Q4-a and Q4-b – the latter constraint ordering is more than twice as fast. Even with precalculated `span/3` facts, the whole corpus and query code uses less than 0.5Gbytes of RAM to run.

| | | | Precalc. spans | |
|---|---|---|---|---|
| | # hits | T.Search | no | yes |
| Loading from source | | | 30 | 50 |
| Loading precompiled | | | 3 | 4 |
| Precalculating `spans/3` | | | 90 | |
| Q1 | 73 | 3 | 1 | |
| Q2 | 65727 | | 1 | |
| Q3 | 152669 | 33 | 10 | 4 |
| Q4-a | 8185 | 200 | 60 | 50 |
| Q4-b | | | | 21 |
| Q5 | 312753 | | 196 | 70 |
| Q7-a | 145737 | 6 | 8 | |
| Q7-b | 119649 | | 6 | |

Table 3: Rounded up wall-clock times in seconds.

To give an impression of scalability, we can report Prolog queries on a 40M tokens, dependency parsed corpus (Bouma et al., 2010). The setup requires about 13Gbyte of RAM on a 64-bit machine. Loading a corpus takes under a minute when precompiled. Due to first-argument indexing, time per answer does not increase much. Handling of larger corpora remains a topic for future work.

## 5 Conclusions

On the basis of six queries designed to highlight strengths and weaknesses of query languages, we have demonstrated that querying syntactically annotated corpora using Prolog is straightforward, flexible and efficient. Due to space constraints, the example queries have been rather simple, and many of the more interesting aspects of using a general purpose programming language like Prolog for corpus querying have not been dealt with, such as querying structures between and above the sentence, result categorization, on-the-fly annotation transformation, and the combination of annotation layers. For examples of these and other use cases, we refer the reader to Witt (2005), Bouma (2008), Bouma et al. (2010), and Bouma (Ms). This paper's Prolog code and further conversion scripts will be available from the author's website.


## Acknowledgements

This research was carried out in the context of the SFB 632 *Information Structure*, subproject D4: *Methoden zur interaktiven linguistischen Korpusanalyse von Informationsstruktur*.


[1] Machine specifications: 1.6Ghz Intel Core 2 Duo, 2GBytes RAM. SWI-prolog (v5.6) on a 32-bit Linux. The TIGERSearch times were taken on the same machine. The TIGERSearch corpus was compiled with 'extended indexing'.

## References


Gerlof Bouma, Lilja Øvrelid, and Jonas Kuhn. 2010. Towards a large parallel corpus of clefts. In *Proceedings of LREC 2010*, Malta.

Gerlof Bouma. 2008. *Starting a Sentence in Dutch: A corpus study of subject- and object-fronting*. Ph.D. thesis, University of Groningen.

Gerlof Bouma. Ms. Querying linguistic corpora with Prolog. Manuscript, May 2010, University of Potsdam.

Thorsten Brants. 1997. The negra export format. Technical report, Saarland University, SFB378.

Stephan Kepser. 2003. Finite structure query - a tool for querying syntactically annotated corpora. In *Proceedings of EACL 2003*, pages 179–186.

Esther König, Wolfgang Lezius, and Holger Voormann. 2003. Tigersearch 2.1 user's manual. Technical report, IMS Stuttgart.

Catherine Lai and Steven Bird. 2004. Querying and updating treebanks: A critical survey and requirements analysis. In *Proceedings of the Australasion Language Technology Workshop*, Sydney.

Torsten Marek, Joakim Lundborg, and Martin Volk. 2008. Extending the tiger query language with universal quantification. In *KONVENS 2008: 9. Konferenz zur Verarbeitung natürlicher Sprache*, pages 5–17, Berlin.

Ulf Nilsson and Jan Maluszynski. 1998. *Logic, programming and Prolog*. John Wiley & Sons, 2nd edition.

Heike Telljohann, Erhard Hinrichs, Sandra Kübler, and Heike Zinsmeister. 2006. Stylebook for the tübingen treebank of written german (tüba-d/z). revised version. Technical report, Seminar für Sprachwissenschaft, Universität Tübingen.

Andreas Witt. 2005. Multiple hierarchies: New aspects of an old solution. In Stefani Dipper, Michael Götze, and Manfred Stede, editors, *Heterogeneity in Focus: Creating and Using Linguistic Databases*, Interdisciplinary Studies on Information Structure (ISIS) 2, pages 55–86. Universitätsverlag Potsdam, Potsdam.

# An integrated tool for annotating historical corpora

**Pablo Picasso Feliciano de Faria**[*]
University of Campinas
Campinas, Brazil
pablofaria@gmail.com

**Fabio Natanael Kepler**[†]
University of Sao Paulo
Sao Paulo, Brazil
kepler@ime.usp.br

**Maria Clara Paixão de Sousa**
University of Sao Paulo
Sao Paulo, Brazil
mclara.ps@gmail.com

### Abstract

E-Dictor is a tool for encoding, applying levels of editions, and assigning part-of-speech tags to ancient texts. In short, it works as a WYSIWYG interface to encode text in XML format. It comes from the experience during the building of the Tycho Brahe Parsed Corpus of Historical Portuguese and from consortium activities with other research groups. Preliminary results show a decrease of at least 50% on the overall time taken on the editing process.

## 1 Introduction

The Tycho Brahe Parsed Corpus of Historical Portuguese (CTB) (Cor, 2010) consists of Portuguese texts written by authors born between 1380 and 1845. Been one of the forefront works among projects dedicated to investigate the history of Portuguese language, it contributed to the renovation of the theoretical relevance of studies about the linguistic change in different frameworks (Mattos e Silva, 1988; Kato and Roberts, 1993; de Castilho, 1998).

This resulted in crescent work with ancient texts in the country (Megale and Cambraia, 1999), and, by the end of the 1990s, the work on Corpus Linguistics has given rise to a confluence between philology and computer science, a relationship not so ease to equate.

### 1.1 Philological and computational needs

In studies based on ancient texts, above all, one has to guarantees fidelity to the original forms of the texts. Starting with a *fac-simile*, a first option would be the automatic systems of character recognition (OCR). For the older texts, however, the current recognition technologies have proven inefficient and quite inadequate for handwritten documents (Paixão de Sousa, 2009). Anyway one cannot totally avoid manual transcription.

There are different degrees of fidelity between the transcription and the original text. In practice, one often prepares a "semi-diplomatic" edition, in which a slightly greater degree of interference is considered acceptable – eg., typographical or graphematic modernization. A central goal of the philological edition is to make the text accessible to the specialist reader, with maximum preservation of its original features.

However, it needs to be integrated with computational and linguistic requirements: the need for quantity, agility and automation in the statistical work of selecting data. The original spelling and graphematic characteristics of older texts, for example, may hinder the subsequent automatic processing, such as morphological annotation. Thus, the original text needs to be prepared, or edited, with a degree of interference higher than that acceptable for a semi-diplomatic edition and that is where the conflict emerges.

### 1.2 Background

The modernization of spellings and standardization of graphematic aspects, during the first years of CTB, made texts suitable for automated processing, but caused the loss of important features from the original text for the historical study of language. This tension has led to the project "Memories of the Text" (Paixão de Sousa, 2004), which sought to restructure the Corpus, based on the development of XML annotations (W3C, 2009), and to take advantage of the core features of this type of encoding, for example, XSLT (W3C, 1999) processing.

A annotation system was conceived and applied to 48 Portuguese texts (2, 279, 455 words), which

* Thanks to FAPESP, n. 2008/04312-9, for funding part of the development of E-Dictor.

† Thanks to CAPES for the scholarship granted during the initial part of this work.



*Proceedings of the Fourth Linguistic Annotation Workshop, ACL 2010*, pages 217–221,
Uppsala, Sweden, 15-16 July 2010. 

allowed keeping philological informations while making the texts capable of being computationally treated in large-scale. Since 2006, the system has been being tested by other research groups, notably the *Program for the History of Portuguese Language* (PROHPOR-UFBA). The system, then, met its initial objectives, but it had serious issues with respect to reliability and, especially, ease of use.

We noted that manual text markup in XML was challenging to some and laborious for everyone. The basic edition process was: transcription in a text editor, application of the XML markup (tags plus philological edition), generation of a standardized plain text version to submit to automatic part-of-speech tagging, revision of both files (XML and tagged). All in this process, except for text tagging, been manually done, was too subject to failures and demanded constant and extensive revision of the encoding. The need for an alternative, to make the task more friendly, reliable, and productive, became clear. In short, two things were needed: a friendly interface (WYSIWYG), to prevent the user from dealing with XML code, and a way to tighten the whole process (transcription, encode/edition, POS tagging and revision).

### 1.3 Available tools

A search for available options in the market (free and non-free) led to some very interesting tools, which may be worth trying:

- *Multext*[1]: a series of projects for corpora encoding as well as developing tools and linguistic resources. Not all tools seem to have been finished, and the projects seems to be outdated and no longer being maintained.
- *CLaRK*[2]: a system for corpora development based on XML and implemented in Java. It does not provide a WYSIWYG interface.
- *Xopus*[3]: an XML editor, which offers a WYSIWYG interface. Some of its funcionalities can be extended (customized) throught a Javascript API.
- *<oXygen/> XML Editor*[4]: a complete XML development platform with support for all major XML related standards. An XML file can be edited in the following perspectives: XML text editor, WYSIWYG-like editor, XML grid editor, tree editor.

Unfortunately, all the cited tools lack the capability of dealing proper with *levels of edition* for tokens (words and punctuations) and an integrated environment for the whole process of edition. Thus, in spite of their amazing features, none of them was sufficiently suitable, specially concerning spelling modernization and normalization of graphematic aspects. In fact, this is expected for the tools are intended to broader purposes.

### 1.4 Solution

Conception and development of a tool, E-Dictor, where the need for a WYSIWYG interface joined a second goal, ie., integrating the tasks of the whole process, which would then be performed inside the same environment, with any necessary external tools being called by the system, transparently.

## 2 Integrated annotation tool

### 2.1 General features

E-Dictor has been developed in Python[5] and, today, has versions for both Linux and Windows (XP/Vista/7) platforms. A version for MacOS is planned for the future. It is currently at 1.0 *beta* version (not stable).

### 2.2 General interface features

As shown in Figure 1, the main interface has an application menu, a toolbar, a content area (divided into tabs: *Transcription*, *Edition*, and *Morphology*), and buttons to navigate throught pages. The tabs are in accordance with the flow of the encoding process. Many aspects of the functioning described in what follows are determined by the application preferences.

In the 'Transcription' tab, the original text is transcribed "as is" (the user can view the fac-simile image, while transcribing the text). Throught a menu option, E-Dictor will automatically apply an XML structure to the text, "guessing" its internal structure as best as it can. Then, in the 'Edition' tab, the user can edit any token or

[1] `http://aune.lpl.univ-aix.fr/projects/multext/`.

[2] `http://www.bultreebank.org/clark`.

[3] `http://xopus.com/`.

[4] `http://www.oxygenxml.com/`.

[5] Available on internet at `http://www.python.org/`, last access on Jan, 21th, 2010. Python has been used in a number of computational linguistics applications, e.g., the *Natural Language Toolkit* (Bird et al., 2009).

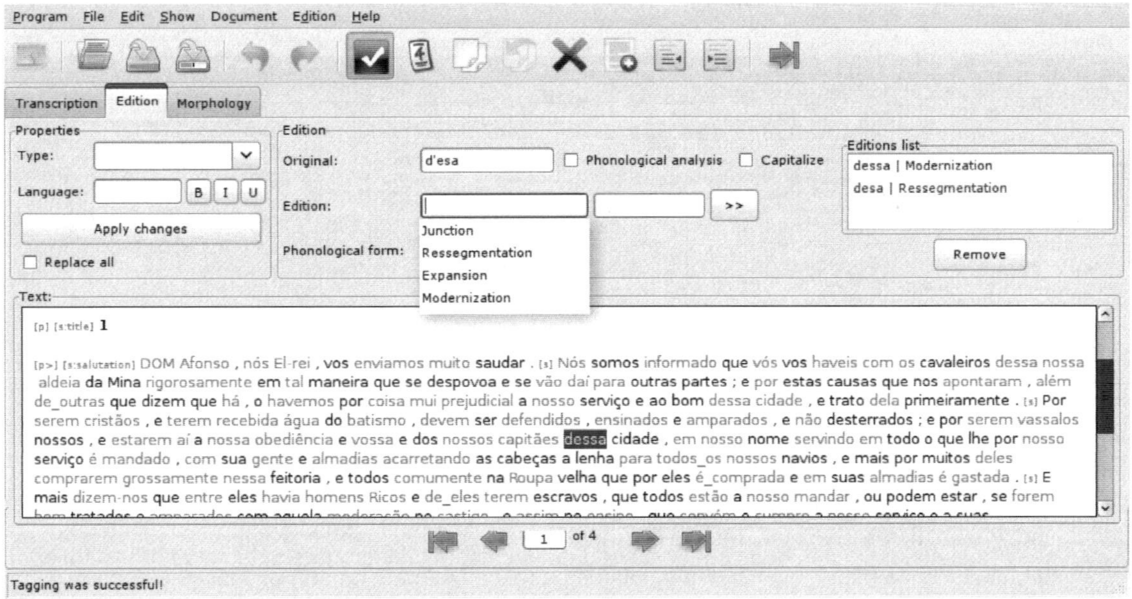


Figure 1: E-Dictor GUI.

structural element (eg., paragraph). Finally, in the 'Morphology' tab, tokens and part-of-speech tags are displayed in token/TAG format, so they can be revised[6].

### 2.3 The XML structure

The XML structure specified meets two main goals: (i) be as neutral as possible (in relation to the textual content encoded) and (ii) suit philological and linguistic needs, i.e., edition must be simple and efficient without losing information relevant to philological studies. In the context of CTB, it was initially established a structure to encode the following information:

- Metadata: information about the source text, e.g., author information, state of processing, etc.
- Delimitation of sections, pages, paragraphs, sentences, headers and footers, and tokens.
- Class of tokens (part-of-speech tags) and phonological form for some tokens.
- Types (levels) of edition for each token.
- Comments of the editor.
- Subtypes for some text elements, like sections, paragraphs, sentences and tokens (eg., a section of type "prologue").

[6]The current version of E-Dictor comes with a POS tagger, developed by Fabio Kepler, accessed by a menu option.

### 2.4 Encoding flexibility

A key goal of E-Dictor is to be flexible enough so as to be useful in other contexts of corpora building. To achieve this, the user can customize the "preferences" of the application. The most prominent options are the *levels of edition* for tokens; the subtypes for the elements 'section', 'paragraph', 'sentence', and 'token'; and the list of POS tags to be used in the morphological analysis. Finally, in the 'Metadata' tab, the user can create the suitable metadata fields needed by his/her project.

### 2.5 Features

Throught its menu, E-Dictor provides some common options (eg., Save As, Search & Replace, Copy & Paste, and many others) as well as those particular options intended for the encoding process (XML structure generation, POS automatic tagging, etc.). E-Dictor provides also an option for exporting the encoded text and the *lexicon of editions*[7] in two different formats (HTML and TXT/CSV).

### 2.6 Edition

To conclude this section, a brief comment about token (words and punctuation) edition, which is the main feature of E-Dictor. The respective interface is shown in Figure 2. When a token is se-

[7]The actual editions applied to words and punctuations of the original text.

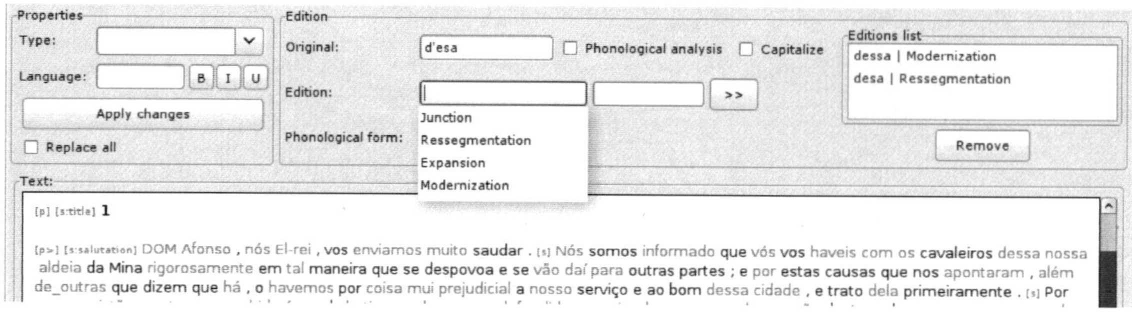

Figure 2: Details of the token edition interface.

lected, the user can: (i) in the "Properties" panel, specify the *type* of the token (according to the subtypes defined by the preferences), its foreign *language*, and *format* (bold, italic, and underlined); (ii) in the "Edition" panel, specify some other properties (eg., phonological form) of the token and include *edition levels* (according to the levels defined by the preferences).

To each token, the user must click on "Apply changes" to effectivate (all) the editions made to it. The option "Replace all" tells E-Dictor to repeat the operation over all identical tokens in the remaining of the text (a similar functionality is available for POS tags revision).

## 3 Discussion

The dificulties of encoding ancient texts in XML, using common text editors, had shown that a tool was necessary to make the process efficient and friendly. This led to the development of E-Dictor, which, since its earlier usage, has shown promising results. Now, the user does not even have to know that the underlying encoding is XML. It is only necessary for him/her to know the (philological and linguistics) aspects of text edition.

E-Dictor led to a decrease of about 50% in the time required for encoding and editing texts. The improvement may be even higher if we consider the revision time. One of the factors for this improvement is the better legibility the tool provides. The XML code is hidden, allowing one to practically read the text without any encoding. To illustrate the opposite, Figure 3 shows the common edition "interface", before E-Dictor. Note that the content being edited is just "Ex.mo Sr. Duque".

Finally, the integration of the whole process into one and only environment is a second factor for the overall improvement, for it allows the user to move freely and quickly between "representations" and

```
<sc id="sc_1">
  <p id="p_1">
    <s id="s_1">
      <w id="s_1#0">
        <o>Ex.mo</o>
        <e t="mod">Excelentíssimo</e>
        <e t="exp">Excelentissimo</e>
      </w>
      <w id="s_1#1">
        <o>Sr.</o>
        <e t="exp">Senhor</e>
      </w>
      <w id="s_1#2">
        <o>Duque</o>
      </w>
```

Figure 3: Example of XML textual encoding.

to access external tools transparently.

### 3.1 Improvements

E-Dictor is always under development, as we discuss its characteristics and receive feedback from users. There is already a list of future improvements that are being developed, such as extending the exporting routines, for example. A bigger goal is to incorporate an edition lexicon, which would be used by the tool for making suggestions during the edition process, or even to develop an "automatic token edition" system for later revision by the user.

### 3.2 Perspectives

Besides CTB, E-Dictor is being used by the BBD project (BBD, 2010), and, recently, by various subgroups of the PHPB project (*For a History of Portuguese in Brazil*). These groups have large experience in philological edition of handwritten documents, and we hope their use of E-Dictor will help us improve it. The ideal goal of E-Dictor is to be capable of handling the whole flow of linguistic and philological tasks: transcription, edition, tagging, *and parsing*.

## References


[BBD2010] BBD. 2010. Biblioteca Brasiliana Digital.

[Bird et al.2009] Steven Bird, E. Klein, and E. Loper. 2009. *Natural Language Processing with Python*. O'Reilly.

[Cor2010] IEL-UNICAMP and IME-USP, 2010. *Córpus Histórico do Português Anotado Tycho Brahe*.

[de Castilho1998] Ataliba Teixeira de Castilho. 1998. *Para a história do português brasileiro*, volume Vol I: Primeiras idéias. Humanitas, São Paulo.

[Kato and Roberts1993] Mary A. Kato and Ian Roberts. 1993. *Português brasileiro: uma viagem Diacrônica*. Editora da Unicamp, Campinas.

[Mattos e Silva1988] Rosa Virgínia Mattos e Silva. 1988. Fluxo e refluxo: uma retrospectiva da lingüística histórica no brasil. *D.E.L.T.A.*, 4(1):85–113.

[Megale and Cambraia1999] Heitor Megale and César Cambraia. 1999. Filologia portuguesa no brasil. *D.E.L.T.A.*, 15(1:22).

[Paixão de Sousa2004] Maria Clara Paixão de Sousa. 2004. Memórias do texto: Aspectos tecnológicos na construção de um corpus histórico do português. Projeto de pós-doutorado – fapesp, Unicamp.

[Paixão de Sousa2009] Maria Clara Paixão de Sousa. 2009. Desafios do processamento de textos antigos: primeiros experimentos na brasiliana digital. In *I Workshop de Linguística Computacional da USP*, São Paulo, 11.

[W3C1999] W3C. 1999. Extensible stylesheet language transformation.

[W3C2009] W3C. 2009. Extensible markup language.

# The Revised Arabic PropBank

**Wajdi Zaghouani[♠], Mona Diab[♣], Aous Mansouri[‡], Sameer Pradhan[◊] and Martha Palmer[‡]**

[♠]Linguistic Data Consortium, [♣]Columbia University,
[‡]University of Colorado, [◊]BBN Technologies

wajdiz@ldc.upenn.edu, mdiab@ccls.columbia.edu, aous.mansouri@colorado.edu,
pradhan@bbn.com, martha.palmer@colorado.edu

## Abstract

The revised Arabic PropBank (APB) reflects a number of changes to the data and the process of PropBanking. Several changes stem from Treebank revisions. An automatic process was put in place to map existing annotation to the new trees. We have revised the original 493 Frame Files from the Pilot APB and added 1462 new files for a total of 1955 Frame Files with 2446 framesets. In addition to a heightened attention to sense distinctions this cycle includes a greater attempt to address complicated predicates such as light verb constructions and multi-word expressions. New tools facilitate the data tagging and also simplify frame creation.

## 1 Introduction

Recent years have witnessed a surge in available automated resources for the Arabic language.[1] These resources can now be exploited by the computational linguistics community with the aim of improving the automatic processing of Arabic. This paper discusses semantic labeling.

Shallow approaches to semantic processing are making large advances in the direction of efficiently and effectively deriving application relevant explicit semantic information from text (Pradhan et al., 2003; Gildea and Palmer, 2002; Pradhan et al., 2004; Gildea and Jurafsky, 2002; Xue and Palmer, 2004; Chen and Rambow, 2003; Carreras and Marquez, 2005; Moschitti, 2004; Moschitti et al., 2005; Diab et al., 2008). Indeed, the existence of semantically annotated resources in English such as FrameNet (Baker et al., 1998) and PropBank (Kingsbury and Palmer, 2003; Palmer et al., 2005) corpora have marked a surge in efficient approaches to automatic semantic labeling of the English language. For example, in the English sentence, 'John enjoys movies', the predicate is 'enjoys' and the first argument, the subject, is 'John', and the second argument, the object, is 'movies'. 'John' would be labeled as the *agent/experiencer* and 'movies' would be the *theme/content.* According to PropBank, 'John' is labeled Arg0 (or enjoyer) and 'movies' is labeled Arg1 (or thing enjoyed). Crucially, that independent of the labeling formalism adopted, the labels do not vary in different syntactic constructions, which is why proposition annotation is different from syntactic Treebank annotation. For instance, if the example above was in the passive voice, 'Movies are enjoyed by John', 'movies' is still the *Theme/Content* (Arg1) and (thing enjoyed), while 'John' remains the *Agent/Experiencer* (Arg0) and (enjoyer). Likewise for the example 'John opened the door' vs. 'The door opened', in both of these examples 'the door' is the *Theme* (Arg1). In addition to English, there are PropBank efforts in Chinese (Xue et al., 2009), Korean (Palmer et al. 2006) and Hindi (Palmer et al., 2009), as well as FrameNet annotations in Chinese, German, Japanese, Spanish and other languages (Hans 2009). Being able to automatically apply this level of analysis to Arabic is clearly a desirable goal, and indeed, we began a pilot Arabic PropBank effort several years ago (Palmer et al., 2008).

In this paper, we present recent work on adapting the original pilot Arabic Proposition Bank (APB) annotation to the recent changes that have been made to the Arabic Treebank (Maamouri et al., 2008). These changes have presented both linguistic and engineering challenges as described in the following sections. In Section 2 we discuss major linguistics changes in the Arabic Treebank annotation, and any impact they might have for the APB effort. In Section 3 we discuss the engineering ramifications of adding and deleting nodes from parse trees, which necessitates mov-

[1] In this paper, we use Arabic to refer to Modern Standard Arabic (MSA).



*Proceedings of the Fourth Linguistic Annotation Workshop, ACL 2010*, pages 222–226,
Uppsala, Sweden, 15-16 July 2010. 

ing all of the APB label pointers to new tree locations. Finally, in Section 4 we discuss the current APB annotation pipeline, which takes into account all of these changes. We conclude with a statement of our current goals for the project.

## 2 Arabic Treebank Revision and APB

The Arabic syntactic Treebank Part 3 v3.1 was revised according to the new Arabic Treebank Annotation Guidelines. Major changes have affected the NP structure and the classification of verbs with clausal arguments, as well as improvements to the annotation in general.[2]

The Arabic Treebank (ATB) is at the core of the APB annotations. The current revisions have resulted in a more consistent treebank that is closer in its analyses to traditional Arabic grammar. The ATB was revised for two levels of linguistic representation, namely morphological information and syntactic structure. Both of these changes have implications for APB annotations.

The new ATB introduced more consistency in the application of morphological features to POS tags, hence almost all relevant words in the ATB have full morphological features of number, gender, case, mood, and definiteness associated with them. This more comprehensive application has implications on agreement markers between nouns and their modifiers and predicative verbs and their arguments, allowing for more consistent semantic analysis in the APB.

In particular, the new ATB explicitly marks the gerunds in Arabic known as maSAdir (singular maSdar.) MaSAdirs, now annotated as VN, are typically predicative nouns that take arguments that should receive semantic roles. The nouns marked as VN are embedded in a new kind of syntactic S structure headed by a VN and having subject and object arguments similar to verbal arguments. This syntactic structure, namely S-NOM, was present in previous editions/versions of the ATB but it was headed by a regular noun, hence it was difficult to find. This explicit VN annotation allows the APB effort to take these new categories into account as predicates. For instance [تكبد]**VN** [-هم]**ARG0** [خسائر كبيرة]**ARG1**, transliterated as takab~udi-, meaning 'suffered' is an example of predicative nominal together with its semantically annotated arguments ARG0 transliterated as -him, meaning 'they' and ARG1 transliterated as xasA}ira kabiyrap, meaning 'heavy losses'.

Other changes in the ATB include *idafa* constructions (a means of expressing possession) and the addition of a pseudo-verb POS tag for a particular group of particles traditionally known as “the sisters of إنّ <in~a 'indeed' ”. These have very little impact on the APB annotation.

## 3 Revised Treebank processing

One of the challenges that we faced during the process of revising the APB was the transfer of the already existing annotation to the newly revised trees -- especially since APB data encoding is tightly coupled with the explicit tree structure. Some of the ATB changes that affected APB projection from the old pilot effort to the new trees are listed as follows:

i. Changes to the tree structure
ii. Changes to the number of tokens -- both modification (insertion and deletion) of traces and modification to some tokenization
iii. Changes in parts of speech
iv. Changes to sentence breaks

The APB modifications are performed within the OntoNotes project (Hovy et al. 2006), we have direct access to the OntoNotes DB Tool, which we extended to facilitate a smooth transition. The tool is modified to perform a three-step mapping process:

a) De-reference the existing (tree) node-level annotations to the respective token spans;

b) Align the original token spans to the best possible token spans in the revised trees. This was usually straight forward, but sometimes the tokenization affected the boundaries of a span in which case careful heuristics had to be employed to find the correct mapping. We incorporated the standard "diff" utility into the API. A simple space separated token-based diff would not completely align cases where the tokenization had been changed in the new tree. For these cases we had to back-off to a character based alignment to recover the alignments. This two-pass strategy works better than using character-based align-

[2] For a complete description of the new Treebank annotation guidelines, see (Arabic Treebank Morphological and Syntactic Annotation Guidelines 2008) at http://projects.ldc.upenn.edu/ArabicTreebank/.

ment as a default since the diff tool does not have any specific domain-level constraints and gets spurious alignments;

c) Create the PropBank (tree) node-pointers for the revised spans.

As expected, this process is not completely automatic. There are cases where we can deterministically transfer the annotations to the new trees, and other cases (especially ones that involve decision making based on newly added traces) where we cannot. We automatically transferred all the annotation that could be done deterministically, and flagged all the others for human review. These cases were grouped into multiple categories for the convenience of the annotators. Some of the part of speech changes invalidated some existing annotations, and created new predicates to annotate. In the first case, we simply dropped the existing annotations on the affected nodes, and in the latter we just created new pointers to be annotated. We could automatically map roughly 50% of the annotations. The rest are being manually reviewed.

## 4 Annotation Tools and Pipeline

### 4.1 Annotation process

APB consists of two major portions: the lexicon resource of Frame Files and the annotated corpus. Hence, the process is divided into framing and annotation (Palmer et al., 2005).

Currently, we have four linguists (framers) creating predicate Frame Files. Using the frame creation tool Cornerstone, a Frame File is created for a specific lemma found in the Arabic Treebank. The information in the Frame File must include the lemma and at least one frameset.

Previously, senses were lumped together into a single frame if they shared the same argument structure. In this effort, however, we are attempting to be more sensitive to the different senses and consequently each unique sense has its own frameset. A frameset contains an English definition, the argument structure for the frameset, a set of (parsed) Arabic examples as an illustration, and it may include Arabic synonyms to further help the annotators with sense disambiguation.

Figure 1 illustrates the Frameset for the verb **استمع isotamaE}** 'to listen'

Predicate: **{isotamaE استمع**
Roleset id: f1, to listen
**Arg0: entity listening**
**Arg1: thing listened**

**Figure 1. The frameset of the verb {isotamaE**

**Rel: {isotamaE, استمع**
**Arg0: -NONE- ***
**Gloss: He**
**Arg1: الى مطالبهم**
**Gloss: to their demands**
**Example: استمع الى مطالبهم**

**Figure 2. An example annotation for a sentence containing the verb {isotamaE**

In addition to the framers, we also have five native Arabic speakers as annotators on the team, using the annotation tool Jubilee (described below). Treebanked sentences from the ATB are clearly displayed in Jubilee, as well as the raw text for that sentence at the bottom of the screen. The verb that needs to be tagged is clearly marked on the tree for the annotators. A drop-down menu is available for the annotators to use so that they may choose a particular frameset for that specific instance. Once a frameset is chosen the argument structure will be displayed for them to see. As a visual aid, the annotators may also click on the "example" button in order to see the examples for that particular frameset. Finally, the complements of the predicate are tagged directly on the tree, and the annotators may move on to the next sentence. Figure 2 illustrates a sample annotation.

Once the data has been double-blind annotated, the adjudication process begins. An adjudicator, a member of the framing team, provides the Gold Standard annotation by going over the tagged instances to settle any differences in the choices. Occasionally a verb will be mis-lemmatized (e.g. the instance may actually be **سَهّل sah~al** 'to cause to become easy' but it is lemmatized under سَهُل sahul-u 'to be easy' which looks identical without vocalization.) At this point the lemmas are corrected and sent back to the annotators to tag before the adjudicators can complete their work.

The framers and annotators meet regularly at least every fortnight. These meetings are important for the framers since they may need to convey to the annotators any changes or issues with the frames, syntactic matters, or anything else that may require extra training or preparation for the annotators. It is important to note that while the framers are linguists, the annotators are not. This means that the annotators must be instructed on a number of things including, but not limited to, how to read trees, and what forms a constituent, as well as how to get familiar with the tools in order to start annotating the data. Therefore, little touches, such as the addition of Arabic synonyms to the framesets (especially since not all of the annotators have the same level of fluency in English), or confronting specific linguistic phenomena via multiple modalities are a necessary part of the process. To these meetings, the annotators mostly bring their questions and concerns about the data they are working on. We rely heavily on the annotator's language skills. They take note of whether a frame appears to be incorrect, is missing an argument, or is missing a sense. And since they go through every instance in the data, annotators are instrumental for pointing out any errors the ATB. Since everything is discussed together as a group people frequently benefit from the conversations and issues that are raised. These bi-monthly meetings not only help maintain a certain level of quality control but establish a feeling of cohesion in the group.

The APB has decided to thoroughly tackle light verb constructions and multi-word expressions as part of an effort to facilitate mapping between the different languages that are being PropBanked. In the process of setting this up a number of challenges have surfaced which include: how can we cross-linguistically approach these phenomena in a (semi) integrated manner, how to identify one construction from the other, figuring out a language specific reliable diagnostic test, and whether we deal with these constructions as a whole unit or as separate parts; and how? (Hwang, et al., 2010)

### 4.2 Tools

Frameset files are created in an XML format. During the Pilot Propbank project these files were created manually by editing the XML file related to a particular predicate. This proved to be time consuming and prone to many formatting errors. The Frame File creation for the revised APB is now performed with the recently developed Cornerstone tool (Choi et al., 2010a), which is a PropBank frameset editor that allows the creation and editing of Propbank framesets without requiring any prior knowledge of XML. Moreover, the annotation is now performed by Jubilee, a new annotation tool, which has improved the annotation process by displaying several types of relevant syntactic and semantic information at the same time. Having everything displayed helps the annotator quickly absorb and apply the necessary syntactic and semantic information pertinent to each predicate for consistent and efficient annotation (Choi et al., 20010b). Both tools are available as Open Source tools on Google code.[3]

### 4.3 Current Annotation Status and Goals

We have currently created 1955 verb predicate Frame Files which correspond to 2446 framesets, since one verb predicate Frame File can contain one or more framesets. We will reconcile the previous Arabic PropBank with the new Treebank and create an additional 3000 Frame files to cover the rest of the ATB3 verb types.

## 5 Conclusion

This paper describes the recently revived and revised APB. The changes in the ATB have affected the APB in two fundamentally different ways. More fine-grained POS tags facilitate the tasks of labeling predicate argument structures. However, all of the tokenization changes have rendered the old pointers obsolete, and new pointers to the new constituent boundaries have to be supplied. This task is underway, as well as the task of creating several thousand additional Frame Files to complete predicate coverage of ATB3.

### Acknowledgments

We gratefully acknowledge a grant from the Defense Advanced Research Projects Agency (DARPA/IPTO) under the GALE program, DARPA/CMO Contract No. HR0011-06-C-0022, subcontract from BBN, Inc. We also thank Abdel-Aati Hawwary and Maha Saliba Foster and our annotators for their invaluable contributions to this project.

## References

Boas, Hans C. 2009. Multilingual FrameNets. In Computational Lexicography: Methods and Applications. Berlin: Mouton de Gruyter. pp. x+352

Carreras, Xavier & Lluís Màrquez. 2005. Introduction to the CoNLL-2005 shared task: Semantic role labeling. In *Proceedings of CoNLL-2005*, Ann Arbor, MI, USA.

3 http://code.google.com/p/propbank/

Chen, John & Owen Rambow. 2003. Use of deep linguistic features for the recognition and labeling of semantic arguments. In *Proceedings of the 2003 Conference on Empirical Methods in Natural Language Processing*, Sapporo, Japan.

Choi, Jinho D., Claire Bonial, & Martha Palmer. 2010a. Propbank Instance Annotation Guidelines Using a Dedicated Editor,Cornerstone. In *Proceedings of the 7th International Conference on Language Resources and Evaluation (LREC'10)*,Valletta, Malta.

Choi, Jinho D., Claire Bonial, & Martha Palmer. 2010b. Propbank Instance Annotation Guidelines Using a Dedicated Editor,Jubilee. In *Proceedings of the 7th International Conference on Language Resources and Evaluation (LREC'10)*,Valletta, Malta.

Diab, Mona, Alessandro Moschitti, & Daniele Pighin. 2008. Semantic Role Labeling Systems for Arabic using Kernel Methods. In *Proceedings of ACL*. Association for Computational Linguistics, Columbus, OH, USA.

Gildea, Daniel & Daniel Jurafsky. 2002. Automatic labeling of semantic roles. *Computational Linguistics*, 28(3):245–288.

Gildea, Daniel & Martha Palmer. 2002. The necessity of parsing for predicate argument recognition. In *Proceedings of the 40th Annual Conference of the Association for Computational Linguistics (ACL-02)*, Philadelphia, PA, USA.

Gusfield, Dan. 1997. *Algorithms on Strings, Trees and Sequences*. Cambridge University Press, Cambridge, UK.

Habash, Nizar & Owen Rambow. 2007. Arabic diacritization through full morphological tagging. In *HLT-NAACL* 2007; Companion Volume, Short Papers, Association for Computational Linguistics, pages 53–56, Rochester, NY, USA.

Hovy, Eduard, Mitchell Marcus, Martha Palmer, Lance Ramshaw & Ralph Weischedel. 2006. OntoNotes: The 90% Solution. In *Proceedings of HLT-NAACL* 2006, New York, USA.

Hwang, Jena D., Archna Bhatia, Clare Bonial, Aous Mansouri, Ashwini Vaidya, Nianwen Xue & Martha Palmer. 2010. PropBank Annotation of Multilingual Light Verb Constructions. In *Proceedings of the LAW-ACL 2010*. Uppsala, Sweden.

Maamouri, Mohamed, Ann Bies, Seth Kulick. 2008. Enhanced Annotation and Parsing of the Arabic Treebank. In *Proceedings of* INFOS 2008, Cairo, Egypt.

Márquez, Lluís. 2009. Semantic Role Labeling. Past, Present and Future . TALP Research Center. Technical University of Catalonia. Tutorial at ACL-IJCNLP 2009.

Moschitti, Alessandro. 2004. A study on convolution kernels for shallow semantic parsing. In *proceedings of the 42th Conference on Association for Computational Linguistic (ACL-2004)*, Barcelona, Spain.

Moschitti, Alessandro, Ana-Maria Giuglea, Bonaventura Coppola, & Roberto Basili. 2005. Hierarchical semantic role labeling. In *Proceedings of CoNLL-2005*, Ann Arbor, MI, USA.

Martha Palmer, Olga Babko-Malaya, Ann Bies, Mona Diab, Mohamed Maamouri, Aous Mansouri, Wajdi Zaghouani. 2008. A Pilot Arabic Propbank. In *Proceedings of LREC 2008*, Marrakech, Morocco.

Palmer, Martha, Rajesh Bhatt, Bhuvana Narasimhan, Owen Rambow, Dipti Misra Sharma, & Fei Xia. 2009. Hindi Syntax: Annotating Dependency, Lexical Predicate-Argument Structure, and Phrase Structure. In *The 7th International Conference on Natural Language Processing* (ICON-2009), Hyderabad, India.

Palmer, Martha, Daniel Gildea, & Paul Kingsbury. 2005. The Proposition Bank: An Annotated Corpus of Semantic Roles. *Computational Linguistics*, 31, 1 (Mar. 2005), 71-106.

Palmer, Martha, Shijong Ryu, Jinyoung Choi, Sinwon Yoon, & Yeongmi Jeon. 2006. LDC Catalog LDC2006T03.

Pradhan, Sameer, Kadri Hacioglu, Wayne Ward, James H. Martin, & Daniel Jurafsky. 2003. Semantic role parsing: Adding semantic structure to unstructured text. In *Proceedings of ICDM-2003*, Melbourne, USA.

Pradhan, Sameer S., Wayne H Ward, Kadri Hacioglu, James H Martin, & Dan Jurafsky. 2004. Shallow semantic parsing using support vector machines. In Susan Dumais, Daniel Marcu, & Salim Roukos, editors, *HLT-NAACL 2004: Main Proceedings*, pages 233–240, Boston, MA, USA.

Xue, Nianwen & Martha Palmer. 2004. Calibrating features for semantic role labeling. In Dekang Lin & Dekai Wu, editors, *Proceedings of ACL-EMNLP 2004*, pages 88–94, Barcelona, Spain.

Xue, Nianwen & Martha Palmer. 2009. Adding semantic roles to the Chinese Treebank. *Natural Language Engineering*, 15 Jan. 2009, 143-172.

# PackPlay: Mining semantic data in collaborative games

**Nathan Green**
NC State University
890 Oval Drive
Raleigh, NC 27695

**Paul Breimyer**
NC State University
890 Oval Drive
Raleigh, NC 27695

**Vinay Kumar**
NC State University
890 Oval Drive
Raleigh, NC 27695

**Nagiza F. Samatova**
Oak Ridge National Lab
1 Bethel Valley Rd
Oak Ridge, TN 37831

## Abstract

Building training data is labor-intensive and presents a major obstacle to advancing machine learning technologies such as machine translators, named entity recognizers (NER), part-of-speech taggers, etc. Training data are often specialized for a particular language or Natural Language Processing (NLP) task. Knowledge captured by a specific set of training data is not easily transferable, even to the same NLP task in another language. Emerging technologies, such as social networks and serious games, offer a unique opportunity to change how we construct training data.

While collaborative games have been used in information retrieval, it is an open issue whether users can contribute accurate annotations in a collaborative game context for a problem that requires an exact answer, such as games that would create named entity recognition training data. We present *PackPlay*, a collaborative game framework that empirically shows players' ability to mimic annotation accuracy and thoroughness seen in gold standard annotated corpora.

## 1 Introduction

*Annotated corpora* are sets of structured text used in Natural Language Processing (NLP) that contain supplemental knowledge, such as tagged parts-of-speech, semantic concepts assigned to phrases, or semantic relationships between these concepts. Machine Learning (ML) is a subfield of Artificial Intelligence that studies how computers can obtain knowledge and create predictive models. These models require annotated corpora to learn rules and patterns. However, these annotated corpora must be manually curated for each domain or task, which is labor intensive and tedious (Scannell, 2007), thereby creating a bottleneck for advancing ML and NLP prediction tools. Furthermore, knowledge captured by a specific annotated corpus is often not transferable to another task, even to the same NLP task in another language. Domain and language specific corpora are useful for many language technology applications, including named entity recognition (NER), machine translation, spelling correction, and machine-readable dictionaries. The An Crúbadán Project, for example, has succeeded in creating corpora for more than 400 of the world's 6000+ languages by Web crawling. With a few exceptions, most of the 400+ corpora, however, lack any linguistic annotations due to the limitations of annotation tools (Rayson et al., 2006).

Despite the many documented advantages of annotated data over raw data (Granger and Rayson, 1998; Mair, 2005), there is a dearth of annotated corpora in many domains. The majority of previous corpus annotation efforts relied on manual annotation by domain experts, automated prediction tagging systems, and hybrid semi-automatic systems that used both approaches. While yielding high quality and enormously valuable corpora, manually annotating corpora can be prohibitively costly and time consuming. For example, the GENIA corpus contains 9,372 sentences, curated by five part-time annotators, one senior coordinator, and one junior coordinator over 1.5 years (Kim et al., 2008). Semi-automatic approaches decrease human effort but often introduce significant error, while still requiring human interaction.

The Web can help facilitate semi-automatic approaches by connecting distributed human users at a previously unfathomable scale and presents an opportunity to expand annotation efforts to countless users using Human Computation, the concept of outsourcing certain computational



*Proceedings of the Fourth Linguistic Annotation Workshop, ACL 2010*, pages 227–234,
Uppsala, Sweden, 15-16 July 2010. ©2010 Association for Computational Linguistics

processes to humans, generally to solve problems that are intractable or difficult for computers. This concept is demonstrated in our previous work, WebBANC (Green et al., 2009) and BioDEAL (Breimyer et al., 2009), which allows users to annotate Web documents through a Web browser plugin for the purposes of creating linguistically and biologically tagged annotated corpora and with micro-tasking via Mechanical Turk, which allows for a low cost option for manual labor tasks (Snow et al., 2008; Kittur et al., 2008).

While the Web and Human Computation may be a powerful tandem for generating data and solving difficult problems, in order to succeed, users must be motivated to participate. Humans have been fascinated with games for centuries and play them for many reasons, including for entertainment, honing skills, and gaining knowledge (FAS Summit, 2006). Every year, a large amount of hours are spent playing online computer games. The games range form simple card and word games to more complex 3-D world games. One such site for word, puzzle, and card games is Pogo.com[1]. According to protrackr,[2] Pogo has almost 6 million unique visitors a day. Alexa.com[3] shows that the average user is on the site for 11 minutes at a time. When the average time spent on the site is propagated to each user, the combined time is equal to more than 45,000 days of human time. Arguably if, the games on Pogo were used to harvest useful data, various fields of Computer Science research could be advanced.

There has been a recent trend to leverage human's fascination in game playing to solve difficult problems through *Human Computation*. Two such games include ESP and Google's Image Labeler (Ahn and Dabbish, 2004), in which players annotate images in a cooperative environment to correctly match image tags with their partner. Semantic annotation has also been addressed in the game Phrase Detectives (Chamberlain et al., 2009), which has the goal of creating large scale training data for anaphora resolution. These types of games are part of a larger, serious games, initiative (Annetta, 2008).

This paper introduces the Web-enabled collaborative game framework, PackPlay, and investigates how collaborative online gaming can affect annotation throughput and annotation accuracy. There are two main questions for such systems: first, will overall throughput increase compared to traditional methods of annotating, such as the manual construction of the Genia Corpus? Second, how accurate are the collective annotations? A successful human computation environment, such as PackPlay, would represent a paradigm shift in the way annotated corpora are created. However, adoption of such a framework cannot be expected until these questions are answered. We address both of these questions in multiple games in our PackPlay system through evaluation of the collective players' annotations with precision and recall to judge accuracy of players' annotations and the number of games played to judge throughput. We show improvements in both areas over traditional annotation methods and show accuracy comparable to expert prediction systems that could be used for semi-supervised annotation.

## 2 Methodology

We empirically show casual game players' ability to accurately and throughly annotate corpora by conducting experiments following the process described in Section 2.1 with 8 players using the PackPlay System. The testers annotate the datasets described in Section 2.2 and results are analyzed using the equations in Section 2.3.

### 2.1 PackPlay Process Flow

Figure 1 shows the average PackPlay process flow that a player will follow for a multi-player game. Assuming the player is registered, the player will always start by logging in and selecting the game he or she wants to play. Once in the game screen, the system will try to pair the player with another player who is waiting. After a set time limit, the game will automatically pair the user with a PlayerBot. It is important to note that the player will not know that his or her partner is a PlayerBot.

Once paired, a game can start. In most games, a question will be sampled from our database. How this sampling takes place is up to the individual game. Once sampled, the question will be displayed to one player or all players, depending on whether the game is synchronous or asynchronous (see definitions in Sections 3.1.2 and 3.2.2). Once the question is displayed, two things can happen.

[1] Pogo. http://www.pogo.com/

[2] Protrackr.com site information and statistics.http://www.protrackr.com/

[3] Alexa: The Web Information Company. http://www.alexa.com/

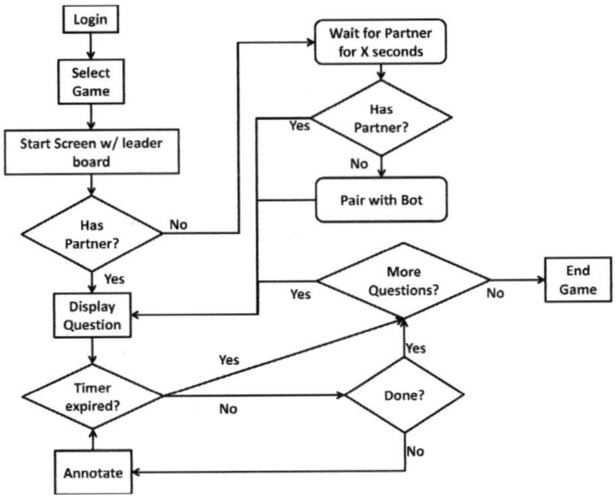


Figure 1: User process flow for PackPlay games.

First, the timer can run out; this timer is set by each game individually. Second, the player may answer the question and move on to the next question. After either one of those two options, a new question will be sampled. This cycle continues until the game session is over. This is usually determined by the game, as each game can set the number of questions in a session, or by a player quiting the game.

### 2.2 Data Sources

To compare named entity results, PackPlay uses sentences and annotations from CoNLL 2003, a "gold" standard corpus (Tjong et al., 2003). We use the CoNLL 2003 corpus since it has been curated by experts and the PackPlay system can compare our players' annotations vs those of 16 submitted predictive models, also refered to as the CoNLL average, in the 2003 conference on natural language learning. This paper will refer to the training corpus as the CoNLL corpus, and we selected it for our evaluation due to its widespread adoption as a benchmark corpus.

### 2.3 Metrics

To measure how thoroughly and accurately our players annotate the data, we calculate both recall (Equation 1) and precision (Equation 2), in which $\alpha$ is the set of words annotated in PackPlay and $\beta$ is the set of words in the base CoNLL corpus.

$$Recall = \frac{|\alpha \cap \beta|}{|\beta|} \quad (1)$$

$$Precision = \frac{|\alpha \cap \beta|}{|\alpha|} \quad (2)$$

Each game module in the PackPlay system has its own scoring module, which is intended to improve the players' precision. For this reason, scoring is handled on a per game level. Each game has its own leader board as well. The leader board is used to motivate the players to continue playing the PackPlay games. This is intended to improve recall for annotations in the system.

## 3 Games

### 3.1 Entity Discovery

#### 3.1.1 Game description

Named entities are a foundational part of many NLP systems from information extraction systems to machine translation systems. The ability to detect an entity is an application area called Named Entity Recognition (NER). The most common named entity categories are Person (Per), Location (Loc), and Organization (Org). The ability to extract these entities may be used in everyday work, such as extracting defendants, cities, and companies from court briefings, or it may be used for critical systems in national defense, such as monitoring communications for people and locations of interest.

To help with the creation of more NER systems, *Entity Discovery* (see Figure 2), a game for annotating sentences with supplied entities was created. The goal of the game is to pair players with each other and allow them to annotate sentences together. While this annotation task could be done by one person, it is a very time consuming activity. By creating a game, we hope that players will be more likely to annotate for fun and will annotate correctly and completely in order to receive a higher score in the PackPlay system.

#### 3.1.2 Implementation

*Entity Discovery* is implemented as a *synchronous* two-player game. A *synchronous* game is one in which both players have the same task in the game, in this case, to annotate a sentence. To have a base comparison point, all players are asked to annotate a random set of 60 sentences to start, for which we have the correct answers. This way we will be able to assess the trustworthiness score in future iterations. After the pretest, the players will be shown sentences randomly sampled with replacement.

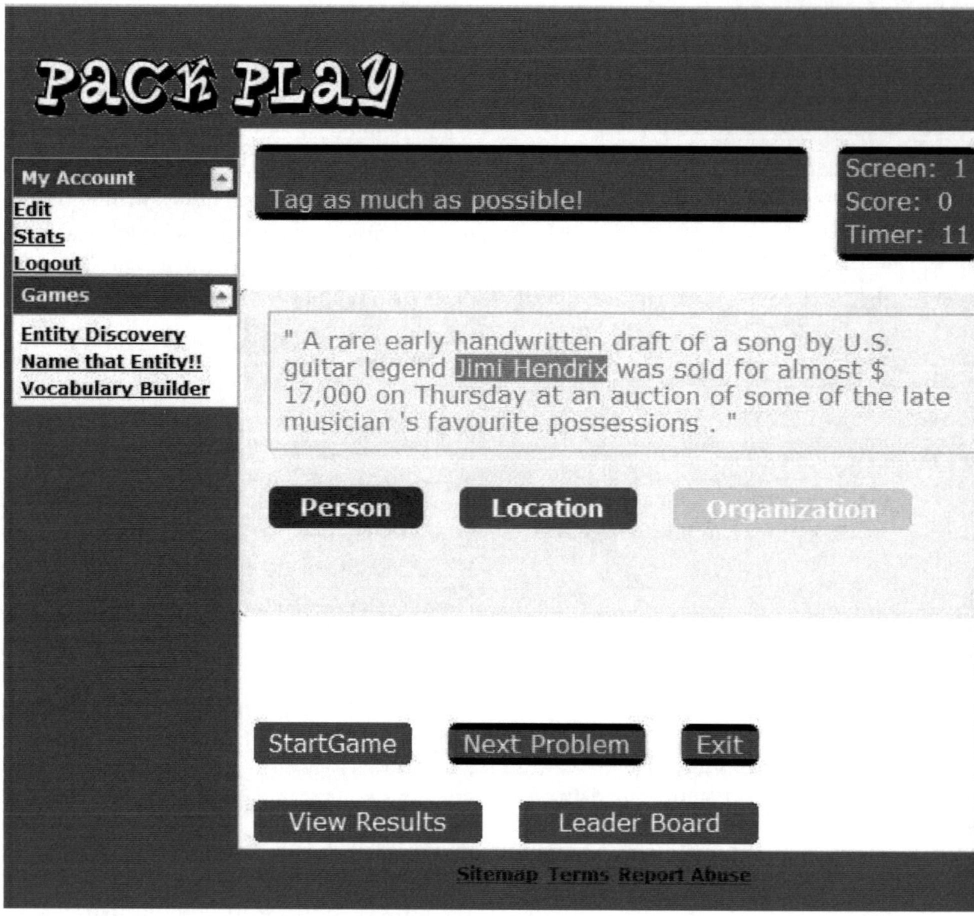


Figure 2: Screenshot of a player annotating the Person entity Jimi Hendrix

In *Entity Discovery*, we made a design decision to keep a player's partner anonymous. This should help reduce cheating, such as agreeing to select the same word over and over, and it should reduce the ability for a player to only play with his or her friends, which might enhance their ability to cheat by using other communication systems such as instant messaging or a cell phone. Since PackPlay is still in the experimental stages, players may not always be available. For this reason, we have implemented a PlayerBot system. The PlayerBot will mimic another player by selecting previously annotated phrases for a given sentence from the database. From the human players' point of view, nothing seems different.

Players are asked to annotate, or tag, as many entities as they can find in a sentence. Players are also told at the beginning of the game that they are paired with another user. Their goal is to annotate the same things as their partner. Our assumption is that if the game is a single player game then the players may just annotate the most obvious entities for gaining more points. By having the player to try to guess at what their partner may annotate we hope to get better overall coverage of entities. We try to minimize the errors, which guessing might produce, in a second game, *Name That Entity* (Section 3.2).

To annotate a sentence, the player simply highlights a word or phrase and clicks on a relevant entity. For instance in *Entity Discovery*, a player can annotate the phrase "Jimi Hendrix" as a Person entity. From this point on, the player is free to annotate more phrases in the sentence. When the player completes annotating a sentence, the player hits "Next Problem." The system then waits for the player's partner to hit "Next Problem" as well. When both players finish annotating, the game points will be calculated and a new question will be sampled for the players.

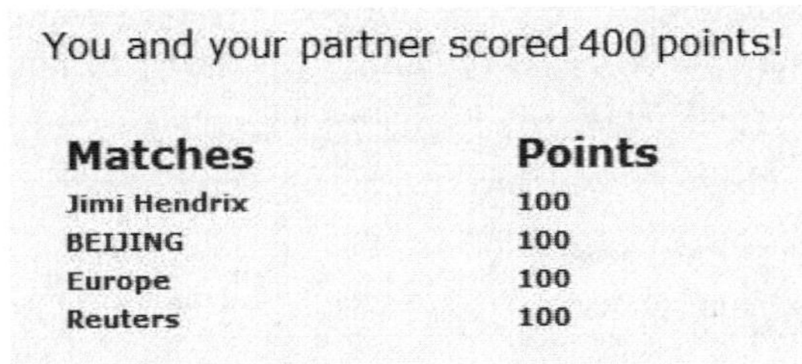


Figure 3: Screenshot of what the player sees at the end of the *Entity Discovery* game

### 3.1.3 Scoring

Scoring can be done in a variety of ways, each having an impact on players' performance and enjoyment. For *Entity Discovery*, we decided to give each user a flat score of 100 points for every answer that matched their partner. At the end of each game session, the player will see what answers matched with their partner. For instance, if both players tagged "Jimi Hendrix" as a Person, they will both receive 100 points. We do not show the players their matched scores after each sentence, since this might bias the user to tag more or less depending on what their partner does. Figure 3 shows a typical scoring screen at the end of a game; in Figure 3, the players matched 4 phrases, totaling 400 points. It is important to note that at this stage we do not distinguish between correct and incorrect annotations, just whether the two players agree.

### 3.1.4 User Case Study Methodology

To examine *Entity Discovery* as a collaborative game toward the creation of an annotated corpus, we conducted a user experiment to collect sample data on a known data set. Over a short time, 8 players were asked to play both *Entity Discovery* and *Name That Entity*. In PackPlay, throughput can be estimated, since each game has a defined time limit, defined as the average number of entities annotated per question times the number of users times the average number of questions seen by a user. Unlike other systems such as Mechanical Turk (Snow et al., 2008; Kittur et al., 2008), BioDeal (Breimyer et al., 2009), or WebBANC (Green et al., 2009), in PackPlay we define the speed at which a user annotates.

Each game in *Entity Discovery* consists of 10 sentences from the CoNLL corpus. These sentences are not guaranteed to have a named entity within them. The users in the study were not

Table 1: Statistics returned from our user study for the game *Entity Discovery*

| Statistic | Total | Mean |
|---|---|---|
| # of games | 29 | 3.62 |
| # of annotations | 291 | 40.85 |

informed of the entity content as to not bias the experiment and falsely raise our precision scores. With only 8 players, we obtained 291 annotations, which averaged to about 40 annotations per user. This study was not done over a long period of time, so each user only played, on average, 3.6 games.

Two players were asked to intentionally annotate poorly. The goal of using poor annotators was to simulate real world players, who may just click answers to ruin the game or who are clueless to what a named entity is. This information can be used in later research to help automatically detect "bad" annotators using anomaly detection techniques.

PackPlay also stores information not used in this study, such as time stamps for each question answered. This information will be incorporated into future experiment analysis to see if we can further improve our annotated corpora based on the order and time spent forming an annotation. For instance, the first annotation in a sentence may have a higher probability than the last annotation. It is possible that if a user answers too fast, the answer is likely an error.

### 3.1.5 Output Quality

Every player completes part of a 60 sentence pretest in which we know the answers. For each game, the questions are sampled without replacement but this does not carry over after a game. For instance, if a player finishes game 1, he or she will never see the same question twice. For game two, no question within the game will be repeated, however, the player might see a question he or she answered in game 1. Because of this, each user will not see all 60 questions, but we will have a good sample to judge whether a user is accurate or not. The ability to repeat a question in different games allows us, in future research, to test players using intra-annotator agreement statistics. This tests how well a player agrees with himself or herself. From this set of 60 questions we have calculated each player's recall and precision scores.

As Table 2 shows, the recall scores for *Entity*

Table 2: Recall and precision for *Entity Discovery* annotations of CoNLL data.

| | Per | Loc | Org | Avg | CoNLL Avg |
|---|---|---|---|---|---|
| Recall (All Data) | 0.94 | 0.95 | 0.85 | 0.9 | 0.82 |
| Precision (All Data) | 0.47 | 0.70 | 0.53 | 0.62 | 0.83 |

*Discovery* in this experiment were 0.94, 0.95, and 0.85 for Person, Location, and Organization, respectively. The overall average was 0.9, which beats out the CoNLL average, an average of 16 expert systems, for recall. *Entity Discovery*'s numbers are similar to the pattern seen in the CoNLL predictive systems for Person, Location and Organization, in which Organization was the lowest and Person was the highest. The precision numbers were quite lower, with an average of 0.62. When examining the data, most of the precision errors occurred because of word phrase boundary issues with the annotation and also players often are unsure whether to include titles such as President, Mr., or Dr. There were also quite a few errors where players annotated concepts as People such as "The Judge" or "The scorekeeper." While this is incorrect for named entity recognition, it might be of interest to a co-reference resolution corpus. The precision numbers are likely low because of our untrained players and because some of the players were told to intentionally annotate entities incorrectly. To improve on these numbers, we applied a coverage requirement and majority voting. The coverage requirement requires that more than one player has annotated a given phrase for the annotation to be included in the corpus. Majority voting indicates that the phrase is only included if 50% or more of the playerss who annotated a phrase, agreed on the specific entity assigned to the phrase.

As Table 3 shows, both majority voting and coverage requirements improve precision by more than 10%. When combined, they improve the overall precision to 0.88, a 26% improvement. This is an improvement to the expert CoNLL systems score of 0.83. The majority voting likely removed the annotations from our purposefully "bad" annotators.

For future work, as the number of players increases, we will have to increase our coverage requirement to match. This ratio has not been determined and will need to be tested. A more successful way to detect errors in our annotations may be to create a separate game to verify given answers. To initially test this concept we have made and set up an experiment with a game, called *Name That Entity*.

Table 3: Precision for *Entity Discovery* annotations of CoNLL data with filtering

| | Per | Loc | Org | Avg |
|---|---|---|---|---|
| Precision (Majority Voting) | 0.56 | 0.79 | 0.65 | 0.72 |
| Precision (Coverage Req.) | 0.69 | 0.83 | 0.63 | 0.73 |
| Precision (Majority Voting + Coverage Req.) | 0.90 | 0.95 | 0.81 | 0.88 |

### 3.2 Name That Entity

#### 3.2.1 Game Description

*Name That Entity* is another game with a focus on named entities. *Name That Entity* was created to show that game mechanics and the creation of further games would enhance the value of an annotated corpus. In the case of *Name That Entity*, we have created a multiple choice game in which the player will select the entity that best represents the highlighted word or phrase. Unlike *Entity Discovery*, this allows us to focus the annotation effort on particular words or phrases. Once again, this is modeled as a two-player game but the players are not playing simultaneously. The goal for the player is to select the same entity type for the highlighted word that their partner selects. In this game, speed is of the essence since each question will ask for one entity as opposed to *Entity Discovery*, which was open ended to how many entities might exist in a sentence.

#### 3.2.2 Implementation

As described above, *Name That Entity* appears to be a two-player *synchronous* game. The player is under the assumption that he or she must once again match his or her partner's choice. What the player does not know is that the multi-player is simulated in this case. The player is replaced with a PlayerBot which chooses annotations from the *Entity Discovery* game. This, in essence, creates an *asynchronous* game, in which one player has the task of finding entities and the other player has the task of verifying entities. This gives us a further mechanism to check the validity of entities annotated by the *Entity Discovery* game.

As with *Entity Discovery*, the player's partner is anonymous. This anonymity allows us to keep the asynchronous structure hidden, as well as judge a new metric, intra-annotator agreement, not tested in the previous game. Since it is possible that a player in PackPlay may have a question sampled that was previously annotated in the *Entity Discovery* game by the same player, we can use intra-annotator agreement. While well-known inter-annotator statistics, such as Cohen's Kappa, evaluate one annotator versus the other annotator, intra-annotator statistics allow us to judge an annotator versus himself or herself to test for consistency (Artstein and Poesio, 2008). In the PackPlay framework this allows us to detect playerss who are randomly guessing and are therefore not consistent with themselves.

#### 3.2.3 Scoring

Since entity coverage of a sentence is not an issue in the multiple choice game, we made use of a different scoring system that would reward first instincts. While the *Entity Discovery* game has a set score for every answer, *Name That Entity* has a sliding scale. For each question, the max score is 100 points, as the time ticks away the user receives fewer points. The points remaining are indicated to the user via a timing bar at the bottom of the screen.

When the player completes a game, he or she is allowed to view the results for that game. Unlike the *Entity Discovery* game, we display to the player what entity his or her partner chooses on the question in which they both did not match. This gives us a quick and simple form of annotator training, since a player with no experience may not be familiar with a particular entity. This was seen with the players' ability to detect an Organization entity. We expect that when a player sees what his or her partner annotates a phrase as, the player, is, in effect, being trained. However, displaying this at the end should not have any affects toward cheating since their partners are anonymous.

#### 3.2.4 User Case Study Methodology

Of the 8 players who participated in the *Entity Discovery* study, 7 also played *Name That Entity* during their game sessions. We did not inform the players, but the questions asked in *Name That Entity* were the same answers that the players gave in the experiment in Section 3.1.4. The basic annotation numbers from our small user study can be seen in Table 4.

Table 4: Statistics returned from our user study for the game *Name That Entity*

| Statistic | Total | Mean |
|---|---|---|
| # of games | 20 | 2.85 |
| # of annotations | 195 | 27.85 |

#### 3.2.5 Output Quality

As *Name That Entity* is not intended to be a solo mechanism to generate annotations, but instead a way to verify existing annotations, we did not assess the recall and precision of the game. Instead we are looking at the number of annotations, unique annotations, and conflicting annotations generated by our players in this game.

Table 5: Types of annotations generated by *Name That Entity*

| Error | Count |
|---|---|
| Annotations | 195 |
| Unique Annotations | 141 |
| Conflicts | 38 |
| Unique Conflicts | 35 |

In Table 5, unique annotations refer to annotations verified by only one user. Of the 195 total verified annotation, 38 had conflicting answers. In the majority of the cases the players marked these conflicts as "None of the Above," indicating that the annotated phrase from *Entity Discovery* was incorrect. For instance, many players made the mistake in *Entity Discovery* of marking phrases such as "German," "English," and "French" as Location entities when they are, in fact, just adjectives. In *Name That Entity*, the majority of players corrected each other and marked these as "None of the Above."

The main use of this game will be to incorporate it as an accuracy check for players based on these conflicting annotation. This accuracy check will be used in future work to deal with user confidence scores and conflict resolution.

## 4 Conclusion

Annotated corpora generation presents a major obstacle to advancing modern Natural Language Processing technologies. In this paper we introduced the PackPlay framework, which aims to leverage a distributed web user community in a collaborative game to build semantically-rich annotated corpora from players annotations. PackPlay is shown to have high precision and recall numbers when compared to expert systems in the area of named entity recognition. These annotated corpora were generated from two collaborative games in PackPlay, *Entity Discovery* and *Name That Entity*. The two games combined let us exploit the benefits of both *synchronous* and *asynchronous* gameplay as mechanisms to verify the quality of our annotated corpora. Future work should combine the players output with a player confidence score based on conflict resolution algorithms, using both inter- and intra-annotator metrics.

## References


Luis von Ahn and Laura Dabbish. 2004 Labeling images with a computer game. ACM, pages 319-326, Vienna, Austria.

Leonard A. Annetta. 2008 Serious Educational Games: From Theory to Practice. Sense Publishers.

Ron Artstein and Massimo Poesio. 2008 Intercoder agreement for computational linguistics. Computational Linguistics, Vol. 34, Issue 4, pages 555-596.

Maged N. Kamel Boulos and Steve Wheeler. 2007. The emerging web 2.0 social software: an enabling suite of sociable technologies in health and health care education. Health information and libraries journal, Vol. 24, pages 223.

Paul Breimyer, Nathan Green, Vinay Kumar, and Nagiza F. Samatova. 2009. BioDEAL: community generation of biological annotations. BMC Medical Informatics and Decision Making, Vol. 9, pages Suppl+1.

Jon Chamberlain, Udo Kruschwitz, and Massimo Poesio. 2009. Constructing an anaphorically annotated corpus with non-experts: assessing the quality of collaborative annotations. People's Web '09: Proceedings of the 2009 Workshop on The People's Web Meets NLP, pages 57-62.

FAS Summit on educational games: Harnessing the power of video games for learning (report), 2006.

Sylviane Granger and Paul Rayson. 1998. Learner English on Computer. Longman, London, and New Yorks pp. 119-131.

Nathan Green, Paul Breimyer, Vinay Kumar, and Nagiza F. Samatova. 2009. WebBANC: Building Semantically-Rich Annotated Corpora from Web User Annotations of Minority Languages. Proceedings of the 17th Nordic Conference of Computational Linguistics (NODALIDA), Vol. 4, pages 48-56, Odense, Denmark.

Jin-Dong Kim, Tomoko Ohta, and Jun'ichi Tsujii. 2008. Corpus annotation for mining biomedical events from literature. BMC Bioinformatics, 9:10.

Aniket Kittur, Ed H. Chi, and Bongwon Suh. 2008. Crowdsourcing user studies with Mechanical Turk CHI '08: Proceeding of the twenty-sixth annual SIGCHI conference on Human factors in computing systems, pages 453-456, Florence, Italy.

Ravi Kumar, Jasmine Novak, and Andrew Tomkins. 2006 Structure and evolution of online social networks. KDD '06: Proceedings of the 12th ACM SIGKDD international conference on Knowledge discovery and data mining, pages 611-617, New York, NY.

C. Mair. 2005. The corpus-based study of language change in progress: The extra value of tagged corpora. The AAACL/ICAME Conference, Ann Arbor, MI.

Paul Rayson, James Walkerdine,William H. Fletcher, and Adam Kilgarriff. 2006. Annotated web as corpus The 2nd International Workshop on Web as Corpus (EACL06), Trento, Italy.

Kevin P. Scannell. 2007. The Crbadn Project: Corpus building for under-resourced languages. Proceedings of the 3rd Web as Corpus Workshop Louvain-la-Neuve, Belgium.

Rion Snow, Brendan O'Connor, Daniel Jurafsky, and Andrew Y. Ng. 2008. Cheap and fast – but is it good?: evaluating non-expert annotations for natural language tasks EMNLP '08: Proceedings of the Conference on Empirical Methods in Natural Language Processing, pages 254–263, Honolulu, Hawaii.

Erik F. Tjong, Kim Sang and Fien De Meulder 2003 Introduction to the conll-2003 shared task: language-independent named entity recognition. Association for Computational Linguistics, pages 142-147, Edmonton, Canada.

# A Proposal for a Configurable Silver Standard

**Udo Hahn, Katrin Tomanek, Elena Beisswanger** and **Erik Faessler**
Jena University Language & Information Engineering (JULIE) Lab
Friedrich-Schiller-Universität Jena
Fürstengraben 30, 07743 Jena, Germany
http://www.julielab.de

## Abstract

Among the many proposals to promote alternatives to costly to create gold standards, just recently the idea of a fully automatically, and thus cheaply, to set up silver standard has been launched. However, the current construction policy for such a silver standard requires crucial parameters (such as similarity thresholds and agreement cut-offs) to be set *a priori*, based on extensive testing though, at corpus compile time. Accordingly, such a corpus is static, once it is released. We here propose an alternative policy where silver standards can be dynamically optimized and customized on demand (given a specific goal function) using a gold standard as an oracle.

## 1 Introduction

Training natural language systems which rely on (semi-)supervised machine learning algorithms, or measuring the systems' performance requires some standardized ground truth from which one can learn or against which one evaluate, respectively. Usually, a manually crafted *gold standard* is provided that is generated by human language or domain experts after lots of iterative, guideline-based training rounds. This procedure is expensive, slow and yields only small, yet highly trustable, amounts of meta data – because human experts are in the loop.

In the CALBC project,[1] an alternative approach is currently under investigation (Rebholz-Schuhmann et al., 2010a). The basic idea is to generate the much needed ground truth automatically. This is achieved by letting a flock of named entity taggers run on a corpus, without imposing any restriction on the type(s) being annotated. The (most likely) heterogeneous results are automatically homogenized subsequently, thus yielding a consensus-based, machine-generated ground truth. Considering the possible benefits (e.g., the positive experience from boosting-style machine learners (Freund, 1990)), but also being aware of the possible drawbacks (varying quality of the different systems, skewed coverage of entity types, different types of guidelines on which they were trained, etc.), the CALBC consortium refers to the outcome of this process as a *silver standard* (Rebholz-Schuhmann et al., 2010a). This procedure is inexpensive, fast, yields huge amounts of meta data – because computers are in the loop – but after all its applicability and validity has yet to be determined experimentally.

The first silver standard corpus (SSC) that came out of the CALBC project was generated by the four main partners' named entity taggers.[2] The various contributions covered, among others, annotations for genes and proteins, chemicals, diseases, etc (Rebholz-Schuhmann et al., 2010b). After the submission of their runs, the SSC was generated by, first, harmonizing stretches of text in terms of entity mention identification and, second, by mapping these normalized mentions to agreed-upon type systems (such as the MESH Semantic Groups as described by Bodenreider and McCray (2003) for entity type normalization). Basically, the harmonization steps included rules when entity mentions were considered to match or overlap (using a cosine-based similarity criterion) and entity types referred to the same class. For consensus generation, finally, simple rules for majority votes were established.

The CALBC consortium is fully aware of the fact that the value of an SSC can only be assessed

[1] http://www.calbc.eu

[2] The CALBC consortium consists the Rebholz Group from EBI (Hinxton, U.K.), the Biosemantics Group from Erasmus (Rotterdam, The Netherlands), the JULIE Lab (Jena, Germany), and LINGUAMATICS (Cambridge, U.K.).



*Proceedings of the Fourth Linguistic Annotation Workshop, ACL 2010*, pages 235–242,
Uppsala, Sweden, 15-16 July 2010. ©2010 Association for Computational Linguistics

by comparing, e.g., systems trained on such a silver standard with systems trained on a gold standard (preferably, though not necessarily, one that is a subset of the document set which makes up the SSC).

In the absence of such a gold standard, the CALBC consortium has spent enormous efforts to find out the most reasonable parameter settings for, e.g., the cosine threshold (setting similar mentions apart from dissimilar ones) or the consensus constraint (where a certain number of entity types equally assigned by different taggers makes one type the consensual silver one and discards all alternative annotations). Once these criteria are made effective, the SSC is completely fixed.

As an alternative, we are looking for a more flexible solution. Our investigation was fuelled by the following observations:

- The idiosyncrasies of guidelines (on which (some) taggers were trained) do not necessarily lead to semantically totally different entities although they differ literally to some degree. Some guidelines prefer, e.g., *"human IL-7 protein"*, others favor *"human IL-7"*, and some lean towards *"IL-7"*. As the cosine measure tends to penalize a pair such as *"human IL-7 protein"* and *"IL-7"*, we intended to avoid such a prescriptive mode and just look at the type assignment for single tokens as (parts of) entity mentions. thus avoiding inconclusive mention boundary discussions.

- While we were counting, for all tokens of the document set, the votes a single token received from different taggers in terms of annotating this token with respect to some type, we generated confidence data for meta data assignments. Incorporating the distribution of confidence values into the configuration process, this allows us to get rid of *a priori* fixed majority criteria (e.g., two or three out of five systems must agree on this token) which are hard to justify in an absolute way.

Summarizing, we believe that the nature of diverging tasks to be solved, the levels of entity type specificity to be reached, the sort of guidelines being preferred, etc. should allow prospective users of a silver standard to *customize* one on their own and not stick to one that is already prefabricated without concrete application in mind.[3]

As such an enterprise would be quite arbitrary without a reference standard, we even go one step further. We determine the suitability of, say, different voting scores and varying lexical extensions of mentions by comparison to a gold standard so that the 'optimal' configuration of a silver standard, given a set of goal-derived requirements, can be automatically learned. In real-world applications, such gold standard annotations would be delivered only for a fraction of the documents contained in the entire corpus being tagged by a flock of taggers. The gold standard is used to optimize parameters which are subsequently applied to the aggregation of automatically annotated data. Note that the gold standard is used for optimization only, not for training. We call such a flexible, dynamically adjustable silver standard a *configurable Silver Standard Corpus* (conSSC). In a second step, we split the various conSSCs, re-trained our NER tagger on these data sets and, by comparison with the gold standard, were able to identify the optimal conSSC for this task (which is not the one (SSC I) made available by the CALBC consortium for the first challenge round).[4]

## 2 Optimizing Silver Standards

In this section, we describe the constituent parameters of a wide spectrum of SSCs. Mostly, these parameters were taken over from the design of the SSC as developed by the CALBC project members. Differing from that fixed SSC, we investigate the impact of different parameter settings on the construction of a collection of SSCs, and, first, evaluate their direct usefulness on a gold standard for protein-gene annotations. Second, we also assess their indirect usefulness by training NER classifiers on these SSCs and evaluate the NERs' performance on the gold standard. Thus, our approach is entirely data-driven without the need for human intervention in terms of choosing suitable parameter settings.

Technically, we first aggregate the votes from the flock of taggers (in our experiments, we used the four taggers from the CALBC project members plus a second tagger of one of the members) for each text token (for confidence-based decisions) or at the entity level (for cosine-based decisions), then we determine the confidence values of these

[3]There may be tasks where a "long" entity such as *"human IL-7 protein"* may be appropriate, while for another task a short one such as *"IL-7"* is entirely sufficient.

[4]`http://www.ebi.ac.uk/Rebholz-srv/CALBC/challenge.html`

aggregated votes, and, finally, we compute the similarity of the various SSCs with the gold standard data in terms of F-scores (both exact and open boundaries) and accuracy on the token level.

### 2.1 Calibrating Consensus

The metrical interpretation of consensus will be based on thresholded votes for semantic groups at the token level (cf. Section 2.1.1) and a cosine-based measure to determine contiguous stretches of entity mentions in the text (cf. Section 2.1.2).

#### 2.1.1 Type Confidence and Type Voting

For each text token, we determine the entity type assignment as generated by each NER tagger which is part of the flock of CALBC taggers.[5] We count and aggregate these votes such that each entity type has an associated type count value.

We then compute the ratio of systems agreeing on the same single type assignment and call this the *confidence* attributed to a particular type for some token. The confidence value will subsequently be interpreted against the *confidence threshold* $[0, 1]$ that defines a measure of certainty a type assignment should have in order to be accepted as consensual.

#### 2.1.2 Cosine-based Similarity of Phrasal Entity Mentions

As the above policy of token-wise annotation decouples contiguous entity mentions spanning over more than one token, we also want to restitute this phrasal structure. This is achieved by constructing contiguous sequences of tokens that characterize a phrasal entity mention at the text level to which the same type label has been assigned. Since different taggers tend to identify different spans of text for the same entity type (as shown in the example from Section 1) we have to account for similar phrasal forms of named entity mentions.

This is achieved by constructing vectors which represent entity mentions and by computing the cosine between the different entity mention vectors. Let $E_1 = T_1T_2T_3$ be an entity mention comprised of three tokens $T_1$ to $T_3$. Let $E_2 = T_2T_3$ be an entity mention overlapping with $E_1$ in the tokens $T_2$ and $T_3$. To decide whether $E_1$ and $E_2$ are considered similar, we first construct two vectors representing the entity mentions:

$$v(E_1) = (f_1, f_2, f_3)^T$$

with $f_i = IDF(T_i)$ being the inverse document frequency of the token $T_i$. We compute the inverse document frequency of tokens based on the corpus which is subject to analysis. Analogously, we construct the vector for $E_2$

$$v(E_2) = (0, f_2, f_3)^T$$

filling in a zero for the IDF of $T_1$ since it is not covered by $E_2$. The entity mentions $E_1$ and $E_2$ are considered equal or similar, if the cosine of the two vectors is greater or equal a given threshold, $\cos(v(E_1), v(E_2)) \geq threshold$.[6] We then compute the number of systems considering an entity annotation as similar in the manner described above. The annotation is accepted and thus entered into the SSC, if a particular number of systems agree on one annotation. This approach was previously developed by the CALBC project partners (Rebholz-Schuhmann et al., 2010a).

The number of agreeing systems and the threshold are the free parameters of this method and thus subject to optimization.

### 2.2 Optimization of Silver Standard Corpora

In the experiments described in the next section, we will consider alternative parametrizations for Silver Standard Corpora, i.e., the required confidence threshold or cosine threshold and the number of agreeing systems. We will then discuss two variants for optimizing this collection of SSCs. The first one directly uses the gold standard for optimization. The task will be to find that particular parameter setting for an SSC which best fits the data contained in the gold standard. Once these parameters are determined they can be applied to the complete CALBC document set (composed of 100,000 documents) to produce the final, quasi-optimal SSC.

In another variant, we insert a classifier into this loop. First, we train a classifier on a particular

[5]Due to time constraints when we performed our experiments, we make an extremely simplifying assumption: From the whole range of possible entity types NER taggers may assign to some token (cf. (Bodenreider and McCray, 2003)) we have chosen the PRotein/GEne group for testing. Still, this assumption does not do harm to the core of our hypotheses. See also our discussion in Section 5.

[6]For final corpus creation, it must be decided which of the matching entity mentions is entered into the reference SSC, e.g. the longest or shortest entity annotation. In our experiments, we always chose the shortest entity mention. However, preliminary experiments showed that the differences to taking the longest entity mention were marginal.

SSC that is built from a particular parameter combination. Next, this classifier is tested against the gold standard. This is iterated through all parameter combinations. Obviously, the best performing classifier relative to the gold standard selects the optimal SSC.

## 3 Experimental Setting

### 3.1 Gold Standard

We generated a new broad-coverage corpus composed of 3,236 MEDLINE abstracts (35,519 sentences or 941,890 tokens) dealing with gene and protein mentions. Altogether, it comprises 57,889 named entity type annotations annotated by one expert biologist. We created this new resource to have a consistent and (as far as possible) subdomain-independent protein-annotated corpus.[7]

MEDLINE abstracts were annotated with (protein coding) genes, mRNAs and proteins. A distinction was made between dedicated proteins as they are recorded in the protein database UNIPROT,[8] protein complexes consisting of several protein subunits (e.g., IL-2 receptor consisting of $\alpha$, $\beta$, and $\gamma$ chain), and protein families or groups (e.g., "transcription factors"). Also enumerations of proteins and protein variants were annotated. Discontinuous annotations were avoided as well as nested annotations (annotations embedded in other annotations). However, gene/protein mentions nested in terms other than gene/protein mentions were annotated (e.g., protein mentions nested in protein function descriptions such as *"ligase"* in *"ligase activity"*). Modifiers such as species designators were excluded from annotations whenever possible. Gene segments or protein fragments were also not annotated.

For our experiments, we did not distinguish between the different annotation classes (see Table 1) but merged all available annotations into one class, *viz.* PRotein/GEne (PRGE).

### 3.2 Automatic Annotation of the Gold Standard

We then asked all four sites participating in the CALBC project to automatically annotate the given gold standard (made available without gold data,

[7]We are aware of other gene/protein-annotated corpora such as PENNBIOIE (http://bioie.ldc.upenn.edu/) or GENIA (http://www-tsujii.is.s.u-tokyo.ac.jp/GENIA/home/wiki.cgi) that will have to be taken into account in future studies as well.

[8]http://www.uniprot.org/

| semantic type | description |
|---|---|
| T028 | Gene or Genome |
| T086 | Nucleotide Sequence |
| T087 | Amino Acid Sequence, Amino Acid, Peptide |
| T116 | Protein |
| T126 | Enzyme |
| T192 | Receptor |

Table 1: Semantic types defining the PRGE group (semantic type codes refer to the UMLS).

of course) using the same type of named entity tagging machinery as was used to annotate CALBC's canonical SSC. The performance results of each group's system evaluated against the gold standard are reported in Table 2. The data of each system constitute the reference data sets and raw data for all subsequent experiments on the configuration and optimization of the silver standard.

The resulting raw material does thus not only contain gene/protein annotations but also any other entity types as supplied by the partners. For our experiments on the gold standard, however, only the entity types subsumed by the PRGE group (see Table 1) were considered and annotations of all other types were discarded. The definition of the PRGE group is identical to the one proposed by Rebholz-Schuhmann et al. (2010a). For the experiments, the specific semantic types (e.g., the UMLS concepts)[9] were not considered, only the semantic group PRGE was.

### 3.3 Evaluation Metrics

The following metrics were used to evaluate how good the silver standard(s) fit(s) the provided gold standard:

- segment-level recall, precision, and F-score values with exact boundaries, the standard way to evaluate NER taggers,
- segment-level recall, precision, and F-score, but with relaxed boundary constraints. This means that two entity mentions are considered to match when they overlap with at least one token and have the same entity type assigned to them,
- accuracy measured on the token level.

These metrics can be considered as optimization criteria.

[9]http://www.nlm.nih.gov/research/umls/

### 3.4 Tokenization

The CALBC partners' data do not necessarily come with tokenization information and, moreover, different partners/systems might have different tokenizations. Since a common ground for comparison is thus lacking we added a new, consistent tokenization based on the JULIE Lab tokenizer (Tomanek et al., 2007b). This tokenizer is optimized for biomedical documents with intrinsic focus to keep complex biological terminological units (such as *"IL-2"*) unsegmented, but to split up tokens that are not terminologically connected (such as dividing *"IL-2-related"* up into *"IL-2"*, "-" and *"related"*). As a matter of fact, entity boundaries do not necessarily coincide with token boundaries. Our solution to this problem is as follows: Whenever a token partially overlaps with an entity name, the full form of that token is considered to be associated with this entity. All data on which we report here (silver and gold standards) obey to this tokenization scheme.

### 3.5 Parameters Being Tested

The following parameter settings were considered in our experiments:

- Four different values for confidence thresholds indicating that 20% (0.2), 40% (0.4), 60% (0.6) or 80% (0.8) of all taggers agreed on the same type annotation, *viz.* PRGE,
- Five different values for cosine thresholds to identify overlapping entity mentions, *viz.* $(0.7, 0.8, 0.9, 0.95, 0.975)$, and two different values for the number $n$ of agreeing taggers, *viz.* $n \geq 2$ and $n \geq 3$,
- Two tagger crowd scenarios, *viz.* one where *all five* systems were involved, the other where subsets of cardinality *2* of these crowds were re-combined.[10]

## 4 Results

As already described in Section 2.2, we performed two types of experiments. In the first experiment (Section 4.1), we intend to find proper calibrations of parameters for an optimal SSC as described in Section 3.5. In the second experiment (Section 4.2), we incorporate an extrinsic task, training an NER classifier on different parameter settings, as a selector for the optimal SSC.

[10]We refrained from also testing combinations of *3* and *4* systems due to time constraints.

### 4.1 Intrinsic Calibration of Parameters

**Full Merger of All Taggers.** In this scenario, we tested the merged results of the entire crowd of CALBC taggers when compared to the gold standard and determined their performance scores (see Table 3). We will discuss the results with respect to the overlapping F-score, if not explicitly stated otherwise.

Looking at the results of the runs involving different *cosine* thresholds, we witness a systematic drawback when more than two systems are required to agree. Although precision is boosted in this setting, recall is decreasing strongly which results in overall lower F-scores. When only two systems are required to agree a comparatively higher recall comes at the cost of lower precision. Yet, the F-score (both under exact as well as overlap conditions) is always superior (ranging between 75% and 73%) when compared to the 3-agreement scenario. Note that the 2-agreement condition for the highest threshold being tested yields, without exception, better scores than the best single system (cf. Table 2).

The best performing run in terms of F-score for the *confidence* method results from a threshold of 0.2 with an F-score of 76%. Note that this F-score lies *4* percentage points above the best performance of a single system (cf. Table 2).

A threshold of *0.2* with five contributing systems results in a union of all annotations. Consequently, this run benefits from a high recall compared with the other runs. However, the run exhibits the lowest precision rating (both for the exact and overlap condition), which is due to the low threshold being chosen. As can also be seen with the confidence method at a threshold of 0.80, a very high precision can be reached (99%) but at the cost of extremely low recall.[11] The methods performing best in terms of overlapping F-score also perform best in terms of exact F-score.

**Selected Tagger Combinations: Twin Taggers.** In this scenario, we evaluated all twin combinations of taggers against the gold standard regarding the confidence criterion. In Table 4 we contrast the two best performing and the two worst performing tagger pairs for the confidence method. The table reveals that there are some cases where the taggers seem to complement each other, e.g., the twins SYS-1 and SYS-3, as well as SYS-3 and

[11]Exactly these kinds of alternatives offer flexibility for choosing the most appropriate SSC given a specific task.

| exactR | exactP | exactF | overlapR | overlapP | overlapF | systems |
|---|---|---|---|---|---|---|
| **0.55** | 0.74 | **0.63** | **0.63** | 0.84 | **0.72** | SYS-1 |
| 0.36 | 0.53 | 0.43 | 0.46 | 0.68 | 0.55 | SYS-2 |
| 0.48 | 0.77 | 0.59 | 0.59 | **0.95** | **0.72** | SYS-3 |
| 0.44 | **0.83** | 0.58 | 0.49 | 0.91 | 0.64 | SYS-4 |
| 0.34 | 0.61 | 0.44 | 0.41 | 0.74 | 0.53 | SYS-5 |

Table 2: Performance of single systems (SYS-1 to SYS-5) as evaluated against the gold standard (best performance scores in bold face). Measurements are taken both for exact as well as overlapping recall (R), precision (P) and F-score (F).

| method | ACC | exactR | exactP | exactF | overlapR | overlapP | overlapF | threshold | agr. systems |
|---|---|---|---|---|---|---|---|---|---|
| cosine | **0.94** | **0.53** | 0.71 | **0.61** | **0.66** | 0.87 | **0.75** | 0.70 | 2.00 |
| cosine | 0.93 | 0.40 | **0.79** | 0.53 | 0.49 | **0.96** | 0.65 | 0.70 | 3.00 |
| cosine | **0.94** | **0.54** | 0.71 | **0.61** | **0.65** | 0.87 | **0.74** | 0.80 | 2.00 |
| cosine | 0.93 | 0.41 | **0.80** | 0.54 | 0.48 | **0.95** | 0.64 | 0.80 | 3.00 |
| cosine | **0.94** | **0.54** | 0.72 | **0.62** | **0.65** | 0.86 | **0.74** | 0.90 | 2.00 |
| cosine | 0.93 | 0.41 | **0.81** | 0.54 | 0.48 | **0.95** | 0.64 | 0.90 | 3.00 |
| cosine | **0.94** | **0.54** | 0.73 | **0.62** | **0.64** | 0.86 | **0.74** | 0.95 | 2.00 |
| cosine | 0.93 | 0.41 | **0.83** | 0.55 | 0.47 | **0.95** | 0.63 | 0.95 | 3.00 |
| cosine | **0.94** | **0.55** | 0.75 | **0.64** | **0.64** | 0.86 | **0.73** | 0.97 | 2.00 |
| cosine | 0.93 | 0.42 | **0.85** | 0.56 | 0.47 | **0.95** | 0.63 | 0.97 | 3.00 |
| confidence | **0.95** | **0.58** | 0.73 | **0.65** | **0.68** | 0.85 | **0.76** | 0.20 | |
| confidence | 0.94 | 0.44 | 0.83 | 0.58 | 0.50 | 0.94 | 0.66 | 0.40 | |
| confidence | 0.93 | 0.32 | 0.88 | 0.47 | 0.35 | 0.97 | 0.52 | 0.60 | |
| confidence | 0.91 | 0.16 | **0.91** | 0.27 | 0.17 | **0.99** | 0.30 | 0.80 | |

Table 3: Merged annotations of the entire crowd of CALBC taggers (best performance scores per parameter setting in bold face). Parameters: threshold (confidence or cosine) and number of agreeing systems (agr. systems).

SYS-4. In both cases, a confidence threshold of 0.2 yields the best F-score. Additionally, these F-scores (81% and 78%) are even higher than the single system's F-scores (+9% up to +14%). This comes with a significant increase in recall over both systems (+13% to +28%) though at the cost of lowered precision relative to the system with the higher precision (−1% to −10%). These results also outperform the best results of the experimental runs where all systems were involved (see Table 3). This indicates that a subset of all systems might yield a better SSC than a combination of all systems' outputs.

## 4.2 Extrinsic Calibration of Parameters

We employed a standard named entity tagger to assess the impact of the different merging strategies on a scenario near to a real-world application.[12] Each SSC variant (and thus each parameter combination) was evaluated with this tagger in a 10-fold cross validation. The SSC and the gold corpus were split into ten parts of equal size. Nine parts of the SSC constituted the training data of one cross validation round, the corresponding tenth part of the gold standard was used for evaluation. This way, we tested how adequate a merged corpus was with respect to the training of a classifier. Because the cross validation has been very time consuming, we did not consider specific combinations of systems but always merged the annotations of all five systems. The results are displayed in Table 5.

Interestingly, the highest recall, precision, and F-score values (both for the exact and overlap condition) are shared by the same parameter combinations which also performed best in Section 4.1. Hence, the use of a named entity tagger supports the evaluation results when comparing the various

[12]This tagger is based on Conditional Random Fields (Lafferty et al., 2001) and employs a standard feature set used for biomedical entity recognition (Settles, 2004).

| ACC | exactR | exactP | exactF | overlapR | overlapP | overlapF | systems | threshold |
|---|---|---|---|---|---|---|---|---|
| 0.95 | 0.62 | 0.69 | 0.65 | **0.76** | **0.85** | **0.81** | **SYS-1 + SYS-3** | 0.20 |
| 0.92 | 0.22 | 0.69 | 0.34 | 0.26 | 0.81 | 0.39 | SYS-2 + SYS-5 | 0.60 |
| 0.95 | 0.55 | 0.75 | 0.63 | **0.67** | **0.91** | **0.78** | **SYS-3 + SYS-4** | 0.20 |
| 0.92 | 0.30 | 0.85 | 0.45 | 0.34 | 0.94 | 0.50 | SYS-4 + SYS-5 | 0.60 |

Table 4: Twin pairs of taggers, contrasting the two best (in bold face) and the two worst performing pairs obtained by the confidence method.

| method | ACC | exactR | exactP | exactF | overlapR | overlapP | overlapF | threshold | agr. systems |
|---|---|---|---|---|---|---|---|---|---|
| cosine | **0.94** | **0.46** | 0.69 | **0.56** | **0.58** | 0.86 | **0.69** | 0.70 | 2.00 |
| cosine | 0.93 | 0.32 | **0.77** | 0.45 | 0.39 | **0.94** | 0.55 | 0.70 | 3.00 |
| cosine | **0.94** | **0.46** | 0.69 | **0.56** | **0.57** | 0.86 | **0.69** | 0.80 | 2.00 |
| cosine | 0.93 | 0.32 | **0.78** | 0.46 | 0.39 | **0.94** | 0.55 | 0.80 | 3.00 |
| cosine | **0.94** | **0.46** | 0.70 | **0.56** | **0.57** | 0.85 | **0.68** | 0.90 | 2.00 |
| cosine | 0.93 | 0.32 | **0.79** | 0.46 | 0.38 | **0.93** | 0.54 | 0.90 | 3.00 |
| cosine | **0.94** | **0.47** | 0.71 | **0.56** | **0.56** | 0.85 | **0.68** | 0.95 | 2.00 |
| cosine | 0.93 | 0.33 | **0.80** | 0.47 | 0.38 | **0.93** | 0.54 | 0.95 | 3.00 |
| cosine | **0.94** | **0.47** | 0.73 | **0.57** | **0.56** | 0.85 | **0.67** | 0.97 | 2.00 |
| cosine | 0.93 | 0.33 | **0.82** | 0.47 | 0.38 | **0.93** | 0.54 | 0.97 | 3.00 |
| confidence | **0.94** | **0.50** | 0.72 | **0.59** | **0.60** | 0.85 | **0.70** | 0.20 | |
| confidence | 0.93 | 0.36 | 0.82 | 0.50 | 0.41 | 0.93 | 0.56 | 0.40 | |
| confidence | 0.92 | 0.25 | 0.87 | 0.39 | 0.28 | 0.95 | 0.43 | 0.60 | |
| confidence | 0.91 | 0.12 | **0.89** | 0.20 | 0.12 | **0.96** | 0.22 | 0.80 | |

Table 5: Performance of an NER tagger trained on an SSC, 10-fold cross validation, and all systems. Parameters: threshold (confidence or cosine) and number of agreeing systems (agr. systems).

SSCs directly to the gold standard corpus. However, this result may be due to our particular experimental setting and should not be taken as a general rule. Instead, this issue should be studied on additional gold standard corpora (cf. Section 5).

## 5 Discussion and Conclusions

The experiments reported in this paper strengthen the empirical basis of the novel idea of a silver standard corpus (SSC). While the originators of the SSC have come up with a fixed SSC, our experiments show that different parametrizations of SSCs allow to dynamically configure or select an optimal one given a gold standard for comparison during this optimization.

Our experimental data reveals that the boosting hypothesis (the combination of several classifiers outperforms weaker single ones in terms of performance) is confirmed for complete mergers as well as selected twin pairs of taggers. We also have evidence that boosting within the SSC paradigm tends to increase precision whereas it seems to decrease recall. This general observation becomes stronger and stronger when the size of the committees (i.e., the number of submitting classifiers) increases. It is also particularly interesting that both the intrinsic evaluation (groups of classifiers *vs.* gold standard), as well as the extrinsic evaluation of SSCs (groups of classifiers trained and tested on mutually exclusive partitions of the gold standard) reveal parallel patterns in terms of performance – this indicates a surprising level of stability of the entire SSC approach.

In our view, the strongest finding from our experiments is the possibility to calibrate an SSC according to requirements derived from the goal of annotation campaigns. In particular, one can adapt parameters to a specific use case, e.g., building a corpus with high precision when compared to the gold standard. Through the evaluation of the parameter space, one can assess the costs of reaching a specific goal. For instance, a precision of 99% can be reached, yet at the cost of the F-score plunging to 30%; only slightly lowering the precision to 97% boosts the F-score by 22 points (see last two rows in Table 3).

Also, when increasingly more annotation sets become available (e.g., through the CALBC challenges) the problem of adversarial or extremely bad performing systems is no longer a pressing issue since with the optimization approach such systems are automatically sorted out when optimizing over the set of possible system combinations.

While our experiments are but a first step towards the consolidation of the SSC paradigm some obvious limitations of our work have to be overcome:

- experiments with different gold standards have to be run as one might hypothesize that different gold standards require different parameter settings for the optimal SSC,
- experiments with different NER taggers have to be run (e.g., we plan to use an NER tagger which prefers recall over precision, while the one used for these experiments generally yields higher precision than recall scores),
- test with crowds of taggers which generate higher recall than precision.[13]

In our approach, a gold standard is needed to find good parameters to build an SSC. A question not addressed so far is how huge such a gold standard must be to offer an appropriate size for the optimization step. Finally, it might be particularly rewarding to join efforts in reducing the development costs for such a gold standards – Active Learning (e.g., Tomanek et al. (2007a)) might be one promising approach to break this bottleneck. Since effective calibration of SSCs is in need of reasonably sized and densely populated gold standards, by combining these lines of research we claim that additional benefits for SSCs become viable.

## 6 Acknowledgments

We wish to thank Kerstin Hornbostel for stimulating and corrective remarks on the biological grounding of this investigation. This research was partially funded by the EC's 7th Framework Programme within the CALBC project (FP7-231727) and the GERONTOSYS research initiative from the German Federal Ministry of Education and Research (BMBF) under grant 0315581D within the JENAGE project.

[13]We used a gold standard in which some unusual entities (e.g., protein families) had been annotated for which most named entity taggers have not been trained. This might also explain the generally overall low recall among the crowd of taggers yielded in our experiments.

## References

Olivier Bodenreider and Alexa T. McCray. 2003. Exploring semantic groups through visual approaches. *Journal of Biomedical Informatics*, 36(6):414–432.

Yoav Freund. 1990. Boosting a weak learning algorithm by majority. In *COLT'90 – Proceedings of the 3rd Annual Workshop on Computational Learning Theory*, pages 202–216.

John D. Lafferty, Andrew McCallum, and Fernando Pereira. 2001. Conditional random fields: Probabilistic models for segmenting and labeling sequence data. In *ICML'01 – Proceedings of the 18th International Conference on Machine Learning*, pages 282–289.

Dietrich Rebholz-Schuhmann, Antonio José Jimeno Yepes, Erik van Mulligen, Ning Kang, Jan Kors, David Milward, Peter Corbett, Ekaterina Buyko, Elena Beisswanger, and Udo Hahn. 2010a. CALBC Silver Standard Corpus. *Journal of Bioinformatics and Computational Biology*, 8:163–179.

Dietrich Rebholz-Schuhmann, Antonio José Jimeno Yepes, Erik M. van Mulligen, Ning Kang, Jan Kors, Peter Milward, David Corbett, Ekaterina Buyko, Katrin Tomanek, Elena Beisswanger, and Udo Hahn. 2010b. The CALBC Silver Standard Corpus for biomedical named entities: A study in harmonizing the contributions from four independent named entity taggers. In *LREC 2010 – Proceedings of the 7th International Conference on Language Resources and Evaluation*.

Burr Settles. 2004. Biomedical named entity recognition using conditional random fields and rich feature sets. In *NLPBA/BioNLP 2004 – COLING 2004 International Joint Workshop on Natural Language Processing in Biomedicine and its Applications*, pages 107–110.

Katrin Tomanek, Joachim Wermter, and Udo Hahn. 2007a. An approach to text corpus construction which cuts annotation costs and maintains corpus reusability of annotated data. In *EMNLP-CoNLL'07 – Proceedings of the 2007 Joint Conference on Empirical Methods in Natural Language Processing and Computational Language Learning*, pages 486–495.

Katrin Tomanek, Joachim Wermter, and Udo Hahn. 2007b. A reappraisal of sentence and token splitting for life sciences documents. In K. A. Kuhn, J. R. Warren, and T. Y. Leong, editors, *MEDINFO'07 – Proceedings of the 12th World Congress on Medical Informatics*, number 129 in Studies in Health Technology and Informatics, pages 524–528. IOS Press.

# A Hybrid Model for Annotating Named Entity Training Corpora

**Robert Voyer, Valerie Nygaard, Will Fitzgerald, and Hannah Copperman**
Microsoft
475 Brannan St. Suite 330
San Francisco, CA 94107, USA
{Robert.Voyer, Valerie.Nygaard, Will.Fitzgerald, Hannah.Copperman}@microsoft.com

## Abstract

In this paper, we present a two-phase, hybrid model for generating training data for Named Entity Recognition systems. In the first phase, a trained annotator labels all named entities in a text irrespective of type. In the second phase, naïve crowdsourcing workers complete binary judgment tasks to indicate the type(s) of each entity. Decomposing the data generation task in this way results in a flexible, reusable corpus that accommodates changes to entity type taxonomies. In addition, it makes efficient use of precious trained annotator resources by leveraging highly available and cost effective crowdsourcing worker pools in a way that does not sacrifice quality.

**Keywords:** annotation scheme design, annotation tools and systems, corpus annotation, annotation for machine learning

## 1 Background

The task of Named Entity Recognition (NER) is fundamental to many Natural Language Processing pipelines. Named entity recognizers are most commonly built as machine learned systems that require annotated training data. Manual annotation of named entities is an expensive process, and as a result, much recent work has been done to acquire training corpora automatically from the web. Automatic training corpus acquisition usually requires the existence of one or more first-pass classifiers to identify documents that correspond to a predetermined entity ontology. Using this sort of approach requires an additional set of training data for the initial classifier. More importantly, the quality of our training corpus is limited by the accuracy of any preliminary classifiers. Each automatic step in the process corresponds to increased error in the resulting system. It is not unusual for NE annotation schemas to change as the intended application of NER systems evolves over time – an issue that is rarely mentioned in the literature. Extending named entity ontologies when using an automated approach like the one outlined in (Nothman, 2008), for example, requires non-trivial modifications and extensions to an existing system and may render obsolete any previously collected data.

Our NER system serves a dual purpose; its primary function is to aid our deep natural language parser by identifying single and multiword named entities (NE) in Wikipedia articles. In addition to rendering these phrases as opaque units, the same classifier categorizes these entities as belonging to one of four classes: person, location, organization, and miscellaneous. These class labels serve as additional features that are passed downstream and facilitate parsing. Once identified and labeled, we then add corresponding entries to our semantic index for improved ranking and retrieval.

We scoped each type in the repertoire mentioned above in an attempt to most effectively support our parser and the end-to-end retrieval task. While this taxonomy resembles the one used in the 7th Message Understanding Conference (MUC-7) NER shared task (Chinchor, 1998), our specification is in fact slightly nuanced. For example, the organization and location classes used in our production system are much more limited, disallowing governmental committees, subcommittees, and other organizations that fall under the MUC-7 definition of organization. Indeed, the determination of types to tag and the definitions of these types is very much dependent upon the application for which a given NER system is being designed. Accurate



*Proceedings of the Fourth Linguistic Annotation Workshop, ACL 2010*, pages 243–246,
Uppsala, Sweden, 15-16 July 2010. 

training and evaluation of NER systems therefore requires application-specific corpora.

Previously, we collected training documents for our system with a more automated two-pass system. In the first pass, we used a set of predefined heuristic rules – based on sequences of part-of-speech (POS) tags and common NE patterns – to identify overlapping candidate spans in the source data. These candidates were then uploaded as tasks to Amazon Mechanical Turk (AMT), in which users were asked to determine if the selected entity was one of 5 specified types. We used majority vote to choose the best decision. Candidates with no majority vote were resubmitted for additional Turker input.

There were a few drawbacks with this system. First and foremost, while the heuristics to identify candidate spans were designed to deliver high recall, it was impossible to have perfect coverage. This imposed an upper bound on the coverage of the system learning from this data. Recall would inevitably decline if we extended our NE taxonomy to include less formulaic types such as titles and band names, for example. One could imagine injecting additional layers of automatic candidate generators into the system to improve recall, each of which would incur additional overhead in judgment cost or complexity. The next issue was quality; many workers tried to scam the system, and others didn't quite understand the task, specifically when it came to differentiating types. The need to address these issues is what led us to our current annotation model.

## 2 Objective

As the search application supported by our NER system evolved, it became clear both that we would need to be able to support additional name types and that there was a demand for a lighter weight system to identify (especially multiword) NE spans without the need to specify the type. The underlying technology at the core of our existing NER software is well suited for such classification tasks. The central hurdle to extending our system in this way is acquiring a suitable training corpus. Consider the following list of potential classifiers:

1. A single type system capable of identifying product names
2. A targeted system for identifying only movie titles and person names
3. A generic NE span tagger for tagging all named entities
4. A generic-span tagger that tags all multiword named entities

Given that manual annotation is an extremely costly task, we consider optimization of our corpora for reuse while maintaining quality in all supported systems to be a primary goal. Secondly, although throughput is important – it is often said that quantity trumps quality in machine learned systems – the quality of the data is very highly correlated with the accuracy of the systems in question. At the scale of our typical training corpus – one to ten thousand documents – the quality of the data has a significant impact.

## 3 Methodology

In general, decomposing multifaceted annotation tasks into their fundamental decision points reduces the cognitive load on annotators, increasing annotator throughput while ultimately improving the quality of the marked-up data (Medero et al., 2006). Identifying named entities can be decomposed into two tasks: identifying the span of the entity and determining its type(s). Based on our experience, the first of these tasks requires much more training than the second. The corner cases that arise in determining if any arbitrary sequence of tokens is a named entity make this first task significantly more complex than determining if a given name is, for example, a person name. Decomposing the task into span identification and type judgment has two distinct advantages:

- The span-identification task can be given to more highly trained annotators who are following a specification, while the relatively simpler task can be distributed to naïve/crowdsource judges.
- The task given to the trained annotators goes much more quickly, increasing their throughput.

In a round of pilot tasks, our Corpus Development team performed dual-annotation and complete adjudication on a small sample of 100 documents. We used the output of these tasks to help identify areas of inconsistency in annotator behavior as well as vagueness in the specification. This initial round provided helpful feedback, which we used both to refine the task specification and to help inform the intuitions of our annotators.

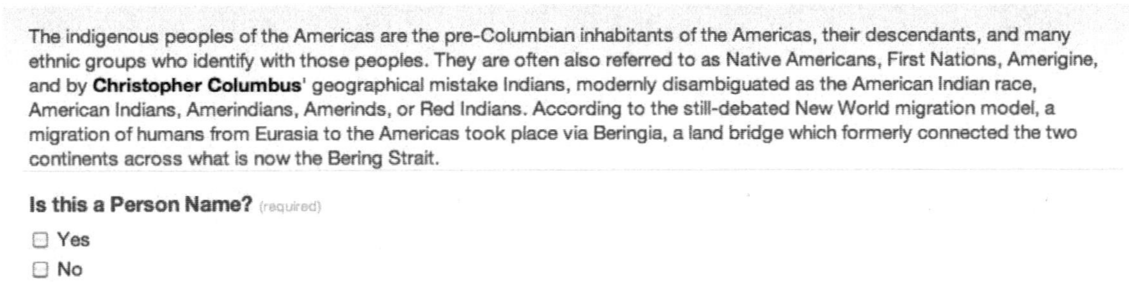


**Figure 1: A NE type task in the Crowdflower interface**

After these initial tasks, inter-annotator agreement was estimated at 91%, which can be taken to be a reasonable upper bound for our automated system.

In our current process, the data is first marked up by a trained annotator and then checked over by a second trained annotator, and finally undergoes automatic post-processing to catch common errors. Thus, our first step in addressing the issue of poor data quality is to remove the step of automated NE candidate generation and to shift part of the cognitive load of the task from untrained workers to expert annotators.

After span-tagged data has been published by our Corpus Development team, in order to get typed NE annotations for our existing system, we then submit candidate spans along with a two additional sentences of context to workers on AMT. Workers are presented with assignments that require simple binary decisions (Figure 1). Is the selected entity of type X – yes or no? Each unit is presented to at least 5 different workers. We follow this procedure for all labeled spans in our tagged corpus. This entire process can be completed for all of the types that we're interested in – person, location, organization, product, title, etc. Extending this system to cover arbitrary additional types requires simply that we create a new task template and instructions for workers.

Instead of putting these tasks directly onto AMT, we chose to leverage Crowdflower for its added quality control. Crowdflower is a crowdsourcing service built on top of AMT that associates a trust level with workers based on their performance on gold data and uses these trust levels to determine the correctness of worker responses. It provides functionality for retrieving aggregated reports, in which responses are aggregated not based on simple majority voting, but rather by users' trust levels. Our early experiments with this service indicate that it does in fact improve the quality of the output data. An added bonus of their technology is that we can associate confidence levels with the labels produced by workers in their system.

This entire process yields several different annotated versions of the same corpus: an un-typed named entity training corpus, along with an additional corpus for each named entity type. Ideally, each NE span submitted to workers will come back as belonging to zero or one classes. How do we reconcile the fact that our existing system requires a single label per token, when some tokens may in fact fall under multiple categories? Merging the type labels produced by Turkers (with the help of Crowdflower) is an interesting problem in itself. Ultimately, we arrived at a system that allows us to remove type labels that do not meet a confidence threshold, while also biasing certain types over others based on their difficulty. Interestingly, agreement rates among crowdsourcing workers can provide useful insight into the difficulty of labeling some types over others, potentially indicating which types are less precisely scoped. We consistently saw inter-judge agreement rates in the 92%–97% range for person names and locations, while agreement on the less well-defined category of organizations often yielded agreement rates closer to 85%.

## 4 Initial Results

As a first level comparison of how the new approach affects the overall accuracy of our system, we trained two named entity recognizers. The first system was trained on a subset of the training data collected using the old approach. System 2 was trained on a subset of documents collected using the new approach. Both systems are trained using only a single type – person names. For the former, we randomly selected 200 docs from our previous canonical training set, with the guiding principle that we should have roughly the same number of sentences as exist in our new training corpus (~7400 sentences). Both systems were evaluated against one of our standard, blind measurement sets, hand-annotated with personal names. The results in table 1 indicate the strict phrase-level precision, recall, and F-score.

It bears mentioning that many NER systems report token-level accuracy or F-score using a flexible phrase-level metric that gives partial credit if either the type classification is correct or the span boundaries are correct. Naturally, these metrics result in higher accuracy numbers when compared to the strict phrase-level metric that we use. Our evaluation tool gives credit to instances where both boundaries and type are correct. Incorrect instances incur at least 2 penalties, counting as at least 1 false positive and 1 false negative, depending on the nature of the error. We optimize our system for high precision.

| System | P | R | F-score |
|---|---|---|---|
| Old system | 89.7 | 70.3 | 78.9 |
| New system | 91.6 | 72.1 | 80.7 |

**Table 1: Strict phrase-level precision, recall, and F-score.**

Our other target application is a generic entity tagger. For this experiment we trained on our complete set of 817 training documents (14,297 sentences) where documents are tagged for all named entities and types are not labeled. We evaluated the resulting system on a blind 100-document measurement set in which generic NE spans have been manually labeled by our Corpus Development team. These results are included in Table 2.

| System | P | R | F-score |
|---|---|---|---|
| Generic span | 80.3 | 85.7 | 82.9 |

**Table 2: Strict phrase-level precision, recall and F-score for generic span tagging.**

## 5 Conclusions

The results indicate that our new approach does indeed produce higher quality training data. An improvement of 1.8 F-score points is relatively significant, particularly given the size of the training set used in this experiment. It is worth noting that our previous canonical training set underwent a round of manual editing after it was discovered that there were significant quality issues. The system trained on the curated data showed marked improvement over previous versions. Given this, we could expect to see a greater disparity between the two systems if we used the output of our previous training data collection system as is.

The generic named entity tagger requires significantly fewer features than type-aware systems, allowing us to improve F-score while also improving runtime performance. We expect to be able to improve precision to acceptable production levels (>90%) while maintaining F-score with a bit more feature engineering, making this system comparable to other state-of-the-art systems.

To extend and improve these initial experiments, we would like to use identical documents for both single-type systems, compare performance on additional NE types, and analyze the learning curve of both systems as we increase the size of the training corpus.

## References


Joohui An, Seungwoo Lee, and Gary Geunbae Lee. 2003. Automatic acquisition of named entity tagged corpus from world wide web. *The Companion Volume to the Proceedings of 41st Annual Meeting of the Association for Computational Linguistics*, pages 165-168.

Nancy Chinchor. 1998. Overview of MUC-7. *Proceedings of the 7th Message Understanding Conference.*

Julie Medero, Kazuaki Maeda, Stephanie Strassel, and Christopher Walker. 2006. An Efficient Approach to Gold-Standard Annotation: Decision Points for Complex Tasks. *Proceedings of the Fifth International Conference on Language Resources and Evaluation.*

Joel Nothman, Tara Murphy, and James R. Curran. 2009. Analyzing Wikipedia and Gold-Standard Corpora for NER Training. *Proceedings of the 12th Conference of the European Chapter of the Association for Computational Linguistics*, pages 612-620.

Joel Nothman, James R. Curran, and Tara Murphy. 2008. Transforming Wikipedia into named entity training data. *Proceedings of the Australian Language Technology Workshop*, pages 124–132.

Lee Ratinov and Dan Roth. 2009. Design challenges and misconceptions in named entity recognition. *Proceedings of the Thirteenth Conference on Computational Natural Language Learning* (CoNLL-2009), pages 147-155.

# Anatomy of Annotation Schemes: Mapping to GrAF

**Nancy Ide**
Department of Computer Science
Vassar College
Poughkeepsie, NY, USA
ide@cs.vassar.edu

**Harry Bunt**
Tilburg Center for Creative Computing
Tilburg University, The Netherlands
harry.bunt@uvt.nl

## Abstract

In this paper, we apply the annotation scheme design methodology defined in (Bunt, 2010) and demonstrate its use for generating a mapping from an existing annotation scheme to a representation in GrAF format. The most important features of this methodology are (1) the distinction of the abstract and concrete syntax of an annotation language; (2) the specification of a formal semantics for the abstract syntax; and (3) the formalization of the relation between abstract and concrete syntax, which guarantees that any concrete syntax inherits the semantics of the abstract syntax, and thus guarantees meaning-preserving mappings between representation formats. By way of illustration, we apply this mapping strategy to annotations from ISO-TimeML, PropBank, and FrameNet.

## 1 Introduction

The Linguistic Annotation Framework (LAF, (Ide and Romary, 2004); ISO 24612, 2009) defines an abstract model for annotations together with an XML serialization of the model, the Graph Annotation Format (GrAF, (Ide and Suderman, 2007)). GrAF is intended to be a pivot format capable of representing diverse annotation types of varying complexity, guaranteeing *syntactic* consistency among the different annotations. GrAF does not address the issue of *semantic* consistency among annotation labels and categories; this is assumed to be handled by other standardization efforts such as ISOCat (Kemps-Snijders et al., 2009). ISOCat provides a set of *data categories* at various levels of granularity, each accompanied by a precise definition of its linguistic meaning. Labels applied in a user-defined annotation scheme should be mapped to these categories in order to ensure semantic consistency among annotations of the same phenomenon.

While the mapping of annotation labels to a common definition, coupled with the syntactic consistency guaranteed by GrAF, takes a giant step towards the harmonization of linguistic annotations, this is still not enough to ensure that these annotations are sufficiently compatible to enable merging, comparison, and manipulation with common software. For this, the conceptual structure of the annotation, in terms of the structural relations among the defined annotation categories, must also be consistent. It is therefore necessary to consider this aspect of annotation scheme design in order to achieve a comprehensive treatment of the requirements for full harmonization of linguistic annotations.

In (Bunt, 2010), a design methodology for semantic annotation schemes is proposed, developed during the ISO project "Semantic annotation framework, Part 1: Time and events" ("SemAF/Time", for short), which is currently nearing completion (see ISO DIS 24617-1, 2009). The methodology includes a syntax that specifies both a class of *representation structures* and a class of more abstract *annotation structures*. These two components of the language specification are called its *concrete* and *abstract syntax*, respectively. A distinguishing feature of the proposed methodology is that the semantics is defined for the structures of the abstract syntax, rather than for the expressions that represent these structures.

In this paper, we generalize the design methodology defined in (Bunt, 2010) and demonstrate its use for generating a mapping from an existing annotation scheme to a representation in GrAF format. By way of illustration, we apply the mapping strategy to annotations from ISO-TimeML (ISO, 2009), PropBank (Palmer et al., 2005), and FrameNet (Baker et al., 1998).



*Proceedings of the Fourth Linguistic Annotation Workshop, ACL 2010*, pages 247–255,
Uppsala, Sweden, 15-16 July 2010. 

## 2 Background

The process of corpus annotation may consist of attaching simple *labels* to textual elements, such as part of speech and syntactic designations and named entity tags. For more complex types of annotation, annotations include a variety of additional information about linguistic features and relations. This is especially true for the kinds of semantic annotation that have recently begun to be undertaken in earnest, including semantic role labeling (e.g., FrameNet and PropBank) and time and event annotation (e.g., TimeML). However, these annotation schemes are not always designed based on formal principles, and as a result, comparing or merging information–even from two schemes annotating the same phenomenon–can be difficult or impossible without substantial human effort.

A major source of difficulties in interpreting annotation scheme content is that information in the annotation is implicit rather than explicit, making (especially) structural relations among parts of the linguistic information ambiguous. This often results from the use of an impoverished representation scheme, which provides only minimal mechanisms for bracketing and association. Consider, for example, the two annotation fragments below, expressed with parenthetic bracketing, taken from a computational lexicon:

```
(1) (SUBC ((NP-TO-INF-LOC) (NP-PP)))
(2) (FEATURES ((NHUMAN) (COUNTABLE)))
```

In (1), the bracketed information is a list of alternatives, whereas in (2), it is a set of properties, but there is no way to *automatically* distinguish the two in order to process them differently. Another example comes from PropBank:

```
wsj/00/wsj_0003.mrg 13 6 gold have.03
vn--a 0:2-ARG0 6:0-rel 7:1-ARG1
10:1-ARGM-ADV
```

Because of the "flat" representation[1], it is impossible to *automatically* determine if the morphosyntactic descriptor "vn–a" is associated with the element annotated as "rel", vs. the "gold" descriptor that is (assumedly) associated with the entire proposition. In both of these examples, linguistically-informed humans have little difficulty determining the structure because of the knowledge they bring to the interpretation. This knowledge is then embedded in the processing software so that the data are processed properly; however, because it is not a part of the representation itself, it is not available to others who may develop software for other kinds of processing.

To avoid these problems, annotation scheme design in ISO projects is split into two phases: the specification of (1) an abstract model consisting of *annotation categories and structures* and (2) specification of (possibly multiple) *representation structures*. An abstract model of annotation structures is typically implemented via development of a "metamodel", i.e. a listing of the categories of entities and relations to be considered, often visualized by a UML-like diagram–i.e., a graph. Schemes described via this method are trivially mappable to GrAF, ensuring that syntactic consistency among the different schemes, whatever their original representation structures may be, is achievable. It also ensures that these schemes are trivially mappable to different representation formats that are used in various software systems, e.g., GATE, UIMA, NLTK, GraphViz, etc.

## 3 Anatomy of an annotation scheme

As specified in (Bunt, 2010), an annotation scheme consists of a syntax that specifies a class of more abstract annotation structures (the *abstract syntax*) and a class of representation structures (the *concrete syntax*), plus a semantics associated with the abstract syntax.

### 3.1 Abstract syntax

The abstract syntax of an annotation scheme defines the set-theoretical structures which constitute the information that may be contained in annotations. It consists of (a) a specification of the elements from which these structures are built up, called a *conceptual inventory*; and (b) *annotation construction rules*, which describe the possible combinations of these elements into annotation structures. The semantics of the annotation scheme components is defined for the annotation structures of the abstract syntax; Bunt (2010) provides a formal specification of the semantics of ISO-TimeML in terms of Discourse Representation Structures (Kamp and Reyle, 1993), and defines the class of concrete representations of the structures defined by the abstract syntax.

For example, a fragment of the ISO-TimeML[2]

[1] In PropBank annotation, this information appears on a single line.

[2] All references to ISO-TimeML are based on the state of the project as documented in ISO 264617-1:2009(E) from

conceptual inventory includes:[3]

- finite sets of elements called event types, tenses, aspects, signatures, cardinalities, and veracities.
- finite sets of elements called temporal relations, duration relations, event subordination relations, aspectual relations, etc.

The annotation construction rules for ISO-TimeML specify how to construct two types of annotation structures: *entity structures* and *link structures*. One type of entity structure, called an *event structure*, is defined as a 6-tuple $\langle e, t, a, s, k, v\rangle$ where $e$ is a member of the set of event types; $t$ and $a$ are a tense and an aspect, respectively; $s$ is a signature (a set-theoretical type that is used for handling quantification over events); $k$ is a cardinality, used for expressing information about the size of a set of events involved in a quantified relation; and $v$ is a veracity, which is used to represent whether an event is claimed to have occurred, or claimed not to have occurred (for dealing with positive and negative polarity, respectively), or to have yet another status such as 'possibly' or 'requested', for handling such cases as *Please come back later today.* A *time-amount structure* is a pair $\langle n, u\rangle$ or a triple $\langle R, n, u\rangle$, where $n$ is a real number, $R$ a numerical relation, and $u$ a temporal unit. The rules also define a link structure called an *event duration structure* as a triple $\langle event\ structure, time\text{-}amount\ structure, duration\ relation\rangle$.

### 3.2 Concrete syntax

The concrete syntax provides the representation of annotation structures defined in the abstract syntax. A concrete syntax is said to be *ideal* for a given abstract syntax if there is a one-to-one correspondence between the structures defined by the abstract syntax and those defined by the concrete syntax. An ideal concrete syntax $\text{RF}_1$ defines a function $F_1$ from annotation structures to $\text{RF}_i$-representations, and an inverse function $F_i^{-1}$ from $\text{RF}_1$-representations to annotation structures. In other words, the abstract and the concrete syntax are *isomorphic*. Since this holds for any ideal concrete syntax, it follows that any two ideal representation formats are isomorphic. Given two

September 2009.

[3]See (Bunt, 2010) for the full specification for ISO-TimeML.

```
<isoTimeML-ICS1rep xml:id="a1">
 <EVENT xml:id="e1" anchor="t2"
    type ="FAST" tense=PAST
    signature="INDIVIDUAL"/>
 <TIME-AMOUNT xml:id="ta1"
    anchor="t4" numeral="2" unit="day"/>
 <MLINK event="e1"
    duration="ta1" relType="FOR"/>
</isoTimeML-ICS1rep>
```

Tokens: $[I_{t1}][fasted_{t2}][for_{t3}][two_{t4}][days_{t5}]$.

Figure 1: ISO-TimeML_ICS1 annotation

ideal representation formats $\text{RF}_i$ and $\text{RF}_j$ we can define a homomorphic mapping $C_{ij}$ from $\text{RF}_i$-representations to $\text{RF}_j$-representations by

(1) $C_{ij} =_D F_j \circ F_i^{-1}$, i.e. $C_{ij}(r) = F_j(F_i^{-1}(r))$ for any $\text{RF}_i$-representation $r$

and conversely, we can define a homomorphic mapping $C_{ji}$ from $\text{RF}_j$-representations to $\text{RF}_i$-representations by

(2) $C_{ji} =_D F_i \circ F_j^{-1}$, i.e. $C_{ji}(r) = F_i(F_j^{-1}(r))$ for any $\text{RF}_j$-representation $r$

These two mappings constitute *conversions* from one format to the other, that is, they constitute one-to-one meaning-preserving mappings: if $\mu(r)$ denotes the meaning of representation $r$, then $\mu(C_{ij}(r)) = \mu(r)$ for any $F_i$-representation $r$, and conversely, $\mu(C_{ji}(r')) = \mu(r')$ for any $F_j$-representation $r'$.

Figure 1 shows a rendering of the sentence *I fasted for two days* using a concrete XML-based syntax for the annotation structures defined by the ISO-TimeML abstract syntax, called the ICS-1 format, as described in (Bunt, 2010).

## 4 GrAF overview

GrAF is an exchange or pivot format intended to simplify the processes of merging of annotations from different sources and using annotations with different software systems. The underlying data model is a directed acyclic graph, which is isomorphic to UML-like structures that may be used to define an abstract syntax for a given annotation scheme, as described in section 3.

GrAF is an XML serialization of a formal graph consisting of nodes and edges, either or both of which are decorated with feature structures. Nodes may have edges to one or more other nodes

```
<node xml:id="fn-n1"/>
<a label="FE" ref="fn-n1" as="FrameNet">
    <fs>
        <f name="FE" value="Recipient"/>
        <f name="GF" value="Obj"/>
        <f name="PT" value="NP"/>
    </fs>
</a>

<edge id="e1" from="fn-n1"
                to="fntok-n5"/>
```

Figure 2: FrameNet frame element annotation in GrAF

in the graph, or they may be linked directly to *regions* within the primary data that is being annotated. The feature structure attached to a node or edge provides the *content* of the annotation–that is, the associated linguistic information expressed as a set of attribute-value pairs. The feature structures in GrAF conform to formal feature structure specifications and may be subjected to operations defined over feature structures, including subsumption and unification. As a result, any representation of an annotation in GrAF must consist of a feature structure that provides all of the relevant linguistic information.

Figure 2 shows a fragment of a FrameNet frame element annotation, serialized in GrAF XML. It consists of a graph node with id "fn-n1" and an annotation with the label "FE"[4]. The *ref* attribute on the <a> (annotation) element associates the annotation with node "fn-n1". The annotation contains a feature structure with three features: *FE* (Frame element), *GF* (Grammatical Function), and *PT* (Phrase Type). An edge connects the node to another node in the graph with the id "fntok-n5" (not shown here), which is associated with annotation information for a token that in turn references the span of text in primary data being annotated.

## 5 Mapping to GrAF

LAF specifies that an annotation representation $R$ is *valid* if it is mappable to a meaning-preserving representation in GrAF, and that its GrAF representation is in turn mappable to $R$. In terms of the definitions in section 3, a *LAF-valid representation* $R$ is one where $\mu(R) = \mu(C_{RG}(R))$ and $\mu(G) = \mu(C_{GR}(G))$, where $G$ is a GrAF representation. We can also define a valid annotation scheme in terms of *conversion transitivity* through GrAF; that is, for two arbitrary annotation schemes R and S, the following holds:

$$\mu(R) = \mu(C_{RG}(R)) = \mu(C_{GS}(S))$$

Our goal here is to provide a formal specification for the mapping function $C_{RG}$, assuming the existence of a formal specification of an annotation scheme as outlined in section 3. To accomplish this, it is necessary to identify the two components of an abstract syntax for annotation scheme $R$: the conceptual inventory and the annotation construction rules that indicate how elements of the conceptual inventory are combined into *annotation structures*–specifically, *entity structures*, which describe annotation objects, and *link structures*, which describe relations among entity structures. Once these are available, a general procedure for establishing a GrAF representation of the annotation structures is as follows: For each type of entity structure $e$:

- introduce a label $L_e$, where $L_e$ is the entity structure type;
- define a set of features $f$ corresponding one-to-one with the components of the $n$-tuple of elements from the conceptual inventory defining entity structure $e$.

A link structure is a triple $\langle E_1, E_2, r\rangle$ consisting of two sets of entity structures and a relational element defining a relation between them. For each type of link structure:

1. introduce a label $L_r$, where $L_r$ is the type name of relation $r$.
2. If $r$ is associated with a set of elements from the conceptual inventory, then features are created as in (2), above.

In GrAF, an annotation $A$ consists of a label $L$ and a feature structure containing a set of features $f$. Annotations may be associated with nodes or edges in the graph. Typically, entity structures are associated with nodes that have links into a region of primary data or one or more edges connecting it to other nodes in the graph. Link structures are associated with edges, identifying a relation among two or more entity structures. In the simplest case, a link structure consists of a relation between two

[4] Note that the value of the *label* attribute is, for practical purposes, a convenience; it is used primarily when generating alternative representation formats.

entity structures, each of a given type; in the corresponding GrAF representation, the link structure label is associated with an edge $d$ that connects nodes $n_1, n_2$, each of which is decorated with annotations labeled $L_1, L_2$, respectively.

For example, for the ISO-TimeML abstract syntax fragment provided in section 3, we define the labels EVENT and INSTANT corresponding to the two entity structures with names *event structure* and *time amount structure*, and a link structure TIME-ANCHORING. Because an event structure is defined as a 6-tuple $\langle e, t, a, s, k, v \rangle$, we define six features *event, tense, aspect signature, cardinality,* and *veracity*.[5] A time-amount structure may be a pair $\langle n, u \rangle$ or a triple $\langle R, n, u \rangle$, where $n$ is a real number, $R$ a numerical relation, and $u$ a temporal unit, so we introduce features *numeral, unit,* and *relType*. Finally, the time anchoring link structure is a triple $\langle event\ structure, time\text{-}amountstructure, duration\ relation \rangle$. In this case, the first two elements of the triple are the entity structures being linked; these will be represented as nodes in the GrAF implementation. The label and features associated with each entity and link structure provide the template for an annotation corresponding to that structure with appropriate values filled in, which may then be associated with a node or edge in the graph.

### 5.1 ISO-TimeML example

The GrAF representation of the ISO-TimeML annotation for the sentence *I fasted for two days* is shown in Figure 3, based on the abstract syntax given in section 3.1.

To create an annotation corresponding to an ISO-TimeML entity structure, a node <node> element) is created and assigned a unique identifier as the value of the XML attribute *xml:id*. An *annotation* (<a>) element is also created, with a *label* attribute whose value is the entity structure name, and which contains a feature structure providing the appropriate feature/value pairs for that entity structure. The annotation is associated with the node by using the node's unique identifier as the value of the *ref* attribute on the <a> element. An edge is then created from the node to another node in the graph (*r2*) that references the data to be annotated–in this case, one or more tokens defined over regions of the primary data.

ISO-TimeML link structures define a relation between two entity structures, and are rendered in GrAF as a labeled edge between the nodes annotated with the entity structure information. In the ISO-TimeML example, an annotation with label MLINK ('measure link') is created with a single feature *relType*. The *from* and *to* attributes on the <edge> element link the node with the EVENT entity structure annotation (node `tml-n1` in the example) to the node with the TIME-AMOUNT annotation (`tml-n2`). This edge is then associated with the MLINK annotation (cf. Bunt and Pustejovsky, 2009; Pustejovsky et al., 2010).

Figure 1 shows the rendering of the ISO-TimeML abstract syntax in the ICS-1 concrete syntax. Following Section 3.2, these two realizations of the abstract syntax for ISO-TimeML are isomorphic.

```
<node xml:id="tml-n1"/>
<a label="EVENT" ref="tml-n1"
  as="TimeML">
 <fs>
   <f name="event" value="fast"/>
   <f name="tense" value="Past"/>
   <f name="signature"
      value="individual"/>
 </fs>
</a>

<edge xml:id="tml-e1" from="tml-n1"
   to="t2"/>

<node xml:id="tml-n2"/>
<a label="TIME-AMOUNT" ref="tml-n2"
   as="TimeML">
 <fs>
   <f name="numeral" value="2"/>
   <f name="unit" value="day"/>
 </fs>
</a>

<edge xml:id="tml-e2" from="tml-n2"
   to="t4"/>
<edge xml:id="tml-e3" from="tml-n2"
   to="t5"/>

<edge xml:id="tml-e4" from="tml-n1"
   to="tml-n2"/>
<a label="MLINK" ref="tml-e4"
  as="TimeML">
  <fs>
    <f name="relType" value="FOR"/>
  </fs>
</a>
```

Tokens: $[I_{t1}][fasted_{t2}][for_{t3}][two_{t4}][days_{t5}]$.

Figure 3: ISO-TimeML annotation in GrAF

[5]The latter three attributes have the default values INDIVIDUAL, 1, and POSITIVE, respectively, and will be omitted in the examples to follow if they have these values.

### 5.2 Reverse engineering the abstract syntax

The previous two sections show how schemes for which an abstract syntax is specified can be rendered in GrAF as well as other concrete syntax representations. However, as noted in section 2, many annotation formats–especially legacy formats–were not designed based on an underlying data model. Therefore, in order to achieve a mapping to GrAF, it is necessary to "reverse engineer" the annotation format to define its abstract syntax. Because of problems such as those outlined in Section 2, this exercise may require some extrapolation of information that is implicit, or not specified, in the original annotation format. We provide two examples below, one for PropBank and one for FrameNet.

#### 5.2.1 An abstract syntax for PropBank

The PropBank format specifies an annotation for a sentence consisting of several columns, specifying the file path; the sentence number within the file; the number of the terminal in the sentence that is the location of the verb; a status indication; a frameset identifier (frame and sense number); an inflection field providing person, tense, aspect, voice, and form of the verb; and one or more "proplabels" representing an annotation associated with a particular argument or adjunct of the proposition. Proplabels are associated with primary data via reference to the Penn Treebank (PTB) node in the syntax tree of the sentence.

Based on this we can specify a portion of a PropBank conceptual Inventory:

- a special proposition type $verb$, designating the verb (replaces PropBank "rel");
- a finite set $PROP = \{ARGA, ARGM, ARG0, ARG1, ARG2\}$ of proposition labels;
- a finite set $FEAT = \{EXT, DIR, LOC, TMP, REC, PRD, NEG, MOD, ADV, MNR, CAU, PNC, DIS\}$, plus the set of prepositions and "null", comprising the set of features;
- a finite set of sets $INF = \{form, tense, aspect, person, voice\}$, where $form = \{infinitive, gerund, participle, finite\}$, $tense = \{future, past, present\}$, $aspect = \{perfect, progressive, both\}$, $person = \{default, 3rd\}$, and $voice = \{active, passive\}$.
- a finite set $FrameSets = \{fs_1, fs_2, ...fs_n\}$ where each $fs_i$ is a frame set defined in PropBank.

An abstract syntax for PropBank could specify the following annotation construction rules:

- a *proposition entity structure* is a pair $\langle f, A\rangle$ where $f$ is a frameset and $A$ is a set of *argument entity structures*.[6]
- an *argument entity structure* is an argument $a \in PROP \times FEAT$.
- a *verb entity structure* is a 5-tuple $\langle f, t, a, p, v\rangle$ where $f \in form$, $t \in tense$, $a \in aspect$, $p \in person$, and $v \in voice$.

Based on this, the PropBank annotation in Section 2 can be rendered into a concrete syntax; in this case, in GrAF as shown in Figure 4. Note that the *to* attribute on `<edge>` elements have as values the reference to PTB nodes from the original PropBank encoding; in GrAF, these values would be identifers on the appropriate nodes in a GrAF representation of PTB. We have also included role names (e.g., "owner") in the annotation, which are not present in the original; this was done for convenience and readability, and the values for the "role" feature could have been given as arg-0, arg-1, etc. instead.

The original PropBank encoding is close to an ideal concrete syntax, as it can be generated from the abstract syntax. However, the round trip back to the abstract syntax is not possible, because it is necessary to do some interpretation of associations among bits of annotation information in order to construct the abstract syntax and, subsequently, map the PropBank format to GrAF. Specifically, in the GrAF encoding the inflection information is associated with the node referencing the verb, but this association is not explicit in the original (and in fact may not be what the annotation scheme designers intended).

#### 5.2.2 An abstract syntax for FrameNet

The FrameNet XML format is shown in Figure 5.[7] The structure and content of this encoding is highly oriented toward a presentation view,

[6] We do not include the bookkeeping information associated with a PropBank annotation in the abstract syntax.

[7] Some detail concerning the html display has been omitted for brevity.

```
<node xml:id="pb-n1"/>
<a label="Proposition" ref="pb-n1"
 as="PropBank">
 <fs>
  <f name="file"
     value="wsj/00/wsj_0003.mrg"/>
  <f name="sentenceNo" value="13"/>
  <f name="verbOffset" value="6"/>
  <f name="status" value="gold"/>
  <f name="frameSet"
     value="have.03"/>
 </fs>
</a>

<node xml:id="pb-n2"/>
<a label="VERB" ref="pb-n2"
 as="PropBank">
 <fs>
  <f name="role" value="rel"/>
  <f name="form" value="finite"/>
  <f name="tense" value="present"/>
  <f name="voice" value="active"/>
 </fs>
</a>

<edge xml:id="pb-e1" from="pb-n1"
   to="pb-n2"/>
<edge xml:id="pb-e2" from="pb-n2"
   to="ptb-6-0"/>

<node xml:id="pb-n3"/>
<a label="ARG0" ref="pb-n3"
 as="PropBank">
 <fs>
  <f name="role" value="owner"/>
 </fs>
</a>

<edge xml:id="pb-e3" from="pb-n1"
   to="pb-n3"/>
<edge xml:id="pb-e4" from="pb-n3"
   to="ptb-0-2"/>

<node xml:id="pb-n4"/>
<a label="ARG1" ref="pb-n4"
 as="PropBank">
 <fs>
  <f name="role" value="possession"/>
 </fs>
</a>

<edge xml:id="e5" from="pb-n1"
   to="pb-n4"/>
<edge xml:id="e6" from="pb-n4"
   to="ptb-7-1"/>

<node xml:id="pb-n5"/>
<a label="ARGM" ref="pb-n5"
 as="PropBank">
 <fs>
  <f name="role" value="adjunct"/>
  <f name="feature" value="adverbial"/>
 </fs>
</a>

<edge xml:id="e7" from="pb-n1"
   to="pb-n5"/>
<edge xml:id="e8" from="pb-n5"
   to="ptb-10-1"/>
```

Figure 4: PropBank annotation in GrAF

intended to support display of the sentence and frame elements in a browser.

A partial abstract syntax for FrameNet derived from this format includes the following conceptual inventory:

- a $Target$, designating the frame-evoking lexical unit;
- a finite set $FE = \{Recipient, Supplier, Means, ...\}$ of frame element labels;
- a finite set $GF = \{Obj, Ext, Dep, ...\}$ of grammatical functions.
- a finite set $PT = \{NP, PP, ...\}$ of phrase types.
- a finite set $LU = \{u_1, u_2, ...u_n\}$ where each $u_i$ is a lexical unit.
- a finite set $POS = \{n, v, a, r\}$ denoting parts of speech;
- a finite set $FrameNames = \{f_1, f_2, ...f_n\}$ where each $f_i$ is a frame defined in FrameNet.

An abstract syntax for this partial inventory could specify the following annotation construction rules:

- a *frame entity structure* is a pair $\langle f, A\rangle$ where $f$ is a frame name, $u$ is a lexical unit, and $F$ is a set of *frame element (FE) entity structures*.
- an *FE entity structure* is a triple $\{f, g, p\}$, $f \in FE, g \in GF, p \in PT$.

The GrAF rendering of the abstract syntax is given in Figure 6, which was generated from the FrameNet abstract syntax using the rules outlined in section 5. Both the FrameNet XML and the GrAF rendering provide an ideal concrete syntax because they are isomorphic[8] to the abstract syntax and, by the definition in section 3.2, are conversions of one another.

## 6 Conclusion

In this paper we outlined a methodology for annotation scheme design and development; demonstrated how schemes designed using this methodology may be easily mapped to GrAF; and demonstrated how "reverse engineering" an annotation

[8]Obviously, in the FrameNet XML additional elements are introduced for display and bookkeeping purposes.

format whose abstract syntax is unspecified can provide the information required to map that format to GrAF. This work was undertaken with two goals in mind: (1) to provide a formal method for mapping to GrAF; and (2) to demonstrate the advantages of a methodology for annotation scheme design that is based on an abstract model, as adopted in ISO TC37 SC4 projects and formalized in (Bunt, 2010). The ultimate goal is, of course, to achieve harmonization of annotation formats, so that they can be merged, enabling the study of interactions among information at different linguistic levels; compared, in order to both evaluate and improve automatic annotation accuracy; and to enable seamless transition from one software environment to another when creating and using linguistic annotations.

```
<annotationSet lexUnitRef="11673"
  luName="provide.v" frameRef="1346"
  frameName="Supply"
  status="MANUAL" ID="2022935">
 <layer rank="1" name="Target">
  <label end="109" start="103"
     name="Target"/>
 </layer>
  <layer rank="1" name="FE">
  <label bgColor="0000FF" ... end="138"
    start="111" name="Recipient"/>
  <label bgColor="FF0000"... end="84"
    start="83" name="Supplier"/>
  <label bgColor="FF00FF"... end="79"
    start="0" name="Means"/>
 </layer>
  <layer rank="1" name="GF">
  <label end="138" start="111"
    name="Obj"/>
  <label end="84" start="83"
    name="Ext"/>
  <label end="79" start="0"
    name="Dep"/>
 </layer>
 <layer rank="1" name="PT">
  <label end="138" start="111"
    name="NP"/>
  <label end="84" start="83"
    name="NP"/>
  <label end="79" start="0" name="PP"/>
 </layer>
...
</annotationSet>
```

Figure 5: FrameNet XML format

```
<node xml:id="fn-as1"/>
<a label="annotationSet" ref="fn-as1"
  as="FrameNet">
 <fs>
  <f name="lexUnitRef" value="11673"/>
  <f name="luName" value="provide.v"/>
  <f name="frameRef" value="1346"/>
  <f name="frameName" value="Supply"/>
  <f name="status" value="MANUAL"/>
  <f name="ID" value="2022935"/>
 </fs>
</a>

<node xml:id="fn-n1"/>
<a label="Target" ref="fn-n1"
  as="FrameNet">
 <fs>
  <f name="name" value="Target"/>
 </fs>
</a>
<edge xml:id="e69" from="fn-as1"
   to="fn-n1"/>
<edge xml:id="e90" from="fn-n1"
  to="fn-t1"/>

<node xml:id="fn-n2"/>
<a label="FE" ref="fn-n2"
  as="FrameNet">
 <fs>
  <f name="FE" value="Recipient"/>
  <f name="GF" value="Obj"/>
  <f name="PT" value="NP"/>
 </fs>
</a>
<edge xml:id="e67" from="fn-as1"
   to="fn-n2"/>
<edge xml:id="e91" from="fn-n2"
  to="fn-t2"/>

<node xml:id="fn-n3"/>
<a label="FE" ref="fn-n3"
  as="FrameNet">
<fs>
 <f name="FE" value="Supplier"/>
 <f name="GF" value="Ext"/>
 <f name="PT" value="NP"/>
</fs>
</a>
<edge xml:id="e46" from="fn-as1"
   to="fn-n3"/>
<edge xml:id="e92" from="fn-n3"
  to="fn-t3"/>

<node xml:id="fn-n4"/>
<a label="FE" ref="fn-n4"
  as="FrameNet">
<fs>
 <f name="FE" value="Means"/>
 <f name="GF" value="Dep"/>
 <f name="PT" value="PP"/>
</fs>
</a>
<edge xml:id="e10" from="fn-as1"
   to="fn-n4"/>
   <edge xml:id="e93" from="fn-n4"
  to="fn-t4"/>
```

Figure 6: FrameNet in GrAF format

## References


Collin F. Baker, Charles J. Fillmore, and John B. Lowe. 1998. The Berkeley FrameNet project. In *Proceed-*

*ings of the 17th international conference on Computational linguistics*, pages 86–90, Morristown, NJ, USA. Association for Computational Linguistics.

Harry Bunt and James Pustejovsky. 2010. Annotation of temporal and event quantification. In *Proceedings of the Fifth International Workshop on Interoperable Semantic Annotation (ISA-5)*, pages 15–22, Hong Kong SAR. City University of Hong Kong.

Harry Bunt. 2010. A methodology for designing semantic annotation languages exploiting semantic-syntactic isomorphisms. In *Proceedings of the Second International Conference on Global Interoperability for Language Resources (ICGL2010)*, pages 29–46, Hong Kong SAR. City University of Hong Kong.

Nancy Ide and Laurent Romary. 2004. International standard for a linguistic annotation framework. *Journal of Natural Language Engineering*, 10(3–4):211–225.

Nancy Ide and Keith Suderman. 2007. GrAF: A graph-based format for linguistic annotations. In *Proceedings of the First Linguistic Annotation Workshop*, pages 1–8, Prague.

ISO. 2009. *Language Resource Management - Semantic Annotation Framework (SemAF) - Part 1: Time and Events*. Secretariat KATS, October. ISO International Standard 24617-1:2009(E)), 11 October 2009.

H. Kamp and U. Reyle. 1993. *From Discourse to Logic*. Kluwer Academic Publishers, Dordrecht.

Marc Kemps-Snijders, Menzo Windhouwer, Peter Wittenburg, and Sue Ellen Wright. 2009. ISOcat : Remodelling metadata for language resources. *International Journal of Metadata and Semantic Ontologies*, 4(4):261–276.

Inderjeet Mani, James Pustejovsky, and Beth Sundheim. 2004. Introduction to the special issue on temporal information processing. *ACM Transactions on Asian Language Information Processing (TALIP)*, 3(1):1–10.

Martha Palmer, Daniel Gildea, and Paul Kingsbury. 2005. The Proposition Bank: An annotated corpus of semantic roles. *Computational Linguistics*, 31(1):71–106, March.

James Pustejovsky, Harry Bunt, Kiyong Lee, and Laurent Romary. 2010. ISO-TimeML: An International Standard for Semantic Annotation. In *Proceedings of the Fifth International Workshop on Interoperable Semantic Annotation (ISA-5)*, Paris. ELDA.

# Annotating Participant Reference in English Spoken Conversation

**John Niekrasz and Johanna D. Moore**
School of Informatics
University of Edinburgh
Edinburgh, EH8 9AB, UK
{jniekras, jmoore}@inf.ed.ac.uk

**Abstract**

In conversational language, references to people (especially to the conversation participants, e.g., *I*, *you*, and *we*) are an essential part of many expressed meanings. In most conversational settings, however, many such expressions have numerous potential meanings, are frequently vague, and are highly dependent on social and situational context. This is a significant challenge to conversational language understanding systems — one which has seen little attention in annotation studies. In this paper, we present a method for annotating verbal reference to *people* in conversational speech, with a focus on reference to conversation *participants*. Our goal is to provide a resource that tackles the issues of vagueness, ambiguity, and contextual dependency in a nuanced yet reliable way, with the ultimate aim of supporting work on summarization and information extraction for conversation.

## 1 Introduction

Spoken conversation — the face-to-face verbal interaction we have every day with colleagues, family, and friends — is the most natural setting for language use. It is how we learn to use language and is universal to the world's societies. This makes it an ideal subject for research on the basic nature of language and an essential subject for the development of technologies supporting natural communication. In this paper, we describe our research on designing and applying an annotation procedure for a problem of particular relevance to conversational language — *person reference*.

The procedure is a coreference annotation of all references to people, and the focus of our scheme is on distinguishing different types of *participant reference* (references to the conversation's participants), the predominant type of person reference in face-to-face multi-party conversation. Participant reference is exemplified by the use of proper names such as *James* or most commonly by the pronouns *I*, *you*, and *we*.

Participant reference plays an essential role in many of the most important types of expressed meanings and actions in conversation, including subjective language, inter-personal agreements, commitments, narrative story-telling, establishing social relationships, and meta-discourse. In fact, some person-referring words are the most frequent words in conversation.[1]

Perhaps contrary to intuition, however, interpreting person-referring expressions can be rather complex. Person-reference interpretation is strongly dependent on social, situational, and discourse context. The words *you* and *we* are especially problematic. Either can be used for generic, plural, or singular reference, as addressee-inclusive or addressee-exclusive, in reference to hypothetical individuals or non-human entities, or even metonymically in reference to objects connected to individuals (Mühlhäusler and Harré, 1990; Wales, 1996). In addition, these and many other issues are not simply occasional problems but arise regularly.

Consider the following utterance from the AMI corpus of remote control design meetings, which is typical of the corpus in terms of complexity of person-reference.

[1]The words *I* and *you* are the most frequently used nominals in several conversational corpora, including Switchboard (Godfrey et al., 1992) and the AMI Meeting Corpus (McCowan et al., 2005). In the British National Corpus they are the two most common of any words in the demographic (i.e., conversational) subcorpus (Burnard, 2007), and Google's Web 1T 5-gram statistics (Brants and Franz, 2006) list *I* and *you* as more frequent even than the word *it*. The word *we* falls within the top 10 most frequent words in all of these corpora.



*Proceedings of the Fourth Linguistic Annotation Workshop, ACL 2010*, pages 256–264,
Uppsala, Sweden, 15-16 July 2010. 

> "Current remote controls do not match well with the operating behaviour of the **user** overall. For example, **you** can see below there, seventy five percent of **users** zap a lot, so **you**'ve got **your person** sunk back in the sofa channel-hopping."

As this example demonstrates, person-referring expressions have many potential meanings and are often vague or non-specific. In this case, "the user" refers to a non-specific representative of a hypothetical group, which is referred to itself as "users." The first use of "you" refers to the addressees, but the second use has a more 'generic' meaning whilst retaining an addressee-oriented meaning as well. The phrase "your person" refers to a specific hypothetical example of the "users" referred to previously.

### 1.1 Purpose of the Annotations

The annotation research we describe here aims at addressing the fact that if conversational language applications are to be useful and effective (our interest is primarily with abstractive summarization), then accurate interpretation of reference to the conversation's participants is of critical importance. Our work looks at language as a means for action (Clark, 1996), and our focus is on those actions that the participants themselves consider as relevant and salient, such as the events occurring in a meeting that might appear in the minutes of the meeting. For our system to identify, distinguish, or describe such events, it is essential for it to understand the participants' roles and relationships to those events through interpreting their linguistic expression within the dialogue. This includes understanding direct reference to participants and recognizing discourse structure through evidence of referential coherence.

Another aim of our research is to increase understanding of the nature of participant reference through presenting a nuanced yet reliable set of type and property distinctions. We propose novel distinctions concerning three main issues. The first distinction concerns vagueness and indeterminacy, which is often exploited by speakers when using words such as *you*, *they*, and *we*. Our aim is to provide a reliable basis for making an explicit distinction between specific and vague uses, motivated by usefulness to the aforementioned applications. The second distinction concerns an issue faced frequently in informal conversation, where words typically used to do person-referring are also commonly used in non-person-referring ways. A principal goal is thus establishing reliable person/non-person and referential/non-referential distinctions for these words. The third issue concerns addressing roles (i.e., speaker, addressee, and non-addressee), which we propose can be a useful means for further distinguishing between different types of underspecified and generic references, beyond the specific/underspecified/generic distinctions made in schemes such as ACE (Linguistic Data Consortium, 2008).

### 1.2 Summary and Scope of Contributions

The work described in this paper includes the design of an annotation procedure and a statistical analysis of a corpus of annotations and their reliability. The procedure we propose (Section 3) is based on a simple non-anaphoric coreference-like scheme, modest in comparison to much previous work. The produced dataset (Section 4) includes annotations of 11,000 occasions of person-referring in recorded workplace meetings. Our analysis of the dataset includes a statistical summary of interesting results (Section 4.1) and an analysis of inter-coder agreement (with discussion of specific disagreements) for the introduced distinctions (Section 4.2).

Though our annotation procedure is designed primarily for multi-party spoken conversation, some of the central issues that concern us, such as addressee inclusion and vagueness, arise in textual and non-conversational settings as well. Our scheme therefore has relevance to general work on reference annotation, though principally to settings where social relationships between the participants (i.e., speakers/authors and addressees/readers) are important.

## 2 Related Annotation Schemes

Previous work on reference annotation has covered a wide range of issues surrounding reference generally. It is useful to categorize this work according to the natural language processing tasks the annotations are designed to support.

### 2.1 Schemes for anaphora and generation

Several schemes have been designed with the goal of testing linguistic theoretical models of discourse structure or for use in the study of discourse processing problems like anaphora resolution and reference generation. These schemes have been applied to both text and dialogue and label discourse references with a rich set of syntactic, semantic, and pragmatic properties. For example, the DRAMA scheme (Passonneau, 1997) and the GNOME scheme (Poesio, 2000; Poesio, 2004) include labels for features such as bridging relation type and NP type in addition to a rich representation of referent semantics. Other schemes label animacy, prosody, and information structure to study their relationship to the organization and salience of discourse reference (Nissim et al., 2004; Calhoun et al., 2005). Recent developments include the explicit handling of anaphoric ambiguity and discourse deixis (Poesio and Artstein, 2008).

Despite the depth and detail of these schemes, participant reference has not been their main concern. The annotations by Poesio et al. (2000; 2004) include dialogue source material, but the rather constrained interactional situations do not elicit a rich set of references to participants. The scheme thus employs simple default labels for words like *I* and *you*. The work by Nissim et al., (2004) is an annotation of the Switchboard corpus (Godfrey et al., 1992), which contains only two participants who are neither co-present nor socially connected. Participant reference is thus rather constrained. Other than labeling coreferentiality, the Nissim scheme includes only a single distinction between referential and generic instances of the word *you*.

### 2.2 Schemes for information extraction

In contrast to the schemes described above, which are mainly driven toward investigating linguistic theories of discourse processing, some reference annotation projects are motivated instead by information extraction applications. For these projects (which includes our own), a priority is placed on entity semantics and coreference to known entities in the world. For example, the objective of the Automatic Content Extraction (ACE) program (Doddington et al., 2004) is to recognize and extract entities, events, and relations between them, directly from written and spoken sources, mostly from broadcast news. The schemes thus focus on identifying and labeling the properties of entities in the real world, and then marking expressions as referring to these entities. Recent work in the ACE project has expanded the scope of this task to include cross-document recognition and resolution (Strassel et al., 2008). In the ACE scheme (Linguistic Data Consortium, 2008), person reference is a central component, and in the broadcast conversation component of the corpus there is an extensive inventory of participant references. The annotation scheme contains a distinction between specific, underspecified, and general entities, as well as a distinction between persons and organizations.

Another closely related set of studies are four recent investigations of second-person reference resolution (Gupta et al., 2007a; Gupta et al., 2007b; Frampton et al., 2009; Purver et al., 2009). These studies are based upon a common set of annotations of the word *you* in source material from the Switchboard and ICSI Meeting corpora. The purpose for the annotations was to support learning of classifiers for two main problems: disambiguation of the generic/referential distinction, and reference resolution for referential cases. In addition to the generic/referential distinction and an addressing-based reference annotation, the scheme employed special classes for reported speech and fillers and allowed annotators to indicate vague or difficult cases. Our work builds directly upon this work by extending the annotation scheme to all person-referring expressions.

## 3 Annotation Method

Our person-reference annotation method consists of two main phases: a preliminary phase where the first names of the conversation participants are identified, and a subsequent person reference labeling process. The first phase is not of central concern in this paper, though we provide a brief summary below (Section 3.2). The primary focus of this paper is the second phase (Section 3.3), during which every instance of person-referring occurring in a given meeting is labelled. We provide more detail concerning the most novel and challenging aspects of the person-referring labeling process in Section 3.4 and present a brief summary of the annotation tool in Section 3.5.

### 3.1 Source Material

The source material is drawn from two source corpora: the AMI corpus (McCowan et al., 2005), which contains experimentally-controlled scenario-driven design meetings, and the ICSI corpus (Janin et al., 2003), which contains naturally occurring workplace meetings. All the meetings have at least four participants and have an average duration of about 45 minutes. In the AMI corpus, the participants are experimental subjects who are assigned institutional roles, e.g. project manager and industrial designer. This helps to establish controlled social relationships within the group, but generally limits the types of person referring. The ICSI meetings are naturally occurring and exhibit complex pre-existing social relationships between the participants. Person referring in this corpus is quite complex and often includes other individuals from the larger institution and beyond.

### 3.2 Labeling Participant Names

The first phase of annotation consists of identifying the names of the participants. We perform this task for every participant in every meeting in the AMI and ICSI source corpora, which totals 275 unique participants in 246 meetings. Despite the fact that the participants' are given anonymized identifiers by the corpus creators, determining participants' names is possible because name mentions are not excised from the speech transcript. This allows identification of the names of any participants who are referred to by name in the dialogue, as long as the referent is disambiguated by contextual clues such as addressing.

To extract name information, the list of capitalized words in the speech transcript is scanned manually for likely person names. This was done manually due to the difficulty of training a sufficiently robust named-entity recognizer for these corpora. Proceeding through each meeting for which any participant names are yet unidentified, and taking each potential name token in order of frequency of occurrence in that meeting, short segments of the recording surrounding the occurrences were replayed. In most cases, the name was used in reference to a participant and it was clear from discourse context which participant was the intended referent. In the AMI meetings, 158 of 223 (71%) of the participants' first names were identified. In the ICSI meetings, 36 of 52 (69%) were identified. While these numbers may seem low, failure to determine a name was generally associated with a low level of participation of the individual either in terms of amount of speech or number of meetings attended. As such, the proportion of utterances across both corpora for which the speaker's name is identified is actually 91%.

### 3.3 Person-reference Annotation

The second, principal phase of annotation consists of annotating **person-referring** — instances of verbal reference to people. The recognition of person-referring requires the annotator to simultaneously identify whether a referring event has occurred, and whether the referent is a person. In practice, this is divided into four annotation steps: markable identification, referent identification, functional category labeling, and co-reference linking. For non-specific references, there is an additional step of labeling addressing properties. For each meeting, annotators label every instance of person-referring in every utterance in the meeting, performing the steps in sequence for each utterance. Section 4 describes the set of meetings annotated. The UML diagram in Figure 1 depicts the formal data structure produced by the procedure.[2]

The first step is markable identification, which involves recognizing **person-referring expressions** in the transcript. Only expressions that are noun phrases are considered, and only the head noun is actually labeled by the annotator — the extent of the expression is not labeled. These identified head nouns are called **markables**. Note, however, that before human annotation begins, an automatic process identifies occurrences of words that are likely to be head nouns in person-referring expressions. The list of words includes all personal pronouns except *it*, *them*, and *they* (these are more likely to be non-person-referring in our dataset) and the *wh*-pronouns (not labeled in our scheme). It also includes any occurrences of the previously identified proper names. Some of the automatically identified words might *not* be person-referring. Also, there may be instances of person-referring that are *not* automatically identified. Annotators do not unmark any of the automatically identified words, even if they are not person-referring. The resulting set of manually and automatically identified words, which may or may not be person-referring, constitute the complete set of markables.

The second step is the labeling of **person referents**. Any people or groups of people that are referred to specifically and unambiguously (see Section 3.4.3 for details) are added by the annotator to a conversation **referent list**. The list is automatically populated with each of the conversation participants.

[2]The diagram may also be viewed informally as loosely reflecting a decision tree for the main annotation steps. A complete coding manual is available from the author's web site.

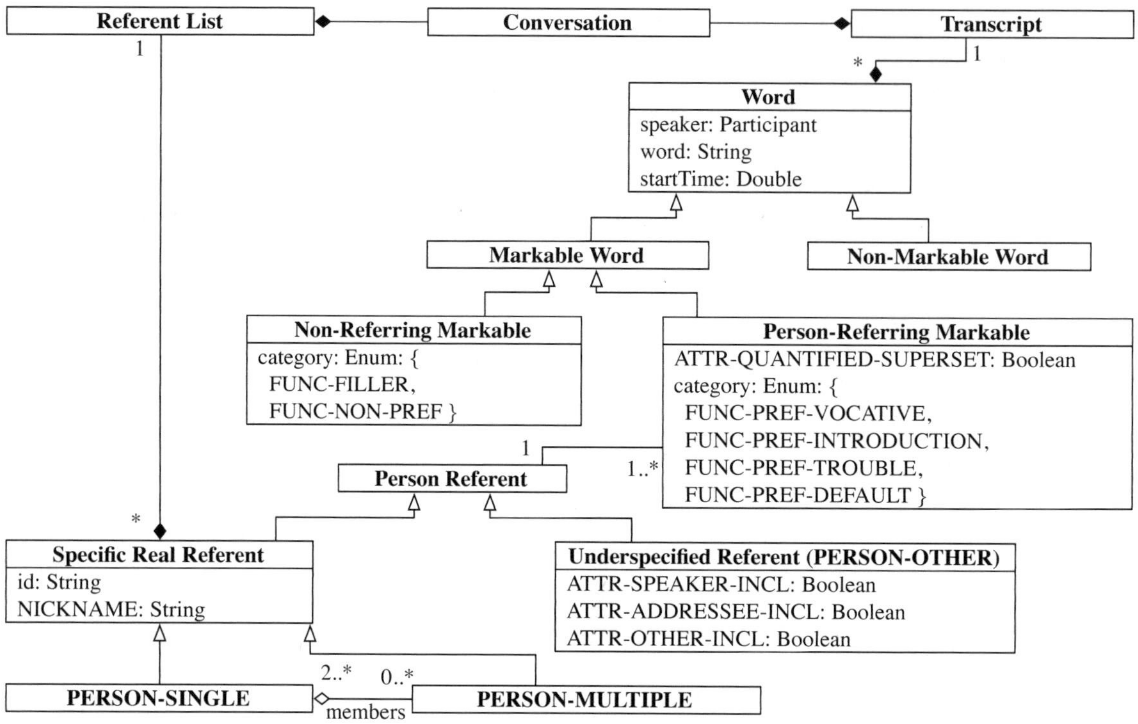


Figure 1: A UML diagram depicting the data structure used to represent and store the annotations.

The third step consists of labeling markables with a **functional category** (FUNC-*). The functional categories serve two main purposes. They are used to distinguish person-referring markables from all others (corresponding to the two main boxes in the diagram), and they are used to distinguish between specific dialogue purposes (the categories listed within the boxes, see Section 3.4.4).

The final step is to link the markables that were labeled as person-referring to the appropriate referent in the referent list. This is only done for specific and unambiguous referring. Otherwise, the referent is said to be **underspecified**, and instead of linking the markable to a referent, it is labeled with three binary **addressing inclusion attributes**. Inclusion attributes label whether the speaker, addressee, or any other individuals are included in the set of people being referred to, given the social, situational, and discourse context (details in Section 3.4.5).

### 3.4 Special Issues

#### 3.4.1 Defining 'person' and 'referring'

To be **person-referring**, an expression must satisfy two conditions. First, the expression's primary contribution to the *speaker's intended meaning or purpose* must be either to identify, label, describe, specify, or address. These are the basic types of **referring**. Second, the referent being identified, labeled, etc., must be a **person**, which we define to include any of the following: a distinct person in the real world; a fictitious or hypothetical person; a human agent, perceiver, or participant in a described event, scene, or fact; a class, type, or kind of person, or representative thereof; a specification or description of a person or set of people; a (possibly vaguely defined) group or collection of any of the above; the human race as a whole, or a representative thereof.

If a noun phrase is used to do person-referring as defined, the associated markable is labeled with one of the four person-referring functional categories (FUNC-PREF-*). If a markable is not person-referring (either non-referring or referring to a non-person referent), it is labeled with the functional category FUNC-NON-PREF. The one exception to this is the use of a pre-defined list of common discourse fillers such as *you know* and *I mean*. When used as fillers, these are labeled with the non-referential FUNC-FILLER category.

#### 3.4.2 Joint action and referring 'trouble'

Annotators are asked to consider occasions of referring to be *joint* actions between the speaker and the addressee(s) of the utterance. The annotator assumes the role of an overhearer and considers as referring any case where the speaker's *intended purpose* is to refer. If the instance of referring is not successfully negotiated between the participants (i.e., common ground is not achieved), but the speaker's intended purpose is to refer, then the annotator marks this as FUNC-PREF-TROUBLE. This is used to identify problematic cases for future study.

#### 3.4.3 Specific, Unambiguous Referring

Only the referents of *specific, unambiguous referring to a person in the real world* (PERSON-SINGLE) are included in the conversation referent list and made the subject of coreference annotation. References to more than one such individual can qualify (PERSON-MULTIPLE), but only if the members are *precisely enumerable* and qualify individually. The motivation for this distinction is to distinguish references that would be directly useful to applications. Coreference for underspecified references is not labeled.

#### 3.4.4 Special Functional Categories

Two functional categories are used to distinguish special uses of person-referring for subsequent use in speaker name induction (the task of automatically learning participants' names). The two categories are FUNC-PREF-INTRODUCTION and FUNC-PREF-VOCATIVE, which specify personal introductions such as "Hi, I'm *John*," and vocative addressing such as "What do you think, *Jane*?" These categories are used only for proper names.

#### 3.4.5 Addressing-based Inclusion Attributes

A major novelty in our annotation scheme is the use of addressing-based distinctions for underspecified referents. Rather than using the labels 'generic' or 'indeterminate', we employ three binary attributes (ATTR-*-INCL) that label whether the speaker, addressee or any other real individuals are members of the set of people referred to.

The use of this distinction is informed by the notion that addressing distinctions are of central importance to the recognition of joint activity type, structure, and participation roles. A generic pronoun, for example, will often have all three categories labeled positively. But as an example of where this scheme creates a novel distinction, consider the phrase "You really take a beating out there on the pitch!", where the speaker is a football player describing the nature of play to someone who has never played the game. This 'generic' use of *you*, used in an activity of autobiographical description, is intuitively interpreted as not including the addressee (ATTR-ADDRESSEE-INCL=FALSE) but including the speaker and others (ATTR-{SPEAKER,OTHER}-INCL=TRUE). These distinctions are hard to motivate linguistically yet critical to identifying useful properties relating to participation in the communicative activity.

#### 3.4.6 Special or Difficult Cases

In some cases, an annotator can determine that a reference is specific and unambiguous for the participants but the annotator himself is unable to determine the identity of the referent. This is generally due to a lack of contextual awareness such as not having adequate video. In such cases, the annotator assigns a special REF-UNKNOWN referent.

Other difficult aspects of our annotation procedure are covered in the annotation manual, including handling of disfluencies, quantification, and identifying lexical heads.

### 3.5 Annotation Tool

The annotations were collected using a software tool we have designed for discrete event-based annotation of multi-modal corpora. The tool uses a simple, low-latency text-based interface that displays multiple streams of discrete events in temporal order across the screen. In our case, the events are time-synchronized words that are distributed to different rows according to speaker. The interface allows keyboard input only and is synchronized with the MPlayer playback engine.

## 4 Results and Analysis

### 4.1 Statistical summary

The dataset consists of approximately 11,000 individually annotated referring expressions in 16 experimentally-controlled, scenario-driven design meetings from the AMI corpus (McCowan et al., 2005) and 3 natural workplace meetings from the ICSI corpus (Janin et al., 2003). Figure 2 shows, for each grammatical type of referring expression, the frequency of occurrence of the five principal markable types, which are defined to consist of the two non-person-referring functional

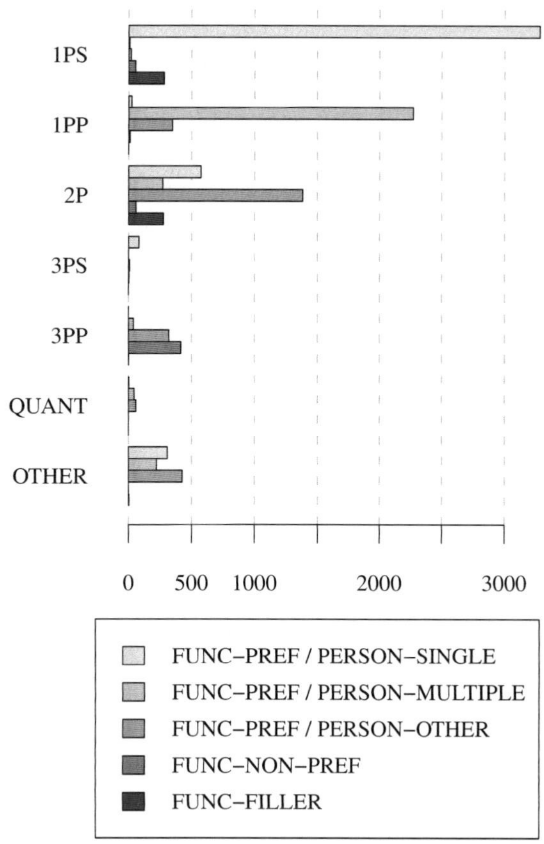


Figure 2: Frequency of occurrence of referring types for the whole corpus, by grammatical type of the referring expression.

categories (FUNC-NON-PREF and FUNC-FILLER), and a breakdown of person-referring according to the type of person referent: a specific individual (PERSON-SINGLE), multiple specific individuals (PERSON-MULTIPLE), or underspecified (PERSON-OTHER). The grammatical types include a grouping of the personal pronouns by grammatical person and number (1PS, 1PP, 2P, 3PS, 3PP), the quantified pronouns (QUANT), and a group including all other expressions (OTHER). Table 1 shows the relative frequency for the grammatical types and the most frequent expressions.

As is usually found in conversation, first-person and second-person pronouns are the most frequent, collectively comprising 82.0% of all person-referring expressions. Of particular interest, due to their high frequency and multiple possible referential meanings, are the 1PP and 2P categories (e.g., *we* and *you*), comprising respectively 24.6% and 23.7% of all person-referring expressions. In Table 1, we show the information entropy of the referring type, given the grammatical category. This measures the uncertainty one has about the type, given knowledge of only the grammatical type of the expression. The analysis reveals that second-person pronouns are a particularly challenging reference resolution problem, with a broad and relatively even distribution across referring types.

| **Gram.** | **Freq.** (%) | **Ent.** (bits) | **Freq. words** |
|---|---|---|---|
| **1PS** | 33.7 | .57 | *I, my, me* |
| **1PP** | 24.6 | .67 | *we, our, us* |
| **2P** | 23.7 | 1.78 | *you, your, yours* |
| **3PS** | .9 | .66 | *he, his, she* |
| **3PP** | 7.2 | 1.25 | *they, them, their* |
| **QUANT** | 1.0 | 1.14 | *everyone, everybody* |
| **OTHER** | 8.9 | 1.57 | *people, guys, user* |

Table 1: A statistical summary of all the markables in the dataset by grammatical type (gram.), showing their frequency relative to all markables (freq.), the entropy of the referring type given the grammatical type (ent.), and a list of the most frequent examples (freq. words).

### 4.2 Reliability and Error Analysis

To show that our annotations are credible and suitable for empirical testing, we must establish that the subjective distinctions defined in our scheme may be applied by individuals other than the scheme developers. To do this, we assess intercoder agreement between two independent annotators on four meetings from the AMI corpus, using Cohen's Kappa (Cohen, 1960). Each of the decisions in the annotation procedure are assessed separately: markable identification, labeling referentiality, labeling specificity of person referents, and labeling addressing inclusion attributes. Because each decision depends on the previous, we employ a hierarchical assessment procedure that considers only instances where the annotators have agreed on previous decisions. This kind of multi-level assessment corresponds to that described and used in Carletta et al., (1997).

**Markables** The first annotation decision of interest is the identification of markables. Markables are either automatically identified occurrences of a pre-defined list of pronouns, or they are identified manually by the annotators. Agreement on this task, assessed only for manually identified words, was very good ($\kappa$=.94). Error analysis shows that the main issue with this decision was not determining lexical heads, but rather determining whether phrases such as "all age *groups*," "the older *generation*," and "the business *market*" should be considered as referring to *people* or not.

**Person referentiality** The next annotation decision is between person-referring and non-person-referring markables. For assessment of this choice, we measure agreement on a three-way categorization of the agreed markables as either FUNC-NON-PREF, FUNC-FILLER, or one of the FUNC-PREF-* categories. Agreement on this task was good ($\kappa$=.77). The only errors occurred on first- and second-person pronouns and between the FUNC-NON-PREF and FUNC-PREF-* categories. Error analysis suggests confusion tends to occur when pronouns are used with semantically light verbs like *go*, *get*, and *have*, for example in phrases such as "there *we* go" and "*you*'ve got the main things on the front." As in the latter example, some of the difficult choices appear to involve descriptions of states, which the speaker can choose to express either from various participants' points of view, as above, or alternatively without explicit subjectivity, e.g., "the main things are on the front."

**Specificity and cardinality** The next choice we assess is the decision between referring specifically to a single person (PERSON-SINGLE), to multiple people (PERSON-MULTIPLE), or as underspecified (also referred to as PERSON-OTHER). Agreement on this choice was very good ($\kappa$=.91), though considering only the difficult 1PP and 2P grammatical categories (e.g., *we* and *you*), agreement was less strong ($\kappa$=.75). Note that due to the hierarchical nature of the scheme, evaluation considered only cases where both annotators labeled a word as person-referring. Errors on this decision often involved ambiguities in addressing, where one annotator believed a particular individual was being addressed by *you* and the other thought the whole group was being addressed. Another common disagreement was on cases such as "*we* want it to be original," where *we* was interpreted by one annotator as referring to the present group of participants, but by the other as (presumably) referring to the organization to which the participants belong.

**Addressing inclusion attributes** For the three inclusion attributes for underspecified referents (ATTR-*-INCL), agreement is calculated three times, once for each of the binary attributes. Agreement was good, though slightly problematic for addressee inclusion (speaker $\kappa$=.72; addressee $\kappa$=.50; other $\kappa$=.66). Disagreements were mainly for occurrences of *you* like the example of autobiography in Section 3.4.5. For example, "it's *your* best friend" was used to explain why a dog is the speaker's favorite animal, and the annotators disagreed on whether the addressee was included.

## 5 Conclusion

We have presented an annotation scheme and a set of annotations that address *participant reference* — a conversational language problem that has seen little previous annotation work. Our focus has been on eliciting novel distinctions that we hypothesize will help us to distinguish, label, and summarize conversational activities. We also address the issues of vagueness, ambiguity, and contextual dependency in participant referring.

Based on analysis of inter-annotator agreement, the major distinctions proposed by the scheme appear to be reliably codable. In addition, our statistical analysis shows that our dataset contains a wide variety of participant references and should be a useful resource for several reference resolution problems for conversation. Our novel method for distinguishing specific reference to real individuals appears to be very reliably codable. Our novel addressing-based distinctions for underspecified reference are less reliable but adequate as a resource for some dialogue structuring tasks.

Further work proposed for this task includes labeling a variety of conversational and non-conversation genres. Our immediate concern is to apply our annotations in the training and/or testing of machine learning approaches to discourse segmentation and abstractive summarization.

## References

Thorsten Brants and Alex Franz. 2006. Web 1T 5-gram, Version 1. Linguistic Data Consortium. Catalog ID: LDC2006T13.

Lou Burnard, 2007. *Reference Guide for the British National Corpus (XML Edition)*. Research Technologies Service at Oxford University Computing Services.

Sasha Calhoun, Malvina Nissim, Mark Steedman, and Jason Brenier. 2005. A framework for annotating information structure in discourse. In *Proceedings of the ACL Workshop on Frontiers in Corpus Annotation II: Pie in the Sky*.

Jean Carletta, Stephen Isard, Anne H. Anderson, Gwyneth Doherty-Sneddon, Amy Isard, and Jacqueline C. Kowtko. 1997. The reliability of a dialogue structure coding scheme. *Computational Linguistics*, 23(1):13–31.

Herbert H. Clark. 1996. *Using Language*. Cambridge University Press, Cambridge.

Jacob Cohen. 1960. A coefficient of agreement for nominal scales. *Educational and Psychological Measurement*, 20:37–46.

George Doddington, Alexis Mitchell, Mark Przybocki, Lance Ramshaw, Stephanie Strassel, and Ralph Weischedel. 2004. The Automatic Content Extraction (ACE) program: Tasks, data, and evaluation. In *Proc. LREC*.

Matthew Frampton, Raquel Fernndez, Patrick Ehlen, Mario Christoudias, Trevor Darrell, and Stanley Peters. 2009. Who is "you"? Combining linguistic and gaze features to resolve second-person references in dialogue. In *Proc. EACL*.

John J. Godfrey, Edward Holliman, and J. McDaniel. 1992. SWITCHBOARD: Telephone speech corpus for research and development. In *Proc. ICASSP*, pages 517–520, San Francisco, CA.

Surabhi Gupta, John Niekrasz, Matthew Purver, and Daniel Jurafsky. 2007a. Resolving "you" in multiparty dialog. In *Proc. SIGdial*, pages 227–230.

Surabhi Gupta, Matthew Purver, and Daniel Jurafsky. 2007b. Disambiguating between generic and referential "you" in dialog. In *Proc. ACL*.

A. Janin, D. Baron, J. Edwards, D. Ellis, D. Gelbart, N. Morgan, B. Peskin, T. Pfau, E. Shriberg, A. Stolcke, and C. Wooters. 2003. The ICSI meeting corpus. In *Proc. ICASSP*, volume 1, pages 364–367.

Linguistic Data Consortium, 2008. *ACE (Automatic Content Extraction) English Annotation Guidelines for Entities, Version 6.5*. Downloaded from `http://projects.ldc.upenn.edu/ace/annotation/`.

I. McCowan, J. Carletta, W. Kraaij, S. Ashby, S. Bourban, M. Flynn, M. Guillemot, T. Hain, J. Kadlec, V. Karaiskos, M. Kronenthal, G. Lathoud, M. Lincoln, A. Lisowska, W. Post, D. Reidsma, and P. Wellner. 2005. The AMI Meeting Corpus. In *Proceedings of Measuring Behavior 2005, the 5th International Conference on Methods and Techniques in Behavioral Research*, Wageningen, Netherlands.

Peter Mühlhäusler and Rom Harré. 1990. *Pronouns and People: The Linguistic Construction of Social and Personal Identity*. Blackwell, Oxford.

Malvina Nissim, Shipra Dingare, Jean Carletta, and Mark Steedman. 2004. An annotation scheme for information status in dialogue. In *Proc. LREC*.

R. Passonneau, 1997. *Instructions for applying discourse reference annotation for multiple applications (DRAMA)*.

Massimo Poesio and Ron Artstein. 2008. Anaphoric annotation in the ARRAU corpus. In *Proc. LREC*.

Massimo Poesio, 2000. *The GNOME Annotation Scheme Manual, Version 4*. University of Edinburgh, HCRC and Informatics.

Massimo Poesio. 2004. Discourse annotation and semantic annotation in the GNOME corpus. In *Proceedings of the ACL 2004 Workshop on Discourse Annotation*, pages 72–79.

Matthew Purver, Raquel Fernndez, Matthew Frampton, and Stanley Peters. 2009. Cascaded lexicalised classifiers for second-person reference resolution. In *Proc. SIGdial*, pages 306–309.

Stephanie Strassel, Mark Przybocki, Kay Peterson, Zhiyi Song, and Kazuaki Maeda1. 2008. Linguistic resources and evaluation techniques for evaluation of cross-document automatic content extraction. In *Proc. LREC*.

Katie Wales. 1996. *Personal pronouns in present-day English*. Cambridge University Press, Cambridge.

# Design and Evaluation of Shared Prosodic Annotation for Spontaneous French Speech: From Expert Knowledge to Non-Expert Annotation

Anne Lacheret[1] Nicolas Obin[1, 2] Mathieu Avanzi[1, 3]

[1] Modyco Lab, Paris Ouest University, Nanterre, France

[2] Analysis-Synthesis team, Ircam, Paris, France

[3] Neuchâtel University, Neuchâtel, Switzerland

anne@lacheret.com, nobin@iracm.fr; Mathieu.avanzi@unine.ch

## Abstract

In the area of large French speech corpora, there is a demonstrated need for a common prosodic notation system allowing for easy data exchange, comparison, and automatic annotation. The major questions are: (1) how to develop a single simple scheme of prosodic transcription which could form the basis of guidelines for non-expert manual annotation (NEMA), used for linguistic teaching and research; (2) based on this NEMA, how to establish reference prosodic corpora (RPC) for different discourse genres (Cresti and Moneglia, 2005); (3) how to use the RPC to develop corpus-based learning methods for automatic prosodic labelling in spontaneous speech (Buhman *et al.,* 2002; Tamburini and Caini 2005, Avanzi, *et al.* 2010). This paper presents two pilot experiments conducted with a consortium of 15 French experts in prosody in order to provide a prosodic transcription framework (transcription methodology and transcription reliability measures) and to establish reference prosodic corpora in French.

## 1 Introduction

In this paper the case of the prosodic annotation of spontaneous French speech is discussed. Ever since the ToBI system was introduced in the international speech community (Silverman *et al.*, 1992), it has been considered by some – irrespective of the language to be annotated[1] - as a standard for prosodic annotation, while others contend that ToBI cannot be regarded as a universal annotation tool, *i.e.* it is not appropriate to capture the prosodic properties of certain languages. This is especially true when dealing with spontaneous speech, for which new methods of annotation must be found. In other words, a better prosodic labelling is essential to improve linguistic analyses of prosody (Martin 2003, as well as research in speech technology (Wightman 2002). Linguistics and speech technology have dealt with prosodic transcription from various points of view, which makes a precise definition of the task difficult. An initial distinction can be drawn between (i) phonological approaches (Silverman *et al.,* 1992; Hirst and Di Cristo, 1998; Delais-Roussarie, 2005; etc.), and (ii) acoustic-phonetic prosodic analysis (Beaugendre *et al.*, 1992; Mertens, 2004). Nowadays, these two approaches still remain problematic. The coding schemes of the former reflect not only a specific, and rather narrow, phonological point of view, but also the phonetic poverty of the transcription (most of the time, only information about the fundamental frequency is delivered, and no information regarding intensity, vocal quality, variations in syllabic length and speech disfluencies is provided). In the second approach, very fine-grained descriptions and modelling have been conducted (House, 1990; Mertens, 2004), but they are too rich to be easily exportable. The question therefore remains: what is the best compromise between an overly detailed phonetic description and a phonological annotation which is too narrow from a theoretical point of view? In an attempt to answer this question, the following prerequisites underpin our approach to prosodic annotation. First, it should be based on a **theory-independent phonological labelling**. To achieve this, we have designed an inductive prosodic processing which does not impose a phonological (generative) mould, but in which various existing notation systems (such as ToBI, Intsint, IVTS, see references below) could be integrated. Second, the annotation proposed by the expert should be easily reproducible by non-expert annotators and finally carried out by computers (in order to reduce the cost of human processing and

[1] For French, see the work of Post (2000) and Jun & Fougeron (2002).



*Proceedings of the Fourth Linguistic Annotation Workshop, ACL 2010*, pages 265–273, Uppsala, Sweden, 15-16 July 2010. ©2010 Association for Computational Linguistics

to avoid the subjectivity and variability of manual treatment).

This paper deals with an initial set of fundamental questions: (i) What does it mean to develop a theory-independent method of annotation? What does it imply in terms of methodological choices? (ii) Can we consider a type of annotation which is based on a categorical processing of prosody as well as continuous judgment, or is the latter too difficult to implement and process in a shared prosodic annotation? (iii) What kind of preliminary analysis is required in order to write a well-documented guideline sharable in the community for French prosody annotation? These three questions led us to conduct two pilot experiments in 2009, which are presented here. Each section is structured as follows: description of the corpus, the task, and the results, and a brief discussion of the experiment in question to explain the final choices made for the reference prosodic labelling summarized in the conclusion.

## 2 Pilot experiment one

This first experiment was conducted on a 63 sec. (335 syllables) recording, consisting in a monologue of spontaneous speech (interview with a shopkeeper in southern France). The recording was processed by 15 expert annotators (native French researchers in phonology and/or phonetics). The goal of this section is to present (§2.1) the task and its different steps, (§2.2) the results of the coding regarding inter-annotator agreement and (§2.3) the major problems revealed by the results concerning the coding method.

### 2.1 The task

The prosodic annotation is based first on the marking of two boundary levels, second on the identification of perceptual prominences, and finally on the labelling of disfluencies and hesitations.

Given our bias neutrality theory, no constraint was set *a priori* regarding prosodic domain and constituents separated by a prosodic break (rhythmic, syntactic or pragmatic units; this point concerns the functional interpretation to be conducted later). Concerning prominences, we considered that prominence was syllabic and had not to be merged with the notion of stress. This means that a prominent syllable is considered as a perceptual figure emerging from its background. Finally, we defined disfluency as an element which breaks the linear flow of speech, whatever the element is: it can be a syllable, a word, a morpheme unit, part of a sentence, etc.

The starting point of the procedure is a semi-automatic alignment processing (Goldman, 2008) conducted under Praat (Boersma and Weenink, 2010 which provides a 3-layer segmentation structure: segmentation within a phones string, syllabic string, and words string. They are all displayed on 3 temporally aligned tiers. Three empty tiers aligned on the syllabic tier have to be annotated (FRONT for marking the prosodic boundaries, PROM for annotating prominences and DYSF for coding disfluencies). Finally, a COMMENTS tier can be used to point out some mistakes in the annotation task and/or errors in the pre-processing (wrong segmentation or transcription, etc). An example of an annotated output file is given in figure 1.

Since the annotators do not have access to the acoustic parameters (melodic and intensity line, spectral information), the identification of prosodic boundaries, prominences and disfluencies is based only on perceptual processing. The coding methodology (categorical scale for the annotation) is structured in the following way: each annotator browses the file from left to right and organises the work in 3 steps.

- **First step: FRONT Tier processing, two degrees of prosodic boundary**

First, each annotator has to identify **breath groups** (henceforth BG, marker '2' at the end of the BG). A BG is defined as follows: it corresponds to a string of syllables bounded left and right by a silent pause, regardless of the function or duration of the pause.

*Example:*

*#C'est clair$_2$#*
*(#it is obvious#)*

Second, in each BG, the expert indicates where he perceives the end of an **internal prosodic group** (IPG, marker '1').

*Example:*
*#mais$_1$ je vais aussi$_1$ leur donner de moi-même$_2$#*
*(#and I will also give them of myself#)*

If the annotator is not sure about the presence of a prosodic boundary, he uses the indeterminacy marker '?'. In this way, two degrees of prosodic boundary are identified (major: BG and minor: IPG). Then, IPG are used to determine internal prosodic segments, which form the new anchor points (coding span) for the following processing steps (prominences and disfluencies annotation).

**• Second step: PROM tier processing**

The marker '1' is associated to syllables perceived as prominent (± terminal: *la* $re_{1}lation_{1}$*: the relationship*), and the indeterminacy marker '?' indicates the locations where the annotator hesitates between the presence and the absence of a prominence.

*Example:*

*La personne*$_{?}$ *va vous ra*$_{1}$*conter sa vie*$_{1}$
*(the man will tell you his life).*

The accentual clash rule (Dell, 1984; Pasdeloup 1990) is not taken into account. In other words, two or more contiguous syllables can be annotated as prominent.

**• Third step: DISF tier processing**

As for the coding of prominences, the experts use the symbol '1' to indicate the disfluencies clearly identified and '?' to point out a hesitation. The latter context is often linked to lengthening and final post-tonic schwa.

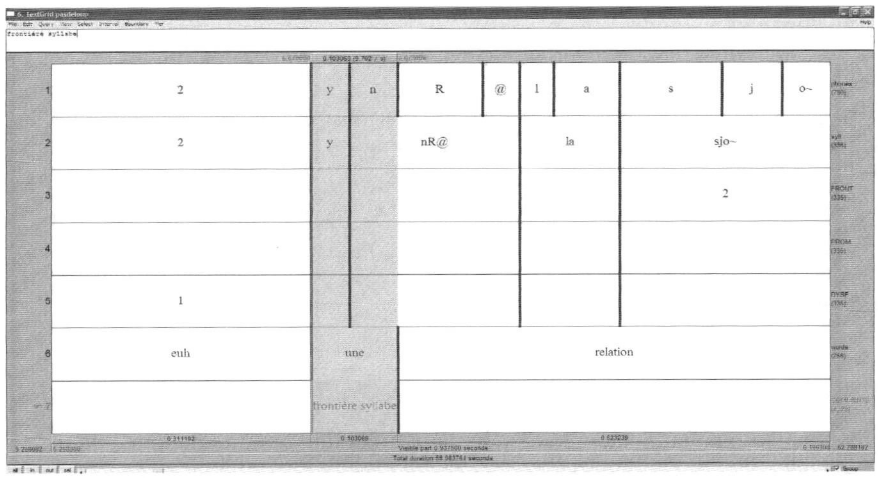


Figure 1. Example of prosodic annotation in pilot experiment one. Tiers indicate, from top to bottom: phones, syllables, boundaries (FRONT), prominences (PROM), disfluencies (DISF), graphemic words and comments. The empty segments correspond to any prosodic events detected in which the comment points out an incorrect syllabic labelling.

## 2.2 Results of the coding: inter-annotator agreement in pilot experiment one

**• Agreement measure**

The kappa statistic has been widely used in the past decade to assess inter-annotator agreement in prosodic labelling tasks (Syrdal and McGory, 2000), and in particular the reliability of inter-annotator agreement in the case of a categorical rating, (Carletta, 1996). Among the many versions proposed in the literature, we selected the *Fleiss' kappa* (Fleiss, 1971), which provides an overall agreement measure over a fixed number of annotators in the case of categorical rating (unlike Cohen's Kappa which only provides a measure of pairwise agreement).

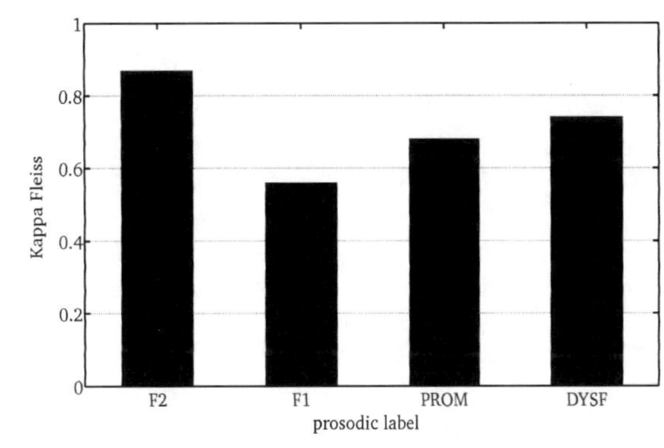


**• Results**

Figure 2 presents the Fleiss' kappa agreement for each prosodic label. Indeterminacy markers were simply processed as missing values and removed from the annotation data.

Figure 2. Inter-annotator agreement for each prosodic label

These results show moderate agreement on prosodic boundaries for FRONT1 (0.56) and FRONT2 (0.86). While agreement on major prosodic boundaries seems to be strong, it should be remembered that this marker was formally imposed on the annotators in the instructions. Consequently, the score questions the relevancy of the task: if a few annotators did not follow it, it is probably because in specific distributions, the end of a BG does not correspond to a major prosodic boundary. Furthermore, experts noticed that a prosodic break could be stronger at the end of an IPG than at the end of a BG where the silent pause is not necessarily due to a prosodic break, especially in spontaneous speech. Prominence labeling provides moderate agreement (0.68), better than FRONT1, and better than the agreement scores found in the literature for other prominence labelling tasks for French speech (Morel *et al.*, 2006)[2]. Finally, disfluency labelling shows substantial agreement, disagreements being mostly due to confusion between the prominent or disfluent status of a syllable.

### 2.3 Conclusion on pilot experiment one

The results of this first experiment call for the following comments. While identification of hesitations and disfluencies seems to be an easy task, the annotation of prosodic boundaries and prominences raises a set of methodological and linguistic questions: (i) Are the concepts sufficiently well-defined to represent the same prosodic reality for each annotator? (ii) How far are the experts influenced by their theoretical background or phonological knowledge? (iii) To what extent does the fixed coding methodology introduce noise in the labelling (for instance, does the end of a BG systematically correspond to a major prosodic boundary)? (iv) Is a 3-step annotation coding too heavy a cognitive task, incompatible with the principle of economy required by a sharable prosodic annotation scheme?

## 3 Pilot experiment two

For this second experiment, we chose the same recording (speaker from southern France, 63 sec. of speech) and a second one that was more difficult because of its interactive dimension and because it contains many speech overlaps and disfluencies (3 speakers of Normandy, 60 seconds of speech, 284 syllables to label). The data were processed by 11 experts. This section follows the same organization as section 2.

### 3.1 The task: focus on prosodic packaging

For this second experiment, we selected to focus the annotation on the most problematic point in the first experiment, namely the coding of prosodic breaks. We conjectured that the lack of agreement derived first from the terminology that the experts were asked to use: the concept of *prosodic boundary*, which is phonologically marked and also theory-dependent, might explain the lack of consensus between experts belonging to different schools. Consequently, each annotator was asked to carry out only one task, called *prosodic packaging*. In this task, the expert had to segment the flow of speech into a string of prosodic packages (Mertens, 1993; Chafe 1998) as far as possible according to his perceptual processing, *i.e.* independently of any underlying functional and formal constraints.

Given the nature of the task, the method of annotation was not imposed, unlike the first experiment. In other words, each annotator fixed his own coding span. Finally the experts were required to carry out a meta-analysis, justifying their coding span and trying to understand and explain the cues they had used for the packaging task (acoustic, rhythmic, syntactic, pragmatic criteria).

Each Praat textgrid is composed of five tiers (see figure 3 below): three tiers are used as anchor points for the annotation (syllables, words and "Loc.", which indicates the speaker changes), and only one tier has to be annotated (prosodic packages); the Comments tier is also displayed with the same function as in experiment one. Four symbols are used for the annotation (continuous scale rating): "?": hesitancy regarding the end of a package; "1": end of a package, weak break with the following package; "2?": indeterminacy regarding the degree of the transition between two packages (weak or strong); "2": strong breaks between two packages.

[2] These better results are probably due to the more stringent method of annotation imposed.

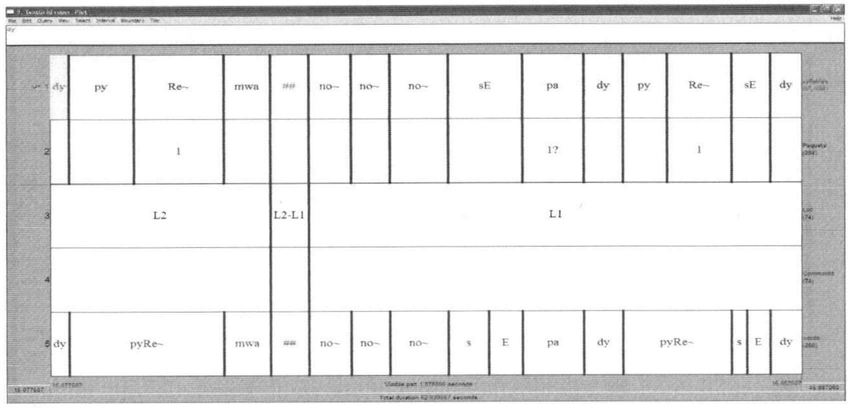


Figure 3. Example of transcription in prosodic packages in pilot experiment 2.Tiers indicate, from top to bottom: syllables, boundaries (FRONT), speakers (LOC, where L1 and L2 mean speaker one and speaker 2, L1-L2 = overlap between the 2 speakers), comments and phonetic words.

### 3.2 Results of the coding: inter-annotator agreement in pilot experiment two

- **Agreement measures**

In addition to the Fleiss'kappa test used in the first experiment, we introduced here the *Weighted Cohen's Kappa* (Fleiss and Cohen, 1973) which provides a pairwise agreement measure in the case of ordinal categorical rating (categorical labels are ordered along a continuous scale). In particular, weighted Cohen's Kappa weights disagreement according to the nature of the disagreed labels. Linear Cohen's Kappa was used in this experiment.

In this second experiment, we addressed three kind of inter-annotator agreement: (i) **Presence of the end of a prosodic package** (PPP), *i.e.* to what extent did annotators agree about the end of a prosodic package? (ii) **Location of the end of a prosodic package**: annotators may agree on a PPP, but disagree on the exact location of this boundary. This was measured by adding a tolerance on the location of the PPP (1-order syllable context). (iii) **Strength of the end of PPP**, *i.e.* how much annotators agree about the degree of a prosodic boundary.

Fleiss' kappa was estimated for the first two problems, and Linear Cohen's Kappa for the last (indeterminacy markers being considered as intermediate degrees).

- **Results**

Figure 4 presents the agreement scores for the three cases mentioned above and for the two corpora used.

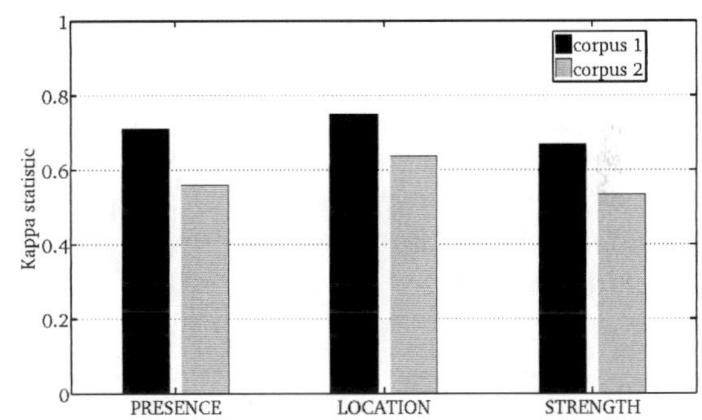


Figure 4. Inter-annotator agreement according to presence, location, and strength of the end of prosodic package.

Overall agreement scores indicate a significantly lower agreement for the second corpus. This is probably related to its higher complexity (low audio quality, high level of interaction, many disfluencies, regional accent) which made the task harder to process. The comparison of **presence** (corpus 1 = 0.71; corpus 2 = 0.56) versus **strength** (corpus 1 = 0.67; corpus 2 = 0.53) of the end of a prosodic package agreements suggests that categorical rating is more reliable than ordinal rating. In other words, annotators appear to perform better at rating the categorical status of a syllable rather than its precise degree. On the **location** problem, it is first interesting to note that the occurrence of such a location shift is significant in the prosodic labelling. In the present study, the location shift represents respectively 12% and 18% of syllables that were rated as PPP by at least one of the annotators (**balance effect**, see figure 5). Thus, merging these shifts leads to a higher agreement score (corpus 1 = 0.75 and corpus 2 = 0.63 after merging).

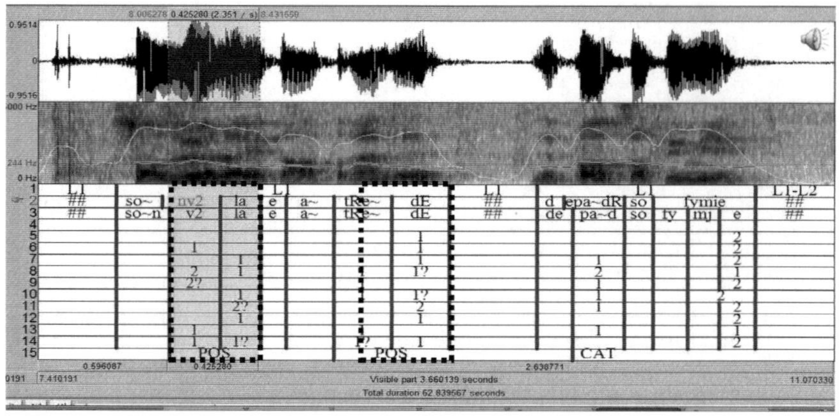

Figure 5. Examples of balance effect in the segment *"son neveu là est en train d'é-"* (*his nephew is there now*)

- **Annotator clustering**

Finally, we investigated whether the experts' phonological models affected the way in which they perceive prosodic objects.

First, annotators were labelled by the authors according to their assumed underlying phonological model. This resulted in 4 groups (3 different phonological models + a residual group: two speech engineers involved in signal processing with no phonological model).

The annotators were then hierarchically clustered according to their agreement score (see figure 6). This hierarchical clustering was achieved through complete linkage on semi-euclidean distance between annotator agreement (see Hastie *et al.*, 2009 for details)

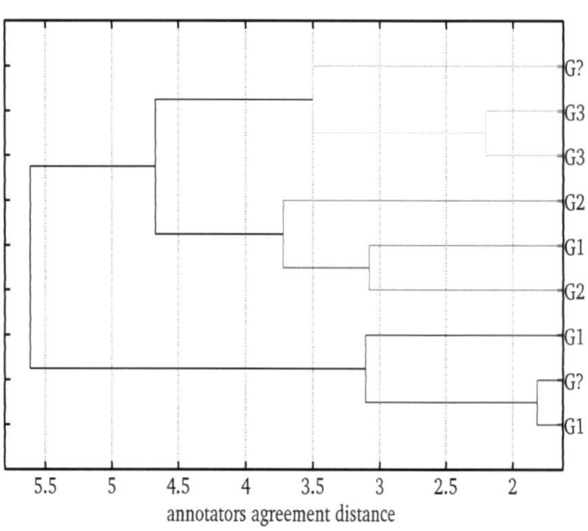


Figure 6. Agglomerative hierarchical clustering of the annotators according to their agreement on both corpora.

Interestingly, this results in three main clusters that significantly match the three previously defined groups for process annotation: (i) A tonal perception (G1) and syntactic functional approach (Mertens, 1993); (ii) Cognitive processing (G2), trying to segment the flow of speech independently of syntactic constraints (Lacheret, 2007; see the notion of flow of thought in Chafe, 1998); (iii) a formal approach (G3) based on prosodic phonology (Nespor and Vogel, 1986) and the problem of mapping between prosodic structure and generative syntax (Selkirk, 1984).

### 3.3 Conclusion on pilot experiment two

Two main conclusions emerge from this second experiment. (i) Even if prosodic constructions are in many respects continuous mechanisms, it seems more realistic for the time being to consider a method based on a categorical annotation. (ii) This second experiment confirms that the experts' phonological models significantly affect annotation and questions the reliability of expert annotation. However further investigation is needed and a comparison with non-expert annotators must be conducted before drawing any definitive conclusions.

## 4 Conclusion

Given the results of pilot experiments 1 and 2, we conclude that neither the static concept of **prosodic boundary**, nor its dynamic substitute **prosodic packaging** leads to a high inter-annotator consensus. In other words, these two concepts are probably too dependent on different levels of processing (syntactic, phonological, and rhythmic) and each annotator, depending on his own definition of the notion (formal or functional) will focus on one aspect or another. Consequently, even if precise instructions are given for annotation, the labelled data still remain heterogeneous. Therefore, these two concepts should not be used as the basis for the development of a shared prosodic annotation method aiming to establish a reference prosodic corpus and annotation software, which are essential tools in handling large volumes of speech data. In contrast, we hypothesize that prominence annotation based on perceptual criteria represents the cornerstone of speech prosodic segmentation, as prosodic structure will be generated from prominence labelling. Although the results of the first pilot experiment are rather poor 0.68), recent experiments have shown that the scores rise (0.86) after training sessions (Avanzi *et al* 2010b). We have therefore decided to focus our annotation guideline on the labelling of prominences (two levels of prominence: strong or weak) and disfluencies (hesitations, false starts, speaker overlaps, post-tonic schwas, etc.). The method does not depend on some abstract property of words or groups of words, as in the case of lexical stress (Martin, 2006; Poiré, 2006; Post *et al.* 2006), but is based on a neutral phonetic definition of prominence, associated with perceptual salience in the context of the speech background. This approach has the advantage of being consensual, whatever the theoretical framework adopted. Based on these criteria, a one day training session has been organized for 5 novice annotators (students in linguistics) in order to annotate 3.30 hours of different speech genres (private, public, professional), over 2 months (from February to April 2010). For each genre a monologal and an interactional sample of around 5 minutes (42 speech files altogether) have to be labelled. Prominences and disfluencies are coded on two independent tiers.

The annotation deliverable will be processed during the spring by five experts who will have to perform four tasks: (i) compute the inter-annotator scores applying the statistical measures used in the two pilot experiments; (ii) diagnose the distributions with the poorest scores for all the samples; (iii) diagnose the genres with the worst scores and (iv) make explicit decisions to provide an output prosodic reference annotation and to enhance automatic prominence detection software (see for French: Avanzi *et al.*, 2010a; Martin 2010; Obin *et al.* 2008a, 2008b, 2009; Simon *et al.* 2008).

## Acknowledgements

This research is supported by the Agence Nationale de la Recherche (ANR-07-CORP-030-01, "Rhapsodie – Corpus prosodique de référence du français parlé"). We would like to thanks our colleagues from LPL (Aix-en-Provence), ERSS (Toulouse), Ircam (Paris), MODYCO (Paris) and also University of Geneve (Switzerland), Louvain-la-Neuve, Leuven (Belgium) to have conduct this work for *Rhapsodie*.

## References

Mathieu Avanzi, Anne Lacheret and Anne-Catherine Simon. 2010. *Proceedings of Prosodic Prominence, Speech Prosody 2010 Satellite Workshop, Chicago, May 10$^{th}$.*

Mathieu Avanzi, Anne Lacheret and Bernard Victorri. 2010a. A Corpus-Based Learning Method for Prominences Detection in Spontaneous Speech. *Proceedings of Prosodic Prominence, Speech Prosody 2010 Satellite Workshop, Chicago, May 10$^{th}$.*

Mathieu Avanzi, Anne-Catherine Simon, Jean-Philippe Goldman and Antoine Auchlin, 2010b. C-PROM. An annotated corpus for French prominence studies. *Proceedings of Prosodic Prominence, Speech Prosody 2010 Satellite Workshop, Chicago, May 10$^{th}$.*

Frédéric Beaugendre, Christophe d'Alessandro, Anne Lacheret-Dujour and Jacques Terken. 1992. A Perceptual Study of French Intonation. *Proceedings of the International Conference on Spoken Language Processing*, J. Ohala (ed.), Canada, 739-742.

Paul Boersma and David Weenink. 2010. Praat: doing phonetics by computer (version 5.1), www.praat.org.

Jeska Buhmann, Johanneke Caspers, Vincent J. van Heuven, Heleen Hoekstra, Jean-Pierre Mertens and Marc Swerts. 2002. Annotation of prominent words, prosodic boundaries and segmental lengthening by non-expert transcribers in the Spoken Dutch Corpus. *Proceedings of LREC2002*, Las Palmas, 779-785.

Jean Carletta, 1996. Assessing agreement on classification tasks: the Kappa statistic. *Computational Linguistics*, 22(2):249-254.

Wallace Chafe. 1998. Language and the Flow of Thought. *New Psychology of language*, M. Tomasello (ed.), New Jersey, Lawrence Erlbraum Publishers, 93-111.

Emmanuela Cresti and Massimo Moneglia, eds. 2005. *C-ORAL-ROM. Integrated Reference Corpora for Spoken Romance Languages*, Studies in Corpus Linguistics 15. Amsterdam, Benjamins.

Elisabeth Delais-Roussarie. 2005. *Phonologie et grammaire, étude et modélisation des interfaces prosodiques*. Mémoire d'habilitation à diriger des recherches, Toulouse.

François Dell. 1984. L'accentuation dans les phrases françaises. *Forme sonore du langage, structure des représentations en phonologie*, F. Dell *et al.* Paris, Hermann, 65-122.

Joseph L. Fleiss. 1971. Measuring nominal scale agreement among many raters. *Psychological Bulletin*, 76(5):378–382.

Joseph L. Fleiss and Jacob Cohen. 1973. The equivalence of weighted kappa and the intraclass correlation coefficient as measures of reliability. *Educational and Psychological Measurement*, 33:613-619.

Jean-Philippe Goldman. 2008. EasyAlign: a semi-automatic phonetic alignment tool under Praat, http://latlcui.unige.ch/phonetique.

Trevor Hastie, Robert Tibshirani and Jerome Friedman, 2009. Hierarchical clustering. *The Elements of Statistical Learning* (2nd ed.). New York: Springer, 520-528.

Daniel Hirst and Albert Di Cristo. 1998. *Intonation Systems: A Survey of Twenty Languages*, Cambridge, Cambridge University Press.

David House.1990. *Tonal perception in Speech*, Lund University Press.

Sun Ah Jun and Cécile Fougeron. 2002. The Realizations of the Accentual Phrase for French Intonation", *Probus*, 14:147-172.

Anne Lacheret. 2007. Prosodie du discours, une interface à multiples facettes. *Nouveaux Cahiers de linguistique française*, 28:7-40.

Philippe Martin. 2003. ToBI : l'illusion scientifique? *Actes du colloque international Journées Prosodie 2001. Université de Grenoble*, 109-113.

Philippe Martin. 2006. La transcription des proéminences accentuelles : mission impossible?, *Bulletin de phonologie du français contemporain*, 6:81-88.

Philippe Martin. 2010. Prominence Detection without Syllabic Segmentation, *Proceedings of Prosodic Prominence, Speech Prosody 2010 Satellite Workshop, Chicago, May 10th*.

Piet Mertens. 1993. Intonational Grouping, boundaries, and syntactic structure in French. *Working Papers Lund University*, 41:156-159.

Piet Mertens. 2004. The Prosogram: Semi-Automatic Transcription of prosody based on a Tonal Perception Model. *Proceedings of Speech Prosody 2004, Nara, Japan*. 549-552.

Michel Morel, Anne Lacheret-Dujour, Chantal Lyche, Morel M. and François Poiré. 2006. "Vous avez dit proéminence?, *Actes des 26èmes journées d'étude sur la parole, Dinard, France*. 183-186.

Marina Nespor and Irene Vogel. 1986. *Prosodic Phonology*, Foris, Dordrecht

Nicolas Obin, Xavier Rodet and Anne Lacheret-Dujour. 2008a. French prominence: a probabilistic framework. *Proceedings of ICASSP'08*, Las Vegas, U.S.A.

Nicolas Obin, Jean-Philippe Goldman, Mathieu Avanzi and Anne Lacheret. 2008b. Comparaison de trois outils de détection automatique de proéminences en français parlé. *Actes des 27èmes journées d'étude sur la parole,* Avignon, France.

Nicolas Obin, Xavier Rodet and Anne Lacheret-Dujour. 2009. A Syllable-Based Prominence Detection Model Based on Discriminant Analysis and Context-Dependency, *Proceedings of SPECOM'09,* St-Petersburg, Russia.

Valérie Pasdeloup. 1990. *Modèle de règles rythmiques du français appliqué à la synthèse de la parole*, PhD, Université de Provence.

François Poiré. 2006. La perception des proéminences et le codage prosodique, *Bulletin de phonologie du français contemporain*, 6:69-79.

Brechtje Post. 2000. *Tonal and phrasal structures in French intonation*. The Hague, Thesus.

Brechtje Post, Elisabeth Delais-Roussarie and Anne Catherine Simon. 2006. IVTS, un système de transcription pour la variation prosodique, *Bulletin de phonologie du français contemporain*, 6:51-68.

Elisabeth Selkirk. 1984. *Phonology and Syntax: the Relation between Sounds and Structure*. Cambridge, Cambridge MIT Press.

Kim Silverman, Mary Beckman, John Pitrelli, Mary Ostendorf, Colin Wightman, Patti Price, Janet Pierrehumbert and Julia Hirschberg. 1992. ToBI: A standard for Labeling English prosody, *Proceedings of the International Conference on Spoken Language Processing (ICSLP)*. 867-870.

Anne Catherine Simon, Mathieu Avanzi, Jean-Philippe Goldman, 2008. La détection des proéminences syllabiques. Un aller-retour entre l'annotation manuelle et le traitement automatique. *Actes du 1er Congrès Mondial de Linguistique Française, Paris*.1673-1686.

Caroline L. Smith. 2009. Naïve listeners' perceptions of French prosody compared to the predictions of theoretical models. *Proceedings of the third symposium Prosody/discourse interfaces, Paris, September 2009*.

Ann K. Syrdal and Julia McGory. 2000. Inter-transcribers Reliability of ToBI Prosodic Labelling. *Proceedings of the International Conference on*

*Spoken Language Processing, Beijing, China.* Vol. 3, 235-238.

Fabrizio Tamburini and Carlo Caini. 2005. An automatic System for Detecting Prosodic Prominence in American English Continuous Speech. *International Journal of Speech technology*, 8:33-44.

Colin W. Wightman. 2002. ToBI or not ToBI?. *Proceedings of Speech Prosody*, Aix-en-Provence, France, 25-29.

# Depends on What the French Say

## Spoken Corpus Annotation With and Beyond Syntactic Functions

**José Deulofeu**
DELIC, Université de Provence
Aix, France.
jose.deulofeu@up.univ-mrs.fr

**Lucie Duffort, Kim Gerdes**
LPP, Sorbonne Nouvelle
Paris, France
lucieduffort@hotmail.com
kim@gerdes.fr

**Sylvain Kahane**
Modyco, Université Paris Ouest
Nanterre, France
sylvain@kahane.fr

**Paola Pietrandrea**
Université Roma TRE / Lattice, ENS
Rome, Italy and Paris, France
pietrand@uniroma3.it

### Abstract

We present a syntactic annotation scheme for spoken French that is currently used in the *Rhapsodie* project. This annotation is dependency-based and includes coordination and disfluency as analogously encoded types of paradigmatic phenomena. Furthermore, we attempt a thorough definition of the discourse units required by the systematic annotation of other phenomena beyond usual sentence boundaries, which are typical for spoken language. This includes so called "macrosyntactic" phenomena such as dislocation, parataxis, insertions, grafts, and epexegesis.

## 1 Introduction

This communication presents the syntactic annotation scheme currently being developed for *Rhapsodie* a project funded by the French National Research Agency (ANR) which aims to study the syntax-prosody interface in spoken French. *Rhapsodie* aims to elaborate a freely distributed corpus, classified into different discourse genres, and doted with prosodic and syntactic annotations elaborated for the study of the relationship of prosody, syntax, and information structure in discourse.

Contrary to what is available in the anglo-saxon world, there is no freely distributed and syntactically annotated corpus of spoken French today. This is what our project aims to provide.

The only tree-bank for French, that we know of, is the Paris 7 Corpus (Abeillé et al. 2003). This is a corpus of newspaper texts, annotated mainly in Penn Tree Bank style and partially with dependency annotations, which is distributed only under highly restrictive conditions.

Some annotated corpora of spoken French nevertheless exist: The CID (Corpus of Interactional Data) (Bertrand et al. 2009) uses an annotation with typed chunks, and the VALIBEL corpus (Dister et al. 2008 ; Degand et Simon 2009) consists of delimiting maximal syntactic units. This notion, allowing segmentation of the text, is essential for any syntactic annotation, a concept we will come back to in section 2. Neither of these corpora is distributed freely and none comes close to the precision and variety of spoken language corpora existing for other languages like English or Dutch.

There is, however, an important tradition of description of the spoken French language, notably at the University of Provence in Aix, where a team led by Claire Blanche-Benveniste coined the two level distinction of "micro-syntax" and "macro-syntax" and proposed a parallel analysis of paradigmatic phenomena ranging from coordinations to disfluencies (Blanche-Benveniste 1990, Berrendonner 1990, Bilger et al. 1997, Guénot 2006, Gerdes & Kahane 2009).

*Rhapsodie*'s innovation stems from a formalization and generalization of this tradition. The parallel annotation of prosody and syntax naturally leads to a syntactic analysis of the text as a whole, including hesitations and disfluencies, whereas other approaches tend to erase these phenomena in order to obtain standard sentences similar to written language where syntactic annotation is well-established. Examples of this latter approach include main reference corpora, for example the English Switchboard corpus (http://groups.inf.ed.ac.uk/switchboard), or the CGN (Dutch Spoken Corpus, http://lands.let.ru.nl/cgn). These types of annotation also commonly exclude phenomena such as colon effects, grafts, and associated illocutionary



*Proceedings of the Fourth Linguistic Annotation Workshop, ACL 2010*, pages 274–281,
Uppsala, Sweden, 15-16 July 2010. ©2010 Association for Computational Linguistics

units, because of their limited conception of sentence boundaries and a focus on written phenomena. The *Rhapsodie* syntactic analysis scheme tends to include all words of the corpus and finds it necessary to take account of all the above phenomena because they are, we believe, intrinsically syntactic.

The original English examples in this paper stem from the Micase corpus (Simpson-Vlach & Leicher 2006), in particular from the segment Honors Advising (http://quod.lib.umich.edu/m/micase) and from interviews that we collected ourselves (ELUI; English Language Use Interviews, Duffort in preparation). Some phenomena are specific to French and we use original examples from the *Rhapsodie* corpus; some other examples, designated as "constructed examples", are simplified constructions of phenomena we only encountered in more complex combinations.

## 2 Annotation

In the analysis of written text, the units of annotation are usually taken to be "graphical" sentences, i.e. the words between two periods, a neither explicit nor homogenous notion that has little or no linguistic relevance. Spoken corpus annotation, on the contrary, has to simultaneously define dependency units and the dependency annotation that we impose on these units. These two questions are not independent: The more phenomena we include in the syntactic analysis, the longer the units will become.

Our first choice concerns syntactic annotation: Functional dependency annotation has proven to be a more challenging task than phrase structure annotation but seems to be more versatile for various languages and more promising as an intermediate syntactic structure between the ordered words and semantics. All dependency based corpora have to choose a set of functions to be used in annotation. This choice is often guided by practical considerations (existing phrase structure annotation, parsers, semantic needs, etc.) but even though few have tried to give a formal and general definition of syntactic functions (Mel'cuk & Pertsov 1987), each choice of a set of functions presumes that two elements (subtrees) that share the same function have something in common: Usually this is thought to be

- the exchangeability of the two elements (at a certain degree of abstraction, excluding, for example, agreement features)
- the coordinability of the two elements

For example, to decide whether *gone* and *the bike* have the same function in *he has gone* and *he has a bike*, it is not sufficient that the two elements can be interchanged; we also need coordinability which in this case is ungrammatical. We will therefore stipulate the existence of two different functions.[1]

(1) *He has gone and a bike.

In other words, a coordination is an orthogonal construction to a head-daughter relation. This also shows in the difficulty in dependency as well as phrase structure approaches to account for coordination. The near-symmetry of coordinations violates basic assumptions of X-bar theory and head-daughter relationships. Contrary to other dependency analyses like the Prague Dependency Treebank (ufal.mff.cuni.cz/pdt) or the Alpino Dependency Treebank (www.let.rug.nl/vannoord/trees), our approach does not include coordinations in our syntactic functions, but these, as well as other paradigmatic phenomena, are encoded in what we call "piles"[2] (see section 2.3).

### 2.1 Dependency Units and Illocutionary Units

We don't consider that syntax can be reduced to dependency, and we have to define the delimitation of functional relations as well as the delimitation of so called "macro-syntactic" phenomena such as dislocation and colon effect that go beyond dependency. Our complete annotation therefore includes units joined by dependency, paradigmatic sub-units, and higher-level relations that are still syntactic and not purely discursive. We propose a well defined distinction between syntax based segmentation, called "dependency units" (DU), and pragmatically based segmentation, called "illocutionary units" (IU).

Applying a bottom-up approach, we first look for rectional (head-daughter) relations, which gives us the DUs: Each DU is a unit, constructed around a syntactic head that itself has no governor. We define a rectional relation using the

[1] Note that this choice is less clear in many cases, such as for example for the distinction between passives and predicative functions, or between full and light verbs.

[2] Of course this can be represented formally equivalently as a specific type of dependency, but we believe that the distinction is linguistically important and limiting the notion of dependency to true head-daughter relations makes the notion of dependency more consistent.

common criteria: i.e. constraints in terms of category, morphological features, and restructuration possibilities (commutation with a pronoun, diatheses, clefting).

In addition to these syntactic units, we define the IUs as unities that demonstrate a discursive autonomy, in other words, that have their own illocutionary force. These terms may seem surprising in formal syntax, but we believe that they are unavoidable for our task. This definition assents to traditional grammarians' intuition of sentences holding a "complete meaning" and Creissels' definition of "sentence" (2004) as a propositional content realizing an enunciation.

Both units, DUs and IUs are relatively independent and complementary and they have their own well-formedness conditions. In general, an IU is a combination of several DUs, but we will show examples ranging from simple interjections to complex embedded DUs. In some cases a rectional relation, and thus a DU can go beyond the limits of an IU.

This opposition of DU and IU reflects Blanche-Benveniste's opposition between microsyntax and macrosyntax (1990): A DU is the maximal microsyntactic unit; an IU constitutes the maximal unit of macrosyntax.

### 2.2 Microsyntax and Dependency Units

In this paper, we will not elaborate further on the dependency annotation itself. We have followed approaches taken by numerous other corpora such as the Prague Dependency Treebank or the Alpino Dependency Treebank (www.let.rug.nl/vannoord/trees/).

Let us consider the following utterance, typical for spoken French:

(2) moi ma mère le salon c'est de la moquette
*me my mother the living room it's carpet*
'My mother's living room is carpeted'

In (2), three elements—*moi,* literally 'me', *ma mère* 'my mother', *le salon* 'the living room'—are paratactically juxtaposed to a predicative unit, *c'est de la moquette* 'it is carpet'. These elements are not syntactically dependent on any element in the predicative unit. We treat them as separate DUs. We will illustrate in 2.4 the treatment we propose for the relation holding between these DUs.

### 2.3 Piles

Beside dependency, we acknowledge the existence of a separate mechanism of syntactic cohesion within DUs: Following Gerdes & Kahane (2009), we call the syntactic relation between units occupying the same structural position within a DU, or, in other words, holding the same position in a dependency tree, a "pile". Coordination is a typical case of piling:

(3) our two languages are {English | ^and French} (ELUI)

We consider that we also have a pile of elements occupying the same structural position in reformulations (4), disfluencies (5) or corrections (6):

(4) did a humanoid species { spring up | or exist } in various places {in the world | {not just in Africa | ^but also in Asia | ^and maybe also in southern Europe }} // (Micase)

(5) { I~ | in~ | including } kind of a general idea of these "uh" (ELUI)

(6) {I | I} have lots of other interests {like "um" | that are a little bit more like} {paleontology | ^or astronomy | ^or international religion | ^or "uh" not religion | international relations | ^so those things {I wanna & | I think I'm gonna concentrate more on} // (Micase)

Our desire to treat coordinations, reformulations and disfluencies as phenomena showing syntactic similarity resides in the fact that, as shown by Blanche-Benveniste (1990) among others, it is not always easy to distinguish between disfluency, reformulation and coordination: As an example, consider (7a), more or less interpreted in the same way as examples (7b,c) which are, respectively, a reformulation and a coordination:

(7) a. she is { a linguist | maybe a technician }
b. she is { a linguist | "um" a technician }
c. she is { a linguist | ^or a technician }
(constructed example)

In all cases of piles, we use the same notation: the segments that occupy the same syntactic position are put between curly brackets { } and they are separated by vertical pipes |. Pipes therefore separate what we call pile layers. These layers may be introduced by pile markers, usually a conjunction. If a pile marker does not play a syntactic role, it is preceded by a caret ^.

Dependencies and piles allow for a complete description of the syntactic cohesion of a DU. In (7), for example, the first layer realizes the position of attribute within the dependency structure. The syntagmatic relation between the two layers entails a paradigmatic relation between linguist and computational scientist. The second layer inherits the structural (attribute) position from the paradigmatic relation within the dependency structure. It should also be noticed that, with the exception of abandoned layers (noted &), layers can be seen as alternatives. It is possible to walk these structures by choosing one layer of each pile, extracting as many utterances as there are paths. Each of these utterances has a complete dependency structure merely containing government and modification relations, for example, (7a) can be reduced to the two DUs in (8), which will constitute the input for the parsing process:

(8) a. she is a linguist
b. she is maybe a computational linguist

Note that *maybe*, though it acts as a pile marker, also plays a syntactic role in the context of the pile, contrarily to a conjunction (*she is or a computational scientist), the latter being marked with the caret to make this distinction.

### 2.4 Macrosyntax and Illocutionary Units

An Illocutionary Unit (IU) is any portion of discourse encoding a unique illocutionary act: assertions, questions, and commands (see Benveniste 1966, Searle 1976). An IU expresses a speech act that can be made explicit by introducing an implicit performative act such as "I say", "I ask", "I order". A test for detecting the Illocutionary Units that make up a discourse consists of the introduction of such performative segments (see below). A segmentation in IUs is particularly important for the study of the connection of prosody and syntax, which is the goal of *Rhapsodie*, because these units are prosodically marked (Blanche-Benveniste 1997, Cresti 2000). We use the symbol // to segment the text in IUs (but see also the symbols //+ in section 3).

It should be noted that there exist IUs that are not made up of Verbal Dependency Units. See examples (9a,b):

(9) a. SPK1: we've heard all of the "you know" big "uh" meteors coming from outer space // SPK2: right // (Micase)
b. ^and then < boom //
(constructed example)

We extend the notion of IU to a unit whose status in terms of illocutionary acts, let alone in terms of propositional structures, may be unclear, but which can form a "complete message": interjections, phatics, feed back particles like *voilà* 'that's it', *quoi* 'what', *hélas!*, 'alas', *tant pis!* 'oh well'. See for instance in the famous critical punt against French writer Corneille (10a) that could be annotated as in (10b).

(10) a. Après l'Agésilas, hélas ! Après l'Attila, holà ! (Nicolas Boileau 1828)
'After Agésilas, alas! After Attila, no more!'
b. après l'Agésilas < hélas // après l'Attila < holà //

In a context such as (11), a single IU is made up of two verbal DUs: I got up in the morning and I was with clients.

(11) I got up in the morning < I was with clients // I ate at noon < I was with clients // I went to bed at night < I was with clients // (translation, *Rhapsodie*)

The relation between the two verbal DUs in (11) cannot be described in terms of microsyntactic dependency. Indeed, *I got up in the morning* is not dependent on the verbal construction of the following DU. Nevertheless, the existence of a macrosyntactic relation can be acknowledged. The first DU in (11), *I got up in the morning*, is not as autonomous from an illocutionary point of view: it cannot constitute a self standing message. In (11) it is not asserted that "I got up in the morning". And (11) can be paraphrased by (12a) but not by (12b):

(12) a. it is said that I got up in the morning I was with the clients
b. # it is said that I got up in the morning and that I was with the clients.

The illocutionary force of (11) is encoded by the DU *I was with clients*, which can be interpreted as an assertion even if uttered in isolation. Whereas the unit *I got up in the morning* does not have in this context any illocutionary interpretation. The subsegment of an IU supporting the illocutionary force of the IU is called the *nucleus*. It can be autonomized. The nucleus and the others segments forming the IU are called the Illocutionary Components (ICs). The ICs are always microsyntactic units and are generally DUs. The nucleus is the unit that is affected by a negation or an interrogation having scope on the IU. See for example the tests in (13) and (14):

(13) A: I got up in the morning I was with clients
B: this is not true (≈ It is not true that you were with clients, # It is not true that you got up in the morning)
(14) A: I got up in the morning I was with clients
B: Is that true? (≈ Is that true that you were with clients)
(# Is that true that you got up in the morning)

ICs preceding and following the nucleus are called pre-nuclear units (Pre-N) and post-nuclear units (Post-N). We use the symbol < to mark the Pre-N and the > to mark the post-N. These tags can be considered as explicit counterparts of commas in writing.

(15) il y a plein de trucs < tu les vois après > en fait > les défauts (*Rhapsodie*)
there are plenty of things < you see them later > actually > the faults

It is possible that, due to a particular communicative structure, the illocutionary force is carried only by a part of a DU and that the nucleus forms a DU with another IC:

(16) to my mother <+ I don't speak anymore (constructed example)
(17) two euros >+ it costs
(translation, Blanche-Benveniste 1990)

The addition of the symbol + indicates that the IC on one and the other side are parts of the same UR.

## 3 More cases of irregularity in the interface between microsyntactic and macrosyntactic units

We will now present a number of structures that were particularly problematic for the syntactic annotation of the *Rhapsodie* corpus and that illustrate the mismatch between DU and IU boundaries well.

### 3.1 DU beyond the IU

Up to now, we have seen a few examples of segmentation of an IU into DUs. We will now show that there are cases, traditionally named epexegesis, where we can consider that it is in fact the DU which is segmented into multiple IU. Let us consider these two examples:

(18) SPK1: he has arrived
SPK2: last night (constructed example)
(19) She speaks French. And very well!
(constructed example)

In these two examples, there are two illocutionary acts: in (18) this is evident as there are two speakers uttering two different assertions. In (19), there are two assertions. In both cases, the second illocutionary act is not (micro) syntactically autonomous. The second IU directly follows the first IU and integrates and completes its syntactic structure, being in a dependency relation with the head of the first IU (the verb *arrived* in (18), the verb *speaks* in (19)). We can therefore paraphrase the preceding examples thusly:

(20) SPK1: he has arrived
SPK2: he has arrived last night
(21) She speaks French and (what is more) she speaks French very well.

Rather than postulating an ellipsis in the second segment (as suggested by Culicover & Jackendoff 2005, among others) we analyze the two IUs as belonging to the same DU. This choice naturally descends from the modular approach we adopted, which distinguishes between illocutionary and syntactic relations. As in the case of a dependency relation crossing the IC border, we add a + symbol to indicate that the illocutionary frontier is not a limit to the DU.

In addition to dependency, piling can also cross IU frontiers, as in (22):

(22) SPK1: How often do you go {there |} //+
SPK2: {| to the States} // (ELUI)

In (22) the argument position of the verb *go* is realized twice: through the segment *there* uttered by the first speaker and through the segment *to the states* uttered as a separate IU by the second speaker. We use the notation {X|}...{|Y} when the pile between X and Y is interrupted by a syntactic frontier, in this case an IU frontier, or a discontinuity.

It should be noted that the piling in (22) does not only cross an IU frontier but it crosses a speech turn frontier as well, as it is realized by two different speakers. We do not consider the speech turn as a limit for the extension of syntactic phenomena, rather we assume that there can be co-construction of semantic content and syntactic structures in dialogues

### 3.2 Inserted IUs

An IU can be inserted into another IU. This is what happens for example in the case of insertions.

(23) a. I woke up (you're going to laugh //) in the morning at five o'clock // (constructed example)
b. { I studied | (sorry//) I studied in college | I studied } international relations // (ELUI)

We propose two equivalent ways to note this, either by placing the inserted utterance between parentheses as in (23) or by using the symbol # to indicate that the utterance is continued later at the following occurrence of #:

(24) a. I woke up #// you're going to laugh //# in the morning at five o'clock //
(constructed example)

These two notations are strict equivalents __"(" = "#//" and ")" = "//#"__, but the symbol # also allows the encoding of more complex cases such as the following example, where SPK1 is interrupted three times by SPK2. This does not keep SPK1 from pursuing a relatively complex utterance, all the while interacting with SPK2 through *yeahs* which punctuate SPK2's interventions. The sequence of //#+ tags indicates that the IU is completed (//), but that the DU continues later on (#+):

(25) SPK1: but but otherwise uh well & // in any case the fundamental research it it remains free //#+
SPK2: yeah yeah //
SPK1: #luckily //#+
SPK2 so yeah // in 2009 //
SPK1: yeah //
SPK2 : we'll have to see later //
SPK1: yeah // # the applied research < less // ^but the fundamental research < yeah //
(translation, *Rhapsodie*)

### 3.3 Embedded IUs

Direct discourse presents a particular difficulty due to the embedding of illocutionary acts. Consider the following example:

(26) he said [ go away > poor fool // ] //
(translation, radio)

The reported speech in (26), annotated with the symbols [ ], has its own illocutionary force, it can be regarded therefore as an autonomous IU. Regardless, the preceding segment (he said) does not form an autonomous illocutionary act or a complete DU. We treat such a structure as an embedded IU. The reported speech is an IU embedded in the IU made up of the whole utterance *he said go away poor fool*.

Another phenomenon that we treat as the embedding of IUs is the graft. We define a graft as the filling of a syntactic position with a segment belonging to an unexpected category (Deulofeu, 1999).

(27) a. you don't have an agenda with [one day I do this // one day I do that //] (translation, Deulofeu 1999)
b. you follow the tram line which passes towards the [I think it's an old firehouse //] // (translation, *Rhapsodie*)
c. I could like take and see {if I & | if it was worth it that I should go into "you know" more depth | ^or if that was just sort of like [ okay {I l- | I like it} // ^but I don't wanna like study that // ^so I don't know //] } //
(Micase)
d. we had criticized the newspaper [I think it was the Provencal #] we had criticized it in relation to (# or the Meridional //) in relation to the death of [what was his name // not Coluche // the other guy //] //
(translation, Blanche-Benveniste 1990)

This phenomenon can be regarded as a rupture of sub-categorization. The grafted segment usually has its own illocutionary force, being in most cases a unit commenting on the lexical choice that should have been done to respect the sub-categorization. In a graft, as well as in reported speech, an IU occupies a governed position inside a DU.

### 3.4 Associated IUs

A number of discourse particles (such as "right", "of course" in English, "quoi", "bon" in French) and parentheticals units (such as "I think", "I guess", "you know" in English, "je crois", "tu vois" in French) are endowed with an illocutionary force. However, these elements do not serve the purpose of modifying the common ground between speakers. They merely have a function of modal modification or interactional regulation. We call these units "associated units", we treat them as non autonomous illocutionary components and we annotate them between quotation marks " ".

(28) it's a really "you know" open field "you know" like all that stuff // (Micase)
(29) he is coming "I guess" // (constructed)
(30) "I mean" English wasn't that helpful itself // (ELUI)

## 4 Levels of annotation

Our annotation strategy rests on the fact that relatively good tools for automatic analysis of French written texts are currently in existence (Bourigault et al. 2005, De la Clergerie 2005, Boulier & Sagot 2005). Adapting these tools to spoken French would constitute a project in and of itself, one much more ambitious than our annotation project (even though we believe that *Rhapsodie* is an essential step towards the development of parsers for spoken language, and that one of the final uses of *Rhapsodie* will be as a contribution to the training and development of these parsers). In other words, we want to use these tools developed for written text without modifying them substantially. In order to do this, we realize a pre-treatment of transcribed text "by hand": We manually annotate every phenomenon typical of the syntax of speech. The result is a pre-treated text that parsers can analyze as written text with minimal error. The segmentation into IUs and DUs described in the previous sections aims at providing such a pre-treatment. As we hope we have shown, our pre-treatment has a theoretical and practical value, and could constitute a satisfying analysis of speech on its own. Regardless, we would like to present all levels of our treatment, as this will allow a greater understanding of the choices that have been made (for example the analysis of piles during pre-treatment).

Our annotation procedure is organized into several steps which alternate regularly between automatic and manual treatment.

**Level 1**: Raw transcription (i.e. without syntactic enrichment) - This consists of orthographic transcription which includes speech overlap, truncated morphemes, etc.

**Level 2**: Simple automatic pre-treatment - Annotation of trivial "disfluencies" (such as word repetition) and identification of potential associated IUs (*um, uh...* but also *like, you know...*). This automatic step is very rough and is to be corrected at level 3.

**Level 3**: Manual syntactic segmentation - This is the annotation presented in the previous sections of this paper, indicating DUs, IUs, ICs, piles, etc. This level is obtained manually starting at level 2. The general idea is that it simultaneously constitutes:

- A coding of everything that we know we are not able to automatically calculate, and which would cause problems for parsers (originally programmed for written text),
- A coding which is satisfactory in itself and permits a preliminary study of the syntax-prosody interface.

A tool has been developed for checking the well-formedness of this level of annotation.

**Level 4**: Parser entry - Existing parsers for French have not been programmed to process simple transcriptions of speech, nor have they been tuned to treat the markup that we have introduced at level 3. However, these tags allow us to automatically segment the text and furnish the parser with sections it is capable of analyzing. The following example will illustrate this point.

(31) are you thinking {of other communicat~ |
"uh" of other functions}
(constructed example)

would give us to two segments:

(32) a. are you thinking of other communicat~
b. are you thinking of other functions.

Certain fragments of text are therefore duplicated and analyzed multiple times. These analyses, if identical, are automatically fused in the ulterior levels. If they differ, a manual treatment is necessary. Another strategy consists of not unpiling but rather perceiving an utterance including a pile as a Directed Acrylic Graph (DAG), that is to say a graph in which the arcs are labeled by words of the text, and which integrate all possible paths in a pile structure. A parser like SxLFG (Boulier and Sagot 2005) can manage a DAG entry, but for the moment it is parameterized to choose the best path in the DAG and not to analyze the entire DAG.

**Level 5**: Parser output - Parsers provide us with a syntactic analysis in the form of a dependency tree. We now have two things left to do: 1) automatically translate these analyses so that they correspond exactly to the desired labels (this is mainly a renaming process of functional labels); 2) apply syntactic annotations computed for the unfolded segments to the original texts (those from level 3), while fusing duplicated syntactic annotations.

**Level 6**: Dependency analysis - This consists of level 5 after automatic reinsertion of analyzed sections and manual correction. The last level is a manual correction of level 5, this is absolutely necessary as the parsers still make many mistakes (we estimate that about 30% of dependencies will have to be corrected) and do not use our same labels. The encoding of level 6 is therefore a complete syntactic analysis of text, which includes microsyntax (functional dependencies) as well as macrosyntax.

## Conclusion

The ongoing process of annotating transcriptions of spoken French with syntactic functions has revealed the necessity of a well-defined text segmentation separated into illocutionary and dependency units. This process is an interesting challenge in its own right as it allows, for the time being, only very limited automated steps, and can be seen as a necessary pre-treatment before the parsing process, relying mainly on tools tuned to work on written data. Linguistically, contrary to the conventional ad-hoc punctuation of written text, our segmentation can be seen as a systematic punctuation process relying on reproducible criteria allowing for a distribution of this process to trained annotators. Moreover, the notion of paradigmatic piles naturally completes the short-comings of head-descriptions in coordinations and other paradigmatic phenomena.

If we want to share tools and resources across languages and theoretical models, it is necessary that annotation norms develop in the field of syntactic annotation of spoken texts, in other words, we need some kind of language-independent punctuation scheme reflecting syntactic and pragmatic segmentation of the text. This is a process that is well on its way for written text. Our work on French and English shows that our annotation scheme proposes criteria that can be applied to different languages while yielding interesting results. We hope this to be a contribution to the development of unified annotation methods in dependency annotation of spoken text and thus to a deeper understanding of functional syntax as a whole.

## References


Abeillé, A., L. Clément, F. Toussenel. 2003. Building a Treebank for French. A. Abeillé (ed) *Treebanks*. Kluwer, Dordrecht.

Benveniste, E. 1966. *Problèmes de linguistique générale*, Gallimard, Paris

Berrendonner, A. 1990. "Pour une macro-syntaxe". *Travaux de linguistique* 21: 25-31.

Bertrand, R., P. Blache, R. Espesser, G. Ferré, C. Meunier, B. Priego-Valverde, S. Rauzy. 2009. Le CID - Corpus of Interactional Data - Annotation et exploitation multimodale de parole conversationnelle. *Traitement Automatique des Langues*, 49(3): 1-30.

Bilger M., Blasco, M., Cappeau, P., Sabio, F. & Savelli, M.-J. 1997. Transcription de l'oral et interprétation: illustration de quelques difficultés. *Recherches sur le français parlé* 14: 55-85.

Blanche-Benveniste, C., M. Bilger, C. Rouget, K. van den Eynde. 1990. Le Français parlé. Études grammaticales. Paris, CNRS Éditions.

Blanche-Benveniste, C. 1997. *Approches de la langue parlée en français*, Ophrys, Paris.

Boullier, P. et B. Sagot. 2005. Analyse syntaxique profonde à grande échelle: SxLfg. *Traitement Automatique des Langues*, 46(2):65-89.

Bourigault D., Fabre C., Frérot C., Jacques M.-P. & Ozdowska S. 2005. Syntex, analyseur syntaxique de corpus, in Actes des 12èmes journées sur le *Traitement Automatique des Langues Naturelles*, Dourdan, France

Creissels D. 2004. *Cours de syntaxe générale*. Chapitre 1, http://lesla.univ-lyon2.fr/sites/lesla/IMG/pdf/doc-346.pdf

Culicover P., R. Jackendoff 2005. *Simpler Syntax*. Oxford: Oxford University Press

Cresti, E. 2000. *Corpus di italiano parlato*. Accademia della Crusca, Florence.

De la Clergerie, E. 2005. DyALog: a tabular logic programming based environment for NLP. *Proceedings of 2nd International Workshop on Constraint Solving and Language Processing*, Barcelona, Spain.

Degand, L., Simon, A. C. 2009. On identifying basic discourse units in speech: theoretical and empirical issues. *Discours* 4 (http://discours.revues.org/index.html)

Deulofeu, J. 1999. *Recherches sur les formes de la prédication dans les énoncés assertifs en français contemporain (le cas des énoncés introduits par le morphème que)*. Thèse d'état, Université Paris 3.

Dister, A., Degand, L., Simon, A. C. 2008. Approches syntaxiques en français parlé: vers la structuration en unités minimales du discours. *Proceedings of the 27th Conference on Lexis and Grammar*, L'Aquila, 10-13 September 2008, 27-34.

Gerdes, K., Kahane, S. 2009. Speaking in Piles. Paradigmatic Annotation of a Spoken French Corpus. *Proceedings of the fifth Corpus Linguistics Conference*, Liverpool.

Guénot M.-L. 2006. La coordination considérée comme un entassement paradigmatique: description, formalisation et intégration, *Proceedings of TALN*, Leuven, Belgique, 178-187.

Mel'cuk, I., Pertsov, N. 1987. *Surface Syntax of English. A Formal Model within the Meaning-Text Framework*, Benjamins, Amsterdam.

Searle, J. R. 1976. A classification of illocutionary acts. *Language in Society* 5:1, 1-23.

Simpson-Vlach, R., & Leicher, S. 2006. *The MICASE handbook*, The University of Michigan Press, Ann Arbor.

# The Annotation Scheme of the Turkish Discourse Bank and An Evaluation of Inconsistent Annotations

**Deniz Zeyrek, Işın Demirşahin, Ayışığı Sevdik-Çallı, Hale Ögel Balaban, İhsan Yalçınkaya**
Middle East Technical University, Ankara, Turkey
**and**
**Ümit Deniz Turan**
Anadolu University, Eskişehir, Turkey

Corresponding author: dezeyrek@metu.edu.tr

## Abstract

In this paper, we report on the annotation procedures we developed for annotating the Turkish Discourse Bank (TDB), an effort that extends the Penn Discourse Tree Bank (PDTB) annotation style by using it for annotating Turkish discourse. After a brief introduction to the TDB, we describe the annotation cycle and the annotation scheme we developed, defining which parts of the scheme are an extension of the PDTB and which parts are different. We provide inter-coder reliability calculations on the first and second arguments of some connectives and discuss the most important sources of disagreement among annotators.

## 1 A brief introduction to the Turkish Discourse Bank

### 1.1 The Data

The Turkish Discourse Bank (TDB) project aims to annotate the 500,000-word-subcorpus of the two-million-word METU Turkish Corpus (MTC) (Say et al, 2002). The subcorpus includes a wide range of texts, e.g. fiction, interviews, memoirs, news articles, etc. reflecting the distribution of the genres in the MTC (Zeyrek et al, 2009). The main objective of the project is to annotate discourse connectives with their two arguments, modifiers and supplementary text spans. Following the Penn Discourse Tree Bank (PDTB), we take discourse connectives as discourse-level predicates taking two (and only two) arguments, called Arg1 and Arg2, which may span one or more clauses and sentences that are adjacent or nonadjacent to the connective (Prasad et al, 2007, Webber, 2004). Discourse relations can certainly be expressed without connectives but we have chosen to annotate discourse relations encoded by connectives since they are more specific about their semantics.

Discourse connectives are identifiable from three syntactic classes, namely, coordinating conjunctions, subordinating conjunctions, and discourse adverbials. As in the PDTB, we take elements belonging to these syntactic classes as discourse connectives when they semantically relate syntactic entitities such as clauses, sentences, sequences of sentences, and nominalizations having an abstract object interpretation i.e., eventualities, possibilities, situations, facts, and propositions (as in Asher, 1993, cf. Webber, et al, 2005). Major departures from the PDTB are, attribution is not annotated, only overt connectives are being annotated, and the nominal arguments of connectives are being annotated where they denote an abstract object. Annotation of implicit connectives is further work.

### 1.2 The annotation cycle

Before the annotation process started, the annotators studied the guidelines, which defined some general principles and illustrated difficult cases. The guidelines were written in a way to allow the annotators enough freedom to reflect their intuitions on the annotations. The annotators were also told to observe the minimality principle (MP) of the PDTB guidelines, which expects them to mark as argument parts of a clause or sentence that are



*Proceedings of the Fourth Linguistic Annotation Workshop, ACL 2010*, pages 282–289,
Uppsala, Sweden, 15-16 July 2010. 

minimally sufficient and necessary for the discourse relation encoded by the connective.

The annotation cycle includes three steps. First, the annotators go through the whole subcorpus to annotate a given connective at a time. Any disagreements are discussed and resolved by the project team. In the second step, the definitions in the annotation guidelines are revised with the new issues that emerged in annotating the connective. Finally, the agreed annotations are checked to ensure they obeyed the annotation guidelines fully. The annotations were created by a tool designed by Aktaş (2008).

The connectives are being annotated for the categories given in the next section by three annotators, who have been in the project since the annotation effort started. The three-step annotation process and the number of annotators we use slow down the task considerably but given the complexity of discourse annotation and the need for annotation efforts in Turkish, we were compelled to target maximum reliability achieved by three annotators.

The inter-coder reliability has recently stabilized and to speed the annotation effort, two annotators have started to carry out their task as a pair, while the other annotator works independently. This annotation style involves two annotators working side-by-side at one computer, continuously collaborating on one connective type at a time to code all its tokens in the subcorpus. One of the annotators carries out the task on the annotation tool, while the other observes her continuously for any defects and problems and suggests alternative solutions. This style of annotation, created by our group independently of pair programming, corresponds to the practice explained in Williams, et al (2000) and Williams and Kessler (2000). It is quite a beneficial and reliable method that also speeds up the process (Demirşahin, et al ms). [1] We give the preliminary results of this procedure in section 2.1.4.

### 1.3 An outline of Turkish connectives and the annotation scheme

We annotate discourse connectives belonging to the syntactic classes listed below, leaving out converbs that may function as discourse connectives.

- Coordinating conjunctions (*ve* 'and', *ya da* 'or', *ama* 'but')
- Complex subordinators (*için* 'for', *rağmen* 'although, despite'), converbs/simplex subordinators (*-Ince* 'when,' *–ken* 'while, now that')[2]
- Anophoric connectives (*bundan başka* 'in addition to/separate from these', *bunun sonucunda* 'as a result of this,' *bunun için* 'due to/for this reason', *buna rağmen* 'despite this') and discourse adverbials (*oysa* 'however', *öte yandan* 'on the other hand', *then* 'sonradan')

In Turkish, coordinators are typically s(entence)-medial, they may also be found s-initially, or s-finally. Coordinators show an affinity with the second clause, as evidenced by punctuation and their ability to move to the end of the second clause. Subordinators take as their second argument a nonfinite clause that contains a genitive marked subject that agrees with the subordinate verb in terms of person and number. The subordinate clause may also be assigned case by the postposition that functions as the connective. The subordinator and its host clause are always adjacent and the subordinate clause may appear s-initially or s-finally. Anaphoric connectives are characterized by an anaphoric element in the phrase and hence they have the ability to access the inference in the prior discourse (Webber, et al 2003). Furthermore, they may take as their first argument text spans that are nonadjacent to the sentence containing the connective (Zeyrek and Webber, 2008).[3] As example (1) illustrates, discourse adverbials can be used with connectives from other syntactic classes, e.g. a coordinating conjunction, *fakat* 'but' may be used with *sonradan* 'then', and in accessing its first argument, the discourse adverbial may cross one or more clauses. In the examples, Arg1 is italicized, Arg2 set in bold, and the connective head is underlined.

[1] Except for *ve* 'and', the statistics reported in this paper reflect the agreement among 3 independent annotators.

[2] The capital letters are used to capture the cases where a vowel agrees with the vowel harmony rules of the language. The vowel rendered by the capital letter I may be resolved as any of the high vowels in the language, i.e., i, ü, ı, u.

[3] In the PDTB, expressions like *after that* are coded as "alternative lexicalization" while coding implicit connectives, i.e., as a "nonconnective expression" (Prasad et al, 2007:22). In Turkish, such phrasal expressions are abundant. They are two-part expressions with one part referring to the relation, the other anaphorically to Arg1 as in English. We decided to take these expressions as connectives because otherwise, we would be missing an important fact about Turkish. Therefore they are being annotated as connectives in the TDB project.

(1)

a. *Bunları açıkladığımız vakit yöneticiler evvela şaşırdılar*
When (we) explained these, the administrators were first surprised.

b. Böyle bir şeyi asla beklemiyorlardı.
(They) were never expecting such a thing.

c. Fakat **<u>sonradan</u> kendilerini toparladılar.**
But **<u>then</u> they gained their composure.**

Largely following the annotation style of the PDTB, we determined the categories that form the annotation of a relation as follows:

**Conn**: This is the connective head of an explicit connective.

**Arg2**: This tag refers to the argument that forms a syntactic unit with the connective.

**Arg1**: This tag is for the other argument that the connective relates semantically to Arg2.

**Sup1/Sup2**: This attribute specifies either the material that makes the semantic contribution of the argument more specific (as in the PDTB), or the clause/sentence where an anaphoric element expressed in the argument is resolved. The Sup tag is not specifically used for anaphor resolution in the PDTB.

**Mod**: This tag specifies the following features: (a) the adverbs that are used along with connective heads, e.g. *<u>tam</u> aksine* '<u>just</u> to the contrary', (b) the focus particle *dE* used together with the connective head (e.g., *ve <u>de</u>* 'and-focus particle 'and'), (c) adverbs showing the determinacy of the relation, e.g. *belki* 'perhaps', *sadece* 'only' etc., (d) polarity of postpositional phrases (e.g. *için değil* 'not for'). In the PDTB, the Mod category is utilized only for adverbs used together with connective heads. The other categories are used to capture aspects of attribution and verbs of attribution.

**Shared**: This attribute identifies the subjects, objects, or any temporal adverbs shared by the arguments of the discourse relation. This category was required for Turkish, which is a pro-drop and free word-order language. In Turkish, subjects, objects or adverbs can appear s-initially, s-medially or s-finally. Subjects and objects are dropped if they are salient in the discourse. This category allows us to capture the variable position of subjects, objects and adverbs shared by the arguments of a discourse relation. The PDTB does not have this feature.

In what follows, we will report on the inter-coder reliability statistics on Arg1 and Arg2 of a set of connectives for which we obtained low inter-coder reliability results and discuss the most common inconsistencies. The remaining categories mentioned above are under use but inter-coder reliability statistics have not been calculated for them.

## 2 A quantitative and qualitative evaluation of the inconsistent annotations in the TDB

So far, 60 types of discourse connectives amounting to 6873 relations have been annotated in the TDB project. We computed the reliability of the coders' agreement for Arg1 and Arg2 of these connectives by means of the Kappa statistic (Carletta, 1996). A value of K agreement coefficient (henceforth K values) between 0.80 and 1.00 shows a good agreement, and a value between 0.60 and 0.80 indicates some agreement (Poesio, 2000). The K values we obtained for Arg1 and Arg2 of most connectives annotated so far range between 0.80 and 1.00 but for the connectives that are in focus in this paper, the K values for Arg1 are less than 0.80 (see Appendix B). It is these connectives that we now turn to.

These connectives are listed below again, along with the K values obtained for their Arg1 and Arg2. Before calculating the K values, all annotated text spans were re-processed in order to express the annotations in (pseudo) categories. During re-processing, for each annotator the annotated text span boundary characters (i.e., the beginning and end characters) were coded as 1 and the remaining text was coded as 0, so that an agreement table could be constructed (Artstein, and Poesio, 2008; Di Eugenio and Glass, 2004). It is on the basis of this table which we measured inter-coder reliability.

| Connective | K value | |
|---|---|---|
| | Arg1 | Arg2 |
| *yandan* 'on the other hand' | 0.523 | 0.645 |
| *ayrıca* 'in addition, separately' | 0.545 | 0.760 |
| *rağmen* 'despite, despite this' | 0.688 | 0.742 |
| *fakat* 'but' | 0.719 | 0.855 |
| tersine 'on the contrary' | 0.741 | 1.000 |
| *dolayısıyla* 'as a result' | 0.759 | 0.930 |
| *oysa* 'however' | 0.767 | 0.913 |
| *amaçla* 'for this purpose' | 0.785 | 0.876 |

Table 1. Eight connectives with K values less than 0.80 (total number of annotations: 554)

For comparison, we provide the K values for two discontinuous connectives in Table 2:

| Connective | K value | |
|---|---|---|
| | Arg1 | Arg2 |
| *ne* .. *ne* 'neither nor' | 0.820 | 0.930 |
| *hem* .. *hem* 'both .. and' | 1.000 | 0.982 |

Table 2. Two discontinous connectives with K values higher than 0.80 (total number of annotations: 126)

As seen in Table 2, inter-coder agreement in discontinuous connectives is high. We argue that discontinuous connectives are maximally different from anaphoric connectives (and discourse adverbials) since they unambiguously draw the boundaries of their arguments. As a result, the inter-coder reliability tests yield good agreements, with K values > 0.80. Anaphoric connectives relate their second argument with another argument adjacent or nonadjacent to the connective, in a way much similar to how definite NPs find their antecedents in the previous discourse. Depending on the relation encoded by the connective, the previous discourse is likely to contain clauses that elaborate and expand a generalization, refute an assertion, list the components of a statement, explain the cause of an eventuality, etc. It may not be an easy task to decide whether one should take all or part of these clauses as Arg1; therefore inconsistencies are expected in drawing the Arg1's boundaries. Arg2, on the other hand, is relatively easier to determine since it is syntactically related to the connective and hence its domain is determined.

Example (2), which shows a relation encoded by the connective *tersine* 'on the contrary', presents one of the most common cases of inconsistency in determining the Arg1 span.

(2)

a. Eyleme değil, karaktere ağırlık veren modern romanda biliyoruz ki roman kişilerinin psikolojisi, iç dünyası, bilinci ve bilinçaltı yazarın dikkatle çözmeye çalıştığı ilginç sorunları içerir.
(We) know that in the modern novel, which emphasizes character rather than action, the novel contains the interesting problems that the writer wants to solve and the characters' psychology, their inner world, consciousness, and the subconscious.

b. Bundan ötürü önemli bir yönünü oluşturur romanın.
For this reason, (it) constitutes an important aspect of the novel.

c. Ama gene biliyoruz ki *halk edebiyatı ürünlerinde önemli olan kişinin iç dünyası değil,*
But we also know that *in folk literature what is important is not the person's inner world,*

d. **tersine, eylemidir.**
on the contrary, **(it) is his action.**

Two annotators selected as Arg1 the italicized part in (2c) while the third one selected as Arg1 the clauses in (2a), and (2c). In fact, a careful analysis of the discourse connective *tersine* 'on the contrary' reveals that in all tokens in the corpus, the speaker introduces an assertion, then refutes some aspect of it with an overt negation and then rectifies it in Arg2. (Turan and Zeyrek, 2010). The third annotator's selection of Arg1 is compatible with this observation, while the other annotators' selection of Arg1 appears to be guided by the MP.

### 2.1 Common Sources of Disagreement

An examination of the 8 connectives for which K values were below 0.80 for Arg1 or Arg2 showed that there were 6 main sources for the inconsistencies. These were (a) no overlapping annotations for Arg1, (b) partially overlapping annotations for Arg1 or (c) Arg2, (d) lack of adequate definitions in the guidelines, (e) annotators' errors in following the linguistic definitions in the guidelines, (f) other inconsistencies, e.g., errors in selecting spaces, leaving characters out, etc. (Appendix A).[4] Among these, partially overlapping Arg1 annotations is the major source of discrepancy observed in 63.98% of the inconsistent cases, followed by partially overlapping Arg2 annotations observed in 10.17% of the cases, and no overlapping annotations in 9.74% of the cases. While errors grouped under the 'other' category is 9.74%, annotators' errors in following the linguistic definitions in the guidelines is negligible (2.97%). The percentage of lacking definitions in the guidelines is also low (3.39%), showing that the coverage is good in the updated guidelines. Let us now turn to the

[4] There were also missing annotations but since we did not calculate inter-coder statistics for them, they are not mentioned in this work.

common sources of disagreement among annotators.

### 2.1.1 Interpretations of the minimality principle

A frequent reason for inconsistent annotations was lack of agreement in determining the exact boundaries of argument spans, which is ultimately related to how the MP is interpreted. For example, in (3), the connective *fakat* 'but' may be taken as linking clauses (3a) and (3b). Yet, the scope of the predicative morpheme (i.e. *–tır* in (3c)) that determines finiteness is shared by the verbs of (3b) and (3c), i.e. this morpheme takes into its scope two consecutive clauses. While two annotators coded only clause (3b) as Arg2, the third annotator tended to interpret Arg2 as the clauses within the scope of the shared predicative morpheme (*-tır*), coding (3b) and (3c) as Arg2. It appears that the disagreement in example (3) stems from different interpretations of the MP coupled with a structural property of Turkish.

(3)

a. Onlara sunulan kurbanlar, başlangıçta insanlardı
At the beginning, it was humans that were sacrified for them.

b. Fakat bu âdet sonraları hafifletilerek, insan yerine hayvanlar kurban edilmeğe başlanmış,
But later on, loosening this tradition, (they) started to sacrifice animals instead of humans,

c. sonunda da bu hayvanları temsil eden bazı şeylerin (…) kâğıt hayvan figürlerinin (…) yahut da bir taşın suya atılmasının yeterli olacağına inanılmıştır.
finally, it was believed that it would be sufficient to throw a stone or paper animal figures to the water, as well as other objects that represent these animals.

The text given in (4) further illustrates a case where the annotators disagreed on the final boundary of Arg2. One annotator selected as Arg2 the span "this is .. noted" (4b), while the other annotators selected the span "this is…. a lost place" ((4b)-(4c)); i.e., they included as Arg2 not only the clause adjacent to the connective, but they also selected the clause that followed where the cataphor is resolved. Faced with such inconsistencies, we decided to annotate the material that is needed for pronoun resolution as supplementary text. In this case, the clause in (4c) is marked as Sup2.

(4)

a. … ikincisindeki ayrıntı bolluğu Recaizade Ekrem'in gerçekçiliğine atfedilmiştir.
*.. the richness of details in the second (novel) was attributed to Recaizade Ekrem's realism.*

b. **<u>Oysa</u> asıl dikkat çekmesi gereken şudur**:
**<u>However</u>, this is what should be noted**:

c. Araba Sevdasının Çamlıca'sı yitik bir Çamlıca'dır.
The Çamlıca described in Araba Sevdası is a lost place.

The inconsistencies that derive from different interpretations of the minimality requirement is particularly interesting from a theoretical perspective. It appears that this principle may be interpreted as syntactic minimality as illustrated in example (3), and as a factor that goes against basic insights of discourse interpretation such as anaphor/cataphor resolution as in example (4). In the former case, the MP pulls the annotators in one direction, and the need to reflect their understanding of the discourse in the annotations pulls them in the opposite direction, especially when there is morphological/syntactic evidence for them to choose more than one clause. In the latter case, the annotators seem to feel they would lose the anaphoric/coreference chains in the discourse if they left out the text span where the anaphor was resolved. After using the Sup label for anaphor resolution/coreference chains, disagreements of the latter sort diminished considerably but this was a methodological approach with a bias towards the MP rather than the desired solution of the role of anaphoric/coreference chains in argument spans. We aim to tackle this issue in further research.

A parenthetical or evaluative clause in the argument span also led to inconsistencies in determining argument boundaries. For example, the annotators gave conflicting decisions as to whether or not they should select parenthetical clauses, especially when they are s-medial, as in (5):

(5)

Kemal, **<u>bir yandan</u>** *askeri bir savaş verirken* **<u>öte yandan</u> yerli işbirlikçilerle** –ki bunların başında da basın- **savaşmak zorunda kalmıştır.**
Kemal, while **<u>on the one hand</u>** *fighting a military war*, **<u>on the other hand</u> (he) had to fight with local accomplices** –which mainly included the media.

Disagreements that arise from parenthetical clauses have diminished after we added a new principle to the guidelines, asking annotators to select the parenthetical together with the argument if it contributed to the meaning of the argument.

### 2.1.2 Ambiguity

Another reason for inconsistent annotations was ambiguity in meaning. Consider example (1) once again, where the contrast relation can be interpreted in three ways: it is not clear whether the contrast is between *to be surprised* in (1a) and *to regain composure* in (1c) or whether it is between *not expecting such a thing* in (1b) and *to regain composure* in (1c). Alternatively, the contrast can be interpreted between (1a) and (1b) on the one hand, and between (1a) and (1c) on the other. We observed that some of the disagreements concerning the span of Arg 1 stemmed from such cases.

### 2.1.3 Type of discourse relation

Yet another type of inconsistency appears to be associated with the type of discourse relation. Sanders and Noordman (2000) and Pitler, et. al. (2008) state that causal (contingency) relations are among the most salient coherence relations. They suggest that the connectives that signal comparison and contingency are mostly unambiguous. Being cognitively salient, causal and contingency relations are more tightly organized than the additive list relation. This is because in causal relations, one target sentence is more important than the other; while in a list relation there is more than one sentence contributing to the discourse. Sanders and Noordman (2000:53) argue that causal relations are more strongly connecting than additive relations. This salience in discourse relations can be universal. In fact, we found that the inter-coder agreement of the causal connective *çünkü* 'because' was high (0.888 for Arg1 and 0.941 for Arg2). However, for the connective *ayrıca 'in addition to',* which encodes the list relation, the inter-coder K value was 0.545 for Arg1, 0.765 for Arg 2. An example of the list reading interpretation of this connective is illustrated in (6) below.

(6)

a. Babanın yaşamı artık derli toplu olmuştu.
The father's life now became orderly.

b. Evde kavgalar da azalmıştı.
The fights at home have diminished

c. __Ayrıca__ yeni bir çevrede de bulunuyorlardı.
**__Besides,__ (they) are now in a new neighborhood.**

In the extract given in (6), the topic under discussion seems to be the list of the family's diminishing problems: Father's having an orderly life, reduced fights at home, etc. While two annotators preferred to select (6b) as Arg 1, the third one preferred to select (6a) and (6b) together. The connective *ayrıca,* marking a weaker relation between its two arguments, is among the connectives that yielded such instances of disagreement.

### 2.1.4 Nominalized arguments

In this section, we will report on some preliminary results about a common inconsistency that occurred while annotating the connective *ve* 'and,' namely the problem of teasing apart nominalized arguments that have an abstract object interpretation and those that do not. We also explain the pair annotation process.

In Turkish, a nominalizing process realized by various inflectional suffixes forms nonfinite clauses. The clauses formed by some of these suffixes are abstract enough to be easily specified as an argument of a discourse relation, e.g. –mAk. On the other hand, some of the suffixes (e.g. –mA, -Iş) are very productive in deriving ordinary nouns referring to actual instances or things. It is these cases where disagreement among the annotators increases. Example (7) illustrates the use of –mAk, where the clauses it forms were easily determined as arguments with abstract object interpretations.

(7)

18. yüzyılın yaptığı, 17. Yüzyılın yarattıklarını *çoğaltmak* ve **yaymaktır**.
What the 18th century did was *to increase* and **to extend** what the 17th century created.

Example (8) shows a difficult case where the annotators were inconsistent in deciding whether the connective's arguments have abstract object interpretations or not. This is because the morphological form of the words *gelişme* (improve-mA) 'improvement' and *yapılaşma* (construct-mA) '(re)construction' are very much the same as the words *bekleme* (wait-mA) 'waiting' and *arama* (search-mA) 'search, searching' shown in (9). The final decision was to annotate (9) only.

(8)

Deprem bölgesinde yeniden [gelişme] ve [yapılaşmanın] planlanması gibi ciddi bir sorun bulunmaktadır.
There is the important issue of planning the [improvement] and [re-construction] of the areas affected by the earthquake.

(9)

Artık onu *beklemenin* **ve** **aramanın** boşuna olduğunu anlamıştır.
He has already figured out that it was futile *to wait for her* **and** **to search her**.

We noticed such inconsistencies in annotating 1/3 of the files for *and*. When we shifted to the pair annotation procedure, we obtained high agreement on Arg1 and Arg2 annotations of *and* because we observed that when done in pairs, resolving any disagreements between the annotations was faster since the members of the pair discussed difficult cases between them and sometimes determined a preferred annotation before presenting the results to the group. Table 3 shows the results for *and* annotations. A repeated measures test shows that the increase in K values is significant ($p< 0.01$).

| Annotators | K value | |
|---|---|---|
| | Arg1 | Arg2 |
| 3 annotators | 0.692 | 0.791 |
| A pair of annotators and an independent annotator | 0.945 | 0.964 |

Table 3 K values for *ve* 'and' of 3 independent annotators, and a pair and an independent annotator

## 3 Summary

In this paper we presented common sources of disagreement we observed in annotating the arguments of discourse connectives in the TDB, a project of discourse-level annotation on written Turkish. We defined our annotation scheme and annotation cycle. We achieved high agreement on argument annotations of discontinuous connectives but agreement on some other connectives was low, particularly for Arg1. Since these connectives belong to different syntactic classes, the inconsistencies cannot be easily explained by the properties of the syntactic class of connectives. We discussed various potential factors affecting inter-coder agreement, including the minimality principle coupled with language specific properties, the structure of discourse (as in the case of our example in *tersine*), cognitive salience of discourse relations, and ambiguity. We discussed inconsistencies resulting form the difficulty of distinguishing the non-abstract object interpretation of a nominalized clause from its abstract object interpretation. We argued that once inter-coder reliability stabilizes, it is beneficial to shift to the procedure where a pair of annotators works together to annotate a specific connective while the third works independently.

## Acknowledgments

We acknowledge the grant form The Scientific and Technological Research Council of Turkey and thank our anonymous referees for comments.

## References

Berfin Aktaş. 2008. Computational Aspects of Discourse Annotation. Unpublished MS Thesis, Cognitive Science Program, Middle East Technical University

Ron, Artstein and Massimo Poesio (2008). Inter-coder agreement for computational linguistics. *Computational Linguistics*, *34*(4). pp. 555-596.

Nicholas Asher. 1993. *Reference to Abstract Objects in Discourse.* Kluwer Academic Publishers.

Işın Demirşahin, İhsan Yalçınkaya, Deniz Zeyrek (ms). Pair Annotation: Adaption of Pair Programming to Corpus Annotation.

Barbara Di Eugenio, & Michael Glass (2004). The Kappa statistic: a second look. *Computational Linguistics*, *30*(1). pp. 95-101.

Eleni Miltsakaki, Rashmi Prasad, Aravind Joshi, Bonnie Webber. 2004. Annotating Discourse Connectives and Their Arguments. In *Proceedings of the HLT/NAACL Workshop on Frontiers in Corpus Annotation*. Boston, MA. 2004.

Emily Pitler, Mridhula Raghupathy, Hena Mehta, Ani Nenkova, Alan Lee, and Aravind Joshi. 2008. Easily Identifiable Discourse Relations *Proceedings of COLING*, 2008. Poster paper.

Massimo Poesio. 2000. Annotating a Corpus to Develop and Evaluate Discourse Entity Realization Algorithms: Issues and Preliminary Results. *Proceedings of LREC-2000*. Athens, May 2000.

Rashmi Prasad, Eleni Miltsakaki, Nikhil Dinesh, Alan Lee, Aravind Joshi, Livio Robaldo and Bonnie Webber. 2007. The Penn Discourse Tree Bank 2.0 Annotation Manual. December 17, 2007.

Ted J. M. Sanders and Leo G. M. Noordman. 2000. The Role of Coherence Relations and Their Linguistic Markers in Text Processing. *Discourse Processes 29*(1): 37–60.

Bilge Say, Deniz Zeyrek, Kemal Oflazer, and Umut Özge. 2002. Development of a Corpus and a Treebank for Present-day Written Turkish. In *Proceedings of the Eleventh International Conference of Turkish Linguistics*.

Ümit Deniz Turan and Deniz Zeyrek. 2010. Context, Contrast, and the Structure of Discourse in Turkish. ms.

Bonnie Webber, Aravind Joshi, Eleni Miltsakaki, Rashmi Prasad, Nikhil Dinesh, Alan Lee, and Kate Forbes. 2005. A Short Introduction to the Penn Discourse Treebank. Copenhagen *Working Papers in Language and Speech Processing*.

Bonnie Webber. D-LTAG: Extending Lexicalized TAG to Discourse. *Cognitive Science*, 28(5). September 2004.

Bonnie Webber, Aravind Joshi, Matthew Stone, and Alistair Knott. 2003. Anaphora and Discourse Structure. Computational Linguistics 29(4). pp. 545-587. 2003

Laurie Williams, Robert R. Kessler, Ward Cunningham, Ron Jeffries. 2000. Strengthening the Case for Pair Programming. *IEEE Software*, July/August 2000, pp. 19-25.

Laurie Williams and Kessler, Robert R. 2000. All I Really Need to Know about Pair Programming I Learned In Kindergarten, *Communications of the ACM*, Vol. 43, No., 5, pp. 108-114, May 2000.

Deniz Zeyrek and Bonnie Webber. 2008. A Discourse Resource for Turkish: Annotating Discourse Connectives in the METU Turkish Corpus. *The 6th Workshop on Asian Language Resources, The Third International Joint Conference on Natural Language Processing (IJNLP)*, Hyderabad, India, January 2008.

Deniz Zeyrek, Ümit Turan, Cem Bozşahin, Ruket Çakıcı, Ayışığı Sevdik-Çallı, Işın Demirşahin, Berfin Aktaş, İhsan Yalçınkaya, Hale Ögel. 2009. Annotating Subordinators in the Turkish Discourse Bank.*ACL-IJCNLP,* In *Proceedings of LAW III Annotation Workshop III*. Singapore, August 6-7, 2009, pp. 44-48.

Appendix A. Sources of disagreement in 8 connectives (Turkish equivalents of 'but', 'however', 'for this reason', 'despite', 'on the other hand', 'for this reason', 'on the contrary', 'in addition')

| **Source of disagreement** | **No.** | **%** |
|---|---|---|
| Partial Arg1 overlap | 151 | 63.98 |
| Partial Arg2 overlap | 24 | 10.17 |
| No overlap of Arg1 | 23 | 9.74 |
| Other | 23 | 9.75 |
| Lack of guidelines | 8 | 3.39 |
| Guidelines not followed | 7 | 2.97 |
| Total | 236 | 100 |

Appendix B. K values of connective types annotated in the TDB project[5]

| | | **K Value** | |
|---|---|---|---|
| **Connective (type)** | **English equivalent** | **Arg1** | **Arg2** |
| ne ..ne | neither .. nor | 1.000 | 0.982 |
| veya | or | 0.942 | 0.980 |
| dolayı | since | 0.892 | 0.957 |
| çünkü | because | 0.888 | 0.941 |
| örneğin | for example | 0.870 | 0.898 |
| ya da | or | 0.843 | 0.974 |
| yoksa | otherwise | 0.837 | 0.938 |
| ama | but | 0.832 | 0.901 |
| karşın | despite, despite this | 0.824 | 0.893 |
| hem .. hem | both .. and | 0.820 | 0.930 |
| dahası | moreover | 0.785 | 0.908 |
| amaçla | for the purpose of | 0.785 | 0.876 |
| için | for, for this reason | 0.776 | 0.915 |
| oysa | however | 0.767 | 0.913 |
| dolayı-sıyla | for this reason | 0.759 | 0.930 |
| tersine | on the contrary | 0.741 | 1.000 |
| fakat | but | 0.719 | 0.855 |
| amacıyla | for the purpose of | 0.700 | 0.912 |
| ve | and | 0.692 | 0.791 |
| rağmen | despite, despite this | 0.688 | 0.742 |
| ayrıca | in addition; separately | 0.545 | 0.760 |
| yandan | on the one hand | 0.523 | 0.645 |

[5] The results about the connective types for which 10 or more relations have been annotated by three annotators are included in the appendices.

# Author Index


Agarwal, Apoorv, 20
Aktaş, Berfin, 202
Alex, Bea, 29
Alm, Cecilia Ovesdotter, 118
Antunes, Sandra, 152
Avanzi, Mathieu, 265

Bada, Michael, 207
Balahur, Alexandra, 1
Beck, Kathrin, 147
Beisswanger, Elena, 235
Bertrand, Roxane, 186
Bhardwaj, Vikas, 47
Bhatia, Archna, 82
Bigi, Brigitte, 186
Blache, Philippe, 186
Boldrini, Ester, 1
Bonial, Claire, 82
Bouma, Gerlof, 212
Bozşahin, Cem, 202
Breimyer, Paul, 227
Bruno, Emmanuel, 186
Buch-Kromann, Matthias, 127
Bunt, Harry, 247

Cela, Edlira, 186
Chiarcos, Christian, 166
Cho, Seong-Eun, 182
Choi, Jinho, 91
Copestake, Ann, 73
Copperman, Hannah, 243

Demirşahin, Işin, 282
Deulofeu, José, 274
Diab, Mona, 222
Dickinson, Markus, 38
Dipper, Stefanie, 182
Dligach, Dmitriy, 64
Duarte, Inês, 100
Duffort, Lucie, 274

Eckart, Kerstin, 166
Eckert, Miriam, 207
Espesser, Robert, 186

Faessler, Erik, 235
Faria, Pablo Picasso Feliciano de, 217
Feldman, Anna, 197
Ferre, Gaelle, 186
Fitzgerald, Will, 243
Fort, Karën, 56

Gerdes, Kim, 274
Ginter, Filip, 137
Goehring, Anne, 192
Gonçalves, Anabela, 100
Green, Nathan, 227
Grover, Claire, 29
Guardiola, Mathilde, 186

Hahn, Udo, 235
Hana, Jirka, 11, 197
Haverinen, Katri, 137
Hellan, Lars, 172
Hendrickx, Iris, 100, 152
Herbelot, Aurelie, 73
Hinrichs, Erhard, 147
Hirst, Daniel, 186
Hülscher, Olaf, 177
Hunter, Lawrence, 207
Hwang, Jena D., 82

Ide, Nancy, 47, 247

Kabadjov, Mijail, 29
Kahane, Sylvain, 274
Kepler, Fabio Natanael, 217
Keßelmeier, Katja, 177
Kiss, Tibor, 177
Korzen, Iørn, 127
Kresse, Lara, 182
Kübler, Sandra, 147
Kumar, Vinay, 227

Lacheret-Dujour, Anne, 265
Laippala, Veronika, 137
Lebani, Gianluca E., 157
Lee, Sun-Hee, 162

Mansouri, Aous, 82, 222

Marek, Torsten, 192
Martin, Jean-Claude, 186
Martínez-Barco, Patricio, 1
Matsuzaki, Takuya, 123
Mazziotta, Nicolas, 142
Mendes, Amália, 100, 152
Merlo, Paola, 113
Miyao, Yusuke, 123
Montoyo, Andrés, 1
Moore, Johanna, 256
Morel, Mary-Annick, 186
Müller, Antje, 177
Murisasco, Elisabeth, 186

Nesterenko, Irina, 186
Niekrasz, John, 256
Nielsen, Rodney, 64
Nygaard, Valerie, 243

Obin, Nicolas, 265
Ögel Balaban, Hale, 282
Ogie, Ota, 109

Paixão de Sousa, Maria Clara, 217
Palmer, Martha, 64, 82, 91, 207, 222
Passonneau, Rebecca, 47
Passonneau, Rebecca J., 20
Pereira, Sílvia, 100
Pianta, Emanuele, 157
Pietrandrea, Paola, 274
Pradhan, Sameer, 222

Rambow, Owen C., 20
Rauzy, Stéphane, 186
Ritz, Julia, 166
Roch, Claudia, 177
Rosen, Alexandr, 11

Sagot, Benoît, 56
Salakoski, Tapio, 137
Salleb-Aouissi, Ansaf, 47
Samardzic, Tanja, 113
Samatova, Nagiza, 227
Samuelsson, Yvonne, 38
Schnurrenberger, Martin, 182
Sevdik-Çalli, Ayişiği, 282
Shen, Rongzhou, 29
Škodová, Svatava, 11
Song, Jae-young, 162
Stadtfeld, Tobias, 177
Štindlová, Barbora, 11
Strunk, Jan, 177

Tan, Ning, 186
Telljohann, Heike, 147
Tomanek, Katrin, 235
Tsujii, Junichi, 123
Turan, Ümit Deniz, 282

Vaidya, Ashwini, 82
van der Plas, Lonneke, 113
Viljanen, Timo, 137
Volk, Martin, 192
Voyer, Robert, 243

Wang, Xiangli, 123
White, Barbara, 132

Xue, Nianwen, 82

Yalçinkaya,, 282
Yu, Kun, 123

Zaghouani, Wajdi, 222
Zeyrek, Deniz, 202, 282